Mystics of the Book

Themes, Topics, and Typologies

Edited and with an Introduction by

R.A. Herrera

PETER LANG
New York • San Francisco • Bern • Baltimore
Frankfurt am Main • Berlin • Wien • Paris

Library of Congress Cataloging-in-Publication Data

Mystics of the book : themes, topics, and typologies / [edited by]
Robert A. Herrera.
   p. cm.
Includes bibliographical references and index.
1. Mysticism—Comparative studies. 2. Mysticism—Judaism.
3. Mysticism. 4. Mysticism—Islam. I. Herrera, Robert A.
BL625.M8975   1993   291.4'22—dc20   92-32887
ISBN 0-8204-2007-7   CIP

Die Deutsche Bibliothek-CIP-Einheitsaufnahme

Herrera, Robert A.:
Mystics of the book : themes, topics, and typologies / edited by Robert
A. Herrera.—New York; Berlin; Bern; Frankfurt/M.; Paris; Wien: Lang,
1993
   ISBN 0-8204-2007-7

Cover design by George Lallas

The paper in this book meets the guidelines for permanence and
durability of the Committee on Production Guidelines for
Book Longevity of the Council on Library Resources.

© Peter Lang Publishing, Inc., New York 1993

Printed in the United States of America.

Mystics of the Book

Acknowledgments

I wish to express my gratitude to Seton Hall University, to Msgr. John Oesterreicher, Director of its Judaeo-Christian Institute, Dean Jerry Hirsch of the College of Arts and Sciences, and Professors David O'Connor and William Radtke of the Philosophy Department for their generous support. I also wish to thank Dr. Carlos del Valle, Director of the Hebraic Section of the Instituto de Filología, CSIC [Madrid], for his kindness and help during my semester's residence, as well as the Librarians at the Consejo Superior, the Firestone Library of Princeton University, and The McLaughlin Library of Seton Hall.

Table of Contents

Introduction

Mysticism, at first viewing, may appear as something vague, vast, sentimental and amorphous, a convenient umbrella for things bizarre, amazing, and strange. William James said as much.[1] The term 'mysticism' is protean and has been used as a catch-all label for such diverse phenomena as spirituality, altered states of consciousness, and psycho-pathological aberrations. A multiplicity of means — spiritual, psychological, and chemical — have been used to prepare the way for or actually induce mystical states. Prayer, meditation, speculation, logic, readings, letters, numbers, music, body postures, breathing techniques and mind-altering substances can be counted among them.

That academic studies of comparative mysticism arose fairly recently — in the Nineteenth Century — illustrates both mysticism's elusive character and its resistance to scholarly probing. Recent scholarship, following in the steps of James, is inclined to reject the view that mysticism is an isolated phenomenon, a rare plant which should be studied in isolation detached from the vicissitudes of everyday life. A consensus has developed which stresses that personal, cultural, and universal factors are interwoven into these mystical states and experiences.[2] A good case can be made that the privileged experience resembles a blank cheque which the mystical writer fills out in accordance with his canon of belief.

St. Bernard writes in Christian theological terms with accents taken from his historical epoch; Ibn 'Arabi in terms of Islamic belief passed through the filtre of NeoPlatonism with embellishments appropriate to Al-Andalus; Abraham Abulafia, the Torah viewed through the prisms of Maimonides and Kabbalah. There is no doubt that a multiplicity of factors converge to spin the web within which these experiences are generated and interpreted. The vague and indeterminate boundaries of the mystical event, its prolixity, and proximity to the strange and bizarre, what one could call its ectoplasmic status, has given it a tarnished reputation. Not without reason did the majority of philosophers from Xenophanes to Lord Russell regard mysticism with undisguised distaste.[3]

Mystical writers responded in kind. Jili's vision of Plato filling the unseen world with light is a decided anomaly[4] as was the tradition which considered Socrates to have been a recluse with contemplative inclinations. But if mysticism is not an ecumenical grab-bag, welcoming all comers indiscriminately, what in fact is it? Can its boundaries be fixed. . . . its characteristics ascertained? Can any of the schema elaborated by scholars or inherited from the religious traditions be accepted outright without unduly widening or narrowing the field? The exorbitant attention given to the esoterica of mysticism adds another impediment to the scholarly enterprise. Extended analysis and prolonged discussion about ecstatic states, trances, visions, 'tastes', 'touches', somatic correlates such as cataleptic rigidity, anesthesia, and kaleidoscopic variations of consciousness, detracts from the principal task.

Typologies are necessary to impose a modicum of order on such an anarchic field. Yet they prove to be elusive. Should Niebuhr be followed, or Stace, perhaps Otto, Schimmel, Lindblom, or countless others who have attempted this important but difficult task? Or should all typologies be rejected and a return made to traditional schema which at least have the advantage of being organic outgrowths of living spiritualities? In any case all those typologies which serve to introduce order and structure into what otherwise is a forbidding chaos can be recommended, if guardedly.

Adding to our difficulties is the uncertain not to say shadowy nature of the origins of mysticism. The Greek *'mustēria'* probably initially referred to the Eleusinian mysteries, in which secret ceremonies were accessible only to the initiates, the 'mystics', who were obliged to maintain secrecy. Philological subtleties are not of much help. Whether the term *'mustēria'* was derived from a Greek root signifying 'to close', or a Hebrew root meaning 'to hide', and whether or not a variant of the term later emerged as 'sacramentum' in primitive Christianity are interesting problems but scarcely to the point at hand and possibly have little to do with the modern usage of 'mysticism'.

However, mysticism cannot be dismissed as a historical conundrum or a mere oddity, a troubling presence larded with insoluble problems. The influence of mysticism on other fields of endeavor is pervasive. Mystical literature has exercised a formative role in the development of language. It has had major resonances on speculative ethics and through ethics on practical life. Professor Dan states that "Jewish mystical-heretical writers produced ethical literature which was accepted and followed by the orthodox majority of the Jewish people".[5] Moreover, science and law, as well as other disciplines, flirted with mysticism and enjoyed lengthy albeit ultimately disappointing liaisons.

This influence was reciprocal. Philosophical ideas were infiltrated into Sufism by Tirmidhi, 'the philosopher'. Abraham Abulafia, one of the first commentators of the *Guide of the Perplexed*,[6] accepted a 'philosophically oriented theology' inspired by Maimonides. Al-Ghazzali's teaching has been considered a 'marriage' between mysticism and law.[7] Meister Eckhart used Thomistic and Aristotelian elements to formulate his mystical doctrine. Many medieval Christian mystics were inspired either by the muted Neoplatonism of Augustine or the radical Neoplatonism of the Pseudo-Denis and themselves influenced the development of future speculation in spirituality, philosophy, and science.

Mysticism has surfaced in the least likely places and persons. Abbot Suger's famous blue, the color of the stained glass windows at St. Denis, was derived from a mistranslated reading of the Pseudo-Denis.[8] Gustav Landauer, a Utopian Socialist, and Robert Musil, the author of the prophetic work, *The Man Without Qualities*, had definite if erratic mystic leanings. Landauer translated and wrote an introduction to extensive elections of Meister Eckhart's mystical works.[9]

Both theology and mysticism are subsumed under the umbrella of religion. What distinguishes the two is mysticism's claim to be uniquely wedded to experience and to teach a deeper mystery, to probe alien heights and depths, to uncover hidden meanings, and transcend the natural order. If we take the mystics at their word they aspire to 'polish the mirror of the soul', ascend Mount Carmel, imitate Christ in a unique manner, spiritually reproduce the Prophet's *Hijra* from Mecca to Medina, "descend" to the divine *hekhalot* (palaces) or *merkavah* (divine chariot). They aspire to arrive at proximity with the Prime Reality, God, even union—'*unio mystica,*' '*devekhut*', a return to the 'Day of *Alastu*' when only God existed. Union can take place with God, His Presence, the Active Intellect, or an assortment of superior beings. These goals can be conflictive, at times putting the religious and philosophical in frank opposition, as instanced by Judah Halevi's *Kuzari*.

The approach to this ultimate experience has been compared to a path to be traversed, a bridge to be crossed, a height to be climbed, a cloud to be entered, and more. Mysticism's point of departure is the human condition, its usual method, moral and spiritual purification, its goal, proximity to or union with the Highest Reality, the Divine, God. The mystical life comprises a unique dialectic between a transcendent belief and a discipline which organizes the lower cravings of sensibility. The contact of the soul with the Divine, at its most intense, is usually called ecstasy. Conceptual thought is silenced while a surge of activity of the soul on a higher level, or complete suppres-

sion of conscious noetic activity, is experienced. The soul is enabled
to come into contract with another realm, present and active, which
permeates both physical and spiritual worlds, infusing them with a
new and higher life.

Although these mystical experiences are ineffable — or so we are
constantly told — the mystical writer, if he desires to communicate his
experience to others is obliged to describe them as best he can by
means of human words, a task for which our everyday language is
found sadly lacking. The mystic is forced to make an attempt to
impregnate language with a new élan so as to extend its range and
enrich its possibilities. This has been attempted in a variety of ways
throughout history, some mystical writers recurring to sacred texts
from which a vocabulary appropriate to the task may be garnered, a
language pointing beyond the earthbound categories of the everyday
world. Often an intermediary stage between the experience itself and
its formuation in discursive language is found to be expedient. For
example, St. John of the Cross first crystallizes the mystical event into
verse before formulating it on the level of discursive language in the
shape of a commentary which 'decodes' this prior stage. Mystical
writers have used imagery, allegory, aphorism, meta-language, even
numbers to constitute this intermediate stage, which acts as the point
of departure for ordinary language.

The importance of canonical — authoritative — texts should not be
underestimated. Jewish mysticism, for example, tends to confirm the
authoritative status of Holy Scripture: the *Torah*, the *Nebhi'im*
[Prophets], and the *Ketubhim* [Writings]. Kabbalah itself designates a
teaching which originates in prophetic revelation and is transmitted
by worthy *Mekubalim* [bearers of tradition]. Gershom Scholem indicated that "all Jewish mystics from the Therapeutae . . . . to the latest
Hasid are at one in giving a mystical interpretation to the Torah."[10]
While Judaism speaks of a 'Torah from heaven', the Koran, at an
early date, was accepted as uncreated and co-eternal with God. Christians, for their part, poured over the two Testaments and other
canonical writings — the 'words of the Word' — while gathering a
wealth of exempla and analogies along together with spiritual inspiration. But inspiration works in wildly disparate ways. The "Song of
Songs", for example, inspired both the esoteric *Shi'ur Qomah* and St.
John of the Cross' *Cantico Espiritual*.

Mysticism, at least as found in the three Religions of the Book [*ahl
al-kitab*], has at times been their its central element, the very core of
spirituality; at times, their dangerous underside, the gateway to
heretical innovation; often a colorful but decidedly tangential
phenomenon. The mystical enterprise and its sequelae carry the

threat of alarming deviations — theological, social, and psychological — not the least being a definite tilt in the direction of antinomianism, to which the watch-dogs of the three religions have been alert. The Islamic masters of Baghdad developed the art of speaking in subtle allusions [*isharat*] in order to lessen the dangers posed by highly charged language.[11] The Rabbi's placed strict, at times draconian, limitations on the study of Kabbalah while Christian theologians cast a jaundiced eye on dogmatic and liturgical innovation often to the detriment of even the unassailably orthodox.

The dangers which accompany the mystical enterprise may, at least in part, account for the surprising number of ascetic and purificatory techniques taught and practiced in Christianity and Islam. Asceticism was not as common in Judaism and the Safed community, in which pentinence was established as a way of life, was a definite exception. As Professor Idel has indicated, in Judaism the full realization of the life of the spirit is not connected with the choice of a way of life markedly different from most of their coreligionists as in Christianity and Islam.[12] Christian monasticism has its parallels in loosely-knit Islamic ascetic communities and the master-student relation in both Islam and Judaism as exemplified by the Hasidic Rebbe and other variations on the theme. The wandering Friar and the later Russian *starets* may have been influenced by the wandering *fakirs* of Islam who travelled from 'spiritual oasis' to 'spiritual oasis' in their quest for illumination and spiritual perfection. Jews, although more tightly anchored to the community, often led a peripathetic existence in spite of themselves because of social and political vicissitudes. Several ended their lives with romantic leaps into the unknown: Judah Halevi's voyage to crusader Jerusalem, Abraham Abulafia's search for the mythical Sambatyon river.

A multiplicity of methods to generate mystical and pseudo-mystical states were formulated, both active and passive, voiding or emptying the soul to make 'space' for Divine activity. Ascetical practices ranged from physical maceration, prolonged silence, meditation techniques, solitude, seclusion, and so on buttressed by vocal gymnastics, music, colors, letter combinations, special garb and intoxicating substances. The Sufis speak of the threefold meaning of *Tasawwuf*; according to *shari'a* [Muslim Law], the *tariqa* [Mystical Path], and the *haqiqa* [Truth], as representing different levels of spiritual purification. This is a "vague parallel" to the traditional Christian division of the spiritual life into purgative, contemplative, and illuminative.[13] The repetition or combinations of Divine Name, words, or numbers, are found in the three religions. The practice of *gematria* in Judaism, the *Dhikr* in Islam, the Jesus-prayer in Orthodox Christianity, often accompanied by preparatory moves, are opposite examples. Mystical dance is found in the convents of the Mevlevis (Whirling Dervishes) as well as in the movements of the Hasidim. There were houses in which Sufis listened to music to induce ecstatic states. In Christian monasteries Gregorian chant — an echo of eternity — prods the soul to rise from the changeable to the unchangeable, from the everyday world to God.

But if there are important similarities there are also glaring discrepancies, not only between the three religions, but among mystical writers themselves. Is the human soul, a 'part' of the Divine? Is the mystical experience a 'déjà vu' of a lost inheritance? Is the human soul created *ex nihilo*, in effect a 'nothing' striving for ever more complete reality and being? Is the physical world an autonomous entity with its own *raison d'être*, a canvas on which the Divine attributes are projected, or a hollow, deceptive facade to be cast aside in the soul's quest for an alien, wholly-other Deity? John Smith may be right in suggesting that mysticism represents a 'pure empiricism' in the attempt of the self to encounter truth and reality,[14] but this view, as every view, brings in its wake a number of fundamental questions which must be faced and, if possible, answered.

We have attempted to mute the difficulties of the present enterprise by restricting the field to those mystical writers belonging to the Religions of the Book, and within this enclave to those who have weathered the tests of time, piety, and criticism. Yet this attempt to introduce a modicum of order and structure into what otherwise is a forbidding chaos may be only partially successful. We are still left with a mixed company which includes Rumi's verse, Meister Eckhart's theosophical ponderings, Abraham Abulafia's *gematria*, Ibn Arabi's mystagogical treatises, Pseudo-Denis' Neoplatonic flights, Rabi'a's outpourings, and a veritable family of mystical tracts generated by the *Sefer Yetzirah*. We have attempted to steer a middle course between the ecumenical and the parochial, keeping to those topics and themes which are considered reputable from a scholarly viewpoint. Although the omission of other 'mysticisms' by arbitrary *fiat* may well be deplored, an 'open house' policy would have extended the area of investigation irresponsibly and served to even further blur the already tenuous boundaries of the topic at hand.

'Mysticism' as we have previously indicated, is a vague term, an overdetermined term, having a multiplicity of sometimes conflicting meanings, pointing to a reality which is itself nebulous. The title *Mystics of the Book: Themes Topics and Typologies*, was selected to reflect these ambivalences. The subject-matter of this volume does not present any strict uniformity. There is no rigid pattern in theme, style, approach or topic. There are brief and lengthy studies, those with few footnotes and those with many studies with varying degrees of academic intensity and literary virtuosity. Some follow the line of 'typologies', while most range further afield. All deal with the mystical.

Included are studies on major mystical writers of the three traditions such as Meister Eckhart, Ibn al-'Arabi, Rabbi Judah the Pious and others. Also discussed are seminal texts such as the *Sefer Yesirah*, the *Tract on Ecstacy*, *Von Abegescheidenheit*, and the *al-Futuhat al-Makkiva*. General trends, particular modes, symbols, metaphors, historical and ideological turns within a chronological range of nearly fifteen hundred years and a geographical range which extends from Spain to Persia and Germany to North Africa are studied.

We have attempted, within our limitations, to concentrate on themes and topics which act as redoubts within an unpacified territory, islands within a troubled sea, charted enclaves able to provide a point of departure for future scholarship. A volume such as the present can serve as an advanced introduction for students of mystical literature, a reference work for the scholar, and weighty if exotic reading for the educated public. Mystical literature is scarcely topical reading as it requires a minimal acquaintance with theological and philosophical speculation as well as a definite religious turn. Once these requirements are satisfied mystical literature is truly superb reading combining the depth of rigorous thought with the excitement of mystery and the aesthetic delight of lyric poetry.

The realization that man stands before the secret of the world which is also the secret of the self and of reality is shared by mystical writers with many others. Perhaps poets are the best example. This was sensed by Boccaccio when he stated in his commentary to *The Divine Comedy* that poetry is theology.[15] But the poet—unless he is also a mystic—merely skims the surface, muting his nostalgia for Paradise, projecting his aspirations on to lesser things. The mystic, perhaps in spite of himself, concentrates on that intense point of transcendent light, the ultimate source, which both suffuses and extends beyond the human soul and the physical universe. He opens a horizon with strange vistas and unfamiliar scenes. Through the mystics, their writings, and writings on their writings, we enter into a new world in which our charts and categories no longer apply and new 'senses' must be acquired.

Notes

1 The *Varieties of Religious Experience* (New York: Modern Library, 1922), pp. 370-371.

2 Refer to Daniel Merkur's helpful study "Unitive Experiences and the State of Trance" which I had the opportunity of perusing prior to publication.

3 On the other hand, Rudolf Otto believed that mystical conceptions lie behind the "higher speculations of modern times" — behind Descartes, Malebranche, Spinoza, Leibniz, Kant, and others. *Mysticism East and West* (New York: Meridian, 1960), Appendix II, p. 233.

4 R. A. Nicholson, *Studies in Islamic Mysticism* (Cambridge, C.U.P., 1921, reprinted 1967), p. 137.

5 Joseph Dan, *Jewish Mysticism and Jewish Ethics* (Philadelphia: Jewish Pub. Society of America; Seattle & London: Univ. of Washington Press, 1986), pp. 2; 76-103.

6 Moshe Idel, *Studies in Ecstatic Kabbalah* (Albany: State University of New York Press, 1988), pp. 1-2.

7 Annemarie Schimmel, *Mystical Dimensions of Islam* (Chapel Hill: Univ. of North Carolina Press, 1986), pp. 95-96.

8 Meredith Parsons Lillich, "Monastic Stained Glass: Patronage and Style". *Monasticism and the Arts*, edited by T. G. Verdon (Syracuse: Syracuse Univ. Press, 1984), pp. 222-225.

9 *Meister Eckhart's Mystische Schriften* (Berlin, 1903) 2 Auflage 1922. Cited by Ruth Link-Salinger, *Gustav Landauer: Philosopher of Utopia* (Indianapolis: Hackett, 1977), p. 60, note 41.

10 *Major Trends in Jewish Mysticism* (New York: Schocken Books, 1961), pp. 13-14. Refer to Eliezer Schweid, *Judaism and Mysticism According to Gershom Scholem* (Atlanta: Scholars Press, 1985), p.27ff.

11 Anne Marie Schimmel, "Sufism and the Islamic Tradition". *Mysticism and Religious Traditions*, edited by Steven T. Katz (Oxford: Oxford Univ. Press, 1983), pp. 130-147; esp. p. 130.

12 Idel, *op. cit.*, pp. 104-105.

13 Schimmel, *Mystical Dimension*, p. 98.

14 John E. Smith, "William James's Account of Mysticism: A Critical Apprasial." *Mysticism and Religious Traditions*, pp. 247-279.

15 Cited by Jacques Maritain, *The Frontiers of Poetry* (New York: Scribner's, 1962), p. 224, note 179.

Section I

Jewish Mysticism

Yeridah la-Merkavah: Typology of Ecstasy and Enthronement in Ancient Jewish Mysticism

Elliot R. Wolfson

I

It has been long recognized, following the pioneering research of Gershom Scholem, that one of the salient features of early Jewish mysticism — known technically as *hekhalot* (palace) or *merkavah* (chariot) speculation — is heavenly ascent.[1] The motif of the heavenly journey is, of course, not unique to Jewish mystical sources, but is found rather in a host of variant texts from the Greco-Roman period.[2] As is to be expected, the phenomenological content of the ascent as it appears in these diverse apocalyptic, gnostic and mystical-magical writings is not identical. In the case of *merkavah* mysticism, as may be gathered from some of the principal texts, the mystic ascends through seven palaces which are located in the seventh heaven, reaching his ultimate destination in the innermost palace where the throne of glory is situated. The culmination of the ascent is a direct vision of the divine glory (*kavod*) or Power (*gevurah*) referred to by various technical expressions including, most prominently, the beholding[3] of the King in his beauty (*yofi*).[4] While several scholars of late have criticized Scholem's identification of the visionary ascent as the essential feature of the *hekhalot* corpus,[5] it nevertheless remains the case that in a significant body of texts included within this corpus the visionary component assumes a central position and functions as the organizing literary principle.

A problem that has plagued the minds of scholars for some time is the seemingly paradoxical way that certain of the texts, primarily *Hekhalot Rabbati* and a fragment from the Cairo Genizah which a copyist has conveniently called *Hotam ha-Merkavah*, "The Seal of the Chariot," but which scholars name the Ozhayah text, refer to the ascent as a descent to the chariot (*yeridah la-merkavah*). In a lengthy article on the subject published in 1893, Philipp Bloch concluded that the journey to the throne of glory was rightfully called a descent

because it involved something akin to an ecstatic fall of the body.[6]
Scholem suggested that the origin of the terminology *yored la-merkavah* is to be found in the liturgical expression *yored lifne ha-teivah* as is attested in the practice of the synagogue.[7] Scholem's conjecture has been accepted by several other scholars, including, for instance, Ithamar Gruenwald[8] and Ira Chernus.[9] Three other theories that have emerged in recent years are noteworthy. The first is that of Joseph Dan who suggested that the term *yeridah* (descent) in this context reflects the influence of Song of Songs 6:11, "I went down to the nut orchard," אל גנת אגוז ירדתי.[10] Underlying Dan's hypothesis is the further assumption that the nut orchard symbolizes the chariot. Evidence for such a symbolic association, however, is found in textual fragments copied and preserved in the literature of the German Pietists of the twelfth and thirteenth centuries. While these texts may indeed be older than their late medieval appearance, as Dan in fact surmised,[11] the fact is that the image of the chariot as a nut does not play a significant role in the main *hekhalot* texts that describe the ascent or descent to the chariot. It thus seems, as Alexander Altmann suggested,[12] that the linkage of the *merkavah* to Song of Songs 6:11 represents a later exegetical reading that connects the technical idiom *yeridah la-merkavah* to the expression "I went down" (*yaradeti*) used in the relevant verse. Another explanation for *yeridah la-merkavah* was offered by Gedaliahu Stroumsa who noted that the expression should be seen as a linguistic analogue to *katabasis* in Greek magical papyri[13] which designates the preparatory rite for a mystical vision.[14] More recently, David Halperin has proposed yet another explanation which is based on a midrashic passage in *Exodus Rabbah* concerning the Israelites who crossed the Red Sea. In that context the Israelites are first called *yorede ha-yam*, "descenders to the sea," and afterwards *'ole ha-yam*, "ascenders from the sea."[15] Halperin is led to propose this passage as a possible source for the peculiar terminology, *yored la-merkavah*, because of the association of the visions of the glory and the crossing of the sea. Indeed in that very passage the Israelites are further described as beholding the divine glory at the sea.[16]

While all the views mentioned above are interesting in their own way, it seems to me that the original conjecture of Scholem can still be defended as the best explanation for the term *yeridah la-merkavah* and related expressions. Nevertheless, Scholem, and others who have followed him, are left with the apparent paradox that an ascent should be referred to as a descent.[17] It is my intention to show in this paper that a careful reading of the relevant passages wherein this term occurs will demonstrate that, in fact, there is no paradox here at all, i.e., the expression *yeridah la-merkavah* does not signify an ascent referred to paradoxically as a descent, but means rather going before the chariot.[18] Henceforth I will thus translate the idiom *yeridah la-merkavah* as entry to the chariot, a connotation that is well attested for the root *yarad* in other contexts in rabbinic sources.[19] By grasping the intended meaning of this expression one can attain a better understanding of the magico-mystical praxis cultivated by these anonymous Jewish writers. To anticipate my conclusion at the outset: in *Hekhalot Rabbati* the *yeridah* to the chariot was a necessary prelude to the mystic's vision of the glory and his liturgical participation in the celestial choir. In the Ozhayah fragment, by contrast, the "seeing of the King in His beauty" is emphasized as the sole goal of the *yeridah la-merkavah*. Moreover, in the case of both sources, but especially the latter, we find the additional element that the *yeridah* results in the mystic being seated alongside or facing the throne of glory. Occupying this seat represents a process of enthronement which signals that the visionary has become a full-fledged member of the throne-world, attaining the rank of the highest angel.

II

A perusal of the places in which the term *yeridah la-merkavah* occurs in *Hekhalot Rabbati* and the Ozhayah text reveals that in the vast majority of cases the *yeridah* does not refer to the entire ascent, as has been previously thought, but refers rather to the culminating stage of the ascent, the last phase of the heavenly journey. To support this rather startling revelation, I would like to cite some of the relevant sources. I will begin with *Hekhalot Rabbati* and will then turn to the Ozhayah fragment.

(1) *Hekhalot Rabbati*

[A] "All these songs R. Akiva heard when he entered the chariot (כשירד למרכבה) and learnt them before the throne of glory, for His angels were singing before Him" (Schäfer, *Synopse*, § 106).[20]

[B] "Let His heart rejoice at the time of the prayers of His children. He seeks out and finds those who enter the chariot (יורדי למרכבה) when they stand before Him, before the throne of His glory" (§ 172).

[C] "He enters (יורד) [the chariot] and beholds the wonderful loftiness and strange lordship, loftiness of exaltation and lordship of pride,[21] which are activated before the throne of His glory three times a day" (§ 200).

[D]   "Those who enter the chariot (יורדי למרכבה) ascend [to the seventh palace] and are not harmed . . . they enter safely (יורדים בשלום), and come and stand and give testimony, and recount the awesome and frightful vision of which there is no equal in all the palaces of mortal kings, and they bless, praise, applaud, glorify, exalt, honor, and attribute glory, splendor, and greatness to Toṭrosiai Lord, God of Israel, for He rejoices at those who enter the chariot" (§ 216).

[E]   "When a person desired to enter the chariot (לירד במרכבה), Anafiel would open up for him the doors [of the] entrance of the seventh palace" (§ 247).

[F]   "The one who is worthy to enter the chariot (לירד במרכבה), when he stands before the throne of glory, he opens and begins to utter song" (§ 260).

There is thus in *Hekhalot Rabbati* a clear linkage between the *yeridah la-merkavah* and the last stage of the ascent at the seventh palace. Although this is implied in all the sources cited above, perhaps it is most striking in [D] and [E]. In the case of the former [D] we find the combination of *'aliyyah* and *yeridah*: the mystic ascends to the seventh palace and then enters before the chariot. The reference at the beginning to the ascent in the words, "those who enter to the chariot ascend and are not harmed," is not to the ascent through all the heavenly palaces. It is such an interpretation which has led scholars to posit that the *yeridah* likewise must refer to the entire ascent. Yet this interpretation is wrong for it fails to note the specific context in which the passage occurs, viz., the mystic has already passed through the first six palaces, and thus is ready to proceed to the seventh, the place where the *yeridah* occurs. This is the meaning of the continuation of the passage, "they enter safely, and come and stand and give testimony, and recount the awesome and frightful vision . . . and they bless, praise, applaud, glorify, exalt, honor, and attribute glory, splendor, and greatness to Toṭrosiai"—all this comes to pass within the seventh palace. It is thus incorrect to interpret the expression used in this context, *yoredim be-shalom*, as referring to the descent from heaven to earth. The recounting and retelling of the vision does not occur below before human beings, but rather above before the divine glory. The narration of the "frightful vision" is a

testimony (*'edut*) offered to God which functions as a means of praise
or glorification, a usage evident in other passages in this redactional
unit.[22] It is only in light of this explanation that one can make sense
of the continuation of this section: "In the same degree that Totrosiai
YHWH, the God of Israel, looks forward to the redemption and the
time of salvation reserved for Israel since the destruction of the last
Temple, He desires and looks forward to [the time] when the one
who enters the chariot will enter, when he will see the loftiness on
high, when he will see the time of the salvation, when he will hear the
time of miracles, when he will see that which no eye has seen, when
he will rise (יעלה) and tell [his experiences] to the 'seed of Abraham,
My friend'[23]" (§ 218). Just as in this context the term *yored* connotes
entry to the chariot, the word *ya'aleh* signifies the departure from
there; hence, the mystic is implored to exit from the throne so that he
may relate his otherworldly experiences to fellow Jews who are
designated by the biblical locution, "the seed of Abraham, My friend."

The reading I have proposed is confirmed by the second passage
[E] where it says explicitly that when a person desired to enter the
chariot the angel Anafiel opened the doors of the entrance to the
seventh palace. The entry to the chariot occurs specifically at the
seventh palace. It is thus no mere coincidence that in one section of
Hekhalot Rabbati (§ 234) the angel of the sixth palace, Dumiel,
announces that "he who enters the chariot does not enter" (אין יורד
היורד למרכבה) if he has not both mastered all forms of Jewish
learning and fulfilled all the commandments. This pronouncement is
especially relevant at this juncture of the journey for one is
approaching the seventh palace where the entry to the chariot will
take place.[24] Indeed, in the continuation of the text (§ 236) the
guardians of the seventh palace are described as covering their faces
when they see "the angels Dumiel, Gabriel and Qaspiel [or, according
to some manuscripts, Qafsiel] coming before the carriage of the
person who merits and enters to the chariot" (אדם שזוכה ויורד
למרכבה).[25] In yet another passage in the same text a figure described
as having the appearance of the Hashmal (based on Ezek. 1:27 which
is explicitly cited) is said to "select from amongst the ones who enter
the chariot those who are worthy of entering and those who are not"
(§ 258). In this case the process of selection occurs not at the sixth
palace (cf. §§ 224-25) but at the seventh palace, at the stage right
before the entry to the chariot.

In the case of [C] the entry is placed in a visionary context, i.e., the
one who enters the chariot is said to have a vision of the various
hypostasized attributes which are before the throne of glory. In still
other cases, such as [B], [D], and [F], the entry is decidedly liturgical

in its orientation. The mystic stands in the place of the angels before
the throne and utters the appropriate testimony or praise to the
glory. Indeed, the wording of [D] describing the *yoredei merkavah*,
"they blessed, praised, lauded, glorified, exalted, honored, and gave
glory, splendor, and greatness to Ṭoṭrosiai, Lord, God of Israel"
should be compared to the *qedushah de-yoṣer* which is the narrative
account of the angelic hymning of God that is recited as part of the
traditional morning service: "And they all opened their mouths in
holiness and purity, in song and melody, and they blessed, praised,
glorified, worshipped, sanctified and enthroned the name of God."[26]
The *merkavah* adept thus takes the place of, or participates with, the
celestial angels, a motif that is repeated throughout these texts. That
is, an essential characteristic of the entry to the throne, which follows
the ascent to the seventh palace, is the utterance of hymns before the
glory. This is implied as well in [A] where R. Akiva is said to have
heard and learnt the songs of praise when he entered the chariot and
stood before the throne of glory. Similarly, in another passage in
Hekhalot Rabbati the entry to the chariot is placed in an obvious
liturgical context: "R. Ishmael said: What is the recitation[27] of songs
that a person chants when he enters the chariot (יורד למרכבה)? He
begins and utters the first of songs, the primary praise . . . and the
first melody which the attendant angels sing each day to the Lord,
God of Israel, and to His throne of glory" (§ 94). The proper
understanding of this passage is predicated on our previous
discussion: the *yeridah* occurs at the seventh palace when the mystic
enters before the throne and joins the angelic choir in uttering song
and praise to the divine glory. The heavenly status of the mystic is
manifest in his ability to sing in accordance with the *hymnologia* of the
angels.[28]

It is quite clear from the lengthy description of the *yeridah la-
merkavah* in *Hekhalot Rabbati* (§ 233ff.) that this occurs at the seventh
palace. There can be no question that the *yeridah* technically refers to
the last stage of the journey and not the whole process of ascent.[29]
Accordingly, it is inaccurate to consider the expression *yored la-
merkavah* paradoxical for, in fact, it refers to one who enters before
the chariot. When it says, then, that R. Neḥuniah ben ha-Qanah sat
before the fellowship of rabbis and arranged (מסדר)[30] before them
matters pertaining to the techniques of *yeridah* and *'aliyyah* (§ 203),[31] it
means the entry before the chariot followed by an exit from it. That
is, in this context the "ascent" does not signify the journey
heavenward, but rather the rising from the immediate vicinity of the
throne after one has entered into that stage of the experience. The
phrase ירידה ועלייה is equivalent, in my opinion, to the Talmudic

expression used in connection with R. Aqiva, "entered safely and exited safely,"[32] or, according to an alternative reading, "ascended safely and descended safely."[33] That is to say, within the framework of *Hekhalot Rabbati* the expression ירידה ועלייה indicates a successful and completed journey to the throne: one enters and afterwards exits.[34] Interestingly enough, in the very first passage of *Hekhalot Rabbati* the expression "enter safely and exit safely" is used in conjunction with the mystical experience of contemplating the chariot: "R. Ishmael said: What are the songs that the one who desires to behold the vision of the chariot, to enter safely and exit safely (לירד בשלום ולעלות בשלום), must say?" (§ 81). The twofold process of *yeridah* and *'aliyyah* is a technical way of referring to the vision of the chariot. Hence, in this case as well the *yeridah la-merkavah* is followed by an *'aliyyah*.[35]

The same meaning seems to be implied in yet another passage that appears only in the longer recension[36] of the text known as *Ma'aseh Merkavah*.[37] The section (§§ 586-91)[38] consists of R. Neḥuniah ben ha-Qanah teaching R. Ishmael five prayers intended to strengthen him so that he may "make use" of the secret (רז),[39] i.e., theurgic use[40] of the divine or angelic names.[41] Before the five prayers are specified R. Ishmael reports: "When R. Nehuniah ben ha-Qanah arranged before me these five prayers, each day I would recite every one with its names, in the entry (ירידה) and in the exit (עלייה), and all my limbs did benefit"[42] (§ 586). It is noteworthy that this locution contradicts the view that is prevalent in other sections of this very text, including the opening passage,[43] where the heavenly journey to the chariot is referred to as an ascent.[44] The fact that in this section the approach to the chariot and/or throne is called *yeridah* is yet another indication that this section is an interpolation inserted by the redactor of the longer recension. The use of the expression ירידה ועלייה suggests the influence of *Hekhalot Rabbati* or a similar text, such as the Ozhayah fragment, that shared this nomenclature. In any event, it is reasonable to conclude that in a given stage in the development of *hekhalot* mysticism the successful experience was referred to as ירידה ועלייה, the former signifying the entry to the throne-world and the latter the subsequent departure from there.[45]

(2) *Ozhayah Text*

When we turn to the other major source wherein the terminology of "descent" to the chariot is employed, the so-called Ozhayah text, we find similar support for the interpretation that I have suggested. In the first instance we read: "It is written on the seal of the chariot (חותם המרכבה) [how] to enter to it [the chariot] to see the King in His beauty" (לירד בה לראות מלך ביופיו).[46] There is here an indisputable link between the *yeridah* and vision of the anthropomorphic form of the divine glory. This is further confirmed in a second passage from the same fragment: "You shall write and place the seal of the entry to the chariot (חותם ירידת המרכבה) for people of the world, for you and for whoever wants to enter to behold the King and His beauty (לירד להציץ במלך ביופיו). Grab this path, enter and see (ירד ויראה), and you will not be harmed for I have given you [the seal] as a scroll."[47] In yet another passage we read of the *yeridah*: "When you desire to enter to the chariot to contemplate the King and His beauty (לירד למרכבה להסתכל במלך וביופיו), you and whoever else desires to enter, whether of your generation or other generations, should mention My name at each and every palace and call Me in a quiet voice; immediately no creature will harm him."[48] Although in this last case the gradual ascent through the various palaces is alluded to, it is clear that the *yeridah* to the chariot refers in this case as well to the ultimate stage in the process and not to the whole journey. This is confirmed by the obvious connection between the *yeridah* and the contemplative vision of the King in His beauty, i.e., the anthropomorphic glory. It is this process that is designated in the same text as the "teaching of the entry to the chariot" (תלמוד ירידת המרכבה) that the angel Ozhayah arranges before R. Ishmael, i.e., the mystic or the recipient of the text, which includes the techniques of how one enters and departs (כך יורדין וכך עולין).[49]

At the end of this fragment there is one of the most vivid descriptions of the visionary's "actual" entry into the throne-world. In this case, moreover, the *yeridah* involves a process akin to enthronement. When R. Ishmael reaches the seventh palace God welcomes him with these words: "Whoever knows that he is pure from sin[50] [and] bloodshed, and possesses Torah, should enter and sit before Me."[51] It is not specified that the mystic who is worthy should sit on a throne, but only that he should sit before God. Nevertheless, from the continuation of the text it is abundantly clear that the *yeridah la-merkavah* is followed by the enthronement of the visionary:

> Look at the youth who comes forth from behind the throne to greet you; Zehubadiah is his name . . .[52] He will take your hand and seat you in his lap.[53] It is not only because you come with his permission; he seats others as well on a seat (מושב)[54] that is fixed before the [throne of] glory.[55] This is the quality [or attribute] of the sign (מדת סימן) for the seventh palace.[56]

The first thing to note is that the angel Zehubadiah is in all probability identical with Metatron, for the name 'youth,' *na'ar*, is a frequent epithet used to describe the latter in *hekhalot* literature.[57] In the seventh palace, then, the highest of all angels takes the mystic in his lap which is compared to his placing others on a seat that is set before the throne of glory. It is of interest to note that the word used in the above passage for seat, *moshav*, is connected in several other sources with the throne of glory; indeed on occasion the words *moshav* and *kisse'* (throne) function as parallel terms. I will mention in this context only some of the pertinent sources. Thus, we find in one of the fragments of the so-called angelic liturgy at Qumran, the 4Q *Serekh Shirot 'Olat Ha-Shabbat* (4Q S1 40 24 4), the expression, "the seat of His glory," *moshav kevodo*[58] which, as scholars have already pointed out, clearly refers to the divine throne or chariot.[59] Similar to this expression is another one widely attested in *hekhalot* literature, *moshav yeqaro*, "the seat of His honor," which likewise is a technical designation for the divine throne.[60] There is yet a third expression, semantically related to the first two, found in *Hekhalot Rabbati* (§ 159) as well as in a *merkavah* hymn (§ 969),[61] which refers to the throne of glory as *moshav hadaro*, "the seat of His splendor." Elsewhere in this literature, in *Hekhalot Rabbati* (§§ 94, 154), in a text which Peter Schäfer has called "Die Beschwörung des sar ha-panim" (§ 634),[62] and in a titleless Genizah fragment,[63] the throne of glory is referred to as *moshav 'elyon*, "the lofty seat." The use of the word *moshav* for the throne may be adduced from other texts as well, such as *Hekhalot Rabbati* (§ 170), *Ma'aseh Merkavah* (§§ 590, 591, 596), a *Shi'ur Qomah* fragment that has been copied as part of *Hekhalot Zuṭarti* (§ 367), and *3 Enoch* or the *Hebrew Book of Enoch* (§§ 34, 72). Finally, in one passage it is stated explicitly that "the throne of glory is the seat of His glory," *we-khisse' kavod hu' moshav kevodo* (§ 373). From all this evidence, then, it may be safely concluded that the word *moshav* in these texts is basically interchangeable with *kisse'*.[64] If that is so, it is reasonable to conclude that the reference in the Ozhayah text to the "seat (*moshav*) that is fixed before the [throne of] glory" is meant to convey the image of a specially designated throne upon which the mystic himself sits. The act of sitting on that seat, therefore, amounts to an enthronement.[65]

That the process of sitting functions here as a kind of enthronement may be gathered from the use of the image of sitting before the throne in other *hekhalot* texts. Before discussing these, however, it is necessary to point out that the majority of texts within this corpus emphasize that the *yoredei merkavah* stand before the throne. Furthermore, in most of these cases the standing before the throne is connected with the liturgical act of uttering hymns and praises before God.[66] Terminologically, this is related to at least two standard themes known from rabbinic literature[67]: first, prayer itself is connected with the act of standing as is attested by the technical expression to begin prayer, *la'amod bi-tefillah*[68] (for the central liturgical unit, the *shemoneh 'esreh*, is called *'amidah*, i.e., the prayer uttered in a standing position[69]), and, second, the angels are characterized as standing before the throne.[70] Evidence of both is to be found in the *hekhalot* literature.[71]   Indeed, on more than one occasion the description of the angels as standing is connected with the specific task of praising God with songs or hymns.[72]   Hence, the description of the mystic standing before the throne conveys the notion of liturgical participation that I mentioned above: the *yored merkavah* stands before the throne and joins the angels in uttering hymns before God.[73]

To appreciate the specific intent of the image of sitting as employed in the Ozhayah text, it is necessary to review briefly the usage of this image in two other *hekhalot* texts, *Hekhalot Rabbati* and *Hekhalot Zutarti*.   I confine my remarks here to only those passages dealing with the experience of the mystic in the celestial realm.[74]   In *Hekhalot Rabbati* there are only a few cases in which the activity of sitting is used to characterize the *yoredei merkavah*.   In one passage, R. Nehuniah ben ha-Qanah, while in a trance-state, is described as sitting before the throne (§ 227).   What is particularly striking about this passage is that at the same time that R. Nehuniah is said to be sitting before the throne he is supposed to be sitting below in the Temple.[75]   In another passage the angel at the sixth palace, Dumiel, is said to receive the mystic and "seats him on a bench of pure stone,[76] and he sits next to him on his right side" (§ 233).   Shortly after that text we read that the angelic gatekeepers of the seventh palace together with the mystic "entered before the throne of glory, and they brought out before him all kinds of melody and song, and they sang until they lifted him up and sat him down next to the Cherubim, the Ophanim, and the holy Hayyot.   He saw miracles and wonders, [the qualities or attributes of] pride, greatness, holiness, purity, fear, modesty, and justice" (§ 236).   According to this text, then, the mystic first takes a seat at the sixth palace on the bench next to Dumiel and then in the seventh palace, presumably on a separate seat or throne but possibly on the chariot itself, alongside the various classes of angelic beings who bear the throne and minister to the glory.   It is instructive to compare this account with an exact parallel in *Hekhalot Zutarti*.   In that text one finds as well an elaborate description of the reception of the mystic by the different angels presiding at the seventh palace: "The mighty Ophanim embraced him, the glorious Cherubim kissed him, the Hayyot carried him, the Nogah danced before him, the Hashmal serenaded him . . . until they lifted him up and sat him down before the throne of glory, and he beheld and saw the King in His beauty" (§ 411). The language in the two texts, *Hekhalot Rabbati* and *Hekhalot Zutarti*, is very close. Both employ the critical phrase, "until they lifted him up (מעלין אותו) and sat him down" (מושיבין אותו). Nevertheless, the differences are also of significance. In the former it is specified that the mystic is given a seat alongside the Cherubim, Ophanim, and Ḥayyot; the reader is not told if the mystic has a seat of his own or if he sits upon the chariot itself.[77] In the case of the latter it is specified that the mystic is placed in front of the throne of glory, apparently on his own seat. Both texts likewise connect the sitting down in the seventh palace with an extraordinary visionary experience, though the immediate object of vision differs in the two accounts. In the case of the former the mystic is said to see wonderful and marvelous things, consisting largely of hypostatized ethical and pietistic qualities, whereas in the case of the latter it is specified that the mystic sees the divine King in His radiant beauty.

It may be concluded, therefore, that sitting before the throne was considered to be an important stage in the ecstatic experience of the *merkavah* mystic. Three major literary units that I have discussed, *Hekhalot Rabbati*, *Hekhalot Zutarti*, and the Ozhayah fragment, provide textual evidence to the effect that the mystic occupied a seat alongside the throne of glory. Although not much detail is given about the process of the mystic being seated before the throne, we have seen that in the relevant passages the act of sitting down was followed by a vision of some sort. I would venture a suggestion and propose that whereas the recitation of hymns and praises on the part of the mystic was accomplished in a standing posture, the visionary experience was facilitated by his sitting down before the throne of glory.[78] This observation corroborates the claim I made above that the sitting of the mystic must be viewed as a kind of enthronement.[79] That is to say, the act of sitting and the consequent vision of things divine indicates that at this moment the mystic has attained the rank of an angelic being and can thus see things which were hitherto invisible from the mortal perspective. To be sure, as I remarked above, standing and not sitting is the salient characteristic of the angels' ontic status. Yet, in this body of literature on several occasions angels are said to be seated upon a throne.[80] The first two examples come from the magical text, *Sefer ha-Razim*, which has great affinity with *hekhalot* mysticism. In the description of the third heaven mention is made of three archons who sit on fiery thrones,[81] whereas in the description of the fifth heaven mention is made of the twelve glorious princes who sit on thrones of splendor whose appearance is likewise characterized as that of fire.[82] A third example is that of the archon of Sabbath (*sar shel shabbat*) who, according to a passage in *Seder Rabbah di-Bereshit*, is said to be placed on the throne of glory by God (§ 852).[83] The fourth example is from a description in *Masekhet Hekhalot* of seven ministering angels, the first born of all created entities, who sit on seven thrones set before the curtain behind which is the throne of glory.[84] The fifth and final example of an enthroned angel, and by far the most important for the purposes of this analysis, is that of Metatron (cf. §§ 13, 20, 856, 894). It has even been suggested by some scholars that the name Metatron itself is based on the Greek $\mu\epsilon\tau\alpha\theta\rho\text{ovo}\varsigma$ which is semantically related to $\sigma\nu\nu\theta\rho\text{ovo}\varsigma$, signifying that Metatron occupied the throne alongside that of God.[85]

That sitting on a throne represents a highly privileged status,[86] indeed one that proximates divinization, is evident from a number of relevant sources, mostly apocalyptic in nature, that describe the enthronement of select figures. In this context I will mention only a few of the most obvious examples: Moses in the *Exagoge* of Ezekiel the Tragedian, 68-76;[87] Sophia according to the apocryphal *Wisdom of Solomon* 9:4 (cf. 8:3, 15),[88] the Son of Man in *1 Enoch* 69:29;[89] Enoch in *2 Enoch* 24:1; Adam in *Vita Adae et Evae* 47:3 (= *Apocalypse of Moses* 39:3), the *Testament of Abraham*, recension A, 11:4-12, and the *Testament of Adam* 3:4; Jesus in Mt. 22:44 (Mk. 12:36, Lk. 20:42-43) and 26:64 (Mk. 14:62, Lk. 22:69), based on an interpretation of Ps. 110:1;[90] and the twenty-four elders in Rev. 4:4 (cf. 3:21 and 20:4).[91] That the righteous in the celestial Paradise occupy thrones is alluded to in some Jewish sources and stated quite explicitly in others.[92] Elsewhere in rabbinic literature Abraham[93] and David[94] are said to occupy thrones in the heavenly realm alongside that of God. The enthronement of Adam also seems to be implied in a statement attributed in *Genesis Rabbah* to R. Hoshaya commenting on the verse, "And God said, 'Let us make man in our image, after our likeness'" (Gen. 1:26). According to R. Hoshaya's interpretation, when God created Adam the angels mistook him for God and desired to say the *Trisagion* before him. In order to make a sharp distinction between divine and human God is said to have caused Adam to sleep so that the angels would know that he is human. This is compared to a king and his servant who ride together in a chariot (קרוכין, from the Greek $\chi\alpha\rho\rho\text{ov}\chi\alpha$). The people of the country wish to bestow honor on the king by proclaiming "Lord" (*domine*) before him but they cannot differentiate between the king and his servant. The king therefore pushes the servant out of the chariot so that all would know who is the king.[95] It is not stated explicitly that Adam occupied a throne or sat on the chariot but it is implied in the notion that the angels wanted to utter the *Trisagion* before him. In this passage not only is Adam depicted as sitting on the throne, but the whole issue is placed in a polemical context which emphasizes that enthronement is a sign of divinity. Thus, commenting on this passage, Saul Lieberman noted that "the people did not realize who is the *synthronos* and who is the master. By being thrown out of the chariot the subordinate position of the *synthronos* was revealed."[96] Lieberman goes further and suggests that the legend regarding Adam is comparable to that of Metatron who is described as sitting and recording the merits of Israel,[97] a position developed in more detail by Moshe Idel.[98] I shall return to the case of Metatron momentarily.

The divine status accorded to sitting upon a throne is also evident from the polemical statements of the rabbis directed against the heavenly enthronement of the angels: "there is no sitting above"[99] or, alternatively, the angels "have no joints."[100] A statement in *3 Enoch* is particularly revealing of the need to emphasize that angels are not enthroned. After describing the two angels, Soperiel and Shoperiel, who act as scribes respectively registering the appropriate record of death and life of individuals, the author reminds the reader: "So that you should not suppose that since the Holy One, blessed be He, sits on a throne, they too sit and write, Scripture states, 'all the host of heaven standing in attendance [to the right and to the left of Him]' (1 Kings 22:19). It does not say, 'host of heaven' but 'all the host of heaven,' which teaches that even the great princes who are without peer in the heavenly height only attend to the needs of the *Shekhinah* while standing" (§§ 28, 864). This polemical stance is also implied in the famous legend which attempts to explain the apostasy of Elisha ben Abuyah (first half of second century C.E.) found in B. Hagigah 15b and in *3 Enoch* (§§ 20, 856) where it is obviously a secondary interpolation.[101] According to this account, Elisha is misled by Metatron's sitting on a throne and writing the merits of Israel into believing that there are two divine powers since a being which occupies a throne must be divine.[102] Interestingly enough, a later authority, the German Pietist, Eleazar ben Judah of Worms (d. ca. 1230), applied the view expressed in *3 Enoch* with respect to Soperiel and Shoperiel, to Metatron himself, also known as the heavenly scribe: "He [Metatron] stands, as it is written, 'all the host of heaven standing in attendance [to the right and to the left of Him]' (1 Kings 22:19), he has no throne upon which to sit. When he writes it appears as if he is sitting, but it is not so in reality."[103] Such a view, which openly contradicts traditions that affirm Metatron's sitting on a throne, is rooted in the other view widely attested in rabbinic sources, viz., only God sits above. Thus, an anonymous midrashist flatly states: "Is there sitting above? You find rather that all [of the angels] are standing . . . No one sits there but the Holy One, blessed be He."[104]

What is relevant to our discussion is that, insofar as sitting most properly characterizes God, or at the very least the vicegerent of God who is His anthropomorphic representative, it follows that the mystic being seated in the throne-world symbolically depicts the narrowing of the gap that separates divine and human nature. It thus makes perfectly good sense that at some stage in the literary development of *hekhalot* mysticism a book such as *3 Enoch* would have been composed in which the prototype of the *merkavah* mystic is Enoch who is transformed into Meṭaṭron, the very angel who occupies a throne alongside that of God. Here the apocalyptic tradition of the apotheosis of Enoch reaches its fullest expression.[105] In the case of the *hekhalot* material discussed above this last step is not taken, for the distinction between God and human in these texts is never fully blurred, as Scholem already observed.[106] It is nevertheless evident that in the key texts examined in this paper one of the features that results from the entry to the chariot is the mystic's being seated upon a throne. This fact, in turn, signifies his elevation to the status of not just an angel, but the highest angel who alone, apart from God, occupies a throne in the seventh palace of the seventh heaven. In that sense, I submit, the enthronement of the mystic should be understood as a form of quasi-deification.[107] While the vision of the divine glory does not make the mystic divine or equal to the glory, as is implied, for instance, in 1 John 3:2,[108] the entry to the chariot does culminate with what may be called a deifying vision. At the very least, it is in virtue of the enthronement that the *merkavah* mystic can see that which is ordinarily concealed from mortal eyes.

III

In sum, it may be said that, contrary to accepted scholarly opinion, the expression *yeridah la-merkavah* according to the authors of *Hekhalot Rabbati* and the Ozhayah fragment, does not refer paradoxically to an ascent, but rather names the last stage in the ascent that actually involves an entry into the throne-world. As we have seen, moreover, the *yeridah* results in the mystic's being enthroned, having a vision of the glory or the divine attributes that surround the throne, and uttering hymns together with the angels before God. Whereas the vision is attained after the mystic has been seated, the liturgical element is only realized when the mystic stands before the glory. Yet, in both respects—the sitting and standing—the model is that of an angel. Within these texts there are clearly two distinct views on the nature of angelic existence, and both provided ideal-types for the mystic.

At the outset of the paper I remarked that the thesis that I would put forth in this paper would strengthen Scholem's conjecture that the term *yeridah la-merkavah* is patterned after the liturgical locution *yeridah lifne ha-teivah*. Although the *yeridah la-merkavah* comprises both a visionary and liturgical component, it seems to me that the language of *yeridah* is in fact based on the liturgical expression that Scholem suggested. On the other hand, it would be wrong to separate these two elements in too sharp a fashion. Here we would do well to consider Schäfer's conclusion that a careful scrutiny of the ascent passages in the *hekhalot* literature demonstrates that "the ascent does not culminate in a vision, but rather in the merkavah mystic's participation in the heavenly liturgy."[109] Schäfer is right in making the distinction between vision and the liturgical act, the recitation of the doxology. The distinctive quality of these two categories does not, however, imply that they can in any meaningful way be isolated. On the contrary, participation in the angelic choir arises precisely in virtue of the mystic's *yeridah* to the chariot and consequent vision of the enthroned glory. One cannot separate the visionary and liturgical aspects of this experience; indeed, it might be said that in order to praise God one must see God.[110] The point was made already by Samuel Leiter in his study on acclamation in rabbinic writings. Leiter cites various rabbinic sources that emphasize that praise of God is dependent on seeing God.[111] One such source worth repeating is a passage in the *Midrash 'Otiyyot de-Rabbi 'Aqiva'* that draws upon chariot imagery: "When the time for the *qedushah* arrives and the Holy One, blessed be He, does not descend from His exalted height and dwell in the chariot, the two (letters that make up the *mem* when written in full) approach one another and say: When will the Holy One, blessed be He, descend from the exalted heights and descend to the chariot[112] so that we will see the image of His countenance and utter song before Him."[113] Leiter goes so far as to assert that the "paradoxical situation" of having to praise an invisible God "stimulated merkavah mysticism. Just as the letters wait to see God on the Merkabah so that they can praise Him, so the mystic's aim is to see the Divine Presence on the Merkabah."[114] While it may be somewhat of an exaggeration to say that this is the theoretical issue that stimulated early Jewish throne-mysticism, it is nevertheless instructive that Leiter has recognized the inherent connection of the visionary and liturgical components of these texts. In this context it is of interest to note the following passage from a German Pietistic commentary on the *merkavah* hymn, *Ha- 'Aderet we-ha-'Emunah,* preserved in manuscript: "The Holy One, blessed be He, shows the angels the greatness of His glory, and the angels must delve into the secret according to the greatness of His glory, how to bless Him . . . According to the greatness that He shows them they give praise."[115] The meaning of the expression *yored la-merkavah* that I have proposed lends considerable support to the view that the twin goals of the mystic ascent, vision and liturgical hymning of the glory, are interrelated.

Notes

* This paper has gone through various permutations. I have benefited from the comments and criticisms of several colleagues who read the different drafts: Moshe Idel, Ithamar Gruenwald, Peter Schäfer, Lawrence Schiffman and Michael Swartz.

1 See, e.g., G. Scholem, *Major Trends in Jewish Mysticism* (N. Y., 1954), pp. 43-50, 72; idem, *Kabbalah* (Jerusalem, 1974), pp. 14-21. Scholem's emphasis on ascent as the essential feature of *merkavah* mysticism is no doubt related to his view that the *hekhalot* literature is an offshoot of Jewish apocalyptism. This thesis has been most fully worked out by I. Gruenwald in his monograph, *Apocalyptic and Merkavah Mysticism* (Leiden, 1980), as well as in other studies; see, e.g., "Priests, Prophets, Apocalyptic Visionaries, and Mystics," in *From Apocalypticism to Gnosticism* (Frankfurt am Main, 1988), pp. 125-44. See, however, the author's more nuanced analysis in the same volume, "Two Types of Jewish Esoteric Literature in the Time of the Mishnah and Talmud," pp. 53-64. See also J. Maier, *Vom Kultus zur Gnosis* (Salsburg, 1964), p. 106. For a critique of the Scholemian approach, see P. Schäfer, "The Aim and Purpose of Early Jewish Mysticism," in idem, *Hekhalot-Studien* (Tübingen, 1988), p. 288, n. 44; D. Halperin, "Ascension or Invasion: Implications of the Heavenly Journey in Ancient Judaism," *Religion* 18 (1988): 47-67; idem, *The Faces of the Chariot* (Tübingen, 1988), pp. 451-52.

2 The scholarly literature on this subject is vast. A classical study of this motif is W. Bousset, "Die Himmelsreise der Seele," *Archiv für Religionswissenschaft* 4 (1901): 136-69, 229-73. For some of the more recent surveys, see A. F. Segal, "Heavenly Ascent in Hellenistic Judaism, Early Christianity and their Environment," in *Aufstieg und Niedergang der Römischen Welt, Principat* II, 23 (1980): 1333-94; M. Smith, "Ascent to the Heavens and the Beginning of Christianity," *Eranosjahrbuch* 50 (1981): 403-29; I. P. Coulianu, *Psychanodia I: Survey of the Evidence Concerning the Ascension of the Soul and Its Relevance* (Leiden, 1983); idem, *Out of This World: Otherworldly Journeys from Gilgalmesh to Albert Einstein* (Boston & London, 1991); M. Dean-Otting, *Heavenly Journeys: A Study of the Motif in Hellenistic Jewish Literature* (Frankfurt am Main, 1984); J. D. Tabor, *Things Unutterable: Paul's Ascent to Paradise in its Greco-Roman, Judaic, and Early Christian Contexts* (Lanham, MD, 1986), pp. 57-111; M. Himmelfarb, "Heavenly Ascent and the Relationship of the Apocalypses and the *Hekhalot* Literature," *Hebrew Union College Annual* 59 (1988): 73-100.

3 Several verbs are used in the *hekhalot* corpus to denote the contemplative vision of God: *lehistakkel, lehasis, leṣappot, lahazot,* and *lir'ot.* I cannot detect any significant variation in meaning or nuance between these different terms.

4   Cf. P. Schäfer, *Synopse zur Hekhalot-Literatur* (Tübingen, 1981), §§ 198, 248, 259, 407, 408, 409, 411, 412, 545; idem, *Geniza-Fragmente zur Hekhalot-Literatur* (Tübingen, 1984), pp. 103, 105. For a comprehensive analysis of this and related expressions, see R. Elior, "The Concept of God in Hekhalot Mysticism," in the "Proceedings of the First International Conference on the History of Jewish Mysticism," *Jerusalem Studies in Jewish Thought* 6 (1987): 27-31 (in Hebrew) [English translation in *Binah: Studies in Jewish History, Thought, and Culture*, vol. 2, ed. J. Dan (New York, 1989), pp. 97-120]. See also S. Leiter, "Worthiness, Acclamation and Appointment: Some Rabbinic Terms," *Proceedings of the American Academy of Jewish Research* 41-42 (1973-74): 143-45. It should be mentioned that in *Synopse*, § 198 the mystic is said to have a vision of eight things that correspond to the eight earthly vices specified in § 199 that the mystic has to master. Cf. N. A. Van Uchelen, "Ethical Terminology in Heykhalot-Texts," in *Tradition and Re-Interpretation in Jewish and Early Christian Literature: Essays in Honour of Jürgen C. H. Lebram*, ed. J. W. Van Henten, H. J. De Jonge, P. T. Van Rooden, and J. W. Wesselius (Leiden, 1986), p. 256.

5   Cf. Schäfer, "The Aim and Purpose," pp. 285-89; Halperin, *The Faces of the Chariot*, pp. 370-75.

6   Cf. P. Bloch, "Die *Yorede Merkavah*, die Mystiker der Gaonenzeit, und ihr Einfluss auf die Liturgie," *Monatsschrift für Geschichte und Wissenschaft des Judenthums* 37 (1893): 25. Cf. Gruenwald, *Apocalyptic*, p. 145, n. 15, where the author explains that the current usage of the verb "to descend" in the *hekhalot* literature means "to enter into the trance of the Merkavah experience." For a criticism of Bloch's view, see *Major Trends*, p. 359, n. 23.

7   G. Scholem, *Jewish Gnosticism, Merkabah Mysticism and Talmudic Tradition* (New York, 1965), p. 20, n. 1. Cf. *Major Trends*, p. 47. Concerning this expression, cf. I. Elbogen, *Der Jüdische Gottesdienst in seiner geschichtlichen Entwicklung* (Leipzig, 1913), pp. 469-76, and 575, n. 1; E. Levy, *Yesodot ha-Tefillah* (Tel Aviv, 1947), pp. 79-82. See also the use of the Aramaic idiom *naḥeit qammeih* in B. Megillah 25a. It is noteworthy that in one place, *Kabbalah*, p. 6, Scholem offers an entirely different explanation, suggesting that the expression *yoredei merkavah* "means those who reach down into themselves in order to perceive the chariot." To the best of my knowledge scholars have not taken sufficient note of this view expressed by Scholem.

8   Gruenwald, *From Apocalypticism to Gnosticism*, pp. 170-73. See, however, Gruenwald's earlier view mentioned above, n. 6. In a private letter to me Ithamar Gruenwald emphasized a key difference between his analysis and that of Scholem: whereas the latter explained the expression *yored la-merkavah* in structural terms, the former stressed its functional usage. To cite the relevant text in *From Apocalypticism to Gnosticism*, p. 171: "according to *Hekhalot Rabbati*, the person who is called 'Yored LaMerkavah' is a kind of public emissary or more precisely: a medium entering into a mystical trance, describing to his fellow mystics that which he sees in heaven."

9   I. Chernus, "The Pilgrimage to the Merkavah: An Interpretation of Early Jewish Mysticism," in *Jerusalem Studies in Jewish Thought* 6 (1987): 5 (English section). See also references to Schäfer and Smith given below, n. 17.

10 J. Dan, *Three Types of Ancient Jewish Mysticism*, The Seventh Annual Rabbi Louis Feinberg Memorial Lecture in Judaic Studies (University of Cincinnati, April 26, 1984), p. 34, n. 29; idem, *The Ancient Jewish Mysticism* (Tel Aviv, 1989), p. 60 (in Hebrew).

11 Cf. J. Dan, "Hokhmath ha-'Egoz, its origin and development," *Journal of Jewish Studies* 17 (1967): 73-83; idem, *The Esoteric Theology of Ashkenazi Hasidism* (Jerusalem, 1968), pp. 207-10, 257-58 (in Hebrew); idem, "On the Development of the Text of Hokhmat ha-'Egoz," *'Ale Sefer* 5 (1978): 49-53 (in Hebrew). Concerning this text, see also A. Altmann, *Studies in Religious Philosophy and Mysticism* (Ithaca, 1969), pp. 161-71; and the comprehensive study of A. Farber, "The Concept of the Merkabah in Thirteenth-Century Jewish Esotericism — Sod ha- 'Egoz and its Development" (Ph. D., Hebrew University, 1986; in Hebrew).

12 Cf. Altmann, *Studies*, p. 161.

13 Cf. H. D. Betz, "Fragments from a Catabasis Ritual in a Greek Magical Papyrus," *History of Religions* 19 (1980): 287-95.

14 Cf. G. Stroumsa's review of I. Gruenwald, *Apocalyptic and Merkavah Mysticism* in *Numen* 28 (1981): 108-09. My thanks to Michael Swartz for calling my attention to this reference.

15 *Exodus Rabbah* 23:15.

16 Halperin, *The Faces of the Chariot*, pp. 226-27.

17 Cf. Schäfer, "The Aim and Purpose," p. 281, n. 17; M. Smith, "Observations on Hekhalot Rabbati," in *Biblical and Other Studies*, ed. A. Altmann (Cambridge, MA., 1963), p. 150; idem, "Ascent to the Heavens," p. 412, n. 29. See also Chernus, "The Pilgrimage to the Merkavah," p. 30, n. 36, who suggests that the term "descent" in the *hekhalot* texts, like other terms in rabbinic literature, "is used euphemistically to denote its opposite." And see, most recently, A. Kuyt, "Once Again: Yarad in Hekhalot Literature," *Frankfurter Judaistische Beiträge* 18 (1990): 45-69, who agrees with Scholem that the term *yarad* in this context denotes an outward journey to the *merkavah*, but disagrees with Scholem by arguing that this usage was in fact the more original one which was at some point changed to *'alah*, i.e., ascend. In this context it is of interest to consider the following comment in the Gnostic treatise, *The Three Steles of Seth* (*VII, 5*), 127, in *The Nag Hammadi Library in English*, ed. J. M. Robinson (San Francisco, 1988), p. 401: "For they all bless these [aeons] individually and together. And afterwards they shall be silent. And just as they were ordained, they ascend. After the silence, they descend from the third. They bless the second; after these the first. The way of ascent is the way of descent." It is curious that in this case the ascent from the third to the first of the aeons is described as a descent. The particular formulation of this text reminds one of the famous remark of Heraclitus reported by Hippolytus, *Refutatio* IX.5: "The way up and down is one and the same." On the possibility that Heraclitus' fragment already dealt with the upward and downward movement of the psyche, see C. H. Kahn, *The Art and Thought of Heraclitus* (Cambridge, 1979), pp. 240-41.

18 See comment of Liebes noted below, n. 33. I do not wish to enter here into the
    larger question if the heavenly ascent is to be construed as veridical or merely
    hallucinatory. On this issue see M. Stone, "Apocalyptic — Vision or Hallucina-
    tion," *Milla wa-Milla* 14 (1974): 47-56. A recent advocate of the second approach
    is D. Halperin. See his "Heavenly Ascension in Ancient Judaism: The Nature of
    the Experience," *SBL 1987 Seminar Papers*, pp. 218-32; *The Faces of the Chariot*,
    pp. 68, 441, 451. Another entirely germane question is to what extent the apoca-
    lyptic and/or mystical texts reflect actual personal experiences of ascent or are
    merely literary accounts. On this issue in the case of Jewish apocalypses, see S.
    Niditch, "The Visionary," in *Ideal Figures in Ancient Judaism*, ed. G. W. E. Nickels-
    burg and J. J. Collins, *Septuagint and Cognate Studies* 12 (Chico, CA, 1980), pp.
    155-63; M. Himmelfarb, "From Prophecy to Apocalypse: The *Book of the Watchers*
    and Tours of Heaven," in *Jewish Spirituality from the Bible through the Middle Ages*,
    ed. A. Green (New York, 1986), pp. 153-54.

19 See the examples collected in Eliezer ben Yehudah, *A Complete Dictionary of
    Ancient and Modern Hebrew*, 8 vols. (Jerusalem, 1959), 3: 2148, s.v. *yarad*; and M.
    Jastrow, *A Dictionary of the Targumim, the Talmud Babli and Yerushalmi, and the
    Midrashic Literature* (New York, 1950), p. 594, s.v. ירד. The same claim can be
    made for the Aramaic root נחת as used in rabbinic sources; cf. M. Sokoloff, *A
    Dictionary of Jewish Palestinian Aramaic of the Byzantine Period* (Bar-Ilan, 1990), p.
    347.

20 Another treatise from this corpus, *Masekhet Hekhalot* ends with a parallel to this
    passage. Cf. *Bet ha-Midrash*, 6 vols., ed. A. Jellinek (Jerusalem, 1967), 2: 47.

21 The word translated as pride is זהיון. Cf. Nathan ben Yehiel, *Aruch Completum*,
    ed. A. Kohut, 8 vols. (Vienna, 1878-1892), 3: 273, s.v. זהיון; E. ben Yehuda, *A
    Complete Dictionary of Ancient and Modern Hebrew*, s.v. זיהיון, 2: 1296. As ben
    Yehuda notes, the term also has the connotation of splendor, which accords with
    the translation of Morton Smith that Ithamar Gruenwald has kindly placed in my
    hands. (I am presently preparing for the Classics of Western Spirituality Series an
    annotated translation of *Hekhalot Rabbati* based on the work of Smith.) In private
    communication Professor Gruenwald reiterated his view that splendor is the
    correct translation of זיהיון. A perusal of the contexts wherein this term appears
    in the *Hekhalot* literature, however, seems to support my translation. Thus, the
    word is coupled with the terms גאוה, גבורה, and רוממה, i.e., pride, power, and
    loftiness. Cf. *Synopse*, §§ 100, 152, 167, 169, 216, 227, 251, 260, 974. See also J.
    Yahalom, *Liturgical Poems of Sim'on bar Megas* (Jerusalem, 1984), p. 85, n. 3 (in
    Hebrew), who renders זהיון as happiness in line with the suggestions of S.
    Lieberman, "Hazanot Yannai," *Sinai* 4 (1939): 245; Z. Ben-Haim, "Samaritan
    Poems for Joyous Occasions," *Tarbiz* 10 (1939): 354, n. 6 (in Hebrew). Cf. J.
    Levy, *Wörterbuch über die Talmudim und Midraschim* (Berlin-Vienna, 1924), 1: 514,
    s.v. זהיינא.

22 Cf. *Synopse* § 164: "Testify to Me concerning the testimony for you see what I do
    to the visage of Jacob, your father which is engraved on my throne of glory." See
    also § 169, and the use of *'edut* in the *Shi'ur Qomah* fragment, § 36 (and § 728).
    Consider too the title of Metatron as the *sara' rabba' de-sahaduta'*, the great angel
    of testimony; cf. M. Cohen, *The Shi'ur Qomah: Liturgy and Theurgy in Pre-*

Kabbalistic Jewish Mysticism (Lanham, 1983), p. 190, n. 3 for discussion and other scholarly references.

23   Isa. 41:8.

24   For another account of testing at the sixth palace from the *Hekhalot Zuṭarti*, that parallels the famous statement in B. Ḥagigah 14b, see Scholem, *Major Trends*, pp. 52-53; *Jewish Gnosticism*, p. 15.   The account of the water episode has been discussed by several scholars; for recent analysis and review of previously expressed views, cf. R. Reichman, "Die 'Wasser-Episode' in der *Hekhalot-*Literatur," *Frankfurter Judaistische Beiträge* 16 (1989): 67-100.

25   Cf. *Synopse*, § 232. For a description of this passage, see Gruenwald, *Apocalyptic*, pp. 166-67.

26   Cf. Elbogen, *Der Jüdische Gottesdienst*, pp. 66-67.   On the relationship of the *qedushah de-yoṣer* to the *qedushah* hymns in the *hekhalot* texts, cf. Bloch, "Die *Yorede Merkavah*" pp. 305-07; A. Altmann, "Liturgical Poems in the Ancient Hekhalot Literature," *Melilah* 2 (1946):   8-10 (in Hebrew).   See also L. A. Hoffman, "Censoring In and Censoring Out: A Function of Liturgical Language," in *Ancient Synagogues: The State of the Research*, ed. J. Gutmann (Chico, Ca., 1981), pp. 19-38.   Cf. M. Bar-Ilan, *The Mysteries of Jewish Prayer and Hekhalot* (Bar-Ilan, 1987), pp. 109-20 (in Hebrew).   For a strikingly close formulation to *qedushah de-yoṣer*, cf. Schäfer, *Geniza-Fragmente*, p. 132.

27   In six of the seven manuscripts utilized by Schäfer the reading here is הפרש, which I have rendered as "recitation." MS Vat 228 reads: פרוש. The translation was suggested by Ithamar Gruenwald in private correspondence. Cf. his *Apocalyptic*, p. 150, where he rendered this expression as "incantations."

28   For references to the notion of angelic language (cf. 1 Cor. 13:1) see, e.g., *1 Enoch* 40; *Ascension of Isaiah* 7:15; *Apocalypse of Abraham* 15:7, 17:1 ff.; and references in rabbinic sources in P. Billerbeck, *Kommentar zum Neuen Testament aus Talmud und Midrasch*, III (Munich, 1926), pp. 449-50. See also P. van der Horst, "The Role of Woman in the Testament of Job," *Essays on the Jewish World of Early Christianity* (Göttingen, 1990), pp. 102-03.

29   The same meaning is implied in other contexts as well; cf. *Synopse*, §§ 108, 204, 218, 672. For a different use of the root *yarad*, see § 123 which should be compared to an aggadic tradition attributed to R. Joshua ben Levi in B. Shabbat 89a that begins: "When Moses descended from before the Holy One, blessed He." See also the *Shiʿur Qomah* fragment, in *Synopse*, § 390: "One Ḥayyah rises above the Seraphim and descends (*yored*) on the tabernacle of the youth [i.e., Metatron; on this expression, see Scholem, *Jewish Gnosticism*, p. 49, n. 20; Cohen, *The Shiʿur Qomah*, pp. 133-34]." See also §§ 399, 488, 961; *Geniza-Fragmente*, p. 117. This imagery is transferred to the letter *kaf* in the *Midrash ʾOtiyyot de-R. ʿAqivaʾ*; cf. *Batte Midrashot*, ed. S. Wertheimer (Jerusalem, 1970), 2: 400.

30   On the technical use of the word סדר in *merkavah* sources, cf. Maier, *Vom Kultus zur Gnosis*, pp. 144-45.

31 Cf. *Synopse*, § 92: לירד ולעלות במרכבה. See, by contrast, ibid., §§ 422-23, where one finds the expression מידת עליית וירידת מרכבה, "the quality [or practice] of ascending and descending the Throne."

32 Cf. the various liturgical formulae in P. Berakhot 9:4.

33 For the variant readings, see S. Lieberman, *Tosefta Ki-Fshutah*, Part V: Order Mo'ed (New York, 1962), p. 1290, n. 21; see also Halperin, *The Merkabah in Rabbinic Literature* (New Haven, 1980), p. 92. Cf. *Synopse*, §§ 345, 672. Cf. Y. Liebes, "The Messiah of the Zohar," in *The Messianic Idea in Jewish Thought: A Study Conference in Honour of the Eightieth Birthday of Gershom Scholen*, (Jerusalem, 1982), pp. 154-55, n. 240, who likewise suggested that the locution *'alah we-yarad* semantically equals *nikhnas we-yaṣa'*, i.e., entered and departed.

34 In § 199 the descenders to the chariot, *yoredei merkavah*, are compared to a man "who has a ladder in his house upon which he ascends and descends" (see also § 237). The locution here may be due to the influence of the description of the angels ascending and descending upon the ladder beheld by Jacob (cf. Gen. 28:12). And cf. the usage of this image in *Seder Rabbah di-Bereshit*, §§ 436, 847, where it is said that the angels are "ascending and descending" upon ladders made by God, ascending to give praise and utter song and descending to propagate peace in the world. See also the mention of the "seal through which they [the angels] ascend and descend" in §§ 384, 485, 729, 957.

35 The more standard way of interpreting the expression employed at the beginning of *Hekhalot Rabbati* is to explain that the *yeridah* refers to the ascent to the chariot and the *'aliyyah* to the descent from the heavenly realm. See, e.g., Dan, *The Ancient Jewish Mysticism*, pp. 63-64.

36 Cf. M. Swartz, *Mystical Prayer in Ancient Judaism: An Analysis of Ma'aseh Merkavah* (Tübingen, 1991), p. 103.

37 The text was published by Scholem in *Jewish Gnosticism*, pp. 101-26, and so-named on the basis of various medieval authorities who referred to the text using this title. See also Schäfer, "Tradition and Redaction in Hekhalot Literature," in *Hekhalot-Studien*, p. 13. Prior to Scholem excerpts of this text, without the title *Ma'aseh Merkavah*, were published by Altmann, "Liturgical Poems," pp. 1-24.

38 For a fuller description of this section, cf. Swartz, *Mystical Prayer in Ancient Judaism*, pp. 95-99.

39 Cf. Swartz, *Mystical Prayer in Ancient Judaism*, p. 81, n. 4, who remarks that the term "secret" (*raz*) in *Ma'aseh Merkavah* denotes "incantation or praxis." Underlying this meaning is the identification of *raz* as the divine names, or the Torah in its mystical sense which is made up of the letters of the divine names, a usage widely attested in the *hekhalot* literature as well as other mystical and magical sources. Cf. *Synopse*, §§ 79, 166, 292, 293, 294, 297, 499, 563, 569, 572, 586, 593, 655, 657, 823; and extended discussion in M. Idel, "The Concept of Torah in Hekhalot and its Development in Kabbalah," *Jerusalem Studies in Jewish Thought* 1 (1981): 24-36 (in Hebrew). On the use of the word *raz* in *hekhalot* literature, see also Elior, "The Concept of God," pp. 35-37; Schäfer, "The Aim and Purpose,"

pp. 291-92. On the technique of employing the name in *Ma'aseh Merkavah* see the discussion in N. Janowitz, *The Poetics of Ascent: Theories of Language in a Rabbinic Ascent Text* (Albany, 1989), pp. 83-99.

40 On the theurgic connotation of the word *lehishtammesh*, see Scholem, *Major Trends*, p. 358, n. 17.

41 Cf. *Synopse*, § 569.

42 The Hebrew reads: והיה רוח לכל אברי. For an alternative translation, see Swartz, *Mystical Prayer in Ancient Judaism*, p. 95: "there was safety for all my limbs." See also Janowitz, *The Poetics of Ascent*, p. 56.

43 *Synopse*, § 544: "R. Ishmael said, I asked R. Aqiva about the prayer that a person recites when he ascends to the chariot."

44 Cf. ibid., §§ 545, 546, 595. An exception to this usage is to be found in § 565 where PNQRS, the Angel of the Countenance says to R. Ishmael: "Descend (רד) and see that if anyone like you descends (ירד) without permission of PNQRS, Lord, God of Israel, he will be killed." In this context the *yeridah* is a *terminus technicus* for the mystical praxis, although it is difficult to ascertain if it names the heavenly ascent in general or the culminating stage of the ascent. Cf. Swartz, *Mystical Prayer in Ancient Judaism*, p. 84.

45 In this context it is of interest to mention the following statement in *Sefer ha-Bahir*, ed. R. Margaliot (Jerusalem, 1978), § 88: המסתכל בצפיית המרכבה ירד ואחר כך יעלה, which I would render: "The one who contemplates the vision of the chariot enters and afterwards departs." See ibid., § 68: "Whoever turns his mind away from worldly matters and contemplates the chariot." Concerning the former passage, cf. Bloch, "Die *Yorede Merkavah*," pp. 22-24. For a later theosophic reading of this bahiric text, see J. Gikatilla, *Sha'are 'Orah*, ed. J. Ben-Shlomo (Jerusalem, 1981), 2: 95. See also Abraham ben Eliezer Halevi, *'Iggeret Sod ha-Ge'ulah*, MS JTSA Mic. 1697, fol. 32b, who describes those who master the spiritual realities as "ascending to heaven and entering the chariot," ויעלו שמים וירדו למרכבה. To be sure, in the continuation of this very passage Abraham Halevi discusses a gradual ascent from grade to grade in the palaces. Yet, it is instructive that the expression "they ascended to heaven" is immediately followed by, according to my reading, the claim that they entered the realm of the chariot.

46 Schäfer, *Geniza-Fragmente*, p. 105; cf. Halperin, *The Faces of the Chariot*, pp. 369-70. The text was first published by I. Gruenwald, "New Fragments from the Hekhalot Literature," *Tarbiz* 38 (1968-69): 356-64 (in Hebrew).

47 *Geniza-Fragmente*, p. 103.

48 Ibid.

49 Ibid.

50 No specific type of transgression is specified but only the generic term for sin, עבירה. It is possible, however, that this word connotes especially sexual immoral-

ity. For this usage in rabbinic literature, see, e.g., B. Sanhedrin, 70a; *Genesis Rabbah* 90:3, ed. Theodor-Albeck, p. 1102. Mention should also be made of the talmudic expression הרהור עבירה which is to be rendered as "sexual fantasy;" cf. B. Berkahot 12b; Yoma 29a (and see commentary of Rashi ad loc., s.v. הרהורי עבירה, which he interprets as "lust for women"). Finally, mention should be made of the parallel passage in *Hekhalot Rabbati* (*Synopse*, § 199) where sins of incestuous and adulterous relations (גילוי עריות) are specified as one class of actions from which the descender to the throne must be purified. Cf. ibid., § 686.

51 *Geniza-Fragmente*, p. 105.

52 Cf. *Synopse*, § 682. According to MS Oxford, Neubauer 1531, Zehubadiah is given as a name of Metaṭron who is frequently designated as the youth (see n. 57).

53 The text as transcribed in Schäfer, *Geniza-Fragmente*, p. 105, reads here: בחי ??. I have suggested to complete the last two letters as קו, thus making the word, בחיקו, i.e., in His bosom. Cf. Gruenwald, "New Fragments," p. 363, who suggested: בח[ן]ימ[ה]. My suggested reconstruction is based on similar expressions in other *hekhalot* texts; cf. *Synopse*, §§ 122, 417.

54 For the use of the term מושב in the sense of seat, see, e.g., 1 Sam. 20:25; M. Kelim 1:5.

55 I have restored the text according to the suggestion of Gruenwald, "New Fragments," p. 363.

56 *Geniza-Fragmente*, p. 105.

57 Cf. Gruenwald, "New Fragments," p. 362, n. 13. On the use of the term "youth" (נער) as a name for Metaṭron, see Scholem, *Jewish Gnosticism*, pp. 49-50; Halperin, *The Faces of the Chariot*, pp. 421-27.

58 Cf. J. Strugnell, "The Angelic Liturgy at Qumran—4Q Serek Sîrôt 'Olat Hassabbat," *Suppl. To Vetus Testamentum*, VII (1959): 336-37; L. H. Schiffman, "Merkavah Speculation at Qumran: The 4Q Serekh Shirot 'Olat Ha-Shabbat," in *Mystics, Philosophers, and Politicians: Essays in Jewish Intellectual History in Honor of Alexander Altmann*, ed. J. Reinharz and D. Swetschinski (Durham, 1982), pp. 34-35 (Schiffman translates the key expression as "His glorious throne"); C. Newsom, *Songs of Sabbath Sacrifice: A Critical Edition* (Atlanta, 1985), pp. 303-306 (Newsom translates: "His glorious seat"). For another important Qumran text (4QM) where reference is made to sitting above upon a throne, see below, n. 65.

59 Schiffman, op. cit., pp. 38-39; Newsom, op. cit., pp. 314-315. See also M. Bar-Ilan, "The Throne of God: What is Under It, What is Opposite It, What is Near It," *Da 'at* 15 (1985): 30, n. 58 (in Hebrew).

60 For references, see Scholem, *Jewish Gnosticism*, p. 28, n. 18.

61 Cf. *Sefer ha-Razim*, ed. M. Margalioth (Jerusalem, 1966), p. 109; *Sefer Raziel* (Amsterdam, 1701), fol. 40a (there the reading is מושב יקרו); S. Musajoff, *Merkavah Shelemah* (Jerusalem, 1921), fol. 42b.

62 P. Schäfer, "Die Beschwörung des sar ha-panim. Edition und Übersetzung,"
    Frankfurter Judaistische Beiträge 6 (1978): 107-45, reprinted in *Hekhalot-Studien*,
    pp. 118-53.

63 Gruenwald, "New Fragments," p. 369; *Geniza-Fragmente*, p. 185.

64 For exceptions, see *Synopse*, §§ 40, 274, 499.

65 The possibility of heavenly enthronement in a Qumran text has recently been
    proposed by M. Smith, "Ascent to the .Heavens and Deification in 4QM," in
    *Archaeology and History in the Dead Sea Scrolls: The New York University Conference
    in Memory of Yigael Yadin*, ed. L. Schiffman (Sheffield, England, 1990), pp. 181-88.
    The critical text as reconstructed by Smith reads as follows: "[El 'Elyon gave me a
    seat among] those perfect forever, a mighty throne in the congregation of the
    gods . . . And none shall be exalted save me, nor shall come against me. For I
    have taken my seat in the [congregation] in the heavens . . . I shall be reckoned
    with gods and established in the holy congregation" (p. 184).

66 Cf. *Synopse*, §§ 1, 126, 172, 216, 251, 260, 306, 558, 565, 585, 882. Occasional
    exceptions are to be found as well; cf. §§ 81, 680.

67 A possible third theme is suggested by the fact that the utterance of song and
    praises before God is considered to be a kind of testimony; see esp. § 216. The
    necessity for witnesses to stand is standard judicial procedure according to
    rabbinic law; cf. B. Shevu'ot 30b.

68 Cf. M. Berakhot 5:1. To be sure, as I. Gruenwald has reminded me, the verb
    עמד, to stand, is already employed in some biblical contexts in a liturgical sense.
    See, e.g., Deut. 10:8, 18:5; 1 Kings 8:11; 2 Chron. 5:4, 29:11.

69 Cf. *Masekhet Soferim*, ed. M. Higger (Jerusalem, 1970), 16:9, p. 295. In this
    connection it is of interest to note the technical use of the expression מעומד, i.e.,
    in a standing position, in a statement in one of the *hekhalot* texts published by
    Schäfer in *Geniza-Fragmente*, p. 167: "This is the seal of R. Ishmael, it should only
    be recited when standing." In the printed text the word מעומד was transcribed as
    משומר (misreading the *'ayin* as a *shin* and the *dalet* as a *resh*), though it is evident
    from inspecting the manuscript that the correct reading is the former. In
    Schäfer's *Konkordanz zur Hekhalot-Literature* (Tübingen, 1988), 2: 526, s.v.,
    עמד, the mistake in transcription has been corrected.

70 The description of the angels as beings who stand is based on biblical statements
    and is reflected in later Jewish and Christian literature. Cf. 1 Kings 22:19; Isa.
    6:2; Zech. 3:4, 7; Job 1:6; Dan. 7:10; Tob. 12:15 (the long recension); Rev. 5:11;
    Ascension of Isaiah 7:14-16; P. Berakhot 1:1; B. Berakhot 10b; Hagigah 15b; *Zohar*
    2:170a, 241b; 3:260a. For counter-examples where angels are described as sitting
    on thrones, see below, n. 80.

71 On the use of expressions related to לעמוד בתפילה, cf. *Synopse*, §§ 1, 132, 143, 320
    (MS Budapest 238), 565, 682. See also §§ 126, 557. On the use of the word
    עמוד to describe the status of angelic beings, cf. §§ 8, 20, 28, 29, 30, 40, 42, 45,
    50, 52, 55, 144, 180, 183, 219, 220, 222, 242, 276, 306, 327, 384, 420, 469, 485,

505, 550, 569, 587, 623, 749, 785, 813, 881, 957; *Geniza-Fragmente*, pp. 105, 142, 143, 151, 153, 156.

72   Cf. §§ 43, 54, 58, 146, 406, 440 (MS Oxford, Neubauer 1531), 546, 558, 592, 714, 745.   In this context it is of interest to consider the statement in the longer recension of *2 Enoch* 22:2 to the effect that there were "choir stalls" surrounding God (*The Old Testament Pseudepigrapha* [hereafter: *TOTP*], ed. J. H. Charlesworth [New York, 1983], 1:136).

73   With regard to this notion there are precedents in Jewish apocalyptic literature as well. See, e.g., *2 Enoch* 22:6 (*TOTP* 1: 138-39). From the context it is abundantly clear that the mortal Enoch is transformed into an angel.

74   In an anonymous fragment in the *hekhalot* corpus sitting down before God is placed in an eschatological context: the one who does not misuse knowledge of the divine names is guaranteed that he will "inherit the Garden of Eden and will sit before [God] like a disciple before his master" (§§ 500, 712). On the notion of a throne for the righteous in the celestial Paradise, cf. *1 Enoch* 108:12; *Apocalypse of Elijah* 1:8, *Ascension of Isaiah* 9:9-10, 24-25 (see also 7:22 where the specific throne for Isaiah "above all heavens and their angels" is mentioned); Rev. 4:4, 20:4 (cf. A. Feuillet, *Johannine Studies*, tr. T. E. Crane [New York, 1965], pp. 182-214; other scholars reject the claim that the twenty-four elders refer to the righteous and suggest that they represent the angelic attendants who surround the throne of God; cf. C. Rowland, *The Open Heaven: A Study of Apocalyptic in Judaism and Ancient Christianity* [New York, 1982], p. 224, and other references on p. 481, n. 24; according to Rev. 3:21 the righteous, or "those who conquer," are said to be granted to sit on the throne of the Son just as the latter sat on the throne of the Father); *'Avot de-R. Natan*, version A, chap. 1, ed. S. Schechter (Vienna, 1887), p. 5 and B. Berakhot 17a (no throne is mentioned in these contexts but the righteous are described in the World-to-Come as sitting with crowns on their heads and being sustained by the splendor of the *Shekhinah*); *Midrash Konen*, in *Bet ha-Midrash*, ed. A. Jellinek (Jerusalem, 1967), vol. 2, p. 29; *Midrash Gedullat Mosheh* in *Batte Midrashot*, 1:284-85; *Midrash 'Otiyyot de-R. 'Aqiva*, in ibid., 2:375: "each and every one [of the righteous in Paradise] sits like a king on a throne of gold;" *'Alfa' beita' shel Metatron*, published by I. Weinstock, *Temirin*, vol. 2 (Jerusalem, 1981), p. 69: "whoever humbles himself in this world merits to sit in Paradise on a golden throne with stones of the finest gold, in the company of King David and Jacob our patriarch, who humbled themselves in this world . . . Jacob merited to be engraved upon the throne of glory and David merited that his throne was set alongside the throne of glory." Concerning David's throne, see below, n. 77; on the motif of Jacob's image engraved on the throne, see E. Wolfson, "The Image of Jacob Engraved on the Throne: Further Speculation on the Esoteric Teaching of the German Pietists" (in Hebrew), *Efraim Gottlieb Memorial Volume* (forthcoming). See also the tradition of the twelve thrones set up for the apostles in order to judge the twelve tribes of Israel in Mt. 19:28 and Lk. 22:30, which should be compared to *Tanḥuma'*, Qedoshim, 1, where the "great men of Israel" are said to sit on thrones (derived exegetically from the plural "thrones" in Dan 7:9) so that they will judge the nations of the world together with God. (Cf. the tradition in the Falasha text *Tĕ'ĕzāza Sanbat* to the effect that God sits upon twelve thrones in order to judge; cf. *Falasha Anthology*, trans. W.

Leslau [New Haven, 1951], p. 18, and p. 147, n. 99; S. Kaplan, "Tě'ĕzāza Sanbat: A Beta Israel Work Reconsidered," in *Gilgul: Essays on Transformation, Revolution and Permanence in the History of Religions Dedicated to R. J. Zwi Werblowsky*, ed. S. Shaked, D. Shulman, G. G. Stroumsa [Leiden, 1987], p. 119.) According to another rabbinic tradition, which had a significant impact upon subsequent Jewish thought, the souls of the righteous are said to be hidden under the throne of glory; see B. Shabbat 152b; *Midrash Debarim Rabbah*, ed. S. Lieberman (Jerusalem, 1964), p. 131.

75 Cf. Idel, *Kabbalah: New Perspectives*, p. 89. Cf. the description of Jesus in the *Gospel of Bartholomew* I, 31-32, where he is said to be simultaneously sitting at the right hand of God (cf. Mt. 22:44 [= Mk. 12:36, Lk. 20:42-43] and 26:64 [= Mk. 14:62; Lk. 22:69] based on Ps. 110:1; see below, n. 90) and teaching the apostles on earth; cf. *New Testament Apocrypha*, ed. W. Schneemelcher, Eng. trans. ed. R. Mcl. Wilson (Phila., 1963), 1: 491.

76 In four of the seven manuscripts published by Schäfer the reading is ליתוק which is the Hebrew corruption of the Greek λιθιχος which means "of stone." Cf. Gruenwald, *Apocalyptic*, p. 166.

77 Cf. Tabor, *Things Unutterable*, pp. 88-89, who discusses this passage from *Hekhalot Rabbati* and duly notes the importance of the enthronement motif. See, by contrast, the description of David in an apocalyptic section which has clearly been appended to the main body of *Hekhalot Rabbati*: "He came and sat on his throne, set parallel to the throne of his Creator . . . David immediately rose and uttered songs and praises that no ear had ever heard" (§ 126). On David's throne see further B. Sanhedrin 38b, *Lamentations Rabbah*, Petihta 23, ed. S. Buber (Vilna, 1899), p. 18; M. Bar-Ilan, "The Throne of God," pp. 30-31. It is likely that the legends concerning David's throne are connected with the view that he is the Messiah; cf. L. Ginzberg, *The Legends of the Jews* (Phila., 1968), 6:272, n. 128. According to *Exodus Rabbah* 14:3 Solomon sat on the divine throne.

78 The connection between enthronement and visionary experience is already evident in the case of the *Exagoge* of Ezekiel the Tragedian, 68-76, where Moses has a vision immediately following his sitting upon the throne. Cf. E. Starobinski-Safran, "Un poète judéo-hellénistique: Ezechiel le tragique," *Museum Helveticum* 31 (1974): 216-24; for other references, see below, n. 87. In this context it is also of interest to note the eschatological tradition found in rabbinic sources, e.g., '*Avot de-Rabbi Natan*, version A, chap. 1 and B. Berakhot 17a, to the effect that in the World-to-Come the righteous sit (!) with their crowns and derive pleasure from the splendor of the *Shekhinah*. That the latter involves a vision of God's Presence is evident from the key prooftext, "They beheld God" (Exod. 24:11). In this case as well, then, the visionary component is related specifically with sitting and not standing.

79 Cf. Smith's discussion of 4QM mentioned above, n. 65. Entirely different is the description in the *Sar-Torah* section of *Hekhalot Rabbati* where the divine voice reportedly says to the different rabbis who were standing before the throne of glory: "Rise up and sit before My throne in the way that you sit in the academy, grab the crown and receive the seal, and learn the order of the Torah, how it is

practiced, how it is interpreted, and how one makes use of it" (§ 298). In this case
the sitting is not an enthronement but a reenactment of the appropriate posture
for study. On the question of whether study requires a standing position or one
of sitting, see B. Megillah 21a. Cf. *Midrash Gedullat Mosheh*, in *Batte Midrashot* 1:
280. After having ascended to the throne of glory in the seventh heaven with the
assistance of Metatron (on the links between Moses and Metatron, see Cohen, *The
Shi'ur Qomah*, pp. 135-36; Ch. Mopsik, *Le Livre Hébreu d'Hénoch ou Livre des Palais*
[Paris, 1989], pp. 65-71; Halperin, *The Faces of the Chariot*, pp. 417-27), Moses is
said to have sat down before Zagzagel, the prince of wisdom and Torah, to learn
the ten secrets. (Parenthetically, it will be noted that the name Zagzagel is composed of six consonants with the first two repeating themselves. The last two, *'alef*
and *lamed*, spell the name of God, whereas the combination of the first two, *zayin*
and *gimel*, numerically equals ten. Perhaps there is an allusion in his name to the
ten secrets — which are not specified — or perhaps later exegetes derived the notion
of ten secrets using this numerological method.)   See also the tradition in
Deuteronomy Rabbah 11:10 that Moses learnt the divine name (*shem ha-meforash*)
from Zagzagel. For alternative spellings of this angel's name, see text published in
Bet ha-Midrash, ed. A. Jellinek, 1:120; see also a magical charm for illumination
extant in MS JTSA Mic. 8115, fols. 133b-134a; and the statement of R. Eleazar of
Worms, Paris, Bibliothèque Nationale, MS héb. 850, fol. 122a. Cf. R. Margaliot,
Mal'akhe 'Elyon (Jerusalem, 1988), pp. 54-55.

80   On the image of enthroned angels, cf. *Apocalypse of Zephaniah*, cited in Clement,
Stromata 5.11.77 (English translation in *TOTP*, 1:508); *Ascension of Isaiah* 7:13
(according to the second Latin and Slavonic versions; see *TOTP*, 2:166). Related
to this notion is the technical use of the word "thrones" to refer to a class of
angels. Cf. Col. 1:16; *2 Enoch* 20:1 (the longer recension); *Testament of Levi* 3:8;
Ascension of Isaiah 7:21; *Apocalypse of Elijah* 1:10, 4:10; *Testament of Adam* 4:8. For
a discussion of angels sitting upon thrones in the apocalyptic literature, with
special reference to *Ascension of Isaiah*, cf. Gruenwald, *Apocalyptic*, pp. 59-60. See
also *Exodus Rabbah* 25:2, where the angels' sitting and standing, as well as various
other traits, is made subordinate to God's will. On sitting on a heavenly throne as
an endowment of spiritual powers, see *The Teachings of Silvanus* (*VII, 4*), 80, 20-90,
2, in *The Nag Hammadi Library in English* p. 383. Concerning this work, see J.
Zandee, "'The Teachings of Silvanus' (NHC VII, 4) and Jewish Christianity," in
*Studies in Gnosticism and Hellenistic Religions presented to Gilles Quispel on the
Occasion of his 65th Birthday*, ed. R. Van den Broek and M. J. Vermaseren (Leiden,
1981), pp. 498-584, esp. 507-08.

81   *Sefer ha-Razim*, p. 92.

82   Ibid., p. 101.

83   For a discussion of this passage, see E. Ginsburg, *The Sabbath in the Classical
Kabbalah* (Albany, 1989), pp. 103-04.

84   *Bet ha-Midrash*, ed. Jellinek, 2:46.

85   Cf. Odeberg, *3 Enoch*, pp. 136-38; Lieberman's appendix to Gruenwald, op. cit.,
pp. 235-41.

86 On the highest status accorded to sitting, see *Exodus Rabbah* 23:1.

87 See reference above, n. 78; cf. Gruenwald, *Apocalyptic*, pp. 128-30; G. Quispel, "Judaism, Judaic Christianity and Gnosis," in *The New Testament and Gnosis: Essays in Honour of Robert McL. Wilson*, ed. A. H. B. Logan and A. J. M. Wedderburn (Edinburgh, 1983), pp. 48-49; P. W. van Der Horst, "Moses' Throne Vision in Ezekiel the Dramatist," *Journal of Jewish Studies* 34 (1983): 21-29, esp. 24-27; idem, "Some Notes on the Exagoge of Ezekiel," *Mnemosyne* 37 (1984): 354-75. Both papers have been reprinted in P. W. van der Horst, *Essays on the Jewish World of Early Christianity* (Göttingen, 1990), pp. 63-93. Cf. H. Jacobson, "Mysticism and Apocalyptic in Ezekiel the Tragedian," *Illinois Classical Studies* 6 (1981): 272-93; idem, *The Exagoge of Ezekiel* (Cambridge, 1983). See also the traditions concerning Moses' enthronement in apocalyptic, rabbinic and Samaritan sources discussed by W. A. Meeks, *The Prophet-King* (Leiden, 1967), pp. 147-49, 184-85, 232-38, 243; idem, "Moses as God and King," in *Religions in Antiquity: Essays in Memory of Erwin Ramsdell Goodenough*, ed. J. Neusner (Leiden, 1970), pp. 354-59. And cf. *Midrash Tannaïm zum Deuteronomium*, ed. D. Hoffmann (Berlin, 1909), p. 19, where Moses' level is contrasted with that of the ministering angels insofar as he was allowed to sit before God and they could only stand. See also B. Megillah 21b. On Moses' dwelling under the throne of glory, cf. *Deuteronomy Rabbah* 11:10. Mention should also be made of another ancient legend concerning Moses' saving himself from the hostile angels by holding on to the throne of God. Cf. *Exodus Rabbah* 42:4; B. Shabbat 88a; Ginzberg, *Legends* 5:417, n. 117; 6:46, n. 247, 53, n. 273. For other traditions regarding Moses' enthronement, cf. M. Bar-Ilan, "Moses' Stone, Seat and Cathedra," *Sidra* 2 (1986): 15-23 (in Hebrew).

88 Cf. Sirach 24:4 where Wisdom is said to dwell in the heavens and its throne to be in a pillar of cloud. See also *1 Enoch* 84:3; *On the Origin of the World* 105:30 (*The Nag Hammadi Library in English*, p. 176); Ireneaus, *Against Heresies*, 1.13.6. For the development of this motif in the medieval period, including iconographic evidence, cf. H. Adolf, "The Figure of Wisdom in the Middle Ages," *Actes du quatrième congrès international de philosophie médiévale, 4th, Montreal, 1967: Arts libéraux et philosophie au moyen âge* (Montreal, 1969), pp. 429-43.

89 Cf. *1 Enoch* 71:14-17. The account of Enoch is probably based on the description of one "like a human being" (lit., "son of man") in Dan. 7:13 who was said to have "reached the Ancient of Days" (who in 7:9 is described as sitting on a fiery throne) and to be "presented to Him." It says further (ibid., 14) that "dominion, glory, and kingship" were given to this man, but it does not say explicitly that he sat on a throne. On the other hand, in 7:9 the plural form "thrones" is used and this may imply that one throne was for the Ancient of Days and the other for the son of man.

90 See also *Ascension of Isaiah* 11:32 and Eusebius, *Historia Ecclesiastica*, II. xxiii. 13. Cf. D. Flusser, "Melchizedek and the Son of Man," in *Judaism and the Origins of Christianity* (Jerusalem, 1988), pp. 27-28; D. M. Hay, *Glory at the Right Hand: Psalm 110 in Early Christianity* (Nashville, 1983). The Christian interpretation of Ps. 110:1 is evident in the Nag Hammadi text, *On the Origin of the World*, which in one context describes Sabaoth as being surrounded by a being called Jesus Christ

on a throne to his right and the virgin of the holy spirit on a throne to his left (*The Nag Hammadi Library in English*, p. 176). Cf. Gruenwald, *Apocalyptic*, p. 186. In yet another Gnostic text, clearly related to the former, *The Hypostasis of the Archons* Sophia (Wisdom) is said to take her daughter, Zoe (Life), and to have her sit to the right of Sabaoth with the angel of wrath upon his left (*The Nag Hammadi Library in English*, p. 168). On the relation of this text to merkavah mysticism, see Gruenwald, *From Apocalypticism to Gnosticism*, pp. 196-200. The similarity between the description of Jesus as God's viceregent sitting on a throne and the description of Metatron has been noted by scholars; see, e.g., D. Neumark, *Toledot ha-Pilosfiyah be-Yira'el* (New York, 1921) 1: 74; A. Murtonen, "The Figure of Metatrôn ," *Vetus Testamentum 3* (1953): 409-11; G. G. Stroumsa, "Form(s) of God: Some Notes on Metatron and Christ," *Harvard Theological Review* 76 (1983): 281-88.

91   Cf. Gruenwald, *Apocalyptic*, pp. 66-67.

92   For references, see above, n. 74.

93   See *'Aggadat Bereshit*, ed. S. Buber (Cracow, 1903), ch. 18, p. 37, where Abraham is described as the סונקנדריס of God seated on His right side. (On the midrashic tradition of Abraham being God's advisor, סונקתדרין, see also *Genesis Rabbah* 49:2, ed. Theodor-Albeck, p. 500; elsewhere Moses' relation to God is compared parabolically to an advisor [סוקתדרו] to the king; cf. *Exodus Rabbah* 43:1). Cf. Bar-Ilan, "The Throne of God," p. 31, who notes that the word סינקתידרין or, in its more corrupt form, סונקדריס, is obviously based on two Greek words, the preposition συν (along with) and the noun καθεδρα (seat). The notion of Abraham's occupying a throne to the right of God is also implied in *Midrash Tehillim* 110:1.

94   See above, n. 77.

95   *Genesis Rabbah* 8:9 (ed. Theodor-Albeck, p. 63).

96   Cf. Gruenwald, *Apocalyptic*, p. 239.

97   Ibid., pp. 239-40.

98   Cf. M. Idel, "Enoch is Metatron," *Jerusalem Studies in Jewish Thought* 6 (1987): 153 and 164, n. 18 (in Hebrew; French translation, "Hénoch c'est Metatron," in Mopsik, *Le Livre Hébreu d'Hénoch*, p. 387).

99   *Genesis Rabbah* 65: 21, ed. Theodor-Albeck, p. 738; B. Hagigah 15a; *Midrash Tehillim*, 1; *Tanhuma'*, ed. Buber, Beshallah, 13; Qedoshim, 6; *Exodus Rabbah* 43:4.

100   *Genesis Rabbah* 65:21; P. Berakhot 1:1; *Leviticus Rabbah* 6:3 (with respect only to angels of destruction); *Midrash Debarim Rabbah*, ed. S. Lieberman, p. 68.

101   See also *Synopse*, § 672. In that case it is difficult to maintain that the thrust of the polemic is against Metatron's sitting inasmuch as the reading is: "above there is no standing and no sitting," suggesting that angelic beings neither sit nor stand. A similar reading is attested in B. Hagigah 15b as well; cf. Rashi ad loc., s.v.,

לא עמידה; Maimonides, *Mishneh Torah, Hilkhot Yesode Torah*, 1:11. On the other hand, it is difficult to maintain the view that angels do not stand as the overwhelming evidence is that this is their unique property. See reference to Liebes' study in following note.

102 Cf. A. Segal, *Two Powers in Heaven* (Leiden, 1977), pp. 60-67. For a different interpretation of this legend, see Y. Liebes, *The Sin of Elisha, The Four Who Entered Paradise, and the Nature of Talmudic Judaism*, 2nd ed. (Jerusalem, 1990), pp. 29-34 (in Hebrew).

103 Paris, MS Bibliothèque Nationale, héb. 850, fol. 83b.

104 *Exodus Rabbah* 43:4.

105 Cf. M. Black, "The Throne-Theophany, Prophetic Commission and the 'Son of Man': A Study in Tradition-History," in *Jews, Greeks and Christians Religious Cultures in Late Antiquity: Essays in Honor of William David Davies*, ed. R. Hamerton-Kelly and R. Scroggs (Leiden, 1976), pp. 56-72. On the ancient Jewish concept of the transformation of human beings into angels, see J. H. Charlesworth, "The Portrayal of the Righteous as an Angel," in *Ideal Figures in Ancient Judaism*, ed. G. W. E. Nickelsburg and J. J. Collins, pp. 135-51. See also the instructive summary by van der Horst, "Some Notes on the Exagoge of Ezekiel," p. 82: "In early post-biblical Judaism there was, in some circles, a tradition in which the highest angel, called 'the angel of the Lord' in the Old Testament, was seen as God's primary or sole helper and allowed to share in God's divinity. It was part of this tradition that a human being, as the hero or exemplar of a particular group, could ascend to become one with this figure, as Enoch or Moses. So these angelic mediators often began as humans and later achieved a kind of divine status in some communities. They had charge over the world and became close to being anthropomorphic hypostases of God himself."

106 Cf. *Major Trends*, pp. 55-56.

107 The divinization of the one who ascends to the chariot is also evident from the description in *Hekhalot Rabbati* of the knowledge granted to such a person as a result of the mystical experience; cf. *Synopse*, §§ 81-86; Dan, *The Ancient Jewish Mysticism*, pp. 64-66.

108 Quispel, "Judaism, Judaic Christianity and Gnosis," pp. 53-54. Other examples of deification through vision are supplied by Quispel, op. cit., pp. 55-58. In this context it is of interest to consider the description in the Nag Hammadi text, *Trimorphic Protennoia* 45:13, in *The Gnostic Scriptures*, ed. B. Layton (New York, 1987), p. 97: "When you enter it [the superior, perfect light] you will be glorified by the glorifiers; the enthroners will give you thrones; you will be given robes by the enrobers, and the baptists will baptize you; so that along with glories you become the glory in which you existed, luminous, in the beginning." See also *Zostrianos (VIII, 1)*, 5, 15, in *The Nag Hammadi Library in English*, p. 405: "I was baptized there, and I received the image of the glories there. I became like one of them."

109 Schäfer, "The Aim and Purpose," p. 286.

110   I am thus in agreement with the following observation of Gruenwald, "Literary
      and Redactional Issues in the Study of the Hekhalot Literature," in *From
      Apocalypticism to Gnosticism*, p. 184: "The main aim of Merkavah mysticism still
      seems to me to be the vision of God." This represents a modification of
      Gruenwald's earlier view; cf. *Apocalyptic*, p. 94: "Despite the daring modes of
      expression one can find in that [Hekhalot] literature about the contents of the
      mystical experience, the possibility of a direct visual encounter with God is
      generally ruled out." On the centrality of visionary experience in the *hekhalot*
      texts, see also I. Chernus, "Visions of God in Merkabah Literature," *Journal for the
      Study of Judaism* 13 (1982): 123-46. See I. Gruenwald, "The Impact of Priestly
      Traditions on the Creation of Merkabah Mysticism and the Shi'ur Komah,"
      Jerusalem Studies in Jewish Thought 6 (1987): 105, n. 7 (in Hebrew), where the
      author explicitly acknowledges the correctness of Chernus' critique (I thank I.
      Gruenwald for reminding me of this passage). See also Smith's observation with
      respect to the heavenly ascent narratives in general in "Ascent to the Heavens," p.
      410. For a different approach by Schäfer, see now his *The Hidden and Manifest
      God: Some Major Themes in Early Jewish Mysticism* (Albany, 1992), p. 155, n. 19.

111   Leiter, "Worthiness, Acclamation and Appointment," pp. 141-48. Leiter does not
      deal with the interpretations of Exod. 33:20 attributed respectively to R. Aqiva
      and R. Shimon ben Azzai in *Sifra'* on Leviticus, 1:12, to the effect that neither the
      celestial beasts who bear the throne nor any of the angels can behold the divine
      glory. Cf. *Siphre ad Numeros*, ed. H. S. Horovitz (Jerusalem, 1966), 103, p. 101.
      Such a view would, of course, render problematic the general thesis of Leiter that
      acclamation or praise is predicated on a prior vision. Gruenwald, *Apocalyptic*, p.
      94, maintains that this view is expressed in the *hekhalot* literature as well. He
      mentions, however, only one passage from *Hekhalot Rabbati*, cf. *Synopse*, § 102,
      which may be read in quite a different way; see Chernus, "Visions of God," pp.
      128-29. See, however, *Synopse*, § 183. It must be pointed out that within various
      hekhalot texts there is a genuine tension between the stated goal of beholding the
      divine glory and the inherent dangers ensuing from such an experience. The
      theoretical issue of seeing God is treated explicitly, for instance, in *Hekhalot
      Zuṭarti*; cf. *Synopse*, §§ 350-52.

112   It seems to me that the expression used here to describe God's action, וירד
      במרכבה, reflects the technical term used in the *hekhalot* texts to describe the
      mystic's activity which forms the focus of this study.

113   *Batte Midrashot* 2: 378, cited in slightly different translation by Leiter, "Worthi-
      ness, Acclamation and Appointment," p. 147.

114   Leiter, op. cit., p. 148.

115   Vatican, Biblioteca Apostolica, MS Cod. ebraici 228, fol. 105b. A version of this
      text, with slight textual variants, is found in the prayer book with kabbalistic
      commentary by Naftali Herz Treves, *Mal'ah ha-'Areṣ De'ah* (Tiengen, 1560).
      Concerning this text, and its relationship to Eleazar of Worms, see J. Dan,
      "Ashkenazi Hasidic Commentaries in the Hymn *Ha-'Aderet we-ha-'Emunah*," *Tarbiz*
      50 (1981): 396-404 (in Hebrew).

The Exegetic Elements of the Cosmosophical Work, Sepher Yeṣirah

Asher Finkel

Introduction

In the contemporary scholarship[1], the cosmosophic work, Sepher Yeṣirah, is enigmatic, in view of its particular language, style and content. Although it is ascribed to the Tannaitic circle of *yorde merkabah*[2], the nature of the work and its dating remain in question. Does it reflect a Jewish gnostic tradition that incorporated neo-Platonic and Pythagorian ideas, magical and cosmogonic elements of Greek and even Persian origins? However, this diminuitive work enjoyed a prominent place in the proto-mystical tradition of the Geonim and it generated reflective commentaries in Rabbinic and Kabbalistic circles, beginning with Saadiah Gaon and his contemporaries. The book itself was transmitted in two versions, a fate shared by other significant writings.[3] Sepher Yeṣirah influenced the cosmogonic view of the philosophical works of Saadiah and Yehudah Halevi. It became the ground text for early mystical Midrash of the "Bahir" and all other major works of Kabbalah cite it. Sepher Yeṣirah indeed influenced the early Hasidic circles at the turn of the millennium. These circles developed neo-prophetic, mystical and meditative systems that were claimed to be rooted in earlier esoteric tradition.

Contemporary scholarship tends to reject their claim of early roots for the mystical tradition, even though a marked difference exists between exoteric and esoteric transmission. Historically, Sepher Yeṣirah already belonged to the earlier period of the Geonim, but it was viewed as an ancient manual of esoteric wisdom. It is to be traced to the first believer, Abraham, and indeed a pseudonymic ascription marks visionary tradition. The epilogue of Sepher Yeṣirah refers to Abraham, in both versions. Although it enjoyed a Midrashic expansion in the longer version, the exegetic elements about Abraham existed in the end of the work, as found in the original version of Saadiah's commentary. Furthermore, its final statement on Abrahamic dual covenant appears also at the beginning of the work, as will be shown. No wonder that Sepher Yesirah enjoys a common tradition with the Tannaitic *"ma'aseh merkabah"* (the work of the chariot) and *"ma'aseh bereshith"* (the work of creation), while echoing the liturgical formulary of numinous hymns. Its formative historical setting belongs to the early centuries, the period of Jewish apocalypticism.

Exegetic-Cosmosophic Elements

Exegetical elements of cosmosophic tradition appear in Sepher Yeşirah. They are linked with liturgical phraseology of the numinous type, that is replete with God's names and doxological terms. It exhibits, therefore, affinity with the early apocalyptic tradition of theosophy and cosmosophy. The numinous liturgy was associated with angelic hymns, that were marked by repetitive and antiphonal forms of address to God, as the sublime Wholly Other. In early Rabbinic tradition it was connected with the Isaianic *Trishagion* or *Kedushah* service, with its doxological refrains. Such numinous liturgy was known during the latter part of the Second Temple period, as is attested by the writings of Qumran and early Christianity. In Tannaitic times, this liturgy was inserted in the Dawn-prayer of *"Yoṣer 'or"*, displaying correspondence to the angelic praise in Heaven, at that experienced time. The purpose was to relate the numinous to the cosmogonic awareness of morning light in prayer experience. This basileomorphic vision of God in the upper expanse of the cosmos is depicted in the apocalyptic writing of the latter part of the Second Temple period.[4]

Apocalypse does not only offer a disclosure of the End-Time, the historiosophical eschatology. It is, moreover, a disclosure of protology, relating to the works of creation and God's appearance on the Chariot. Such a vision resulted from a meditative reflection and pietistic discipline. Its meditative point of departure[5] was the Holy Scripture, as the case was with Daniel reflecting on Jeremiah's words concerning the seventy years of Babylonian exile (Dan 9:2). In protological disclosure, the points of departure are the account of creation (Gen 1) and the account of the chariot (Ezek 1). Such visions necessitate angelic guidance to interpret the esoteric meanings of letters, numbers and configurations, that are captured in God's words. This is the experience described in Daniel and in Enoch. Thus, angelic guidance marks the proto-mystical writings of Hekhaloth, that depict a mystical ascent of the Tannaim (the *yorde merkabah*). Only in the company of a heavenly guide can the seeker gaze into the works of creation. This is stipulated in Mishnah Hagigah 2,1 and it is corroborated by Origen in his introduction to the Commentary on Canticles.[6]

Apparently Sepher Yeṣirah emerged out of such exegetic cosmosophical reflection, that the early esoteric circles of Provence Ḥasidim recalled in view of their transmitted tradition of meditative practice. This is described in the *"Rokeaḥ"* by R. Eleazar of Worms,[7] a disciple of Rabbi Yehudah the Ḥasid. He also authored a commentary to Sepher Yeṣirah and an exegetical guide to mystical interpretation of the Scriptures and prayers.[8] His account is corroborated by the Nasi Rabbi Yehudah of Barcelona, who was highly acquainted with the Geonic tradition. He also wrote a commentary to Sepher Yesirah. Both cite earlier Geonic sources and variants. They write[9] that Sepher Yeṣirah evolved out of the meditative reflection by Abraham, the first believer. They conclude with the following account: "When Abraham was all alone, meditating on the works of creation but could not comprehend, God appeared to him and told him to seek out a *ḥaver* (a guiding partner), namely Shem, the son of Noah. Together you will gaze and understand and at the end of three years of reflection, you will be able to "sketch" (*laṣur*) the cosmos".

In view of Sepher Yeṣirah, God creates the world through the word in three distinct ways, that are captured in the threefold reading of *sepher, sephor* and *sippur*. These represent the graphic configuration of letters, their numerological value and their spoken form. Rabbi Eleazar of Worms offers the mystical keys of exegesis (*sode raze*), as they open the gates of esoteric knowledge in the reflection of God's words of the Torah. According to his view, the meditative exercises that are defined in Sepher Yeṣirah of *"da', haŝov* and *ṣor"*, were practiced by Abraham (as described in the above legend), with regard to the configuration, number and spoken forms of letters.

"Sepher Yeṣirah" is also designated by Nasi Rabbi Yehudah of Barcelona as "Sepher de Otioth of Abraham". This designation recalls a similar ascription to an early medieval work of proto-mystical tradition, that is known as "Sepher Otioth de Rabbi Akiba".[10] This work focuses also on the graphic configuration, the numerological value and speech forms of letters, incorporating exegetic-cosmosophical materials. For this common tradition affected the mystical approach of early Ḥasidim, that gave rise to letter mysticism. The theurgic use of letters, as related to the divine employment of Hebrew alphabet in creation and its corresponding use in building the microcosmic Tabernacle, was known in early Rabbinic times.

The exegetical understanding of a mystical view of letters is connected with multifaceted seeing and hearing the consonantal words, that offer various vocalization, combinations, transpositions and permutations. One word and its relatedness to other words produce many sparks for visionary understanding. Sepher Yeṣirah opens with a similar reading of the Biblical story of creation. The last letter of the Pentateuch is *"lamed"* and the first letter of Genesis is "beth". Together they produce the numerical value of 32.[11] The reading of the opening verse, then becomes *"lb r'š ytbr'"* which means "through 32 (paths) of wisdom was it created." This is the opening line of Sepher Yeṣhirah, which reflects then on the next word of the Biblical text. The word is "Elohim", or God representing creative power, which is employed 32 times in the account of creation. Thus Sepher Yeṣirah relates that there are 32 creative forces. These are represented in the Biblical text by ten references to speech, *vayo'mer* (He spoke), and twenty-two references to becoming *"yehi-vayehi"* (let it become; and it became). Such an exegetical understanding provides the key to Sepher Yeṣirah. The cosmos is issued by ten "sephirot" and it formed by twenty-two letters. Thus, the nine "sephirot" that generate from the Holy Spirit[12] produce the configurations *"'mr"* and *"yhu"*. The first configuration represents the acronym *'eš, Mayim* and *Ruah* (fire, water and air), the primordial forces of God's speech. The second configuration represents six permutations of the graphic letters *"yhw"*, that denote the six vectors of becoming in space. The synchronic reading of the words *"vayo'mer"* and *"yehi-vayehi"* governs the understanding. For this reason, Sepher Yeṣirah does not cite the Biblical verse, as it is found in Rabbinic Midrash. It offers only the resultant visionary reading of the Biblical text. This phenomenon has puzzled the researchers and comes to distinguish between the proto-mystical work and its Midrashic accretions in the epilogue.

The use of God's Name in prayer also elicits exegetic-cosmosophical explanations to insure proper intention (*"kavannah"*) in prayer. Aside from the meditational significance of the six points of *Iaw* (God's Name), Sepher Yeṣirah offers an exegetical account of God's other names. A similar account appears in the interpretative account of the seventy names of God in Midrash Canticle Zuṭṭa. In the longer version of Sepher Yeṣirah, the exegesis ends with a depiction of the *"Kedushah"* service of the angelic hosts. For this concludes the introductory trilogy of praise in daily prayer, which opens with an address to God. This address offers attributes and names that were revealed to Abraham and Moses. Similar names appear in Sepher Yeṣirah and even the doxological refrain is preserved. There is no question that this composition was anchored in the practice of visionaries, who used numinous liturgy.

The Epilogue on Abraham

The apocalyptic backdrop to Sepher Yeṣirah is most striking in the concluding paragraph that describes the epiphanic reply to Abraham's search for the Creator. God's revelation to Abraham results in two covenantal expressions. One seals his organ of speech and the other circumcises the reproductive organ. This theme appears also in the beginning of the work: "The covenant of the Unique One is directed towards the middle (of the person) in the word of the tongue and in the circumcision of the organ" (ch. 1,3). The Biblical texts cited in the expanded epilogue shed light on the meaning. They refer to the covenant of pieces (Gen 15) and the covenant of circumcision (Gen 17). The latter chapter refers to the change of Abraham's name, which designates him "a father of many nations". However, Sepher Yeṣirah (including the original version) explains the divine intention as a prophetic commission, "I placed you a prophet to the nations" (alluding to Jer 1:5). Apparently, the motifs of prophetic reception, divine relevation and covenant-making were stressed in the original epilogue. Abraham is the model of the first person who sought God the Creator in a world of nature worship and polytheism. He enjoys a covenantal relationship to God through speech and circumcision. The former governs the esoteric knowledge and the latter the exoteric. Sepher Yeṣirah guides the initiated Jew into the dual way of Abraham.

The primordial event of God's revelation to a person is captured in early legends about Abraham.[13] For he becomes an ideal type for any person of faith, who takes a journey in his religious philosophical quest for the Creator. However, in the apocalyptic tradition Abraham's encounter with God as the first prophetic experience was at the "covenant of pieces".[14] The apocalyptic view of history is determined by millennial cycles; for a millennium is but one day of God (Ps 90:4). Thus, the first encounter follows the first two thousand years of chaos and opens the historical period of revelation over the next two thousand years. The last two millennia represent the Messianic Times, leading to the final thousand years of the perfect Sabbath.

At the age of seventy, Abraham is engaged by God at the "Covenant of pieces". He receives a historiosophical disclosure about his descendants in bondage ending in exodus and a return to the promised land. In the early rabbinic tradition, the disclosure included the eschatology on successive empires, Temples and the final messianic redemption. Rabbi Yochanan ben Zakkai and Rabbi Akiba even claim[15] that the world to come and resurrection following the

End were revealed to him. In his tradition, the first disclosure to Abraham was all inclusive. It not only embraced historiosophy and eschatology but also protology, the cosmosophic and theosophic traditions. Sepher Yeṣirah offers the latter disclosure. Abraham's new name is now associated with creation and not only with proselytization in human history. The opening verse of the second story of Creation reads: "This is the genesis of heaven and earth when they were created". The last words translate the Hebrew "behibar'am". Through a transpositional reading of the Hebrew word[16] as *"be'abraham"*, the verse states; "This is the genesis of heaven and earth through Abraham." A scribal rendition of a petit *"he"* in the Torah scroll reflects the change of the name from Abram to Abraham.

In early circles of apocalyptic thought, such as in the circle of maskilim who issued the Book of Jubilees, the "covenant of pieces" is associated with first covenant of speech. The creative use of the Hebrew alphabet was made known to Abraham. "He took then the books of his ancestors, Shem and Noah, which were written in Hebrew. He copied them and meditated through them and all the complexities were revealed to him" (12:12). Most significantly this covenant was performed on the Day of Pentecost in accordance with the fixed calendar of the sun, that determines it on the fifteenth day of the month of Sivan, which always falls on Sunday (the "Morrow of the Sabbath"). "On that day", it continues, "a covenant with Abraham was cut, as the one that Noah entered in the same month (refer to ch. 6) and which prefigured the covenant made with Israel at Mount Sinai".

Such a covenantal event was instituted for the Day of Pentecost in perpetuity, according to the Book of Jubilees of the Second Century B.C.E. It is most remarkable that this tradition governed the covenantal life at Qumran and its fixed seasonal calendar. The period of initiation, in accordance with the Maskil's instruction, culminates with the event of covenant making on Pentecost. This is clearly stipulated in the recent finding of 4Q244, a variant of Damascus Document. It is apparent that during the latter part of Second Temple period, a dual covenant with Abraham was known.

The Dual Covenant and the Apocalypse of Abraham[17]

The early tradition on the dual covenant with Abraham, the covenant of pieces on speech and the covenant of circumcision was known to the author of Sepher Yeṣirah. A mystagogic covenant kept the cosmosophic and theosophic knowledge secret. Thus, Sepher Yeṣirah (1,8) declares: "Keep your mouth shut and your mind from reflecting; concerning this matter a covenant was cut." Hekhalot literature also relates such a practice among the Tannaim and Mishnah Ḥagigah 2:1 restricts the study of the esoteric tradition.[18]

The Tannaitic tradition relates[19] that "Moses was sanctified through entering the cloud", upon ascending Mount Sinai to receive God's law. This portrays a particular initiation that prepared Moses for a spiritual encounter with God's speech. The rabbis determine this to be a period of seven days of sanctification to be distinguished from the three days of separation (*hagbalah*) required of the people in facing God's presence at Mount Sinai. In rabbinic historiography the ascent of Moses occurred on the Sabbath, the seventh day of Sivan. Thus, that day provided the setting for initiation, following a period of discipline in esoteric circles of Tannaim. In the early Christian tradition (Acts 2) the event of glossolalia is associated with Pentecost. It was the day on which a new *ecclesia* was established, which eventually dismissed the covenant of circumcision in view of the new covenant of sanctification through the spirit.

In light of this background, Sepher Yeṣirah indeed shared common exegetic-cosmosophical elements with the Apocalypse of Abraham, a pseudepigraphic work to be dated in the early Tannaitic period. The Slavonic Apocalypse from the original Hebrew utilizes the Greek word "*stoicheion*" for element and letter, as in Sepher Yesirah "*otiot-yesod*". It also refers to fire, water and air, the very primordial elements associated with "*'mš*" in Sepher Yeṣirah. The Apocalypse opens with the known Targumic and Midrashic tradition on Abraham, who seeks the true God, smashes the idols of his father's shop and then is cast into the furnace of fire. His doubting brother Haran is also thrown into the furnace but he dies. This legend explains the scriptural juxtaposition of Haran's death with the first trial of Abraham in Ur, meaning "furnace", that led to Abram's departure to Canaan (Gen 11:28).

In the Apocalypse, the above legend is now related to the initial epiphanic experience. "As I was thinking about the elements of fire, water and air, about the luminaries of the sun, moon and stars, then the voice of El Shaddai came down from heaven in a stream of fire, saying: 'Abraham, Abraham' and I said 'Here I am'. God said 'You are searching for the God of gods, the Creator of all, in the understanding of your heart. I am He (*Ani Hu*) depart from Terah (Gen 12:1). Then the voice said 'It is I, fear not for I am your shield (15:1), take the sacrifices of pieces, and through these sacrifices I will set down a covenant' (15:18)." Apparently this vision in the Apocalypse is connected with covenant-making that came to seal Abraham's organ of speech upon initiation into the divine mystery. Thus the Apocalypse continues: "I will announce to you guarded things (Gk "*synteremēna*" Heb: "*neṣurim*") and you will see great things."

Abraham is first asked to abstain from food, drink and ointment for forty days, i.e. the period of initiation.[20] Then he brings the sacrifice on the High Mountain, namely on Mount Horeb (the site of Sinaitic theophany). Consequently God shows him "things made from ages ago by my word, which I affirmed, created and renewed". This disclosure of cosmogony necessitates an angelic interpreter for the apocalypticist. In the cosmosophic tradition, it is Iawel, who is identified with the Metatron in the Rabbinic tradition.[21] He represents the supreme angel who sits at God's throne in the Seventh Heaven, as described in the Apocalypse of Abraham. For he is charge of the angelic hosts of hayyot and cherubs, who offer daily praise. Thereupon, Abraham addresses God with his revealed names of El Shaddai, Elohim hayyim, Holy Sabbaoth and Iaw. These very names appear in the opening paragraph of Sepher Yeṣirah.

In the Apocalypse of Abraham, God is described as "the One who makes the light shine before the morning light appears on the creation". This is God of creation, who issued light on the first day, before He creates the luminaries on the fourth day. This distinction governs the exegetic-cosmosophical tradition. For it comes to separate the upper realm of angelic pleroma in God's eternal light from the lower realm of earthly life under the luminaries. Thus, the eternal Almighty says to Abraham: "Look from the High at the stars below". This is the Apocalypse's cosmosophical rendering of Gen 15:15. The apocalyptic Midrash of Canticles[22] describes the climactic experience of ascent in the last verse of the Song of Songs. It interprets "Flee my beloved" (8:14), as "soar high, my beloved Abraham (see Isa. 41:8) and become like deer or young gazelle upon the elevated realm in Heaven." "*Hare beśamim*" of Canticles is read as "*Hare baśammaim*".

Through the ascent experience, the apocalypticist views the world below and its historical development from beginning to end. According to the early formulation of Mishnah Hagigah 2:1, cosmosophical gazing includes "what is above and what is below". This describes the vertical dimension of ascent experience, as the two worlds are separated by a cosmic veil (the *Belon*). "What is in front and what is in back". The Tosefta (ibid 2:1) explains it represents the horizontal dimension of cosmic history, namely what happened before the creation and what will happen after the End. Thus, the Mishnah concludes with the warning: "Anyone who gazes in these four areas, it is pity for him that he came into this world". Such an admonition points to extra caution requiring a special guide and to the restriction of the covenant of the lips for the initiated.

The Apocalypse of Abraham offers the cosmosophic vision through the angelic guide, Yaoel. "Look from on the High at the stars and then look beneath the firmament and understand the creation that was sketched (*skiagraphen* = Heb. *ṣar*) of old on the expanse." Sepher Yeṣirah presents the sketch of the divine creation, in view of the particular understanding of Isa 26:4 (*beyah YHWH ṣur 'olamim*). It translates the verse to mean, "through the Tetragrammaton, God sketched the [two] worlds". In the view of Sepher Yeṣirah and the Apocalypse, Abraham not only gazed on "what is above and what is below" but also on "what is in front and what is back". The Apocalypse concludes that Abraham is led at the Covenant of Pieces to see what God has decreed was to exist and already has been previously at the time of creation. Then Abraham saw what happened since then until the end of time.

Sepher Yeṣirah has related the exegetic-cosmosophic elements to Abraham's initial revelation at the Covenant of Pieces. For it stressed the Covenant of the lips for the initiated, who also had entered into the covenant of circumcision as the "son of Abraham". God has called Abraham his beloved and the initiated is called "my son, the beloved". The cosmosophic tradition of the creative use of the holy Hebrew letters, as determined by configurations, number and speech, is offered to the initiated, who already undergone circumcision and now committed himself to the covenant of the tongue. Through the dual covenant Abraham became the model in Tannaitic circles of esoteric discipline and thought, as found in Sepher Yeṣirah. However, under the influence of Paul and his followers, who claimed apocalyptic experiences, early Christians sought to separate these two covenants. They placed the stress on the former "covenant of pieces," in which God reckoned Abraham's faith as righteousness, to seal the faith experience through the spirit. Sepher Yeṣirah's linkage to the Apocalypse of Abraham and their common view of the dual covenant offers a most significant background that guided Talmudic and Geonic thought on exoteric and esoteric knowledge.

Notes

1 Refer to the recent studies of G. Scholem, *Major Trends in Jewish Mysticism* (New York: Schocken, 1946) lecture 2; *Kabbalah* (New York: Quadrangle, 1974) p. 21ff; *Reshith Hakabbalah* (Jerusalem: Akadamon, 1969) p. 19ff. Y. Dan, *The Ancient Jewish Mysticism* (Hebrew) (New York: Ktav, 1978) ch. 3.

2 The so-called "riders of the divine Chariot" were engaged in a mystical discipline and their circles produced cosmosophic and theosophical works. Their practice is described in Hekhalot literature (see in particular Hekhalot Rabbati ed. Wertheimer in Bate Midrash).

3 Refer to the discussion in A. Kaplan, *Sepher Yetzirah* (York Beach, Maine: Weiser's Book, 1990) XXIIIff. and Appendix I. Consult also A. Epstein, *Miqadmonioth Hayehudim* (Jerusalem: Mosad Harav Kuk, 1957) pp. 38ff and 179ff.

4 See note 2 and consult H. Odeberg's edition of the Third Enoch and its new rendition by P. Alexander in James H. Charlesworth, *Old Testament Pseudepigrapha* (New York: Doubleday, 1983) vol. I p. 223ff.

5 On the meditative discipline, see A. Kaplan, *Meditation and the Bible* (New York, 1978).

6 Refer to the discussion in G. Scholem, *Jewish Gnosticism, Merkabah Mysticism and Talmudic Tradition* (New York: Jewish Theological Seminary 1960) ch. 2, 3, and the Appendix by S. Lieberman (Hebrew).

7 See Harokeah Hagadol, Jerusalem, 1977, p. 19.

8 See *Perush Harokeah 'al Hatorah* (Bnei Berak, 1986) introduction and *Perush Siddur Hatefillah Larokeah* (Jerusalem, 1992) 2 volumes.

9 See their commentaries in the Collection of Sepher Yeṣirah (Jerusalem, 1962). It contains also several versions. However, the original commentary of Saadiah Gaon and his version are to be found in the recent translation from the Arabic by Y. Kafih, *Sepher Yeṣirah Hashalem* (Jerusalem, 1972).

10 See E. Lipiner, *The Metaphysics of the Hebrew Alphabet* (Jerusalem, Magnes Press, 1989 (Hebrew)) chs. 5, 6, 7.

11 See Bahye ben Asher Commentary on the Torah, final verse, New York: Keter, 1948.

12 Sepher Yeṣirah, ch. 1, 9-14. The first 'sephirah' is the Holy Spirit, from which emanate *Ruah*, *Mayim*, and *'esh* and they are followed by the six directional points of the permuted name Iao.

13 See L. Ginsberg's *Legends of the Jews*, volumes I and V, notes.

14 See Seder Olam Rabbah 3, Pirke de R. Eliezer 48 and Palestinian Targum Exod 12:40.

15 See Midrash Genesis Rabbah 15 (par. 44).

16 See Bahye's commentary on Gen. 2:4; Midrash Hagadol Gen 2:4 (p. 72).

17 See Translation and Introduction by R. Rubinkiewicz in James Charlesworth (ed.), *Old Testament Pseudepigrapha* I, p. 681ff.

18 Compare Paul's description in II Corinthians 12:2-4. Upon his ascent into Paradise (compare, Tannaitic *"Nikhnas lapardes"*), he received words that were forbidden to utter. This also explains the coming of Nicodemus to Jesus at night (John 3).

19 The opening chapter of *Aboth de Rabbi Nathan*, ed. S. Schechter, versions A and B.

20 Compare the account of Jesus' trial in the wilderness in Mark 1:13 and parallels.

21 On the Metatron, refer to G. Scholem, *Kabbalah*, part 2, 17 and refer to Alexander's introduction to Hebrew Third Enoch.

22 See Midrash Genesis Rabbah 15:5 (par. 44, 12).

The Emergence of Jewish Mysticism in Medieval Germany

Joseph Dan

I

The last two or three decades of the 12th century present a most perplexing problem before the historian of Jewish religious phenomena: During these decades, so it seems, European Jewry produced several sects of mystics, both in Southern Europe and in the center of the continent, while during the centuries before this period the mystical dimension seems to have been almost absent from Jewish European culture. In the centuries following the end of the 12th century Jewish mysticism developed mostly in a linear fashion, each stage based on the previous one, following it or contradicting it, but no radical new beginnings "ex nihilo" seem to have occurred. The last decades of the 12th century are the only period in the history of European Jewish mysticism in which circles of mystics seem to come into being independently of each other, in various parts of the continent, and producing original systems of symbols and expressions of profound religious experiences. If this picture is historically correct, then these few decades are unique in Jewish medieval history, and the reasons underlying this phenomenon should be studied in great detail.[1] The present paper is intended to analyze only a specific part of this problem, the appearance of Ashkenazi Hasidic mystical circles, though the wider problem should always remain in the background and be taken into account.

The two main centers in which the emergence of Jewish medieval mysticism took place were, one, in southern France, the Provence, together with Catalonia, especially Barcelona and Gerona[2], and the other in the Rhineland, especially Mainz, Worms and Spier, but also including Regensburg and a few other towns. The three most important mystical circles which appeared in this period in the south-European region are, first and foremost, the Sefer ha-Bahir, the earliest text which contains the kabbalistic symbolism of the ten divine hyposthases, which became a corner-stone of kabbalistic speculation throughout the many centuries of the development of the kabbalah.[3]

The second was the appearance of the school of mystics surrounding Rabbi Abraham ben David, the Ravad, late in the 12th century, and the main writer of this school was the Ravad's son, Rabbi Isaac the Blind, who wrote the first kabbalistic treatise written by a known author which reached us.[4] The relationship between the authorship of the Book Bahir and the school of the Ravad is not clear, and merits further study, but it can be stated that it is not certain that this school was aware of the existence of the Book Bahir, and it is possible that these two schools developed their very similar symbolisms independently of each other.[5] The third mystical circle which emerged in southern Europe approximately at the same time was the Iyyun circle, so called because of its central text, the Sefer ha-Iyyun ("Book of Contemplation"), and several other mystical works which present a symbolism radically different from the previous two, but still containing very strong mystical-neo-Platonic characteristics.[6] The teachings of all these three circles became united in the works and ideas of the Gerona school of kabbalists in the first half of the 13th century; the works of Rabbi Ezra ben Shlomo, Rabbi Azriel, Nachmanides and others reveal the clear influence of the Sefer ha-Bahir, Rabbi Isaac the Blind and some elements of the Iyyun circle terminology, all combined.[7] From then onwards, the kabbalah in Spain developed stage by stage, generation after generation, each deriving its ideas and symbols from the previous ones and developing its original—and often radically different—mystical systems on the basis of the teachings of the previous schools and circles, and creating the spiritual-mystical alternative to the ruling Jewish ideology in Spain—rationalistic philosophy.

At the same time, in the second half of the 12th century, an established rabbinic school in Germany, that of the Kalonymus family, whose roots stretch all the way to 8th-century Italy, begins to lean towards mystical expression of religious ideas, creating what became known later as the Ashkenazi Hasidic school of esoteric religious speculation and ethical thought.[8] This family produced the three great writers of Ashkenazi Hasidism—Rabbi Samuel son of Kalonymus, known as the "Pious, Saint and Prophet"[9]; his son, Rabbi Judah the Pious, the most influential thinker of the school (died in 1217); and the latter's disciple, Rabbi Eleazar ben Judah ben Kalonymus of Worms, the main writer of Ashkenazi Hasidic literature (died c. 1230). These three scholars, whose works are the core of Ashkenazi Hasidic teachings, created a body of esoteric works presenting a new Jewish conception of religious worship, a new understanding of biblical and talmudic traditions, a revival of ancient Jewish mystical works, and a new interpretation of the Jewish prayers; but they are especially

known for their works in the field of ethics. The Sefer Hasidim —
"The Book of the Pietists", is the major contribution of German
Jewry to Jewish ethics in the Middle Ages[10]; it was written mainly by
Rabbi Judah the Pious, though possibly some portions of it were
written by his father, Rabbi Samuel. Rabbi Eleazar of Worms's
ethical ideas were incorporated in the two opening chapters of his
halachic work, the Sefer ha-Rokeah.

While the centrality of the Kalonymus school in Ashkenazi
Hasidism cannot be doubted, it was not the only one to emerge at
about the same period, and it seems that several groups and individuals were creating new esoteric and mystical systems without being in
touch, or even without being aware, of the Kalonymus school. The
most important among these circles is the anonymous group which
created the pseudepigraphical mystical body of works attributed to
the traditions of Joseph ben Uzziel, a fictional figure who is described
as the grandson of Ben Sira (Ecclesiasticus), who in turn is described
as the son of the prophet Jeremiah.[11] This circle created and interpreted a short text called "The Barayta of Joseph ben Uzziel", and
several other works closely related to it, the best-known among them
being the so-called "PseudeSaadia Commentary on the Sefer Yezira".
The one author of this circle whom we know by name was Rabbi
Elhanan ben Yaqar of London, who wrote in the first half of the 13th
century two commentaries on the Sefer Yezira and a theological
work, Sod ha-Sodot ("The Secret of Secrets"), in which he often
quotes the earlier traditions of this circle.[12] These writers put
forward an original system of symbols, based on their own understanding of the ancient Sefer Yezira, without revealing any familiarity
with the works of the Kalonymus school on the same subject, or
indeed any subject.

Another meaningful work of religious thought, which shows
elements of an original approach to basic Jewish religious questions
and presenting new terminology is the anonymous work Sefer ha-
Hayyim ("The Book of Life"), which was written probably around
1200 (It is quoted in Rabbi Moses Taku's Ketzv Tamim, written about
1220, who attributes the work to Rabbi Abraham Ibn Ezra, whose
influence indeed is discernible in this work)[13]. The author of this
book deals with theological, anthropological, psychological and
ethical problems as if he were the first medieval scholar to study
them, revealing no knowledge of any other school or circle of esoteric
or mystical thought. It seems to be the work of an individual, isolated
theologian of some mystical tendencies. A similar phenomenon can
be found in the Sefer ha-Navon "The Book of the Wise", written in
the first half of the 13th century by an isolated thinker, dedicated to a

commentary on the Shema Yisrael, the declaration of divine unity, and to an interpretation of the ancient mystical work, the Shiur Komah.[14]

These facts present the historian with a two-fold problem when searching for the origins and trying to explain the appearance of each of these schools: He cannot do it only by isolating each of them and trying to understand the reasons for their appearance; he must also take into account the fact that the one he is describing was not the only one, and that others appeared at the same time in other places and reflected other historical circumstances. He must, at the same time, deal both with the specific and the general; to understand the detail as well as the wider picture; to explain the specificity of each phenomenon and to deal with the larger problem of the uniqueness of the period as whole. Even if we understand, for instance, the reasons for the appearance of the Kalonymus school of mystics, we still have to explain why it appeared at the same time that five other schools and circles emerged and created ideas surprisingly similar to it. On the other hand, no general answer can cover and explain the emergence and the nature of all these six separate phenomena; it must be a combination of specific study and comparative study which will lead us to the understanding of this central and unparalleled phenomenon in the history of Jewish mysticism.

It is impossible in the framework of this paper to deal with the complete complex of problems just described. It is my wish here to present the material relevant to the appearance of the Kalonymus school of Jewish mystics, combined with a comparative study of its relationship to the kabbalistic schools in southern Europe. I hope that this will serve as a contribution towards a wider study of the emergence of Jewish mysticism in Europe in the second half of the 12th century.[15]

II

The term "mysticism" does not have a Hebrew equivalent, and therefore no Jewish mystic ever defined himself as a mystic, nor did any Jewish author define himself as a non-mystic. The appellation "mystic" is an arbitrary modern one, which scholars attach to various phenomena, motivated each by his own understanding of the nature and characteristics of mysticism. In the end of this paper I shall try to point out the elements which seem to justify, to some extent, the use of the term "mysticism" for the Ashkenazi Hasidic circles, but the basic analysis should rest on the ways in which they described themselves and understood their own work, in which this term, of course, did not and could not play any role. But while the term "mysticism" is completely absent, another one is prominent: The term Sod, or esoteric. The Ashkenazi Hasidim viewed themselves as presenting to themselves, and to others in some cases, something that was hidden and regarded secret until now. A common title which appears at the beginning of several paragraphs in the writings of Rabbi Elahan ben Yaqar states: "Here you are given the meaning of things which have been secret until today". The works of Rabbi Eleazar of Worms abound with references to great secrets, and the same is true about most of the other works relevant to our subject.[16] There can be no doubt that a common denominator to all the early Jewish mystics at the end of the 12th century was a deep perception that they are dealing with esoteric problems, something that was hidden from the esoteric works of their predecessors and should be hidden now and in the future from anyone who does not belong to the select few who deserve to know it.

Rabbi Eleazar of Worms dedicated his most important work of esoteric knowledge to the meaning of the divine names, and called it Sefer ha-Shem, "The Book of the Name". In this work, which has not been published and is found in several manuscripts[17], Rabbi Eleazar gave several interpretations of the name of four letters (yod ha vav ha) and other, more esoteric, names of God. To this detailed work he added a preface, in which he described a special ceremony to be performed before the secret of the holy name is transmitted by the teacher to his disciple.[18] The ceremony included standing in front of running water, and reciting biblical verses and benediction concerning the holiness and mysteriousness of the divine name. This ceremony undoubtedly reflects an old tradition of transmitting secrets from generation to generation, probably practiced by the Kalonymus family.

There is a constant paradox involved in reading works which state and emphasize the secrecy of the material included in them: If it is so secret, why was it written down for anyone, including the modern historian, to read? There can be no doubt that many secrets which were regarded as such did not reach us because they were never written down. But in the case of Rabbi Eleazar, we do have his answer to this question. It is included in his personal, autobiographical preface to his book Sefer ha-Hochma ("The Book of Wisdom"), which he wrote in 1217, as he clearly states in this preface.[19] Rabbi Eleazar explains that now, after the death of Rabbi Judah the Pious earlier that year, and after his own son had died (probably of wounds sustained during one of the Crusaders' attacks on the Jewish communities in the Rhineland), he, Rabbi Eleazar, remained alone with the traditions he received from his father and from his teacher, without children or disciples to whom he can transmit these secrets. He decided to write, so he says, so that these traditions will not be completely lost. In other words, he states that though this material should never be written, the force of unusual circumstances makes it imperative for him to write them down.

We have two reasons to doubt whether Rabbi Eleazar revealed the complete truth when writing this preface. One is, the fact that his teacher, Rabbi Judah the Pious, has already done this, and wrote several works of esoteric traditions, of which Rabbi Eleazar himself made extensive use in his own writings. Many sections of Rabbi Eleazar esoteric works are either copies of Rabbi Judah's works, or paraphrases and abbreviations of them.[20] He knew very well, therefore, that he was not the first to commit these secrets to paper. The second reason for doubt is that we know that Rabbi Eleazar did have disciples who continued to study esoteric lore after him. The most important among them was Rabbi Abraham son of Azriel, called "from the elders of Bohemia", the author of the encyclopaedic commentary on the piyyutim (religious hymns), Arugat ha-Bosem.[21] Rabbi Abraham quotes Rabbi Eleazar as his teacher over a hundred times in his work[22], and he also quotes Rabbi Judah the Pious, whom he knew and from whom he also received secret traditions.[23] This means that Rabbi Abraham started his studies before 1217, when this preface was written, and Rabbi Eleazar clearly disregarded him when stating that he had no disciples.

It is very difficult to explain what Rabbi Eleazar meant exactly when expressing his deep feeling of loneliness and making this the reason for writing down the works of esoteric teachings. It is clear that he regarded Rabbi Judah's works as insufficiently organized and unclear; it seems that in his own works he intended to systematize and present in a clearer way his master's teachings.[24] We do not know what were the exact relations between Rabbi Eleazar and Rabbi Abraham berabi Azriel. But it seems that this preface is characteristic of the eternal tension in the heart of the student of esoteric material: The strong drive to preserve the secrecy of the tradition, conflicting with the equally strong drive to present the treasures at his disposal at least to a chosen, deserving few.

A very similar problem faced the kabbalah very early in its history. G. Scholem discovered and published a letter sent by Rabbi Isaac the Blind from Provence to the Rabbis of Gerona (the recipients were Rabbi Moses Nachmanides and Rabbi Jonah of Gerona).[25] In this epistle Rabbi Isaac complains that rumors have reached him that in Gerona kabbalah is talked about in the streets and in the markets, and that books were written expounding it. He states emphatically that these secrets should never become public, and that books should not be written, because, as he says, "a book already written — there is no cupboard in which it can be hidden".[26] Obviously Rabbi Isaac believed that kabbalistic works should not be written, because once written there can be no hope of keeping them secret. Of course, one may ask, if Rabbi Isaac was so emphatic on this point why did he himself write the commentary on the Sefer Yezira? (It is possible that he did not write the work himself, but that one of his disciples wrote it down, but there is no proof of this). This might be another example of the basic conflict between revelation and esotericism.

This concept of esotericism, characteristic of both Ashkenazi Hasidism and early kabbalah, is combined with another element: The claim that the authors do not reveal anything new; all they are doing is to pursue and develop traditions which they have received from antiquity. Significant efforts have been made both by the kabbalists and by the Ashkenazi Hasidim to present their teachings as revelations of ancient esoteric lore, sometimes emphatically described as having been revealed by God to Moses on Mount Sinai.[27] Concerning the problem of the emergence and beginnings of mystical speculation in medieval Germany, this point should be examined in detail, because it is most relevant to the question of this beginning and its reasons.

To a very large extent, there can be no doubt that the first Jewish mystics in medieval Europe were indeed the followers and revealers of ancient traditions. One of the most meaningful characteristics of Ashkenazi Hasidic mysticism is the re-discovery and revival of ancient Jewish mystical sources, the Hekhalot and Merkavah mysticism of the Talmudic period. Large sections in the works of Rabbi Judah the Pious and Rabbi Eleazar of Worms are nothing but a presentation, sometimes in paraphrase, of several of the works of the Hekhalot mystics. It seems that several Hekhalot texts have reached us only in editions prepared by the Ashkenazi Hasidim.[28] There was a group among them which specialized in presenting such texts with commentaries which are themselves selections from Hekhalot literature, like the commentaries known as Sefer ha-Heshek ("The Book of Desire")[29], and the commentary on the hymn from Hekhalot Rabbati ("The Greater Book of Hekhalot"), Ha-Aderet veha-Emunah ("The Garment and the Faith").[30] A work of this sort was preserved in the Mussajjof manuscript of Hekhalot mysticism[31], and another was composed by Rabbi Moses, the grandson of Rabbi Judah the Pious.[32] The second book in Rabbi Eleazar's magnum opus, Sodey Razaya

("The Secrets of Secrets"), is dedicated to a presentation of the celestial realm by quotations from Hekhalot literature.[33]

We can validate the Ashkenazi Hasidic claim to base their Hekhalot speculation on early traditions for several generations, probably even centuries. We have a document which describes the culture of the Kalonymus's family ancient roots in Italy, going as far as the 8th century: The Megilat Ahimmaz, the family traditions written down by Ahimmaz and including historical and fictional material concerning the life of several of the Kalonimides' ancestors.[34] In this document it is stated that Hekhalot mysticism was studied by these old masters[35], and this fact is supported by the frequent references to Hekhalot material in the piyyutim of Italian and early Ashkenazi religious poets. It seems, therefore, that the reliance on Hekhalot mysticism was not a new discovery by the late 12th century writers, but that they followed a tradition going back for many generations.

On two specific subjects the indebtedness of the early Jewish mystics in Germany to ancient traditions is most prominent: The image of God, and the creation. The image of God was presented in the greatest detail and the most profound mystical and mythical manner in the ancient work, Shiur Komah ("The Measurement of the Height" = of the divine figure).[36] This work was known to other Jewish non-mystical authors, and caused them much embarrassment, because of the stark anthropomorphism it seemed to express; Saadia Gaon, for instance, probably believed that it was a forgery, pseudepigraphically attributed to the ancient sages Rabbi Akibah and Rabbi Ishmael, but he could not completely disregard it and explained that it referred to a created angelic power (a very difficult explanation, because this figure is clearly called within the work "Our Creator").[37] The Ashkenazi Hasidim adapted the myth of the Shiur Komah and made it central to their conception of the divine world[38]; the figure described is a divine one, though not the supreme God, but an emanated power derived from the "divine fire" or "divine light", which serves as a subject for the revelation to the prophets. In this case, at least, the claim that they follow and reveal ancient traditional secrets seems to be entirely correct. To support this one can mention the fact that the Shiur Komah was known even to non-Jewish scholars, who sometimes used it in order to denounce Jewish faith.[39] This was also done by Karaitic polemicists, who saw here a rare opportunity to attack the two great sages of the mishnah, Rabbi Akibah and Rabbi Ishmael.[40]

A similar, though not identical, situation can be found in the early kabbalah. The Sefer ha-Bahir and other early kabbalistic works adopted the Shiur Komah anthropomorphism to present the

Godhead in terms of a combination of symbols derived from human physiology. The difference is, that the Shiur Komah myth was combined by the kabbalists with another set of symbols, that of the ten divine emanations (the sefirot), thus the ancient text was for them a source for symbolism as well as a living myth to follow.

A somewhat similar situation can be found concerning the speculations about the creation, though there are also some differences. The Sefer Yezira became, in the works of the early European mystics, the most important source for symbolism and speculation. A collection of the commentaries written by them to this work will be a most central anthology of medieval mysticism. The impact of this very brief and enigmatic work can be equalled only to the book of Genesis itself. It is one of the greatest riddles of the history of Jewish books how a work, written probably in the third or fourth century by an author who did not belong to the mainstream of Talmudic-Midrashic schools, and which was not mentioned for many centuries in Jewish traditions, suddenly, in the tenth to the thirteenth centuries, became a cornerstone for all Jewish ideologies: Rationalistic philosophers and their opponents, kabbalists and Ashkenazi Hasidim – all dedicated their best efforts to its study and composed commentaries on it; sometimes, even when not writing a commentary, a work will be written which actually is such a commentary. Such examples can be found all the way from Rabbi Judah ha-Levi's Kuzari (chapter 4), to Rabbi Elhanan ben Yaqar's Sod ha-Sodot.[41]

When the early Jewish mystics in medieval Germany wrote their works based on Sefer Yezira they were confident that they were following ancient traditions, revealed by God to Abraham. Yet, the book itself is so brief, and its terminology so unique and enigmatic, that every commentator, in fact, was not revealing a tradition but presenting his own views. Every term in the Sefer Yezira received a new meaning by every commentator. The claim that they had an ancient tradition concerning the true meaning of this work – a claim clearly made by Rabbi Eleazar in his own commentary on the book, which is the fifth part of Sodey Razaya[42] – must be regarded with care. The wealth of material that we have concerning the interpretation of this work from the 10th century onwards seems to indicate that the Jewish scholars of the Middle Ages did not have any previous tradition concerning this book, and that each of them – Shabbatai Donolo in 10th century Italy, Rav Saadia in 10th century Babylonia, Donash ben Tamim, Judah ha-Levi, Judah ben Barzilai in 12th century Barcelona, and others, all treated the work on their own original terms, except when relying on each other. Rabbi Eleazar is certainly correct when he states that he received traditions from

Donolo and other medieval sources, but we have no proof of any ancient tradition but the enigmatic text itself.

The basic historical question concerning the appraisal of the Ashkenazi Hasidic claim to be the followers of ancient tradition is, in fact, whether the most essential aspects of their doctrines, the ones which characterize them and differentiates them from previous Jewish thinkers, were indeed derived from these sources. The answer to this question, from the modern historian's point of view, should be a negative one. In most respects it can be proven that the ideas which are basic to the essence of Ashkenazi Hasidism developed in the 12th century, and cannot be shown to be derived from ancient traditions. They often had sources — which we can follow and analyze — but these were medieval ones, like the works of Rav Saadia Gaon, Rabbi Judah ben Barzilai of Barcelona, Rabbi Abraham Bar Hijja, Rabbi Abraham Ibn Ezra, Shabbatai Donolo and others which they used in a creative manner, often disagreeing with them or developing original concepts based on these medieval sources. A few examples will be given in the following pages.

Another reason for such a negative answer is that when using the wealth of material at their disposal from ancient Jewish mystical works, the Ashkenazi Hasidim either intentionally disregarded, or just did not know about, the active mystical aspects of these traditions, namely the actual practice of the "descent to the chariot".[43]   No exhaustive study has been made as yet concerning the exact library of Hekhalot texts which were used by the Ashkenazi Hasidim. It is certain, however, that the two most important ones for them were the Shiur Komah and Sefer Hekhalot ("Third Enoch" or the "Hebrew Book of Enoch"). How much material from Hekhalot Rabbati and Hekhalot Zutarti, the two main texts which describe the ascension of Rabbi Ishmael and Rabbi Akibah respectively, was available to them and actually used by them cannot be ascertained in an accurate manner. It is significant, however, that their works do not deal in any detail with these central episodes, which are the most important element in the ancient mystical tradition. In this the Ashkenazi Hasidim are one more example of a common medieval attitude, shared by writers ranging from Rav Saadia to Rabbi Judah ben Barzilai, who all either neglected, or were unaware, of this meaningful aspect of the Hekhalot mystical tradition.

This point is crucial concerning the assessment of the nature of the reliance of the mystics of medieval Germany on ancient Jewish mystical works. If we take out of the ancient tradition the descriptions of the mystical ascensions of Rabbi Akibah, Rabbi Nehunia ben ha-Kanah and Rabbi Ishmael, what is left, in essence, is a description of the celestial worlds, validated and sanctified by the ancient sages, but including no element of active mystical ascension of a particular person. Gershom Scholem, when describing this school of mystics in medieval Germany, raised the question whether they only studied, copied and commented upon the works of the Hekhalot mystics, or whether they also followed their mystical practices.[44] It seems that the absence of the descriptions of the mystical ascensions from Ashkenazi Hasidic writings can be interpreted in one of two ways: Either they did not know about it and therefore could not follow it, or they knew about it and did follow it but kept it a secret even in their own esoteric works. It seems to me that the first possibility is closer to the truth; it is very difficult to imagine a "conspiracy" in which all these writers, in the several schools of Ashkenazi Hasidism, decided to reveal everything but this section of the traditions that reached them (it should also be emphasized that the south European mystical sources as well do not include references to the mystical ascensions of the Hekhalot sages; it is possible that these texts reached Europe later than the more descriptive material, though this explanation raises many difficult textual problems concerning the history, recensions and transmission of the Hekhalot texts). Be that as it may, Ashkenazi Hasidic contentions that all their teachings are based on ancient traditions from the east cannot be regarded as accurate descriptions of the actual situation in the second half of the 12th century.

In southern Europe, Hekhalot traditions and the Sefer Yezira serve as a central and meaningful source for the works of the early kabbalists. Rabbi Isaac the Blind presented his kabbalistic description of cosmogony and cosmology, and mainly the process of the emanation of the divine hyposthases, in the framework of a commentary on the Sefer Yezira.[45] The Book Bahir used several sections of this work and included them in the book, introducing into them meaningful changes which transformed the ancient cosmological work into a mystical description of the divine world. The Iyyun circle, more than any other early kabbalistic school, based its terminology and symbolism on a new understanding of this ancient work. It were the mystics of the Iyyun circle, more than any other group, who demonstrated their attachment to the mystical Hekhalot tradition both in the pseudepigraphical framework of some of their works (especially the Sefer ha-Iyyun itself), and the content of their speculations; a majority of the thirteen divine hyposthases described in Sefer ha-Iyyun are derived from Merkabah speculations.[46] The Sefer ha-Bahir also includes several sections which are based on Hekhalot terminology, and its indebtedness to the ancient mystics is obvious (it should be noted, however, that the Gerona circle, while continuing the tradition of reliance on Sefer Yezira, used very little of the Hekhalot tradition).   In this case too, therefore, the parallelism between the development of Ashkenazi Hasidic esoteric traditions and the kabbalah is clear and striking.

Another aspect of the problem of ancient traditions is the Ashkenazi Hasidic insistent claim that they had specific, direct lines of traditions from which they received ancient eastern esoteric traditions. Usually these claims were accompanied by stories describing the circumstances in which these secrets were transmitted.   One such story which involves the legends concerning Jeremiah, Ben Sira and Joseph ben Uzziel is obviously fictional, having its origin in the group of legends known as the "Pseudo Ben Sira", originating from Babylonia in the 9th or 10th century.[47]   Another vague tradition claims that the origin of esoteric traditions was a certain Yossef Maon, who was among those exiled by Titus when the second temple was destroyed.[48] Again, this is obviously a legend, which is not repeated in any other source.

The most serious tradition of this kind is the well-known one ascribing Ashkenazi Hasidic esoteric traditions to a chain of transmission which began with the visit of Rabbi Aaron ben Samuel of Baghdad (sometimes called Abu Aharon), who belonged to a Babylonian gaonic family, to Italy, where he revealed his secrets to the forefathers of Ashkenazi Kalonymus family.   There is no doubt that some historical foundation can be found to this story, which is preserved in two independent sources—a tradition by Rabbi Eleazar of Worms and the Chronicle of Ahimaaz, though most of the historical details, including the exact chronology of the events described, are unclear.[49] It should be noted that Rabbi Eleazar clearly states in his version of this tradition that the secrets brought by Rabbi Aaron of Baghdad concerned mainly "the secrets of the prayers and other secrets"; the centrality of the "secrets of the prayers" concerning the emergence of Jewish mysticism in Germany will be discussed below.

The claim that ancient traditions served as a basis for medieval mystical speculations is, of course, common to Ashkenazi Hasidism and the kabbalah in the Provence and in Spain.   The Sefer ha-Bahir, the earliest work of the kabbalah, was written in the form of a midrash, and attributed to ancient mishnaic sages, like Rabbi Nehunia ben ha-Kanah, Rabbi Akibah and others.   This sort of clear, blatant pseudepigraphy is similar to the one found in the works attributed to Joseph ben Uzziel on the one hand and to the writings of the Iyyun circle on the other[50], where ancient sages, from the mishnah, Hekhalot literature or gaonic figures are used as authoritative sources of secrets.   And like the Ashkenazi Hasidism, not all kabbalists tolerated this kind of pseudepigraphy: The schools of Rabbi Isaac the Blind and of the kabbalists of Gerona did not use pseudepigraphy, like the Ashkenazi mystics of the Kalonymus family, who argued among themselves whether one should emphasize his authorship of a work or not[51], but never dreamed of attributing their own works to earlier sages. The parallels between the schools of Jewish mystics in the late 12th century seem, therefore, to be present in many aspects of their works, and even the variations seem to follow the same general lines.

III

The importance of these similarities concerning "external" characteristics between central-European and south-European circles of mystics, as indications denoting the circumstances and nature of their origins, should not be minimized, but they are undoubtedly secondary to other elements, which reflect more directly the essence and nature of their mystical speculations. Here, I believe, lies the most important key to the understanding not only the similarities but also the differences, and therefore it can be essential for the quest for the origins of Ashkenazi Hasidic mysticism. The most important idea to emerge from all these schools, and which constitutes the main reason for their being called "mystics" is the revolutionary conception of the divine world as comprised of several, structured, emanated forces, each having its own distinct personal image, even though they represent together the unity of God.

The various symbolisms of the ten sefirot, which together constitute the divine world, are the basic characteristic of the mysticism of Sefer ha-Bahir and the school of kabbalists in the Provence, led by Rabbi Isaac the Blind. The new concept of the divine world as comprised of ten emanated layers, each of which being a divine personality described in a specific set of symbols, is the essence of the medieval symbolism of the kabbalah. The origin—or origins—of this new system of symbols is unknown, and the rapidly increasing attempts to discover it (or them) has, up to now, added very little to our knowledge. The Iyyun circle, however, used both the numbers 10 and 13 as indicating the inner structure of the divine world, using terminology which is well-rooted in the ancient and medieval sources that were common to all Jewish medieval mystics. The basic problem concerning these circles, as well as their parallels in Ashkenazi Hasidism, is: What motivated them to depart from traditional Jewish conceptions of the unity of God, and adapt the mythological notion of the divine world as structured from several emanated powers?

The actual development of the Ashkenazi Hasidic concept of the divine world is fairly well documented in the sources available to us. They put in the center of their speculations concerning the divine world the term kavod, the divine glory, which they usually identified with the rabbinic concept of the Shekhinah, a term denoting God in His relationship to the temple in Jerusalem and to the people of Israel.[52] It was Rav Saadia Gaon (probably following previous norms adapted by the Aramaic translators of the Bible, who, to avoid stark anthropomorphism in their translations sometimes introduced the term "divine glory" instead of a direct reference to God[53]; it is also possible that there were some Karaitic speculations of similar kind among the early theologians of this sect)[54], who first formulated clearly the concept that the power revealed to the prophets, and the one described in the anthropomorphic verses of the bible and the sayings of the talmud, was the divine glory, which is a created, angelic power, which was called Shekhinah by the talmudic sages.[55] In this way Saadia removed the danger of anthropomorphism from prophetic revelation, but at the same time put this peak of religious experience on a much lower level; the prophets did not see God himself, even when they stated this explicitly (Isaiah 6:1); all they had seen was a created angel, which God entrusted with the duty of appearing in certain shapes before the prophet as a sign that what they were going to hear was indeed coming from a divine source, and not an earthly, magical delusion.

This was a neat, simple and satisfactory solution to a very serious problem; probably, much too neat, for it neglected most of the really important religious factors involved. Rav Saadia himself had to depart from it when he was facing the necessity, imposed on him by the polemics of his Karaitic opponents, of explaining the nature of the enormous divine figure, called "our creator", whose astronomical measurements are given in the ancient mystical tractat, Shiur Komah, which is attributed to the two great sages of the mishnah, the oral law (which the Karaites did not accept)—Rabbi Akibah and Rabbi Ishmael. Saadia was undoubtedly inclined to dismiss this text as pseudepigraphical, but could not do that wholeheartedly because he was facing the Karaites who claimed that the whole mishnah was a pseudepigraphy. He therefore added a theological explanation of the Shiur Komah to the suggestion that the work was not authentic. In this explanation he stated, that there was another divine glory above the one revealed to the prophets, one created by God in order to be revealed to the angels, the celestial powers and to the revealed divine glory, and this superior glory was the one described in the Shiur Komah.[56] Saadia thus had to postulate a succession of created divine glories, one above the other, and later formulations of the same idea, especially by the talmudic commentator Rabenu Hananel, summarized this Saadian concept in terms which may indicate that there was an infinite succession of such divine glories, one greater than the other and one above the other, the higher ones so brilliant and sacred that they are beyond the comprehension of even Moses, the greatest prophet.[57]

When the simplicity of the Saadian statement was broken by the author himself, the door was open for later developments which added to the dimensions of this celestial figure, the divine glory, and increased its religious significance. It seems that the crucial step was taken by the great neo-Platonic philosopher and biblical commentator, Rabbi Abraham ibn Ezra. When discussing the revelation of God to Moses (Ex. 33), both in his commentary to the Torah and in his brief ethical and theological treatise, Yesod Morah ("The Foundation of Worship")[58], Ibn Ezra stated that the divine glory has two "faces", one directed towards creation, which is revealed to the prophets, and one hidden from everything, because it is turned towards God himself, and is "united" with Him. The terminology used by Ibn Ezra is not completely clear, but it seems evident that what he was stating was that the divine glory is emanated from God, and that its relationship to the reality below it is also one of emanation.[59] The Saadian concept of a divine glory which is not divine but created, has been rejected by Ibn Ezra, and substituted by one in which the glory is indeed divine, part of the succession of divine powers emanating from God.

Rabbi Judah the Pious not only knew Ibn Ezra's commentary, but he himself wrote a commentary on the section of Yesod Morah dealing with the emanation of the divine glory[60], and while there may be some doubt concerning the exact meaning of Ibn Ezra's statement, there is none concerning Judah the Pious's understanding of it. The Ashkenazi mystic saw the divine glory as an emanated power, divine in its nature and having many functions in the divine governing of the cosmos. The most important addition which Rabbi Judah the Pious brought to the concept of the divine glory was the inclusion of the task of accepting the prayers of the people of Israel among the tasks of the glory. A created power cannot be the target of human prayers; praying to a created being is the definition of idolatry. By the addition of this task to the divine glory Rabbi Judah the Pious clearly introduced the mystical concept of a succession of personalized divine powers emanating from the Godhead.

A very similar development has occurred in the Ashkenazi mystical circle which based its traditions on the Barayta attributed to Joseph ben Uzziel. These anonymous mystics of the late 12th century and the beginning of the 13th were even more outspoken and less hesitant in their descriptions of the various powers within the divine realm. The most important contribution which they added to the theory of the divine glory was to go one more step away from the Saadian concept, and declare, very emphatically, that the divine glory as a whole was completely remote from human perception and could not even be revealed to the prophets.[61] Thus a power which Saadia, who started its "medieval history" as a created angel revealed to the prophets, has become a supreme, hidden divine power, which, according to this circle of mystics, should never be described in any corporeal terms, and therefore cannot be the image to which biblical and rabbinic anthropomorphic phrases should be related; the Shiur Komah, perforce, cannot be the kavod or the Shekhinah. An answer to the problem of anthropomorphism has become an intensification of the question: If the kavod is so divine and hidden, what did the prophets perceive?

The answer of this circle of mystics to this problem follows the lines of development that have occurred elsewhere: Another divine power has to be added to the hierarchy of supreme forces in order to serve this purpose. This power was called by them ha-keruv ha-meyuhad ("The Special Cherub"), who was described, according to them, in the revelations to Isaiah and Ezekiel, and the "creator" of the Shiur Komah is indeed this "cherub". These works insist that the Cherub is an emanated power, derived from the divine "fire" in a way which is not similar to the creation of angels and other celestial beings who were made out fire, but not emanated from the divine spirit, which is also described symbolically as fire. Paradoxically, this "special cherub" is described as sitting on the kise ha-kavod, "the throne of glory". As the term itself clearly indicates, the "throne of glory" was, originally, the throne of the kavod, the divine glory. These mystics could not accept that, because the kavod, the glory, cannot be described as "sitting", as it does not have any corporeal form; it is the special cherub, the revealed divine power, which sits on the throne, which the theology of this circle forced the glory to vacate.

Why did the authors of these mystical works feel it necessary to add another power to the divine realm, a power which is not mentioned in any previous source, and represents their departure from old, reliable traditions? It is quite clear from their writings (especially one brief tractat pesaq ha-yirah veha-emunah, "Decision Concerning Faith and the Fear of God"), that the motivation for this development came from their conception of the prayer.[62] The enormous religious meaning of the constant proximity between Man and God, represented by the Jewish prayers, could not be directed towards a power which has a corporeal form, even if it is emanated and divine in nature. The prayers, they believed, should be dedicated and directed to a more supreme force, which cannot be revealed, cannot "sit" and cannot be described in the anthropomorphic terms of the Shiur Komah. The religious force of the need to pray to a supreme divine power made them disassociate the divine glory from the task of being revealed to the prophets, and serving as an answer to the problem of anthropomorphism, and to the addition of a specific, new divine figure to serve this purpose. The "pesaq" is an emphatic demand, phrased in halachic legal terms, that prayers should not be directed towards the "special cherub" but to the divine hidden glory alone.

It should be emphasized that as far as the evidence in our disposal can show, there was no connection between the circle of mystics which produced these texts and the central Ashkenazi Hasidic school of the Kalonymus family. The development of the concepts of revealed divine powers, and ones designated to accept the prayers, occurred independently in these two groups. A part of their terminology is derived from previous sources common to both, like Saadia and Ibn Ezra, but the actual mystical concepts of the divine emanated powers is expressed in terminology and symbolism unique to each of these circles.[63] The differences are meaningful enough to prove that none of these writers relied on another from the second group. This seems to prove how necessary, from a religious point of view, were these ideas and symbols to Jewish Ashkenazi scholars in the end of the 12th century, so much so that they developed them independently but on closely parallel lines.

The development of these mystical notions did not stop when the problems of divine revelation, anthropomorphism and the divine power which accepts the prayers have been answered. Rabbi Elhanan ben Yaqar, who followed the traditions of the Joseph ben Uzziel circle (and was probably unaware of the works of Rabbi Judah the Pious and Rabbi Eleazar of Worms), added another dimension in his theological tractat Sod ha-Sodot.[64] The first part of this work is dedicated to an analysis of the story of the creation as presented in the beginning of the book of Genesis, and Rabbi Elhanan describes a central role for the kavod, the hidden divine glory, in the process of the creation. According to him, the actual creation in the first six days was the result of the emanation and separation of the glory from the supreme Godhead. The completion of the process on the seventh day signifies the re-uniting of these divine powers, when the full spiritual divine force of the supreme Godhead was given to the glory, and they became, in Rabbi Elhanan's original terminology, "like twins".[65] As proof to his description Rabbi Elhanan relies on the different names of God used in this section of Genesis. The holy name of four letters, YHVH, is, according to him, the name of the glory, while Elohim is the name of the supreme God (this notion is based on Sefer Yezira, where, according to this circle's commentaries on that work this name signifies the supreme Godhead). When, in the end of the process of the creation the names are united (YHVH-Elohim), they signify the re-unity of the divine source and the emanated power. When the name YHVH, which is so central both in the bible and in Jewish faith and worship, is attributed to a secondary divine power, an emanated one, a scholar may definitely conclude that the simple unity of the conception of God has been broken, and mystics using such symbolism indeed perceive the divine realm as multi-layered.

Other Jewish mystics who wrote in the same period in Germany reveal the same basic tendencies, even though they did not create such elaborate systems as did the two schools, of the Kalonymus family and the circle following the traditions of Joseph ben Uzziel. The Sefer ha-Navon, for instance, is partially dedicated to a commentary on the Shiur Komah, who is perceived as divine, not created, power.[66] In Sefer ha-Hayyim it seems that the old dictum that there is a succession of divine glories each above the other was accepted and made a basis for a theological system; the author describes seven such divine glories constituting the celestial "ladder" between the divine realm and the earth.[67]

One point should be added, in order to put in the proper historical perspective these religious developments in the circles of the Ashkenazi Hasidim. In order to put forward such ideas they had to overcome two meaningful obstacles. One was, the great prestige of Rav Saadia, who was not only an ancient and revered figure as head of the Sura academy in Babylonia, but also as a master of esoteric theology. All these writers were familiar with the old, poetic Hebrew paraphrases of Saadia's philosophical work, Emunot ve-Deot[68], and of his commentary on Sefer Yezira. They believed that these works incorporated eastern esoteric traditions, and it was very difficult to contradict ideas expressed in them. Yet, they did; Rabbi Judah the Pious clearly states that the correct view is not the one that Rav Saadia espoused.[69] The second obstacle was the fact that not only Rav Saadia presented the view that the divine glory was a created power for the benefit of prophetic revelation. There was a closer author who put this idea forward—Rabbi Judah ben Barzilai of Barcelona, who in his commentary on Sefer Yezira dedicated many dozens of pages to the emphatic statement and elaboration of Saadia's views.[70] Unlike Saadia, Judah ben Barzilai analyzed in great detail talmudic sayings and made them support this view. The great prestige of Rabbi Judah ben Barzilai was thus added to that of Rav Saadia to make it very difficult to depart from their views, especially as both were great authorities in halachah. The fact that the Ashkenazi Hasidic mystics did not hesitate, and described their mystical contradiction to Saadia's rationalistic approach in unmistakable terms, seems to indicate the importance and the centrality of these problems in their religious and intellectual world and the necessity to present new answers to them.

IV

A comparison between the development of the theology in which the divine realm contains several emanated divine powers in Ashkenazi Hasidism on the one hand and the kabbalah is Provence and Spain on the other, can be helpful to the understanding of the emergence of this idea in medieval Germany. The sequence of developments which lead from Rav Saadia Gaon's concepts of the kavod, through his refutation of the Karaitic charges concerning the Shiur Komah, via the formulations by Rabenu Hananel and Rabbi Judah ben Barzilai, the possibility of a concept of emanation in Ibn Ezra's commentary, and then the stages of development inside the movement — Rabbi Judah the Pious, the Baraita of Joseph ben Uzziel, Rabbi Eleazar of Worms and Rabbi Elhanan ben Yaqar — cannot be done concerning the system of the ten divine emanations in the Bahir and the works of Rabbi Isaac the Blind. The direct line leading from the questions concerning divine revelation, anthropomorphic verses and rabbinic sayings, and the meaning of the prayers to the concepts of divine powers who are revealed to prophets, carry anthropomorphic images and accept and answer the prayers and participate in the process of creation, is completely unknown to us concerning the beginning of the kabbalah.

The reasons for the formulation of the concept of the "special cherub" in Ashkenazi Hasidic mysticism are relatively clear; the reasons why the kabbalistic system should contain the powers of Nezah, the severnt sefirah, or Yesod, the ninth, are not. The tradition originating in the Sefer Yezira demands that there will be "ten sefirot, ten and not nine, ten and not eleven"[71]; this was known in the same degree to the mystics in Germany and the Provence. Yet the former paid no attention to it when formulating their symbols concerning the emanated divine powers, and the kabbalists put it in the center of their system (with the exception of the Iyyun circle, where the number 13 played a meaningful role).[72] We know many of the sources that served the kabbalists, yet no theological explanation of their system of symbols can be derived from their analysis.

The conclusion to be reached from this fact is, that though the similarity between the development of the concept of God as comprised from various emanated powers is surprisingly similar in both Germany and Spain-Provence, it is erroneous to assume that exactly the same spiritual forces were acting in both areas, and that this similarity is the result of an identical set of circumstances. We must enquire a little deeper into this problem before formulating any conclusion.

A factor which should serve to point out both the similarities and the differences between central and southern Europe is the attitude towards Jewish philosophy, which was the dominant spiritual force among Jewish intellectuals in the Arabic-speaking world since the 10th century. In the late 12th century and the early 13th, both kabbalists and Ashkenazi Hasidim were united in the struggle against it. Rabbi Jonah of Gerona was one of the leading figures in the attempt to excommunicate the works of Maimonides in 1232, and it is possible that Ashkenazi Hasidic leaders supported the move[73], at least it is certain the Nahmanides thought that they did, and referred to Rabbi Eleazar's works in his discussion of the problem.[74] There are several denunciations of the dialectical method in Ashkenazi Hasidic literature[75] (though the term "philosopher" was not associated by them with the rationalism which they rejected; it was used by them as a title for any learned scholar).[76]

While the opposition to the rationalistic movement in Judaism, and especially to Maimonides's Guide to the Perplexed, unites the two groups of mystical circles, it is a fact that this opposition did not hinder both of them from being influenced by rationalistic sources and ideas. Philosophical terms abide in the works of the Gerona circle, but can be found also in the traditions of Rabbi Isaac the Blind and the Bahir itself. The Bahir, despite its atmosphere of an ancient mystical midrash, most probably used terms and ideas derived from the works of Rabbi Abraham bar Hijja, Rabbi Abraham Ibn Ezra and even the Hebrew translation of Bahya Ibn Paquda's Hovot ha-Levavot ("The Duties of the Heart"), a translation written by Rabbi Judah Ibn Tibbon in the Provence in the last third of the 12th century.[77] There was no ban of any sort by the kabbalists against philosophical literature and ideas. Neoplatonism plays a central role in the mysticism of the Iyyun circle, and the kabbalistic notions concerning divine emanation and several other subjects are impossible to imagine without the impact of this central school of medieval thought, which had a profound influence on Christian, Moslem and Jewish mysticism alike.

The Ashkenazi Hasidim, on their part, used extensively the works of Rav Saadia, Rabbi Abraham bar Hijja, Rabbi Judah ben Barzilai and Rabbi Abraham ibn Ezra.[78] It is true that they did not regard them as rationalists, but rather as esoteric writers who received important and truthful secret traditions from previous generations. But it does not change the fact that basic ideas – even the neo-Platonic system of worlds as used by Bar Hijja[79] – were accepted by these Jewish-German mystics. Rabbi Eleazar reveals the extent of neo-Platonic influences on his thought when interpreting some key terms in the Sefer Yezira.[80] It is wrong, therefore, to assume that Ashkenazi Hasidism was vehemently opposed to rationalistic Jewish philosophy in a total manner.

This can be demonstrated by the fact that when a true and complete opponent to rationalism appeared in Germany, he became the opponent of Ashkenazi Hasidism no less than of the Jewish philosophers. The halachist Rabbi Moses Taku wrote, around 1220, the most thorough and unqualified denunciation of rationalism in Ashkenazi culture in his book Ketav Tamim ("The Book of Honesty").[81] In it he attacked Maimonides (only the Sefer ha-Mada in Mishneh Torah; he did not know as yet the Guide to the Perplexed), Rav Saadia Gaon (who is the main target of the attack), and Rabbi Abraham ibn Ezra (to whom he wrongly attributed the Sefer ha-Hayyim). But with them he attacked Rabbi Judah the Pious, the Shir ha-Yihhud ("Poem of Divine Unity", which was written in Ashkenazi Hasidic circles in the second half of the 12th century)[82], the "Books of Worms", probably referring to Rabbi Eleazar of Worms, and the Sefer ha-Hayim. All these together were regarded by Rabbi Moses Taku as speakers of a new, heretic religion, equivalent to Christianity and Karaitic heresy, which began with Saadia's Emunot ve-Deot and his commentary on the Sefer Yezira. He is not completely wrong when, compared to his own version of traditional orthodoxy, both rationalists and mystics are heretics in the same degree.

Rabbi Moses Taku, in his fierce polemics, proves one central point: Jewish rationalistic philosophy, exactly like Ashkenazi Hasidism, was seeking answers to new religious problems that Jews were facing in the Middle Ages. Traditional talmudic answers did not suffice any more, and new concepts had to be discovered in order to enable intellectual, spiritually-inclined Jews to continue in their traditional worship. The conception of God had to be changed if His commands should continue to be followed. Rabbi Moses Taku was wrong, therefore, when he attributed the new ideas of the philosophers or the Ashkenazi Hasidim to heresy, comparable to other movements which started within Judaism and then were separated from it, and developed new concepts concerning the performance of commandments. Saadia, Maimonides and Judah the Pious shared the conviction that the practical side of Judaism is to be preserved completely without any change. Their new ideas were directed to give new explanations and new motivations to the performance of the old commandments.

Can the kabbalists in southern Europe be included in this picture? Can they be also characterized as forming new ideas and new symbols in order to preserve the traditional Jewish practices? It seems that the answer can be a positive one, once we omit the words "in order". The kabbalists indeed did that: Their new symbols and new mystical interpretations of old tradition undoubtedly assisted in the preservation of the Jewish adherence to their traditional way of life. Later in the 13th century the kabbalists developed a whole system of taamey mitsvot, explanations of the practical commandments, which used mystical symbolism to give new meaning to the performance of the commandments. Beginnings of this endeavor can be found in the Book Bahir and other early kabbalistic works. So the orthodox impact of the revolutionary new ideas and symbols of the kabbalists is undeniable. The difference is, that we do not find, as we do concerning Ashkenazi Hasidism, the element of purpose, the deliberate connection between questions and answers that we find in Ashkenazi Hasidism and to a very large extent in Jewish rational philosophy. It is as if the kabbalists supplied answers to contemporary religious problems without intending to, as an offshoot of their original concepts, while the other schools demonstrate an intense connection between questions and answers.

This difference becomes much more emphasized if we take into consideration the distinct possibility that the Ashkenazi Hasidim had at their disposal some traditions which were remarkably similar to those that gave the kabbalah its distinctive character, but did not make any use of them. As Scholem had shown, the book Raza Rabba ("The Great Secret"), was one of the sources of the Book Bahir[83]; essentially it was a work closely related to Hekhalot mysticism, but its symbolism had some of the more daring, revolutionary characteristics later found in the kabbalah. This work is partially known to us today only from quotations found in Ashkenazi Hasidic literature, though admittedly in a later stratum—the works of Rabbi Moses, the great-grandson of Rabbi Judah the Pious, who wrote at the end of the 13th century. It is, however, a legitimate possibility that this work was known to earlier Ashkenazi Hasidic writers, but made no impact on their ideas or choice of symbols, while it may have had a shaping influence on the Book Bahir and kabbalistic symbolism.

Another example of the same phenomenon is to be found in a commentary on one of the esoteric holy names of God, attributed to Rav Hai Gaon, which was included by Rabbi Eleazar of Worms in his Sefer ha-Hokhmah, written in 1217.[84] This pseude-Hai commentary includes a portion which describes the ascension of prayer in the celestial realm, in a most dynamic and mythological way, including some terms which have become basic symbols of the kabbalah, like keter, atarah and "malkhut asirit".[85] It is not known whether kabbalists had in their traditions the same commentary, though some connection to the works of Rabbi Isaac the Blind can be imagined. Rabbi Eleazar, however, copied this commentary, but never used its symbols or ideas in any way in his extensive works. The centrality of the problem of the prayers for the Ashkenazi Hasidim has already been mentioned, and will be discussed further below; yet Rabbi Eleazar did not find a place for such an unusual and provocative treatment of the subject in any other of his works. He wrote an extensive commentary on the prayers, to which he dedicated many years; he may have written it in three different versions, but none of them contains any reference to the pseudo-Hai dynamic description of the ascension and the divine status of the prayer.

We can conclude, therefore, that even though the new concept of the divine world as comprised of several emanated powers appeared in about the same time in Germany and in Spain-Provence, and there are close similarities between the circles in southern and central Europe, the Ashkenazi Hasidic phenomenon carries a much more distinct contemporary character than the kabbalistic one. Ashkenazi Hasidism can be described as a response to the urgent needs of the time; the kabbalah seems to be revealing eternal truth, which always existed and will always be true, without revealing any special eagerness, at least in the Bahir and the Provence school, to confront the specific theological conflicts of the time in which it emerged.[86]

V

If we analyze the characteristics of all these esoteric and mystical circles and compare them to the dominating school of rationalistic philosophy in southern Europe and traditionalist orthodoxy in France and Germany in the second half of the 12th century and the early 13th, the most obvious fact to emerge, I believe, is that almost all the mystical circles are united in a new attitude towards the Jewish prayer. The earliest two commentaries on the prayers which reached us are those of Rabbi Eleazar of Worms on the one hand, probably in three original versions[87], and the one written by Rabbi Azriel of Gerona. But even those mystics who did not write such extensive, specialized works on the prayers, revealed in their mystical speculations a keen interest in the nature of the prayers themselves and in the mystical significance of the God-Man meeting during the prayers. An important discussion in the Book Bahir is dedicated to the subject[88], and the problem of the nature of devekut, adherence or communion with God, is one of the new subjects treated in depth by Rabbi Isaac the Blind, following his father, the Rabad.[89] A new interest in the text of the prayers characterizes one of the most important works by Rabbi Judah the Pious.[90] On the other hand, Jewish rationalistic philosophy almost completely ignored this central element of Jewish worship[91], while traditional orthodoxy, dealing mainly in halachic problems, had no new message concerning the prayers to its followers.

It seems, therefore, that when trying to understand the emergence of Jewish medieval mysticism as a whole, this phenomenon should be central to our analysis. The emergence of Jewish philosophy, and especially the ethical literature which followed the basic rationalism of this movement, is often described, correctly, I believe, as a process of spiritualization of Jewish religious life, of bringing a new emphasis to the non-practical, rational and emotional element within Judaism.[92] It is wrong to assume that this process was limited to Jews living in Moslem countries and being influenced directly by Arabic spiritualistic works. Jews in Christian countries as well underwent the same process, though their ways of expressing it were radically different.

Two elements should form the connection between the emergence of mysticism and the more general process of spiritualization. One is the attitude towards prayers, as mentioned above. The other is the meaningful parallel found between Ashkenazi Hasidism and early kabbalah in the fact that both movements produced, side by side with their mystical works, a body of ethical literature, which was directed towards the general public. While both movements, in their different ways, preserved the structures of esotericism concerning their mystical works, both had a message which, they felt, should be directed to the public as a whole, and help shape its every-day worship. I have described in some detail the process in which the Gerona kabbalists began to write ethical works[93]; their message was completely orthodox, but it undoubtedly contained the basic premise that religious life should be rich in their spiritual and emotional dimensions; the fact that they relied on traditional sources when proclaiming this does not diminish its adherence to 13th-century spiritual needs.

Ashkenazi Hasidism is better known for its ethical works than for its mystical ones. Both Rabbi Judah the Pious in Sefer Hasidim (probably following his father, Rabbi Samuel ben Kalonymus), and Rabbi Eleazar of Worms, dedicated a central place in their works to the ethical message they had for the public. They even developed a special literary genre, on the borderline between theology and ethics, dedicated to expounding in an exoteric manner their teachings concerning the unity of God and the intentions of the prayers.[94] The creation of this specific literary genre is another demonstration of the deep interest and commitment of the Ashkenazi Hasidism to bring their new concept of spiritual worship to the attention of German Jewry as whole, and to re-shape its religious attitudes. This is a clear indication that they perceived their new ideas as relevant and constructive concerning the religious situation in their time; the kabbalists of the 13th century felt the same, when they produced the body of traditionalistic ethical literature in the first half of the 13th century, when faced with the controversy concerning the study of philosophy, and wishing to present the public with an alternative spiritual way to follow traditional Judaism. But was this new, spiritual way, a mystical one?

The application of the term "mystical" to a religious phenomenon is always difficult; the definitions of this term are many, and a productive use of it depends usually on the specific context. In the framework of this survey, we can use the term in a comparative, not an absolute one, that is, as a comparison of the mystical element in Ashkenazi Hasidism on the one hand and in the works of the early kabbalah on the other. Such a comparison shows without any doubt, that the mystical element in the symbolism of the early kabbalah is much stronger than that of the Ashkenazi Hasidic esoteric theology. But more than that: It seems to me that such a comparison shows clearly the great difference between these two schools concerning their attitude to contemporary religious needs.

We do not find in Ashkenazi Hasidism any parallel to the new kabbalistic idea of the bi-sexuality of the divine pleroma, of the existence of divine feminine counterpart to the masculine system of the divine powers. We do not find in the works of the mystics in medieval Germany, before they were influenced by the kabbalah in the middle and second half of the 13th century, the concept of the divine "tree" which includes ten dynamic divine figures, which are in constant movement and changing inter-relationship. We do not find any Jewish-German parallel in this period to the kabbalists deep commitment to the theurgic notion, that the religious deeds of man have a meaningful impact on the well-being of the divine pleroma, a commitment found only in a vague way in the Book Bahir, but developed into a central theme of the kabbalah in the Provence and subsequent schools. The subject of the powers of evil, and the possibility of their being able to develop an independent pleroma opposing the holy one, which is evident in the kabbalah in the second half of the 13th century, has some roots in the Bahir and other early kabbalistic works, but not in Ashkenazi Hasidic works. These mystical dimensions, which gave the early kabbalah its great mythological drive, and had a great impact on the imagination and emotions of the kabbalists, are completely absent from Ashkenazi Hasidic speculation; but they are also absent from the popular ethical literature written by the kabbalists.

The mystical elements which are found in Ashkenazi Hasidism are, first and foremost, the new concept of the Godhead as comprised from a series of emanated powers which have distinct functions. In the second place it is found in the new discovery, and deep adherence, to ancient, Hekhalot mystical works, and especially to the myth of the gigantic Shiur Komah anthropomorphic figure. The third element is the new, mystical attitude towards the prayers, evident in the works of Rabbi Judah the Pious and Rabbi Eleazar of Worms, both concerning the sanctity of every word and every letter of the prayers, and concerning the direction of the prayers to an emanated divine power. A hint of mystical attitude can be found also in some aspects of Ashkenazi Hasidic ethics.[95] All these elements, without exception, have parallels in the works of the early kabbalists, and in all cases they are much stronger, richer in symbolism and in religious impact then their presentation in Ashkenazi Hasidic works.

The conclusion which is suggested here, as a result of this analysis, is the characterization of the appearance of mystical elements in the works of Jewish-German pietists in the late 12th and early 13th centuries as a result of contemporary spiritual needs: The movement towards the spiritualization of Jewish religious life, the need to confront rationalistic ideas, the need to re-establish the religious meaning of the prophecy and of the daily prayers, the search for a more intimate contact with the divine world, and to share those elements which are relevant to the wide public with them by the means of popular and ethical works. All this is found in the kabbalah, and characterizes the creative activity of the early kabbalists as well. The great difference between the two schools is, that the kabbalah is all this, and much much more besides; the "answers" the kabbalah supplied to contemporary spiritual needs are much greater than the questions; the clear balance between a problem and its spiritual response, which can be found in Ashkenazi Hasidism to a very large extent, is absent in the works of the kabbalists: Their intense, mythical and mystical symbolism far transcends contemporary needs.

It can be stated, therefore, that the emergence of mysticism in medieval Germany in the schools and circles of Ashkenazi Hasidism can be explained by a historical analysis of the spiritual circumstances of the age. To this, of course, should be added the personal inclination towards mystical speculation and expressions, which, probably, exists potentially within every religious group in every age; it is the circumstances which make it express itself and give it legitimacy in the cultural atmosphere of the age. The kabbalah, while also being such an answer, is also the expression of some much deeper motives and cultural undercurrents which added to historical needs a new dimension of intensity, variety and richness. The examination of these specific forces which made the kabbalah so different from Ashkenazi Hasidism and allowed it to create independently of current spiritual needs, cannot be done here; suffice it to say, that it is the irony of history in its attitude towards its faithful servants that it is the kabbalah which had the upper hand in Jewish spirituality and mysticism in the end of the 13th century and subsequent periods. The relevant and balanced Ashkenazi Hasidic response to history was superseded by the much less restrained but much stronger force of kabbalistic mysticism.

Notes

1 A brief attempt to present and analyze this problem was made in several sections of my book "Early Kabbalistic Circles", published by Academon, Jerusalem 1977 (in Hebrew).

2 The main analysis of the early kabbalah is found, of course, in Gershom Scholem's masterly study of the problem in his Ursprung and Anfänge der Kabbala, Walter de Gruyter, Berlin 1962. This was Scholem's third publication of the same material. The first was an essay, Hathalot ha-Kabbalah, published in Hebrew in Kneset le-Zecher Bialik, vol. 10, Tel Aviv 1947, pp. 179-228. This essay, with many additions, was published as a book, Reshit ha-Kabbalah, Schocken Publishing House, Jerusalem-Tel Aviv 1948. In the years just before and just after the publication of the book in an extended and corrected form, considerably enlarged, in German, Scholem gave, for four years, courses on that subject at the Hebrew University. These were edited by R. Shatz and Y. Ben Shlomo, published by Academon, Jerusalem 1960-1965. The last version of this work was recently published in English, The Origin of the Kabbalah, edited by R. J. Zvi Werblowsky (Princeton, 1987).

Compare also the chapter on the early kabbalah in my book: "Gershom Scholem and the Mystical Dimension in Jewish History", New York University Press, New York 1987, pp. 147-187. The chapter was separately published in Modern Judaism, vol. 5 (1985), pp. 39-66. See also J. Dan, R. Kiener, The Early Kabbalah, Paulist Press, New York 1986.

3 G. Scholem, Das Buch Bahir, Leipzig, W. Drugulin, 1923. An analysis of this work is presented in Scholem, Ursprung, pp. 43-174. Compare Dan, Kiener, The Early Kabbalah, pp. 57-70.

4 Rabbi Isaac's Commentary on Sefer Yezira was published by Scholem as an appendix to Ha-Kabbalah bi-Provence, the second volume in the Hebrew version of Ursprung (above, n. 1, Academon, Jerusalem 1962). On the recensions of this work see H. Wirszubsky's analysis in Scholem's Jubillee Volume (Tarbiz vol. 27), Jerusalem 1958 pp. 257-264. And see Ursprung, pp. 219-272; The Early Kabbalah, pp. 71-86; G. Scholem, Kabbalah, Keter Publishing House, Jerusalem 1974, pp. 45-47.

5 This is one of the most difficult subjects concerning the history of the early kabbalah, which cannot be treated here in detail. Suffice it to say that if indeed Rabbi Isaac did not use the Bahir, the whole concept of the ten sefirot will then be one which has been developed in two different, but almost unbelievingly similar, Jewish traditions. An exhaustive study of the problem will be published elsewhere.

6   G. Scholem presented a list of possible works belonging to this circle in Reshit ha-
    Kabbala (1948, see note 2) pp. 255-262, and an analysis of them pp. 162-175, and
    compare Ursprung, pp. 273-323. Recently Dr. M. Verman concluded a Ph. D.
    thesis (Harvard University, 1984) dealing with the textual and historical problems
    concerning this circle, and presented an edition of the various versions of Sefer
    ha-Iyyun (see also The Early Kabbalah, pp. 43-56). Dr. Verman reached the
    conclusion that the Sefer ha-Iyyun and the other works of this circle were written
    in the second half of the 13th century, and were based on the works of Rabbi
    Azriel of Gerona. A similar attitude to the question of the relationship between
    Sefer ha-Iyyun and Rabbi Azriel is to be found in I. Tishby's edition of Rabbi
    Azriel's Commentary on the Talmudic Legends (Jerusalem, 1944, Hebrew).
    However, no explanation was given how is it possible that mystics writing a
    generation after Rabbi Azriel and using his terminology in some cases could
    completely ignore the concept of the ten sefirot and all the symbols connected
    with that, and disregard not only the major theme in Rabbi Azriel's works but also
    those of the Bahir, Rabbi Isaac the Blind, Rabbi Ezra ben Shlomo, Nachmanides
    and many others. It seems therefore more probable that this circle's central works
    preceded Rabbi Azriel and other kabbalists, and the latter used some of the
    terminology found in Sefer ha-Iyyun. It should be noted that the Scholem list
    includes 32 works, but only a few of them actually belong to the original Iyyun
    circle. The others are kabbalistic works which used this circle's symbolism and
    terminology. See now: M. Verman, The Books of Contemplation, New York:
    SUNY Press, 1992.

7   On the Gerona circle see Scholem, Ursprung, pp. 324-406; I. Tishby, Hikrey
    Kabbalah u-Shluhoteha, Magness Press, Jerusalem 1982, pp. 3-35; The Early
    Kabbalah, pp. 78-150. Concerning Rabbi Azriel's commentary on the Prayers see:
    G. Sed-Rajna, Azriel de Gerone Commentaire sur la Liturgue quotidienne,
    Leiden, E. J. Brill, 1974.

8   The modern study of the esoteric theology of Ashkenazi Hasidism was started by
    G. Scholem with the third chapter of his Major Trends in Jewish Mysticism
    (Schocken, New York 1941 pp. 80-118). My two volumes on the subject are
    Toarat ha-Sod shel Hasidey Ashkenaz (The Bialik Institute, Jerusalem 1968) (=
    Torat ha-Sod); A summary of this book is to be found in: Die esoterische Lehre
    des Deutschen Chassidismus, Tr. E. Hanker, Hebraische Beitrage zur
    Wissenschaft des Judentums, vol. 1, ed. M. Graetz, Heidelberg 1985, pp. 153-185;
    and Iyyunim be-Sifrut Hasidey Ashkenaz (Massada, Ramat Gan 1975) (=
    Iyyunim).

9   The biography of Rabbi Samuel and a list of his writings were complied by A.
    Epstein, re-published in the collection of his studies ed. by A. M. Haberman, vol.
    1, Mosad ha-Rav Kook, Jerusalem 1950, pp. 245-269.

10 The literature on Ashkenazi Hasidic ethics is growing very fast, and cannot be
    presented here in detail. A recent important collection in Hebrew is I. G. Marcus
    (ed.), Dat ve-Hevra be-Mishnatam shel Hasidei Ashkenaz, Jerusalem 1986; to
    which should be added: H. Soloveitchik, Three Themes in the Sefer Hasidim, AJS
    Review 1 (1976), pp. 311-357, and I. G. Marcus: Piety and Society, Brill, Leiden
    1981; idem, The Devotional Ideals of Ashkenazic Pietism, in: A. Green, ed.,

History of Jewish Spirituality, vol. 1, Crossroads, New York 1986, pp. 356-366. Concerning Sefer Hasidim itself, the book was first published in Bologna, 1538; a longer version was found in Parma Ms. 3280, and first published by J. Wistinetzki in Berlin, 1891. The same work, with a detailed introduction and index, was published by J. Freiman, Frankfurt A/m 1924 (with several subsequent printings). Recently I. G. Marcus published a facsimile edition of the Parma Ms., with an introduction (Jerusalem 1985).

11   This circle of mystics was described and an attempt was made to list their works and their inter-relationship in my paper published in Tarbiz, vol. 35, 1966, pp. 349-372. The text of the Barayta of Joseph ben Uzziel was published by A. Epstein (above, n. 9, vol. 2, 1957, pp. 226-250). A recent survey of the problem is presented in: J. Dan, Pseudepigraphy in Medieval Jewish Mysticism in Germany, in: Falschungen im Mittelalter, Monumenta Germaniae Historica Schriften Band 33, V, Hannover 1988, pp. 519-532. Concerning the legend on which this circle based its tradition, see below, n. 47.

12   G. Scholem mentioned the importance of Rabbi Elhanan's works in Major Trends, p. 85, 376 n. 114. G. Vajda published a study of the relationship of his works to some medieval non-Jewish works (Archives d'Histoire Doctrinale et Littéraire du Moyen Ages, 1961, pp. 15-34), and then published one of his commentaries on the Sefer Yezira in Kovetz Al Yad, vol. 16 part 1, Jerusalem 1966, pp. 147-197. The Sod ha-Sodot and the second Commentary were published by me in Esoteric Texts of Ashkenazi Hasidic Theology, Akademon, Jerusalem 1975 (in Hebrew).

13   Sefer ha-Hayyim appears in the annals of Jewish scholarship in an unusual manner: When G. Scholem presented his plans of the study of kabbalah to the poet H. N. Bialik in a letter written in 1925 (published in Devarim Bego, Tel Aviv, Am Oved, 1976, pp. 59-63), he placed Sefer ha-Hayyim as the first among the mystical texts which should be published in critical editions. He frequently used it in Major Trends and in the Ursprung. See also my Torat ha-Sod, pp. 143-156. The book was copied in my Esoteric Texts of Ashkenazi Hasidic Theology (above, n. 12). It still awaits a scholarly edition.

14   Sefer ha-Navon was published by me, based on several manuscripts, in Kovetz Al Yad vol. 16, part 1, Jerusalem 1966, pp. 199-223.

15   I am preparing a detailed study of this subject as a part of the History of Jewish Mysticism which is in preparation.

16   The Ashkenazi Hasidim had a concept dividing all knowledge into 73 parts (the numerical value of the Hebrew hochmah, wisdom), and two books in our possession are structured according to them; a prominent place among these "gates of wisdom" is given to Sha'ar ha-Sod, the Gate of Esoteric Knowledge. The two books are: Rabbi Eleazar of Worms's Sefer ha-Hochmah, The Book of Wisdom, which also gives the list of these "gates". Parts of it were published by me in Zion, vol. 29 (1964), pp. 168-181 and reprinted in Iyyunim, pp. 44-57. The second book is an extensive commentary on the torah, found in a Bodleian ms., and described in: J. Dan, The Ashkenazi Hasidic "Gates of Wisdom", Homage a Geroges Vajda, ed. G. Nahon et C. Touati, Louvain 1980, pp. 183-189. This commentary was subsequently published as "Peirush ha-Roqeah al ha-Torah", in

three volumes, Bnei-Berak, 1978-1981, attributing it to Rabbi Eleazar, without any foundation, and adding it to the text of the Sefer ha-Hockmah. See my note concerning this in Kiryat Sefer, vol. 50, 1984, p. 644. In both works, however, a large part is given to Sha'ar ha-Sod, interpreting the biblical verses according to the esoteric method.

17 Rabbi Eleazar's Sefer ha-Shem is found in manuscripts which contain the full five works which comprise together his magnum opus, Sodey Razaya. It is the third book in this collection. The best manuscripts are British Museum 737 and Munich 81.

18 G. Scholem noted the text describing this ceremony in: On the Kabbalah and Its Symbolism, pp. 136-138; (= Zur Kabbalah und ihere Symbolik, Rhein Verlag, Zurich 1960, pp. 182-183), and compare Torat ha-Sod, pp. 74-76.

19 See above, note 16 (Iyyunim, pp. 44-57).

20 Among Rabbi Eleazar's many works, the ones in which he seems to have used his teacher's writings most extensively are the Sod ha-Merkavah (The Secret of the Chariot, published as Sodey Razaya by Israel Kamelhar, Rhysza, 1930), Hochmat ha-Nefesh ("The Wisdom of the Soul", i.e., psychology, printed in Lwow, 1876 and Safed, 1883), and his Commentary on Sefer Yezira, Premiszla 1883; these are the second, fourth and fifth parts of Sodey Razaya collection.

21 This work was published in a most detailed scholarly edition, with a comprehensive introduction, by E. E. Urbach, Mekizei Nirdamim, Jerusalem 1939-1963 (4 volumes).

22 Many of these references to Rabbi Eleazar are taken from the latter's Commentary on the Prayers, which was Rabbi Abraham's major source.

23 Rabbi Abraham berabi Azriel seldom mentions Rabbi Judah the Pious by name, in contradiction to his constant efforts throughout the book to quote authorities ancient and contemporary, Spanish and Ashkenazi, in full. The reason seems to be that Rabbi Judah the Pious objected to the practice of writing an author's name on a book, for fear that this will cause him, or his descendants, to commit the sin of pride; this is mentioned several times in the Sefer Hasidim. Rabbi Judah was, however, completely alone among his followers in this; everybody else, including Rabbi Eleazar, prominently placed their names on their works (Rabbi Eleazar probably added, in deference to his teacher, the term ha-katan, "the small", to his name, expressing thus the required humility). As a result, Rabbi Abraham quotes Rabbi Judah's Sefer ha-Kavod ("Book of Divine Glory") about 40 times as if it were an anonymous work, not wishing to transgress Rabbi Judah's wishes. He had, however, a special problem which he solved in a unique way. Rabbi Moses, Rabbi Judah's son, wrote after his father's death a commentary on the Torah, based on his recollections of the conversations and arguments that he and his father had about the weekly portion of the torah. Rabbi Judah's statements in this work could not be quoted by Rabbi Abraham anonymously, so he used a special title: Reah Bosem Nihoah, being the acronym of Rabbi Judah the Pious son of Samuel, and nihoah has the same numerical value as "hasid". Thus he obviously quoted Rabbi Judah, without having mentioned his name explicitly.

24   An example of this attitude may have been his Commentary to the Prayers; see below, note 87.

25   G. Scholem, Teudah Hadasha le-Toeldot Reshit ha-Kabbalah, Sefer Bialik, Tel Aviv 1934, pp. 141-162. See also Ursprung, pp. 219-230. Compare now: J. Dan, Jewish Mysticism and Jewish Ethics, Seattle and London 1986, pp. 28-36 and: idem, The Ideological and Social Background to the Emergence of Rabbinic Ethical Literature in the 13th Century, in: S. Pines Jubilee Volume (ed. M. Idel, Z. Harvey, E. Schweid), part 1 (= Mehkerey Yerushalayim be-Mahshevet Yisrael vol. 7), Jerusalem 1988, pp. 239-263.

26   *sefer ha-nichtav ein lo aron.*

27   The most detailed tradition was written by Rabbi Eleazar of Worms in his Commentary on the Prayers (not, as sometimes is mistakenly stated, in the treatise Sodot ha-Tefilah, which was not written by Rabbi Eleazar but by another disciple of Rabbi Judah the Pious; the latter copied it into his treatise, but there is no doubt that the original source is in the Commentary; Ms. Paris 772 is a most complete version of Rabbi Eleazar's extensive work). Some versions of this tradition extended it explicitly to Moses (see H. Gross, MGWJ vol. 49, 1905, pp. 692-700), but the inference exists in the shorter versions as well. See the bibliography on this subject in Torat ha-Sod, pp. 15-17.

28   The problem of the relationship between the Ashkenazi Hasidim, and other European mystics, and the texts of the Hekhalot literature is a most difficult one. A few sentences about it are included below. The core of the problem is how much of what is presented in the seven manuscripts which served as a basis for P. Schafer's Synopsis (Tübingen, 1981) was known to the Ashkenazi Hasidim. There is, on the one hand, evidence that at least some of these manuscripts were based on traditions from Ashkenazi Hasidic schools. On the other hand, some sections are never used or mentioned in the works of these mystics. A detailed study of the exact material used by European writers up to the middle of the 13th century is most important task that should be undertaken.

29   See: J. Dan, The Seventy Names of Metatron, Proceedings of the Eighth World Congress of Jewish Studies, vol. III, Jerusalem 1982, 19-23.

30   The problem was discussed in detail in my study: Perushey ha-Aderet veha-Emunah shel Hasidey Ashkenaz, Tarbiz Jubillee Volume (vol. 50), ed. E. E. Urbach, Jerusalem 1981, pp. 396-404.

31   Mussajoff, Merkavah Shelemah ("A Complete Chariot", a publication of his own manuscript of Hekhalot mystical texts), Jerusalem 1927. Rabbi Judah the Pious and Rabbi Joel the Pious are mentioned there by name.

32   This work was published by G. Scholem as an appendix to his Reshit ha-Kabbalah, Jerusalem 1948, pp. 220-238.

33   This part of the work was published by I. Kamelhar under the title Sodey Razaya (see above, note 20).

34   The work was published by Benjamin Klar, Jerusalem 1944. The stories on Rabbi Aaron begin there on page 13. See Torat ha-Sod, p. 18, and now the detailed historical analysis by R. Bonfil, Bein Eretz Yisrael u-Bavel, Shalem vol. 5, 1987, pp. 1-30.

35   See my analysis of this section in Torat ha-Sod, p. 12. Z 36 G. Scholem dedicated an important and innovative discussion to this work in his Jewish Gnosticism, Merkabah Mysticism and Talmudic Tradition, New York, The Jewish Theological Seminary, 1960; revised edition, 1965. S. Lieberman added an analysis of the pertinent talmudic and midrashic sections in his Mishnat Shir ha-Shirim, published as an appendix to Scholem's book (pp. 118-126). Another study of the subject is included in Scholem's paper on the Shiur Komah concept, in: Von der mystischen Gestalt der Gottheit, Rhein Verlag, Zurich 1962, pp. 7-48. The texts of this work were collected and published by M. S. Cohen, in two volumes: The Shiur Komah, Liturgy and Theurgy in Pre-Kabbalistic Jewish Mysticism, University Press of America, Latham, New York, London, 1983; The Shiur Komah: Texts and Recensions, J. C. B. Mohr, Tübingen 1985. See also: J. Dan, The Concept of Knowledge in the Shiur Komah, Studies in Jewish Intellectual History Presented to Alexander Altmann, ed. S. Stein, R. Loewe, Alabama 1979, pp. 67-73.

37   Rav Saadia's discussion of this subject, which was probably part of the now lost Saadian answer to Solomon Ben Yeruhim (see below, n. 40), was preserved in Rabbi Judah ben Barzilai ha-Brazeloni, Commentary on the Sefer Yezira, ed. by S. J. Halberstam, Berlin 1885, pp. 20-22.

38   The work was included in Rabbi Eleazar's Sod Ma'aseh Bereshit ("The Esoteric Meaning of the Creation"), which was partly published in the Sefer Raziel, Amsterdam 1701 (the section dedicated to it is there on pages 37a-38b). A new, more complete edition of the work was recently published in Jerusalem, 1988.

39   The very famous example is found in Bishop Agobard's of Lyons testimony; see the new study of it by R. Bonfil.

40   Solomon ben Yeruhim, Milhamot ha-Shem ("The Wars of the Lord"), ed. I. Davidson, New York 1934. This work is a satirical treatment of the traditions of the talmudic rabbis in rhymed prose, personally attacking Saadya Gaon for believing in them. The first half is dedicated to halachic points of controversy between the Karaites and their Rabbinic opponents, and the second—to a presentation of the Shiur Komah and other sections of Hekhalot mystical literature as absurdities believed by the Rabbis.

41   Concerning the works of Elhanan ben Yaqar on Sefer Yezira, see above, note 12.

42   Published in by the Hasidic author, Rabbi Zevi Elimelech of Dinow.

43   See above, note 28. Concerning the practice itself, see G. Scholem's studies in Major Trends, pp. 46-79 and Jewish Gnosticism (above, note 36), pp. 14-30. The possibility that a similar practice was known to Paulus was raised by Scholem, and rejected by P. Schafer; see: Hekhalot-Studien, J. C. B. Mohr, Tübingen 1988, pp.

234-249. And compare: J. Dan, Three Types of Ancient Jewish Mysticism, Cincinnati 1985, pp. 8-16.

44 There is a possibility that though the known works of the Kalonymus school do not mention such a practice, other Ashkenazi Hasidic mystical authors, whose works were not preserved, did follow them. The possibility exists especially concerning Rabbi Yoel Hasid and Rabbi Nehemia ben Shlomo.

45 See above, note 4.

46 The text was printed (from the edition prepared by M. Verman) in J. Dan, R. Kiener, The Early Kabbalah (see above, note 6).

47 This work of fiction is a literary satire of some basic Jewish beliefs, especially those concerning the afterlife and redemption, and various Jewish biblical figures, including Abraham and David, and often of God himself. See my study of it included in The Hebrew Story in the Middle Ages, Keter Publishing House, Jerusalem 1974 (in Hebrew), pp. 69-78. The text was published in many traditional editions and is found in an unusually large number of manuscripts. M. Steinschneider printed an edition of it (Berlin, 1858), and recently a scholarly edition by E. Yassif was published, Magnes Press, Jerusalem 1985. See my review of this edition in Kiryat Sefer, vol. 60, pp. 294-297. It is still a mystery why did this circle of Ashkenazi mystics choose their heroes from a work of fiction, which should have been regarded by them as heretical and rude.

48 In ms. Adler 1161, at the Jewish Theological Seminary in New York, there is a collection of material which combines kabbalah and Ashkenazi Hasidic traditions, including the one concerning Yosef Maon.

49 This tradition has been recently studied in great detail by A. Grossman, who devoted most of his efforts to the problem of the chronology of the emigration of the Kalonymus family from Italy to Germany (Zion, vol. 40, 1975, pp. 85-154). It seems that Grossman's analysis rejecting all previously suggested dates as impossible because of conflicting evidence concerning the lives of the figures mentioned, is correct. His alternative suggestions seem to me to raise too many new difficulties. For instance, to reject Rabbi Eleazar's very detailed tradition as completely unreliable is very difficult, because it is derived from a school and a family which took great care to preserve such traditions; mistakes undoubtedly can be found in it, but it cannot be regarded as completely fictitious. Another difficult problem is the one concerning "King Karl" mentioned by Rabbi Eleazar as the monarch who initiated the move of that family. Grossman tends to view this statement as evidence to the existence of legends concerning Karl the Great, and that Rabbi Eleazar was following the 12th century custom of tying this emperor to many legendary traditions. The difficulty here is, that no other Ashkenazi Hasidic authentic source ever mentioned Karl the Great; in the many volumes of Rabbi Eleazar's works he is not mentioned at all. He may have appeared in the later legends on the Ashkenazi Hasidim, which, though preserving some authentic material, undoubtedly reflect a different period and attitude. It is inconceivable that when referring to Karl the Great a 13th century author will just say "King Karl"; this is more correctly interpreted as an emphasis

that it is not Karl the Great, whose name included the "great" as an integral part in European languages. It seems to me, therefore, that an attempt to connect this event with one of the Carolingian emperors might still prove fruitful.

50 See above, note 11, and compare: J. Dan, The Problem of Pseudepigraphy in Early Kabbalah, Studies in Kabbalah and Jewish Ethical Literature Presented to I. Tishby, ed. J. Dan and J. Hacker, Jerusalem 1986, pp. 111-138. Another example of kabbalistic pseudepigraphy can be found in the many "sources" and fictitious stories included in the works of Rabbi Isaac ha-Cohen, a kabbalist from Castile in the beginning of the second half of the 13th century. See G. Scholem, Kabbalot Rabbi Yaakov ve-Rabbi Yitzhak, Madaey ha-Yahadut vol. II, 1927, pp. 244-264; and compare: J. Dan, Samael, Lilith and the Concept of Evil in Early Kabbalah, AJS Review vol. V, 1980, pp. 17-40.

51 Above, note 23.

52 In rabbinic traditions the Shekhinah is one of the many names for God, and only in the Middle Ages there is a beginning of a concept which sees it as separate power, and later as a feminine divine power. See G. Scholem, Zur Entwicklungsgeschichte der kabbalistischen Konzepzion der Schechina, Eranos Jahrbuch 21 (1952), pp. 45-107.

53 While the exact dating of the old Aramaic translations is uncertain, there can be no doubt that the practice preceded considerably Saadia's works.

54 A. Altmann, Saadia's Theory of Revelation, Its Origin and Background, Saadia Studies, ed. Rosenthal, Manchester 1943, pp. 4-25.

55 Rav Saadia dedicated to this problem the second half of the second chapter in his philosophical work, Emunot ve-Deot (Leipzig 1859, p. 63 ss.).

56 This is quoted by Rabbi Judah ha-Barzeloni (above, note 37). Rabbi Judah himself, who wrote this commentary in the middle of the 12th century, did not repeat Saadia's view concerning a multiple system of glories. On the other hand, he was somewhat dissatisfied with the basic Saadian explanation of the process of prophecy, though he relies on it and repeats it frequently. Thus, for instance, he rejects emphatically a reponsum by Rav Hai Gaon, who identifies the glory with an angel (pp. 137-138), and states that the glory is much more than an angel—but he does not explain in what way.

57 The relevant section from Rabenu Hananel, and many other sources dealing with the same subject, were collected and presented by Rabbi Abraham berabi Azriel in his Arugat ha-Bosem (above, note 21), vol. I, pp. 197-202.

58 Yesod Mora, Ch. 12.

59 Ibn Ezra uses the verb "dvk" (to adhere, to unite) instead of the verb "azl" which was adopted by the kabbalists, and Rabbi Judah the Pious followed his usage. There seems to be a good basis to the supposition that Ibn Ezra meant it to be a better expression of the idea of emanation. I. Tishby pointed out the possibility that Rabbi Shabbatai Donolo adopted this idea—but not the terminology—in the

10th century, in his commentaries on the verse "Na'aseh Adam be-Zalmenu" and on Sefer Yezira.

60   This section of Rabbi Judah the Pious's work was published in Iyyunim, pp. 158-167.

61   J. Dan, Kavod Nistar, in: Dat ve-safah, edited by M. Halamish and A. Kasher, Bar Ilan University, Ramat Gan 1982, pp. 71-79.

62   This text was translated and analyzed in my paper: "The Emergence of the Mystical Prayer", in: J. Dan, F. Talmage (ed.), Studies in Jewish Mysticism, Cambridge, Mass., 1981, pp. 85-120; I.Dan, Pesaq ha-Yirah veha Emunah and the Intention of Prayer in Ashkenazi Hasidism, Frankfurter Judaistische Beiträge 19 (1991/92), 185-215; idem, Prager as Text and Prayer as Mystical Experience, Torah and Wisdom, Essays in Honor of Arthur Hyman, ed. Ruth Link-Salinger, New York: Shengold 1992, pp. 33-47.

63   For instance, this circle of mystics does use the Hebrew term for emanation (azl), which is not used by the Kalonymus school (see above, note 59).

64   See above, note 12.

65   In Hebrew: Nitomemu, an unusual usage of the name "twins" as a verb.

66   See above, note 36.

67   On the kavod theory in the Sefer ha-Hayyim see Torat Ha-Sod, pp. 143-156.

68   The characteristics and chronology of this important medieval work were recently studied by Ronald C. Kiener, The Hebrew Paraphrase of Saadiah Gaon's Kitab al-Amanat wa'l-I'tiqadat, AJS Review vol. XI, 1986, pp. 1-26.

69   Rabbi Judah attributes the view that the glory was created to the "third stage" in a fictitious trialogue which he presents (the first sage represents the rationalistic view that revelation is a psychological process, by which God gives illusionary images to the prophet. The second sage represents Rabbi Judah himself), and he states clearly that the words of this sage are those of Rav Saadia. The text was published in Iyyunim, pp. 163 ss.

70   The introduction to Judah ben Barzilai's Commentary on Sefer Yezira (pp. 1-105) is dedicated mainly to this subject.

71   Sefer Yezira Ch. 1, section 4 (in the traditional editions; Paragraph 4 in I. Gruenwald's commentary, Some Critical Notes on the First Part of Sefer Yezira, Revue des Etudes juives, CXXXII (4), 1973, p. 488), and the same in P. Hayman's translation (Shadow, vol. 3 no. 1, June 1986, p. 28).

72   In 13th-century kabbalah the problem of the relationship between the numbers 10 and 13 was an important one, because of the tradition of 13 divine attributes of mercy. A famous kabbalistic work of this period, attributed to a responsum by Rav Hai Gaon, explains that the ten sefirot have 3 supreme roots within the Godhead, thus reconciling the two numbers.

73 See: E. E. Urbach, Helkam shel Hachmei Ashkenaz ve-Zarfat ba-Pulmus al ha-Rambam ve-al Ketavav, Zion vol. 12, pp. 149-159.

74 This is found in Nachmanides's early epistle concerning the controversy over the writings of Maimonides, known by its first sentence, Be-Terem Eaneh Ani Shogeg. In the last section of this epistle Nachmanides quotes a few lines from a work by Rabbi Eleazar of Worms which describes the unity of God in terms which may seem almost identical to the philosophical ones. Nachmanides, who at that time tried to restore peace among the various parties, tried to show that differences were not that great between them. It is obvious, however, that he believed Rabbi Eleazar to be an opponent of Maimonidean philosophy. See Shevel's edition of the works of Nachmanides, vol. II, Jerusalem 1963, p. 346.

75 Both in Sefer Hasidim and in Rabbi Eleazar's book on psychology, Hochmat ha-Nefesh, the term "dialectics" is used as an equivalent to heresy.

76 Rabbi Judah the Pious used the term "philosophers" to describe Jewish sages when presenting conflicting ideas. See Iyyunim, pp. 31-33.

77 G. Scholem alluded to the Bahir's indebtedness to Rabbi Abraham bar Hijja (Ursprung, p. 54-55); concerning Ibn Ezra, it seems that the use of the verb "dvk" denoted his influence (see paragraph 129 and parallels). The influence of the Hebrew version of Bahya's ethical work is evident in the Bahir's adaptation of a parable presented in the end of the preface to Hovot ha-Levavot, concerning a king's gift of cloth to his servants. This was used in the Bahir in a different way, in the explanation of the process of the gilgul. Scholem analyzed medieval influences on Rabbi Isaac the Blind, and I. Tishby pointed out the philosophical terminology of the Gerona school (see above, note 4).

78 See Torat ha-Sod, pp. 114-116, 204.

79 G. Scholem, Reste neuplatinischer Speculation bei den Deutschen Hasidim, MGWJ, 75 (1931), pp. 172-191. The concept of the four divine worlds, based on Bar Hijja neo-Platonic formulation, is found, for instance, in the Pesaq ha-Yirah veha-Emunah.

80 See Torat ha-Sod, pp. 99-100. Rabbi Eleazar explains, for instance, the Sefer Yezira concepts of the dimensions of good and evil as referring to matter and spirit.

81 This work was first published by R. Kircheim in Ozar Nehmad, vol. 3, Vienna 1863, pp. 57-99. A facsimile edition of the Paris manuscript, the only one we have of this work, was published in Jerusalem, 1984, to which a detailed introduction and analysis by me was added.

82 See J. Dan, Introduction to the facsimile edition of Shir ha-Yihhud, Magnes Press, Jerusalem 1985.

83 Sections of this work were published by G. Scholem (above, note 32).

84 G. Scholem translated this section in Ursprung, pp. 162-165. The Hebrew text was published and discussed in Torat ha-Sod, pp. 118-125; and also: J. Dan, Hugey ha-Mekubalim ha-Rishonim, Academon, Jerusalem 1977, pp. 159-165; and

in English: J. Dan, The Emergence of the Mystical Prayer (above, note 62). This text was carefully studied by A. Farber-Ginat in a Ph. D. thesis: The Concept of the Merkabah in 13th Century Jewish Esotericism—Sod ha-Egoz and Its Development, Jerusalem 1986, pp. 231-244 et passim. Compare: M. Idel, Kabbalah—New Perspectives, Yale University Press, New Haven and London 1988, pp. 195 ss.

85　These terms, which denote the most supreme sefira (keter) and the tenth and lowest (atara, malchut), are presented in this text as synonyms to the prayer when it reaches the divine realm.

86　The problem of the emergence of the kabbalah and its relationship to Jewish rationalistic philosophy was presented by G. Scholem in the opening pages of his Ursprung. He discussed there the attitudes of previous scholars, especially Neumark and Graetz, to the same problem. A further discussion of this problem is presented below.

87　The differences between the three main manuscripts of this work (Paris 772, Oxford 1204 and Vienna 108) seem to indicate that the author himself re-edited his own work several times.

88　A discussion of this section of the Bahir can be found in: J. Dan, The Dawn of Midrash in the Kabbalah, in: Midrash and Literature, ed. G. H. Hartman and S. Budick, Yale University Press, New Haven and London, 1986, pp. 127-140. And compare: Early Jewish Mysticism, pp. 61-66.

89　See Scholem, Ursprung, pp. 264-273 and compare: J. Dan, The Emergence of the Mystical Prayer (above, note 62).

90　Rabbi Judah the Pious wrote an extensive commentary on the prayers, which was not preserved. Many quotations from it are included in a brief treatise, found in many manuscripts, called Sodot ha-Tefilah ("The Secrets of the Prayers"), written by one of his disciples. According to these quotations, the main purpose of Rabbi Judah was to show that the version of the prayers known to him is the only true one, and that every change, even of one letter, will destroy the intrinsic, mystical harmony of the text. See: J. Dan, The Historical Rabbi Judah the Pious, in: Culture and Society in Medieval Jewry, Studies Dedicated to the Memory of H. H. Ben-Sasson, ed. M. Ben-Sasson, R. Bonfil and J. Hacker, The Historical Society of Israel, Jerusalem 1989, pp. 389-398; and see above, note 62.

91　A definitive analysis of the attitude of Maimonides, and of Jewish philosophy in general, to the prayers, was presented by Marvin Fox in his paper: The Prayer in Maimonides's Philosophy, in: Prayer in Judaism, Continuity and Change, ed. G. H. Cohen, Ramat Gan 1978, pp. 142-167.

92　This process has been described in my Hebrew Ethical and Homiletical Literature, Keter Publishing House, Jerusalem 1975, pp. 47-68, and detailed bibliography included there. Compare: J. Dan, Jewish Mysticism and Jewish Ethics, pp. 1-75.

93　See above, note 25.

94 A list of the works belonging to this genre, and a description of their content, is found in my study on the Sifrut ha-Yihhud in Kiryat Sefer, vol. 41, 1966, pp. 533-544.

95 An example can be found, for instance, in Rabbi Eleazar's description of the love of God in his preface to the Sodey Razaya (Sefer Raziel, Amsterdam 1701, 9a), in which this love is metaphorically described as equal to the erotic drive of a youth in sexual intercourse (see J. Dan, The Ashkenazi Kabbalah: A New Examination, Proceedings of the Second International Conference on the History of Jewish Mysticism, ed. J. Dan, Jerusalem 1987, pp. 125-139, especially p. 136 note 29).

Defining Kabbalah: The Kabbalah of the Divine Names*

Moshe Idel

I Kabbalah as Theosophy in Modern Scholarship

The medieval form of mystical Judaism known as Kabbalah[1] is known mainly as a theosophical doctrine related to the ten *sefirot*. This theologically oriented description recurs often in modern scholarship, as we can learn from several scholarly discussions regarding the nature of this lore, mainly those following the lead of G. Scholem. The prevailing assumption in the academic field is that a relatively homogenuous mystical phenomenon, more theoretical than practical, underlies the entire range of Kabbalistic literature, as it has already been proposed by the late Prof. Gershom Scholem. Let me start with one of his more explicit descriptions of Kabbalah:

> "the mystical interpretation of the attributes and the unity of God, in the so-called doctrine of the Sefiroth, constituted a problem common to all Kabbalists, while the solution given to it by and in the various schools differ from one another."[2]

Despite this scholarly attempt to propose the existence of a common core-question for all the Kabbalistic schools, which responded to it in various ways, we may safely assert that it would be much more cautious to see the theosophical question as one of the important ones, addressed by many, though not by all the Kabbalists. However, the absence of the theurgical element in this description may leave the impression, that is corroborated by the reading of the opus of this scholar, that theosophy is not only a central issue shared by "all" the Kabbalists, but it is also the single most important question in medieval Jewish mysticism. In other words, the gnosis of the divine attributes, rather than the experiential involvement in processes connected with them, by the means of theurgical, and sometimes mystical-theurgical performance of the commandments, was preferred by the abovementioned description.

Let us adduce another instance of Scholem's description of Jewish mysticism, which is, indeed, very representative of his vision of Kabbalah; just before the above quote, after indicating that Jewish mysticism is shaped by the positive content and values recognized by Judaism, Scholem writes on the Jewish mystics as follows:

> "Their ideas proceed from the concepts and values peculiar to Judaism, that is to say, above all from the belief in the Unity of God and the meaning of Hid revelation as laid down in the Torah, the sacred law. Jewish mysticism in its various forms represents an attempt to interpret the religious values of Judaism in terms of mystical values. It concentrates upon the idea of the living God who manifests himself in the act of Creation, Revelation and Redemption. Pushed to its extreme, the mystical meditation on this idea gives birth to the conception of a sphere, a whole realm of divinity, which underlies the world of our sense-data and which is present and active in all that exists."[3]

The meditation on an idea, namely on the special nature of the deity as creative, revealing and redeeming, is conceived of as the source of the theosophical Kabbalah. In principle I agree to this view though I would propose a more variegated description of the Kabbalistic lore, which would be less theologically oriented. The theoretical approach to Kabbalah, prevalent in modern scholarship, has tended to conceive this mystical lore in more theological rather than experiential terms.[4] So, for example, we learn from R. J. Zwi Werblowsky, that "the fact remains, nevertheless,[5] that the discursive and even dialectical elements are so prominent in kabbalistic literature that we may almost speak of an intellectualistic hypertrophy. It often looks as if the sole difference between talmudic and kabbalistic literature resides in the different subject-matter."[6]

Though this stand seems to implicitly diverge from Scholem, "nevertheless", it seems that Scholem himself would subscribe to Werblowsky's view; indeed, in one of his latest formulations of his stand, Scholem has insisted that theosophical speculations

> "occupy a large and conspicuous area in kabbalistic teaching. Sometimes their connections with the mystical plane becomes rather tenuous and is superseded by an interpretative and homiletical vein with occasionally even results in a kind of Kabbalistic pilpul. [casuistry]"[7]

The same emphasis on the centrality of the role of theosophy for the definition of Kabbalah is conspicuous in Isaiah Tishby's presentation of the Zoharic thought, and even of Kabbalah in general:

> "At the very core and foundation of this teaching[8] is one particular subject of investigation: the mystery of the knowledge of the Godhead. The great themes of the Creation and the Chariot, the existence and activity of the angels, the nature of the spiritual worlds, the forces of evil in the realm of Satan, the situation and destiny of Man, this world and the next, the process of history from the days of creation until the end of time—all these topics are no more than the boughs and branches of the mighty tree of the mystery of the Godhead. The knowledge

of this mystery, which depends on man's spiritual level and on the root of his soul, is the basis of religious faith as seen by the Kabbalah."[9]

It should be noticed that the core of Kabbalah is not related, according to the above quote, to a mystical experience or to a mystical performance of the commandments, that can be designated as theurgical activity. A certain form of gnoseology, or a mystical theology, is conceived of as being the mystical core of Kabbalah. In a very similar vein we learn from the otherwise perceptive book of R. J. Zwi Werblowsky:

> "until the advent of Lurianism, the doctrine of sefiroth necessarily formed the core and bulk of almost all Kabbalistic writings . . . the mystery of the sefiroth remained the unfaltering centre of their speculations and the absorbing focus of their contemplative exercises . . . nothing could ever compete with the theological significance and compelling fascination of that highly complex and dynamic image of the deity: the sefirotic pleroma."[10]

We may, therefore, summarize the above discussions as rotating around the theosophy as a defining moment in Kabbalistic lore. The modern vision of Kabbalah as proposed by the Scholemian school is therefore concerned with the Kabbalistic treatments of theosophical issues, which are part of a large picture of Kabbalah as a mythocentric type of lore generated by Gnostic and Gnostic-like types of religious mentalities. In the following discussions I would like to draw the attention to another view of Kabbalah, marginalized or totally ignored by most of the modern definitions of Kabbalah, as the esoteric tradition concerning the divine name[s] as well as to the emergence of the esoteric use of the term Kabbalah in this context. These discussions will serve as introduction to a discussion of Abraham Abulafia's different views of Kabbalah as being a lore focused upon divine names and—less crucial for our discussion here—as an experiential lore, which was presented as distinct and superior to the Kabbalah of the *Sefirot*. The following discussions are intended to serve both as a corrective and a complementing proposal to the present scholarly overemphasis on the theosophical, and therefore more theologically, oriented vision of Jewish mysticism.

II. Kabbalah and Transmission of the Divine Name: Earlier Sources

The Name of God is conceived as an esoteric issue already in archaic religions.[11] Its knowledge was understood as enabling one to have some power on the divine being, because of the possible link between the name and the designated entity. Indeed, in line with these remarks, it is conspicuous that one of the most esoteric topics in ancient Jewish thought was the precise pronunciation, or the correct vocalization of the consonants of the divine names.[12] The assumption that the divine name stands for much more than the conventional appellation seems to underly the awe that is related to its pronunciation. In the most concentrated Talmudic text on this issue we read, inter alia, that

> "Rab Judah said in Rab's name: The Forty-two lettered Name[13] is entrusted only to him who is pious,[14] and meek, of middle-aged, free from bad temper, sober, and not insistent on his rights. And he who knows it, is heedful thereof and observes it in purity, is beloved above and popular below, feared by man and inherits two worlds, this world and the future world."[15]

Indeed, the divine names were revered, and the pronunciation of the Tetragrammaton constituted the peak of the most sacred of the Jewish rituals; in the day of Atonement the High Priest would pronounce it, according to some sources, in a way that was not so distinct to those present, in order to preserve its precise vocalization from the wicked and from the vulgus.[16] Already in the *Heikhalot* literature the revelation of the divine names are part of the secrets from above, and in my opinion, there was a certain reading of the Torah in according to the divine names that can be extrapolated by various devices from the regular sequel of the letters in the biblical verses.[17] Moreover, these divine names are also part of the ancient Jewish magical and mystical techniques.[18] However, despite the ambiance of secrecy that surrounds the topic of the divine names, no detailed rite of transmission is detectable in ancient Judaism, and no specific term is known in connection to the traditions related to divine names. Though it may be assumed that the transmission of the pronunciation of the divine name, which according to another Talmudic text, took place once in seven years,[19] must have involved some solemn rite, the extant material does not permit a meaningful reconstruction of such a hypothetical initiation rite.

It is therefore of special importance, from our point of view, to notice that the first known uses of the term *Qabbalah* in connection to esoteric issues, is related to divine names. As pointed out very briefly already by Naftali Tur-Sinai[20] and B-Z. Dinur[21] it is reasonable to assume that the earliest cases of the use of the term *Qabbalah* as an esoteric lore can be traced to the gaonic period. However, this view was apparently not accepted by Gershom Scholem, though he did not refer to it explicitly. Instead, Scholem has offered another solution[22] namely that the term was definitively understood as involving mystical traditions in the writings of the students of R. Isaac Sagi Nahor, who was, hypothetically,[23] the master who inspired his student to this effect. It would, therefore, be worthwhile to inspect again the extant texts, those adduced by Tur-Sinai, and others, in order to clarify the possibility that a secret doctrine related to the pronunciation of the divine names was designated as *Qabbalah* long before the first references to this term in relation to the doctrine of ten *sefirot*.

R. Hai Gaon, a tenth-century leading halakhic figure, who was not inclined to mysticism[24] indicates in one of his responses that:

> "The explicit name[25] is that which consists of forty-two letters and it is still found in [our] academy by the way of an [esoteric] tradition[26], and it is known to the Sages."[27]

The last phrase, assumes that this is an elitist issue, not open to the public, but cultivated in an important academy in the East. Since another spiritual activity was also related by Hai to the divine name, *Kavvanah*, without revealing the precise nature of it,[28] it may be assumed that the existence of an esoteric tradition dealing with the divine name might have been known by this author. In any case, even if we accept the assumption, found in the other responsum, that he did not know the pronunciation of the divine name, we still have there a fascinating description of the way of transmitting the name, which anticipates, at least in its atmosphere, the ritual of the Hasidei Ashkenaz.[29] I assume that despite the fact that the term *Qabbalah* does not occur, the details of the transmission may reflect the content of this term in the first quote. Let me adduce this highly interesting passage:

> "We have already explained above that we do not know how to pronounce and recite correctly[30] it[31] and it was not transmitted to us[32] [by way of] a Rabbi from the mouth of another Rabbi, who, [at his turn] has received it from another Rabbi, a triple tradition[33] but we have heared it in an incidental manner[34] from the mouth of those who are divided[35] on its reading but not by [the way of] transmission.[36] And he needs the transmission and the Kavvanah, which is involved in it, and he transmits to him in purity, in holiness, in a fixed[37] transmission[38] and Kavvanah. And whoever did not receive in this order, is considered as if he does not know it."[39]

Unfortunately, the meaning of some of the key terms in this passage is not as clear as we would like: what exactly is a "constant" versus an "incidental" transmission? Or what is the meaning of *Kavvanah* in this context? However, the oral component of the process is crucial here, and the authoritative factor, "Rabbi from the mouth of a Rabbi"[40] together with the assumption found in the first quote that the tradition is found in a *Yeshivah* and is transmitted to the sages, is obvious. Does this last quote define the meaning of *Qabbalah* in the first one? If such a conclusion could be drawn, we would be in the position of having an important insight into the esoteric nature of the term *Qabbalah* long before the emergence of the European Kabbalah.

In another text of the same author, he mentions that the pronunciation of the Tetragrammaton is "transmitted from one to one"[41] while the name of forty-two letters, though its consonants are known, its pronunciation and recitation is not transmitted by *Qabbalah*[42,43]

This text was known to a 12th century author in Barcelona, who quotes it almost *verbatim*; it is found in the *Commentary on Sefer Yeṣirah*[44] by R. Yehudah ben Barzilai that we encounter, probably for the first time in Europe, this nexus between the term *Qabbalah* as an esoteric tradition and the divine name.   However, according to another passage in this text, to which David Neumark[45] and G. Scholem[46] have drawn attention, some metaphysical issue, namely the creation of the Divine Spirit or the *Shekhinah*, is introduced as follows:

> "The sages did not deal with it explicitly in order that men would not come to speculated concerning "what is above" and many other things related to it, and that is why they were transmitting this thing in whisper and in secret,[47] as an esoteric tradition to their pupils and their sages."[48]

Therefore, already by the middle of the 12th century the esoteric understanding of *Qabbalah* is related to two different topics: the divine name and the first creation, namely that of the Divine Spirit. Interestingly enough, the author assumes that the Rabbinic sources have spoken in an esoteric manner and it is he who explicates the meaning of their statements in an explicit manner.

It is therefore not a great surprise that R. Eleazar of Worms, has adduced in the name of this Gaon a short discussion related to the divine names as part of *Qabbalotav*, namely "R. Hai Gaon's traditions".[49]   Given the fact that the Ashkenazi master mentions this tradition in his voluminous book on the divine names, it is possible that some material on the subject reached him from the East.[50] Indeed, the Ashkenazi Hasidic masters were immersed in numerous and diverse speculations and practices related to pronunciations of the divine names and R. Eleazar himself mentions the pronunciation of "depth[51] of the names" as connected to revelatory experiences.[52] However, what is more important is the existence of a relatively detailed description of a ritual for transmitting the divine name, which was preserved by an Ashkenazi master.[53] Though Dan assumes that this rite has a theological aspect alone, I would prefer to allow, on the basis of the mentioning of the ecstatic uses of the divine names by R. Eleazar, that the transmission of the divine names was part of an initiation into a more mystical form of practices.[54] Therefore, it seems that in so far as this topic is concerned, there is no reason to doubt the fact that an oral medium was used in order to impart some forms of esoteric knowledge regarding the divine name. I would therefore propose to see in the Ashkenazi texts, and in their earlier antecedents, one of the major sources of the esoteric understanding of the term Kabbalah. In the 12th century Provencal Kabbalah the term seems to be absent and Scholem's assumption,[55] — actually inspired by D. Neumark,[56] — that the possible transition to an esoteric understanding of the term in an interesting text of R. Yehudah Barceloni[57] seems to me very doubtful.

III. Early Kabbalistic Views

A younger contemporary of R. Eleazar of Worms, R. Moshe ben Nahman known as Nahmanides, indicates that he was acquainted with a tradition, referred to by him as *Qabbalah*, which asserts that the Torah is composed, on a more esoteric level, of divine names.[58] What is pertinent for our analysis here is the very fact that Kabbalah is understood as dealing with divine names.

By the middle of the 13th century, R. Hai and his father are mentioned in connection with magical and mystical traditions, apparently spurious, by R. Isaac ben Ya'aqov ha-Kohen in Spain. What seems to me to be relevant in this instance is the occurrence of the idea of oral transmission in phrases that are reminiscent of the above quotes from Hai Gaon:

> "according to the *Qabbalah*, that was transmitted to the masters of this wisdom from the mouth of ancient sages. We have known that indeed R. Sherira and R. Hai,[59] blessed be their memory, were competent and have received this wisdom, as a tradition transmitted in their hands,[60] a Rabbi from the mouth of a Rabbi, an old man [*zaqen*] from the mouth of an old man, a Gaon from the mouth of a Gaon, all of them have used the magical practice of *Heikhalot Zuṭartei*, namely the *Shimmusha de-Sheidei*, in order to climb by its means the ladder of the prophecies and its powers [*sullam ha-nevu'ot ve-kohoteiah*".[61]

Though the divine names were not mentioned here I have no doubt that it was assumed that the magical books were based upon the magic of divine names.

Interestingly enough, still at the end of the 13th century, an esoteric tradition related to the divine name was presented as *Qabbalat Ashkenaz*; R. Bahya ben Asher wrote in his *Commentary on the Pentateuch* on the vocalization of the divine name, which is apparently the content of the Ashkenazi Kabbalah which he has received it in a "whisper".[62] This quote, which is corroborated by some similar instances in R. Isaac of Acre's *Me'irat Eynayim*, wherein encounters with Ashkenazi masters are mentioned in connection to the divine names. Bahya, a resident of Barcelona, may be an important example of the arrival of Ashkenazi esoteric material to the city. He wrote his commentary in the 90's of the 13th century. Two decades beforehand, R. Abraham Abulafia has studied there Kabbalah, including some Ashkenazi esoteric texts.[63] Apparently in Castile, an anonymous compiler of *Sefer ha-Ne'elam*, mentions a tradition regarding the transmission of Qabbalah:

> "from Daniel to Hillel, the father of Hillel the Old, and from the generation of Hillel the Old they [the sages] have begun to completely close up the issues of Kabbalah, and all these *Qabbalot* concerning the divine name, which is also the very hidden name, let the Glory of His Name be blessed for ever and ever. But when the sages of the Mishnah came, they have begun to explain the hints of *Qabbalah* concerning the secret of each and every name, with the exception of the divine name."[64]

Therefore, the Kabbalah of the divine names started, again, with the committing to writing of the oral Torah, the *Mishnah*.

IV. Theosophical Understandings of the Divine Name

Among the first Kabbalistic traditions extant from Provencal Kabbalah, a short text, introduced as the *Qabbalah* of R. Ya'aqov the Nazirite of Lunel, the letters of the divine name are interpreted as symbols of the Sefirotic system.[65] R. Isaac the Blind, one of the important masters of early Kabbalah, emphasized the importance of the mystical intention, *Kavvanah*, during prayer, especially when the Tetragrammaton is pronounced.[66] When inspecting the antecedents of this nexus between the Tetragrammaton and *Kavvanah*, it is possible to point out some parallels found in contemporary, though unrelated texts, and therefore establish that even one of the first Kabbalists did not invent it, and we can easily predate it by a few generations.[67] Moreover, according to the recent findings of Haviva Pedaya, the divine name, more precisely, the rupture between its various letters reflect, symbolically, the historical state of exile, and their reunification will reflect that of redemption.[68] The symbolical-theosophical and theurgical understandings of the divine name became, since the Geronese Kabbalah, topoi of a continuously growing literature. Immersed in theosophical speculations the Castilian

Kabbalists of the last decades of the 13th century envisioned with explicit suspicion a Kabbalah that will deal with the divine names; nonetheless eventually even they would approve some of the ecstatic implications of the practice of divine names.[69]

It is against the background of these views that an interesting definition of the divine name as symbolic of the theosophical structure is to be better understood; R. Todros ben Joseph ha-Levi Abulafia wrote in the eighties of the 13th century as follows:

> "You should know that all the foundation of the true Kabbalah and all its corner-stones, are based on this Great and Holy Name, by the means of which the perfect unity is explicated, and this is the reason that it was called Shem ha-Meforash namely because it is explicated and displayed in its inner powers, and they become reified and they are unified in the essence of his holy and pure unity. Know that by the knowledge of the innerness of the structure of its letters, all the secrets of the Torah and the prophets[70] will be explained and revealed to whomever will know it, each one in accordance with what he will be announced from heaven, to understand one thing from another, and to return the thing to its [proper] essence. Happy is he who will be able to understand even one of the thousand of thousands of the mysteries and allusions that are inscribed in the innerness of the letters of the [divine] name for [the sake of] those who know. Oh for us, people who see and do not understand what we do see.[71] All the ancient and late masters of Kabbalah have sworn not to hint at issues [of Kabbalah] but they hint to their modest[72] disciples the notes of the chapters."[73]

According to another text of the same Kabbalist, we learn about a rather different attitude to the doctrines related to the divine names:

> "There is no need to the words of those who allude to the seventy-two names in connection to 'Av 'Anan,[74] despite the fact that it is known to the masters of Kabbalah that seventy-two names surround the seat of glory.[75] This issue is distant from our intention concerning the hints which we have hinted, as west is distant from East. The Kabbalah of the sages of the divinity, [Ḥakhmei ha-'Elohut] regarding the secrets of the Torah is separated from the Kabbalah of the knowers of the names, except those that are not to be erased."[76]

The author explicitly acknowledges the existence of two different types of Kabbalah: one concerning the nature of the divinity and another one, concerned with the divine names, apparently those names which are not to be found in the Bible, and whose erasure is interdicted in the Talmudic prescriptions. Therefore, we may assume, on the basis of the two quotes from the same book that the theosophical understanding of the divine name, namely the Tetra-grammaton, was conceived as the quintessence of Kabbalah, whereas the speculations about the diversity of divine names were conceived as a different kind of lore.

A much less liberal attitude is expressed in a contemporary of the abovementioned Todros Abulafia; in R. Isaac ibn Abu Sahulah's *Commentary on the Song of Songs* it is said that

> "The illuminati should not pay attention to the words of the ignorant of their generations, who boast saying that they possess a Kabbalah of names [Qabbalat Shemot] and issues they have invented, by the means of which they have attained the knowledge of the future."[77]

The distancing from the Kabbalah of names is conspicuous in these two texts; they were composed in the early eighties of the 13th century, no more than a decade after Abraham Abulafia's visit in Castile. These Kabbalists seem to be reacting to the attempt he made to disseminate the ecstatic Kabbalah in this region. Part of this propagandistic effort concerned an unsuccessful attempt to teach his peculiar type of Kabbalah to R. Moshe of Burgos, the teacher of Todros Abulafia in matters of Kabbalah, and an acquaintance of ibn Abu Sahulah.[78] In any case, Abraham Abulafia's firm view as to the superiority of his Kabbalah based on practices of pronunciations of letters of the divine names, to which we shall turn immediately, was not shared by those who cultivated a more theosophical-theurgical one, namely the reigning Kabbalah in Castile since the beginning of the eighties. However it should be emphasized that both those who accepted the view of Kabbalah as related to the divine names or those who were reticent or even rejected it, were acquainted with such a view. It is therefore reasonable to assume that even in the theosophical Kabbalah the view of the divine name as a symbol of the divine structure is but an interpretation of an older esoteric tradition dealing with Kabbalah as concerned with the divine name[s].

V. Abraham Abulafia's Kabbalah of Divine Names

If Nahmanides' description of Kabbalah as oral esoteric tradition is the most influential text on the later Kabbalists,[79] the following definitions of the younger contemporary of this Kabbalist, R. Abraham Abulafia, had some impact on some of the scholarly definitions of this lore. An inspection of Abulafia's earlier Kabbalistic writing demonstrates that at the beginning of his Kabbalistic activity he was not eager to delineate his special vision of Kabbalah as substantially distinct from that of the other Kabbalists. Different as his Kabbalah was from the most important sorts of 13th century Spanish Kabbalah,[80] the founder of ecstatic Kabbalah did not engage in a phenomenological comparison for its own sake but as the result of a bitter controversy.[81] As part of a response to the fiery assault of R.

Shlomo ben Abraham ibn Adret, Abulafia undertook the most elaborate exposition of his Kabbalah versus that of his opponent. In the first part of his epistle, the ecstatic Kabbalist indicates the existence of two types of Kabbalah as part of a more complex epistemological discussion. Each information is acquired either by sensual [*murgash*] or intellectual [*muskkal*] channels. The former are the five senses. The latter involves two different types of sources: the received one, *mequbbal*[82] and the wide-known [*mefursam*].[83] It is only when attempting to describe the two kinds of Jewish received tradition that he offers an explicit distinction between the two kinds of Kabbalah:

> "It is not necessary to elaborate here about all kinds of receptions, but only about that of the persons of the Torah from among our nation alone, because for the reason of their receiving that tradition they were called masters of the [esoteric] Reception [Ba'alei ha-Qabbalah]. I shall indicate that this Kabbalah is unknown to the multitude of the Rabbis, who are immersed [only] in the wisdom[84] of the Talmud. It is divided into two parts: the one is that part that deals with the knowledge of God by the way of the ten Sefirot known as branches [neṭi'ot]; whoever uproots them is called the cutter of the branches [meqazzez bi-neṭi'ot][85]; these [branches] are revealing the secret of the unity. The other part [of Kabbalah] consists in the knowledge of God by the means of the twenty-two letters, out of which, and out of whose vowels and cantillation-marks, the divine names and the seals [hotamot][86] are composed. They [the names and the seals] are speaking with the prophets in their dreams, in the Urim and Tummim,[87] in the Divine Spirit and during prophecy.[88]"

Abulafia's definition is ostensibly derived from the first paragraph of *Sefer Yezirah*, where the creation of the world is presented as accomplished by the agency of thirty-two paths: the ten *Sefirot* and the twenty-two letters. The definition of the first type of Kabbalah as focused on the ten *Sefirot* reflects a great amount of Kabbalistic material that deals with the ten divine manifestations. The second type of Kabbalah is basically that of the divine names. However, artificial as this distinction may seem, it reflects a crucial phenomenological difference between forms of thirteenth-century Kabbalah. The language as the main prime-matter for Kabbalistic manipulations is represented here by its less semantically active aspect: divine names and seals. Its main target is the transformation of the human mind, which is to be united with God's thought. This anthropocentric move diverges from the strong theosophical emphasis of the Kabbalah based on the ten *Sefirot*. While the theosophical Kabbalist unifies the upper, divine powers between themselves, the human intellect is the main object of transformation according to the ecstatic Kabbalist. The emphasis on mystical metaphysics, that can be called theosophy, so widespread in the main stream of Kabbalah, as well as the centrality of the mystical intention during the performance of the commandments[89] have been drastically marginalized by the ecstatic Kabbalist in the favour of the manipulation of language, that manipulates the soul.

Elsewhere in the same epistle, Abulafia proposes a three-stage division of speculative knowledge: philosophy, the Kabbalah of the *Sefirot* and the Kabbalah of the divine name. The relations between these three stages of study are compared by the Kabbalist to the relationship between the vegetal soul to the animal and the human, namely rational soul. According to the medieval concepts of these three souls, especially in its Aristotelian version of psychology, all the three souls are present in the higher one, while in the lower stages the higher souls are absent. Consequently, to follow this comparison, a good Kabbalist who believes in *Sefirot* must have passed through the study of philosophy. *Prima facie* such a view may appear as non-representative; indeed the first Kabbalists would hardly accept such a view. However, during the generation of Abulafia some of the most important Kabbalists, including the two most influential theosophical Kabbalists, R. Moses de Leon and R. Joseph Gikatilla, had started as students of more philosophical types of knowledge, and their earlier Kabbalah is deeply indebted to Aristotelian thought.[90] Other Kabbalists, like Abulafia and an anonymous ecstatic Kabbalist, underwent a philosophical stage before they became ecstatic Kabbalists. At least one of Abulafia's contemporaries, and someone acquainted with Abulafia[91], R. Moses ben Shimeon of Burgos, described Kabbalah as standing on the top of philosophy.[92] Therefore Abulafia's description of the hierarchy between the two types of thought reflects a certain historical process of transition from the medieval philosophy to different forms of Kabbalah. The conceptual nexus between the two kinds of lore is the fact that they do provide ways to understand God: philosophy—by the means of his creatures, the Sefirotic Kabbalists—by the means of his attributes.[93] According to another important passage of Abulafia:

> "Kabbalah does not contradict what the wisdom reveals because there is no [difference] between wisdom and Kabbalah, but [the fact] that Kabbalah was expressed from the mouth of the Agens Intellect, in a more profound manner than that in what the wisdom was expressed, though both were expressed from its mouth, nevertheless it [Kabbalah] is more subtle."[94]

VI. Two Types of Kabbalah

However, from our vantage point the description of the relationship between the two different types of Kabbalah is much more important.

The Sefirotic one is allegorized as the vegetative soul when compared to the higher, ecstatic Kabbalah, the counterpart of the human soul. Though the medieval psychology would acknowledge a certain continuity between the two souls, the superiority of the human over the animal soul is not only a matter of degree but also of quality. It is a quantum jump that distinguishes the two; nevertheless, it is incumbent upon the ecstatic Kabbalist to study at the beginning of his Kabbalistic career, the Sefirotic one, before embarking upon the study of the higher form of Kabbalah. However, the feeling is that Abulafia assumes that there are no organic links between the two kinds of mystical discipline; while speaking about the *Sefirot* as part of the divine entity, he describes this topic as the lore of the others, *lefi darkam*, leaving the distinct impression that he does not agree to this stand.[95]

Another simile helps also to understand the relations between the three levels of study: each of these levels is compared, respectively, with the three degrees of the Jewish persons: Israel, Levi and Kohen. This simile may imply again the definitive superiority of the ecstatic Kabbalah. In another, earlier instance, in his *Sefer Shomer Mitzvah* Abulafia used the same simile of the Israel, Levi and Kohen in order to exemplify the relations between the three souls and three types of knowledge: that of the plain sense of the Scriptures, that of the philosophers and finally that of the Kabbalists.[96] The absence of the distinction between the two types of Kabbalah demonstrates that the emergence of this distinction is part of a later development, namely a religious struggle, an attempt to show the superiority of his Kabbalah over that of his detractor. Indeed in comparison to the calm tone of the book written in 1287, the epistle we shall analyze below betrays a much more belligerent spirit, which reaches its peak in a sharp critique of the Sefirotic Kabbalah, or at least one of its major forms. According to Abulafia:

> "The masters of the Kabbalah of the Sefirot have thought that they will unify the Godhead[97] and evade the faith in Trinity; but [instead] they have caused His Decadization[98]. Just as the gentiles say that He is three and the three are one, so also some of the Kabbalistic masters believe and say that the Godhead is ten Sefirot and the[se] ten are one. Therefore they have multiplied God at its maximum, and they composed Him in the most extreme manner, since there is no multiplicity greater than ten."[99]

It may well be that this is the more extreme critique of the Kabbalistic theosophy coming from the pen of another Kabbalist.[100] The danger of introducing multiple divine powers was conceived as especially pertinent in connection to the Kabbalistic thought represented by Nahmanides' school, whose main exponent was no other than Abulafia's critique: R. Shlomo ibn Adret. The view of the *Sefirot* as the essence of God, that was the fundamental theosophy of Nahmanides' school seems to be the major target of the above critique.[101] It is obvious that Abulafia does not attack all the theosophical Kabbalists, since he indicates that only "some of the Kabbalistic masters" are prone to fall into the theological "error"; therefore we may assume that other Kabbalists, I assume those who believed that the *Sefirot* are not the essence of the Divinity but His instruments,[102] are less endangered by their concept of the divine.

What are the fundamental differences between the two kinds of Kabbalah as Abulafia defined them? While the Sefirotic Kabbalah is conceived as a preliminary step, necessary for the advance to the higher one, the latter is radically different from the former. The lower, Sefirotic lore is the patrimony of those who are "prophets for themselves"[103] who, like the philosophers, possess a knowledge that is not imparted to the others. Their thoughts are sometimes illuminated by a feeble light, but they do not attain the experience of receiving the speech, *ha-Dibbur*.[104] It is the achievement of the higher Kabbalah, the ecstatic one, to ensure such an experience, by the means of the recitation of the divine names. Indeed, as Abulafia acknowledges, also the Sefirotic Kabbalists make use of the divine names, in order to point at the divine manifestations, the *Sefirot*. However, the ecstatic Kabbalist uses them in order to unite the human thought with the divine one.[105] While according to the first Kabbalah, especially as it was systematically exposed by Abulafia's former student R. Joseph Gikatilla,[106] the divine names are symbols of the divine attributes, hinting at the supernal divine reality and serving as epistemological tools, these names are intended by the ecstatic Kabbalist to bring about an ontic identification between the human and the divine.[107]

Abulafia's emphasis upon the divine names as the core of his Kabbalah recurs also in other instances.[108] However in his writings there are also other attempts to define Kabbalah, in purely linguistic terms, especially those related to the constitutive elements of language. So, for example he describes the three principles of Kabbalah as follows:

"The names of those principles are letters, combinations [of letters] and vowels. Their acronym is 'AZN,[109] which can be permuted as Zo'N[110] . . . The combination turns the letters and the vowels turns the combinations and the spirit of man, given by God, turns the vowels until they will cause the emergence and the illumination of the concept[111] that is proper to any intelligent Kabbalist."[112]

In fact, as it becomes clear from the sequel of the above text, it is the regular use of Abulafia's mystical techniques that are portrayed here as the principles of Kabbalah. Though indeed the acquaintance with these three principles of Kabbalah are involved here, there would be very unlikely that a theoretical approach is the main gist of Abulafia's Kabbalah. In fact, in many of his handbooks Abulafia proposes a very practical involvement in those practices. Though the definition of Kabbalah as proposed in the above quote has nothing to do with the experience itself, the latter is expressly mentioned as the result of the use of the techniques described there.

VII. Three Sources of Kabbalah

In his *Sefer ha-Ḥesheq*,[113] Abulafia adduces the three different channels of receiving Kabbalah, as complementary ways:

> "In order to understand my intention regarding [the meaning of] Qolot [voices] I shall hand down to you the known Qabbalot, some of them having been received from mouth to mouth from the sages of [our] generation,[114] and others that I have received from the books named Sifrei Qabbalah composed by the ancient sages, the Kabbalists, blessed be their memory, concerning the wondrous topics;[115] and other [traditions] bestown on me by God, blessed be He, which came to me from ThY[116] in the form of the Daughter of the Voice, [Bat Qol], these being the higher Qabbalot ['Eliyonot]."[117]

Written in 1289, this passage is perhaps the first confession of a Kabbalist to the effect that contents revealed to him are Kabbalistic traditions higher than any others, received orally or extracted from written documents. However, it seems that we can propose a certain scale of authority of these three different channels; they can be arranged in an hierarchical order, the oral traditions being conceived as the lower one, and therefore referred as "known".[118] Apparently, Abulafia was well-aware of the importance of the oral traditions in the circle of Nahmanides' student; the traditions understood from Kabbalistic documents being conceived as higher; and, finally, the direct revelation as the highest source. We can assume that the strong personality of Abulafia comes to the fore by the assumption that *his* own experiences and their contents, rather than the *known* mystical traditions, were considered as a higher form of Kabbalah. Apparently, this discussion is part of the confrontation between him and R. Shlomo ibn Adret, the representative of the theosophical-theurgical Kabbalah, which he conceived, as we have seen above, as inferior to his own lore, namely the ecstatic Kabbalah.[119] The superiority of the revealed content, which reaches the mystic in a distinct form, *Bat Qol*, reflects Abulafia's vision of his Kabbalah as conducive to the hearing of a speech, *Dibbur*.

In another, earlier text, Abulafia writes about the "human Kabbalah", [*Qabbalah 'enoshit*] then about the intellectual speculation, and finally about the influx descending from above.[120]

VIII. The "Easy" Kabbalah

A *leitmotif* permeating Abulafia's views of his Kabbalah is the emphasis upon the easy access to extraordinary experience and knowledge that his Kabbalah allows; this peculiar view is worthwhile of a more detailed inspection. The ecstatic Kabbalist indicates that

> "We and all these who follow our intellectual Kabbalah [Qabbalah muskkelet],[121] [attaining] prophecy by the means of the combinations of letters, he will teach us the essence of reality as it is, in an easier way in comparison to all the way in existence in the world, despite the fact that the knowledge of the essence of reality which is apprehended by much thought. What brings about it [the knowledge] is the combination [of letters][122], and this combination induces it [the knowledge] as immediately as a youth studies the Bible, then the Mishnah and Gemara, he will indubitably achieve it quickly, with perseverance, being better than any thought."[123]

Again, in a very concise way, Abulafia defines the goal of the Kabbalah that is based on the Torah [*Qabbalah Toriit*] as follows:

> "to attain by it the knowledge of God. And it is known that Kabbalah is easy to be studied, more than any other intellectual study. God has intended to perfect us in an easy way, which is congenial to human nature."[124]

This emphasis on "easiness" or the accessibility of the experience is related, at least partially, to the medieval conception that transmitted tradition, sometimes referred as *Kabbalah*, is a much easier way to learn some issues, whose study would otherwise take a long time.[125]

The easiness of attaining an experience and its apprehension, the latter being but a result of the encounter with the agent intellect, is to be understood both in itself, as a genuine self-understanding, and as part of a propagandist effort. In itself, the proposal of a mystical technique which short-circuits the lengthy curriculum of the philosophers assumes that the combinations of letters is a higher form of logic, which is congenial to the study of the canonic scriptures, while the logic of the philosophers as being pertinent to the order of nature.[126] Abulafia's conception of Kabbalah was oriented toward contemplation and manipulation of linguistic material, whose results were conceived as been immediate. In comparison to the lengthy way of the Sefirotic Kabbalah, which involves both the study of details of the commandments and both the intricacies of the theosophical system, Abulafia insists that his method is indeed the easy way.

To a certain extent, we can compare these two types of Kabbalah, and their respective mystical practices, to what Eliade and Staal designated as easy and difficult ways.[127] The Sefirotic way, with its nomian techniques, is a perfect example of a difficult path, in the manner that this type of mysticism was described by these two scholars. However, despite Abulafia's own use of the term "easy", in fact he proposes an anomian technique which is very complex, indeed one of the most complex mystical techniques I am acquainted with.[128] In lieu of the assumption proposed by Eliade, that the easy ways are vulgarizations or decadences of the difficult ways, in the case of Kabbalah the two ways stem from differently historical and phenomenological religious phenomena. In order to avoid prejudices of moral or religious kind, which apparently have affected Eliade's evaluation of the easy ways, like the drugs for example,[129] I propose to regard Abulafia's Kabbalah as an attempt to force the regular psychosomatic system of the mystic by the means of intensive and complex exercises which are indifferent towards the common Jewish way of life.

In conclusion, let me draw attention to what may be one of the implications of the above discussions. The emphasis on another content of the core of Kabbalah, the divine names and the permutations of their letters instead of the *Sefirot*, changes the more onto-theologically oriented vision of Kabbalah in modern scholarship, relying as it is solely on the theosophical Kabbalah. The turn toward language, that is so conspicuous in many of the above quotes, is reminiscent of the modern linguistic turn.[130] However, though this is somehow indeed implicit in the above discussions, we shall not be oblivious of the fact that the divine name, a linguistic entity indeed, is nevertheless conceived as being instrumental in revealing, or helping to reach a revelatory experience of its signified, God.

Notes

* This study is part of a much more comprehensive survey of the various definitions of Kabbalah in the writings of medieval Kabbalists, Renaissance thinkers and modern scholars. This project evolved from an attempt to delineate the differences between Abraham Abulafia's Kabbalah and that of the theosophical-theurgical Kabbalah found in my Ph. D. thesis, *Abraham Abulafia's Works and Doctrines* [Hebrew University, Jerusalem, 1976] pp. 434-449. [Hebrew]

1 On the term Qabbalah see the very important observations of Gershom Scholem, *Kabbalah* [Jerusalem, 1974] pp. 3-7.

2 *Major Trends in Jewish Mysticism*, [New York, 1967] p. 13.

3 *ibidem*, pp. 10-11. The emphasis is mine.

4 See David Biale, "The Jewish Mysticism in the Sixteenth Century" in ed. Paul Szarmach, *An Introduction to the Medieval Mystics of Europe*, [SUNY, Albany, 1984] p. 314. See, however, Elliot R. Wolfson, "Circumcision, Vision of God, and Textual Interpretation: From Midrashic Trope to Mystical Symbol," *History of Religions* 27 (1987): 189-215, esp. concluding statement on p. 215; idem, "The Hermeneutics of Visionary Experience: Revelation and Interpretation in the *Zohar*," *Religion* 18 (1988): 311-345. In both of these studies Wolfson has emphasized the experiential underpinning of theosophical gnosis.

5 Werblowsky refers to the views expressed by Scholem in *Major Trends*, pp. 15-16.

6 See his *Joseph Karo, Lawyer and Mystic*, [JPS, Philadelphia, 1977] p. 40; compare also *ibidem*, pp. 158-159.

7 *Kabbalah*, p. 4.

8 That of the book of the Zohar.

9 *The Wisdom of the Zohar*, [Oxford University Press, Oxford 1989] vol. I, p. 229.

10 *Joseph Karo*, p. 189.

11 *L'Analyse du langage theologique*: *Le Nom de Dieu* [Editions Montaigne, Aubier, 1969], pp. 135-144.

12 *BT, Sanhedrin*, fol. 90b. See also J. Petuchowski, "Judaism as "Mystery" — The Hidden Agenda?" *Hebrew Union College Annual*, vol. L11 (1981) pp. 141-152.

13 See Lawrence Shiffman, "A Forty-Two Letter Divine Name in the Aramaic Magic Bowls" *Bulletin of the Institute of Jewish Studies*, vol. I [1973] pp. 97-102.

14 *Zanu'a*: this term and those stemming from the same root are connected to the
secret transmission in some ancient and medieval texts; see e.g. on the same page
in the Talmud, in Ivan Marcus, *Piety and Society*, [Leiden, 1981] p. 85; *Sefer ha-
Manhig*, ed. I. Raphael, [Jerusalem, 1978] vol. I, p. 85; and see note 47 below.

15 *BT, Qiddushin*, fol. 71a; Tr. H. Freeman [London, 1966].

16 See note 12 above.

17 See M. Idel, "The Concept of the Torah in the *Heikhalot* Literature and Its Meta-
morphoses in Kabbalah" *Jerusalem Studies in Jewish Thought* vol. I [1981] pp. 23-
84. [Hebrew]

18 See M. Idel, *The Mystical Experience in Abraham Abulafia* [SUNY, Albany, 1987] pp.
14-15; idem, *Golem: Jewish Magical and Mystical Traditions on the Artificial Anthro-
poid* [SUNY, Albany, 1990] pp. 11, 13, 30-32.

19 *Qiddushin*, fol. 71a.

20 E. ben Yehuda, *A Complete Dictionary of Ancient and Modern Hebrew* vol. XI, [1946]
p. 5700 notes 1, 3. Tur Sinai has suggested also an affinity between the magical
term *Qiblah* and *Qabbalah* but this second suggestion was rejected by Gershom
Scholem, *Origins of the Kabbalah*, tr. A. Arkush, ed. R. J. Zwi Werblowsky
[Princeton, Philadelphia, 1987] p. 38 note 64.

21 *Israel ba-Golah*, [Jerusalem, 1969] vol. II, 4 p. 418 note 40.

22 *Origins of the Kabbalah*, pp. 38, 261-262 see also above note 20. Scholem's reliance
on R. Meir ibn Avi Sahulah's 14th century description of Kabbalah as dealing with
Sefirot and commandments cannot mitigate the importance of the Gaonic and
Ashkenazi texts to be discussed below.

23 As Scholem has mentioned, *ibidem*, p. 261 this term is not found in Sagi Nahor's
extant writings.

24 See Moshe Idel, *Kabbalah: New Perspectives*, [New Haven, London, 1988] p. 90:
idem, *Golem*, pp. 48-49.

25 *Shem ha-Meforash*.

26 *Be-Qabbalah*.

27 *Otzar ha-Geonim*, [Jerusalem, 1934] ed. B. Levin, vol. VI, pp. 18-19; See also
another text of R. Hai, where he indicates that the elders and pious men of his
generation knew the names and used them for magical purposes; cf. Idel, *The
Mystical Experience*, pp. 15, 42 note 3. See also another text attributed, correctly in
my opinion, to R. Hai Gaon, printed in *ibidem*, p. 21: "[the high priest] was
pronouncing explicitly the name of twenty-two letters and it was arranged
[*messudar*. According to Tur Sinai (note 20 above) this is a mistake, for the form
masur, since in Hebrew the difference between the two forms being minimal] by
Qabbalah to the head of the Yeshivah." Therefore, again we have the idea that
Kabbalah, divine name, and elite are connected to each other.

28   See *Otzar ha-Geonim*, vol. IX, to be quoted below beside note 39; Idel, "R. Isaac Sagi Nahor's *Kavvanah* of *Shemoneh Esreh*".

29   See below note 53.

30   *Be-'emunah*.

31   The divine name.

32   *Lo masru be-Yadeinu*.

33   *Masorah Meshuleshet*.

34   *Ela 'aray*.

35   *Mi-pi ḥaluqim be-Qeriato*.

36   *Lo bi-mesirah*. This term is crucial for the understanding of the whole text. At its end, a phrase indicates that without the event of transmission there can be no licit pronunciation; see *Otzar ha-Geonim*, vol. IX, p. 177: *mesirah me'akkevet*.

37   Or constant.

38   *Masoret qeva'*. In classical Talmudic texts, the opposition between *'aray* and *qeva'* is well known.

39   See B. Levin, *Otzar ha-Geonim*, [Jerusalem, 1940] vol. IX p. 176; idem, [Jerusalem, 1931] vol. IV p. 23; Eliezer Ashkenazi, *Ta'am Zeqenim*, [Frankfurt, 1885] p. 57.

40   This issue is to be compared to Nahmanides' introduction to his *Commentary on the Torah*, ed. Ch. D. Chavel, [Jerusalem, 1961] vol. I pp. 15-17.

41   *masur me-eḥad le-eḥad*.

42   *'Eino masur . . . be-Qabbalah*.

43   *Otzar ha-Geonim*, ed. B. Levin, [Jerusalem, 1931] vol. IV, p. 23.

44   [Berlin, 1885] p. 128.

45   *Geschichte des juedische Philosophie* [Berlin, 1907] vol. I p. 192.

46   *Origins of the Kabbalah*, pp. 47, 261-262.

47   *Uvezin'ah*; see above note 14 and beside note 72 below.

48   *Commentary on Sefer Yeẓirah*, p. 189; my translation differs from the rendering found in Scholem, *ibidem*.

49   See Scholem, *Origins of the Kabbalah*, p. 262 n. 139, where he mentions also another instance of using the term *Qabbalah* by this author in connection to the angelic names. The divine names quoted by R. Eleazar in his *Sefer ha-Shem*, Ms.

Munich 81, fol. 233b are found in the magical tract named *Sefer ha-Yashar*, Ms. Escorial, G. III 14, fol. 1b, and to Abraham Abulafia, *Sefer Otzar 'Eden Ganuz*, Ms. Oxford 1580, fol. 16a.

50 It is interesting to note that also in another case, discussions of the divine name of forty-two were mentioned by R. Eleazar as traditions of R. Hai, as well as theosophical issues. See Scholem, *Origins of the Kabbalah*, pp. 185-186; Joseph Dan, *The Esoteric Theology of Ashkenazi Hasidim*, [Jerusalem, 1968] pp. 119-128 [Hebrew]; idem, "The Emergence of Mystical Prayer" *Studies in Jewish Mysticism* eds. J. Dan - F. Talmage [Cambridge, Mass. 1982] pp. 112-115; Idel, *Kabbalah: New Perspectives*, p. 195. Nevertheless I doubt very much the attribution of the magical names to a tradition stemming from Hai Gaon. In any case, at least the cultural image of the Gaon was informed by his authentic discussions of divine names.

51 On this term see Marcus, *Piety and Society*, p. 85 note 53; Moshe Idel, "Maimonides and Kabbalah" *Studies in Maimonides* ed. 'I. Twersky [Harvard University Press, Cambridge, 1990] pp. 57, 62.

52 See Idel, *The Mystical Experience*, pp. 16-17; See also the tradition that connected R. Eleazar to the mystical experience of R. Ezra of Montcontour, adduced by Scholem, *Origins of the Kabbalah*, p. 239.

53 See Gershom Scholem, *On the Kabbalah and Its Symbolism*, [New York, 1973] pp. 135-136; Dan, *The Esoteric Theology*, p. 74; Marcus, *Piety and Society*, pp. 84-85. Also this quote is part of *Sefer ha-Shem*.

54 See Dan, *ibidem*, p. 75 and Idel, *Kabbalah: New Perspectives*, pp. 99, 323 note 171. For other forms of revelatory experience cultivated by the Haside Ashkenaz, see Elliot R. Wolfson, "The Mystical Significance of Torah-Study in German Pietism," in *Jewish Quarterly Review* (forthcoming). On another tradition about the divine name in Haside Ashkenaz, connected especially to the phallus, see Elliot R. Wolfson, "Circumcision and the Divine Name: A Study in the Transmission of Esoteric Doctrine," *Jewish Quarterly Review* 78 (1987): 77-112, esp. 85-96.

55 *Origins of the Kabbalah*, pp. 259-260.

56 *ibidem*, p. 47.

57 *Commentary on Sefer Yeẓirah*, p. 189, discussed by Scholem, *ibidem*, p. 262 is indeed very fascinating, but it does not deal with the divine names as the content of the Kabbalah, while Rav Hai Gaon's text, not mentioned by Scholem, seems to be somehow related to the Ashkenazi tradition both from the point of view of the content and by the dint of mentioning the name of the Gaon.

58 Idel, "The Concept of the Torah" pp. 52-53.

59 On the traditions adduced by this author see our discussions above.

60 On this phrase in the context of the transmission of Kabbalah see Moshe Idel, "We Have No Kabbalistic Traditions on This" *Rabbi Moshe Naḥmanides [Ramban]:*

Explorations in His Religious and Literary Virtuosity ed. I. Twersky, [Cambridge, Mass., 1983] pp. 52-54.

61   Printed by Gershom Scholem in R. Isaac ben Ya'acob ha-Kohen's *ha-'Azilut ha-Smalit, Mada'ei ha-Yahadut*, vol. II [Jerusalem, 1930] p. 90. See also Scholem, *Le-Heqer Qabbalat R. Isaac ha-Kohen* [Jerusalem, 1934] pp. 119-120.

62   On Numbers 6, 27, ed. Ch. D. Chavel, p. 34. See also Bahya's discussion in his commentary on Leviticus 16, 30, where a view similar to the Ashkenazi rite of transmission is found. See also Scholem, *ibidem*, p. 136 note 1.

63   See Adolf Jellinek, *Bet ha-Midrasch* [Leipzig, 1855] vol. III, p. XLII.

64   Ms. Paris, Biblioteque Nationale 817, fol. 56a. An interesting discussion about the transmission of the divine names from Moses to the later generations is found in one of the writings of R. Moshe of Burgos, see Gershom Scholem, *Tarbiz*, vol. V [1934] p. 52 and note 6.

65   See Scholem, *Reshit ha-Kabbalah* [Tel Aviv, 1948] pp. 73-74 [Hebrew]; *Origins of the Kabbalah*, pp. 209-210.

66   See M. Idel, "R. Isaac Sagi Nahor's Mystical Intention of the *Shemoneh Esreh*" *Ephrayim Gottlieb's Memory Volume*, eds. M. Oron – A. Goldreich [Jerusalem, 1993] [forthcoming]. [Hebrew].

67   *ibidem*.

68   See her "'Flaw' and 'Correction' in the Concept of Godhead in the Teaching of Rabbi Isaac the Blind" *The Beginnings of Jewish Mysticism in Medieval Europe* ed. J. Dan, [Jerusalem, 1987] pp. 157-285. [Hebrew].

69   See Scholem, *Kabbalah*, p. 179.

70   See also *Otzar ha-Kavod*, fol. 19d.

71   This form of exclamation is characteristic of the Zoharic style.

72   *Zenu'im*. See notes 14, 47 above.

73   *Sefer Otzar ha-Kavod* [Warsau, 1879] fol. 13d; quoted by R. Meir ibn Gabbai, *Sefer 'Avodat ha-Qodesh*, [Jerusalem, 1963] fol. 16d.

74   Cf. Exodus 19, 9. The word *'Av*, namely cloud, has the numerical value of seventy-two; the biblical divine epiphany in the cloud was transformed into a revelation by the means of the divine names.

75   This view of the ontological status of the divine names is found already in the Kabbalistic school that has influenced Todros Abulafia's thought, in the *Commentary on the Merkavah* of R. Ya'aqov ha-Kohen.

76   R. Todros ben Joseph ha-Levi Abulafia, *Sefer Otzar ha-Kavod*, fol. 11c.

77 Ed. Arthur Green, "R. Isaac ibn Sahola's Commentary on the Song of Songs" *The Beginnings of the Jewish Mysticism in Medieval Europe*, ed. J. Dan, [Jerusalem, 1987] p. 412 and his note to line 22. See also Gershom Scholem, *Peraqim be-Toledot Sifrut ha-Kabbalah* [Jerusalem, 1931] pp. 60-61. By mentioning the knowledge of the future, the Kabbalist may hint at Abraham Abulafia's claim that he is a prophet. In any case, it seems that some concepts related to the technique of attaining a mystical experience by means of music, crucial in ecstatic Kabbalah, were known to ibn Avi Sahulah; see Idel, *The Mystical Experience*, pp. 59-60.

78 See Jellinek [note 63 above].

79 On this issue see his introduction to his *Commentary on the Pentateuch*, note 40 above.

80 For the phenomenological divergences between Abulafia's ecstatic Kabbalah and the theosophical-theurgical one see Idel, *Kabbalah: New Perspectives*, pp. XI-XIV, 200-210; idem, *Studies in Ecstatic Kabbalah*, pp. 18-20; idem, *Language, Torah and Hermeneutics in Abraham Abulafia*, pp. X-XVI.

81 I hope to devote elsewhere an elaborate study to this forgotten controversy which shaped the path of the development of Spanish Kabbalah.

82 See also below notes 114, 118.

83 *Auswahl kabbalistischer Mystik*, [Leipzig, 1853] pp. 14-15.

84 *Hokhmat ha-Talmud*.

85 On this phrase and its sources see Scholem, *Origins of the Kabbalah*, p. 394.

86 The seals are different combinations of the letters of the Tetragrammaton, conceived, according to *Sefer Yezirah*, as stamping the extremities of the universe.

87 On this technique of revelation as understood by Abulafia see Idel, *The Mystical Experience*, pp. 105-108, 158-160; idem, *Studies in Ecstatic Kabbalah*, pp. 125-126.

88 *Auswahl*, p. 15, corrected according to Ms. New York, JTS, 1887, fol. 98b.

89 On this issue see Scholem, *Origins of the Kabbalah*, p. 38 as well as the scholarly description of Kabbalah adduced above.

90 See I. Twersky, "Religion and Law" *Religion in a Religious Age*, ed. S. D. Goitein [Cambridge, Mass., 1974] p. 74.

91 Idel, "Maimonides and Kabbalah" pp. 56, 61.

92 As quoted in R. Isaac of Acre's *Meirat Eynayim*; see Scholem, *Major Trends*, p. 24.

93 *Auswahl*, pp. 17-18.

94 *Sefer Mafteah ha-Hokhmah*, Ms. Parma, de Rossi 141, fol. 19a; Scholem, *Major Trends*, pp. 143-144, 383 n. 90.

95   *Auswahl,* p. 20, corrected according to Ms. New York, JTS 1887, fol. 99b; Ms. Cambridge, Add. 644, fol. 3a; the version as printed by Jellinek is here very erroneous.

96   Ms. Paris, Biblioteque Nationale 853, fols. 49a-50a.

97   See above his definition of the Sefirotic Kabbalah.

98   *'Issruhu.*

99   *Auswahl,* p. 19.

100 See the analysis of the critique of another topic that is important for the Sefirotic Kabbalah, the Kabbalistic symbolism, in Abulafia's last book in Idel, *Kabbalah: New Perspectives,* p. 202.

101 See Idel, *ibidem,* pp. 138-139.

102 *ibidem,* pp. 141-146.

103 *Auswahl,* p. 16.

104 On the reception of the mystical speech see Idel, *The Mystical Experience,* pp. 83-95; idem, *Language, Torah and Hermeneutics,* pp. 106-107.

105 On this issue see Idel, *Studies in Ecstatic Kabbalah,* pp. 5-8.

106 See especially his *Sefer Sha'arei Orah.*

107 *Auswahl,* pp. 16-17. On ontic versus epistemological union see Idel, *Kabbalah: New Perspectives,* pp. 46-49.

108 Idel, "Maimonides and Kabbalah" pp. 67-68; *Sefer Imrei Shefer* printed in Jellinek, *Philosophie und Kabbala* [Leipzig, 1853] vol. I p. 36, etc.

109 *'Otiot, Nequddot, Zeruf.*

110 Namely sheep.

111 *Ziyyur;* on this medieval concept see H. A. Wolfson, "The Terms *Tasawwur* and *Tasdiq* in Arabic Philosophy and Their Greek, Latin and Hebrew Equivalents" The Moslem World, [April, 1943] pp. 1-15.

112 *Sefer Hayyei ha-'Olam ha-Ba,* Ms. Oxford 1582, fol. 45b. See also Idel, *Language, Torah, and Hermeneutics,* pp. 3-11. On the influence of this quote on R. Mordekhai Dato's description of R. Moses Cordovero's Kabbalistic activity see Idel, *Studies in Ecstatic Kabbalah,* p. 137.

113 Ms. New York, JTS 1801, fol. 4b.

114 This is one of the few instances where Abulafia explicitly mentions the reception of oral traditions from some masters. On the reception of esoteric traditions concerning the secrets of Maimonides' *Guide of the Perplexed* see Idel, "Maimonides

and Kabbalah" pp. 58-59 and note 90; p. 69. For the Renaissance misunder-standing of the identity of Abulafia's master as Maimonides himself see Chaim Wirszubski, *Pico della Mirandola's Encounter with Jewish Mysticism*, [Harvard University Press, Cambridge, Mass., 1988] pp. 87-88, 91-98.

115 A list of ancient mystical books appears in a similar context in his epistle *Sheva' Netivot ha-Torah*, p. 21.

116 In the Ms. *MHTY*; it is possible that this is one of the many errors of the copyist of this manuscript that is, unfortunately, a unicum. If so, we should read the sentence as follows; "which came to me in the form of *Bat Qol*." However, it is possible that Abulafia alluded to the Greek form *THY*, namely God, and then *MTHY* would mean "from God". Abulafia uses the form *THYV* in order to point to God already in his earlier *Sefer Get ha-Shemot*, see Idel, *Language, Torah, and Hermeneutics*, p. 24.

117 Compare to his epistle *Sheva' Netivot ha-Torah* p. 21, where he counts the revela-tion from the Agent Intellect as higher than the secrets he learned from various esoteric books. Cf. Idel, "Maimonides and Kabbalah", pp. 57-58.

118 I wonder whether the oral transmission as lower is connected also to Abulafia's own teachings to his Kabbalistic students. In one instance he mentions the "external Kabbalot", *Qabbalot Ḥiẓoniot*, in the context of the oral traditions concerning the mystical interpretations of the *Guide of the Perplexed*: See *Sefer Otzar Eden Ganuz*, Ms. Oxford 1950, fol. 164b.

119 The above quote is to be compared to another pertinent discussion of Abulafia, translated by Scholem in *Major Trends*, pp. 140-141. Though there are some divergences between them, the variety of channels for receiving Kabbalah is accepted also in this other, earlier, Kabbalistic text.

120 *Sefer Ḥayyei ha-'Olam ha-Ba*, Ms. Oxford 1580, fol. 52a.

121 See Yoḥanan Alemanno's view of Kabbalah as "understood by the intellect" in his ideal curriculum, cf. M. Idel, "The Study Program of R. Yohanan Alemanno" *Tarbiz*, vol. 48 [1978] p. 309. [Hebrew] See also below note 123.

122 *ẓeruf*.

123 *Sefer Otzar Eden Ganuz*, Ms. Oxford 1580, fol. 90a. See also *ibidem*, fol. 136a: "We have Kabbalistic ways which are bringing us to the *intelligibilia* in a easy way [*be-qalut*], without their [the philosophers'] ways". See also above note 121.

124 Abulafia's untitled text, Ms. Sassoon 290, p. 234. Compare also to the pseudo-Maimonidean *Epistle of the Secrets*, which stems from Abulafia's circle, where "the science of Kabbalah" has ways that enable someone to reach in a very easy way [*be-qalut nimraẓ*], whatever is within the scope of human apprehension; according to the epistle, this was the way of the prophets. Cf. *Ḥemdah Genuzah*, ed. Z. E. Edelman, [Koenigsberg, 1856] fol. 43a. See also Idel, "Maimonides and Kabbalah" p. 75, note 160.

125 See the views of R. Sa'adiya Gaon and R. Yehudah ha-Levi on the oral tradition as analyzed by respectively Harry A. Wolfson, *Studies in the History of Philosophy and Religion*, eds. I. Twersky and G. H. Williams [Harvard University Press, Cambridge, Mass., 1973] vol. I pp. 584-597, Raphael Jospe, "The Superiority of Oral over Written Communication: Judah Ha-Levi's *Kuzari* and Modern Thought", *From Ancient Israel to Modern Judaism, Intellect in Quest of Understanding, Essays in Honor of Marvin Fox*, eds. J. Neusner, E. S. Frerichs, N. M. Sarna [Scholars Press, Atlanta, Georgia, 1989], vol. III, 127-156.   On R. Yehudah ha-Levi's view of mysticism see Elliot R. Wolfson, "Merkavah Traditions in Philosophical Garb: Judah Halevi Reconsidered," *Proceedings of the American Academy for Jewish Research*, vol. LVII [1991] pp. 179-242.

126 See M. Idel, "*Ma'aseh Merkavah*:   A Case of Intercultural Translations" [forthcoming].

127 See Mircea Eliade, *Shamanism: Archaic Techniques of Ecstasy* [London, 1964] p. 401; idem, *Images & Symbols, Studies in Religious Symbolism* [Sheed and Ward, New York, 1969] pp. 54-55; Frits Staal, *Exploring Mysticism* [Penguin Books, Harmondworth 1975] pp. 100-101, 155-156.

128 See Idel, *The Mystical Experience*, pp. 13-52.

129 See Staal's critique *ibidem*, pp. 100-101.

130 See Idel, "Ma'aseh Merkavah" [note 126 above].

Human Hands Dwell in Heavenly Heights: Contemplative Ascent and Theurgic Power in Thirteenth Century Kabbalah

Seth L. Brody

A. Tending the Garden: The World of the Kabbalist.

In one of the *Zohar's* most charming and witty narratives, two students of R. Shimon bar Yoḥai, Rabbis Isaac and Judah, encounter a child prodigy in the village of Siknin (III. 186a - 191b). Before sitting down to eat with him, the two sages wash their hands in accordance with rabbinic law. When washing, R. Judah recites the liturgical formula "Praised are You, Lord our God, King of the universe, who has sanctified us by His commandments and commanded us concerning the washing of the hands" before performing his ritual ablution. In this reversal of normative practice, R. Judah is praising God while his hands remain dirty.

Appalled, the child states: "If you are students of R. Shemaayah the Ḥasid (R. Shimon bar Yoḥai), you would not have blessed with filthy hands. One who blesses with filthy hands should be put to death!"

This alarming contention is justified via an exegetical discourse on Exodus 30:20 concerning the significance of laving.

> The child opened and said:
> "When they enter the tent of Meeting
> they will wash with water so they will not die..."
> (Ex. 30:20)
> We learn from this verse that one who is not careful and appears in the presence of the King with filthy hands should be put to death.
> Why?
> Because the hands of a human being inhabit the height of the world.[1] (*Zohar* III 186a)

---

forthcoming in *Visions of God: Typologies of Mystical Experience*, Robert Herrera, editor

The youngster's choice of Ex. 30:20 as a prooftext and springboard is fraught with profound significance. The rabbinic practice of ritual washing is rooted in the Temple cult. Just as the priests washed their hands before engaging in the sacrificial service of the altar, so too must a Jew lave before sitting at the table which constitutes his own private altar. This ritualized washing evolves out of the Pharisaic movement's attempt to model Jewish life upon the paradigm of the Temple cult, to sacramentalize all aspects of daily existence and transform Israel into a priestly people in the fullest sense.[2] The emphasis placed by the child upon laving and its presentation within a sacerdotal framework reflect traditional rabbinic sensitivities.

However, where the youngster's association of the secular act of breaking bread with priestly offering is rooted in Talmudic tradition, his final statement reflects a distinctively Kabbalistic spirituality. It is not merely the cultic priest who courts death if he approaches the altar in a state of impurity. The priest is an archetype. Any Jew who enters into the Presence of God to offer blessing like a priest, merits death if he does so with dirty hands. "For the hands of a human being inhabit the height of the world." The influence of human hands extends into spiritual realms; an individual's actions possess causal efficacy in the worlds above.

The power inherent in a Jew's ritual activity, i.e. the capacity inherent in his intention, word and deed to touch worlds far beyond his own, derives from the fact that the essential structures of human existence are modeled upon and consequently mirror divine reality. Coalescing in late twelfth and thirteenth century Provence and Spain out of a welter of Neo-Platonic, Midrashic and Gnostic influences, the Kabbalistic worldview is an emanational one. The Kabbalistic imagination envisages the cosmos as a hierarchy of interlocking and inter-penetrating realms, in which the structures of our phenomenal universe mirror the forces and dynamics of "higher", spiritual worlds and embody their energies.

Animating this new mystical tradition is a revolutionary vision of Divinity, expressed in a rich and subtle symbolism. The transcendent Godhead, described as the *Ilat ha-Ilot* (Causa Causarum) and *Ein Sof* (Infinite) eludes all human comprehension and definition. The Kabbalists instruct us that concerning the *Ein Sof* "there is no intimation, either in the Torah, Prophets or Writings or in the words of the Rabbis. However, the Masters of Prayer have received some intimation."[3] From out of its depths, unknowable divinity emanates a tenfold hierarchy of energies, inherent within it like flames within a coal. Kabbalistic literature describes these forces with a wide array of names: Powers (*Koḥot*), Lights (*Orot*), Channels (*Naḥalin*), Words

(*Dibburim*) and Crowns (*K'tarim*). The term that quickly achieves prominence is *Sefirot*. The *Sefirot* must be understood as differentiated modes of infinitude, through which the boundless power and being of divinity enter into the realm of particularization and distinguishable function.

Within this tenfold hierarchy of divine being, Kabbalists distinguish two modes of existence and activity. The first three *Sefirot* take the form of an intellectual triad, constituting the realm of divine volition and intellection. These give rise to a lower septet of cosmogenerative powers, envisioned as the archetypal days of Creation figured in Genesis 1, through which God creates and acts in the universe. Straddling these twin domains of divine thought and action stands the third *Sefirah*, Binah (Understanding), symbolized by the *tohu va-vohu*, the formless and shapeless void of the Creation narrative, which serves as the seedbed of the cosmos.

Ein Sof's first emanation, named Keter Elyon (Supernal Crown) or Ratzon (Will), constitutes the realm of divine Volition, the primal stirrings of outward movement and revelatory drive within the inner life of Divinity. The creative ground of all being, Keter is also paradoxically described as *Ayin* or Nothing. It is that ineffable realm transcending all differentiation and positive predication. Keter gives rise to Ḥokhmah (Wisdom) and Binah (Understanding), which together comprise the divine consciousness. Ḥokhmah is a state of nondifferentiated awareness, bearing within itself the embryonic seeds of the remaining eight *Sefirot* and serving as the ultimate source of the highest elements of the human soul. Binah or Understanding is that level of consciousness in which content moves towards definition and manifestation. Within her fertile womb rest the roots of "heaven and earth": the world forming Sefirotic powers of the "Days of Creation", forces of Love and Justice mediated by divine Compassion and manifested through the *Shechinah*, God's nurturing immanence in the world.

It is this lower Sefirotic septet, emanated from Understanding, that constitutes the domain of God's creative activity. The Sefirotic forces comprising this septet are distinguished by their differentiation into principles of cosmic compassion and justice, symbolized by the powers of right and left, which produce a subtle dialectic of opposition and resolution within the life of Deity. From the hidden depths of Binah flow the light and radiant energy of Ḥesed (Love), the unbounded and unfocused force of divine benevolence and creativity. Ḥesed's emergence sparks the emanation of its polar opposite: Din or Gevurah, God's Justice or Might, which acts to structure and channel (and if unchecked, choke) the efflux of Love. These contrasting and even contradictory movements in divine life attain resolution in a mediating force which combines and harmonizes the energies of both. Kabbalistic writings refer to this force as either Tiferet (Splendor) or Raḥamim (Compassion). This dialectical process of opposition and resolution repeats itself in the emanation of a further triad of Netzaḥ (Eternity), Hod (Majesty) and Yesod (Foundation). Netzaḥ and Hod channel prophetic vision to the adept while Yesod is described as the world of souls. The emanational process culminates with the revelation of the lowest *Sefirah*, the *Shechinah* – God's immanent presence, which permeates and animates the cosmos. Just as all waters gather into the sea, so too does the *Shechinah* gather the light and generative energies of the *Sefirot* and spin them into the phenomenal universe.[4]

On an ontological level, the divine and phenomenal realms constitute a single interlinked continuum. In a wedding sermon, R. Moshe b. Naḥman, the great thirteenth century Kabbalist, exegete and legist, claimed: "Everything that was created above was created below. For it is written: (I Chron. 29:11) 'Everything that is *in* the Heavens and *in* the Earth." Corresponding to the *Ein Sof*, manifest in the form of a noetic Sefirotic triad and a cosmogenerative septet, are the earth's four corners (the sum of one and three), which are crisscrossed by seven climactic zones. Just as the seventy names of God radiate from the seven lower *Sefirot*, so too do the seventy nations of the world inhabit the world's seven climactic areas. Moshe b. Naḥman argues that these same cosmic archetypes find expression in the history of Israel. Noah, via his third son Shem, engenders seven patriarchs and matriarchs. These give rise to Israel, who descended to Egypt seventy strong and were ruled by the seventy sages of the *Sanhedrin*. Every aspect of Israelite existence mirrors this cosmic order, from the arrangement of their camp in the wilderness to the vestments of Aaron the High Priest. Garbed in seven vestments, resplendent with two onyx stones on his shoulders and a golden frontlet attached to his miter, Aaron wears twelve precious stones on his breastplate, corresponding to both the twelve tribes of Israel and the twelve permutations of the Tetragrammaton, God's ineffable four letter name.[5]

These correspondences which structure the world and human history are more than carefully crafted allegorical signs, a speculum through which "videmus nunc. . . in aenigmate". Our physical universe emanates from and reflects its Sefirotic sources. Thus Kabbalistic spirituality in its totality, from its conceptualization of mystical experience to its analysis of the power of human intentionality and moral action, is founded upon the conviction that the entirety of reality is inextricably interlinked on an ontic level. This is particularly the case of the soul and human consciousness, which are literally born in the process of divine emanation, originating in the *Sefirah* of Hokhmah (Wisdom). R. Ezra of Gerona (fl. 1220 - 1230's), one of the founding fathers of Spanish *Kabbalah* and senior colleague of Nahmanides, asserted " . . . a human being . . . contains all of the *Sefirot* and his soul is bound to the Supernal Soul (the *Shechinah*). It is accordingly written in the Torah: (Lev. 19:2)"Be holy for I am holy" and (Lev. 11:44; 20:7) "Sanctify yourselves and be holy"."[6] Writing some sixty years later, de Leon states in the *Zohar* (III 48a): "It is taught: 'When the human was created, all was perfected. All that is above and below was included in the human.'" A parallel passage (I 52a) describes the first human as standing in "the wisdom of the supernal light" and as being bound to the Tree of Life, interpreted as symbolizing Tiferet, the locus of divine compassion.

Even in the world's current fallen state, the human being retains this divine image. Human consciousness and even corporeality reflect and participate in the dynamics of Divine Self-revelation. In a discussion of ritual washing in his commentary to the Talmudic *aggadot*, R. Ezra's contemporary and neighbor, R. Azriel of Gerona, states that the hands must be clean if one wishes to praise God. For the ten digits of the human hand correspond to the ten Sefirotic utterances with which God created the world.[7] Underlying R. Azriel's words is the conviction that human hands are tenfold because the inner life of God unfolds in ten stages. Consequently, Moshe de Leon, who undoubtedly knew R. Azriel's statement, depicted the youngster as instructing Rabbis Isaac and Judah on the need to praise God with clean hands for *"kol da it baho"*: "all that"—the Sefirotic worlds and their energies "are within them" in a very real if mysterious sense. A human being originates in the upper worlds and his physical being resonates in accord with divine archetypes. Consequently, a person bears within himself the potentiality of embodying and manifesting the creative power of his source. The right modes of human consciousness and action can energize the cosmos and bring blessing to the worlds and the Divine Name, the Sefirotic pleroma. The hands of a human being truly inhabit heavenly heights.

We see the that Kabbalists envision the human being as constituting a microcosmic image of the emanational process, whose life and activity influences the entirety of the universe. For what purpose then was the human being created? How does the Kabbalistic vision of *takhlit ha-Adam*, the purpose of human existence, condition their understanding of the nature of mystical experience and the transformations of consciousness and behavior which it induces?

The evolving Kabbalistic tradition of thirteenth century Spain focuses upon the mystery of *Maaseh Bereishit*, "the work of Creation".

This is the process whereby *Ein Sof*, transcendent Deity, manifests itself through the emanation of both the Sefirotic and phenomenal universes. This fascination with creation is shared with the philosophical tradition with which *Kabbalah* coexists. The high Jewish tradition of the Mediterranean world is distinguished by a profound cosmological focus. The disparate theologies of such Neo-Platonists as Solomon ibn Gabirol (ca. 1020 - ca. 1057) and Abraham ibn Ezra (1089 - 1164) and Aristotelians such as Moses b. Maimon (1135 - 1204) argue that the religious seeker arrives at the knowledge and love of God through the systematic and rational analysis of the natural world. In particular, Aristotelian thinkers like Maimonides believe that the resultant intellectual love of God bears the potential of culminating in a state of conjunction with the Active Intellect (Arab. *ittisall* Heb. *devekut*), in which the universe is revealed to the mind in all of its intelligibility and interconnectedness. In Maimonides' eyes, this state of illumination, identified with prophecy, spurs its bearer to renewed activity within the world and human society. The philosopher-illuminate must reconstruct society in accordance with the harmonious and orderly patterns perceived as pervading the cosmos.[8]

Thirteenth century Kabbalists recreate this essential paradigm within a profoundly mystical and contemplative framework in which illumination is conjoined with a deeply rooted sense of cosmic stewardship. The quest for illumination and the maintenance of the cosmos become the twin foci of religious endeavor.

Kabbalistic exegetes find their emanational ontology and cosmology reflected in the creation narrative. Gen. 3:10 "A river goes forth from Eden to water the garden, from whence it separates into four tributaries" is read as esoterically intimating the emanation of the *Sefirot* from Divine Wisdom (Eden) and the infusion of their energies (symbolized as the river) into the Divine Presence, the creative and nurturing garden.[9] From the *Shechinah*, these energies shine forth and take on the shape of the extradivine universe. The four tributaries are interpreted as representing the four angelic camps surrounding the divine throne of Ezekiel's vision, from which the lower worlds derive. Although Kabbalistic thinkers envision our universe as the product of conscious design and willful emanative action upon God's part, possessing its own unique reality and significance, the line of demarcation separating the two realms can be quite blurred, for ours is a cosmos suffused with the divine energy. Similarly, Kabbalists point to Ḥokhmah, the divine realm of unitive consciousness containing the seeds of all being, as the human mind's point of origin. Human thought is at times described as attaining a unity of identity with this source in language as nondualistic as any found in the East.

The purpose of human existence is the integration of both the cosmos and human consciousness into God.   Mind and the commandments are tools which open the portals of emanation so that the world might be suffused with God's light and energy and the divine and mortal realms function as a unified continuum, enabling divinity to be as manifestly present in the lower worlds as it is in the upper.   In his *Shaarei Orah* (wr. ca. 1291), one of the first works of systematic Kabbalistic theology, Joseph Gikatilla explains:

> Know that at the beginning of creation, the *Shechinah's* primary manifestation was in the lower worlds, for the arrangement of the created orders corresponded to the structure of the *Sefirot*; the celestial worlds corresponding to the higher grada- tions of divinity and the terrestrial realms to the lower. Consequently, the *Shechi- nah* was present in the lower realms and as the *Shechinah* was below, Heaven and Earth were united.   This is the meaning of the verse: (Gen. 2:1) "Heaven and earth were completed (*vayekhulu*) and all of their host"—they were included (*nishtakhlelu*) in each other and filled by each other.   The channels and sources were functioning perfectly and were being drawn forth from above to below. God, be He praised, was immanent in all, from above to below.   Your prooftext: (Is. 66:1) "The heavens are My throne and the earth My footstool."   God was equally present in the upper and lower worlds . . . [10]

The first humans were created to preserve and maintain this primor- dial unity.   The unfolding process of emanation, in which infinite Being manifests Itself as distinct and definable *Sefirot* and creates a cosmos, is placed into the hands of a being who combines both infinity and finitude, the celestial and terrestrial, within his structure. God cannot attain a full "dwelling in the lower worlds", the infinite cannot become completely manifest in the finite, without the aid of a consciousness which can straddle both realms.

This mystery was believed to be intimated in Gen. 2:15: "The Lord God took the human being and placed him in the Garden of Eden to work and preserve it."   Biblical Hebrew uses the verb *la-avod* (to work) to designate both physical labor and the sacrificial worship of God.   Some Midrashic commentators accordingly interpret Adam's primordial labor as consisting of sacrificial worship.   Seizing upon this interpretation, Kabbalistic writers depict Adam as the world's primor- dial priest and cosmic steward, offering sacrifice to tie heaven and earth into a unified whole, permeated with blessing and life.   The vision of Adam's priestly vocation is lucidly enunciated by Moshe b. Naḥman's discussion of Gen. 3:15 in his Torah commentary.

> They said in Genesis Rabbah (16:5): "'To work (*le-ovdah*) and preserve (*ule- shomrah*) it.' These are the sacrifices. As it says: (Ex. 3:12) 'Serve (*taavdun*) God'

and (Num. 28:2) "Take care (*tishmeru*) to offer to Me in due season." Their intention in this . . . is that the plants and all living beings are in need of the primary powers (*koḥot rishonot* — the *Sefirot*), from whom come (the power of) generation. From the sacrifices, an efflux of blessing comes to the upper worlds and from them to the plants of the Garden of Eden. They will derive their being from them and live eternally, by means of the rains of favor and blessing through which they grow . . . [11]

It is not simply the terrestrial garden that is blessed and suffused with divine energy but the supernal garden, the feminine *Shechinah*. This mystery is intimated by the fact that while the word *gan* (garden) is a masculine noun, Gen. 3:15 treats it as possessing feminine gender, the phrase "*le-ovdah ule-shomrah*" being literally translatable as "to work and preserve her." Adam, as primordial priest, is to engage in a worship which will sustain the unity of the entire emanational process, so that the nine upper *Sefirot*, the *Shechinah* and the physical universe might be bound together as a creative, lifefilled whole.

This organic and manifest unity of creation's dawn, in which the world was filled with a heavenly radiance through which Adam could see from one end of the world to the other, has been shattered by human sin. The mystical literature of this period presents several contradictory accounts of Adam's prelapsarian nature and transgression. Moshe b. Naḥman envisions Adam as an embodied being, comprised of an etherialized matter on the order of the heavenly spheres, transparent to the light of divinity which he guides into the world. His older contemporary, R. Ezra, depicts him as immaterial intellect on the order of an angel. Adam's fall not surprisingly consisted of a movement towards egocentric differentiation culminating in physical embodiment and entanglement in material desires.[12] R. Ezra's view entranced many Catalonian Kabbalists and was lucidly expressed at the end of the century by R. Baḥya ibn Asher, who describes the first human, prior to his sin, as "an angel of the Lord of Hosts, purely intellectual, lovely without blemish, worthy of living forever like the celestial servitors. When he sinned and was drawn towards physical desires, he was divested from the intellectual and clothed in matter. He was banished from the Garden and given herbs to eat like a beast, as it says concerning him (Gen. 3:18): 'You shall eat the herbs of the field.'"[13]

Similarly, these early Kabbalistic authors tell contradictory stories concerning the nature of Adam's sin. However, the explanation proffered by Rabbi Ezra won the widest acceptance by the late thirteenth century and gained the endorsement of the increasingly influential *Sefer ha-Zohar*. This account depicts Adam as separating the Tree of Knowledge (the *Shechinah*) from the Tree of Life (Tiferet) as the result of a contemplative error in which he worshipped her apart from the *Sefirot*. Seeing the lights of the other divine aeons manifested in the *Shechinah*, he focused his contemplative intentionality upon her alone. As a result of his error, the primordial unity of the *Sefirot* was shattered and the channels conveying their cosmogenerative powers into the universe were blocked. Cast into exile, the *Shechinah's* manifest light was extinguished on earth. To quote Gikatilla's discussion of the fall in the *Shaarei Orah*, "The first human came and sinned, the ranks were damaged, the conduits shattered, the fountains ceased, the *Shechinah* departed and the tie was broken."[14]

In a world marked by the *Shechinah's* exile, the goal of the spiritual seeker is to restore the primordial unity shattered in Adam's sin. This is achieved firstly on the level of the reintegration of individual consciousness into the life of divinity. The image of God within humanity has not been destroyed. The devotee is thus capable of uniting his consciousness with Divine Wisdom. As we shall shortly see, Kabbalistic practitioners engaged in contemplative prayer achieved altered states of consciousness in which human mind merges with the Divine. However, the devotee's goal is not merely the attainment of his own personal illumination and liberation. When human mind merges with divine wisdom, the devotee is transformed into a channel drawing God's presence, light and blessing into the world. The mantle of Adam's priestly vocation is once again assumed and both humanity's primordial dignity and the world's primal unity brought closer to final restoration. Although the enterprise of *tikkun*, world restoration, does not grip the Spanish Kabbalistic imagination with a power comparable to that with which it animates the Lurianic tradition in the late sixteenth century, even at this early date Jewish mystics are acutely attuned to the horrors and suffering of history. They live in a world that they know to be incomplete and imperfect. The light lying at the heart of the cosmos has been dimmed by humanity's abuse of its freedom. It is only through the proper use of human consciousness and action that this divine light will again shine into the universe and God and His Name become one as they were at the beginning of time.

Spanish Kabbalists understandably present Jewish history as a process of restoration in which the *Shechinah* is drawn back into the world and the rifts in the cosmos mended. Gikatilla transforms the salvation history of Scripture into a process of redemption directed as much for the benefit of God as humanity.

The came Abraham, Isaac and Jacob. They began to draw (the *Shechinah*) down and prepared three thrones for her. They draw her down partially, making their bodies thrones for her presence. But the *Shechinah* was not brought down into the world permanently, but only in a transient manner . . . Concerning this the Sages said: "The patriarchs are the Chariot". The *Shechinah* in their day was hovering in the air, finding no rest in the world as it formerly had at the beginning of Creation.

Moses arose and all of Israel with him. They made the Tabernacle and all of its utensils, repaired the damaged channels, ordered the ranks and mended the fountains, drew living waters from out of the House of Water Drawing. They returned the *Shechinah* to a dwelling place in the terrestrial realm—a tent, but not on the earth itself as at the beginning of creation. This is the esoteric meaning of the verse (Ex. 25:8): "Make Me a sanctuary so that I might dwell among them". The *Shechinah* was like a guest at an inn, moving from place to place. For this reason the verse says: "that I might dwell among them" and not "that I might dwell below." . . . That is to say: "Wherever Israel will go, I will go. I will go with them and dwell among them, but not in a fixed place.[15]

Gikatilla, when presenting a Kabbalistic rendition of Israel's history, is attracted in particular to the figure of Abraham, "who began to plant the shoots cut by the first human"[16]. This process of restoration, which reached its preMessianic climax with the construction of Solomon's Temple, has been temporarily thwarted by the destruction of Jerusalem and Israel's (and the *Shechinah*'s) return to exile. It is this profound and uniquely Jewish sense of exile that accounts for the activism of the Kabbalistic tradition and its deep-seated commitment to both the illuminative and theurgic sides of spiritual life. In a fractured universe, Kabbalists are striving to restore both soul and cosmos to a lost state of primal unity and effect a redemption as much God's as Israel's. It is this sense of the power and cosmic significance of Israel's worship and action that inspires the *Zohar*'s exquisite imagery of human hands dwelling within—that is shaping—the heights of the world.

The conviction that human hands inhabit heavenly heights transforms the Kabbalistic understanding of mystical adhesion to God, generally designated as *devekut* (lit. cleaving or adhesion). In that contemplative intentionality shattered the cosmos' primal unity, it is contemplative intentionality conjoined with *mitzvah*, Scripturally ordained commandment, which will restore it. Our *Zohar* text expresses this insight powerfully. The youngster substantiates his claim for the heavenly power of human hands by referring to the arms of the priests outstretched in blessing and Moses' rod raised heavenwards during Israel's war with Amalek. de Leon's predecessors regarded both situations as paradigmatic examples of profound contemplative absorption in God. This state empowers the devotee, enabling him to both perform the theurgic functions of uniting heaven and earth and to draw energies of blessing from the ground of

Divine Will and Wisdom into the lower *Sefirot* and the physical universe. By juxtaposing his claim for the theurgic power of human action with the imagery of the Temple priesthood and Moses engaged in contemplative prayer, de Leon is arguing that human hands dwell in heavenly heights because mind, in its mystical ascent, leads them there. The Kabbalists' sensitivity to history and their painful experience of exile, create a spirituality in which contemplative and theurgic intentionality, illuminative insight and empowerment, are inextricably intertwined. Having described the fundamentals of the Kabbalistic worldview, it is now time to examine in detail the primary manner in which this tradition conceptualized mystical experience so that we might better understand the spirituality producing the claim that human hands dwell in heavenly heights.

B. *Maḥashavah Devekah*: 'Adhesive Consciousness' and Theurgic Empowerment in Thirteenth Century Kabbalah.

During its evolution in thirteenth century Spain, the Kabbalistic tradition branches into two fundamental schools of thought and practice. The first school, originating in the Provencal disciplic circle of the great legist R. Asher b. David of Posquiere and his son R. Isaac the Blind, is brought by their students to the Spanish cities of Gerona and Barcelona by the 1220's. These students, R. Ezra and R. Abraham the Ḥazan, along with R. Azriel and R. Jacob bar Sheshet, establish a uniquely Catalonian Kabbalistic tradition flourishing into the next century and marked by a strong Neo-Platonic bent. Around midcentury, a second Kabbalistic circle coalesces in Castile, distinguished by a profound mythological *tendenz*. To the Provenco-Catalan doctrine of the *Sefirot*, the Castilians add a passionate fascination with angelology and disquieting speculations concerning the origin of evil. It is within this circle that Moshe de Leon received his spiritual formation. His magnum opus, the *Zohar*, is a brilliantly executed vehicle for the exposition of its teachings.[17]

The generic term most often used to describe mystical experience in both circles is *devekut*, from the root *dvk*, meaning to cleave or adhere. The root itself possesses a venerable Biblical pedigree. It appears in verbal form in Deuteronomy (10:20; 11:22; 30:20), where Israel is commanded to love, revere and adhere (*davek*) to God. There the primary connotation of the term seems to be Israel's obligation to adhere loyally to the covenant and eschew the worship of other deities. However, in rabbinic sources, the verb has acquired a clearly experiential valence. In *Sanhedrin* 64a, Israel is said to cleave (*davek*) to God like two datepalms growing together out of a common trunk and "adhering to each other". Similarly, Ketubot 111a quotes Deut. 4:4 "You shall cleave to the Lord, your God" and asks: "Is it possible for a human being to adhere (*davek*) to God? It is written: (Deut. 4:24) The Lord your God is a consuming fire". Concerning such denials of the possibility of humanity's consummating communion with divinity, *Sanhedrin* 64a quotes Deut. 4:4 "You shall cleave to the Lord, your God" and retorts: "Truly adhering".[18] It is this experiential understanding of the word that engenders its adoption as the Hebrew equivalent for *ittisal*, conjunction with the Active Intellect, by Neo-Platonists such as Abraham ibn Ezra and the great twelfth century Provencal translators of the Judeo-Arabic philosophical classics, Judah and Samuel ibn Tibbon. It is the ibn Tibbons who take the abstract form *devekut* and indelibly fix its meaning in medieval Jewish consciousness as experiential perception of the divine.

Careful analysis of thirteenth century Kabbalistic sources reveals that the term *devekut* functions as a general rubric for a wide array of spiritual experience and consequently covers and even masks several distinct typologies of mystical experience. One of the most important of these typoi in terms of the history of Jewish mysticism appears in the early 1200's in the writings of R. Isaac the Blind and his successors, the Gerona circle, Rabbis Ezra, Azriel and Jacob b. Sheshet. It is developed further by a wide range of influential thirteenth century Spanish Kabbalists, including the Castilian R. Joseph Gikatilla and the anonymous author of the *Iggeret ha-Kodesh*, a work on Kabbalistic sexual ethics. It plays a significant, if secondary role in the *Zohar*, informing the text opening this essay. In this typos, *devekut* is presented as a process of *mahashavah devekah* — "consciousness which adheres to Divinity", in which the Kabbalistic adept engages in a contemplative ascent into the Sefirotic realm in order to unite his thought and volition with their supernal counterparts, Divine Wisdom and Will, Hokhmah and Keter. The mystic's attainment of unio sparks a downward surge of creative energy from Keter into the *Sefirot* and the cosmos, which are channeled into the natural order via the meditative concentration of the Kabbalistic adept. The goal of mystical life is thus two-fold: the union of the mind and will with God and the simultaneous evocation of energies of blessing and life into the emanated and phenomenal realms. Consequently, it is impossible to distinguish the illuminative and theurgic foci of mystical experience in Kabbalistic spirituality and literature, for they are inextricably intertwined. To this highly Neo-Platonized vision of *mahashavah devekah*, de Leon in the *Zohar* adds two other fundamental typoi of *devekut*, derived from the Castilian tradition. As we shall presently see, visionary experience plays an honored role in the Catalonian tradition, R. Azriel speaking of the perception of *Ein Sof* with "the eyes of the heart". The Castilians, in turn, are unabashed visionaries. They place profound emphasis upon the Kabbalist as seer, who is able to spiritually perceive the unfolding process of Sefirotic emanation, described with such exquisite imagery in the *Zohar*. de Leon furthermore works with an understanding of *devekut* as a process of theosis, in which the adept attains identification and even union with one particular aspect of the Sefirotic pleroma and takes on its functions in the worlds above. In these modalities of *devekut*, the illuminative and theurgic foci of mystical experience are again intermingled. These Castilian modes of *devekut* possess a complexity warranting separate study.[19] Consequently, the remainder of this essay will focus upon the conception of *mahashavah devekah*, considering the profound role it plays in a wide range of thirteenth century texts produced by both schools and the manner in which it exemplifies the fundamental values and concerns of Kabbalistic spirituality outlined in the first part of this essay.

Any discussion of mystical experience in a Kabbalistic context must commence with a brief summation and analysis of Gershom Scholem's views on the subject. Working from a small sample of sources, Scholem, in his essay "*Devekut* or Communion with God" presents a monlithic vision of *devekut* as an essentially anti-social and non-eschatological experience, coming as the apex of a long and arduous spiritual ascent. Scholem furthermore argues that *devekut* falls short of a true union with God, in which the devotee's sense of possession of an identity distinct from deity is annihilated.[20]

As a subjective experience attained by an individual in this life, Scholem argues that *devekut* is devoid of eschatalogical value. Scholem finds the anti-social nature of *devekut* to be exemplified by Moses b. Naḥman's description of the saintly as those "who abandon the affairs of the world and pay no regard to this world at all, as though they were not corporeal beings, but all of their intent and purpose is fixed on their creator alone, as in the case of Elijah and Enoch, who live on forever in body and soul, after having attained communion of their souls (*behidabek nafsham*) with the Great Name."[21] Scholem's description of *devekut* as the final telos of the spiritual path is based upon the mystico-pietistic literature of the Safed renaissance, where it is indeed presented as being accessible to a mere handful of spiritual athletes. Eliezer Azikri, the author of the *Book of the Tremblers*, for example, depicts *devekut* as an ultimate value to be cultivated only by the saintly, who have retreated from society and practice ascetic denial.[22]

Scholem's model of *devekut* has been extensively critiqued by Ephraim Gottleib and Moshe Idel over the past three decades. Both Gottleib and Idel have demonstrated convincingly that Scholem's discussion fails to adequately describe the richness of spiritual experience evidenced by thirteenth century Kabbalistic literature. Working from the extensive and highly valuable writings of R. Isaac of Acre, (fl. late 13th to early 14th century), Gottleib has uncovered a wealth of information indicating that *devekut* was conceptualized as a contemplative discipline in which a Kabbalist engaged from the onset of his career and which concludes with a true unio mystica in which the soul experiences itself as being absorbed and annihilated in God.[23] In his *Meirat Einaim*, R. Isaac argues that the path culminating in the attainment of the Holy Spirit, *commences* with *devekut*. This is described as a contemplative focusing of the mind upon God, achieved, in part, through visualization of the letters of the Tetragrammaton — a practice accessible to the learned and simple alike.[24] Another such exercise calls for the visualization of the *Sefirot* arrayed like a ladder. R. Isaac's mystical diary, *Otzar ha-Haim*, makes it abundantly clear that such mental exercises produced altered states of consciousness in which the devotee experienced himself as grounded in *Ein Sof*.[25] Such experiences are described by R. Isaac with the terminology of annihilation and unification — the image of water poured from a jug into a stream being one such example.[26]

Our understanding of *devekut* has grown profoundly in recent years due to the labor and insight of Moshe Idel. His work constitutes the first serious attempt to chart the parameters of unio mystica within the Kabbalistic tradition and identify its various typologies. Studying *Kabbalah* in terms of its intellectual context, the worlds of Neo-Platonic spirituality and Aristotelian epistemology, Idel finds that the motifs, concepts and imagery descriptive of *devekut* derive from three primary sources. These are the Neo-Platonic vision of the soul's heavenly ascent to the One, Aristotelian notions of the mind's noetic union with the Active Intellect and hermetic discussions of the invocation and conjuration of heavenly spirits.[27] The Neo-Platonic model of the soul's heavenward ascent to union with the celestial Oversoul is evidenced in a wide range of thirteenth century Kabbalistic sources, extending from R. Ezra to the early fourteenth century Italian mystic Menaḥem Racanati, often in the context of discussions of prophecy.[28] It is Idel's contention that in Gerona, this vision of the soul's heavenly ascent merged with Aristotelian notions of union with the Active intellect, to produce the concept of *maḥashavah devekah*, "consciousness adhering to Divinity". Through *maḥashavah devekah*, human consciousness merges with the *Sefirah* of Ḥokhmah, Divine

Wisdom, in order to be filled with an efflux of energy and wisdom from the highest *Sefirah*, "the Negation of Thought".[29] Modes of *devekut* can also be distinguished according to their final goals, whether it is the attainment of union with God, mediation for one's fellows as is the case with the priests uttering *Birkat Kohanim* (the Priestly Benediction of Num. 6:22-27) or the unification of the *Sefirot*.[30]

My own extensive work with Kabbalistic notions of contemplative worship indicates that in the practice of *mahashavah devekah*, the primary mode of *devekut* in the Catalonian tradition, facets of all three of these great spiritual movements have been gathered together to produce a new and unique mode of mystical endeavor and conscious-ness. The Kabbalist is an individual thirsting for the experience of God and convinced that his soul and mind originate in heavenly realms. He is equally intent on drawing the light and vivifying power of Divinity back into the world, in order to sustain the cosmos and undo the damage caused by the sin of the original human. Drawing upon all of the intellectual resources available to him, he creates a spiritual path and epistemology enabling him to simultaneously achieve both of his goals, the reintegration of self and cosmos into God and the restoration of a scattered and diminished primal unity. Mind is united with its primal source in divine Wisdom, in an ascent described in terms of language culled from both the Aristotelian and Neo-Platonic traditions. Human consciousness is described as ascending and uniting with its divine source. This unified mind then is transformed into a conduit for the manifestation of vital energy and blessing within both the Sefirotic pleroma and the physical universe. The Kabbalist engaged in the discipline and experience of *devekut* does not differentiate between his desire to commune with God, to unify the *Sefirot* and raise them back to their sources in the realm of divine Wisdom, and the need to invoke an influx of "blessing-energy" into the cosmos. To him, all of these activities are part and parcel of the same quest and act, a process of cosmic ascent which simultane-ously confers personal illumination and sustains the world. The Kabbalistic adept is not simply a devotee but a cosmic steward, the *tzaddik yesod olam*, the righteous foundation of the world (Prov. 10:25). Although *devekut* commences as a personal experience of the highest order it is equally an act of love and compassion directed towards the entire universe.

It is within the writings of Rabbis Ezra and Azriel of Gerona (fl. ca. 1220's - 1230's) that we find the first complete articulation of the vision of *devekut* as *mahashavah devekah*: a process of contemplative ascent and adhesion (if not downright union) to the Wisdom of God, in order to draw an effluence of divine energy and blessing into the visible cosmos. This understanding of *devekut* is grounded within the fundamental teachings of Kabbalistic ontology and serves as the foundation of its prophetology. In the *"Mystery of the Tree of Knowledge"*, attributed in many of our manuscript sources to R. Ezra, we find:

> You already know that a human being contains the entirety of the *Sefirot* and that his soul is bound to the Supernal Soul. It is written in the Torah: (Lev. 19:2) "You shall be holy for I am holy" and (Lev. 11:44; 20:7) "Sanctify yourselves and be holy". Therefor, the righteous person causes his pure and pristine soul to ascend to the holy, supernal soul. He unites {*mitahed*} with it and knows future events. This is the prophetic nature and way, for the evil inclination does not dominate him, to separate him from the Supernal Soul. Therefor, the prophet's soul unites with the Supernal Soul in a perfect unity and he fulfills the Torah in his intellect for they (the commandments: Scholem) are contained within it. Thus the sages said: (Kid. 82a) "The patriarchs fulfilled the Torah mentally {*besikhlam*}" and they said: (Gen. Rab. 47:8) "The patriarchs are the chariot." So their children after them, each and every person like them. Concerning this it is written: (Ex. 29:45) "I shall dwell among the children of Israel." For the Holy Spirit rests upon them and joins them. When a person walks in evil ways, which are the Satan, he cuts the soul off {*mekatzetz*} and separates it from the Supernal Soul. Concerning this it is written in the Torah: (Lev. 26:30) "My soul loathes you", (referring to) the distancing and separation of soul from Soul. This is the "cutting off" {*kitzutz*}.[31]

Prophecy is envisioned as a spiritual ascent. The prophet directs his soul (the Sefirotic image) upwards to adhere to its roots in the Supernal Soul (in this literature most often a symbol for the *Shechinah*[32]). The soul's adhesion is described as the attainment of unio: "he unites to her" (*yitahed imah*); "he unites with her in a perfect unity" (*nefesh ha-navi mityahedet im ha-neshamah ha-elyonah yihud gamur*). This unio mystica with the Supernal Soul/*Shechinah* confers both a knowledge of future events and of the contents of the Torah, which are transferred from divine to human consciousness. The revelation of the Torah and its commandments is conflated with mystical illumination, for the *mitzvot* are part and parcel of divine being and the vision of God necessarily brings with it knowledge of His ways.

In this text, we encounter a fascinating combination of the language of ascent and descent. Upon his unification with the Super-soul, the devotee is vouchsafed an efflux of prophecy from the Holy Spirit, which rests upon him. It is possible that this source is doing no more than uniting two distinct terminologies. R. Ezra uses the language of medieval Jewish Neo-Platonism to describe the soul's ascent to the Supernal Soul, which has been identified with the *Shechinah*. He then slips into the time honored Talmudic model of the descent of the Holy Spirit in order to convey his point that the experience of unification confers upon the adept intuitive knowledge of the Torah and the future. However, it is possible that he views *devekut* as a process in which the attainment of unity with God draws an illuminating and empowering influx of divine light and insight into the human soul.

This depiction of prophecy as a process of contemplative ascent and unification with God is developed further by Ezra's colleague and possible son in law, R. Azriel, in his *Commentary to the Talmudic Aggadot*. In Azriel's discussion, it is consciousness which ascends rather than soul.

> . . . the prophet would isolate himself, focus his mind and cause his thought to adhere above, and according to his prophetic adhesion {*devekut ha-nevuah*}, he would see and know what would be in the future. Prophets are distinguished in their grades according to their knowledge and adhesion {*devekut*} and they would speak the words as if they were receiving them from above, as if caught by the word {*Dibbur*}, like a fish caught on a hook.[33]

The prophet enters and in a sense experiences himself as being seized by the prophetic word.

This process of ascent and unification is possible because the human person contains the entirety of the Sefirotic realm within his being. Ezra informs us: "You already know that the human contains within it all of the *Sefirot* (*Devarim*) and that his soul is connected to the Supernal Soul." It is for this reason that the righteous individual can cause "his holy and pure soul" to ascend to God, while the sinner "cuts off and separates (his soul) from the Soul above."

In Gerona, this ontology becomes the foundation for an overarching theory of contemplation. If the human soul contains the entirety of the Sefirotic pleroma, then human consciousness must also possess its roots in the world of divine thought. If one works within a worldview predicated upon the premise that like will attract like, one must conclude that it is the nature of human thought to yearn to return to its source. Spiritual life and praxis will center around the cultivation of *mahashavah devekah*, in which mind will 'rise toward' and unite with its heavenly root, Divine Wisdom.

> A person who prays must see himself as if God were speaking with him and guiding him. He should receive his words in dread and awe, trembling and sweat and consider all the words that God teaches a person to be infinite. Thought, however, expands and ascends to the place of its origin. When it reaches there, it stops and cannot ascend higher . . . The saints of old would raise their thought to its point of origin. They would recite the commandments and the words (of prayer). Through their recitation and adhesive thought {*mahashavah devekah*} which was of the highest order, the *Sefirot* were blessed and enhanced and in

receipt (of energy) from the nullification of thought, like a man who has opened a channel of water, which spreads hither and yon. For thought that adheres is the source, the fountain and the font which has no end. Therefor, he who causes his thinking to adhere to an evil thought is punished on account of the thought, sinful thoughts being graver than the sin (*Yoma* 29a), and thoughts concerning (performance of) the commandments greater than the commandment.

Concerning this it is said: (*Cant. Rabbah* 1:10) Ben Azzai was sitting and teaching and fire was burning around him. R. Akiba came to him.

Ben Azzai said to him: "Why is this day different from any other day?"

Akiba said: "I heard that you were sitting and teaching and that fire was burning around you." I said: "You have descended to the chambers of the celestial chariot."

Ben Azzai said to him: "Words of Torah are compared to fire, as it is said: (Jer. 23:29) 'Behold — My words are like a fire declares the Lord.'"

Because he was sitting and teaching and causing his thought to adhere above, the Supernal Words were engraved in his heart. And from that emanation and adhesion of thought, the *Sefirot* are increased and augmented and from that joy revealed to him.[34]

R. Azriel has conflated three ostensibly distinct spiritual activities: prayer, study and the quest for prophetic illumination, presenting each as an example of *mahashavah devekah*. Each activity serves to bind human consciousness to its point of origin in Supernal Wisdom, thereby grounding it in its transcendental source. When words of prayer and Torah are spoken in a state of adhesive thought, in which the mind ascends to its root, the devotee attains a direct and unmediated perception of divinity. The "Supernal Words" — the *Sefirot* — are engraved in the devotee's heart and revealed to him. Although this is not directly stated, the devotee is most probably treating the words of prayer and Scripture as symbolic cyphers, representing various Sefirotic "addresses", meditated upon and entered during his contemplative ascent. The recitation of *devarim*, the human words of prayer, is thus an act of meditating upon the *Devarim*, the Supernal Words or Sefirotic pleroma, which are revealed to the Kabbalistic adept as he achieves union with Divinity and his heart (i.e. consciousness) is infused with their presence.[35]

This perception of the *Sefirot* through "the eye of the heart" is presented as constituting the soul's true source of sustenance. In *Lev. Rabbah* 20:10, the third century sage R. Yoḥanan describes the nurturance drawn by the righteous in the World to Come from their vision of the light of the *Shechinah* as "true eating", in accord with the words of Prov. 16:15: "In the light of the King's countenance is life". Concerning this midrashic statement, R. Azriel comments: "Material food, which derives from one source after another, receiving this from this and that from that, nourishes and sustains a person. How much the more so is one who adheres to and sees the Causa Causarum with the heart's eyes nourished and gladdened. This is the authentic and essential (act of) eating."[36]

The repercussions of *devekut* transcend the narrow confines of personal, mystical experience. The devotee's unification with God is fraught with cosmic significance. The transformation of the inner man sparks an equally profound awakening in the inner life of divinity. When human thought unites with its source in Divine Wisdom, that very Wisdom is blessed and enhanced (*mitbarekh ve-mitvasef*) by an efflux of creative energy from its source, Keter, designated in Azriel's terminology as both "the Naught" and the "Nullification of Thought". This effluence of emanational power (*meshekh*) then pours out of Ḥokhmah into the other *Sefirot*, as well as into the adept's "heart" and the world.

Of particular moment is the emphasis placed by Azriel on the power and cosmic import of the human contemplative act. It is not the "Nullification of Thought" which is defined as the "source, foundation and font which has no end" but rather *maḥashavah devekah*, the contemplative consciousness of the Kabbalistic adept. Through its reintegration with divine Wisdom, the human mind sparks and channels an infusion of vivifying energy into both the Sefirotic pleroma and the universe it creates. An individual's mystical experience becomes a fundamental vehicle for the maintenance of the cosmos.

This Geronan model of *devekut*, emphasizing contemplative integration with Divine Wisdom and glorifying the power of the mind, shapes the spirituality and meditative practice of a wide array of Kabbalists throughout the thirteenth century in both Catalonia and Castile. Among them are such significant figures as R. Joseph Gikatilla and R. David b. Judah the Ḥasid and even R. Moshe de Leon, although his extraordinary creativity causes him to elude easy classification.

One of its most charming and influential expressions is found in the *Iggeret ha-Kodesh*, a work dealing with the mystical dimensions of sexuality. Like several pivotal early Kabbalistic works, we know precious little about its composition. The oldest manuscripts date from the early fourteenth century. The Kabbalistic tradition of the late 1300's ascribes it to Naḥmanides, an attribution decisively refuted by Gershom Scholem. In his *Reishit ha-Kabbalah*, Scholem describes its fundamental teachings as being in consonance with those of the

Gerona circle, but internal stylistic evidence led him to tentatively attribute the work to Gikatilla.[37] All that can be stated with reasonable certainty is that the text probably dates from the late thirteenth century and that is expounds the typos of *devekut* under consideration with great eloquence and lucidity.

The penultimate chapter of this short work is an expanded and highly creative gloss on the Azriel text which we have just discussed. Building upon the Geronan description of *maḥashavah devekah* as a process which opens the fonts of blessing, our anonymous author depicts the Kabbalistic adept as an individual whose altered consciousness serves as a channel for the manifestation of divine energy into the world.

> And now I am enlightening your eyes concerning these matters, and others like them, which the Talmud presents in an unclear manner. Our sages say: (*Lev. Rab.* 16:4) "Ben Azzai was sitting and teaching and fire was burning around him". "R. Eliezer was sitting and expounding and his rays of light were like those of Moses, our rabbi." You must realize that a single intention underlies all of these matters, which I am expounding to you. Know that a fountain of water, which is drawn from a high to a low place, possesses the ability to rise to another high place, corresponding to the elevation from which it has come forth. Similarly, the masters of *Kabbalah* know that a person's thought (derives) from the place of the rational soul drawn from the upper worlds. Thought has the power to expand and rise up to its point of origin. Then it adheres to that Supernal Mystery from which it is drawn and they become one entity. When thought returns from above to below, it forms everything into the likeness of one ray {*kav*}. That supernal light is drawn forth below through the power of the thought that draws it downwards. The *Shechinah* is present below. Then the bright light is drawn out and spreads in that place where the thinker {*baal ha-maḥashavah*} resides. Thus, the sages of old caused their thoughts to adhere to the upper worlds and would draw down some of that light, and from this the *Sefirot* were augmented and blessed, according to the power of that thought.[38]

A central concern animating the *Iggeret* is the issue of human intentionality. R. Azriel argues that through *maḥashavah devekah* the font of blessing opens, seemingly automatically. In the *Iggeret*, we find an example of that spiritual state which later Hasidic teachers label *ratzo ve-shov*, that is a unification with divinity followed by an eventual return to dualized consciousness. Human consciousness possesses the ability to annihilate itself in its divine source to the point that the two become one entity. This union, however, cannot be sustained indefinitely. The reemergence of egocentric consciousness both parallels and reinvigorates the primordial and ever renewed process of divine emanation, through which the Non-dual gives rise to the differentiated Sefirotic powers and the universe. Because both distinct human consciousness and the emanational outflow reappear simultaneously, the adept can unite himself with and direct the emanative energy, drawing the Divine Presence and her vital power into the mortal realm.   Indeed, the *Shechinah*'s energy radiates into the cosmos from the focal point of the contemplative's home.   The Kabbalist has become the simultaneous locus and transmitter of celestial blessing in the world.

The Kabbalistic adept, moreover, is capable of seeking out, uniting with and channeling distinct Sefirotic forces, according to his personal will.   For example, the highest aspect of the soul, the *neshamah*, originates in divine Wisdom (Hokhmah), and enters the embryo at the moment of conception.   The quality of an individual's soul is determined by the general spiritual status of his/her parents and their particular mental state during intercourse.   If the husband is a Kabbalistic adept and has entered into a state of *mahashavah devekah*, he can draw a sanctified soul into his sperm which is then planted into his wife's womb.

> . . . when a man unites with his wife and his thought adheres to the upper worlds, that thought draws the supernal light downwards, and it rests upon that drop upon which he is contemplating and thinking . . . and that drop is connected to the radiance in the bright light.   This is the meaning of the verse: (Jer. 1:5) "Before I formed you in the womb, I knew you".   For at the time of intercourse, he was already connected to the clear light in the seminal drop of the righteous. For the thought concentrating upon it was connected to the super worlds and it draws the clear light below.   Understand this very well and from it you will comprehend a great secret concerning the nature of the God of Abraham, the God of Isaac and the God of Jacob.   This is the secret—their thought was not separated from the Supernal Light for even one hour or minute.   The Patriarchs were like those servants who are acquired by their master for eternity and therefor it says: "the God of Abraham, the God of Isaac and the God of Jacob".   The Sages said: "When they were occupied with eating, drinking, intercourse and their bodily functions, what became of their words of Torah?"   The answer is that also with regards to their bodily functions, their entire intention was for the sake of heaven and their thought did not separate from the supernal light for even one minute.   For this reason, Jacob our Father merited fathering twelve tribes, all of them perfectly righteous, without perverseness or obstinacy.   All were worthy of being in the likeness of the world order {*bedimayon seder olam*}, bearers of God's armaments, for their thought did not stray from its celestial adhesion even at the time of intercourse.[39]

Within the *Iggeret*, we witness a profound and creative expansion of the Geronan tradition out of which our author is working. *Mahashavah Devekah*, the experience of *devekut* itself, is not restricted to the holy of holies of prayer and study or mirabile dictu— contemplative sex!   Instead, *devekut* encompasses every aspect and moment of human life.   In his *Guide for the Perplexed* (III.51), Maimonides depicts

the Patriarchs as having reached such a perfect state of union with the
Active Intellect that they communed with it even when engaged in
their daily occupations. Inspired by this passage, the *Iggeret*'s author
describes the patriarchs as living a life of permanent "adhesive
thought", bound to the upper worlds through their unflagging
contemplation. Such a life will culminate in the radical transformation of its practitioners' innermost being. Not only is Jacob able to
bring twelve virtuous souls into our world who establish a holy nation.
His children embody within themselves the very structure of the
cosmos while their minds never suffer separation from their celestial
source.

This vision of a life rooted in contemplative union with God is not
relegated to the dim recesses of antiquity. In the context of interpreting Proverbs 3:6: "Know Him in all of your ways and He will
make all of your paths straight", our author spurs the Kabbalist to
strive for the attainment of *devekut temidit*, a constant mental attachment of God which will cause the divine light to adhere to his deeds.

> Thus, in his . . . parables, Solomon said: "Know Him in all your ways and He will
> make all of your paths straight." Our Sages said: "In all of your ways know
> Him—even in all of your bodily needs, great and small". (based upon *Ber.* 63a)
> As for his statement "Know Him": you already know the meaning of the term
> "knowledge", that it is the conjunction of the rational soul and its adhesion to the
> supernal light. As the union of a man and a woman is called knowledge, so too is
> the adhesion of the soul with the World of the Intellect called knowledge, as a
> person is not said to know a particular thing until the intelligizer adheres to the
> intelligible. Understand this. If so, contemplate the mystery of the statement:
> "Know Him in all your ways" and its conclusion: "He will make all of your paths
> straight". For the Supernal Light will adhere to his deeds and all of them will be
> in order {*beseder*} and established. This is their statement: (Avot 2:12) "All your
> deeds will be for the sake of Heaven."[40]

The author of the *Iggeret* has provided us with a statement of remarkable depth and radicality. His words go beyond a call to the adept to
root his consciousness in God's Wisdom so that the resultant divine
efflux might be manifest in his deeds. Our author is contending that
Solomon has called upon the Jew to attain a state of nondualized
consciousness.

This contention takes its foundation in a daringly mystical reinter-
pretation of Neo-Aristotelian epistemology. Knowledge is a process
in which mind, as pure form, extracts and takes on the form of the
object of cognition. We understand terrestrial entities because our
minds have united with and become the inner intelligible essences of
those things. Similarly, our author argues, the adept knows God
when his thought unites with its source (often referred to as the

Clear/Supernal Light), so that the two become one entity. This unified consciousness transforms both thought and deed. The adept's deeds are permeated with the presence of divine light; they are the product of an individual whose mind and hands inhabit heavenly heights. The actions of such individuals are thus said to be *beseder*, "ordered". This most likely means that they, like Jacob's sons, are *bedimayon seder olam*, "in the likeness of the world order", in consonance with the underlying spiritual harmonies and structures of the universe.

To the best of current knowledge, the *Iggeret*'s call for continuous *devekut* is extraordinarily rare this early in the history of the Kabbalistic tradition. In general, formative Kabbalistic sources present *devekut* as a religious value finding primary expression within the discipline of contemplative prayer.[41]

The Kabbalists' understanding of prayer, as theorized and practiced in Gerona and by the great late thirteenth century adept, R. Joseph Gikatilla, is permeated with the spirit of the mystical experience which we have been discussing. It is through prayer that the Kabbalistic devotee enters into the living dynamis of the Sefirotic worlds. The Kabbalist ascends in contemplation to Hokhmah and sparks the movement of a vivifying efflux of divine energy into the universe. Kabbalistic literature accordingly comes to distinguish between two stages in the life of prayer: unification and blessing. Unification is the movement upwards, in which the mind ascends to its source and draws the *Sefirot* back to Hokhmah or even Keter. Blessing is movement in the opposite direction, in which creative energy is channeled downwards into the world. Among the Catalonians, the recitation of *Keriat Shema* (Deut. 6:4) — the central affirmation of Jewish faith in the unity of God, can be used as a technique to enter into either mode of consciousness and activity. On the other hand, the *Amidah*, the eighteen benedictions recited three times daily as the heart of the liturgy, is generally viewed as a means of drawing energy down into the phenomenal universe.[42]

The Catalonians present the first step in prayer as a contemplative ascent of the Sefirotic ladder. They found a classic rabbinic basis for this contention in the statement of Rav Hisda (*Ber.* 8a): "Let a person always step forward (the width of) two portals and pray". In his *Commentary to the* Aggadot, R. Azriel quotes Rav Hisda and states enigmatically: "You already know that the two portals are a hint to what is above."[43] Such a terse statement is of little value to the uninitiated reader. Parallel sources in the Geronan tradition reveal that these two portals are Hesed and Din, the *Sefirot* of Love and Justice.[44] The ascent of prayer commences with the *Shechinah*, the immanent presence who is the entrance way to the Sefirotic pleroma. Through her, the Kabbalist ascends and enters into the gates of Love and Justice. The master of prayer must not be content to rest here but is instead obligated to continue his climb upwards, towards Ḥokhmah, Divine Wisdom. Commenting on Rav Ḥisda's statement, R. Jacob b. Sheshet, a prominent member of the Geronan circle, explains:

> We must say that through his hint, Rav Ḥisda's intention was to inform us concerning the matter of prayer and how it procedes. His statement (means): "Let a person always enter" to draw forth and emanate blessing and will into that matter which is drawn forth and emanated . . . from fountain to fountain . . . like a candle lit from a candle. So too a person should enter within these two portals (Din and Ḥesed) . . . and afterwards let him pray in thought and humility from the (letter) *yod*, which hints at the quality of humility (Ḥokhmah), as is seen from its small and bent form . . . [45]

Yet not even transcendental Wisdom, Ḥokhmah itself, serves as the ultimate telos of the Kabbalist's contemplative intention. Ḥokhmah is symbolized by the letter *yod*, the first letter of the Tetragrammaton. The *Yod*'s minute, twisted shape, surmounted by an upward reaching 'crown', reveals that Ḥokhmah too originates and derives its being from yet a higher source. This is Keter, designated by bar Sheshet as "reverence", following Ps. 111:10: "The Beginning of Wisdom is reverence for God". When adhering to Ḥokhmah, the devotee must "draw forth the power of Reverence into Wisdom" and from thence into the entire Sefirotic chain.[46]

A prooftext for this conception of prayer as a process of ascent and return, unification and blessing, is provided by Ps. 145:1: "I will extol You (*aromimkha*) my God and King/ and bless (*va-avarkha*) Your name forever and ever." The Geronan exegetes see the word *rom*—height as constituting the root of the verb *romem*—extol. *Rom* is not merely a metaphoric term for the lofty or heavenly. It serves as one of the epithets of Keter, Supernal Will, the source of divine and human thought, the font of blessing and grace. The adept must cast his mind as far as it is capable of ascending, to that lofty and ineffable point where Transcendent Wisdom emerges from *Rom*, in order to invoke an effluence of emanative energy into the Sefirotic pleroma. Azriel comments:

> This is the esoteric meaning of the verse: "I will extol You my God and King", which concludes: "And bless Your name." I will extol you in my thought, which rises with all of its power to its source at the very boundary of thought. From that source blessing {*berakhah*} flows forth, like a fountain {*bereikhah*} flowing without end.[47]

Similarly, bar Sheshet states: "When a person comes to praise the Holy One, Blessed be He, he must first cause his mind to ascend to the very end of anything which can be given dimension or measure. Afterwards, let him bless. As David said: (30:7) "I will extol You, O Lord, for You have raised me up." This point beyond dimension or measure, which is activated by the mind through its ascent to Wisdom, is defined by bar Sheshet as the *"romemut ad en sof"* — "the exaltation (extending) infinitely".[48]

The highest point reached by the mind in its contemplative ascent would then seem to be that locus wherein Divine Wisdom arises out of Will (Keter). Communion with Wisdom either sparks an efflux from Will or serves as a base from which to channel its power into the second *Sefirah*.

R. Azriel reveals no qualms or hesitation in defining this state of the conjunction of mind with Wisdom as one of unio.

> Know that every place in Scripture in which you find the term "holy" refers on an esoteric level to supernal Wisdom. This is the meaning of the verse: (Jer. 2:3) "Holy is Israel to the Lord, the first fruits of His harvest." And it says: (Ps. 134:2) "Lift up your hands to the holy place and bless the Lord." Look at this verse. How very powerful it is. How clearly it refers to the point from which blessing begins to emanate. This is the meaning of: (Eccl. 7:12) "Wisdom gives life to its possessors" and (Prov. 7:4) "Say *to* Wisdom, You are my sister (and you shall call understanding a kinswoman). The verse informs us that one should cause one's thought to adhere (*davek*) to Transcendent Wisdom, so that thought and Wisdom become one entity (*lihyot hi ve-hu davar ehad*). The "to" (in "Say *to* Wisdom") intimates all (of the *Sefirot* contained in potentia in Ḥokhmah).[49] One should draw out the effluence of Wisdom and cause this effluence, called kinswoman {*moda*} to emanate into Understanding. This is the esoteric interpretation of "You shall call {*k'ra*} understanding a kinswoman". This is to be interpreted according to the meaning of Ps. 50:1: "God, the Lord God spoke and called {*va-yiKRA*} the world from east to west."[50]

R. Azriel has produced an exegetical tour-de-force. The text is woven out of two primary verses. Ps. 134:2, "Lift your hands to the holy (place) and bless the Lord" proves that Ḥokhmah, divine wisdom, is the font of all blessing. This conclusion is based upon a set of Midrashic associations, not all of which are evinced in the passage. Jer. 2:3 describes Israel as being "holy" to God, for they are His first fruits (*reishit tevuato*). This sparks an immediate association with Prov. 8:22, which describes primordial Wisdom as the beginning of God's way (*reishit darko*). Holiness and Wisdom are consequently equated. It is thus to this holy place of Ḥokhmah that the adept must ascend if he is to draw forth energies of life and benediction. Prov. 7:4: "Say to Wisdom: "You are my sister" and call understanding a kinswoman" encapsulates this entire process of contemplative ascent and theurgic activity. The dative preposition "to" in "Say to Wisdom" esoterically reveals Hokhmah to be the fecund ground of Sefirotic being while the verb *kra* (call) is revealed by its usage in Ps. 50:1 to be a cipher for the emanational process. For God has "called"—that is emanated—the world from east to west. Through prayer, the adept is to unite with Wisdom and 'call'—draw its creative energy into Understanding, the next stage in the chain of Sefirotic manifestation. The adept thereby renews the emanational process.

This vision of prayer as the mind's ascent of the Sefirotic ladder to the realms of divine thought and volition finds significant proponents throughout the thirteenth century, both in Catalonia and Castile. One of the most eloquent of these in the late thirteenth century is Joseph Gikatilla. In his *Shaarei Orah*, an encyclopedic compendium of Sefirotic symbols, Gikatilla describes prayer as a process wherein the contemplative, in a state of profound concentration, ascends the emanational chain from the *Shechinah* to Keter, in order to draw an influx of vivifying energy back into the universe. This proves to be the esoteric meaning of Ps. 130:1: "From out of the depths I have called You, O Lord". From out of the depths of the divine Will, the "mystery of the crownlet of the *Yod* of the Tetragrammaton", the contemplative calls forth energies of blessing and life.

> Since a person must concentrate in his prayer and ascend from *Sefirah* to *Sefirah* and Desire to Desire, until he arrives in his consciousness (*libo*—lit. heart) to the source of that Supernal Desire called infinity,[51] David said: (Ps. 130:1) "A Song of Ascents: From out of the depths have I called You." The meaning of "From out of the depths have I called You, O Lord" refers to the Supernal Source called Infinity, which is *Deep*—the mystery of the crownlet of the *yod* of the Tetragrammaton . . . (it refers to the manner) in which he directs his intentionality on the path of (the) rungs from below to above, entering into the final *heh* of the Name (the *Shechinah*) and ascending from attribute to attribute and from *Sefirah* to *Sefirah*, until his thought ascends to the crownlet of the *yod*, to Keter called Infinity. This is the esoteric dimension of "from out of the depths". Therefor, he said: "A Song of Ascents: From out of the depths have I called You O Lord". Think not that the term "Depth" refers to everything lowly and (descending) deep below, containing no other thing. Rather, everything mysterious and hidden and difficult to comprehend is called Deep, as it says: (Eccl. 7:24) "That which was is far and deep, deep—who can find it?" The great mystery containing everything (Ps. 92:7) "How deep are Your thoughts."[52]

The contemplative must consequently center himself and inwardly focus this thought "until he arrives with perfect intention at the Source of Desire . . . which is the Depth of Thought."

> By means of this prayer, properly performed, all the *Sefirot* are united and an overflow (*shefa*) drawn forth from above to below. The worlds above and below

are blessed on account of this praying individual. His prayer is accepted and he is beloved above and pleasant below . . . concerning him it is said: (Ps. 145:18) "God is near to all who call upon Him, to all who call upon Him in truth".[53]

Such a master of prayer was Moses, who during Israel's moment of most dire need, "raised his thought to the place of the decree's nullification" and banked the flames of God's Justice with the higher and ontologically prior forces of heavenly forgiveness, rooted in the *Sefirah* of Binah, divine Understanding.

Prayer, then, is the highest and most complete expression of *devekut* available to the Kabbalist. Through it, he attains union with Divine Wisdom and manifests its life giving force in the cosmos. The Geronan sources discuss this process in surprisingly warm and even familiar terms. The adept has achieved true intimacy with God. By unifying the *Sefirot*, he has entered God's house and become a member of the celestial household. More importantly, God comes to dwell with him below. Through this bestowal of blessing in the world, a deep seated desire of God is fulfilled and in a profound sense, grace has been bestowed upon Divinity as well.

R. Ezra speaks quite touchingly about the high level of intimacy existing between God and the adept in his *Commentary on Canticles*.

> You must know the mystery of the blessings and their necessity. Blessing is an emanation of superabundant effluence from the Negation of Thought (Keter), which is the source of life. As it says: (Ps. 68:27) "Praise God, the Lord, from the Source of Israel." Therefor David ordained one hundred blessings, corresponding to the ten *Sefirot*, in each one of whom are (all) ten. The wise are zealous and careful to (daily) complete their number. For God desires blessing and according to the spiritual state and perfection of the one blessing, He draws near and comes to his home . . . Thus God says: "If you come to My house, I will go to your house". As it says: (Ex. 20:24) "In every place I will cause My name to be mentioned, I will come to you and bless you." The verse begins: "You shall make an earthen altar and sacrifice upon it". "If you come to My house"—that is, if you know how to unify the Tetragrammaton and cause blessing to emanate upon it. For we have found that God's name is called a house, as it says: (Prov. 24:3) "God, in Wisdom, will build a house" and (Ps. 93:5) "Holiness befits Your house". "Then I will come to your house, to fulfill the needs of your body". By means of the benediction emanated into the Name of the Holy One, Blessed be He, blessing benefits the world. This is "Every place I cause My Name to be mentioned, I will come to you to bless you."

We find that the Holy One is very much desirous of this blessing. The Sages say in the tractate *Shabbat* (89a): "When Moses ascended on high, he found the Holy One, Blessed be He, attaching crowns to the letters. He asked Moses: "Is there no greeting (Lit. peace) in your city?"

Moses answered: "Master of the Universe, does a servant greet his Master?"

God replied: "You should have aided Me".

Immediately Moses said: (Num. 14:17) "May the power of God now be magnified".

Concerning this the Sages said in the tractate *Berakhot* (32a): "(Num. 14:21) "Behold as I live and as the glory of God fills the world". Rabba said: "You have given Me life through your words."[54]

Through prayer and the recitation of blessing formulae, the Kabbalistic adept lives a life of intimate contact with God. He ascends into the Sefirotic Temple, the House of the Divine Name, built by Wisdom, and blesses God. As a result of his *devekut,* God in turn dwells with him and grants him blessing.

R. Ezra tells us that God is deeply desirous that humanity bless Him. As proof, he quotes an *aggadah* from *Shabbat* 89a, describing Moses' ascent on high, where the prophet confers benediction upon God. In so doing, Moses reveals himself to be the archetypal Kabbalist. He has ascended the heavenly worlds, entered the presence of his Creator and aided Him in His creative enterprise through engagement in an act of blessing, which magnifies the power of God in the world. During his illumination experience, God teaches the prophet that the goal of his *devekut* is not merely unitive absorption in Divine Being. This is but one pole in the mystic's career. Rather, the adept bears on his shoulder a heavy burden of responsibility for both God and cosmos. Through his *devekut,* he is to bless, that is to draw "an emanation of superabundent effluence from the Negation of Thought", into the Divine Name and world. He is a cosmic citizen and steward, a priest serving in the Sefirotic sanctuary on high, who enables the Divine Presence to become fully manifest below.

The Kabbalistic vision of mystical experience as a process of *mahashavah devekah* attains some of its most lucid formulations in Kabbalistic analyses of the Temple priesthood and cult. If the Kabbalist has become a priest, bestowing blessing upon the world, the priest in turn has become a Kabbalist. In his short treatise, "The Mystery of the Sacrifice", Rabbi Azriel writes:

When the priest offers the sacrifice, he binds his soul to the altar. His soul ascends ever upwards in an upward movement. And he is called an angel, as it says: (Mal. 2:7) "The lips of priests shall preserve knowledge, they will seek instruction from his mouth, for he is an angel of the Lord of Hosts."[55]

The altar to which the priest binds his intentionality is not merely the physical altar in the Temple, but the *Shechinah,* the portal and place of offering in the Sefirotic sanctuary. Binding his soul to the *Shechinah*, he begins his contemplative ascent.

During this mental ascent, it is not simply the consciousness of the priest that is restored to its primordial source. Rather, every aspect of the phenomenal world and the *Sefirot* themselves are restored to their primordial unity.

> . . . although (each) sacrifice is distinct and different and its limbs and innermost parts are different from each other, yet it has one function—to revitalize and strengthen the individual who consumes it. Thus, when he draws near to it and adheres to it, it is as if they were one entity . . . and his prayer is accepted . . . For he has united the offerer and the offering into one intention, to return that which is separated at its source and the branch to the root, to acknowledge that the owner and the owned possess one root and that they return to Him in the end. If they are distinct in appearance and different, they come from and return to one principle. Thus, the priest must know the contemplative intention needed to draw each kind of limb, fat and blood to its essential origin.[56]

In an act of contemplative intention, the priest identifies himself with his offering and restores both it and himself to their respective Sefirotic sources. In so doing, he comes to realize that all things "come from and return to one principle." Sacrifice provides both a means to recreate and directly experience the world's primordial unity in God.

This contemplative ascent bears with it a reciprocal ability to channel divine energy back into the world. Through a merger of his individual will with God's, the priest unites the sacrifices/cosmos with their Sefirotic ground and restores the divine Powers in turn to their primordial font in Keter, divine Volition. Through his personal mystical ascent, intentionality and action, the entire universe achieves a reditus to its Source. This accomplished, he is himself charged with the vivifying forces of creative blessing which his activity invokes. "And he is called an angel, as it says: (Mal. 2:7) "The lips of priests shall preserve knowledge . . . for he is an angel of the Lord of Hosts." Dubbed by Azriel a *malakh be-taḥtonim*, "an angel in the lower worlds", he is transformed into a source of energy, blessing and atonement for his flock.

The power which he absorbs as the product of his contemplative ascent finds its manifestation in three-fold Aaronide benediction (Num. 6:22-27), pronounced daily after the Continual (*tamid*) Offering by those "who cause their souls to adhere above and bless the people (*ha-madbikim nafsham le-maalah u-mevarkhim et ha-am*)". While bestowing this benediction, the priest again ascends the Sefirotic ladder, whose energies radiate through his person and words. The ascent commences with the *Shechinah* and culminates with Binah. The first verse of the blessing: "The Lord bless you and keep you (*yishmerekha*)" refers to the *Shechinah*—who is the *Shomer Yisrael*, the Guardian of Israel. The second verse: "The Lord shine his Countenance (*Panav*) upon you" refers to Tiferet, the Shining Countenance (*Panim Meirot*). The final verse, the request for peace, manifests the power of Binah, the supernal mother. This blessing is pronounced with arms extended and fingers outstretched, for the soul is absorbed into the upper worlds and the body transformed into a vehicle for the revelation of God's life-giving power[57]. Thus in the *Zohar*, the youngster informs Rabbis Isaac and Judah: "All of the priest's blessings depend upon the fingers" (III 186b).

It is this image of the priest with outstretched arms and fingers pronouncing blessing in a state of contemplative absorption that creates the exquisite image of human hands dwelling in heavenly heights and spurs the *Zohar*'s statements concerning the theurgic power of human hands. Commenting on Lev. 9:22: "And Aaron raised his hands over the people and blessed them", the *Zohar* speaks of ten angelic powers who are awakened by the outstretched arms of the individual at prayer, which raise his words and requests to the upper worlds and channel their energy back into the world.

> Wondrous mysteries reside in this stretching out of the hands. When a person raises them and lifts them above . . . he is found worthy of unifying the Mystery of the Ten Words,[58] so as to unify all and bless the Holy Name as is fitting . . . (and) to unify the Inner Chariots (the *Sefirot*) and the Chariots Without (the extra-Sefirotic heavenly worlds) so that the Divine Name might be blessed from every side and everything, above and below, might be unified. (III. 67a)

Parallel discussions of Lev. 9:22 reveal that this process of unification is rooted in the priest's contemplative intention. When raising his hands, the priest must intend to confer blessing above (II. 57a). And when speaking of such theurgically charged actions as the uplifting of hands in prayer, de Leon concludes: "Worthy is Israel in this world and in the world that is coming, for they know how to adhere to the Holy King, to arouse the heavenly host and to draw the holiness of their Lord upon them, as it is written: . . . . (Deut. 4:4) "All of you, who adhere to the Lord your God, are alive this day". (III. 92b)

This sense of thought and body caught up and transformed by contemplative absorption in Divinity is lucidly expressed by the *Zohar*'s discussion of the Priestly Benediction. In this act, the contemplative intentionality of the priest soars to the realm of Keter Elyon, Divine Volition, which Castilian Kabbalists define as the realm of *Raḥamim Gemurim*, Absolute Compassion free of all admixture of judgement. It is the energies of Absolute Compassion and their lower manifestations in Tiferet that the priest invokes and draws forth in the act of blessing. Concentrating his attention upon them, he enables all of the worlds to be infused with blessing "from the side of compassion that is drawn forth from the most Ancient, Hidden and Concealed of all" (III. 147a). As a result, the *Shechinah* herself rests upon the priests' hands, although, as a spiritual entity, she remains invisible. Consequently, R. Yosi states: "When the priest extends his hands, it is forbidden for the people to gaze upon him for upon his hands the *Shechinah* rests." R. Isaac retorts that such a practice would seem unnecessary, given that the *Shechinah*'s spiritual nature causes her to elude mortal sight. R. Yosi responds that "the Holy Name finds intimation in the fingers of the hand and a person must be in awe." (III. 147a)

Because human hands, fueled by the power of contemplative intentionality, inhabit heavenly heights, the Divine Presence can radiate its beneficent presence from mortal finger tips. The Kabbalist's goal is to become a living bridge, uniting heaven and earth, so that God may become equally manifest above and below, for the healing and redemption of all. That, to the Kabbalist, is the essence of the mystical quest.

Notes

1 The translation of this *Zohar* passage is that of Daniel Matt. v. Daniel Matt, *Zohar: The Book of Enlightenment* (New York: Paulist Press, 1983), 170-1. Unless otherwise noted, all further translations from primary sources are my own.

2 A lucid discussion of Pharisaic "table fellowship" in comparison to the practices of the Qumran community and the nascent Christian movement is provided by Jacob Neusner, *From Politics to Piety: The Emergence of Pharisaic Judaism* (New York: *KTAV* Publishing House, 1979), 82-90.

3 *Maarekhet Elohut* (editio Mantua, 1558), 82b.

4 This discussion of the chain of emanation is based upon the presentation of the *Maarekhet Elohut*, 90b-94b. For a fuller discussion of the fundamentals of Sefirotology, see Gershom Scholem, *Major Trends in Jewish Mysticism* (New York: Schocken Books, 1961), 205-243 and Isaiah Tishby, *Mishnat ha-Zohar* (Jerusalem: *Mosad Bialik*, 1971), 131-161.

5 Nahmanides' wedding sermon is published with extensive notes by Haim Chavel in *Kitvei ha-Ramban* (Jerusalem: *Mosad ha-Rav Kook*, 1978), Vol. 2, 133-8.

6 This text, taken from R. Ezra's "Mystery of the Tree of Knowledge" is published by Scholem in his essay "*Sitra Ahra: Ha-Tov veha-Ra be-Kabbalah*," chap. in *Pirkei Yesod be-Havanat ha-Kabbalah ve-Simleha*, ed Y. ben Shlomo (Jerusalem: *Mosad Bialik*, 1976), 195. Two extensive biographico-bibliographical essays on Ezra and Azriel have been written by Isaiah Tishby. "*Ha-Mekubbalim R. Ezra ve-R. Azriel u-Mekomam be-Hug Gerona*" and "*Kitvei ha-Mekubbalim R. Ezra ve-R. Azriel*," chaps. in *Hikrei ha-Kabbalah u-Sheluhoteha* (Jerusalem: Magnes Press, 1982), 3-30.

7 *Perush ha-Aggadot le-R. Azriel*, ed. Isaiah Tishby (Jerusalem: Magnes Press, 1982), 89.

8 The Maimonidean vision of the philosopher—illuminate, directing human affairs in the light of a heavenly paradigm, is insightfully discussed by David Hartman, *Maimonides: Torah and the Philosophical Quest* (Philadelphia: Jewish Publication Society, 1986), 187-214.

9 v. Joseph Gikatilla, *Shaarei Orah*, ed. Y. ben Shlomo (Jerusalem: *Mosad Bialik - Sifriyat Dorot*, 1970), Vol. 1, 65-66. For an introduction to Gikatilla's Kabblistic thinking, see Ephraim Gottleib, *Ha-Kabbalah be-Sof ha-Meah ha-Shelosh Esrei*, ed. Y. Leibes (Jerusalem: *Akademon* Press, 1969).

10 *Shaarei Orah*, 65.

11 Nahmanides' discussion of Gen. 3:15 appears as part of his analysis of Gen. 3:8 "The Lord God planted a garden in Eden in the East". v. *Perush ha-Ramban la-Torah*, ed. Haim Chavel (Jerusalem: *Mosad ha-Rav Kook*, 1959), Vol. 1, 31. For R. Azriel's discussion of Adam's priestly role in the Garden of Eden, see R. Isaac of Acre, *Sefer Meirat Einaim*, ed. Amos Goldreich (Jerusalem: Publications for the Institute of Advanced Studies, 1984), 141.

12 A detailed analysis of the views of Nahmanides and R. Azriel on Adam's sin is provided by Bezalel Safran, "R. Azriel and Nahmanides: Two Views on the Fall of Man" in *Rabbi Moses Nahmanides (Ramban): Explorations in His Religious Creativity*, ed. Isadore Twersky (Cambridge: Harvard University Press, 1983), 75-106. R. Ezra's views are set forth in his "Mystery of the Tree of Knowledge", published in Scholem, *Pirkei Yesod*, 194-6.

13 *Rabbeinu Bahya: Beur al ha-Torah*, ed. Haim Chavel (Jerusalem: *Mosad ha-Rav Kook*, 1974), Vol. 2, 519.

14 *Shaarei Orah*, Vol. 1, 66. For the *Zohar's* presentation of Adam's sin, v. *Mishnat ha-Zohar*, Vol. 1, 221-3.

15 *Shaarei Orah*, Vol. 1, 66-67.

16 *ibid.*, Vol. 2, 54.

17 The most detailed and lucid discussion of Provencal and Catalonian Kabbalah is found in Gersham Scholem, *Origins of the Kabbalah*, trans. A. Arkush (Philadelphia: Jewish Publication Society/Princeton University Press, 1987), 199-308, 365-460. A comparable study of the Castilian school remains a major desideratum. Scholem published most of the significant writings of its "founding fathers", the brothers Rabbis Isaac and Jacob ha-Cohen in *Madaei ha-Yahadut* 2 (1927), 165-293. A sampling of this material is available in English translation in Joseph Dan and Ronald Keiner, *The Early Kabbalah* (New York: Paulist Press, 1986), 151-182. The finest study of the *Zohar* remains Isaiah Tishby's magisterial two volume *Mishnat ha-Zohar* (Jerusalem: *Mosad Bialik*, 1971), now available in the English translation of David Goldstein, *The Wisdom of the Zohar* (Oxford: Littman Library/Oxford University Press, 1989). The English speaking reader should also consult Scholem, *Major Trends*, 156-243.

18 Abraham Joshua Heschel, *Torah min ha-Shamayim be-Ispaklaryah ha-Dorot* (London: Soncino Press, 1962), Vol. 1, 153-5.

19 For discussions of visionary experience in the *Zohar*, see Elliot Wolfson, "Circumcision, Vision of God and Textual Interpretation: From Midrashic Trope to Mystical Symbol," *History of Religions* 27 no. 2 (Nov. 1987): 187-215 and "The Hermeneutics of Visionary Experience: Revelation and Interpretation in the *Zohar*" in *Religion* 18 (1988): 311-345. For Tishby's discussion of love and *devekut* in the *Zohar*, see *Mishnat ha-Zohar*, Vol. 2, 280-306.

20 Gershom Scholem, "*Devekut* or Communion with God" in *The Messianic Idea in Judaism* (New York: Schocken Books, 1971), 203-227. The analysis on pages 203-8 is of particular relevance to our discussion.

21   Scholem, *Messianic Idea*, 204. The translation of the passage from Naḥmanides is Scholem's.

22   *ibid.*, 206-7.

23   R. Isaac of Acre studied with Naḥmanides, who spent his final years in the Land of Israel. In the early fourteenth century, Isaac traveled extensively in Spain, where he met such significant Kabbalists as Moshe de Leon, who offered to show him the "original" manuscript of the *Zohar* but died before doing so. In Spain, Isaac amassed a wide array of mystical teachings which he transcribed in his *Sefer Meirat Einaim*, an encyclopedic supercommentary on the Kabbalistic comments included by Naḥmanides in his Torah commentary, and in his spiritual diary *Otzar ha-Haim*, thereby preserving a wealth of earlier sources. For Isaac's meeting with R. Moshe de Leon, v. *Mishnat ha-Zohar*, Vol. 1, 28-32. His contemplative techniques and experiences are discussed by Gottleib in his study "*Hearot, Devekut ve-Nevuah be-Sefer Otzar ha-Ḥaim le-Rabbi Yitzhak de-Min Akko*", published in his *Mehkarim be-Sifrut ha-Kabbalah* (Tel Aviv: Tel Aviv University, 1976), 231-47.

24   *Meḥkarim*, 235.

25   *ibid.*, 236.

26   *Otzar ha-Ḥaim*, 111a, quotes in *ibid.*, 237.

27   Moshe Idel, *Kabbalah: New Perspectives* (New Haven: Yale University Press, 1988), 39-42.

28   *ibid.*, 42-5.

29   *ibid.*, 46-7.

30   For *devekut* as a means of mediation, see Idel, 53 and as a means of unifying the *Sefirot*, 53-5.

31   The Hebrew original of this text has been edited and published by Scholem, v. *Pirkei Yesod*, 195. Words in parentheses were added to the original by Scholem for the sake of clarity. It is important to note that *Kiddushin* 82a reads simply "Abraham our Father observed the entire Torah before it was given." The claim that the patriarchs observed the commandments "mentally" is R. Ezra's contribution. For a thorough analysis of thirteenth century Kabbalistic readings of Kiddushin 82a, see Arthur Green, *Devotion and Commandment: The Faith of Abraham in the Hasidic Imagination* (Cincinnati: Hebrew Union College Press, 1989), 39-42; 85, n. 84.

32   For the *Shechinah* as Supernal Soul (*ha-Nefesh ha-Elyonah*) and the source of the Holy Spirit, see *Perush ha-Aggadot le-Rabbi Azriel*, ed. Isaiah Tishby, 22a, 111.

33   *Perush ha-Aggadot*, 17a-b, 102-3.

34   *ibid.*, 16b-17b, 101-3. The text concludes with the discussion of prophecy quoted immediately above.

35   Scholem, *Origins*, 242-6.

36   *Perush ha-Aggadot*, 6a, 77.

37   See Scholem's early work, *Reishit ha-Kabbalah* (Jerusalem: Schocken Press, 1948), 148 and Origins, 388 n. 58. Full arguments are presented in "*Ha-Im Hibber ha-Ramban et Iggeret ha-Kodesh?*" in *Kiryat Sefer* 21 no. 3 (Oct. 1944): 179-186. Scholem notes there that the *Iggeret's* first manuscript appearance is in a compilation produced in Laredo in 1328 (Ms. Florence, Plut. II, Cod. 41). There is no attribution to Nahmanides in the text. The *Iggeret* is distinguished from authentic Nahmanidean works in terms of both content and style. Containing no uniquely Nahmanidean teachings, it is instead based upon the vision of *mahashavah devekah* taught by Rabbis Ezra and Azriel. Terminology and stylistic techniques such as the constant use of the term "*sod*" (Mystery) and stock phrases such as "gates of light" and "a great key" for the understanding/interpretation of assorted Kabbalistic mysteries are highly reminiscent of the style of Joseph Gikatilla. Scholem consequently dates the text to the period of 1290-1310 and suggests Gikatilla or an imitator as its author. There are two editions of the Hebrew text: 1) Haim Chavel, *Kitvei ha-Ramban*, vol. 2, 321-337 and 2) Seymour Cohen, *The Holy Letter* (New York: *Ktav*, 1976) with accompanying translation. Both Chavel and Cohen use JTS mss. 839 (Halberstam 444) as their master text, to which Cohen has annotated variant readings in his critical apparatus from British Mus. Add. 17,807 and Paris 769. I have consulted both editions when preparing my translations. Cohen's translation is unfortunately unreliable.

38   Chavel, *Kitvei ha-Ramban*, vol. 2, 333; Cohen, *The Holy Letter*, 121-5.

39   Chavel, 333-4; Cohen, 125-7.

40   Chavel, *ibid.*; Cohen, 129-131.

41   In the *Zohar*, de Leon does raise the possibility of a more or less constant adhesion to Divinity through the performance of the Commandments. See Tishby, *Mishnat ha-Zohar*, vol. 2, 303-04.

42   For a reading of *Keriat Shema* as outlining both a contemplative ascent of the *Sefirot* from the *Shechinah* to the *Ein Sof* and the corresponding emanation of the divine pleroma from the depths of the *Ein Sof*, v. R. Jacob bar Sheshet, *Sefer ha-Emunah ve-Bitahon*, in *Kitvei ha-Ramban*, ed. Haim Chavel, Vol. 2, 360. bar Sheshet interprets Ps. 51:17: "Lord, open my lips (*safatai*) and let my mouth speak Your praise", whispered at the beginning of the recitation of the *Amidah*, as outlining a process of Sefirotic ascent and reconstitution in *Ein Sof* which sparks a consequent efflux of creative energy into the universe. This is channeled into the world by the Kabbalistic adept during the recitation of this prayer. bar Sheshet's reading is founded upon a twofold Midrashic pun. The term *safah* (lip) also denotes anything possessing border or boundary. The "lips" opened at the beginning of the recitation of the *Amidah* thus symbolize the primordial Sefirotic powers which ascend to their point of origin in Divinity. The verb *yagid* (to speak) is interpreted as sharing the same root as the Aramaic *ngd* –"to flow forth". The praise spoken by the adept's mouth is the renewed emanation of the Sefirotic realm. v. *Sefer ha-Emunah ve-ha-Bitahon*, 368. bar Sheshet's analyses of these two

liturgical texts are available in English translation in Dan and Keiner, *Early Kabbalah*, 117-122; 124-132.

43 *Perush ha-Aggadot*, 4b, 73.

44 *ibid.*, n. 9.

45 Jacob bar Sheshet, *Sefer Meshiv Devarim Nekhohim*, ed. George Vajda (Jerusalem: Israeli Academy of the Arts and Sciences, 1968), 366.

46 *ibid.*

47 *Perush ha-Aggadot*, 24b, 54.

48 *Sefer ha-Emunah ve-ha-Bitahon* in *Kitvei ha-Ramban*, vol. 2, 160.

49 I am here following Tishby's suggested reading of this difficult passage. v. *Perush ha-Aggadot*, 82, n. 12.

50 *ibid.*, 7b-8a, 82.

51 The Supernal Desire named infinity (Ein Sof) to which the devotee ascends is Keter. v. *Shaarei Orah*, 165, n. 37.

52 *ibid.*, 165-6.

53 *ibid.*, 168.

54 R. Ezra, *Commentary to the Song of Songs* in *Kitvei ha-Ramban*, ed. H. Chavel, Vol. 2, 526-7. R. Ezra's *Commentary to Canticles* has been translated into French with extensive analysis by George Vajda. *Le Commentaire D'Ezra De Gerone Sur Le Cantique des Cantiques*, trans. Georges Vajda (Aubier: Montaigne, 1969).

55 R. Azriel's "*Sod ha-Korbanot*" ("The Mystery of Sacrifice") is preserved in two recensions in over half a dozen manuscripts: including Moscow Ginzberg 131/3; Parma 1420/19; Vat. 211/5; JTS Halberstam 444; Ox. Bod. 2456.1. A complete and reliable text is also transmitted in R. Isaac of Acre's *Sefer Meirat Einaim—Parashat Vayikra*, providing an early and significant witness. References are to Amos Goldreich's critical edition of this work. v. *Sefer Meirat Einaim*, ed. Amos Goldreich (Jerusalem, 1984), 53b, 140.

56 *ibid.*, 56b, 144.

57 *ibid.*, 53b, 140.

58 R. Abraham Galante, a student of the great sixteenth century Kabbalist R. Moshe Cordovero of Safed, defines these ten transcendent Words as constituting the roots of the ten *Sefirot* hidden in the depths of divine Wisdom. Through his contemplative activity and outstretched hands, the priest unites the *Sefirot* in their transcendent mode of existence. In so doing, he unites their manifest mode in the World of Emanation as well and brings blessing to all worlds. v. *Or ha-Hamah* (Przemysl, 1896-8), Vol. 2, 79b.

Abraham Ibn Ezra's Mathematical Speculations on the Divine Name

Carlos del Valle

The technique of *gematria*[1] is an exegetical tool often used by Kabbalists to decipher Scripture, a tool employed in Israel from ancient times. Basically it consists in reducing the letters of each word to its numerical value, then interpreting it by means of a different word of the same value.[2] Maimonides refers to an interpretation by gematria of Gn 42:4 which he received "from his father, who received it from his father, and so on successively until the beginning of the exile from Jerusalem"—which is to say, from the foundation of the first Jewish settlement in Spain. According to this interpretation, the word *rĕdû* [*rdw*—"*descend*"] of Gn 42:4 has a numerical value of 210, signifying the 210 years of Israel's residence in Egypt.[3] This interpretation by gematria is already found in one of the most ancient exegetical midrashim, the *Genesis Rabbah*,[4] in the mouth of R. Abba ben Kahana, an Amora of the third generation (fourth century).[5]

Numbers have an important role in Jewish mysticism, probably on the basis of influences emanating from Pythagorian doctrines. This trend is operative in *gematria* and reaches its highest development in the Kabbalah, though here it is closely related to the notion of the special sanctity and creative significance of the sacred Hebrew letters. Eleazar ben Yehuda of Worms (early thirteenth century) provided the impetus for a new development. With the aid of *gematria* he discovered new combinations of letters gifted with special powers. The *Sepher ha-hokmah* [on *gematria*] is attributed to another Ashkenazi kabbalist, Yehuda ha-Hasid (cir. 1150-1217). Abraham Abulafia (1240-cir. 1291) made extensive use of *gematria*, and one of his disciples, Yosef ben Abraham Chiquitilla (1248-cir. 1325), wrote a work dedicated to a detailed explanation of *gematria, notarikon,* and *temurah.* As a general rule all the great kabbalists utilized *gematria*.[6]

Abraham Ibn Ezra, in the two introductions to his commentary on the Pentateuch (in its two redactions, long and short),[7] includes an excursus on the different exegetical methods used throughout history, giving special emphasis to the method he prefers. Five methods are given: (1) the purely allegorical method ascribed to the Christians; (2) that of the Karaites who reject tradition as an exegetical method;

(3) that of the great Jewish scholars of Islamic lands who introduce into exegesis many alien elements taken from the sciences; (4) that of the Jewish sages who dwell in Christian lands and comment on Scripture—at times literally, at times in a midrashic or allegorical sense; (5) the method of *pēsat*; literal interpretation based on grammatical knowledge of the language.[8]

It is the fifth method, that of *pēsăt*, that Ibn Ezra attempts to introduce in his commentaries, as follows: "Fifth way: I shall place the basis of explanation in duly clarifying all of Scripture, its grammar, its literal sense . . . . In each section I shall first explain each complex word grammatically."[9] It is clear that in this type of method, one based on grammar, *gematria* as such has no place. In fact, Ibn Ezra's commentary on Gn 14:14 formally rejects the exegesis by gematria which had been employed by other commentators. For example, Rashi (1040-1105) interpreted the 318 servants to mean Eliezer, since the numerical value of "Eliezer" is 318.[10] Ibn Ezra rejects this interpretation on the grounds that Scripture "does not speak with gematria." "The calculation of the letters for Eliezer," he says, "is midrashic. Scripture does not speak with gematria because in this way whoever so wished could interpret a name correctly or incorrectly."[11]

This statement of principle by Ibn Ezra gives us a point of departure for the interpretation of his mathematical speculations regarding the divine Name. What is at issue is not a logical usage of the techniques of *gematria* to deduce new doctrines or to make surprising identifications. The object proposed by the sage of Tudela in these speculations is simply to describe the unfathomable mysteries which surround the divine Name.

The Divine Names

Abraham Ibn Ezra, taking advantage of his expertise in mathematics,[12] speculated about the mathematical mysteries of the divine Name. Three principal works harbor these speculations: the *Sepher ha-Šem* ("Book of the Name"),[13] the commentary on the Pentateuch (especially to Ex 3:15),[14] in both the long and short redactions; and the *Yēsod Mora'* ("The Foundation of Awe").[15] In addition to these three works there is also a small treatise, an explanation of the mathematical speculations on the divine Name, found in a commentary on Ex 33:21 which the manuscripts ascribe to Ibn Ezra. This is what is known as the *Midraš ha-Šem* ("Commentary on the Name"),[16] or the *Ma'ămar Šem ha-'esem* ("Treatise on the Proper Name"),[17] or the *Sod ha-Šem ha-mikbad* ("Mystery of the Glorious Name").[18] Although this small work was the object of later elaborations,[19] it is possible that its nucleus came from the hand of Ibn Ezra himself.[20]

According to Ibn Ezra, there are three proper names (*Šem-ha-'esem*) of God: Yah, Ehyeh, and YHWH. "The prophets", he declares, "established the name of the two letters [Yah], that of the four letters [YHWH], and the name Ehyeh [as] the proper names of the Most High. . . . The remainder of the divine names found in the Bible are adjectives [*šemot ha-to'ar*]".[21] In the commentary on Ex 3:15 he expressly states, "These three names are proper names."[22]

Ibn Ezra attributes the same derivation to the three proper divine names: Yah, Ehyeh, and YHWH.[23] Obviously he is thinking of the root *hayah* ("to be," "to exist") as the ultimate root from which the three names are derived. It is precisely this derivation which explains some of the anomalous forms which he detects in YHWH and Yah. As he observes, *ehyeh* is a common form in Hebrew (the first person singular of the future tense: "I shall be," or "I am"). So that this common form will not be confused with the divine Name, the *yod* is transformed into a *waw*; the Tetragrammaton is no longer pronounced *yihyeh* ("he will be"), but *yhwh*. As a clarifying, illustrative example Ibn Ezra mentions the name of Eve (*hawwah* — "the living"). According to him, this should be *hayyah* but is transformed into *hawwah* so that it cannot be confused with *hayyah* ("beast," "animal").[24]

The name Yah should be the abbreviation of the apocopated form of the future tense, *yĕhî* ("he shall be"). But this is complicated by two factors: the introduction of a patah under the *yod* (*yĕhî* > *yahî*) because of the guttural, and the dropping of the final *yod* (*yahî* > *yah*) "because of another mystery by reason of number."[25]

In Ibn Ezra's interpretation, Ehyeh ("I am") signifies or expresses the Being of necessary existence: "All substances and accidents require one which provides them with consistency, which, as such, would be eternal and changeless. He is true Being. Apart from Him, every other being is what it is through His causality. Because of this it is written: *ehyeh ăšer ehyeh* ('I am He who is' — Ex 3:14). Why does He call Himself by this name? Because the present is not eternal, without external change."[27]

Whereas Yah and Ehyeh are pronounced just as they are written, the Tetragrammaton is written but not pronounced.[28] Ibn Ezra provides a singular explanation of this Jewish custom. According to him, "the name of the two letters [Yah] was received by those venerable beings who do not possess bodies (the angels), as was the name which begins with *aleph* [Ehyeh]. Because of this any man can pronounce it in any place such as it is written."[29] In contrast, the name of YHWH possesses a unique sanctity and excellence. It is for this reason that the Hebrews refuse to mention it directly. "Because of its dignity and high grandeur," states Ibn Ezra, "they did not wish to mention [the sacrosanct Name] in an impure place and were constrained to name Him with the word Adon (Lord), in the plural (Adonay), after the manner of Elohim."[30] Nevertheless, Moses, when he communicated the name of God of Israel to Pharoah, used the Tetragrammaton such as it is written, without using any substitute, "because he was holy."[31] In another passage of the *Sepher ha-Šem*, Ibn Ezra indicates that to pronounce the sacrosanct Name such as it is written was also the custom of ancient Israel: "Perhaps they began to use a substitute [instead of pronouncing the sacrosanct Name] because they were in an impure land."[32]

As to the correct pronunciation of the Tetragrammaton, Ibn Ezra is certain that anyone who knows grammar knows what it is.[33] Be that as it may, even apart from the question of correct pronunciation the Tetragrammaton admits of different readings as the vowel combination changes. In the *Sepher ha-Šem* Ibn Ezra declares that "if we were to place a mobile *šěwâ* below the first letter, its readings would surpass two hundred."[34] In his short commentary on Exodus he asserts that the different readings reach a total of 320.[35]

YHWH, the proper name of God, was revealed to some patriarchs and other just men prior to the time of Moses.[36] Abraham and Jacob knew it; Job did not.[37] It was Moses, however, who made the divine Name known in its completeness.[38] It is surprising that Ibn Ezra affirms that the patriarchs knew the name YHWH as a proper name but not as an adjective.[39] This when in various places he states that the Tetragrammaton, apart from being a proper name, is on some occasions an adjective.[40] According to him, it is an adjective whenever it is used as a genitive in the construct state.[41] This occurs, for example, in the expressions YHWH Elohim ("YHWH of the gods" [Gn 2:4]) and YHWH *sěba'ot* ("YHWH of the armies" [Is 1:9]), which are similar in construction to the expression Elohe ha-Elohim ("God of the gods" [Dt 10:17]).

Ibn Ezra attempts to reach a metaphysical justification for the use of YHWH as an adjective. God is the absolute Being, the eternal Being, subsistent in Himself. But equally He is the Being in which everything subsists, on which everything depends. The name YHWH signifies this dependence of all beings on the absolute Being. YHWH Elohim signifies YHWH who gives consistency to the Elohim, that is to say, the angels; Him who is in the midst of the angels. YHWH Sěba'ot signifies YHWH who is with the heavenly armies and who provides them with consistency and permanence.[42]

In the Bible, Elohim appears as the name of God in the first creation narrative (Gn 1:1-2:3). Afterwords, the name of YHWH Elohim is used, and then, beginning with Cain's birth, only YHWH.[43]

According to Ibn Ezra, the use of the different names stems from the fact that in the first moment of the period of creation the situation of the world was varied and multiple, and use of the divine Name corresponded to that state. At that time Elohim, with its connotation of plurality, was the adequate name for that state of things — a full name in a full world.[44] The name of YHWH could not be received by man until he no longer ate of the tree of knowledge and until he had engendered a son.[45] YHWH is the name of the Most High in relation to the concrete world, be it understood personally or collectively — the Name which communicates and transmits power to the individual Israelite or to the people of Israel as a whole.[46]

The Tetragrammaton and Mathematical Speculation

The Tetragrammaton is, as the word implies, composed of four letters — the venerable letters *yod, he, waw, he* — although only three of the letters are different. Each letter has a numerical value. *Yod*=10, *he*=5, and *waw*=6. Ibn Ezra attempts to justify the use of these three letters, and only these three, from the perspectives of linguistics,[47] orthography,[48] and numerical value.[49]

Ibn Ezra advances speculations concerning the various numerical values of the Tetragrammaton — the letters taken either conjointly or individually. In some cases he discovers surprising identifications, and in most, he discovers the unfathomable mysteries of the holy Name. I will now indicate, in numerical order of the integers upon which they are based, the principles of his mathematical speculations concerning the divine Name:

10. If the sum of the first and second letters is squared [$(y + h)^2 = 15^2 = 225$] and the product is added to the sum of the first three letters squared [$(y + h + w)^2 = 21^2 = 441$], the result is 666, which subtracted from the square of the complete name [$(y + h + w + h)^2 = 676$] comes to 10, which is the numerical value of the first letter, *yod*.[50]

15. The first two letters, yh, add up to 15. With 5 at the center, the nine unit numbers can be arranged in a square such that the sum of the three units in any direction will always be 15.

4	9	2
3	5	7
8	1	6

[51]

If you add the first five unit numbers, the product will also be 15 [1 + 2 + 3 + 4 + 5 = 15].[52]

25. The value of the first two letters when the first is doubled [10 + 10 + 5 = 25] coincides with the value of the square of the second [$h^2 = 5^2 = 25$].[53]

26. The numerical value of the complete Name is 26 [10 + 5 + 6 + 5], which corresponds to the number of planetary conjunctions.[54] If the numerical value of yh [15], such as it is written, is added to the numerical value of this half of the Name, such as it would be pronounced [ya = 11], the sum is 26, equal to the value of the entire Tetragrammaton.[55] If one adds to square of the first unit number [$1^2 = 1$] to the square of the middle number [$5^2 = 25$] the sum is 26, the value of the entire Tetragrammaton.[56]

72. The number 72 represents the numerical value of the divine Name when all its integral parts are added together [y + yh + yhw + yhwh = 10 + 15 + 21 + 26 = 72]. Four verses of Scripture, each containing 72 letters (Ex 14:19, 20, 21; Ez 1:1) refer to the divine Name.[57]

120. The sum of the squares of all the even numbers corresponding to the order of units is 120 [$2^2 + 4^2 + 6^2 + 8^2$ = 4 + 16 + 36 + 64 = 120], which coincides with the sum of integers in half of the Name [Yh: 1 + 2 + 3 + 4 + 5 + 6 + 7 + 8 + 9 + 10 + 11 + 12 + 13 + 14 + 15 = 120].[58] The same number [120] is obtained if the numerical value of the first two letters is multiplied by the sum of half of that value and half of 1 [15 × (7.5 + .5) = 120].[59] Moreover, the number of the conjunctions of the seven planets is also 120. It is also true that the sum of the numbers by which 120 can be evenly divided is exactly its double [1 + 2 + 3 + 4 + 5 + 6 + 8 + 10 + 12 + 15 + 20 + 24 + 30 + 40 + 60 = 240].[60]

125. The sum of the squares of the first two letters [$(y + h)^2 = 10^2 + 5^2 = 125$] is equal to the value of the second letter elevated to the cube [$5^3 = 125$].[61] If the first letter is squared [$y^2 = 10^2 = 100$] and the product is subtracted from the square of the first two letters [$(y + h)^2 = 15^2 = 225; 225 - 100 = 125$], the result coincides with the value of the second letter elevated to the cube [$h^3 = 5^3 = 125$]. Thus the *he* alone can be used as the divine Name.[62]

165. If the first half of the Name is multiplied by the second [(y + h) × (w + h) = 15 × 11 = 165], the product is the same as the sum of the squares of the odd numbers of the order of units [$1^2 + 3^2 + 5^2 + 7^2 + 9^2$ = 1 + 9 + 25 + 49 + 81 = 165].[63]

The same number is obtained if the first half of the Name as written is multiplied by the way it would be pronounced [yh = 15; ya = 11; 15 × 11 = 165].[64] The sum is also 165 if the first nine units are added to 120 [1 + 2 + 3 + 4 + 5 + 6 + 7 + 8 + 9 + 120 = 165.)[65]

216. If yh is squared [15^2 = 225] and yhw is also squared [21^2 = 441], and then the one sum is subtracted from the other [441 − 225 = 216], the result is identical to the third letter elevated to the cube [$w^3 = 6^3 = 216$].[66]

340. The sum of the multiplication of the first letter of the Tetragrammaton by each of the four letters is 260 [y × y (10 × 10) + y × h (10 × 5) + y × w (10 × 6) + y × h (10 × 5) = 260]. If the product of the multiplication of the second letter by the first and the third is added [y × h (10 × 5) + w × h (6 × 5) = 80], the result is 340, which is the numerical value of *šem* ("The Name").[67]

385. The sum of the squares of the first ten integers is 385 [1^2 + 2^2 + 3^2 + 4^2 + 5^2 + 6^2 + 7^2 + 8^2 + 9^2 + 10^2 = 1 + 4 + 9 + 16 + 25 + 36 + 49 + 64 + 81 + 100 = 385], which corresponds to the numerical value of the *šěkhynah*.[68]

390. If the first half of the Name [yh (15)] is multiplied by the complete Name [yhwh (26)], the result is 390—exactly the numerical value of *samayim* [s(300) + m(40) + y(10) + m(40) = 390].[69]

1500.If we multiply the first two letters [y × h (10 × 5)], and the product by the third letter [w (6) × 50 = 300], and this in turn by the fourth letter [h (5) × 300], the result is 1,500, which is like the value of the name Yah [15].[70]

Conclusions

The mathematical speculations of Abraham Ibn Ezra on the divine Name, the Tetragrammaton, are not grounded as such on gematria, that exegetical technique based on the numerical value of letters or words. The mathematical speculations concerning the Name of YHWH are for Ibn Ezra not a technical means of attaining new exegetical identifications. They are, above all, concerned with discovering a portion of the unfathomable mysteries surrounding the divine Name. Evidently Ibn Ezra draws upon very ancient traditions in Israel, fundamentally of a mystical tendency, concerning speculations on letters and numbers.[71] The sage of Tudela, buttressed by his basically Neoplatonic conceptions and respectful of traditional trends as documented in the *Book of Creation*, attempts to evidence the harmony of the universe on all levels, a harmony which is reflected in the divine Name itself.[72]   He is quick to point out that 26 is both the value of the entire name of YHWH and the number of the conjunctions of the five planets,[73] and that 120 is both half the value of the Name as it would be pronounced and the number of conjunctions of the seven planets.[74] If there are nine numbers there are nine spheres; with the addition of a tenth that represents the divine dwelling place, just as there are ten fingers, ten categories of discourse and ten commandments.[75]

Mathematical speculations on the divine Name have nothing to do with theurgy or magical practices. Ibn Ezra, at the beginning of the *Sefer ha-Sem*, makes a highly significant observation: "Given that [the Name] is not a substance, no effect is produced by the union of its letters. The words of the [snake] charmers produce no effect by themselves but do so only insofar as they emerge from the charmer's mouth [just as] human saliva, before [the act of] spitting, cannot kill the scorpion."[76]   In his commentary on Ex 3:13 he clarifies these words, stating that the changes which can be made in a name have no influence at all on the essence of the thing named. He immediately adds: "Because of this, those who say they perform great works with the Name do not know the Name. God preserve me from those who say that the Name was engraved on [Moses'] staff and that with it he parted the sea." Ibn Ezra is obviously referring to the incident in which Moses raised his staff, extended his hand, and parted the Red Sea so that the Israelites could pass (Ex 14:16). In Ibn Ezra's opinion this prodigy was not caused by the magical power of the divine Name engraved on the staff; it was effected by the power of God. This observation provides us with an adequate framework for his speculations on the divine Name.

The Midraš Ha-Šem

I hereby append the *Midras ha-Šem*, according to ms. Add 396, fol. 11a-12a of the Cambridge University Library. The small work appears here without any title, although in other manuscripts it is known under the name of *Midraš ha-Šem, Ma'ămar Šem ha-'esem* or *Sod ha-Šem ha-nikbad*.[77]

The treatise is an additional commentary to Abraham Ibn Ezra's commentary on Ex 33:21. The Cambridge manuscript attributes it directly to him. Although, as we have previously stated,[78] this opuscle was actually elaborated after the fact, in its simple form it could derive from Ibn Ezra himself.

(מדרש השם)

1. אמר אברהם המחבר: כי השם הנכתב ואינו נקרא. ככה הוא שם
העצם. והעצם הוא הכבוד. פירוש השם של ד' אותיות, הנכתב בתורה
ואינו נקרא כמו שנכתב הוא שם העצם של הקבה. ומהו העצם? הוא
שם שנבדל משם התאר מכמה דברים המבוארים בספרי הדקדוק.
והעצם הוא הכבוד. פירוש וכאשר אנו אומרים ברוך שם מלכותו וכונה
היא על שם בן ד' אותיות שאינו נקרא ככתבו והוא העצם והוא
הכבוד.

2. וכאשר תחבר מספר כל האותיות יעלו ע"ב. פירוש כי האות הראשון
עולה עשרה ושתים הראשונות עולים ט"ו ועוד שלשה הראשונות עו-
לות כ"א וארבעתם עולות כ"ו וכשתחבר הכל יחד יהיו ע"ב.

3. וכאשר תחבר מרובע ראשון אל מרובע אמצעי באמת יהיה כמחבר
השם. פירוש יש לך לדעת שכל המספרים הם אי בי גי די הי וי זי חי
טי שלעולם יתגלגל בהם החשבון, כי אי דומה לעשרה ולמאה ולאלף
ולרבוא וכן בי לעשרים ולמאתים ולאלפים ולרבואתים וכן השאר.
ומרובע הראשון בחשבון הוא אחד ומרובע האמצעי בחשבון שהוא ה'
עולה כ"ה. חבר עמהם האחד יהיה הכל כ"ו כמספר אותיות השם של ד'
אותיות. גם כן מחברות כוכבי לכת. פירוש הם שבתאי צדק מאדים
נגה ככב שפעמים הם שנים במזל אחד ופעמים שלשה ופעמים ארבעה
ופעמים עשרה ופעמים יתחברו כל החמשה יחד ועולים כל המחברות
שיחברו כ"ו כמספר השם להודיע שבכח הי יתי יתחברו וישימו
משמרם בארץ.

ובאור הכ"ו מחברות הוא זה. שבתאי צדק, שבתאי מאדים, שבתאי
נגה, שבתאי ככב, שבתאי צדק מאדים, שבתאי צדק נוגה, שבתאי צדק
כוכב, שבתאי צדק מאדים נוגה, שבתאי צדק מאדים כוכב, שבתאי
צדק מאדים נוגה כוכב, צדק מאדים, צדק כוכב, צדק נוגה, צדק
מאדים נוגה, צדק מאדים כוכב, צדק מאדים נוגה כוכב, מאדים נוגה,
מאדים כוכב, נוגה כוכב, נוגה שבתאי מאדים, נוגה שבתאי כוכב, נוגה
שבתאי מאדים כוכב, כוכב שבתאי מאדים, כוכב צדק נוגה, כוכב
מאדים נוגה, כוכב צדק נוגה.

4. גם בחברך האותיות שיבטא האדם בחצי השם יהיו כמספר השם. פי'
חיצי השם הוא יהי והאותיות שיבטא האדם בהם באותו חצי השם הם
יוד הא ועולים כ"ו כמספר להורות שאין חלוק ופירוד בעניין השם.

5. ובחברך מרובעי הזוגות ההם במעלה הראשונה יהיו כמספרים המחוברים
מחצי השם. פירוש מעלה הראשונה שבחשבון הם מא' ועד טי
והמספרים אשר הם זוגות אשר במעלה הזאת הם בדו"ח ומרובעים
עולים ק"כ כי מרובע בי די ומרובע די יוי ומרובע וי ל"ו ומרובע חי

ס"ד ובין הכל עולים ק"כ וזה יהיה כמספרים המחוברים מחיצי השם. פירוש חיצי השם עולה ט"ו וכאשר תחבר כל המספרים מתחלת החשבון שהוא אחד ועד ט"ו והם בכלל יעלו ק"כ גם כן.

6. וכאשר תכפול חיצי השם הראשון על חיצי השם השני.   פירוש כשתכפול ט"ו על י"א שעולים קס"ה, אז תמצא מרובעי הנפרדים. פירוש הם המספרים שאינם זוגות שהם א ג ה ז ט כי מרובע א' הוא א י' ומרובע ג' הוא ט' ומרובע ה' הוא כ"ה ומרובע ז' הוא מ"ט ומרובע ט' הוא פ"א ובין הכל הוא קס"ה גם כן.

7. וכאשר תחסר מרובע האות הראשון שבשם שעולה עשרה והמרובע שלו מאה מן מרובע השנים כלומר מן השנים מרובעות שעולות ט"ו ומרובעם רכ"ה אז ישאר קכ"ה והוא כחשבון מעוקב האות השני. פירוש קורא מעוקב אל חשבון מרובע באורך ורוחב ועומק והאות השני שבשם מספרם חמשה והי פעמים, הוא רבועה, עולה כ"ה. כפול עוד זה המספר בחמשה להיות לו קומה, יהיה קכ"ה.

8. ואם תחסר מרובע השנים שהוא רכ"ה כאשר אמרנו מן מרובע הג' אותיות שהם כ"א במספר ומרובעם ד"י מאות ומ"א, ישאר רי"ו שהוא כחשבון האות השלישי מעוקב שבשם שהיא ו', כי ו' פעמים ו' עולים ל"ו ו' פעמים ל"ו עולים רי"ו.

9. ואם חברנו מספר הראשון עם הראשון והשני, כלומר, אם חברנו עשרה אל ט"ו יעלה כ"ה ואז יהיה המספר המחובר הזה כמרובע האות השני[ן] שבשם שהוא ה' , שמרובע ההי עולה כ"ה.

10. ואם חסרנו מרובע השנים אותיות שבשם שעולה רכ"ה וכן נחסר מרובע של שלשה אותיות שבשם שעולים תמ"א מן מרובע הגדול שהוא כ"ו. וכ"ו פעמים כ"ו עולים תרע"ו שאז ישאר עשרה כמספר האות הראשון שבשם וקורא לו מרובע הגדול בעבור שהמספר הזה נעשה מכל אותיות השם.

11. ואם נערוך הראשון אל השני על מחברת השנים האחרים.   פירוש אם תכפול האות הראשונה שבשם על השניה יעלה חמישים וזה החמשים על האות השלישי יעלה שלש מאות. ואלו שלש מאות יכפול על מספר האות הרבעית יעלה המספר אלף ות"ק והיא דומה לחשבון השם. פירוש יעלה זה ט"ו מאות שהוא דומה לחשבון הי כלומר יהי שזה עולה ט"ו אחדים וזה עולה ט"ו מאות.

12. ואם ערכנו השם שהיא חיצי השם על כלו עולה כמנין שמים, כלומר, אם כפלנו ט"ו על כ"ו יעלה ש"ן וזה הוא כמספר אותיות השמים והוא אס־ מכתא למה שאנו מכנים שמו של הַקָבָה כמלת שמים כמו ויהי מורא שמים עליכם.
תם זה הפירוש.

Notes

* This study has been written under the auspices of a research program of HEBREW AUTHORS OF AL-ANDALUS subvented by the DIRECCION GENERAL DE INVESTIGACIÓN CIENTÍFICA DEL MINISTERIO ESPAÑOL DE EDUCACIÓN Y CIENCIA.

1   *Gimatriyya*, is a Greek word. It signifies calculation or number [Elias Levita. Tisbi. Lexicon Hebraicum. Basileae, 1557, ad loc.] "Gematria figura kabbalistica circa aequipollentiam numerorum in dictionibus occupata". Knorr von Rosenroth, *Kabbala Denudata* . . . . Sulzbach, 1677, I, ad loc.; reprinted in Hildensheim, 1972).

2   Christian D. Ginsburg, *The Essenes, their History and Doctrine. The Kabbalah. Its Doctrine, Development, and Literature.* London, 1863, 131 (reprinted 1956). The techniques of *gematria*, in their different modalities and combinations, are eloquently described in a late treatise which presents itself as an Italian translation [only the introduction is in Latin] of a work of Ibn Ezra (*De arte cabalistica*), Ms. 258 of the Kaufmann collection in Budapest. Assuredly, the work is not by Ibn Ezra. But, given the attribution, it is fully justified to reproduce the introduction of the opuscle: "De arte cabalistica. Quid sit haec scientia, ad quid attinet. Elapsis temporibus vocabatur celestis et divina, que data fuit populo Israel, qui propter sua scelera privatus fuit, quamvis credebat et denuo credit istam habere, etsi non habeat.   Tunc erat celestis, modo terrena, id est, humana unde quilibet qui numerare non ignorat potest esse huius capax scientiae, dummodo habeat caracteres quos in clave describit, que clavis ignota, aut sub silentio manere debet, aliter universus orbis capax esset huius tante scientia et gloriose.   Hec tamen celestis traditio fuit que fit per caracteres divinos, sine qua latione nulla est scientia.

Cabala enim est scientia salutaris,sancta, bona, scientifica: salutaris dico, quia innuat omnibus illis qui eam imitant per se et per omnes, viam bonam malis docet, damna fugat, pericula demonstrat et ad ea fuganda docet, occultas cogitationes patefacit, insidiam aperit, offensiva dettegit, et tuto ad omnes felicitates et infelicitates arguit atque nemo inveniri potest cabalista qui non teneatur mirabilis, et regali veste dignus, seu encomio, sed necesse est quod sit secretus, fingendo eam nescire.

Hec est illa scientia que gloriosos facit homines semper, tum in virtutibus, tum im armis, tum in omnibus occasionibus, dum istam capiant et per evidentiam certam scimus neminem unquam huius scientie possessorem fuisse aliis subiectum.

Hec tamen tota fundata est super dispositiones numericas et super se habet 54 regulas, quas facilius aprehendunt docti, sed in eas disponendo, et simul associando, necessaria est clavis caracterica tota, qua mediante divinum elementum totum se complet feliciter, ut in sequentibus regulis videbimus, quoniam in illis est felicitas magna: e pure combinate non rivoltano, se prima non si traslasciano con l'elemento, atteso quello é l'elemento e la radice di tutta la pianta naturale et epilogando la scienza divina avuta divinamente che all' umana cognizione é tradotta e per ciò si dice cabala umana.   Questa disponiamo dichiarare con permissione divina, ponendo le regole con questa disposizione ordinate (per) facilità come qui a basso si dimostra".

3   Letter from Yemen (XXIII:38). I cite my Spanish translation: *Cartas y Testamento de Maimonides*. Cordoba, 1989, 171). In the same letter, Maimonides, basing himself on *gematria*, refers to a tradition in which prophecy, as a pre-messianic event, would be restored in 1216 (XXIII:38) and notes the interpretation of Gen. 17:20 made by a dissident, which is applied to Mohammed according to *gematria*.

4   *Berešit Rabbah* 91.2 (Ed. A. A. ha-Levi. Tel Aviv, 1956, 698).

5   Hermann L. Strack, *Einleitung in Talmud und Midrasch*. München, 1921, 142; H. L. Strack - G. Stemberger, *Introducción a la literatura talmúdica y midrásica*. Valencia, 1988, 143. The definitive redaction of the *Midraš Rabbah* to Genesis is usually placed in the same period as the final redaction of the Jerusalem Talmud.

6   S. A. H., *"Gematria"*. *Encyclopedia Judaica*. Berlin, 1931, VII:170ff.

7   The two have recently been edited by Asher Wiezer [*Ibn 'Ezra Pěruše ha-Torah*. Jerusalem, 1977). M. Friedlaender published the brief redaction in *Ibn Ezra Literature. Essays in the Writings of Abraham Ibn Ezra*. London, 1877, Hebrew appendix, pp. 1-9. D. Rosin edited the Hebrew text of the exegetical methods with a German translation ("Reime und Gedichte des Abraham Ibn Ezra". *Jahressbericht des jüdisch-theologischen Seminars Franckel' sch Stiftung*. Breslau, 1885, I:23ff.) A Latin translation was provided by Joseph de Voysin ("Opus rythmicum R. Abraham Abben Ezrae de modis quibus Hebraei legem solent interpretari". *Disputatio cabalistica Israel filii R. Mosis de anima*, Paris, 1635, 151-167) and Schickard (*Bechinathhapperuschim, hoc est, Examinis Commentationum Rabbinicorum in Mosen Prodonius*. Tubingen, 1624).

8   Bacher's study remains one of the most important on the methods described by Ibn Ezra in the introduction to his commentary to the Pentateuch "Abraham Ibn Ezra's Einleitung zu seinem Pentateuch — Commentar als Beitrag zur Geschichte der Bibelexegese". *Sitzungsgeschichte der kaiserlichen Akademie der Wissenschaften, Philosophisch-Historische Classe* 81 (1875), 361-444.

9   A. Wiezer, *op. cit.*, *Běrešit* 141. All quotations made, from this point on, from the Commentary of Ibn Ezra to the Pentateuch, will be based on Wiezer's edition.

10   *Le pentateuque . . . . acompagné du commentaire de Rachi traduit en francais par Joseph Bloch - Israël Salzer, Elie Munk, Ernest Cugenheim*. Paris, 1964, ad loc.

11   Commentary to Genesis, ad locum.

12   His most important mathematical works are the *Sepher ha-Mispar*, edited by Moritz Silberberg with German translation [*Sepher ha-Mispar. Das Buch der Zahl . . . .* Frankfurt, 1895] and the *Sepher ha-Ehad . . . .* Odessae, 1867, re-edited by Israel

Levin, *Abraham Ibn Ezra Reader*. New York-Tel Aviv, 1985, 397-416. To these works the *Sepher Yĕsod Mispar* on numerals should be added. Edited by S. Pinsker. [*Einleitung in das Babylonische-Hebräische Punktationssystem . . . . nebst einer Grammatik der hebraischen Zahlwörter (Jesod Mispar) von Abraham Ibn Ezra . . . .* Wien, 1863.]

13 In the *Yĕsod Mispar* he cites it under the name of *Sepher ha-Šem ha-Nikbad* (Ed. S. Pinsker, *op. cit.*, 140). It was first edited by G. H. Lippmann [*Sepher haschem oder das Buch über den vierbuchstabigen Namen Gottes von Rabbi Abraham Aben Ezra. Furth*, 1834]. Israel Levin has prepared a new edition [Abraham Ibn Ezra Reader. New York-Tel Aviv, 1985, 417ff]. Lippman's commentary continues being the most complete. Among the commentaries of the *Sepher ha-Šem* with which I am familiar, I shall cite those of Šabtay ha-Cohen (Ms. of Kaufmann; B 150 of the Leningrad Orientalism Institute; Mardoqueo ben Eliezer Comtino (Paris ms. 681, 2); Šĕlomoh ben Eliyyah Šarbit ha-Zahab (Vatican 105/3): Eliezer of Norzi (Paris, 1092/8). I follow Lippman's edition in the quotations of the *Sepher ha-Šem*.

14 The commentary to the Pentateuch was edited by A. Wiezer (refer to note 7). M. Friedlaender, in the Hebrew appendix to his *Essays on the Writings of Abraham Ibn Ezra* (London, 1877) includes an additional commentary to Ex. 3:15 (pp. 72-78) which develops three questions: (1) the numbers are nine under one aspect, ten under another; (2) Equality and the resemblance between one and ten; (3) Qualities of the numbers 5 and 6.

15 Chapter XI and XII. Edited by M. Creizenach accompanied by a German version [*Jesod Mora. Grundlage der Gottesverehrung oder Untersuchungen über das mosaische Gesetz und die Grundprinzipien der israelitischen Religion von Abraham Ibn Ezra.* Frankfurt A/M - Leipzig, 1840). Israel Levin has re-edited it (*op. cit.*, 313-374). Following Creizenach's edition he will be cited under the siglum YM.

16 Casanatense I.V.II; 3104/10, fol. 47-51.

17 Casanatense H.IV.17; 3152/, fol. 108-109f.

18 Paris 825, 6, fol. 207 V.

19 Such is the case in the version to which witness is given by manuscript Ebr IA 98 of the Leningrad Firkovitch Collection which includes an incomplete enumeration of the 70 names of Metraton which states: "these things I have garnered from the words of the great luminary, the Rab, our master Menachem, disciple of Rab, our master, Eliezer of Worms".

20 A study of this opuscle is recommended. Aside from the mss. cited, it is found in Casanatense (I.II.9; 3087/15, fol. 96-10a; Vat 36/3 [*AIE mathematicis rationibus ostendere nititur necessitatem quatuor literarum quibus nomen Dei ineffabile componitur, ita ut nec plures nec pauciores esse potuerint*]. El Ms. 707, 4 of Paris has the explanation of Yosef ben Moše's calculations of AIE in relation to the Tetragrammaton.

21 *Sepher ha-Šem*, 2.

22   He mentions Elohim, Adonay, Šadday, and Ṣěba'ot among the divine names as always being adjectives (*Sepher ha-Šem*, 2.)

23   Com. to Ex. 15:20.

24   *Sepher ha-Šem*, 8; Com. to Ex. 15:2. The basis of the change is the permutability of the letters aleph, he, waw, and yod (*Sepher ha-Šem*, 2), a property on which he insists in his grammatical works [*Sepher Ṣahot*, 11, 14 et passim. Ed. C. del Valle. Salamanca, 1977; *Šěfat Yeter* 134 (Ed. N. Allony, *Yěsod diqduq* . . . . Jerusalem, 1984); *Šafah Běrurah* 22b (ed. G. Lippmann, Fürth, 1839). Based on the permutability of the letters aleph, he, waw, and yod, *Yehuda Hayyūq* (X century) arrived at the principle of trilateralism on which the scientific grammar of Hebrew is grounded [J. W. Nutt, *Two Treatises on Verbs containing Feeble and Double Letters* . . . . London, 1970, 16ff.; 24ff.

25   Com. to Ex. 15:2. The mystery of the number consists in that with the removal of the yod only two letters remain (yh) which, when computed numerically according to their pronunciation (ywd h'), add up to 26, the numerical value of the complete name of Yhwh ($10+5+6+5 = 26$).

26   Menahem ben Saruq (died cir. 970) interpreted Ehyeh as a proper divine name: "I am He who is . . . . Ehyeh has sent me to you (Ex. 3:14). It is the Holy Name, venerable and most glorious. This word is not derived from other words. The interpreters say it is derived from *hawiya, lihyot* (being). When God said to Moses: I am he who is, it seems as if He had said: I have existed from always, I exist now, and will exist eternally. However, when He repeats the word for the second time saying Eyheh (I am) sent me to you, it is done as a word without meaning". [*Mahberet*. Ed. A. Filipowski. London, 1854, ad loc.]

27   *Sepher ha-Šem*, 8.   Šabtay ha-Cohen endorses the same interpretation (Commentary to the *Sepher ha-Šem*, Ms. 271 of the Budapest Kaufmann collection, fol. 59: "The meaning of ehyeh is as explained: (I am) he who is. This is because no being subsists but God or in God".

28   The Jewish custom of not pronouncing the Tetragrammaton and substituting it by Adonay is documented from at least the third century, BCE. Refer to L. F. H., "Names of God" in *EJ*, Jerusalem, 1972).

29   *Sepher ha-Šem*, 8.

30   *Sepher ha-Šem*, 2. The use of *ădoní* (my Lord) occurs in common speech so it would be incorrect to apply it to God. Because of this, the majestatic plural is used (Com. to Ex. 3:15).

31   Com. to Ex. 3:15.

32   *Sepher ha-Šem*, 8.

33   Short com. to Ex. 3:13. It is, in any case, a problem to establish the pronunciation of the Tetragrammaton such as he understood it. In the same commentary he states that "Eliyahu the prophet is a master of justice. This is a mystery". This

allusion is clarified by a further allusion in the *Sepher ha-Šem*, 7: "In times past, I thought that (the word) Eliyáhu (= my God is Yah) could serve as proof until I found wĕ-gasmú-omer (what Gasmu says)". The author of the *Ohel Yosef*, additional commentary to Ibn Ezra's commentary on the Pentateuch, believes that if the pronunciation of Eliyáhu, with accent on the penultimate, were to be transferred to the Tetragrammaton, the pronunciation *yehî wa-hu* (is and will be forever) would result. Cited by G. H. Lippmann, *Sepher haschem*. Fürth, 1834, 17b, n. 12).

34 *Sepher ha-Šem*, 7.

35 "The illustrated man who knows the foundation of the unmoved and the mobile knows the ways of the Name, knows how it is pronounced". Short Com. to Ex. 3:13). In the different pronunciations of the divine Name AIE collects ancient traditions of a mystical character. Yosef ben Abraham Chiquitilla (1248-cir. 1325), a distinguished kabbalist, alludes to the different pronunciations of the Tetragrammaton: "To Yahweh are ascribed 54 compound names, in the combination of *yhwh*. They add up to 216 letters. These 54 names are the mystery which extends (divine) power to everything that exists in the world . . . . In these 54 names all the things of the world are contained. It is these which supply what is necessary to all creatures by means of Adonay". [*Sepher ša'arê orâ*. Cracovia, (1600), cap. 1]. Refer to the combinations in Knorr von Rosenroth, *Kabbala denudata*. Salzburg.

36 Thusly we AIE opposed to R. Yesua', the Karaite, who affirmed that Israel had a tradition received from the fathers according to which the saviour of Israel (= Moses) revealed a new name which had previously not be heard. [Com. to Ex. 3:13].

37 This Name was unknown in the world except for a few men until Moses. "Don't you realize it cannot be found in any of Job's replies nor in those of his companions?" [*Sepher ha-Šem*, 8.]

38 Com. to Ex. 3:13.

39 "Because the fathers knew this Name (Yhwh) as a proper name, but did not know that this Name is an adjective". [Ex. 6:3].

40 *Yĕsod Mora*, 12; Com. to Ex. 3:15; *Sepher ha-Šem*. The same is said about Ehyeh (YM, 12).

41 AIE gives great significance to the use of Yhwh as an adjective. In fact, the entire second chapter of the *Sepher ha-Šem* is dedicated to distinguish proper name and adjective. Four differences are given: the adjective has verbal derivation while the proper name does not; the adjective admits the plural, determinate article, construction, the addition of suffixes while the proper name does not. Nevertheless, one should keep in mind that a common name - such as man - is understood by Ibn Ezra as an adjective. Refer to Com. to Ex. 3:15.

42 Com. to Ex. 3:15; *Sepher ha-Šem*, 2. Concerning Elohim, he states in the Com. to Ex. 3:4, that it "embraces all sanctity which is not a body nor a potency in a body".

Contrast Abner of Burgos' interpretation of El-Sadday: "Esto es el su sepparamjento que muestra el vjerbo Saday que quier dezir que es abondable en ssj de ssjn aver mester para su sostenjmjento a otra ninguna cosa sjno a ssi mismo". [*Libro de la Ley*, Spanish ms. 43, Paris. There, the work appears, in the first instance, without a title.

43   Com. to Ex. 3:13; YM 12.

44   YM 12. Yosef ben Abraham Chiquitilla also searched for an explanation of the various names of God found in the Pentateuch: "The venerated and most glorious Name, Yhwh, you will find in the Torah in various ways and usages. Sometimes, in the greater part of the Torah, you will find it alone. Thus it is written: Yhwh said . . . . Other times you will find it joined with other holy names, as in the work of creation: These are the generations of the heavens and earth when they were created, the day in which Yhwh Elohim made heavens and earth . . . . I am obliged make known to you the meaning of this. You should know that Yhwh is perfect and complete and fills all the measures . . . . In Him all things are consummated and ended . . . . It was not necessary to mention this in the work of creation as the world and its creatures did not as yet exist as a finished work. The world was not yet in plenitud but was in the process of being made. But when the creation of the world was terminated, when things were consummated with full completion, then (the name) of Yhwh Elohim is mentioned. [*Sa'ăre orâ*], cap. 5].

45   *Sepher ha-Šem*, 8. "Except in one unique place, the name Elohim is never found in Moses' words, only the venerable Name". [Com. to Ex. 3:13].

46   YM 12.

47   They are the easiest letters to pronounce and also matres lectionis, which abound in proper names. Refer to Com. to Ex. 3:15; YM 11.

48   The *yod* is like a semicircle which embraces everything within its interior. It signifies totality. The *he* is composed of two tracts which signify duality: matter and form, substance and accident. The *yod*, with a numerical value of 10 and equivalent to one, is the symbol of the absolute unity of one. Because of this it opens to the Tetragrammaton. The *he*, with its two tracts, signifies the dismemberment of unity into matter and form in creatures. Refer to the *Sepher ha-Šem* and the commentary of G. H. Lippmann [*Sepher haschem* . . . . 31). The *waw* has the form of a hook and signifies union [*Sahot* 54]. The *Zohar*, in the treatise of *The Secrets of the Letters of the Divine Name*, describes the *yod* as a nutshell which covers the occult. Although the parallel with the simile of AIE (the semicircle) is evident, they do not have the same meaning. Refer to the edition of Stephen G. Wald, *The Doctrine of the Divine Name*. Atlanta, 1988, 153.

49   The four numbers which represent the letters composing the Tetragrammaton (10, which is like the one; 5; 6; 5) have a common property in that when they are squared their own number always appears in its base ($5^2 = 5 \times 5 = 25$; $6^2 = 6 \times 6 = 36$; $1^2 = 1 \times 1 = 1$) [*Sepher ha-Šem*, 3]. Because of this, Ibn Ezra calls 5 and 6 circular numbers; as in a circle, each returns to its base [*Sepher ha-Šem*], 3; YM 11]. "These numbers, the 1, 10, 5, 6, guard themselves. [Anonymous Additional Commentary to the Commentary of Ex. 3:15]. The one has only one

lateral, 2, while all the other numbers have two laterals, one to the right and one to the left. The laterals of 3 are 2 and 4. This property of 1 demonstrates that it depends on nothing and everything depends on it.   [Com. to Ex. 33:21; Additional Commentary to Ex. 3:15, Friedlaender, 75]. The 5 is the sum of the prime numbers that precede it (2 + 3 = 5) [YM, 11]. The 6 is the sum of its divisible wholes (3 + 2 + 1 = 6). [Com. to Ex. 3:15]. The *waw*, valued as it is pronounced, with double *waw*, is equivalent to 12. If its divisible parts are added the sum is 28 (1 + 2 + 3 + 4 + 6 + 12 = 28) which, surprisingly, is the only number in the twenties whose whole divisibles add up to the same number (1 + 2 + 4 + 7 + 14 = 28). The 10, the mighty one, is the basis of all calculation, similar to the 1. If on the one hand the numbers are nine, on the other they are ten. [Anonymous Additional Commentary to the Com. on Ex. 3:15, Friedlaender, 72ff.].

50   *Sepher ha-Šem* 5; *Midraš ha-Šem* 10 (according to the attached edition).

51   YM 11.

52   *Sepher ha-Šem* 3.

53   *Sepher ha-Šem,* 5; *Midraš ha-Šem* 9.

54   Com. to Ex. 33:21.

55   Com. to Ex. 3:13; *Midraš ha-Šem* 4.

56   Com. to Ex. 33:21; *Midraš ha-Šem* 3.

57   *Sepher ha-Šem* 5; Com. to Ex. 3:13 and 33:21; *Midraš ha-Šem* 2.

58   Com. to Ex. 33:21; *Midraš ha-Šem* 5; *Sepher ha-Šem* 5.

59   *Sepher ha-Šem* 5.

60   *Sepher ha-Šem* 5.

61   Commentary to the Tetragrammaton, Ms. Ebr. IA98, fol. 196 of the Firkovitch collection at Leningrad.

62   *Midraš ha-Šem* 7; Com. to Ex. 33:21.

63   Com. to Ex. 33:21; *Sepher ha-Šem* 5.

64   *Midraš ha-Šem* 6.

65   YM 11.

66   YM 11; Com. to Ex. 33:21; *Midraš ha-Šem* 8. The consequence is that the *waw* signifies the entire divine Name.

67   *Sepher ha-Šem* 5.

68   Commentary on the Tetragrammaton, Ms. Ebr. IA98, fol. 20a of the Firkovitch Collection. Hence the *yod* signifies the *šĕkkinah*, the divine Presence.

69   *Sepher ha-Šem* 5: *Midraš ha-Šem* 12: "This is the convention by which God is designated by the name of *šamayim* (heavens)". [*Midraš ha-Šem* 12.]

70   Given that in the system of tens there is an essential parallelism between the different orders [*Midraš ha-Šem* 11; *Sepher ha-Šem* 5].

71   Speculations which appear in the *Sefer Yĕsirâ*. Regarding his observations on numbers 10 and 1, Ibn Ezra depends directly on Dunas ben Tamim (IX Century) in his commentary on the *Book of Creation*. [*Sefer Yĕsirah*. . . . with Commentary by Dunash ben Tamim. London, 1902. Ed. M. Grossberg].

72   Refer to H. Greive, *Studien zum jüdischen Neuplatonismus. Die Religions-philosophie des Abrahams Ibn Ezra*. Berlin, 1973; C. del Valle, "El Hay ben Meqis de Abraham Ibn Ezra". *Cuadernos salmantinos de filosofía* 4 (1978), 99-125.

73   Com. to Ex. 33:21.

74   Com. to Ex. 33:21.

75   *Sepher ha-Šem* 3; Com. to Ex. 3:15. To document Ibn Ezra's proclivity to discover the harmony between all the levels of the universe, refer, for example, to *Sahot* 2, 4, 12.

76   *Sepher ha-Šem* 1.

77   Refer to footnotes 16, 17, and 18.

78   Refer to footnote 19.

Section II

Christian Mysticism

Temple and Community: Foundations for Johannine Spirituality

Lawrence E. Frizzell

I. Review of Scholarship

The spiritual riches of the Johannine tradition (the Fourth Gospel and three epistles) have been recognized as a treasure by Christian theologians and spiritual writers since the early centuries.[1] But may we speak of *mystical* doctrine in John? A discussion of definitions must precede any effort to answer this question.

The term "mystical" may be described as "involving or having the nature of an individual's direct subjective communion with God or ultimate reality". Mysticism, then, is "the belief that direct knowledge of God, spiritual truth or ultimate reality can be attained through subjective experience".[2]

Some scholars object to the term "Johannine mysticism" because they stress that the definition implies direct apprehension of God by the human mind. "St. John is strongly anti-mystical . . . He is emphatic that no man hath beheld God at any time (1:18); that saying repudiates that essentially mystical experience . . . ."[3]

However, if one allows an experience of God mediated through the Word made flesh (Jn. 1:14) to be considered mystical, then the Fourth Gospel may be considered as the most complete interpretation and record of the early Church's experience whereby it felt itself to be in Christ, and through Christ, in God. The relation of the Father with the Son, understood as a mystical relation, becomes the key to illuminate the Christian life.[4]

In the early decades of this century many critical scholars considered John to be the Gospel most influenced by Hellenism.[5] In his influential study of Paul's mysticism, Albert Schweitzer situates the Fourth Gospel in the second century; along with Justin Martyr, John continued the work of Ignatius, Bishop of Antioch, introducing into the Hellenistic mysticism of communion with Christ the theory of Jesus Christ bearer of the Logos.[6]

The discovery of the Qumran scrolls in 1947 and subsequent years has shown that elements in John that seemed "Hellenistic" were already part of the Jewish traditions in the Holy Land of the late Second Temple period.[7] Although few scholars would follow J. A. T. Robinson, who considers John to be the *earliest* Gospel, its traditions do fit into the world of Judaism before 70, when the Temple was destroyed.[8]

"John is certainly different from the mystical religions which flourished in the environment of the Gospel". With these words, the English scholar C. K. Barrett completes his contrast between contemporary general conceptions about mysticism and the message of the Fourth Gospel. According to Rudolf Otto the term "mystical" tends to stress non-rational or supra-rational elements in religion; Barrett states: "John, on the contrary, showed a marked concern for the intellectual content of the Christian faith".[9]

A fine essay by James McPolin, S. J. entitled "Johannine Mysticism" looks carefully at the theme of communion with God as an essential constitutive principle of the Christian life.[10] He presents many of the texts and themes of the Fourth Gospel that will be treated in this study as well. However, McPolin does not investigate the background of the evangelist's teaching, so our approaches are complementary.

In a recent work on phenomenological and theological reflections concerning mysticism, the authors entitle the section on the biblical heritage "Experience of God".[11] The chapter on John notes that there is no emphasis on extraordinary spiritual phenomena (such as the charisma described in Paul's letters). Rather, John offers a profound account of the Christian experience, focused on Christ and radiating from him. Communion with the Father of Jesus is not described in terms of asceticism or contemplation, but by the commandments to believe in God and to practice love. There is no elitist attitude that salvation is for a small group of initiates. Faith is required because no one can see God directly in this life. This faith is grounded on apostolic witness, for which the Gospel comes to the community, and is manifested through fraternal love. The mediation of the apostolic tradition and the community of believers is essential. Communion with God the Father through Jesus is a reality for each person, but is not individualistic; it takes place within a community in imitation of the Trinitarian mystery (Jn. 17:20-24), an introduction into the circle of knowledge and love that constitutes the very life of the three divine persons in the one God.[12]

Not all scholars nuance the tension regarding individual and community as carefully as McPolin and Maggioni. In a recent study we read: "'Eternal life' allows John to make more personal and individualistic the corporate concept of 'Kingdom of God' . . . Life is a 'mystical' or perhaps 'spiritual' conception, a description of internal experience or of the ultimate destiny of one's soul".[13] The thesis of my essay is rather that the Johannine corpus, rooted deeply in the biblical heritage and the Jewish tradition, indeed stresses the personal and interior dimensions of the Christian experience; however this fact should not be interpreted as promoting individualistic piety or theology to the detriment of the group. The community setting is essential, as one would expect in a work emerging from the biblical worldview.

The major purpose of the evangelist in composing his work is indicated in the first ending to the Gospel. "These (signs) are written so that you may believe that Jesus is the Christ, the Son of God, and that believing you may have life in his name" (20:31). As with all New Testament texts, this Gospel was composed to be proclaimed aloud, so the verb forms are often in the second person plural. Of course, the text lends itself marvelously to personal meditation and provides foundations for a theology of Christian spirituality.[14] The tendency has been to focus on passages that resonate well for a given group and historical period. This approach should be tested against the way in which these texts are integrated into the entire Gospel and its use of the biblical heritage.

II. Covenant in Jewish Tradition

As Maggioni has indicated, communion with God is described by John within the framework of the commandments to believe in God and to practice love. As stated, his point should be applied to the entire corpus of the Jewish Scriptures; to be specifically Johannine he should have added that belief comes *through Jesus* and love is to be practiced *in imitation of him*. For our purpose it is necessary first to review the biblical tradition.

How can faith and love be presented as commandments? Does not the gift of self in freedom better connote the mystery of love?

In its division of the Decalogue, the Jewish tradition limits the first commandment to the statement of Exodus 20:2. "I am the Lord your God, who brought you out of the land of Egypt, out of the house of bondage". Thus a statement of faith is seen to be the basis for the response required in the subsequent commandments. If those belonging to the people believe, their faith should prove itself in acts of faithfulness.[15]

Because the Decalogue and other commandments of God's Torah (instruction) were to guide Israel's life as a political community in the land promised to them, the emphasis in many laws is on the social order.[16] However, the last commandment of the Decalogue points to the necessary of inner self-discipline. The prohibition of covetousness demanded at least that a person not express desires, and probably advocated the need for inner self-control. During the Exile (after the destruction of Jerusalem in 587 B.C.E.) the people were under Babylonian civil and criminal law, so the prophets and other teachers stressed the personal and interior dimensions of God's Torah. It remained valid for the people at a level deeper than the social order alone.

The Decalogue and all other commandments are given within the context of the initial gift of the Covenant. "If you obey my voice and keep my covenant, you shall be my own possession among all the peoples, for all the earth is mine, and you shall be to me a kingdom of priests and a holy nation" (Ex. 19:5-6). The call of Abram and Sarai (Gen. 12:1-3) and the revelation of the divine Name to Moses (Ex. 3:13-15) are clearly events wherein God took the initiative. One may recognize that faith as a divine gift is implicit in such experiences; the human response involves an act of acceptance which then requires a continuing activity of faithful obedience in acts of love.[17] The synthesis of faith-and-love in the thought of Paul and John in the Christian Scriptures stands within the ancient biblical message and its interpretation in Jewish circles in the Second Temple period.

The Sinai covenant is presented by the biblical writers as a reciprocal relationship, with responsibilities on both sides. God called the people of Israel his first-born son (Ex. 4:22) to show the intimacy of love which they are privileged to share. He promised protection and guidance on condition that the people submit to the divine will by keeping the commandments. Even after they worshipped the golden calf (Ex. 32:1-6) and Moses executed judgment on the guilty (32:25-29), commandments were bestowed again (34:1-4). In this context the meaning of the divine Name was revealed to Moses more fully than in the burning bush (Ex. 3:1-15), in which God's Name is revealed as "I am who am".[18] "The Lord passed before Moses and proclaimed: 'The Lord, the Lord, a God merciful and gracious, slow to anger and abounding in steadfast love and faithfulness, keeping steadfast love for thousands, forgiving iniquity and transgression and sin, but who will by no means clear the guilty . . . . " (34:6-7). The rabbis counted thirteen attributes of God in this passage and probably John's statement "God is love" (1 Jn. 4:8, 16) summarizes the meaning of the divine Name as revealed to Moses. If so, the theological insight of John derives from the covenant experience of Moses and Israel.[19]

In the priestly tradition the reciprocal nature of the covenant is expressed in the statement "I will be your God and you shall be my people" (Lev. 26:12, see Ex. 6:7). The same formula is part of Jeremiah's promise of a new covenant to those who survived the destruction of Jerusalem (Jer. 31:31-34, see Ez. 36:22-30). Later, Zechariah proclaimed God's message in similar terms. "Thus says the Lord of hosts: 'Behold, I will save my people from the east country and from the west country, and I will bring them to dwell in the midst of Jerusalem, and they shall be my people and I will be their God, in faithfulness and righteousness" (Zech. 8:7-8, 2:11; 8:20-23 for extension of this reality to the nations).

The renewal of God's covenant with the survivors of Judah, Benjamin and Levi took place in the context of Haggai's and Zechariah's mission that resulted in the rebuilding of the Temple. Although by 100 B.C.E. some groups rejected the priestly leadership of the Hasmoneans (and the Sadducees at the time of Jesus), it is an invalid generalization to state that the cult was moribund in Second Temple times, as one scholar does.[20]

The centers of focus for the spiritual life of most Jews during those centuries were the Torah (and the other parts of the Scriptures) and the Temple, the place where God revealed himself to his people and where sacrificial worship was offered. The three great pilgrimage feasts (Deut. 16:1-17) were the context for large multitudes to seek communion with God; the experience was personal but shared within the community.[21] Many drew strength from the rhythms of worship that consecrated each day and week to God, with the sabbath in home and synagogue constituting a profound experience of peace with God and neighbor.[22] The psalter provided inspiration for each generation, as it continues to do so for both Jews and Christians today.

As devout lay people who were educated in understanding the Scriptures, the Pharisees maintained that the entire community of Israel was "a kingdom of priests, a holy nation" (Ex. 19:6). They extended and adapted the ideals of priestly holiness in the context of a life in Temple service to their synagogues and homes. Meals were framed by prayer and became an opportunity for family and friends to sense God's presence in their midst.

Male Jews used *tefillin* (phylacteries) and fringes as daily reminders "to remember all the commandments of the Lord, to do them . . ." (Numbers 15:39-40). The *tefillin* and the *mezuzah* on the doorpost contained texts of Torah that stressed total commitment to the service of God (Deut. 6:4-9, etc.). As in practices of any religion, there may have been a tendency for some people to fall into routine but many in each generation must have profited by the numerous occasions in which God's covenant and teachings were presented.   Prayers preserved in the deuterocanonical books, the pseudepigrapha and the Qumran Scrolls give eloquent testimony to the vitality of Jewish spirituality during these centuries.[23]

Offering a blessing to God at the occasion of numerous events in daily life is a practice rooted in the ancient traditions of Israel. Certainly by the early rabbinic period this was a means of reminding the person of God's presence in every facet of daily life. It became customary as well to recite a blessing before performing any of the 248 positive commandments. This conscious effort to make ordinary, familiar things and occurrences the occasion for experiencing God has been called "normal mysticism".[24] It may be difficult to show how widespread this practice was before the destruction of the Second Temple. However, there are many texts from Qumran (which are dated to this period) that show a profound spirituality that might be designated "mystical".

We may conclude that the Jews who were attracted to the teaching of Jesus, of the apostles and others in the first decades of Christianity need not have been deprived spiritually. Rather, many of them would have had a personal experience in prayer and liturgy that provided an excellent foundation for appreciating the Christian message. It is beyond the scope of this paper to discuss the variety of their responses to Jesus and Christianity.

III. Aspects of the Biblical Heritage in John

The Christian experience of the divine mystery in human life, as described by John, is mediated by the person and work of Jesus, and his work, consummated in his "hour". This "hour" is the series of events from the Last Supper, passion and death to the resurrection and sending of the Holy Spirit, considered in their profound unity. A Greek verb rendered "to be lifted up" was used to show that the humiliation of crucifixion is but the negative prelude to the positive exaltation that allows Jesus to release the Spirit upon the world (see 7:39). "As Moses lifted up the serpent in the wilderness (Num. 21:9), so must the Son of man be lifted up so that whoever believes in him may have eternal life" (3:14, see 8:28; 12:31-33). Thus faith, as a divinely-given insight and a human response, is associated intimately with eternal life. John states: "This is eternal life, that they may know you, the only true God, and Jesus Christ whom you have sent" (17:3). The Hebrews experienced God's presence and work in their midst within the covenant framework and especially in the Temple. Because John presents Jesus within the matrix of the Judaism of his day, it is important to discuss his references to these realities of Jewish life.

a. The Temple

The prologue (Jn. 1:1-18) moves from a reflection on the creation hymn of Genesis (1:1-2:4) to the Word's presence as light and life among the chosen people (1:9-13). "The Word became flesh and pitched his tent among us, full of grace and truth; we have seen his glory, glory as of the only Son from the Father" (1:14). In these statements the poet draws heavily on themes from the book of Exodus.[25] He explains the Incarnation of the Word by referring to the tent of meeting constructed in the wilderness to house the ark of the covenant. The phrase "grace and truth (fidelity)", which may constitute a hendiadys "faithful loving-kindness", is associated with the covenant and the divine attributes revealed to Moses (Ex. 34:6-7). The title "glory" designates the impressive, illuminating presence of God in the tent of meeting (see Ex. 40:34-40). Thus, John harks back to the Sinai experience of Israel in order to describe the impact of Jesus upon "those who believe in his name" (1:12).

The intimacy of the Word with God (1:1-2) is now understood as a father-son relationship. Taking flesh (human nature), this unique Son has made the Father known in a new way (1:18). A solemn statement develops this theme for the community of those following Jesus. "Amen, amen, I say to you (plural), you will see heaven opened, and the angels of God ascending and descending upon the Son of man" (1:51). This text alludes to Jacob's dream (Gen. 28:12), after which the patriarch recognizes a particular place to be "the house of God (Beth-El), the gate of heaven" (28:17). John teaches that the new place for the ministry of angels is the Son of man, whose task is twofold: to make the Father known and to offer life to all, after making reconciliation through the forgiveness of sin (1:29). "When I am lifted up, I will draw all human beings to myself" (12:32).

The Fourth Gospel frequently uses the Temple as the frame of reference for understanding the mission of Jesus. As "Lamb of God", he is the victim to be offered (1:29); Jesus declares that his body is the Temple (*naos*, sanctuary) that he himself will raise up (2:19-22). As good shepherd, Jesus exercises a priestly function on behalf of his flock. "I lay down my life that I may take it up again . . . . " (10:17-18). On the feast of Hanukkah, commemorating the rededication of the Temple and consecration of a new altar in 164 B.C.E. (1 Maccabees 4:41-51, see Jn. 10:22), Jesus states that the Father consecrated him and sent him into the world (10:36, see 17:19). The sabbath and several great feasts celebrated in the Temple become the

occasion for John to present facets of Jesus' mission. John situates the
death of Jesus at the time the lambs were offered in the daily sacrifice
for the forgiveness of sin. The paschal lambs were sacrificed at this
time in preparation for the Passover meal. Like them (Ex. 12:46) not
one of his bones would be broken (Jn. 19:36). To understand what
John wishes to teach about Jesus, his signs and teachings as well as his
"hour", one must know the practices associated with Temple worship,
wherein the majority of Jews of the day found intimacy with God.[26]

As this outline shows, the Temple is the scene for several sections
of the Fourth Gospel, and allusions are made to its practices
elsewhere. In contrast, the term "covenant" is never used by John
and only in recent years have scholars noticed the importance of this
theme for Johannine theology.

b. The Covenant

In an important study on the mystery of divine Love, André Feuillet
investigates the doctrine of covenant in the Jewish Scriptures; he
remarks that, as lived by prophets and psalmists, it implies mutual
possession and joy full of love that makes one think of the "most
authentic Christian mysticism". This experience of the covenant
unites harmoniously the desire to possess God and to enjoy his presence and the desire to serve God by working for the realization of the
divine plan of salvation.[27] Because we have access to these ancient
times only through prophets, psalmists and sages, it should be noted
that many must have followed their lead, striving consistently for this
deep communion with God as they grappled with the ambiguities and
temptations of their age. Unlike the tendency of some to escape from
"the world" by seeking an other-worldly salvation in the divine, the
teachers of Israel tried to unite contemplation and action. The call of
Moses and the other prophets to experience intimacy with God is
always completed by a mission to revive fidelity to the covenant and
its commandments among their contemporaries.

Feuillet notes that, in biblical times, relations between God and
people are first communitarian, whereas the Johannine writings are
above all personal. Then he balances this observation by commenting that, among these Jews, piety evolved toward "personalism" – and
John's personalism does not lose sight of the Church.[28]   One
presumes that the last clause is intended as an understatement! By
positing two sources for John, Rudolf Bultmann and his disciples have
tried to show that the ecclesial and sacramental themes that pervade
the Fourth Gospel derive from a later stage of the Gospel's redaction.
However, when one moves away from a search for Hellenistic,
Gnostic and Mandaean parallels (the background of John according

to Bultmann) to a setting for John within the matrix of Palestinian Judaism, it becomes inconceivable to pit the individual against the community. Jews knew that the community provided the authenticating context for interpreting the Scriptures and living the divine mandate to "be holy as I, the Lord your God, am holy" (Lev. 19:2). There were great differences among those aspiring to leadership during the century before the Romans destroyed the Temple; some groups indeed called for a re-commitment to *their* model of living the covenant (e.g. the Qumran community) but no one is recorded as advocating a hermetic existence. John knew that "salvation is from the Jews" (4:22); from these roots he challenged his listeners (readers) to be born from above (3:3-8) so that they would belong to the family that will "worship the Father in spirit and truth" (4:23). This phrase "spirit and truth" is a hendiadys which points to the Spirit of truth, "the Paraclete whom the Father will send in my name, who will teach you (plural) all things . . . " (14:25-26), see 16:15). John certainly stresses that each person is called to experience the mystery of divine love in a profound, interior way. He also teaches that this Trinitarian indwelling must lead to a life of obedience to the new commandment, which is social. The challenge "Love one another" in imitation of Jesus' love and self-giving is followed by another statement. "By this all men will know that you are my disciples, if you have love for one another" (13:34-35; see 15:12). In the "high priestly prayer" of Jesus at the Last Supper the Christian community is called to live in imitation of the unity that is God. Jesus gives the reason for this life of harmony: "so that the world may believe that you have sent me" (17:21).[29]

Feuillet offers a very important insight when he posits that the reciprocal formula of the covenant is the background for the Johannine clauses of mutual exchange between God and the faithful. As we noted, "I will be your God and you shall be my people" is found in the promises of Jeremiah (31:31-34) and Ezekiel (36:22-30), upon which the Qumran and New Testament theology of a new covenant draws. During the Exile, when the Torah was not the basis for the public life of Jews to the extent it had been in the First Temple period, the prophets emphasized its value for developing sensitivity of conscience. Each person was responsible for his or her own lot, based on obedience to the commandments or rejection of their demands (see Ez. 18:1-32). Thus the Torah became the basis for growing maturity of the community and its members in God's service. A new experience of the spiritual order was described as "putting my Torah within them" (Jer. 31:33) or as a new heart and a new spirit (Ez. 36:26).[30]

Very appropriately, John's first use of the reciprocal formula occurs in the discourse of Jesus on "the bread of life". This takes place at Passover time (6:4) when Jesus' sign of multiplying loaves and fishes evokes memories of the divine gift of manna. This discourse moves from a call for faith that brings intimacy with Jesus (6:35-50) to hints about a meal wherein the sacrificial self-giving of Jesus will be experienced (6:51-58). At that time the disciples and other listeners were ignorant of the way this would be accomplished. The words are shocking: "He who eats my flesh and drinks my blood remains in me and I in him" (6:56). The only other passage where precisely this reciprocal formula occurs is in the context of the allegory of the vine and the branches (probably evoked by the "blessing for the fruit of the vine" in the Jewish meal). "Remain in me and I in you. As a branch cannot bear fruit by itself, unless it remains in the vine, neither can you, unless you remain in me . . . . " (15:4-10).[31]

The Greek word "and" in John 15:4 should be understood as making a comparison: "Remain in me *as* I in you". The priority of Jesus' presence in the disciples is thus emphasized; he makes their presence in him possible. As in the Jewish Scriptures, the Gospel postulates that a moral response must flow from this covenant bond.[32] The fruit of good works will redound to the Father's glory (15:8). The Father's love is the pattern for Jesus' love of his disciples and their response must be modelled on the obedient love of Jesus. "If you keep my commandments, you will remain in my love, just as I have kept my Father's commandments and remain in his love" (15:10). The parallel between Jesus' intimacy with the Father and the call for the Christian community to initiate this dynamic life of love within the mystery of divine unity is possible because "they are in us" (17:21). Jesus explained to Jude: "If someone loves me, he will keep my word, and my Father will love him, and we will come to him and make our home in him" (14:23).[33]

Because of the similar vocabulary, McCaffrey links John 14:2-3 and 23; this verse, "in my Father's house are many rooms. . . . I go to prepare a place for you" (14:2), is a promise of the disciples' unity with Jesus in the Father. "The activity of Jesus in Jn. 14:2-3 is directed solely to the disciples as a group, or to the community which they represent . . . In Jn. 14:23, however, Jesus will come with the Father to make his dwelling (*monē*) in every believer. As believers have dwelling-places (*monai*) with the Father in union with Jesus in Jn. 14:2-3, so Jesus and the Father have an abiding-place (*monē*) in every believer in Jn. 14:23. The plural form *monai* of Jn 14:2-3 emphasizes the individuality of the places which all believers have with Jesus in the Father. Inversely, the singular of Jn. 14:23 emphasizes the dwelling-place of the Father with Jesus in each disciple individually. In Jn. 14:2-3 the Father becomes the spiritual area where the whole community of believers dwells individually in union with Jesus; in Jn. 14:23 each individual believer becomes the spiritual area where the Father dwells in union with Jesus."[34]

Because the immediate context (14:18-20 and 25-26) has the second person plural, it is presumed that McCaffrey uses the term "individual" without a nuance of separateness from the community. The response to the mystery of divine love must indeed be personal and focused on the Father giving his only Son (3:16), yet this life with God is experienced in communion with others, now as well as in the fullness of eternal life. John uses this term "eternal life" to describe both the indwelling of God in the faithful (14:23) and for its eschatological fulfillment precisely because the psalmists and prophets had grasped that the deepest meaning of "life" is communion with the living God. Perhaps the Hebrews remained vague about the human situation after physical death because their neighbors had contaminated their natural human hope with idolatrous practices. However, from the second century B.C.E. the predecessors of the Pharisees and Essenes (with whom the Qumran Scrolls are associated by most scholars) proclaimed resurrection of the body and/or immortality.

c. The Commandments

In a careful examination of the Johannine teaching concerning Torah (the Greek translation *nomos* means "Law"), Severino Pancaro shows that "keep my word (words)" in John 14:23 relates directly to faith, whereas "keep my commandments" refers to love and its obligations. "When Jesus asks his disciples to keep his word, he is asking them not to abandon the 'truth' they have accepted, but to cling to it and allow it to permeate and transform their lives; when he asks them to keep his *entolai* (commandments), he is referring to his *entolē* of brotherly love and asks them to allow the love he has made possible to radiate in all their actions . . . . Faith and love cannot be separated.[35] As divine gift and human response, faith is the foundation for Trinitarian indwelling in the community of Jesus' followers.

The Jewish understanding of morality is based on imitation of God, expressed as a commandment (Lev. 19:2) and presented in narrative as the ideal (Ex. 34:6-7). Because the God of Israel is known only after the revelation associated with the covenant, the divine mystery must be approached in the Torah and other parts of the Bible. The commandments in the Torah of Moses provide the practical norms whereby people structure their lives and teach their children. Thus people know where to go in serving God (*halakhah*). The other part of .

God's instruction is the record of divine dealings with the patriarchs and matriarchs and subsequent generations of Israelites. This narration (*haggadah*) presents insights that assist listeners to imitate God's righteousness and love.

The New Testament writers follow this pattern of offering practical principles for responding to the challenges of life and, by focusing on the person, deeds and teachings of Jesus, they present the ideal for imitating God. Thus, the Fourth Gospel shows how Jesus fulfills the Father's commandment (10:18; 12:49-50; 14:30-31; 15:10) and then, in the Last Supper discourses, he challenges his disciples (13:34-35; 14:15, 21; 15:10, 12, 14, 17).

The universality of divine love is shown in the declaration that "God sent his Son into the world, not to condemn the world, but that the world might be saved through him" (3:17). This deliverance from evil is a gift that must be accepted freely; the response of faith brings each person into the light, "that it may be seen clearly that his deeds have been done in God" (3:21). Born from above of water and the Spirit (3:5), each believer requires spiritual nourishment through the living bread (6:48-50), shared in the sacrificial banquet of the new covenant. The sacrificial self-giving of Jesus brings the community to understand the meaning of his statement "the bread which I shall give for the life of the world is my flesh" (6:51). Although a new commandment might be given without allusion to covenant, this would seem unlikely for those steeped in the Jewish way of life. The servant's task of washing a guest's feet before a meal was performed by Jesus (13:1-20) and the meal was underway when Jesus proclaimed: "A new commandment I give to you, that you love one another; even *as I have loved you*, so you should love one another" (13:34).[36] The many acts whereby Jesus served others must be consummated on the cross before the gift of the Spirit can come upon the community of Jesus' followers (see 7:37-39). Then they will be enabled to imitate the pattern of the Master's love in their lives.[37] The death of Jesus manifests the extent of the Father's love for the world (3:16) and the total response made by Jesus to the divine will (4:34; 6:38, etc.) for love of humanity (12:32-33). The narration of Jesus' ministry and passion provides insights for the community of believers concerning the manner in which mutual love must be practiced. The reciprocation of loving service with the covenant community should have a unique quality, complementing the outgoing love demanded by the Torah (Lev. 19:18) and the early Christian tradition of Jesus' teaching concerning enemies. John's silence concerning love of enemies could not be attributed to ignorance (see Ex. 23:4-5) and one may presume that his community knew at least some aspects of Jesus's teaching on this topic. It was impossible to record everything that Jesus did or taught (21:25). The exhausting demands of the Gospel as Christians face the world at large cannot be faced alone; each person should be assured of the replenishment of spiritual energies from within the community of faith, first through the sacraments and prayer and secondly through experiencing and sharing love that strives to imitate Christ's self-giving. Although the ideal of mutual love should be part of married and family life for all peoples, its consistent achievement requires the presence and gifts of the Holy Spirit. The Christian tradition sees Jesus' gift of the Spirit to be fulfillment of Ezekiel's oracle: "I will put my spirit within you and cause you to walk in my statutes and be careful to observe my ordinances" (Ez. 36:26-27, see Jn. 14:25-26; 16:12-15; Romans 8:2). Strength to keep the commandments comes from the Spirit.[38]

d. The New Covenant

Both Jeremiah (31:34) and Ezekiel (36:25) proclaim that God's new bestowal of life will be accompanied by the forgiveness of sin. To be capable of responding to the Torah and its commandments from interior, personal conviction the burden of the believer's previous sins must be removed. John teaches that this is accomplished by Jesus (1:29) and is experienced through the ministry of those imbued with the Holy Spirit (20:22-23)[39] The tremendous responsibility of those called to continue Christ's ministry of forgiveness is clear from the authority he bestowed on them. "If you forgive the sins of any, they are forgiven; if you retain the sins of any, they are retained" (20:23). The community ministers to its members at times when reconciliation is needed.

Jeremiah's promise of the new covenant, with the Torah written upon the hearts of the people, emphasizes the direct manner in which God's word will be communicated to each person. "No longer shall each man teach his neighbor and each one his brother, saying: 'know the Lord'. For they shall all know me, from the least of them to the greatest, says the Lord" (31:34). According to the Hebrew tradition this knowledge is a personal experience of intimacy with God, so profound that the marriage relationship is its best analogue in the human order.

This may be one of the texts to which reference is made in John's Gospel: "It is written in the prophets, 'And they shall be taught by God'" (Jn. 6:45). The Johannine allegory of the good shepherd, which draws heavily upon motifs in Jeremiah and Ezekiel, explains that the sheep know the voice of their shepherd, who calls each by name (10:3), and they follow him in trust. "The good shepherd lays down his life for the sheep" (10:11). After the second declaration "I am the good shepherd," Jesus introduced the reciprocal nature of the bond with his followers. "I know my own and my own know me, as the Father knows me and I know the Father" (10:14-15). The personal intimacy of this relationship is indicated in the post-resurrection scene when Mary Magdalene recognized Jesus only after he called her by name (20:16). The covenant and the knowledge of the Lord that it offers is understood to be patterned after the very manner in which the Father and Son know each other. Thus does the Son reveal the Father (1:18), enabling those who believe in his name to become children of God (1:12); they have eternal life, which is the gift of lasting communion with God. Just as the Son, dwelling in the bosom of the Father, reveals him, so too does the typical Christian manifest Christ to the world. Perhaps this is one of the reasons for the anonymity of the Beloved Disciple. He exemplifies the person whose union with the Master in the meal is the basis for communicating the divine message of forgiveness and reciprocal love (see 13:23).

Long after the tribes of the Northern Kingdom had been deported and lost, Jeremiah expressed the hope that the new covenant would be with the house of Israel *and* the house of Judah (31:31). Other prophets explicitly taught that foreigners would be integrated into God's people (e.g. Isaiah 56:3-7; Zechariah 2:15; 8:22-23; 14:16-21). Like the Qumran community, the disciples of Jesus recognized that the twelve tribes were represented symbolically by their leaders (see Matthew 19:28; Luke 22:29-30). Although this symbolism is clear in the Johannine Apocalypse (7:1-10); 21:10-14), the Fourth Gospel does not seem to play with it. However, both the ingathering of God's people and the inclusion of Samaritans and Gentiles in the new covenant can be traced from the prologue (1:1-18) to the commission of Peter to nurture sheep and lambs in Christ's name (21:15-17). Fields are ripe for the harvest (4:35-37), sheep beyond the fold must hear the Good Shepherd's voice (10:16) and the dispersed children of God will be gathered into one (11:51-52). This is clearly another aspect of the Johannine teaching of unity, important because it shows the outgoing nature of Christian spiritual and moral life. Whereas others might seek profound communion with God to be different from the common lot of humanity, John presents Jesus as one who reveals God's gifts to all. The vocation of Abraham and the prophetic vision for the future might be interpreted differently by others but John's insistence on the witness of a believing community has a special value. Oral presentation of a believer's faith must be accompanied by a life of mutual love within the context of a shared experience. "By this is my Father glorified, that you bear much fruit and become my disciples" (15:8). Thus is enthusiasm to preach *about* the ideal balanced by an insistence that discipleship is a life-long process and the new commandment an ongoing challenge.

Conclusion

John's message about union with God, prayer and their implications for the Christian life contain riches that require further exploration. Two important points can be made from this study: 1.) The same spiritual blessings are open to all, mediated through the paschal mystery of Jesus. 2.) They are explained in terms of typically Jewish institutions and symbols. Whether or not we apply the term "mystical" to the Christian experience described by John, we maintain that he offers a profound and comprehensive teaching, one capable of offsetting elitist tendencies that may plague various other systems of spirituality. While John has a universality that touches a common chord with Buddhist and other ways of pursuing perfection, the roots of his message are in the biblical heritage. This strongly suggests that John can be appreciated most fully when seen in the light of this background. Moreover, a deep sense of continuity can be noted as one investigates the Jewish use of the ancient biblical traditions and then moves to the spiritual message of the Fourth Gospel.

Notes

1   See Maurice Wiles, *The Spiritual Gospel: The Interpretation of the Fourth Gospel in the Early Church.* (Cambridge University Press, 1960). While acknowledging the importance of the Epistles, I limit my study to the *Gospel* of John.

2   Definitions are taken from *Webster's Ninth New Collegiate Dictionary* (Springfield: Merriam-Webster, 1983) p. 785. See John Welch, "Mysticism", *New Dictionary of Theology* (ed. J. Komonchak). Wilmington: Michael Glazier, 1987, p. 694.

3   William Temple, *Readings in St. John's Gospel* (First and Second Series). (London: Macmillan, 1950) p. xx, see p. 91.

4   Adolfo Omodeo, *La Mistica Giovannea: Saggio Critico.* (Bari: Laterza, 1929) p. 4, note 1.

5   Benjamin W. Bacon, *The Gospel of the Hellenists.* (New York, 1933). See the review of shifts in the search for sources in J. A. T. Robinson, *The Priority of John.* (London: SCM, 1985) p. 36-122, with extensive bibliography.

6   Albert Schweitzer, *La Mystique de l'Apôtre Paul* (Paris 1962), p. 282-316.

7   See James H. Charlesworth (ed), *John and Qumran.* (London: Geoffrey Chapman, 1972) and C. K. Barrett, *The Gospel of John and Judaism.* London: SPCK, 1975.

8   J. A. T. Robinson, *Redating the New Testament* (London: SCM Press 1976); see Francis J. Moloney, "The Fourth Gospel's presentation of Jesus as 'the Christ' and J. A. T. Robinson's Redating," *Downside Review* 95 (1977) p. 239-253.

9   C. K. Barrett, *The Gospel according to St. John* (London: 1978) p. 86.

10 *The Way* 18 (1978) p. 25-35.

11 Ermanno Ancilli and Maurizio Paparozzi (ed.), *La Mistica: Fenomenologia e riflessione teologica* (Rome: Citta Nuova Editrice, 1984), two volumes.

12 Bruno Maggioni, "La mistica di Giovanni Evangelista", *La Mistica* I. p. 223-250.

13 Marianne M. Thompson, "Eternal life in the Gospel of John", *Ex Auditu* 5 (1989) p. 36. See C. F. D. Moule, "The individualism of the Fourth Gospel", *Novum Testamentum* 5 (1962) p. 171-190 and J. A. T. Robinson, op. cit. p. 325-329. Robinson would prefer to talk of the personalism rather than of the individualism of John. John O'Grady's essay "Individualism and Johannine ecclesiology", *Biblical Theology Bulletin* 5 (1975) p. 227-261 is too strong in pitting the individual against the community. He discusses "Johannine Mysticism" on p. 238-240.

14   See William J. Fulco, *Maranatha: Reflections on the Mystical Theology of John the Evangelist.* (Ramsey: Paulist Press, 1973), L. William Countryman, *The Mystical Way in the Fourth Gospel: Crossing Over to God.* (Philadelphia: Fortress, 1987) and George A. Maloney, *Entering into the Heart of Jesus: Meditations on the Indwelling Trinity in St. John's Gospel.* (New York: Alba House, 1988).

15   The relation between faith and love as commandments is clear in the great prayer of Jews taken from Deuteronomy 6:4-5. "Hear, O Israel: the Lord our God is one Lord and you shall love the Lord your God with all your heart, and with all your soul, and with all your might." The call to exclusive faith in the God of Israel is followed by a comprehensive commitment to his service. See Kurt Hruby "The proclamation of the unity of God as actualization of the Kingdom", *Standing Before God* (ed. A. Finkel and L. Frizzell. New York: Ktav, 1981) p. 183-193.

16   See my article "Law at the service of humankind", *SIDIC* (Rome) 19 (n. 3 - 1986) p. 4-7.

17   Aspects of this statement are discussed in my article "Commitment in the Hebrew Bible: Moses, Elijah and Jeremiah," *Journal of Dharma* 12 (1987) p. 218-227.

18   Originally this would be understood, not as stressing a metaphysical reality, but as an assurance of God's presence with his people. See Pamela Vermes, "Buber's understanding of the divine Name related to Bible, Targum and Midrash", *Journal of Jewish Studies* 24 (1973) p. 147-166.

19   The covenant framework for understanding John is presented at length by André Feuillet, *Le Mystère de l'Amour divin dans la Théologie johannique.* (Paris: Gabalda, 1972) and Edward Malatesta, *Interiority and Covenant: A Study of einai en and menein en in the First Letter of John* (Rome: Biblical Institute Press, 1978). However, neither posits Ex. 34:6-7 as background to Johannine theology of love and the covenant theme. Feuillet stresses Hosea and the Song of Songs.

20   Fulco, op. cit. p. 5. The failings of priestly leaders in the time of Jesus and the early Church are discussed by Craig A. Evans, "Jesus' action in the Temple: cleansing as portent of destruction?" *Catholic Biblical Quarterly* 51 (1989) p. 237-270.

21   See my article "Pilgrimage: a study of the biblical experience", *Jeevadhara* 12 (1982) p. 358-367.

22   See Asher Finkel, "Sabbath as the way to *shalom* in the biblical tradition", *Journal of Dharma* 11 (1986) p. 115-123.

23   See James H. Charlesworth (ed), *Pseudepigrapha of the Old Testament.* (Garden City: Doubleday, 1983 and 1985).

24   Max Kadushin, *The Rabbinic Mind.* (New York: Blaisdell, 1965), 194-272.

25   See A. T. Hanson, "John 1:14-18 and Exodus 34", in *The New Testament Interpretation of Scripture* (London: SPCK 1980) p. 97-109.

26 For a recent discussion of pertinent texts, see James McCaffrey, *The House with Many Rooms: The Temple Theme of Jn. 14, 2-3)* (Rome: Pontifical Biblical Institute, 1988). See A. T. Hanson, "The theme of Christ as the true Temple in the Fourth Gospel" in *The New Testament Interpretation of Scripture.* (London: SPCK 1980) p. 110-121 and Gale Yee, *Jewish Feasts and the Gospel of John* (Collegeville: Liturgical Press, 1989).

27 Feuillet, op. cit. p. 99.

28 Ibid. p. 100.

29 See my article based on John, "A Catholic reflection on mission", *Journal of Dharma* 6 (1981) p. 141-150. Feuillet discusses Christian fraternity as the ultimate goal of divine love on pages 109-111.

30 See Malatesta, op. cit. for a complete study of the biblical theme of "interiority".

31 Besides Feuillet and Malatesta's works, the theme "to remain" is studied by David Mealand, "The language of mystical union in the Johannine Writings", *Downside Review* 95 (1977) p. 19-34. He cites Lev. 26:12 as background for John's reciprocal phrase but does not note that it is a covenant formula.

32 This paragraph draws on Feuillet, op. cit. p. 101.

33 See Royce G. Gruenler, *The Trinity in the Gospel of John: Thematic Commentary on the Fourth Gospel.* (Grand Rapids: Baker House, 1986).

34 McCaffrey, op. cit. p. 165.

35 S. Pancaro, The Law in the Fourth Gospel (Leiden: E. J. Brill, 1975) p. 450. See Urban von Wahlde, *The Johannine Commandments:* 1 John and the Struggle for the Johannine Tradition (Mahwah: Paulist Press, 1990).

36 Explanations concerning how this commandment is "new" are listed by W. Schrage, *The Ethics of the New Testament* (Philadelphia: Fortress, 1988) p. 314-319.

37 See Alphonse Humbert, "L'observance des commandements dans les écrits johanniques", *Studia Moralia* 1 (1963) p. 187-219.

38 A thorough investigation of Johannine pneumatology is offered by Gary M. Burge, *The Anointed Community: The Holy Spirit in the Johannine Tradition* (Grand Rapids: Eerdmans, 1987).

39 On this theme, see Martin Hasitschka, *Befreiung Von Sünde nach dem Johannesevangelium: eine bibeltheologische Untersuchung.* (Innsbruck: Tyrolia Verlag, 1989).

Vision and Death at Ostia

G. R. Evans

In Book IX of his *Confessions*, Augustine describes the mystical experience he shared with his mother at Ostia, where he and his companions were resting before they embarked for Africa.[1] The episode
occurred at an obvious turning-point in Augustine's life. After his
conversion he and his friends had retired for a time to Cassiciacum,
where they had lived in the "philosophical retirement" Augustine had
always coveted, and spent their time in conversation about such
subjects as order in the universe and the nature of eternal bliss.
When they felt themselves ready, Augustine, his friend Alypius and
his natural son Adeodatus returned to Milan, where they were
baptized (ix.vi.14). Now they were to go back to the region of north
Africa from which Augustine had come to live a monastic life there, as
he proposed. He was, in other words, now embarking upon the
Christian life for which he had hitherto been preparing. He describes
the mood of serenity and joyfulness in which he and his mother stood
side by side, leaning over the window-sill which overlooked the court-
yard of the house where they were staying (ix.x.23). It was a moment
for taking stock, for consciously putting the past behind one and
looking forward (Philippians 3:13).
    Several aspects of this famous moment of mystical experience are
peculiarly its own, and I want to try to set them in context here. It
was shared. It took place in the course of conversation. It is related
to us by an Augustine who was to lose his mother within days of the
event, entirely without warning, from a fever of which she showed no
signs when they had their talk. The experience is therefore colored
for ever for him, and for his readers, by subsequent events.
    As to the conversation: Augustine says that his account in the
Confessions is not given in the exact words they spoke; he has merely
tried to convey the essence of what was said. That is important,
because his description of what happened is full of phrases and echoes
of Plotinus,[2] and we cannot think his mother to have been capable of
exchanging philosophical tags with him. Yet he gives the impression
that the talk was not one-sided. Undoubtedly Augustine led the way,

but he constantly says 'we', 'our thoughts', 'we spoke', as though there was a real exchange of shared experience. The theme with which they began was one which they had discussed at Cassiciacum, that is, the nature of the blessed life. Augustine says that they began by agreeing that no bodily pleasure, however great, could be comparable with the happiness of that life. Then they followed the neoplatonic way of ascending in thought through all the 'degrees' of the material world, up to the heavenly bodies. As they climbed they reflected in increasing wonder and with growing ardour on the marvel of creation. That brought them to the contemplation of their own souls, and to the point where it seemed possible to 'pass beyond' themselves and to reach out towards the eternal Wisdom by which all things are made. For a moment, says Augustine, so great was their longing, they touched it. Then they found themselves back in the world of sense, where the words they spoke were heard and understood in an ordinary way, not as the Word of God is heard.

He does not say how they compared notes or were able to be sure that both had had the same experience. There seems simply to have been a strong common sense of having been in the same place. Perhaps Augustine, at the remove of several years, and with his philosopher's conception of what had happened, is giving us his own picture and assuming his mother's to have been the same. He was working on the *De Genesi and Litteram*, in which he gives his mature account of the mutual intellectual contemplation of God and the soul which is heavenly bliss, at the time when he finished the *Confessions*, and there had certainly been much progress and refinement in his own thinking in this area since he and his mother had shared the actual experience at Ostia. But he tells us that some progress was made at the time. The return to ordinary language did not bring the experience to an end. They went on talking. Suppose, they said, all these aids to understanding and pointers to God which we see and hear around us in the world were silent, and the soul itself could cease to attend to the clamour of its own thoughts and pass beyond itself, so that we might hear God speak to us directly, not through his creation; suppose that this state of direct communication with God were to continue, the brief moment Augustine and his mother had known extended for eternity; would not this be itself the bliss of heaven?

This shared, conversational mystical experience is conveyed by Augustine — unavoidably — in words, but with an art which seeks to put words in their place, that is, to show their inadequacy for their high purpose here. This sense that words would not do may account in part for his willingness to reconstruct their conversation in his own words; he clearly did not feel that the actual words they used were important, or themselves the vehicle of the experience, or even the means of their sharing it.

If that is the case, it may perhaps be accounted for in part by Augustine's loss of his mother so soon afterwards. Verbal communication was broken within days, and broken for ever in this life. But Augustine was left with a strong sense of something accomplished and completed. At the end of their talk, Monica had said, and here he reports her exact words, that she herself had a sense that her work in this world was done, and that she had no more to hope for here. Her only reason for wanting to go on living had been to see Augustine become a Christian. God has granted her wish; she sees him now God's servant, despising this world's allurements. 'What is left for me to do in this world?' she asked him (ix.x.26). The emphasis Augustine gives to this exchange in the context of the vision they have just shared shows that it stuck in his mind as a significant part of the whole experience.

It is the more notable, in contrast to this confidence in a continuing union in God, which goes beyond words and does not depend on their meeting in this life again; and this assurance that Monica herself was ready to die and her life fulfilled; that he should give us so many following paragraphs about his struggle to come to terms with her death. Here we are given the counterpart to the shining experience at the window, and the setting in which it remained for Augustine in the years to come. The philosopher largely falls away. After an edifying word about Monica's willingness to die in Italy, where she could not be buried as she had always wished, beside her husband, which is seen as showing that she had been able to renounce even this last 'vain desire' (ix.xi.28). Augustine describes the common experiences of the bereaved in any age and culture. He was bewildered to find that a death which he feels he should, in the circumstances, have been able to accept with more than equanimity, with joy, should have caused him so much pain.

The first task was to comfort Adeodatus, for the boy was young enough to show his grief in tears without restraint (ix.xii.29). Augustine says he wanted to cry like a child, too. But he held back the tears because they seemed inappropriate to the great hope into which they were all confident his mother had now entered. Friends and fellow-Christians came to offer their condolences, and Augustine kept up a conversation with them in which he believes he entirely hid his grief from them (ix.xii.31). Inwardly he was fighting the waves of sorrow which swept over him. His Christian pride was hurt. He says that he was grieved by his own weakness (ix.xii.31). He was able to keep from weeping while the body was carried out for burial and during

the Eucharist which was offered for her at the graveside before she
was lowered into the earth. He tried praying for comfort and seemed
to get no answer. He went to the baths, in the hope that the act
would purge his mind of its anxiety. He came back in the same state
as before. Only after he had slept and woken up unguarded, and
found that he was now able to enter again into his feelings for his
mother, did he begin to weep. He did not weep for long, and he
confesses it as a sin (ix.xii.33).

He tried to analyse the reasons for this sorrow, which he continued
to feel shameful. His loss had been sudden, and he was suffering
from shock. He had lost, not only the person but the preciousness of
life together. He was bereft of all the comfort he had had from his
mother's presence and her kindnesses to him. In short, he was
grieving for himself, and he took ordinary human comfort from the
kinds of thought the bereaved draw on in any society. He had done
for her in her last illness all that he could. She had said that she could
not remember his having said any hard word to her all his life. Thus
he sought to reassure himself where she could no longer reassure him
(ix.xii.30).

Now, at the end of this last autobiographical book of the
Confessions, he stands away to the distance of years where he now lives,
and reflects on the value of Christian endeavour for the souls of the
dead. He knows that although his mother lived a good life, she
cannot have lived without sin from the moment of her baptism. He
knows that in strict justice God must condemn her, but he trusts that
in mercy he will not. So there is a place for prayer for her sins, and
for remembering her in the Eucharist, as she herself devoutly wanted
him to do, wherever he was in the world (ix.xi.27).

To take the vision at Ostia out of its relation to Augustine's account
of his mother's death is to take it entirely out of context. Augustine
himself could not separate the two. He sets side by side for us the
ideal of the Christian hope, in the language of the highest intellectual
skills of his day; and the reality of coping with death, with its muddle
and confusion and the difficulty of seeing the hope clearly at all in the
conflict of contrary emotions. The resolution Augustine offers is to
trust himself and his mother to 'our Catholic mother the Church'
(ix.xiii.35); he has found and still finds the common citizenship of the
City of God the best practical comfort, and the sacraments a practical
working bond of love.

Notes

1   See Peter Brown, *Augustine of Hippo* (London, 1967), p. 129 and Henry Chadwick, *Augustine* (Oxford, 1986), p. 69.

2   Chadwick, loc cit.

Francis of Assisi: Nature, Poverty, and the Humanity of Christ

Ewert H. Cousins

In Christian mysticism Francis of Assisi holds a distinctive place. His vision on Mount La Verna in Tuscany in 1224 – of a six-winged Seraph in the form of Christ crucified – was the most celebrated Christian mystical experience in the Middle Ages. It was given a prominent place not only in his biographies, but in art history as well from Giotto into the Renaissance. The vision, along with the accompanying stigmata, was looked upon in early Franciscan literature as God's seal upon Francis' holiness and the life of poverty which he proposed to his Friars.

This vision was by no means an isolated event. It was the climax of a life of visionary mysticism in which images of Christ on the cross evoked in Francis a deep compassion for human suffering and led him to a mystical identification with the crucified Savior. There is reason to claim that Francis' visionary mysticism had more influence in shaping the history of Christian spirituality than any other mystical experience in history. For it brought the humanity of Christ to a central position in Christian consciousness, gave impetus to a method of meditating on the life of Christ, and stimulated a revolution in art and devotion – thus transforming the religious sensibilities of Western Christianity.[1]

Francis' stature as a mystic is not confined to visionary mysticism. At the present time he is probably best known as a nature mystic. In fact, he is looked upon as the prime example of a nature mystic in the entire Christian tradition. The image of Francis as a nature mystic is well supported by the many accounts in his early biographies of his love for God's creatures – for lambs, birds, and even insects. His nature mysticism reached a climax in his composing *The Canticle of Brother Sun*, in which he praised God for, by, and through creatures. It is not surprising, then, that with our emerging ecological consciousness Francis should be declared the patron saint of ecology.[2]

In this study I will examine Francis as both a visionary mystic and a nature mystic. At first glance these two types of mystical experience might seem radically disparate because his visions were of the humanity of Christ and not the cosmic Christ. However, I believe they are deeply related, especially if seen within the dynamics of Francis' spiritual journey. To these two types, I will add a third: Francis' mysticism of poverty. I believe that in Francis and the Franciscan tradition, poverty is not merely a pragmatic factor in the lifestyle of a religious order. For Francis it the primary gateway into the life of renunciation and the primary means of identifying with Christ. As such, it takes on the qualities of mystical consciousness. Moreover, poverty can be seen as the major link between Francis' visionary mysticism and his nature mysticism.

Although I will be focusing on Francis, I will also treat Bonaventure (1217-1274), the great Franciscan theologian, who was Minister General of the Franciscan Order for seventeen years at a critical time in its history. He wrote the most influential biography of Francis, interpreted Francis' mysticism in his own spiritual treatises, and integrated Francis' experience into the tradition of Christian Neoplatonism, which flowed through the Fathers of the Church and medieval theologians. The relation of Francis and Bonaventure is unique in Christian history. Here is a case where one of the greatest mystics had one of the greatest spiritual writers as his authoritative interpreter.

Visionary Mysticism

In dealing with Francis, I am taking the term "visionary mysticism" in a broad sense: to include the wide range of images—both external sense images and internal images from the imagination—which manifest the divine or lead the subject along his or her spiritual journey. It is clear from the latter part of the description that these images differ from ordinary everyday sense images in that they participate in the divine realm, either by directly manifesting it or by activating those deeper energies of the human spirit that draw one towards the divine. These images, then, include dreams and waking fantasies, if they meet the above criteria. In the category of visionary mysticism, I will include auditions, or the hearing of sounds in the context of mystical consciousness. As we shall see, Francis' visions were at times accompanied by auditions, in which God spoke to him, either externally or internally.

As the early biographers witness, throughout his spiritual journey Francis was guided by dreams and visions. Shortly before his conversion to a religious way of life, he was considering setting out on a military career.   He had a dream in which, as his biographer Bonaventure describes, "God in his goodness showed him a large and splendid palace full of military weapons emblazoned with the insignia of Christ's cross." According to Bonaventure, when Francis asked to whom these belonged, "he received the answer from heaven that all these things were for him and his knights."[3]

Unskilled at interpreting such a dream, Francis took it to mean that he should become a soldier; so he set out for Apulia to join a certain count, hoping to win the glory of knighthood. But when he had gone only as far as the next town, he heard during the night, as Bonaventure recounts, "the Lord address him in a familiar way, saying: 'Francis, who can do more for you, a lord or a servant, a rich man or a poor man?'" Francis answered that a lord and a rich man could do more. Then God asked him: "Why, then, are you abandoning the Lord for a servant and the rich God for a poor man?" Bonaventure continues: "Francis replied; *'Lord, what will you have me do?'* (Acts 9:6) *And the Lord answered him: 'Return to your own land'* (Gen. 32:9), because the vision which you have seen foretells a spiritual outcome which will be accomplished in you not by human hands but by divine planning." Bonaventure concludes the episode: *"In the morning* (John 21-4), then, he returned in haste to Assisi, joyous and free of care; already a model of obedience, he awaited the Lord's will."[4]

As we will see below, this is very similar to the incident, recorded in *The Legend of Perugia*, that occurred on the night before Francis composed *The Canticle of Brother Sun*. In both cases it is not clear whether the conversation between God and Francis takes place in a dream or in a waking state and whether God's voice was perceived as an external or an internal communication.[5]

According to Bonaventure, the dream and its interpretation was a turning point in Francis' spiritual journey, for "from that time on he withdrew from the bustle of public business and devoutly begged God in his goodness to show him what he should do." It was during this period of intense prayer that Francis had his first vision of Christ crucified. Bonaventure describes it as follows: "One day while he was praying in such a secluded spot and became totally absorbed in God through his extreme fervor, Jesus Christ appeared to him fastened to the cross."[6]

With great spiritual sensitivity, Bonaventure describes the effect of this vision: "Francis' *soul melted* (Cant. 5:6) at the sight, and the memory of Christ's passion was so impressed on the innermost recesses of his heart that from that hour, whenever Christ's crucifixion came to his mind, he could scarcely contain his tears and sighs, as he later revealed to his companions when he was approaching the end of his life."[7] This was a crucial vision in Francis' spiritual life since it opened the depths of compassion in his spirit and gave direction to his subsequent spiritual journey. It was equally significant in the history of spirituality, for through Francis compassion for the suffering Savior became the hallmark of Western Christian spirituality.

The next mystical experience that Bonaventure records is the audition which Francis heard as he prayed before the crucifix in the church of San Damiano, a short distance outside the walls of Assisi. "While his tear-filled eyes were gazing at the Lord's cross, he heard with his bodily ears a voice coming from the cross, telling him three times: 'Francis, go and repair my house which, as you see, is falling completely into ruin.'"[8]

Bonaventure is very explicit that Francis heard an exterior, not merely an interior voice. He also states that the words produced in Francis an ecstatic mystical state: "Trembling with fear, Francis was amazed at the sound of this astonishing voice, since he was alone in the church; and as he received in his heart the power of the divine words, he fell into a state of ecstasy. Returning to his senses, he prepared to obey."[9] As in the case of the dream of the weapons, Francis responded literally, setting out to repair San Damiano, which was, in fact, falling into ruin. However, as Bonaventure indicates, the injunction was directed principally to Francis' role in building up the Church spiritually.

In addition to these three visionary experiences, Bonaventure lists three other mystical visions of the cross which his Friars had in relation to Francis. Brother Silvester saw a golden cross coming from Francis' mouth, and Brother Pacificus saw Francis' body signed with two flashing swords in the form of a cross. When Francis could not be physically present at a chapter meeting in Arles, Brother Monaldus had a vision of him at the doorway, lifted above the ground with his arms extended on a cross. Bonaventure interpreted the three visions of Francis and the three visions of his Friars as stages leading to the climactic vision of Francis' life: the Six-winged Seraph in the form of Christ crucified. "Behold," Bonaventure says, "these seven visions of the cross of Christ, miraculously shown and manifested to you or about you at different stages of your life. The first six were like steps leading to the seventh in which you have found your final rest."[10]

Francis' vision of the Seraph occurred on Mount La Verna in Tuscany two years before his death. Before the vision he had been fasting for a lengthy period and devoting himself to prayer. Because of the importance of the details of the vision, I will give Bonaventure's account in full:

> On a certain morning about the feast of the Exaltation of the Cross, while Francis was praying on the mountainside, he saw a Seraph with six fiery and shining wings descend from the height of heaven. And when in swift flight the Seraph had reached a spot in the air near the man of God, there appeared between the wings the figure of a man crucified, with his hands and feet extended in the form of a cross and fastened to a cross. Two of the wings were lifted above his head, two were extended for flight and two covered his whole body. When Francis saw this, he was overwhelmed and his heart was flooded with a mixture of joy and sorrow. He rejoiced because of the gracious way Christ looked upon him under the appearance of the Seraph, but the fact that he was fastened to a cross *pierced his soul with a sword* of compassionate sorrow. (Luke 2:35)[11]

After describing the vision, Bonaventure gives a detailed account of Francis' reception of the stigmata:

> As the vision disappeared, it left in his heart a marvelous ardor and imprinted on his body markings that were no less marvelous. Immediately the marks of nails began to appear in his hands and feet just as he had seen a little before in the figure of the man crucified. His hands and feet seemed to be pierced through the center by nails, with the heads of the nails appearing on the inner side of the hands and the upper side of the feet and their points on the opposite sides. The heads of the nails in his hands and his feet were round and black; their points were oblong and bent as if driven back with a hammer, and they emerged from the flesh and stuck out beyond it. Also his right side, as if pierced with a lance, was marked with a red wound from which his sacred blood often flowed, moistening his tunic and underwear.[12]

Although at La Verna Francis had an external mystical vision, the power of this vision penetrated his soul to the point that he had a mystical identification with Christ which manifested itself in the appearance of the stigmata. In *The Soul's Journey into God*, Bonaventure describes this mystical identification as follows: "There is no other path but through the burning love of the Crucified, a love which so transformed Paul into Christ when he *was carried up to the third heaven* (2 Cor. 12:2) that he could say: *With Christ I am nailed to the cross. I live, now not I, but Christ lives in me*" (Gal. 2:20). Bonaventure continues: "This love also so absorbed the soul of Francis that his spirit shone through his flesh when for two years before his death he carried in his body the sacred stigmata of the passion."[13]

Although this identification took place on La Verna in a miraculous way, the previous visions, as Bonaventure pointed out, as well as Francis' way of life led to this climax. For example, drawing from his imagination, Francis dramatized scenes from the life of Christ. In 1223 he created a Christmas crib for midnight Mass in Greccio: "He had a crib prepared, hay carried in and an ox and an ass led to the place.   The friars are summoned, the people come, the forest resounds with their voices and that venerable night is rendered brilliant and solemn by a multitude of bright lights and by resonant and harmonious hymns of praise." Bonaventure continues: "The man of God stands before the crib, filled with affection, bathed in tears and overflowing with joy. A solemn Mass is celebrated over the crib, with Francis as deacon chanting the holy Gospel."[14]

This kind of imaginative dramatization led to a cultivation in the Franciscan milieu of a new form of meditation on the life of Christ, which I have termed "the mysticism of the historical event."[15] This form of meditation was latent in the New Testament. In the twelfth century it was cultivated in the monasteries by Anselm of Canterbury, Bernard of Clairvaux, and Aelred of Rievaulx. However it reached its full development through Francis' inspiration in the Franciscan milieu—in Bonaventure's *Tree of Life* and the anonymous *Meditations on the Life of Christ*. In this kind of meditation one vividly imagines an event in Christ's life, observes it as an eye-witness, and even enters into it as an actor in the drama. For example, Bonaventure guides the reader to become an actor in the event surrounding Christ's nativity! "Now, then, my soul, embrace that divine manger; press your lips upon and kiss the boy's feet. Then in your mind keep the shepherds' watch, marvel at the assembling host of angels, join in the heavenly melody, singing with your voice and heart: *Glory to God in the highest and on earth peace to men of good will*" (Luke 2:14).[16] What we have here is a spiritual exercise that parallels on the level of active imagination Francis' visionary mysticism. Its goal is the same, a progressive identification with Christ, although not on the ecstatic mystical level that Francis achieved.

Mysticism of Poverty

This progressive identification with Christ is achieved and expressed in Francis and the Franciscan tradition by what I call the "mysticism of poverty." Poverty, both external and internal, has been an essential element in monasticism since its inception. Monks, mendicants, and hermits live lives of detachment from possessions just as they renounce the way of the householder, marriage, and family. These renunciations along with the practice of obedience have been the hallmarks of the "religious" vocation, taken in a restrictive and technical sense. What, then, is special about Franciscan poverty? Why speak of a mysticism of poverty? I believe that Franciscan poverty differs from that of Benedictines, Dominicans, and Jesuits. Granted that on the level of interior detachment, all these religious orders practice a similar poverty, although the external practice might differ. The external poverty of Francis was radical, it is true, but I do not hold that its distinctive quality lies there. Rather I believe that its uniqueness consists in a particular mystical dimension. By this I mean that Francis' spirituality was channeled through the practice of poverty—in his case radical—which served as a kind of sacramental symbol that drew him into a deep identification with the poor and humble Christ. It functioned as a kind of externalized mantra that focused his attention and drew him into deeper levels of the mystery of Christ. Because it is closely linked to these deeper levels of consciousness, I believe that it can be rightly called mystical and that together with his visionary Christ mysticism and his nature mysticism it forms an integral component of his mystical life.[17]

In typical fashion he dramatized poverty in crucial events in his life: for example, in his stripping of his clothes before his father in the presence of the Bishop of Assisi and in his request to have his body laid naked on the ground after his death. In each case Bonaventure interprets these exercises of poverty as linked to the poverty of Christ: "In all things he wished to be conformed to Christ crucified, who hung on the cross poor, suffering and naked. Therefore at the beginning of his conversion, he stood naked before the bishop, and at the end of his life, naked he wished to go out of this world."[18]

Nature Mysticism

A mystical sense of belonging to the family of nature permeated Francis' life. He preached to birds and befriended lambs. In all creatures he perceived a reflection of God. I will concentrate here on the account of the composition of his *Canticle of Brother Sun*, in the *Legenda Perugina*.[19] Just as La Verna marked the climax of his visionary mysticism, so *The Canticle of Brother Sun* marked the climax of his nature mysticism.

According to the *Legenda Perugina*, on the night before he composed the *Canticle*, God described to Francis the earth transformed into gold, rocks into precious stones, and the rivers into perfume. Here is another example of a visionary mystical experience, but note that it is not the customary vision of the suffering Christ, but the earth itself. This image has resonances in medieval alchemy and can be seen as marking a key transformation from the Christ mysticism of La Verna to the nature mysticism of the *Canticle*. The text of the *Legenda* in the translation of Rosalind Brooke reads as follows:

St. Francis lay there [at San Damiano] for fifty days and could no longer see in the daytime the light of day, nor at night the light of the fire, but always remained in the house and in the little cell in darkness. Moreover, he had great pain in his eyes day and night so that at night he could scarcely rest or sleep, which was very bad for him and greatly aggravated the sickness of his eyes and his other infirmities. Also, if at any time he wished to rest or sleep, there were many mice in the house and in the little cell where he lay, which was a lean-to made of rushes attached to one side of the house. The mice ran backwards and forwards over him and around him, and so did not let him go to sleep. They even hindered him considerably at the time of prayer. Not only at night but even by day they so tormented him that even when he ate they got up on to the table, so that his companions and he himself considered it must be a temptation of the devil, as indeed it was.[20]

On one occasion Francis was so tormented by these sufferings that he prayed to God in his distress as the *Legenda* tells us: "One night St. Francis was thinking about how many tribulations he had and began to feel sorry for himself, saying inwardly: 'Lord, come to my help and look on my infirmities so that I may be able to bear them patiently.'[21]

At this point he heard God speak within himself, promising him eternal happiness in the kingdom of heaven. However God did not merely state this gift directly but expressed it through the image of the earth transformed into gold:

Immediately it was said to him in spirit: 'Tell me, brother: if anyone were to give you for your infirmities and tribulations such a great and precious treasure that, if the whole earth were pure gold, all stones were precious stones, and all water were balsam [si tota terra esset purum aurum, omnes lapides essent lapides pretiosi, et tota aqua esset balsamum], yet you would consider all this as nothing, and these substances as earth, stones, and water in comparison with the great and precious treasure given to you, surely you would rejoice greatly?'[22]

The *Legenda* continues:

St. Francis replied: 'That would be a great treasure, Lord, and worth the seeking, truly precious and greatly to be loved and desired.' He said to him: 'Therefore, brother, rejoice, and rather be glad in your infirmities and tribulations, since henceforth you are as secure as if you were already in my kingdom.'[23]

According to the text, when Francis arose in the morning, he told his companions of the assurance God had given him and how he should rejoice and give thanks to him. The text continues:

'Therefore I want for his praise and my consolation, and the edification of our neighbors, to make a new song of Praise of the Lord for his creatures, which we use daily and without which we could not live. In them the human race greatly offends the Creator and daily we are ungrateful for such grace, because we do not praise our creator and giver of all good things which we ought.' Sitting down, he began to meditate and afterwards began: 'Altissimo, omnipotente, bon Signore.' He made a song on the creatures and taught his companions to recite it.[24]

Interpretation of the Symbol

At first glance the image of the transformation of the earth may not seem to be especially significant in this context. For it is not focused upon directly, and on the surface it seems to function merely as a comparison to highlight the greatness of the gift of the kingdom of heaven. Yet from several points of view, it can be seen to play a much greater role. From the standpoint of the psychology of C. G. Jung, it can be seen as an archetypal symbol, employed by the medieval alchemists, to signify the transformation of consciousness. From this perspective the symbol can throw light upon the specific type of nature mysticism Francis experienced and also highlight a purification which he underwent to reach this stage of nature mysticism at the final stage of his life. It can also help relate his nature mysticism to his visionary Christ mysticism which reached its climax in his ecstatic experience on Mount La Verna.

On the structural-logical level, the symbol does establish a comparison/contrast between the earth and the gift of eternal life. However the comparison is more complex than one would expect. For it really establishes a threefold hierarchical structure: the earth in its natural state, the earth transformed into gold, and the kingdom of God. If one were to take the transformation of the earth in its archetypal-psychological meaning, as we will soon see, the threefold structure of the comparison would correspond to the threefold hierarchical structure of the Neoplatonic universe: matter, spirit, divinity, which provides the fundamental structure of Bonaventure's *Soul's Journey into God* and the basis of his interpretation of Francis' nature mysticism through his metaphysics of exemplarism and epistemology of illumination.

C. G. Jung saw medieval alchemy as having a double concern: the chemical search to transform base metal into gold and the psychological transformation symbolized by the chemical processes, which paralleled Jung's own psychotherapeutic process of individuation. "The entire alchemical procedure," Jung wrote, " . . . could just as well represent the individuation process of a single individual, though with the not unimportant difference that no single individual ever attains to the richness and scope of the alchemical symbolism."[25] Such symbols as treasure (*thesaurus*), gold (*aurum*), stone (*lapis*), and water (*aqua*), found in the above text from the *Legenda Perugina*, feature prominently in alchemy, where they are part of the process of the transformation of consciousness.

The transformation of the base metals of the earth into pure gold symbolizes the process of the differentiation of what Jung calls the Self, the God image at the center of the psyche. This involves what the alchemists called *separatio* — the separation of the spirit from the material body through a process of purification or *mortificatio*. This is not a final state, but is followed by the *conjunctio*, in which the opposites are brought together in an integration.[26]

We find all of these elements in Francis' experience. In the affliction of his senses, especially sight, he suffers what could be called a "dark night," in the later terminology of John of the Cross, especially since it deprives him of his former mystical experience of the presence of God in the physical world. But it is also a purifying suffering since it can separate his spirit from his bodily senses so that he can experience God as pure gold in the depths of his soul. This is the way charted by Bonaventure in his *The Soul's Journey*.

The *separatio* reaches an extreme when Francis is assured of the kingdom of heaven, or the beatific vision of God. At this point we would expect Francis to rejoice in his liberation from the material world. If he were to compose a mystical melody, it should be in an apophatic key, using the negations of *The Mystical Theology* of the Pseudo-Dionysius, the "letting go" of Eckhart, or the *nada* of John of the Cross. On the contrary, Francis sings a kataphatic song, dancing up the ladder of creatures, rhapsodizing on God's presence in and through the sun, the moon, and the stars, earth, air, fire, and water, even calling upon all creatures to join in his song of praise.

We can find the resolution of this paradox in alchemical symbolism, for the final stage in the alchemical process is not *separatio*, but *conjunctio*: the coincidence of opposites: in this case spirit and matter, God and the world. After being assured of heaven, Francis returns to the earth, but it is an earth transformed into pure gold. Through his heightened consciousness, now transformed by the *mortificatio* and *separatio*, he can see the earth in its true reality — transformed by the *conjunctio* of the pure gold of the divine presence.

A further implication of the *conjunctio* can be found if we compare the two poles of Francis' mysticism: his visionary mysticism of the Seraph and his nature mysticism of the transformed earth. The heavenly or sky realm of the Seraph is not joined to the pure gold of the transformed earth. At the center of this *conjunctio* is the figure of Christ Crucified, whose death on the cross is the symbol linking the two realms through the *mortificatio* and *separatio* of his death which is completed in the *conjunctio* of his resurrection.

What does this mean for Francis' nature mysticism? In the process of his life, it means that after the sky experience of La Verna he needed a further purification of his nature experience to bring his nature mysticism to its climax so that *The Canticle of Brother Sun* could stand in conjunction with the heavenly vision of the six-winged Seraph. In the typology of Francis' nature mysticism, the *conjunctio* reflects the coincidence of opposites that we find in Bonaventure's interpretation of Francis' nature mysticism through the metaphysics of exemplarism and the epistemology of contuition, in which one simultaneously perceives a sense object and intuits its *ratio aeterna* in the eternal Word.

In the light of this interpretation through the symbol of the transformation of the earth, I would like to present the text of *The Canticle of Brother Sun* in the original Umbrian Italian along with an English translation:[27]

IL CANTICO DI FRATE SOLE

1 Altissimu onnipotente bon signore,
2 Tue so le laude, la gloria e l'onore et onne benedictione.
3 Ad te solo, altissimo, se konfano,
4 Et nullu homo ene dignu te mentovare.
5 Laudato sie, mi signore, cun tucte le tue creature,
6 Spetialmente messor lo frate sole,
7 Lo qual'e iorno, et allumini noi per loi.
8 Et ellu e bellu e radiante con grande splendore,
9 De te, altissimo, porta significatione.
10 Laudato si, mi signore, per sora luna e le stelle,
11 In celu l'ai formate clarite et pretiose et belle.
12 Laudato si, mi signore, per frate vento,
13 Et per aere et nubil et sereno et omne tempo,
14 Per lo quale al e tue creature dai sustentamento.
15 Laudato si, mi signore, per sor aqua,
16 La quale e multo utile et humile et pretiosa et casta.
17 Laudato si, mi signore, per frate focu,
18 Per lo quale enn' allumini la nocte,
19 Ed ello e bello et iocundo et robustoso et forte.
20 Laudato si, mi signore, per sora nostra matre terra,
21 La quale ne sustenta et governa,
22 Et produce diversi fructi con coloriti flori et herba.
23 Laudato si, mi signore, per quelli ke perdonano per lo tuo amore,
24 Et sostengo infirmitate et tribulatione.
25 Beati quelli ke'l sosterrano in pace,

26 Ka da te, altissimo, sirano incoronati.
27 Laudato si, mi signore, per sora nostra morte corporale,
28 Da la quale nullu homo vivente po' skappare.
29 Guai a quelli, ke morrano ne la peccata mortali:
30 Beati quelli ke travara ne le tue santissime voluntati,
31 Ka la morte secunda nol farra male.
32 Laudate et benedicete mi signore,
33 Et rengratiate et serviateli cun grande humilitate.

THE CANTICLE OF BROTHER SUN

1 Most high omnipotent good Lord,
2 Yours are the praises, the glory, the honor and all blessing.
3 To you alone, Most High, do they belong,
4 And no man is worthy to mention you.
5 Praised be you, my Lord, with all your creatures,
6 Especially Sir Brother Sun,
7 Who makes the day and through whom you give us light.
8 And he is beautiful and radiant with great splendor,
9 And bears the signification of you, Most High One.
10 Praised be you, my Lord, for Sister Moon and the stars ,
11 You have formed them in heaven clear and precious and beautiful.
12 Praised be you, my Lord, for Brother Wind,
13 And for the air — cloudy and serene — and every kind of weather,
14 By which you give sustenance to your creatures.
15 Praised be you, my Lord, for Sister Water,
16 Which is very useful and humble and precious and chaste.
17 Praised be you, my Lord, for Brother Fire,
18 By whom you light the night,
19 And he is beautiful and jocund and robust and strong.
20 Praised be you, my Lord, for our sister Mother Earth,
21 Who sustains and governs us,
22 And produces various fruits with colored flowers and herbs.
23 Praised be you, my Lord, for those who give pardon for your love
24 And bear infirmity and tribulation,
25 Blessed are those who endure in peace,
26 For by you, Most High, they will be crowned.
27 Praised be you, Lord, for our sister Bodily Death,
28 From whom no living man can escape.
29 Woe to those who die in mortal sin.
30 Blessed are those whom death will find in your most holy will,
31 For the second death shall do them no harm.

32 Praise and bless my Lord and give him thanks
33 And serve him with great humility.

As indicated above, Bonaventure interpreted the nature mysticism of the *Canticle* within the philosophical and theological worldview of Christian Neoplatonism. One can experience God in nature through "contuition"—a contemplative insight that accompanies our sense experience of the material world.[28] When, for example, we see the sun, we can be drawn by its beauty to intuit, along with our sense image of the sun, its ontological ground in the divine mind. All things have flowed out from the Father in the Trinity and can draw us back to union with him. From all eternity the Father has generated his Son as his Word and Image, in whom are contained the divine ideas of all he can create. Thus creation begins with the Father, proceeds through the Son and is completed in the Holy Spirit, who draws all things back to the Son and the Father. When Francis saw the beauty of creation, he was drawn back to the Son as their divine Exemplar, and through the Son to the Father.[29]

In conclusion, we can attempt to see an integration of Francis' three types of mysticism: the mysticism of Christ, poverty, and nature. Bonaventure provides such an integration from the standpoint of Christ in the first of *The Collations on the Six Days*, which is entitled "Christ the Center of All the Sciences."[30] Here he presents Christ as the center of the Neoplatonic worldview. His thought is too complex to explore here. Instead, I will use a simpler integrating model: the allegory of Francis' love for Lady Poverty taken from the *Sacrum Commercium*, written very likely one year after Francis' death. In this allegory Francis and his friars are searching for Lady Poverty, who had been the wife of Christ during his life on earth. She has remained a widow for many centuries since no suitors were attracted to her because of her destitution. Learning of her whereabouts, Francis and his companions run up the mountain where she resides. There she teaches them the excellence of the virtue of poverty and in gratitude they prepare a meal for her. But in their own poverty, they can give her only a little bread and water. She is delighted and asks them to show her their cloister. They bring her to the edge of the mountain top and, pointing to the panorama of nature, proclaim: "This, Lady, is our cloister."[31] Thus through the allegorical imagination we see symbolized the spiritual process by which one is drawn to identification with Christ through a mystical relation with his spouse Lady Poverty, which in turn frees one to enjoy the mystical possession of the entire world.

Notes

1   See my article, "The Humanity and Passion of Christ," in *Christian Spirituality: High Middle Ages and Reformation*, edited by Jill Raitt, in collaboration with Bernard McGinn and John Meyendorff, Vol. 17 of World Spirituality: An Encyclopedic History of the Religious Quest (New York: Crossroad Publishing Company, 1987), pp. 375-391.

2   Lynn White, "The Historical Roots of the Ecological Crisis," *Science* (1967), 1403-7.

3   Bonaventure, *Legenda maior*, I, 3. All English translations of Bonaventure are taken from *Bonaventure: The Soul's Journey into God, The Tree of Life, The Life of St. Francis*, trans. Ewert Cousins (New York: Paulist Press, 1978).

4   Ibid.

5   See the passage cited below, notes 22 and 23.

6   Ibid., I, 5.

7   Ibid.

8   Ibid., II, 1.

9   Ibid.

10   Ibid., XIII, 10.

11   Ibid., XIII, 3.

12   Ibid.

13   Bonaventure, *Itinerarium mentis in Deum*, prologue, 3.

14   Bonaventure, *Legenda maior*, X, 7.

15   See note 1, above; also my article, "Francis of Assisi: Christian Mysticism at the Crossroads," chapter of a book entitled *Mysticism and Religious Traditions*, edited by Steven T. Katz (New York: Oxford University Press, 1983), pp. 163-191.

16   Bonaventure, *Lignum vitae*, 4.

17 On this aspect of Franciscan poverty, I am indebted to the work of Lyn Scheuring, "The Poverty of Francis of Assisi According to Bonaventure and Its Relation to Poverty in John of the Cross" (Ph. D. dissertation, Fordham University, 1989).

18 Bonaventure, *Legenda maior*, XIV, 4.

19 For the text of the *Legenda Perugina*, I am using *Scripta Leonis, Rufini et Angeli Sociorum S. Francisci*, ed. and trans. Rosalind B. Brooke (Oxford: Clarendon, 1970).

20 *Legenda Perugina*, 43.

21 Ibid.

22 Ibid.

23 Ibid.

24 Ibid.

25 C. G. Jung, *Memories, Dreams, Reflections*, ed. A. Jaffe (New York: Pantheon, 1963), p. 205.

26 On the psychological aspects of alchemy, see Edward F. Edinger, *Anatomy of the Psyche: Alchemical Symbolism in Psychotherapy* (La Salle, IL: Open Court, 1985).

27 The Umbrian text of the canticle is from the critical edition of Kajetan Esser, OFM, *Opuscula Sancti Francisci* (Grottaferrata: Editiones Collegie S. Bonaventurae, 1978), pp. 84-85. The English translation is my own from the volume cited in note 3 above, pp. 27-28.

28 Bonaventure, *Quaestiones disputatae de scientia Christi*, q. 4.

29 See Bonaventure, *In Hexaemeron*, I.

30 Ibid.

31 *Sacrum Commercium*, 63.

Ramon Llull: Mystic Polymath

R. A. Herrera

The tumultuous and agitated existence of Ramon Llull must be pieced together from many sources. The principle document is the *Vida coetanea*, written in 1311, probably dictated by Llull to an unknown monk of the Charterhouse of Vauvert, located in Paris at the site now occupied by the Luxembourg gardens. To this can be added documents in the archives of Mallorca and Barcelona, notes which, beginning in 1290, Llull would place at the end of his treatises [giving place and date of composition], and the massive testimony of his works, most of which tilt to the autobiographical.[1] To this must be added, if only to reject them as historical fact, the many legends which gathered around his elusive figure in life and the cycles of myths which clustered about him after death. One legend has Llull discovering the philosopher's stone, transmuting base metal into gold, and writing the famous alchemical tract, the *Testamentum*.[2] No wonder that some scholars speak of the three Llulls.

Once fact is detached from fiction a reliable sketch of his life, albeit with significant lacunae, can be ascertained. Ramon Llull belonged to the nobility of Mallorca. His father had participated in the conquest of the island by Jaume el Conqueridor and was rewarded accordingly. The *Vida* has nothing to say about his infancy and childhood. We know that Ramon was born in the Ciutat de Mallorques [Palma] around 1235. At the age of fourteen he became a page in the service of king Jaume and later accompanied him on his travels gaining first hand knowledge of the political and court life of the times. He probably received the education of a gentleman: the practice of arms softened by the graces of the 'trobador'. Llull is appointed 'preceptor' of the Prince, the future Jaume II of Mallorca, and in 1257 marries Blanca Picany by whom he has a son and daughter. According to the *Vida* his youth was spent frivolously, given over to sensuality and lust. In the early *Libre de contemplació* he castigates himself for succumbing all to easily the capital sins.[3]

But there were other austere even radical influences at work. Catalonia and Mallorca had become the refuge of Franciscan Spirituals, Joachimites of all stripes, as well as of Cathars. Voluptuousness struggled, at times merged, with the asceticism of the Pure, an aristocratic sense of hierarchy confronted by radical levelling. Llull's skimming the surface of gratification was abruptly ended by a series of five visions of Christ crucified. He experienced a conversion in which pursuit of sanctity replaced his quest for feminine beauty.[4] Some years later, during an emotional nadir, Llull wrote, in his *Desconhort*, that Christ had rescued him from '*carnalitat*' so that he would be loved and made known throughout the world.[5] After his conversion he lived at home with wife and children dedicating himself to penance, prayer, and works of charity.

A sermon on the life of St. Francis was the catalyst which brought about a more radical change of life. He decided to sell part of his holdings and go on pilgrimage to holy places. It is probable he went to Rocamador [France] and to the great shrine of St. James at Compostela. On return he continued living with his family while exercising himself in pious works and study. He studied Latin, probably with the Cistercians at the monastery of Santa Maria de la Reial, and Arabic from a Muslim slave. These studies continued for some nine years. At the end of this period he wrote the bulky *Libre de contemplació en Deu*, judged by Hillgarth to be "a truly seminal work, which, in a sense, anticipates all the major features of his subsequent works",[6] as well as a compendium of Al-Ghazzali's *Māqaṣid*. This was not merely a resume but a '*compendi novell*' of the work.[7] Both were originally written in Arabic.

Ramon Llull had a conflictive personality with swings of mood which at times left him verging on depression. In his youth the symptoms were muted. Conversion radically transformed his manner of life, while newly found intellectual aspirations – [a visit to Paris was frustrated on the advice of Ramon de Penyafort] – took its toll. His wife requested and obtained an administrator of the family patrimony to protect them from what must have been viewed as Ramon's irresponsibility. His slave teacher, prodded by Ramon's religious zeal, became incensed, attacked him, and while detained committed suicide by hanging. At the time Llull was at Santa Maria asking for guidance.[8]

While on retreat at his property on Mount Randa Ramon was visited by an exceptional experience. He believed that God had illuminated his intelligence and given him with the 'form' and 'order' for the writing of books. He went down to Santa Maria la Reial and, in the words of the *Vida*, wrote, "without effort, a book against the infidels", the first *Ars Magna*.[9] He remained at Miramar for about three years directing a school for the study of Arabic which had been set up by Jaume II, alternating prayer and study, while writing works such as the *Libre de l'ordre de cavalleria* and the *Doctrina Pueril*

dedicated to his son Domenech. This hiatus was to end with Llull
initiating a public career which would span some forty years and take
him—at least in legend—beyond the limits of the known world.
Centered on the Art and its miraculous character, his many plans and
projects sent him scurrying wildly about the world consulting,
imploring, advising, preaching, debating, trying his best to influence
Popes, Kings, and other dignitaries.

His travels begin with a visit to the Pope, then to Paris and Montpellier where he gives public lectures on his Art. In 1290 he leaves
Montpellier and travels to Genoa where he undergoes a profound
crisis. In the *Vida* he states clearly that this 'serious temptation' was
caused by *"tement per la sua pel"*.[10] Very simply, his projected voyage
to Tunis with its dangers overwhelmed him. It is hardly a coincidence
that other events at the time, such as his choice of habit, are frankly
psychopathological.[11] He finally embarks, arrives in Tunis, recovers
his health, engages in controversy, and is consequently expelled. He
ends up in Naples where he petitions Pope Celestine V ['il gran
rifuto'], then joins Jaume II at Perpignan, and later Phillip the Fair
[Felip le Bel] at Paris. That he had high hopes for the king's favor is
reflected in his fulsome praise of Phillip. Llull presented him with
several books over the years including *L'Arbre de filosofia d'amor* in
Latin during this visit. Years later he would dedicate *De natali pueri
parvuli Christi Iesu* to the king pleading with him to suppress the
'Averroist' heresy.

On his way back to Mallorca he receives from Jaume II at
Barcelona authorization to preach in Synagogues and Mosques of
Aragon (Oct, 1299). Some of these sermons will be incorporated into
his *Liber praedicationis contra Iudaeos*. Off to Mallorca for controversies
with Muslims, to Cyprus spurred by an unfounded rumor of the occupation of Syria by the Tartars, disputes with cismatics and heretics.
He visits Aias in Armenia and Limissol, property of the Grand Master
of the Temple, then returns to Europe arriving at Lyon [1305] where
he is received by Pope Clement V: to Bugia [Africa] where he
debates, preaches, provokes the fury of the Islamic crowd, is stoned,
beaten and imprisoned. He begins to write the *Disputatio Raymundi
Christiani et Hamar Sarraceni* but is released because of the influence of
Catalan and Genoese merchants. Expelled, Llull survives a shipwreck
and reaches Pisa lodging at the Franciscan convent of San
Domnino.[12] Nearly a century before an Abbot of the order founded
by Joachim of Fiore took refuge in the same convent. In 1254,
Gerard of Borgo San Donnino, a Francisan who had lived at Pisa,
published his *Introduction to the Eternal Gospel*, an edition of Joachim's
three major works with introduction and glosses. This was to initiate

a veritable epidemic of utopian enthusiasm that was still percolating during Llull's life time, concentrated, to some extent, within the Franciscan Order.

He returns for the last time to Paris and he attacks the 'Averroists', possibly Jean de Jandun, giving public lectures which are attended by masters and students. Forty masters of the Sorbonne approve his Art. The Chancellor of the university reviews his works and declares them orthodox. But his success is transitory. The same university issued an official document between 1395 and 1402 prohibiting the teaching of Llull's Art in the Faculty of Theology.[13] Notwithstanding, the council of Vienne saw the triumph of several of Llull's long-frustrated aspirations. It authorized several of the ten propositions given in his *Petitio Raymundi*. A surprising exception is the condemnation of 'Averroistic' philosophy, which, in spite of Llull's prodding, was not implemented until the Lateran Council of 1511.

Advancing into old age but scarcely diminishing in enthusiasm, Ramon returns to Mallorca, and, in less than a year, write 15 works. On April 26, 1313, he makes his will and distributes his works, copies going to the Charterhouse of Vauvert, his friend Perceval Spinola, and the Franciscan convent at Ciutat de Mallorques [Palma].[14] He returns to Tunis by way of Messina where he preaches publically and enters into debate with Islamic sages. After what must have been an eventful stay in Tunis he dies. His death is clothed in mystery. The traditional account has him expiring as a martyr. Near death after having been stoned by a mob Llull is taken on board a Genoese ship bound for Mallorca and either dies on shipboard or immediately after having viewed the beautiful island. This supposedly occurred June 29 1315, on the feast of the martyrdom of saints Peter and Paul. This ideal death is probably a posthumous tribute, not a historical account. Some scholars, taking their lead from the Dominican Inquisitor, Nicolau Eymerich, who fanatically pursued Llull's memory, contend that he died after having returned to the island, some time in 1316.[15]

As poet, 'trobador' and 'joglar' Llull was both worldly and profane; the poet of secular love was also the 'joglar' of God. It was the latter who wrote the hauntingly lovely *Plant de la Verge* and the stately *Hores de Nostra Dona*. But in spite of high moments, Llull's poetry tends to stall, as do some of his other works, because of his didactic enthusiasm. Llull seems to be unable to hold himself in check. He is compelled to teach, expound, preach, never leaving well enough alone, hardly ever attaining to the light and holy such as does St. John of the Cross. Llull's poetic and literary work is subordinated to the Art which is itself a function of his conversionary vocation. First, convert the 'infidel', and then, by a sort of reflux, spiritually transform Christendom. There is a marked pathos to his efforts, the clue to which is possibly found in the enchanting *Felix* or *Book of Marvels*. He indicates that the most surprising and incomprehensible 'marvel' is that men have ceased loving and desiring to know God. This ingratitude was to him incomprehensible. But even this 'mystical book of chivalry'[16] is somewhat flawed by the overabundance of apologetical arguments [*apolegs*] which he calls '*exemplis*'.

As a 'trobador', Ramon must have been influenced to some extent by the cult of courtly love with its Islamic and Cathar connections. The classic *Roman de al Rose* was finished by Jean de Meun between 1270 and 1280. The milieu of Llull's day was permeated by Cathar ideology and had been for some time. Many Aragonese nobles were Cathars and King Pere I of Aragon, though orthodox, died in 1213 at the head of a partly Cathar army.[17] Ramon was often at Montpellier, birthplace of both Jaume el Conqueridor and Jaume II, which was a gathering place for various sects of enthusiasts. Ramon Llull was acquainted with the Franciscan Spirituals and exercised his apostolate in several places frequented by them, for instance, Ifriquiya. [Tunisia and part of Libya], the refuge of the Fratricelli in 1317 and later of the Freres de Narbonne et de Beziers.[18] The long reign of Jaume II was doubtless influenced by the Spirituals and Llull was very much aware of the euphoria produced by Arnau de Vilanova's *De Tempore adventus Anti-Christi et fine Mundi* which predicted the impending appearance of the Anti-Christ and strongly urged Church reform. Arnau, though he habitually savaged philosophy, thought highly of Llull, "the standard bearer of the spiritual reform of Christianity".[19]

Llull was a man of protean interests. He was historian in spite of himself. Hillgarth lumps him together with Alfonso X as presenting the most comprehensive portrait of the Iberian peninsula in the 13th century.[20] He wrote on astrology, medicine, pedagogy, rhetoric, political theory, and much else. Like Roger Bacon he envisioned a universal Christian *respublica*. He was also a writer on spirituality running from the *Libre de contemplació en Déu* to gems such as the *Libre d'Amic e Amat* and the *Art de Contemplació*, both of which were incorporated into his allegorical novel, *Blanquerna*. He was the first important writer in Catalan, the first to use the vernacular as a vehicle for philosophy and poetry. It is largely due to him that Catalan preceded other European languages as a literary and scholarly medium. As Allison Peers noted some years ago, *Blanquerna* precedes most of European prose fiction.[21] It is almost contemporary with Dante and a century older than Froissart's *Chronicles*, Chaucer's *Canterbury Tales*, and Wycliffe's translation of the Bible.

Llull's Art, developed and refined from the first *Art* [1274] to the final *Ars generalis ultima* [1308], is the centerpiece of his thought. Though greatly indebted to the NeoPlatonic hierarchies, it is an original and radical variation on the theme. The *Art* claims to structure all domains and to be a 'logic' of life, not one of mere abstract concepts. It is not one of causality but of congruence. As Llull indicated to his disciple, Thomas Le Myèsier, the *Art* is universal, meant for all men and Christianity is present only implicitly.[22] It is designed to *excite* the powers of the soul: memory, understanding, and will and is an *ars inveniendi veritatem*, an art of finding truth. This is ultimately reducible to a search for congruence between the created world and the Divine Perfections.

Many different influences converged to produce the 'Phantasticus', perhaps quirky but methodical. Few influences can be determined with precision apart from Llull's overarching debt to various strands of the NeoPlatonic tradition. Augustine and Anselm among Christians, perhaps Scottus Eriugena. Of Muslims, al-Ghazzali, perhaps Ibn Hazm, together with Sufi spirituality and prayer-techniques. Of Jews, aside from a doubtful link with Judah Halevi, intimations — noted by Pico della Mirandola — of Kabbalah, especially the *Zohar* and *Bahir*. He may have been influenced by the Sefirotic Tree and the '*ets ha-hayim*', the ideal model studied by the initiate.[23]

Some years ago Carreras y Artau provided an evaluation of Ramon Llull's place in Medieval thought.[24] He is viewed as the most dramatic example of the medieval obsession with conversion, the personification of the chivalric spirit, a Catalan Don Quijote. Firmly persuaded that his Art was received by means of a 'divine illustration', Llull saw himself as a defender of the faith, especially the fundamental dogmas of Trinity and Incarnation, a faith he was obliged to defend against Islam, Judaism, and Aristotelian philosophy. In doing so he made the most notable attempt to realize the 'pure idea' of Christianity.[25]

It comes as no surprise that Llull was also a spiritual writer of distinction. As noted previously, his conversion was due to a series of five visions of Christ crucified, his apostolic life to a sermon on the conversion of St. Francis. Moreover, there is an intimate connection between the mechanisms of the Art and spirituality, as attested to by his two overarching principles: the convertibility of the Divine Dignities or attributes, and his theory of first and second intention. It is through prayer that these Divine Dignities stamp their likeness on the human virtues. As stated in the *Felix*:

" . . . when a person devoutly and with sincere intention meditates on God, then God's goodness instills its own likeness in that person's goodness insofar as that person is good through the prayer he formulates in meditating on God".[26]

The point of departure both for Llull's thought and his spirituality is the *Libre de Contemplació en Déu* written around 1272 at Mallorca. This bulky work alternates speculation with the elaboration of mystical techniques. Beginning with the Dignities it goes on to consider the created universe, centers on man, discusses love and prayer, finally ending with a spate of allegories, which have since been a source of puzzlement to his interpreters.

As in many other works philosophical speculation and spirituality are found in tandem perhaps subordinated only to Llull's veritable obsession with method. He writes works dealing with a method to induce contemplation, one to generate love according to the mode and principles of the *Art*, a method to preach, and so forth. An acute interpreter of Llull's work, Father Platzeck, believed that there was not the slightest doubt that the Art, in its original and genuine sense, was a method of contemplation for personal use.[27] But it also was or soon became a method by which human reason is rectified and hence a conversionary tool.

An interesting though lengthy text from the *Felix* is very much to the point:

"In the days of the prophets it was proper to convert people on the strength of *belief*, because people believed more easily, and in the times of Christ and the Apostles *miracles* were quite fitting, since people did not have a solid basis in Scripture, and therefore liked miracles, which are physically visible demonstrations of things. Now we have reached a time when people prefer *necessary reasons*, since they are well grounded in the great sciences of philosophy and theology; and therefore peoples who through philosophy, have fallen into errors contrary to the Holy Roman faith, should be conquered by means of necessary reasons, and their false opinions refuted by means of necessary reasons".[28]

Llull's Art revolves around God, the 'A' of creation, one with His Dignities, which signify both God Himself and God in reference to His creation.[29] The Dignities are absolute because of their ontological placement in the absolutely first principle and descend in a Neoplatonic mode to created being itself structured in different levels which differ in degrees of reality and existence.[30] An admirer of Llull, Nicholas of Cusa, put it simply: "Primum fundamentum artis est quod omnia quae Deus creavit et fecit, creavit et fecit ad similitudem suarum dignitatem".[31]

Llull is found in the company of Gregory the Great and others in advocating a spirituality of light in which menacing shadows recede into the background, and this in spite of the probable influence of Scottus Eriugena and through him the Pseudo-Denis. He is strangely myopic regarding the *via negativa*, his spirituality strangely lacking in darker shades and apophatic turns.   We find no dense cloud of unknowing, no nights of sense and spirit, no torturous processes of purification. He seems to restrict himself to the *via positiva*. There is a correspondence between God and His creation which permits the human soul to ascend from the perfections found in creatures—faint echoes of the Dignities—to the summit where God Himself dwells.

Though the menacing shadows are relegated to the periphery, there is no dearth of asceticism, at times verging on the harsh, in Llull's spirituality. He indicates that the ascent to God—the experience of progressive illumination—is not without suffering.   Each elevation of spirit contains a quantum of pain.[32]   Not only aware but highly susceptible to the vicissitudes of the human condition, Ramon Llull experienced a multiplicity of ills, both physical and psychological, and bore then with greater resignation than most men. Perhaps influenced by Islam he proposed the wandering penitent as the human ideal, advising the solitary not to neglect contemplating the Beloved mired in the world, burdened by grief and tribulation.[33]

In the first of a numbing variety of arguments for the existence of God which Llull presents in the *Gentil*, he argues that if finite goodness, which is in accord with non-being, exists, how much more fitting that an infinite good, in accord with infinite being, exist.[34]   Whatever objections can be raised against this argument—against all the arguments 'by equivalence'—it has the advantage of revealing a constant of his thought, one of inestimable importance to his spirituality. The more the Dignities inform human perfections, the more human potentiality for the divine is enhanced, and the swifter the soul is elevated to God.   Llull forges a spirituality in which man is fully immersed in human life yet surrounded by an unchanging realm which he can become conscious of and which has the power to transform both the human soul and the world at large.

The importance of Llull's spirituality is illustrated by the fact that even scholars who have grave reservations concerning his philosophy, the Art itself, nevertheless urge that the Art, as applied in the *Libre d'amic e amat*, provides a useful method of arriving at contemplation.[35]   This elevation of the human soul to understanding, contemplation, or both, is a constant theme with surprising ramifications. When Felix complains that examples provided by a sage seem to miss the point he is told:

"I consciously gave you these examples so that you would elevate your intellect in the effort to understand: for the more obscure the example, the greater is the understanding of the intellect which understands it".[36]

In this delightful though at times exasperating work [*Felix*], most of its characters are either encountered while in meditation, attempting to meditate, or preparing themselves for meditation. A wise hermit — a favorite type — declares that he is wandering through the forest observing trees and herbs, to be able to meditate on God "according to the art of philosophy and theology, which is written in a work entitled *The Book of Articles*, and organized according to the order of the *Ars Demonstrativa*".[37] The realms of nature and grace intersect. At one point Felix makes a valient but unsuccessful attempt to understand. Stalemated, he asks God for the grace appropriate to understanding and forthwith receives it.[38]

Llinares is correct in pointing to the oscillation between intellect and affect in Llull's mysticism.[39] Both trends, the head and the heart, are reflected in his voluminous novel *Blaquerna* which contains two brief treatises, the *Libre de amic e amat* and the *Art de contemplació*. They come together to promote the main enterprise of mending the world, a world which together with the human beings who comprise it and the callings they engage in are not what they should be, failing to reflect the purpose for which they were established. This shattered world still reveals, albeit in disguised form, the presence of God and, once transformed, will restore mankind to its proper status. When the present chaos is reduced to order a unity of language, customs, law and religion will eventually arise.

Here we do not have an Unamunian *agonía*, a struggle between head and heart, but an attempt at making head and heart move in tandem. The *Art de contemplació* and the *Libre d'amic e amat* are not at odds but are meant to complement each other. The former gives a method to arrive at contemplation, a 'combinatoria' simplified to the bare bones, by means of which the Divine Dignities or attributes are considered through a variety of distinct perspectives, the purpose being to etch the Dignities on the three 'faculties' of the soul.[40] This method is found in several of Llull's works. A good though perhaps bizarre example is his *Liber de decem modis contemplandi Deum* in which Llull proposes to contemplate God by means of the Dignities, the Trinity, the Incarnation, the resurrection, the eucharist, glorification, grace, mercy, honor, and the Virgin Mary.[41]

In the *Art de contemplació* he centers on the Dignity of goodness [Divine Goodness] and views it in two complementary ways: goodness as found in the other Divine Dignities; the other Dignities as found in goodness. Once this method is put into operation and all the 'powers' of the soul are centered on the Divine Good, the soul is then elevated to it, which, in language with Kabbalistic intimations, is compared to a lightening bolt with six dimensions.[42] Although in the *Art de contemplació* sixteen Dignities are mentioned the number of Dignities seems to change according to the work at hand. The *Ars inventiva veritatis* lists seven, the *Gentil*, nine. The oscillating number of Dignities is one of the constant difficulties of Llullian scholarship though as long as they comprise a sort of Parmenidean One — as long as they are convertible in God and issue logically into one another — the number may well be irrelevant.

Llull was very much interested in the psychosomatic aspect of prayer and thought. Because of this some of his works seem to be rather contrived with physical actions being all too closely matched by their psychical accompaniment. He could simply not think in the departmentalized not to say schizoid fashion we inherited from Descartes. For Llull affects, attitudes, postures, emotions, physical traits are direct signs of spiritual dispositions. To explain the transition between spiritual levels he indicates in the *Art de contemplació* that by persevering in meditation the heart begins 'to take fire' and the eyes to 'water'.[43] When the ascending movement is interrupted the somatic effects become muted and stall.

There are also downward movements, breaks, falls, and descending spirals, when the understanding falls to the level of the imagination. Llull recommends a strategm to detach the understanding from the imagination. Attentively consider that the Supreme Good is infinite in perfection and therefore possesses every Dignity in a perfect manner. This thought will inflame the heart and generate the gift of tears.[44] Another example. When the proposition "God is good" is denied, "God is not good because of the evil in the world", a loss of knowledge and devotion takes place. The solution. Repeat the affirmation "God is good" but now on a higher level. This will clear the deck of negativities and produce an increase of love and knowledge in contemplation.[45]

The *Libre d'amic e amat* is a decidedly affect-oriented work very much influenced by Islamic spirituality. It presents 360 or so sayings which, when repeated with fervour, generate affective reactions, lead the worshipper to make practical resolutions, bring God to mind, and induce contemplation. Like flicks of a whip they prod the soul to recall its Divine origin. These sayings include aphorisms, epigrams, narratives, puzzles, questions and exclamations. Through the medium of these sayings Llull believes that it is possible to learn to meditate and propel the soul to higher levels of contemplation.[46] The Lover [Amic] and the Beloved [Amat], the human soul and God as Christ, Godhead, or Trinity are the protagonists. These emphatic often euphoric outpourings contrast the delights and afflictions which emerge from the Lover/Beloved intercourse.

Llull distinguishes between 'acquired science', the fruit of study and intellect, and 'infused science' acquired through acts of the will, devotion, and prayer.[47] As has been noted, while the *Art de contemplació* can easily be subsumed under the first, constructing a method of meditation, the *Libre d'amic e amat,* as it speaks to the affects and provides sparks to enkindle the soul, should be included under the second. The rigorous mechanism of the Art organizes, controls, and directs the affective effusions of the sayings. In spite of the novel character of Llull's approach to spirituality several constants of the literature are nevertheless encountered. The 'cloud' but here it is transparent, the 'light' by which the Beloved illuminates the Lover, the mirror-image analogy, the notion of '*sobria ebreitas*', and more are found.[48] Mystical phenomena are mentioned albeit charily.

The *Libre del Gentil* is an unusually good source to probe for information regarding Llull's philosophical method and consequently about his spirituality of it be accepted that contemplation was the primary goal of the Art. As it was written for laymen [*homens lais*], obscure and convoluted terminology is kept to a minimum. Instead of presenting the Art in its logico-mathematical nudity he employs the attractive symbolic guise of five trees with a combined total of 179 flowers which represent the Divine Dignities together with their possible combination of human virtues and deadly sins. 'Lady Intelligence' provides the method of disputation. Each tree is subject to two 'conditions' or rules; the assemblage to two 'meta-conditions'. These rules are not restricted to the noetic realm. By following them it is also possible to 'escape infinite pain' and 'achieve everlasting peace'.[49]

The Divine Dignities are reduced to seven in the *Gentil*, perhaps, as Bonner suggests, to more easily combine them with the seven virtues and the seven deadly sins.[50] Identified in God they are reflected in creation according to different degrees of intensity. The more the multiplicity of created virtues in man is reduced to unity, the more being/reality is possessed, and the higher the soul ascends to God. The contrary is also true. The more man embraces evil and hence non-being the more he falls into nothingness. Llull—as Anselm before him—uncritically accepts that being is superior to non-being, good superior to evil, greater being superior to lesser being. Not to do so would insult God, entail a woefully erroneous notion of human nature and lead to an ontological monstrosity by identifying Being with Non-Being.

But the soul, according to Llull, aspires to more than mere unity.
The unique characteristic of his mystical speculations is its Trinitarian
emphasis, an emphasis reflected to some extent in what could be
called his philosophy and in the Art itself.[51] Ramon Llull insisted, in
terms which tended to become more forceful, that God's principal
work was not creation but His eternal activity of loving, understanding, and glorying in Himself.[52] This 'inner work' is far superior to
that 'outer, external work'. As this inner life escapes the categories of
the speculative mind philosophers are not able to take it into account
and so project God's eternity on to creation. This is both a stunning
instance of the superiority of the Christian faith over unredeemed
reason and a subtle explanation of the infatuation of philosophy with
the notion of an eternal universe.

The goal of the mystic is then to participate in God's inner activity,
so to speak, in His private life. The Divine Dignities which pullulate
throughout creation draw the mystic towards his transcendent goal,
participation in the Trinitarian life. Whatever the influence of
Neoplatonism, filtered not only through Augustine but Scottus Eriugena, the mystical ascent as portrayed by Llull is definitely not a
disembodied *noesis* but a fully human endeavor in spite of the geomet-
ric figures and logical formulae in which it is often formulated.

If it were not for his enthusiasm and powers of recuperation
Ramon Llull could be considered a tragic figure. His best formulated
plans, his most elaborate projects, went awry. Only at the end of his
life did he enjoy a brief period of success. His many visits to the Papal
and French courts, to a multiplicity of other dignitaries proved to be,
on the whole, futile. Both his *Desconhort* [1296] and *Cant de Ramon*
[1299] are exercises in *Shadenfreud*. His missionary efforts were
largely ineffective. The Art, from which so much was expected, was
shunted aside or treated as an oddity by the intellectual community.

Most of his contemporaries anticipated Hegel's judgement,
centuries later, that Llull was incoherent and eccentric. Ramon was
aware that he was an outsider and looked upon as an eccentric. His
Disputatio Petri Clerici et Raymundi Phantasticum presents a dialogue
between a 'prudent man' and a 'fantastic man'. As Lola Badia has
noted, from a worldly viewpoint Llull is hyperfantastic and his
program a complete failure.[53] Aside from localized spurts of interest
and short-lived resuscitations, the intellectual community on the
whole has followed the critical path. This trend reached its apex in
the contempt with which Llull was treated by 19th century scholars
such as Prantl and Littre.

There is a more positive view of Llull reflected in Leibniz' praise
on crediting him with discovering the *ars combinatoria*[54] and

Mersenne's suggestion to Descartes that he consider Llull's Art as a possible key to universal knowledge.[55] Moreover, philosophers of the caliber of Gassendi, Bruno, and Hobbes were considered to be 'Lullist' in their day. Today, Llull's reputation has, to some extent, been rehabilitated, though the Art seems to remain a philosophical conundrum. There are centers of study such as those at Palma and Freiburg im Breisgau dedicated to his work and a steady increase in research and publications. His anticipation of modern symbolic logic and the computer has made him relevant to a generation which otherwise would have dismissed him as another medieval grotesque. Dame Frances Yates' evaluation of Lullism can no longer be considered outrageous: "[it] is not an unimportant side-issue in the history of Western civilization. Its influence over five centuries was incalculably great".[56]

Although the many Llull legends added fuel to the fire, whatever influence he did in fact exercise was due principally to his Art, its interpretations, misinterpretations, and mystifications. How the Art may have conflicted with or continued and expanded scholastic modes of thought is a theme of contemporary scholarship. The Art, that privileged instrument given through divine illumination so as to rectify the human mind and bring about the conversion of the world, grounds his work providing it with structure and method. In itself it is simply an impressive mechanism of gargantuan proportions, infused with life through Llull's hyperkinetic dynamism. He considered himself the most rational of men, but a reason restored to its primitive status will doubtless seem strange to most men and its practitioner very odd indeed. Though a tardy convert to the crusading ideal, Llull never renounced his view that brute force alone was insufficient to convert the 'infidel'. He remained true to the words spoken by Abbot Blanquerna: "knowledge and reason are spiritual weapons with which man conquers evil and error".

Over 260 of Llull's works survive, the great majority preserved in Latin versions, though most may well have originally been written in Catalan.[57] In addition to all his eccentricities and flaws, obsessiveness and lack of discretion, Ramon Llull was, in many ways, a sign of contradiction. He refused to abandon his Arabic mode of speech when prodded to do so by the Masters of the Sorbonne, tried to reinstate the old idea of the unity of the sciences when it had been discarded and attempted to prove the existence of a new sense '*affatus*',[58] at a time when such speculation was of negligible scholarly interest. But above all, he made a heroic attempt to restore the lustre of God's attributes to a humanity which living in a world which reflected them, had lost its capacity to perceive their glory.

Notes

1 Refer to Jordi Rubió i Balaguer, *Ramon Llull i el Lulisme*, próleg de Lola Badia (Barcelona: Pub. de L'Abadia de Montserrat, 1985), pp. 35-72. Also Armand Llinarès, *Ramon Llull*, trad. Miguel Adrover (Barcelona: Ediciones 62, 1987), p. 57ff.

2 Father Colomer notes that Nicholas of Cusa was studying the *Testamentum* at Coblenz in May, 1435. It was the work of a Catalan residing in London and was translated into English around 1443-1446. Eusebio Colomer, S. J., "Novesdades Entorn del Lulisme de Nicholau de Cusa". EL, No. 73, Vol. XXV, Fasc. 1, [1981-1983] pp. 67-91. Refer also to M. Pereira, "La Leggenda di Lullo-Alchemista". EL, No. 75, XXVII, Fasc. 2, 1987, pp. 145-163.

3 *Libre de contemplació*, c. 132,27.

4 *Vida coetanea*, 2-4. A Latin/Catalan text in *Ramon Lull, Obras Literarias* (Madrid: BAC, 1948), pp. 43-78.

5 *Desconhort*, 2. A Latin/Catalan text in *idem*., pp. 1094-1147.

6 J. N. Hillgarth, *Ramon Lull and Lullism in Fourteenth Century France* (Oxford: Clarendon Press, 1971), p. 8.

7 Jordi Rubió i Balaguer, "La Logica del Gazzali posada en Rims per Ramon Llull". *op. cit.*, pp. 113-114.

8 *Vida coetanea*, 13.

9 *Ibid.*, 14.

10 *Ibid.*, 20.

11 *Ibid.*, 21-24.

12 Llinarès, *op. cit.*, p. 88.

13 *Ibid.*, p. 89. Hillgarth, *Ramon Lull*, p. 269j.

14 Llinarès, *op. cit.*, pp. 91-92.

15 J. Tarre, "El darrer quinquenni de la vida de R. L.". SMR 14 (1955), pp. 33-42.

16 Refer to Rubió i Balaguer, "Proleg al Llibre de les Bèsties". *Op. cit.*, pp. 315-316.

17 J. N. Hillgarth, *The Spanish Kingdoms* [1250-1516] (Oxford: Clarendon Press, 1976-1978), I, p. 153, note 1. A fascinating view on the Cathars is provided by Dame Francis A. Yates, *Lull and Bruno: Collected Essays* (London: Routledge and Keegan Paul, 1982), p. 114ff.

18 Dominique Urvoy, *Penser L'Islam: Les présupposés Islamiques de L'Art de Llull*. (Paris: J. Vrin, 1980), pp. 119-121; 128-129.

19 Llinarès, *op. cit.*, p. 39.

20 Hillgarth, *The Spanish Kingdoms*, I, pp. 45-47.

21 E. Allison Peers, *Ramon Lull: A Biography* [Reprint] (New York: B. Franklin, 1969), p. 167ff.

22 Hillgarth, *Ramon Lull*, p. 161. 23 Luis Sala Molins, *La Philosophie de L'Amour chez Raymond Lulle*, preface de V. Jankelevitch (Paris: Mouton, 1974), p. 21ff.; pp. 59-69. Also J. Millàs Vallicrosa, "Algunas relaciones entre la doctrina Luliana y La Cabala". *Sefarad*, XVIII (2), 158, pp. 241-253. Mario Satz, "Raymond Lulle et la Kabbale dans l'Espagne du XIII siecle". *Lulle: Les Actes du Colloque sur Raymond Lulle* (Universite de Fribourg, 1984) (Fribourg: Editions Universitaires, 1986).

24 Tomas Carreras i Artau, *Estudios Filosoficos* (Barcelona: CSIC, 1966-1968), 2, pp. 49; 56; 72-76.

25 *Ibid.*, pp. 122; 127.

26 *Selected Works of Ramon Llull*, ed. & trans. by Anthony Bonner (Princeton: PUP, 1985). *Felix or The Book of Wonders*, VIII, 105. Vol. 2, pp. 1040-1041. Catalan edition. *Obres Selectes de Ramon Llull* (Mallorca: Editorial Moll, 1989).

27 Erardo W. Platzeck, OFM, "La Combinatoria Luliana: Un Nuevo Ensayo de Exposicion e Interpretacion de la misma a la luz de Filosofia General Europea". *Revista de Filosofía* [Madrid], No. 13 (1953), pp. 576; 584. Also "La Vida Eremitica en las Obras del Beato Raimundo Lulio". *Revista de Espiritualidad* [Madrid] (1942), p. 128ff.

28 *Felix*, I, 12. SW 2, pp. 717-718.

29 Platzeck, "La Combinatoria", No. 13 [1953], p. 135, note 16.

30 *Ibid.*, No. 14 [1954], p. 126.

31 Cited by Platzeck, *Ibid.*, p. 135, note 16.

32 *Libre d'Amic e Amat*, No. 244. Spanish translation by M. Batllori and M. Caldentey, *Ramon Lull: Obras Literarias*.

33 *Ibid.*, No. 56.

34 *Selected Works*, 1, pp. 119-120.

35 Platzeck, *op. cit.*, No. 14 (1954), p. 161.

36 *Felix* II, 14. SW, 2, p. 722.

37 *Ibid.*, V, 9. SW, 2, p. 756.

38 *Ibid.*, VIII, 100. SW, 2, p. 1025.

39 Llinares, *op. cit.*, p. 276f.

40 *Art de Contemplació*, prol. 3-4. Spanish translation in *Obras Literarias*.

41 Refer to Llinares, *op. cit.*, pp. 284-285.

42 *Art de Contemplació*, I, 4.

43 *Idem.*

44 *Ibid.*, I, 4-6.

45 *Ibid.*, V, 3.

46 *Libre d'Amic e Amat*, prol. 1.

47 *Ibid.*, 241.

48 *Ibid.*, 43; 50; 100; 123; 283; 284; 364.

49 *Gentil*, prol. SW, 1, pp. 113-116.

50 *Ibid.*, prol. SW, 1, p. 118, note 21.

51 Refer to my *"Proslogion* V as Point of Departure for Llull's Art", to be published in *Acta*, Colloque International du CNRS: Saint Anselme, Penseur d'Hier et D'aujourd'Hui, (Julliet), 1990.

52 Refer to *El 'Liber Predications contra Judeos' de Ramon Llull*. Primera edicion critica. Intro. y notas por Jose Ma. Millàs Vallicrosa (Madrid/Barcelona: CSIC, 1957), pp. 50-54. Note the arguments given in the *Gentil* III, SW, 1, pp. 193-217. Also P. M. Batllori, SJ, *Ramon Llull en el món del seu temps* (Barcelona: R. Dalmau, 1960), pp. 54-56. R. D. Pring-Mill, "The Trinitarian World Picture of Ramon Lull". *Romanistische Janrbuch*, VII (1955-1956).

53 Lola Badia, "Estudi de *Phantasticus* de Ramon Llull". EL, No. 74, Volo. XXVI, Fasc. 1 (1986), p. 15ff.

54 Cited in Gottfried Martin, *Leibniz: Logic and Metaphysics*, trans. by R. J. Northcott & P. Lucas (Manchester: MUP, 1964), p. 24ff.

55 J. N. Hillgarth, *Ramon Lull*, p. 297.

56 Yates, *op. cit.*, p. 67.

57 Bonner, in a recent article, speaks of the number of Llull's works as numbering 265 at last count. Anthony Bonner, "The Current State of Studies on Ramon Llull's Thought". *Catalonia Review* 2 [Barcelona, June, 1989], p. 139.

58 According to Llull's disciple Le Myèsier *affatus* consists in "the power of uttering with the voice those ideas conceived in the mind". Hillgarth, *Ramon Lull*, p. 227.

Meister Eckhart on the Union
of Man with God

Cyprian Smith, O.S.B.

It is important for us to realise that Eckhart's doctrine, even at its most abstract and metaphysical, is essentially *mystical*, in the sense that it is aimed at furthering the union of man with God. This means also, of course, that it is not merely a theory but also a practice and if we examine Eckhart's writings at all closely, we shall always find that even his seemingly most abstruse statements are profoundly relevant to spiritual life as it is actually lived. We should beware, however, of saying that Eckhart, instead of merely philsophising about God, is concerned rather with the *experience* of God, for his mysticism is not properly speaking a quest for experiences. It is fatally easy for us, in the twentieth century, to see the mystical union in psychedelic terms, on a par with the expansion of consciousness obtained through drugs; Aldous Huxley, despite the keenness of his intelligence, seems to have fallen into this trap in his work *The Doors of Perception*. Mysticism as understood by Eckhart is not necessarily a matter of ecstasy or bliss, for it can, on the contrary, involve very real suffering and a sense of abandonment. What it is really about is this: a total surrendering of self and self-will, the creation within oneself of a certain void or nothingness. *Niht.* It is true that he predicts an explosion of light within that void, the mysterious *gottes geburt* or birth of God within the soul, and that such a birth is in a sense blissful—but we must be careful not to use "blissful" here in its normal sense, where it has the inevitable correlate "painful". The bliss he is speaking of is a transcendent reality, non-dual, beyond the polarities of pleasure and pain which is intrinsic to our normal human state in a fallen, divided world.

If we fail to understand this, we shall be in danger of interpreting Eckhart's doctrine as a kind of spiritual hedonism, saying: "Do this, and you will find happiness". Nothing could be further from his meaning. Perhaps we shall find happiness, indeed it is certain we shall, but with the qualifications outlined above. In any case, the mystical quest will be vitiated at the outset if it makes happiness its goal, however exalted and "Spiritual" our notion of happiness may seem to be. The mystic as Eckhart conceives him seeks union with God, not because he hopes it will make him happy, but simply because it is the right thing to do: it is the will of God for His creature, the end for which the creature was made. Eckhart is one of those mystics who are ready to endure the pains of hell if this is according to God's Will, and such an attitude is far removed from hedonism in any of its forms. The word *abegescheidenheit* which plays such a central role in his thought, has many meanings, but one of them is "disinterestedness". If we call his doctrine ecstatic — and indeed, he has been named "Doctor Ecstaticus" — we must understand this word primarily in the strict sense of *going out from self*, a movement towards transcendence. Questions of pleasure and pain are only secondary, and in the final analysis not very meaningful.

In our present study we shall attempt to expound a little of Eckhart's teaching on the union of man with God. We shall begin by showing *how* this union is possible, through grace and a certain natural affinity between the human soul and God; proceeding next to discuss the *path* which man must tread in order to attain to this union, through non-attachment and renunciation of self, and concluding with some analysis of what Eckhart tells us about the *goal* of the quest, namely the *gottes geburt* or birth of God within the soul, discussing the question of how far such a union may be expected to go, and to what extent the distinction between creature and Creator may be transcended. In the course of all this we shall have occasion to refer periodically to Nicholas Berdyaev, a thinker whose insights resemble those of Eckhart in certain particulars, and therefore are helpful in our attempt to grasp the thought of the earlier theologian.

Beginning, then, with the question of how it is that union with God is possible at all, we must say that it is based upon divine grace and upon a certain natural affinity between God and the human soul. Since Eckhart does not lay a great deal of stress on the first prerequisite — divine grace — it is necessary for us to take note that he nevertheless fully recognized it, and was not attempting to construct a "Pelagian" mysticism whereby man might expect to attain to the supreme union by his own natural powers alone. In his treatise *Von Abegescheidenheit*, where he is discussing which human virtue brings us closest to God, he states clearly at the outset that such a union is the work of grace and not of nature:

> I have read many writings both of the heathen masters and the prophets and from the Old and New Testaments, and I have earnestly and with great care sought to find which is the highest and the best virtue whereby man may draw closest to God and whereby man may become by grace what God is by nature.[1]

Here Eckhart is only following the teaching of his great master, the pseudo-Denis, who also emphasises the fact that *theosis* or deification is entirely the work of God and not dependent upon any natural power of the creature. [Indeed, there is no reference whatever in Denis to the divine spark in the soul, the *synteresis* or *funkelin* which is so central to Eckhart's thinking].

We might therefore ask why, if Eckhart recognizes the necessity of divine grace, he does not make more frequent references to it, thereby defending himself in advance from any changes of pantheism which might otherwise be levelled at him. There is no definitive answer to this but we may be justified in making an intuitive leap where conclusive evidence is wanting. Eckhart may have felt, on the one hand, that a mystical theology which stresses grace continually is unbalanced and does not do justice to that other truth of revelation, namely, the Divine Image and Likeness in man. Here Eckhart's thought is paralleled by that of Berdyaev, and also that of Pascal, who felt it is necessary to always balance human *misère* and *grandeur*. But there is also another reason why Eckhart may not have felt it necessary to stress grace heavily at all times. If there were any hint in his theology of any kind of Pelagian spirituality, this would need to be corrected by some emphasis on grace. But in fact Pelagianism is totally undermined by Eckhart's peculiarly delicate and paradoxical notion of the Divine Likeness in man.

The true nobility of the soul only emerges when it abases itself totally, withdraws from externals into itself, frees itself from images, and approaches the state of nothingness, *niht*. Only when it is nothing can it be transformed into the All which is God. This is the mystical or esoteric understanding of the tract "He who humbles himself will be exalted". Human grandeur, or likeness to God, is grounded upon human lowliness and nothingness. Only when we go out of self, can God come in. This is certainly not Pelagianism. It is one of those central paradoxes in Christianity which are totally missed by any one-sided theological view which cannot accept the paradoxical, stressing grace to the detriment of nature, or vice versa. But Eckhart, far from avoiding the paradox, places it right at the centre of his thought. It is precisely our lowliness which is most Godlike. The Image of God is obscured in us until we become Nothing.

This question of the "nothingness" of the human soul is of primary importance in Eckhart's notion of the mystical union, and needs to be examined somewhat more closely. We need to establish first of all in what sense the soul can be called "nothing", since it is, after all, a creature of God, possessing being, and therefore by no means equivalent to non-being. Having done this, we must seek to understand the mysterious and paradoxical way in which it is precisely this "nothingness" which makes the soul most like God and renders union with God possible.

The first reason why the soul can be called "nothing" is that it is created by God out of nothing; all creatures are in this position, having no being of their own, but entirely dependent upon the being of God, which means that considered in themselves, distinct from God and in comparison with God, they are pure nothing:

> I don't say that they are small; they are pure nothing. That which has no being is nothing. All creatures have no being.[2]

The second reason why the soul is in a certain sense "nothing" is that in its innermost essence it is beyond all names, attributes or functions. Eckhart was well enough aware, of course, of the Scholastic doctrine which states that the soul is the form of the body and is its life-principle. He was far from denying any of this, but at the same time, he swept it all aside by drawing a distinction between the soul as form of the body and the soul in its innermost essence or ground:

> One master says: the word 'soul' does not mean the ground or nature of the soul. One master says; whoever writes of mutable things does not touch upon or comprehend the nature or ground of the soul. Whoever wants to name the soul according to its unity and purity, as it is in itself, he can find no name for it.[3]

On the basis of this distinction we may say that the soul as form of the body is something, but in its essence it is nothing, "no thing", having no connection or relation to anything.

The mystery in all this lies in the fact that the soul, being "nothing" in its essence, thereby is seen to have a clear affinity with the transcendent, Godhead or *Gotheit*, which Eckhart also calls "nothing", since it is above and beyond being. Only in a certain sense are we right in calling God "Being"; in another sense we must deny Him this name, this first of names, since that which is the Cause of Being must itself be beyond being. Thus, like the ground of the soul, God is not Being but Nothing:

> If I say that God is being: that is not true. He is transcendent being: a transcendent nothingness.[4]

Nameability and Being are really one reality, and God and the ground of the soul are alike in that they are beyond both:

> God, who is nameless, is ineffable: he has no name. In the ground, it (i.e., the soul) is as unspeakable as He is.[5]

One might object at this point that the soul and God are not "nothing" in the same sense, however. God is nothing in the sense that he is above being and transcends it, whereas the soul is not above being and is only nothing in the sense of being created from nothing. To this we reply that the soul, also can be said to be above being, since it certainly possesses being – not being equivalent to absolute nothingness – and yet is nameless and transcendent, undefinable by functions or attributes. To name the soul according to these is not to touch it in its essence:

> It is as if you were to name someone a carpenter; you are not calling him 'soul' or 'man' or Henry or anything according to his own proper being; you are naming him only according to his proper work or function.[6]

In this it resembles God, for He too is not nothing in the sense of not possessing being, but in the sense that through possessing it in its fullness He transcends it utterly:

> When it is said that God is not a being and that he is above being, I have not thereby denied him being, I have exalted being in him.[7]

Eckhart would not deny, of course, that there is this difference: that what being the soul has, it does not possess by nature, but is conferred upon it by the creative Will of God, whereas God's Being is His by nature. But it is precisely here where the paradox lies. When we consider the soul as "being", then the distinction between it and God becomes most sharp, for in the soul being is conferred, whereas in God being and Essence are the same. Yet when we consider the soul as "nothing" then the distinction begins to fade away, and we find ourselves speaking of the soul in the same way that we speak of God, as nameless and transcendent. Once the creature affirms its own being, it sets itself up in opposition to God, who alone truly has being; once it denies its being, its affinity with God shines forth, and it is its nothingness which is the truest image of God.

This gives us the key to another perplexing problem, namely that of the soul's "uncreatedness". We note hastily that Eckhart never said that the soul is uncreated *tout court*, but there is that in it which is uncreated. But even this statement is disquieting enough, and we need to understand how Eckhart, who believed as an orthodox Christian and Dominican Friar that God was the creator of all things, could maintain that there is something in the soul which is not God but is nevertheless uncreated. We have not discovered any attempt in Eckhart's extant writings to deal with the problem clearly and unambiguously. But perhaps the clue to it lies precisely in this doctrine of the soul's nothingness, and here the writings of Berdyaev can assist us greatly. Like Eckhart, Berdyaev sees an affinity between the radical nothingness of the soul, and the transcendent Godhead. He then goes on, however, to draw a daring parallel between the Godhead as transcendent to God as Creator, and the nothingness of the soul which, so to speak, makes its creation possible by "freely consenting" to the being which God confers upon it. This passage deserves to be quoted in full:

> The Divine Nothing or the Absolute of the negative theology cannot be the Creator of the world. This has been made clear by German speculative mysticism. It is the burden of Eckhart's doctrine of the *Gottheit* and of Boehme's conception of the *Urgrund*. The creation of the world by God the Creator is a secondary act. From this point of view it may be said that freedom is not created by God: it is rooted in the Nothing, in the *Urgrund* from all eternity. Freedom is not determined by God: it is part of the nothing out of which God created the world. . . . Man is the child of God and the child of freedom — of nothing, of non-being, *to meon*. Meonic freedom — consented to God's act of creation; non-being freely accepted being. . . . Out of the abyss, out of the Divine Nothing is born the Trinitary God and He is confronted with meonic freedom. He creates out of nothing the world and man and expects from them an answer to His call — an answer from the depths of freedom.[8]

The similarity with Eckhart (whom Berdyaev clearly knows to some extent) is striking and illuminating. On the one hand we have the transcendent Nothingness of the Godhead, from which is born God as Trinity and Creator; on the other hand we have the pre-cosmic *to meon* from which are born the world and the human soul by an act of free consent. This makes the analogy between the "nothingness" of the soul and the "nothingness" of God abundantly clear. It is clear, too, that *to meon*, not being a "something" lies outside God's creative act, and that the ground of the soul, inasmuch as it partakes of that "nothingness" is also uncreated. It is not Being, which would have to be created; it is Not-Being, which has merely a potentiality for being. According to strict logic, of course, this statement makes very little sense. Nothingness is nothingness, and as such has no "potentiality" for anything. But neither is it an obstacle to anything, there is nothing in it which might resist God's creative call to "be". It is as it were a void in which God is free to act. In this sense it does have a potentiality to be, and also a potentiality to return to itself through decay and destruction. Hence Berdyaev is also justified in seeing it as the source of freedom and basing his daring ethic of creative freedom upon it. This preoccupation with freedom is, of course, characteristic of our own century, and Eckhart does not treat of freedom explicitly or give it anything like the same stress or prominence in his thought. We believe it is present, however, by implication, and we shall have occasion to refer to it again later on, in connection with the Way by which the soul attains to mystical union.

This analogy between the "nothingness" of the soul's essence and the transcendent Godhead, which Berdyaev also clearly perceives, is the basis of the affinity between the soul and God, and it is perhaps the most important of the conditions which make mystical union possible. We are not sure that Vladimir Lossky has altogether understood this, when in his otherwise excellent *Mystical Theology of the Eastern Church*[9], he criticises Western mysticism in general, and Eckhart in particular, for undervaluing the Trinity of Persons as the essence in which the Three are One. Lossky's contention seems to be that God revealed to us in the Judeo-Christian revelation is a Personal God, concrete and alive, rather than some cold, impersonal abstract Essence. Only with the Personal Trinity is it meaningful to talk of mystical union. A transcendent Essence is really just a philosophical notion, so a mysticism centered on perception of the Divine Essence is not truly Christian but a form of Gnosticism. Whether the "Gnostics" really held the notions which Lossky attributes to them is a question we cannot discuss here. We believe, however, that Lossky is much mistaken if he considers Eckhart's *Gottheit* as a cold, impersonal, intellectual notion, a concept belonging to philosophy rather than to the religion of Abraham, Isaac and Jacob. The *Gottheit* as understood by Eckhart is a truly *mystical* notion, in that it is concerned with the union of God and man in actual fact, and not with merely theoretical explanation. That much should be clear from what we have said earlier in this study, and it should become clearer still as it continues.

Secondly, if we speak of the Divine Essence as "transcending" the Trinity of Persons, we must be careful not to misunderstand this by imagining that Eckhart is "undervaluing" the Trinity or the Divine Personality. The power, the life, the infinite love and self-giving of the Three Persons is not obliterated or cancelled out by the unity of Essence; it is on the contrary heightened and brought to its fulfillment. The Essence is not the denial of Divine Personality but its ground, its origin, and its goal; the Persons are born from the Essence, and this return to the essence in order to find their fulfillment. Berdyaev understands the Trinity well when he says that it is a mystery of communion and self-giving, which is only possible between Persons. But Eckhart's insight leads him to see that so long as we speak only of "communion", and not of "unity", then we have not attained the heart of the mystery. So long as the Persons are seen only in their distinctness and intercommunion, they are only tending towards union; they are "like" instead of being "one". We can only speak of *oneness* when there no longer appears any distinction between the lover and the loved one, between subject and object.

This has profound implications for practical mysticism seeking union with God. The Persons are not merely "like" and do not merely "commune"; they are One; and it is in their common Essence that their Oneness is grounded. Similarly, Eckhart does not see the goal of mysticism as merely communion with God but oneness with God, which is why his mysticism is a mysticism of intellect rather than love, since as we have shown in our previous studies, love only *tends* towards its object, whereas intellect actually *unites* with it. Thus the *Gottheit*, like the essence of the soul, is not the denial of Personality, but its ground and fulfillment. We have already quoted Eckhart as saying that when he affirms God to be above Being, he is not denying Him Being, but exalting Being in Him. He could just as easily have said that when he affirms God to be more than Person he is not denying Him Personality but exalting and perfecting Personality in Him. God would not be Person unless He were more than Person. He would not be God, unless He were more than God.

The way in which the Three Persons emerge from the Nameless Essence and unite within it also has its analogue within the human soul and is part of that affinity between God and Man which makes mystical union possible. Looking first at God, we distinguish in Him two "emergings". The first is God emerging as Trinity from the Godhead; in Berdyaev's words: "Out of the abyss, out of the Divine Nothing is born the Trinitary God". The second emerging is that of God as Creator of the world, calling Nothingness into being and Communion finding Himself "confronted with meonic freedom" as Berdyaev puts it. In a certain sense we may say that God, by creating the world, is "going out from Himself", and yet at the same time he remains with Himself as God. He does not lose his Transcendent Godhead by creating; it remains inviolable as his innermost essence. The inviolability of the transcendent essence makes it possible to speak of God's "detachment": or *abegescheidenheit*. Since this virtue is, according to Eckhart, that which brings men closest to God, it is important for us to see its archetype in the Divine Nature. In God, detachment is precisely this inviolability of the Divine Essence, which would not be lost by the act of Creation, nor even by the Incarnation. This is why Eckhart is so anxious to stress that when God became man this was a work of love and humility, not of detachment for this last remained unaffected:

> Now you must know that lovable humility brought God to the point in which he lowered himself into human nature; yet detachment remained unmoved in itself when he became man, as it did when he created heaven and earth.[10]

The essence or ground of the human soul is similarly inviolable and is not in any way compromised by the soul's being also the form of the body and thereby obliged to relate to the external, material world. It retains its inner superiority and inviolability, containing the body as a principle contains its manifestation or the cause its effect:

> One master says: as little as the eye has to do with singing and the ear with perceiving color, likewise has the soul in her nature to do with all that is in this world. Therefore, our best masters about nature say that the body is in the soul rather than the soul in the body, the one holds the other within itself, — as the vessel holds the wine rather than the wine contains the vessel. Thus the soul contains the body within itself rather than the body the soul.[11]

God, by the act of creation, which is a going out, *ussgān*, affirms Himself as God and superior to that which He creates, and thus remains in Himself, *blibet in im selbst*. The soul, by the act of informing and vivifying the body, affirms itself as different and superior, and thus maintains its inviolability — unless it forgets its true nature and identifies with that which is beneath it. This, of course, is sin, and exactly what happens in a fallen world; yet even in these circumstances the soul cannot completely deny its own essence, which remains what it is despite ignorance and sin.

The passage we have just quoted speaks of the soul "containing the body, as a vat contains the wine which is in it". God "contains" the universe which He has created in a similar way, by being the Principle which it manifests. But there is another sense, too, in which God can be said to contain the universe, and this also has its analogue within the human soul. Eckhart, following the Neoplatonist theory of Dionysius, maintains that the universe is created according to the Ideas of it which are contained in the Divine Mind. These Ideas, inasmuch as they are in God, are not distinct from God; they *are* God. They are outside space and time; they have existed in God from all eternity. It is only inasmuch as they are realised in a creation distinct from God that they are subject to time, space, decay, and death. According to Eckhart created things as they are in God are incomparably superior to what they are in themselves. A gnat as it is in God is incomparably superior to an angel as it is in itself. The universe as it is in the mind of God is as far above the universe as it is in itself as an image made out of gold surpasses an image made out of coal:

> The image that is made of gold is far better than an image in coal; God has made all things as if out of coal.[12]

> Tell me how all the things of this corporeal world might stand in (the mind of) some angel, hanging incorporially in a certain light of the intellect, brilliant and

radiant according to the needs of the angelic recipient; for all things are more beautiful in proportion to the nobility of their matter, just as an image is more lovely in silver or gold than in coal.[13]

One master says: the natural perfection of the soul and of her nature is that she becomes in herself an intellectual world whereby God has imprinted in her the images of all things. Whoever says that he has got into his own true nature will find this, that he discovers in himself all things imaged in the purity which they have in God not as they are in their own nature, but as they are in God.[14]

We are drawing attention to this particular analogy between the human soul and God for the following reasons. First, it is another aspect of that basic affinity between man and God which makes mysticism possible. Secondly, it throws further light on the tantalising question of the soul's "uncreatedness". The soul as it is in itself is created and temporal but as it is in the mind of God it must *be* God, uncreated and existing for all eternity. The Pythagorean and Platonic belief in pre-existence and transmigration, like the Hindu belief in reincarnation, are not acceptable to the Christian mind in the form in which they are couched, but Eckhart's perspective may show the truth that underlies these unacceptable expressions. Berdyaev, too, has noticed this:

. . . the Christian view does not make clear the mystery of the genesis of the soul. The presence of the eternal element in the soul means eternity not only in the future but in the past as well. That which has an origin in time cannot inherit eternity. If the human soul bears the image and likeness of God, if it is God's idea, it arises in eternity and not in time, in the spiritual and not in the natural world.[15]

The third point we wish to make is the following. The Idea, eternally existing in the mind of God, is not only the beginning of the soul's career; it is also its goal. Transfiguration, glorification, deification— what all these terms mean is simply the perfect conformation of man to that Idea of him which has existed in the mind of God from all eternity. It is a return to that which has always been. This is the very goal of the mystical quest, which is why Eckhart on his spiritual pilgrimage, finds it necessary to search for the supreme virtue:

. . . that supreme virtue whereby a man would become most like that image which he had in God (in which there was no distinction between him and God) before God made the creatures (created the universe).[16]

The greatest of virtues, which will lead to man's perfect conformity with the Divine Image, is, of course, the celebrated *abegescheidenheit* or non-attachment, and this leads us to the next part of our study, concerned with the Way the mystical union is to be achieved.

The Way to God for Eckhart, as for any Christian, lies in the practice of virtue, the fulfilling of the Law of Christ. But we must be careful not to misunderstand what is meant by "virtue" here. It is not to be seen as obedience to a set of external moral norms imposed on us from without; not even though these norms be backed up by Divine authority, as was the case with the old Jewish law, and is still the case in a slightly different way with the canonical laws laid down by the Church insofar as she functions as a social organization. Laws of this kind, however necessary they may be for humans in a fallen world not yet transformed fully by Divine grace, are not what the Kingdom of God, as revealed by Christ, is all about. The Law of Christ is not concerned with conforming to external rules, but with an inner transformation of the heart. It is not so much what we do, as what we are, that matters. The Beatitudes taught by Christ on the mountain are not, like the ten commandments, rules for behaviour, they are an expression of a state of *being*. This has been seen very clearly by Berdyaev:

> The Gospel appeals to the inner, spiritual man, and not to the outer man, a member of society. It calls not for external works in the social world but for the awakening and regeneration of the spiritual life, for a new birth that is to bring us into the Kingdom of God.[17]

It is also Eckhart's position, stated clearly and unambiguously in numerous texts, such as the following:

> People shouldn't think so much about what they do, they should think more about what they are. If people and their mode of being were good then would their works immediately shine forth. If you are just, then all your works will be just. We shouldn't think of holiness as grounded on deeds, we should think of holiness as grounded on a way of being. Our works do not make us holy, but we should make our works holy . . . . . so far as we are and have being, to that extent we make holy all our works such as eating, sleeping, keeping vigil or whatever.[18]

This criticism of "justification by works" differs from Luther's in that this inward holiness, contrasted with merely external virtue, is not based simply on a conviction of man's hopeless corruption which can be remedied only by faith in the redemptive power of God. It is based upon a real ontological transformation in man's *being*, so that he is not merely *saved* but *deified*. Holiness is not imputed to him, but imparted. It is not simply that God, in his infinite mercy, chooses to overlook our corruption and consider us as good; we actually cease to be corrupt. Luther could not accept that there was any real transubstantiation, — that is, ontological transformation either in the Eucharist or in the soul of man. Eckhart not merely accepted this truth; it lies at the very centre of his mystical doctrine. On this point, at least, he cannot be regarded as a precursor of the Reformers.

This means that that virtue is highest and best, and unites us most closely to God, which is grounded upon our inward essence rather than on any relation to externals, whether these be other people or material things, or even God Himself considered as external "object" of our strivings. Therefore Eckhart does not consider love to be the highest virtue, as many Christian writers do, for love always involves some relation to externals. It is communion rather than union, — a distinction we have met with before. *Abegescheidenheit*, however, has no relation to externals, and leads to real union with the essence of God. Hence it is a higher virtue than love:

> . . . I praise detachment above love, for love forces me to endure all things for God's sake, but detachment causes me to be receptive of nothing save God. Now it is a far nobler thing to be receptive of nothing save God than to endure all things for God's sake. For in enduring, a man has some regard to the creature which is causing him suffering, but detachment stands free of all creatures.[19]

That in us which is most Godlike is our inward essence, which is nothingness, *niht*, as we have seen before *Abegescheidenheit* is the only virtue that brings us to this:

> Now detachment is so close to Nothingness that nothing but God alone is sufficiently subtle to be contained within detachment. Therefore detachment is receptive of nothing apart from God.[20]

Other virtues, such as humility and compassion, turn out to be the same. Excellent and necessary though they are, they involve some degree of externality and do not remain within the inner essence where alone can God be found. They belong to the will rather than to the intellect, they lead to communion but not oneness. Suffering, too, has a great and important part to play in our path towards union; one which we have not so far done justice to and which we shall perhaps have occasion to discuss more fully in future studies. A spritual path which took no account of suffering would not be based on life in the real world, where suffering is built into the very structure of things; neither could such a path be called Christian, since crucifixion is for the Christian the essential condition for renunciation and transfiguration.

But even suffering, though horribly and inescapably real, does not touch the essence of the soul nor its union with God. The value of suffering lies in the fact that it strips us of self and of the inclination to rely upon externals, by knocking away the props on which we are accustomed to lean, forcing us to retreat into our inward essence and lean upon God there. But once we do that we have got beyond love and sacrificial suffering, and have attained to perfect *abegescheidenheit*. Eckhart maintains that this is what Christ did upon the cross, so that in the midst of all the torments He endured out of love for the Father and the human race, His *abegescheidenheit* remained pure and unaffected, for it belonged to His Divine Essence, which could not be touched by temporal pain. It belonged to the inner, not the outer man:

> Now you must know that the outer man can be in a state of travail while the inner man can be entirely free and unchanging. Now in Christ too there was an outer man and an inner man and also in Our Lady, and whatever Christ and Our Lady ever said about outer things had reference to the outer man and the inner man remained in unchanging detachment. And it is in this sense that Christ was speaking when he said "My soul is troubled even unto death".[21]

The time has come for us to define this *abegescheidenheit*, this highest of virtues which brings us into our own essence, our own nothingness where we can be made one with God. The word *abegescheidenheit* seems to have been invented by Eckhart himself, for it is not found in any German writings before him, though it is clearly formed from the verb *scheiden*, to separate or split off. In Eckhart it acquires a richness and importance which makes it impossible for us to translate it by any single word. We have already suggested "non-attachment" in previous studies; but Blakney is also right in seeing "disinterestedness" as an essential part of its meaning. It is, in fact, the virtue of total selflessness, the state of one who has totally gone out from self and from all things. Fortunately, Eckhart has left us a clear definition of it in his own words:

> Now you might ask: 'what is detachment if it is so noble in itself?' Here you must know that true detachment is quite simply that the spirit remains as unmoved by all accidental pleasure and pain, honour, humiliation, and burden as a mountain of lead is moved by a tiny breeze. The unchangeable detachment brings man into the greatest likeness with God. For the fact that God is God he has from his unmovable detachment and from his detachment he has his purity and his singleness and his unchangingness.[22]

This shows why it is that *abegescheidenheit* is divine; it is so because it is a participation in God's immutability, purity, and oneness. It should be clear from what we have said above that it does not mean a kind of stony insensitivity, rendering a man incapable of warm human sentiment such as love, compassion, joy and pain. Christ's love and suffering on the cross were not in any way lessened by his non-attachment; on the contrary they were heightened and intensified by it, since it was his non-attachment that enabled Him to go through with the whole terrible business and drink the bitter cup to the dregs. We said earlier that the Divine Nothingness, the Transcendent Essence of the Godhead, does not lessen the infinite self-giving and communion of the Three Persons; it gives rise to it and fulfills it. The same is true of non-attachment, which is the soul's analogue to the nothingness of the Godhead. It is not the denial of personality, love, or warm feeling; it transcends them only by being their origin and their goal. It is not ruled by feeling, and especially not by any hedonistic pursuit of happiness or avoidance of pain. But feeling remains, in its highest and most intense form.

Since it is not "ruled" by anything, *abegescheidenheit* therefore represents *freedom* in its highest form. An adjective which Eckhart often applies to the non-attached soul is *ledig*, meaning "free and untrammelled". This brings us back to Berdyaev and the question of freedom which is so crucial for us in the twentieth century. On this matter the centuries which separate us from Eckhart roll away, and he speaks to us, not with a medieval but a contemporary voice. The ontological root of the non-attached soul, *lediges gemuet*, is its nothingness as we have seen; and this brings us close, not only to Berdyaev but also to Heidegger and Sartre. The freedom which springs from the ground of the soul liberates a man from all external conditioning factors, whether physical, social, political, or religious. It is easy to see from Eckhart's writings that he was in no sense a political or social drop-out; he was not a revolutionary or agitator but a good citizen, an exemplary friar utterly obedient to the Church and its authority.

The outer man in him respected society, the Church and their conditioning. The inner man in him, however, was free from all this, and transcended it, enabling him to think boldly and creatively, revealing depths within the Christian revelation which others had barely hinted at, so that in a sense he not only transcended the medieval world but even Christianity itself insofar as "Christianity" is encapsulated in solid, traditional formulas; this is why he is virtually the only Christian thinker whose statements make perfect sense to Hindus, Buddhists and Moslems (at any rate, to those Moslems who follow the mystical tradition of the Sufis). Eckhart's freedom is exemplified further by his creative use of the German language, which he did not merely accept in its given form but moulded and reshaped according to his own inner vision. This is "authenticity" in the existentialist sense, and it springs from *abegescheidenheit*. There is an important message here for us in the twentieth century who are apt to become engrossed in the political and social aspects of freedom, which, however important and urgent, are not its essence. True freedom, as Eckhart shows us, is essentially an inward thing, and unless we achieve it within we cannot hope to achieve it without. No amount of political revolution or re-distribution of the world's resources can ever free us so long as we remain inwardly enslaved to self. Action on these more contingent levels is indeed urgent and necessary, but unless it springs from a non-attached spirit, *lediges gemuet*, it cannot hope to accomplish much in the end.

We cannot end our discussion of *abegescheidenheit* without alluding to that in it which is most mysterious and paradoxical. Earlier on we said that it belongs to the inner man, the essence wherein he is most "himself". Yet at the same time it is the point where Self fades out and God takes over. Thus we must say that it is the work of grace rather than nature:

> And if a man is to become equal with God, in so far as a creature can have equality with God, then it must be brought about by detachment. This brings about a likeness or equality between God and man and this likeness must come about through grace: for grace detaches a man from all temporal things and purifies all transient things. And you must know that to be empty of all creatures is to be full of God, and to be full of all creatures is to be empty of God.[23]

This means that it is not a virtue which we should attempt to *cultivate!* Being so simple and untrammelled, it cannot possibly be the *object* of any man's strivings. To strive for it would mean losing it. Striving belongs to the will, and *abegescheidenheit* is above will, being above self. We may strive for love, humility, compassion, whatever other virtue we will, but never for non-attachment. This is why Eckhart, having extolled the excellence of *abegescheidenheit* throughout his famous treatise on the subject, concludes by saying we must not attempt to aim at it. Humility, *dimuetecheit*, abasement of self—this is what we should aim for. The rest is the work of grace. *Abegescheidenheit* comes only when there is nothing left of self and only God remains.

We shall conclude this rather superficial study by some brief remarks on the *goal* of the mystical quest, and how far it is really possible for man to be transformed into God. First we shall make a couple of fairly obvious points, and end with one which is much deeper and more mysterious.

Our first point is that Eckhart's spirituality is not noticeably very corporate or ecclesial. "Togetherness" is not a prominent element in his thought. Did he therefore underestimate the corporate character of Christian salvation, and forget that we are saved as members of a body, the Body of Christ? Is his mysticism really like that of Plotinus, a flight from the alone to the Alone? We believe that this question is answered by reference to what we have already said about the distinction between *union* and *communion*. The communion of the Persons within the Trinity is transcended and perfected in the Godhead wherein they are all one. Similarly the communion of the human person with God as Person, together with the communion with the other members of the Mystical Body, is not denied but perfected by the ineffable union within the ground of the soul. True communion or *sobornost*, as Berdyaev has shown, does not come simply from fraternising or merging oneself in a collective mentality — even the mentality of so-called "Christendom". True communion is rooted in free consent, and freedom is rooted in the ground, in the *lediges gemuet*. If we are not one in the Ground, we shall not be one in that community which is the Church. There is no communion without freedom; freedom is the esoteric reality of which communion is the exoteric manifestation. Without the freedom within the Ground, what we shall have is not communion but mere fraternisation.

Our last point is the most mysterious, and it is the question of how deep and how real our transformation in God can hope to be. It is possible to understand the Neo-Platonic theory of Divine Ideas in a totally dualistic way, creating an irrevocable gulf between spirit and matter. Created earthly things are but a pale reflection of their Ideas in God. The Ideas are eternal but the earthly things themselves are temporal, coming into being and passing away. Thus all talk of their "issuing forth" from God and "returning" to God might only be a metaphor, not implying that they undergo any real ontological change. It might simply be a poetical way of saying that they are born and die; only their Ideas remain forever. We do not think ourselves that this is Eckhart's conception. His thought, as we have said on many occasions, is not dualistic, and therefore it admits of no sharp distinction between spirit and matter. This means that real transformation is possible.

The issue at stake here is central to Christianity, for it concerns the Resurrection and what it means. On this matter Christians seem to divide sharply, depending on whether or not they think that a material, physical body can be "glorified". On the one hand there are those who hold that the Resurrection was simply an event in the minds of the disciples, a sudden realization that despite the crucifixion Jesus' life had "meant something" after all. A similar opinion is voiced by those who hold that if anything of Jesus survived His death, it can only have been his soul, the "spiritual" part of Him. In either case there can be no question of the physical body escaping the fate of decay and dissolution which rules over all matter. This view is perfectly sensible and coherent, although if it is true there seems no reason why we should prefer Christianity to Gnosticism or one of the Asian religions.

The early Church, however, seems to have thought differently, and so did the mediaeval church to which Eckhart belonged. Like others of his time, he believed in the possibility of a real transformation of matter. There is a movement from the spiritual world into the material world, and back into the spiritual world again; a movement which remains continuous although it implies real ontological change. All this is implicit in a "non-dual" way of looking at things. Another consequence of it is that the end of the process will be analogous, but not identical, to the beginning. Man will not be quite the same being on his return to God as he was when he first came forth. But as yet we have not found anything in Eckhart to suggest what the nature of that difference might be, though modern thinkers such as Berdyaev have speculated on the question.

Once the wheel has turned full circle, however, and the whole process of emanation and return is over, it makes no more sense to speak of endings or beginnings; there remains only that which has always been in God. Is it really possible for man, created from the dust of the earth, to be raised to such a state, of *identity* with God? In his Latin notes for a sermon on John 12, 25, Eckhart observes:

> Nota: anima in mundo isto solum est amore. Nam ubi amat, ibi est, qualia amat, talis est. Aug(ustinus) super id (novicam) io (amoris) om (ilia); terra amas, terra es; deum amas, quid dicam? Deus eris non audeo dicere ex me. Scripturas audiamus: ego dixi: dii estis, etc.[24]

However daring Eckhart's notion of deification may be, he is not saying anything that has not been said before him by the Scriptures and by St. Augustine. As Coplestone remarks:

> Phrases like man becoming God or the transformation of the soul into God can be found in the works of writers of unquestioned orthodoxy. If the mystic wishes to describe the mystical union of the soul with God and its effects, he has to make use of words which are not designed to express any such thing. For example, in order to express the closeness of the union, the elevation of the soul and the effect of the union on the soul's activity, he employs a verb like "transform" or "change into". But "change into" denotes such processes as assimilation (of food), consumption of material by fire, production of steam from water, heat from energy, and so on, whereas the mystical union of the soul with God is *sui generis* and really requires an altogether new word to describe it.[25]

But of course, as Coplestone goes on to say, no such word is available in any known language, so the mystic has to use expressions from everyday use, and leave it to intuition to effect the necessary transposition. Not all who read mystical works are able to do this; hence the unfortunate misunderstandings. One thing, however, we can be sure of: when the terms employed by the mystics are properly understood, they will be found to mean *more*, and not *less*, than they do in ordinary language. Transformation, as Eckhart understands it, is a deeper and more real thing than the physical processes alluded to by Coplestone, which are only a metaphor for it. This is perhaps a suitable thought on which to end this essay.

Notes

1   Adolf Spamer, *Texte aus der Deutschen Mystik des 14 and 15 Jahrhunderts* (Jena, 1912), p. 152. [Translations by author].

2   *Ibid.*, p. 136.

3   *Ibid.*, pp. 48-49. The "master" is Avicenna.

4   Franz Pfeiffer, *Meister Eckhart. Deutsche Mystiker des 14 Jahrhunderts*, Bd. 2, 4th. edition (Gottingen, 1924), p. 319.

5   Spamer, *op. cit.*, p. 53.

6   Pfeiffer, *op. cit.*, p. 269.

7   *Idem.*

8   Nicholas Berdyaev, *The Destiny of Man* (London, 1959), pp. 25-26.

9   Vladimir Lossky, *Mystical Theology of the Eastern Church* (London, 1957), pp. 64-65.

10   Eduard Schaefer, *Meister Eckhart's Traktat "Von Abegescheidenheit"* (Bonn, 1956), pp. 159-160.

11   Spamer, *op. cit.*, pp. 55-56.

12   *Ibid.*, pp. 57-58. The original has "pendente" but this is surely a mistake.

13   *Ibid.*, p. 50.

14   *Ibid.*, pp. 56-57.

15   Berdyaev, *op. cit.*, p. 257.

16   Schaefer, *op. cit.*, pp. 152-153.

17   *Ibid.*, pp. 123-124.

18   J. A. Bizet, *Mystique Allemande du XVe. Siecle* (Paris, 1957), p. 127.

19   Schaefer, *op. cit.*, p. 155.

20   *Ibid.*, pp. 155-156.

21 *Ibid.*, pp. 175-176.

22 *Ibid.*, pp. 164-165.

23 Spamer, *op. cit.*, pp. 165-166.

24 *Ibid.*, p. 53.

25 Frederick Copleston, S. J., *A History of Philosophy* (Garden City, 1962), Vol. 3 Part I, pp. 205-206.

Hopkins on Self and Freedom:
On the Possibility of the
Mystical Union

Jorge García-Gómez

My intent here is to come to terms, in principle, with mysticism, and yet I propose to do so paradoxically, for, instead of dealing with this form of experience directly, I am going to look away from it, so to speak, in order to grasp its significance. Now, this procedure is not as strange as it first sounds, for what I have in mind is the examination of matters relevant thereto in a way which is strictly *metaphysical*.

Consistent with this decision, I mean, first of all, to free these remarks from the weight of any conclusion deriving either from the consideration of the causes, motives, components, and effects of mystical experience, or from the presentation of the descriptive features proper to mysticism and the essence they constitute. I am setting aside the first sort of questions not because they are inherently illegitimate — were that my reason, I would have had to have already established it as a necessary fact, which is far from being the case. My justification is simply that, in raising them, one *takes for granted* something that has not been proven, to wit: the genuine *existence* of a special set of facts and events, which are seen as endowed with a *nature* of their own. Coming to this realization should lead one to adopt the alternative approach already identified, and yet this move is also to be suspended on similar grounds, for in it one would assume occurrences and manners of lawfulness not in evidence, namely, that mystical phenomena form a realm *sui generis*, that is to say, that they integrate a province of facts and events set off from (and somehow abidingly connected with) the all-encompassing universe. But this *presupposition* is precisely the subject to be validated in an antecedent investigation which is properly metaphysical in style, for it consists in determining the fundamentals on the basis of which any thing or kind of thing, any manner of lawfulness, and the totality of all there-is (*complicatio omnium*) are rendered possible. Now, this is just the sort of inquiry concerning mysticism I envisaged above, inasmuch as one therein would simply address oneself to the ultimate foundations of the universe and experience, in order *retrospectively* to see whether the phenomena belonging to mysticism—or anything else, for that matter—would in some fashion arise therefrom and become established. However appealing this *radical* procedure may appear at first blush, it is nonetheless an enterprise of vast proportions, indeed a veritable gigantomachy about reality,[1] for which the space available to me here will no doubt be insufficient, and in which I would prove no worthy contender. Given such constraints, it is reasonable to limit one's musings to a few basic matters and relationships, particularly to questions that may be raised within the confines of a special but relevant context, namely, that of the dialectic of freedom and necessity as it is actually operative in human experience. Moreover, on the basis of the kind of familiarity about this area that is characteristic of my personal stock of knowledge, I will interpret this context exclusively from a Christian vantage point, even if I am to examine it only philosophically, not theologically. Now, that signifies that what is to follow will not even be a satisfactory rehearsal of the principles of a *metaphysica generalis*; it will more likely amount to a preliminary formulation of anthropologico-metaphysical problems relevant to mysticism. Hence, any clarification of the subject here under scrutiny that would be arrived at on such a basis must needs be incomplete and at best hypothetical, and yet it will, I hope, pave the way for more ambitious and decisive analyses.

As a first step in that direction, let me try to present, in very broad strokes, the entire sweep of human experience. At one end, man would be found acting and suffering—bodily, mentally, and spiritually—in terms of all the powers and limitations inherent in his nature pure and simple. This is what I wish to call *mere natural experience*.[2] At the opposite end, man would be seen undergoing the many-sided experience that has been named, from the point of view of its intellectual dimension, the *beatific vision*, and which has been accordingly characterized, following Benedict XII's definition, as "*visio intellectiva et facialis* of God's essence".[3] Between these two extremes, the various forms of experience of which man is capable would be modalized,[4] so far as their belief-contents and foundations and the subjective correlates thereof are concerned, under the influence of faith, hope, and charity. Such an influence would begin to be exerted (and the resulting modalizations to become identifiable) already at the ordinary levels of the believer's everyday life, which would thus be transformed into "a sort of experiential knowledge and familiarity that is possible only among those who love one another",[5] but the transmutation in question could eventually progress into the very depths of one's life, at which point one would have reached the *mystical* form of experience proper.

In my opinion, this *aperçu* should in due course lead us to the very heart of the matter under examination, namely, to the problem of mysticism *ut sic*. To appreciate this point, one must at least provide a definition of mystical experience, one that is here advanced only heuristically and hypothetically. To put it in the words of Jacques Maritain, mysticism is a "fruitive experience of the absolute".[6] Now, if by this formula one grasps the essence of this sort of experience, one must then distinguish between two necessarily complementary sides thereof, a point which is suggested by the different senses the words "experience" and "fruitive" have, for they signify, respectively, the contemplative and unitive dimensions of mysticism. The contemplative aspect of the mystical experience (insofar as it is intimately bound up with the fruitive) displays a highly paradoxical visage, for it indicates that mysticism involves an inclination and desire to see or regard the Divine, and yet it manages to do so only as a qualified failure, which, although it is "explainable" in terms of the dialectic of finitude and infinity and the arcanum of personhood, here gains expression as a function of objectivation. Accordingly, one could say that contemplation is characterizable in this context as the attempt to know by which man, when he directs his eyes to the Divine, seeks to become connatural to or familiar with God Himself, precisely insofar as He is a reality that is not *"open to conceptual objectivation"*, to use Maritain's own expression.[7] In other words, mysticism is man's endeavor to see God *qua* invisible (or as He truly is Himself), an assertion that obviously does not refer to any human attempt to see the invisible (a *contradictio in adiecto*), but rather signifies the realization that God in principle escapes all human ideative or conceptual understanding. It would be hard, however, to distinguish this manner of experience from the form of thinking of God that is called *negative theology* (i.e., the conceptual study of God *via negationis*),[8] were the idea of mysticism not immediately linked with that of *fruition* (or with the notion of the fulfillment and enjoyment of the union with God). Now, let us be clear about the fact that the concept of fruition does not denote another phase of the mystical experience that would follow — however instantaneously — the moment of contemplation, but, properly speaking, it designates the other, positive side of one's sustained performative realization that the nature of the living God is non-conceptualizable. Or equivalently stated: grasping God as invisible is co-extensive with seeking Him as the *"terminus of objective union"*.[9] In this sense, one would have to assert that mystical contemplation is after union or fruition, that it is a movement towards man's fulfillment in God Himself as the source of man's being,[10] and that it progresses in the direction of a manner of living in which man would become divine by God's own personal presence to him.[11] Or to use Maritain's blunt but insightful formula: mystical experience is "fruitive unknowing" of God.[12] Accordingly, one must say that the mystical experience is the context in which, by the agency of God Himself, the finitude of man is sublated, however provisionally and inadequately, while we are still *in via*, for the sort of union in which this will come to pass would be a genuine joining with God in *this* life, an event that shall preserve and enhance the human condition defined in Christianity as being in this world but not of it,[13] for it is only "an imperfect foretaste of the [beatific or] blessed vision of God in eternity",[14] however intense or enduring it may prove at times to be.

All this notwithstanding, the classical theological emphasis on the contemplative nature of mysticism, even if the experience is conceptually placed in the perspective of fruition, can be highly misleading and even become a source of error, unless one keeps alive to the complexity of the mystical life. In a genuine mystical experience belonging to a man who is continually open and directed to the fruitive contemplation of God, there is, no doubt, knowledge and vision of God, insofar as man is joined with God by His virtue, and yet this realization fails to do full justice to the mystical life, for it is too much concerned with facets and conditions of experience, while it leaves out of account the overriding fruitive interest by which such a man would seek one and only one thing, namely, union with God. Now, should someone want conceptually to measure up to this decisive and fundamental sense of the mystical life, he would at least have to find a means to overcome the multiplicity of states and phases present in the history of the mystic's life. And yet no indiscriminate choice of means, however lofty they may turn out to be, is allowable for this purpose; only a means that is immanent in the multiplicity of the inner life of the mystic will do, that is to say, exclusively a means that would itself be effecting life's unification from within is pertinent to that task. But that can be no other than the mystic's inherent *télos* insofar as it is ordered to the transcendent God as He encompasses the man in personal familiarity. Perhaps one way of formulating the grounds on the basis of which the unity of the mystical life originates is to say, with Wulf, that "mysticism, in the theological sense, is . . . the charismatic gnosis possessed by the perfect spiritual, a gnosis enveloped by the love of charity".[15] Here we are at last at the heart of the matter, for what in the final analysis counts is the love that guides man and beckons him toward union with God, a love by which his life is ultimately one and unified, for, as Maritain well put it, "the supernatural love of charity alone is capable of rendering the soul connatural to the Divinity".[16]

Let me now turn to a segment of the spectrum of human experience that I described above, a stretch I would again characterize as the everyday form of living of the ordinary Christian, insofar as it is "modalized . . . under the influence of faith, hope, and charity".[17] In other words, I would like to focus upon the examination of what I called *mere natural experience*,[18] but only by bearing in mind the extent to which it appears transformed under the influence of supernatural gifts. I will endeavor to do this, however, by leaving out of account both the mystical form of earthly Christian experience and the beatific vision; here is the source, then, of the paradoxical character of this step, of which I have already spoken,[19] and yet this is no impediment, I believe, to my dealing with mystical experience by strict implication, that is, in terms of some of the conditions that would render it possible. To this end, I would like to avail myself of Gerard Manley Hopkins's concept of *pitch*, keeping in view, as it will eventually become apparent, a most important experiential context, one to which I have already alluded, namely, the field of moral action insofar as it is established by means of the dialectic of freedom and necessity.[20] In my opinion, Hopkins's concept, and some of its principal applications, will prove most useful for my purposes, especially if I try to take full advantage of his originality of expression, a fact that is not reducible to mere linguistic inventiveness, for indeed it is the incarnation of genuine philosophical thought.

To begin with, any appeal to the sense or senses of the word "pitch" may be disconcerting, since the "notion" behind the term does not apply to man alone. As Hopkins says, *pitch* is a manner of being, or a *distinctive* placement in the universe.[21] But what does this highly abstract idea exactly mean? As a first approximation, let us gather our clues from the significations of the locution as actually used, at least from those that are compatible with Hopkins's employment of it. *As a noun*, it connotes "a place at which one stations oneself or is stationed, a position of ground selected by or alloted to a person for residence, business, or any occupation . . .",[22] or a "position taken up and maintained", including "a fixed position or resolution",[23] or the ". . . supreme point or degree; acme, climax . . .",[24] or the "comparative height or intensity of any quality or attribute . . .",[25] or, finally, the "quality of musical sound which depends on the comparative rapidity of the vibrations producing it; [the] degree of acuteness or graveness of tone . . ."[26] On this basis, it is suggested that pitch is the relative degree of being of any natural entity, a measure that allows it to take up and hold its ground in the world by establishing thereupon its abode or residence as a result of its own proper activity. *As a verb*, "pitch" acquires the additional and most important signification of casting or flinging forward.[27] Accordingly, one may entertain the hypothesis that pitch is that relative degree of being by which an entity casts itself or is cast or flung toward some intrinsic acme, constantly to achieve and endeavor to hold its abode or residence in the universe.

In a most interesting passage, Hopkins connects this concept with the Aristotelian notion of *enérgeia* or actuality, which, in his own words, is "the stress . . . of the intrinsic possibility"[28] an entity is or has. Now, what the Greek philosopher understood by *enérgeia* can only be adequately grasped in relation to what he meant by its pair, namely, *kínesis*. As Aristotle said, *kínesis* is an entity's manner of change which consists in the "functioning [*entelékheia*] . . . of what is potential, when there is actually some thing being realized [*enérgeia*], not as itself but as movable . . ."[29] In other words, something is changing in the way of *kínesis* when it is *actually* a potentiality to be something definite (as the bronze is with regard to a statue),[30] in the sense of having a goal or *télos* in the manner of being *de-prived* of it. In this light, one can say that *kínesis* is a process, and not an activity or *enérgeia*, inasmuch as the former is incomplete or not yet at its *télos*,[31] while the latter is the state in which an entity is self-possessed, being already at its essential *télos*, in the sense of being itself as itself at work, or at the *érgon* that consists in the actual performance of its own intrinsic *télos*.[32]

At a first reckoning, one may say that the pitch or *enérgeia* of an entity is highly paradoxical in nature, for it is at once restful and never at rest: it is, on the one hand, a state or condition of being that allows the thing its own self-identity, and, on the other hand, it is an anticipation of itself that consists in flinging itself forward toward itself (i.e., in the direction of its intrinsic acme). This is what Aristotle characterized, in the case of man, as self-progress towards self *qua* actuality.[33] One could then say, perhaps daringly, that the entity is the self-performance of its own identity.

Let me now focus on man as he is concretely found in the wealth of immediate experience, i.e., as I live myself in my own life, both as human nature and as an individual.[34] Basically there is no difference between myself and other subsisting entities of this world, for I meet myself always as "something most determined and distinctive, at pitch . . .";[35] there is only a qualitative distinction founded on the varying degrees of *enérgeia* exhibited by the manifold kinds of entity.[36] But how is it then that I appear to myself? Hopkins argues that I find myself as the natural system of

> ... my pleasures and my pains, my powers and my experiences, my deserts and guilt, my shame and sense of beauty, my dangers, hopes, fears, and all my fate, more important to myself than anything I see ... [37]

In sum: I am the concrete unfolding, anticipation, recollection, and outcome of my encounter with the world, a fact that not only establishes me as *primus inter pares* in the universally graded context of *enérgeia*, insofar as I am "more highly pitched, selved, and distinctive than anything in the world",[38] but as well determines, by virtue of this very reason, that I should find myself " . . . more important to myself than anything I see . . ."

Here then we witness a reversal in approach, indeed one we may experience as a paradox, for the *objective* stance adopted at first by Hopkins is now turned about and displaced by a *subjective* interest. And yet the position where he now places himself is something other than solipsism. At every point, I matter to myself insofar as I am at stake at the world in regard to others, including undoubtedly the Other *par excellence*.[39] And if "this throng and stack of being"[40] is to me the most important component and dimension of reality when I regard it cosmologically, it is even more so when I approach it in all its wealth, as it is disclosed in the immediacy of my experience, i.e., of "my selfbeing, my consciousness and feeling of myself",[41] for there I meet with myself not only without mediation, but also in an *incommunicable* fashion, a realization he was able to formulate to himself early in life and put it to us most disarmingly this way: "as when I was a child I used to ask myself: what must it be to be someone else?"[42] No wonder, then, that Hopkins chose a different turn of expression to convey his point, for now he no longer speaks in terms of *vision* but of *taste*.[43] In his judgment, *I ultimately am to myself as I taste myself*, and this flavor of myself that I am to myself is "more distinctive than the taste of ale or alum, more distinctive than the smell of walnutleaf or camphor . . ."[44] The paradox resolves itself, then, in a *lógos* that points *negatively* at the other (although, mind you, not in the form of "I am not he", but rather in that of "he is not me", since I am the "standard" or main referent of comparison in experience), while it *positively* underscores myself, for I already am *me* in the immediacy of flavor lived. Or to put it in his own words: "Nothing else in Nature comes near this unspeakable stress of pitch, distinctiveness, and selving, this selfbeing of my own".[45]

What is at work here, it seems to me, is Hopkins's awareness of the performative dual unity which is characteristic of every form of experience. In other words, it is clear that he is alive to the reciprocity of self and world in spontaneity, or to what Husserl later would describe as the noetico-noematic nexus of consciousness.[46] This unity structurally allows for its being underscored in different ways as the varying interests of living motivate, for at times (in fact, usually) it is the *objective* side that prevails (but always with a subjective twist and "taste" to it), inasmuch as consciousness is inherently intentional or other-directed, but, on occasion, it is the *subjective* concern that overrides all (but even then it is given as the way of access to the objective). It is precisely this transition and *disclosure* that Hopkins is emphasizing here by means of that "subjective" turn of experience called *reflection*, where an already felt identity, i.e., myself, shows itself now as an "object" endowed with an unsuspected visage of "unspeakable stress".[47] Hopkins's faithfulness to experience, as he displays it here and continually, should commend itself to the reader, especially in those cases in which he is speaking no longer of the looks of the outer world or of the readily available aspects of the inner life, for he is then engaged in the practice of metaphysical analysis at full, while managing nonetheless to proceed on the same basis.

At the root of what anything is, Hopkins finds an intrinsic reference to the Godhead, to the extent that He is the transcendent summit of the universe *qua* "system" of *enérgeiai*. A thing, understood as pitch, depends essentially for what it is on the infinite or universal mind. And yet this position can be easily misrepresented as if it were reducible *simpliciter* to expressing a relationship to a principle (as if Hopkins's thesis belonged to a mere logic), when it rather is the foundation of a cosmic totality which is only taken properly as the unfolding of the *essential but free history of being*. There is in fact an important section where the difference I have in mind is illustrated by the application of the notion of pitch to the moral life of man. This is what Hopkins has there to say:

> God can shift the self that lies in one to a higher, that is . . . better, pitch of itself; that is to a pitch of determination of itself on the side of the good.[48]

Now then, this means not only that man is a definite pitch in the *melody of being*,[49] but as well that, within that definite value, he can *modulate* it at various levels within his own range, that is to say, from good to evil. Furthermore, the pitch of man, its range, and its various possible modulations result from God's *internal* presence to man's being, whether consciously or not. Important though this may be, Hopkins does not rest his case here, but he continues as follows:

But here arises a darker difficulty still; for how can we tell that each self has, in particular, any such better self, any such range from bad to good? In the abstract there is such a range of pitch and conceivably a self to be found, actually or possibly, at each point in it, but how can *each* self have all those pitches?, for this seems contrary to its freedom . . . [50]

As posed, the problem of the universal validity of Hopkins's theory of pitch finds in man its *instantia crucis*. Stated bluntly, the *aporia* is this: if man is essentially free, how is it possible that I be *all* these pitches, i.e., every actual and possible modulation within my range?, for, if I am thus and so, then I am substantially determined and unfree. Here we seem to have reached an impasse, for, on the one hand, I feel myself to be free in immediate experience, and, on the other, an analysis of the structures and foundations of my being appear to characterize it as an entity *ab alio*.

In order to come to terms with this grave difficulty, Hopkins introduces a notion that at first blush flies in the face of his theory of pitch. On the one hand, in the sway of its unmitigated universality, he holds the thesis that anything in this world is selved or pitched; on the other hand, he speaks of some human states as characterized by an "absence of pitch".[51] In the same breath, he employs the phrase "indifference of pitch" as a synonym of the latter, thereby suggesting he may have the Scholastic concept of *libertas indifferentiae* in mind, the meaning of which idea conjoins a classical Greek thesis with a Christian medieval position. First of all, it signifies that no man desires anything but the good, for even evil itself must appear to man *sub specie boni*, if it is to be pursued by him;[52] secondly, nothing is or is good[53] to such a degree that it would of its own power necessarily determine the will of a man to assent to his desire for it. As long as a man leads his life in the world in terms of the wordly, he cannot find anything as good as God or Goodness itself, which alone can determine him absolutely *if confronted as such*. Accordingly, man has sovereignty over his life or enjoys an inner sort of freedom — in the parlance of the Scholastics, he is indifferent to the alternatives he is faced with.

Against this medieval position, Hopkins argues as follows:

. . . it cannot be believed, as the Thomists think, that in every circumstance of free choice the person is of himself indifferent towards the alternatives and that God determines which shall [he], though freely, choose.[54]

Behind Hopkins's reasoning here lies a fundamental premise, to wit: indifference or absence of pitch is not an originary condition of human *enérgeia*, but is, in his own words, "in the nature to be superadded".[55] Or to express it bluntly and paradoxically at once: what is superadded to actual pitch is the absence of pitch. In other words, in such cases man's pitch would become a *neutralization* of the originary pitch, which is the area of good and evil is man's directedness to the good. Indifference or the absence of pitch is a modalization of the basic human *enérgeia* which delivers man consciously to freedom.

Let me at this point attempt, however briefly and inadequately, to render precise the meaning of the expressions I have just been using, namely, "originary condition of human *enérgeia*", "originary pitch", and the like.[56] This is an important task not only in order for us to be capable of making a valid transition to further questions, but also for the purpose of coming face to face with Hopkins's ultimate position in these matters and thereby to be able to confront human reality itself. One way of doing it is perhaps to take up once again his apparently inconsequential remark to the effect that I, this *singular* human being, meet myself always as "something now determined and distinctive, at pitch . . ."[57] It is to be noted, first of all, that he employs the expression "at pitch", and not words like "pitched" or "endowed with pitch", which he could have used in view of his basic tenets and the analyses to follow. This is in itself suggestive, if not revealing. By saying that I am always "at pitch", he seems to imply a hierarchy of pitches, i.e., an ordering of *enérgeia* in the "system" of the universe, for he is addressing the human condition by means of a musical concept, as one does, for example, when one refers to an instrument being tuned according to a standard. Something (i.e., anything natural and therefore man too) is "at pitch" when it is *self-coincident*, that is to say, when it is engaged in the performance of its (defining) *télos* or essential goal. Or, in Aristotle's parlance, it is what it is insofar as *enérgeia* is *entelékheia*, or to the extent that it is at work (*érgon*) in the actual realization of its *immanent* and proper goal, as "an end that coincides precisely with the consummation of the act",[58] for *enérgeia* is an "activity which is an end in itself, and therefore radically different from . . . *po[í]esis* [making] or *kínesis* [process]".[59] This is consistent with a meaning of pitch I referred to above,[60] namely, the quality of a musical sound as a function of the relative rapidity of the vibrations producing it, or the degree of acuteness or graveness of tone.[61] If one *metaphorically* avails oneself of this notion and applies it to the *analogical* spectrum of cosmic *enérgeia*, one would then be able to formulate Hopkins's radical position by means of a threefold thesis:

1. The universe is an essentially graded or articulated whole consisting of discrete pitches or actually existent essences engaged in self-performance.

2. But if the universe is ultimately *harmonia mundi*, so is human essence if it is analogically considered, for it too is a bounded range of essential and accidental pitch-values.

3. And so is every individual man a harmony in the making as well, indeed a possible symphony patterned on the basis of an organizing, intrinsic referent, namely, his singular, essential *télos*.

Accordingly, whenever a man *coincides* with his defining *télos* (whether he is "regarding" it *in genere* or—eventually and more appropriately—in an individual way by means of modulations of his universal range as he directs himself to his singular essence *in via*), one is to say not only that he is "pitched" or "endowed with pitch", but also that he is "at pitch", i.e., that he is living at the level of human *enérgeia* I have characterized as his "originary condition" or "originary pitch", which, paradoxically, is the result of striving (or of *conatus*, insofar as it involves man's achievement and preservation of its own acme *in fieri* by way of rational projection).[62] It is only in terms of these distinctions, it seems to me, that it is possible to be fair to both Hopkins's thought and the facts of human life as actually experienced. Furthermore, one is at the same time able to avoid flying in the face of Aristotle's dictum that "substance does not admit of a more or a less", a judgment exemplified by him when he said that "a man is not called more a man now than before, nor is anything else that is substance",[63] for expressions like "basic" or "originary pitch", "originary condition", and the like are meant to convey what—to use Aristotle's term—"substance" is, whether considered *in genere* (insofar as all men are of the same universal nature) or *individually* (to the extent that somehow I am always of the same individual nature), provided, of course, Aristotle's concept of substance and related notions are suitably re-interpreted so as to de-reify them and render them formal. It is as if all men were coincident or identical in respect of the originary or basic pitch of their universal nature, and as if every individual man were coincident or identical with himself in regard to the originary or basic pitch of his individual nature. This can be asserted as true only on condition that nature be understood as a range of possible values or modulations which are gathered "in view" of a proper or inherent acme (which, in the case of man, is to be constituted and decided upon freely, not only at the moral level, but also, more fundamentally, on the plane of being). Moreover, utterances of that sort, consistent with these qualifications, allow for the phenomena of decadence or decay when a "substance" (man included) is considered *in genere*, and for the various "pitchings" or modulations of a self-identical individual nature (whether they be constructive or destructive). The universal and individual aspects of human nature are then to be understood as arising to establish an endowment that demarcates a performative range of values which are unified with reference to a base pitch or acme, whether such possible modulations come down from it or seek to *exceed* it, as it would be the case if an impossible (because infinite) desire were to take hold of his heart and will as an offering in freedom.[64]

When one is taking into account both the universal and individual aspects of man's being and their reciprocity, it may be helpful to keep in mind Hopkins's thesis about the nexus of individuality and incommunicability, a matter I brought up earlier in a different context.[65] One may approach it now by dealing with such questions in terms of the relationship between pitch and Scotus' notion of *haecceitas*, a connection Hopkins himself hinted at when he said: "Is not this pitch or whatever we call it then the same as Scotus' *ecceitas*?"[66] If one adopts Hopkins's stance, one could then say not just that anything in *this* world is individual or a *haec*, but as well—insofar as it is pitch or *enérgeia*—that it consists in being that self-exercise which progresses towards itself by means of *inlaw*.[67] In other words, the *haecceitas*, thisness, or principle of individuation is the result of concretion and is thus variable, incommensurable, and incommunicable. And this is so because every natural entity's uniqueness is always "on its way", or is being constituted by the entity's own accomplishment in self-performance. This view is applicable to the whole range of the universe of things and events (and hence it is a properly metaphysical hypothesis in verification), for it is certainly not a contention restricted to matters mental or spiritual. Accordingly, consistent with Hopkins's position and his reference to Scotus, one could say that every thing in this world is a *haec*, that its being a *haec* is an *immanent* outcome of its own self-exercise, and that *haecceitas* or the inherent principle by which it individuates itself is—as meant—but an empty *formalitas*, which is being filled at every turn as the pitch, modulation of being, or degree of perfection or complexity (*com-plicatio*)[68] it has thus far achieved in its self-performance. If *enérgeia* or the self-exercise of essential function (*érgon*) is *entelékheia*, or being at the (performance of the) end, then one must assert that being performatively at the end is never being at an end, even if the entity in question meets with destruction or death (as the case may be). Consequently, I contend that *enérgeia* is individuality and the principle of individuation itself, insofar as it is immanently in the making and the essential outcome of self-accomplishment (and further, in the case of man, an activity fundamentally mediated by freedom, if the latter is understood not just as a moral power, but above all as an entitative upsurge).[69]

Let me now resume the discussion of the nexus of pitch and freedom. Hopkins does not rest his case with his consideration of the aspect of moral action I characterized above as "neutralization".[70] He moves one step further, for the notion of *libertas indifferentiae*, however appropriate it may be to express a basic fact about *agere*, is really beside the point, either as presenting the originary form of moral consciousness or as disclosing the essential sense of human freedom as relevant to the moral life. This is how Hopkins makes his point:

> The difficulty does not lie so much in . . . [the person's] being determined by God and yet choosing freely, for on one side that may and must happen, but in . . . [the person's] being supposed equally disposed or pitched towards both [alternatives] at once. This is impossible and destroys the notion of freedom and of pitch.[71]

If I understand him aright, he means to say that freedom, taken radically as that upsurge of my being of which indifference is just a modalization, is *already determined at every turn* as inclination towards, or aversion from, a certain (at least) apparent good or evil (respectively). Such a "specification", as Hopkins asserts, is an effect of God from within ourselves, because it is constituted in terms of my acting it out in my response to God's summons, whether I opt for the good, avert evil, or neutralize the good in "indifference". It is in fact the *sine qua non* for my freedom's exercise, for there is no real freedom which is not some definite self's. As I see it, this is the reason why Hopkins denies there is any contradiction between being determined by God and choosing freely, and at the same time why *liberum arbitrium* is irreducible to *libertas indifferentiae*. We are then, at every turn, identical with what *most* interests us, and yet at the same time we find ourselves creating a hiatus between our determined being and what we want by means of the position we freely adopt with regard to ourselves. The alternatives we are confronting and the "valence" with which they are lived are the objective correlates of the subjective determination God effects in us by way of special pitching or selving, but this does not pre-establish our living free choice, even as we are inclined positively or negatively with respect to some good or evil (respectively), as God Himself does it from within us in His summons. Man's being determined by God is not prior or subsequent to free choice, but is the *enabling* condition of man's free self-constitution, for it allows him to grasp the alternatives by way of feeling, eventually to take them as thus and so, and to accept, reject, or neutralize them, which is the final outcome of deliberation and the first motion towards implementation in living action. The reduction of freedom to, or at least its being grounded in, *libertas indifferentiae* would therefore only destroy, as Hopkins finally remarks, "the notion of freedom and of pitch".

Pitch, modulation, choice: these are three aspects that are to be brought to synthesis for the sake of the unity of man. In a text both rich and suggestive in meaning, Hopkins offers us clues for this work. This is what he has there to say:

> . . . in that "cleave" of being which each of his creatures shews to God's eyes alone (or in its "burl" of being . . . uncloven) God can choose in the strain (or countless cleaves of the "burl") where the creature has consented, does consent, to God's will in the way above shewn . . . [72]

This is God's privilege, one of the prerogatives of omniscience and omnipotence born of love full and constant, to wit: always to have access to me in a way in principle denied to me, and yet one without which I would be unable to be myself as pitch or self-performance in freedom. He grasps me at every turn in my "'burl' of being . . . uncloven", that is to say, in the roundness and fullness of my being.[73] At best, and on my own, I am available to gain myself at any juncture as "one cleave",[74] or the modulation of my pitch where I presently live. But God has me whole, actual and possible and in terms of "the end of . . . [my] being, which is selfsacrifice to God and . . . [my] salvation".[75]

Bluntly stated: to be is to be regarded in this manner that gathers and directs from within even as it discriminates. As a unifying strain for the sake of my wholeness, God takes up my better self and shows it to me modalized in a curious way, in the only fashion in which it is possible to do justice to a being rational and free, and yet consistent with Himself as love perfect and abiding. He *surrenders it to me* in the temporality of a future perfect subjunctive — before the fact, but as if I had lived it, and as an offering to which I would have consented. Indeed, He thus allows me to stress my *imaginative powers* in a guise uniquely human — not memorative, or reproductive, or dreamingly active, or objectively poetic, but self-creative.[76] In this manner, He promotes in me a cleavage between higher and lower, better and worse selfhood in a "system" of mutual implication, a rift that gives me the opportunity creatively to constitute myself, for my better self "may be away, may be very far away, from the actual pitch [of mine] at any given moment existing".[77]

This shift in subjectivity is rooted in God's presence to me as pitch. Hopkins calls it *grace*, both natural and supernatural, which he defines as "any action, activity, on God's part by which in creating or after

creating, he carries the creature to or towards the end of his being
. . ."[78] In total faithfulness to Himself, God is loyal to His works as
meant by Him from all eternity, and this includes a nature rational
and free like man's, even when what is involved is the highest gift of
all, i.e., salvation or one's abiding participation in His inner life
according to one's measure. Hence, this "clothing of . . . [my] old self
for the moment with a gracious self"[79] does not annihilate the old,
i.e., the present self or modulation of my pitch, or even suspend it in
the sense of bringing its level of *enérgeia* to nought. He only prompts
me, within myself and for my sake, to a degree of stress of myself
passively determinable in me, and He thus transforms me into a
fitting, possible dweller of a possible, better world. *Grace thus shifts me
in my imagination*, to ready me for the free exercise of my will in self-
determination, expressible by a performative yeah, nay, or
neutralization, as the case may be, an unfolding of my possibilities
which is geared to the unique, virtual, and yet complete *justice* of my
self to myself which is known by the classical name of *eúdaimonía*, or
happiness complete and abiding, for

> . . . the just man justices;
> Keeps grace: that keeps all his goings graces;
> Acts in God's eye what in God's eye he is —
> Christ. For Christ plays in ten thousand places,
> Lovely in limbs, and lovely in eyes not his
> To the Father through the features of men's faces . . .

as Hopkins chose to put it in the second stanza of his poem, "As kingfishers catch fire".[80] The infinite and creative goodness of the Father
can be and is returned to Him by Christ, the perfect mirror of His
goodness, in the case of each and every man, provided that the
instancings of human *enérgeia* be transmuted by supernatural grace.
It is only when a man is actualized as an *infinite passion* that all his
"goings" may become "graces" or be transformed into all they can
be — acts human yet utterly divine. Only then is man truly open to
ripeness and fullness, by way of anticipation (in regard to the beatific
vision), as well as participatorily (in terms of the mystical life proper,
if such is the charism granted to him). Man's genuine apotheosis
takes place only when he "Acts in God's eye what in God's eye he is —/
Christ". Once turned about by grace, a man's deed acquires a new
significance and direction, but it nevertheless continues to flow from
himself naturally, i.e., spontaneously and according to his proper
inlaw, just as "kingfishers catch fire", or "dragonflies draw flame", or
as "tumbled over rim in roundy wells / Stones ring", or "like each
tucked string tells, each hung bell's / Bow swung finds tongue to fling

out broad its name . . ."[81] The concept of *inlaw* just mentioned (and used in passing before) is crucial to the understanding of Hopkins's basic cosmological position as well as to that of his application of it to man. The *inlaw* of something, say, of a mind, whether divine or finite, is the law both expressing and governing its "distinctive being".[82] In other words, it is the *intrinsic* principle according to which it is what it is, or the gathering source of its *enérgeia* or pitch. In the case of man, or any spiritual monad (God included), one could perhaps assert that it is the *inmost* circle about which the contents of the monad's "world" are organized.[83] Unfortunately, I cannot go here into the analysis of the different meanings of "world", or of "monad" as the center of worldly reference, as one proceeds in thought from the finite to the infinite, nor, for that matter, can I carry out a detailed examination of the dialectic of freedom and necessity (*inlaw*), despite the great importance of these problems.[84] Suffice it to say that freedom is not incompatible with necessity, for freedom does not essentially involve the continual arbitrary replacement of one regimen of lawfulness by another, or require the existence of two strata of performance, namely, a manner of self-determination according to choice and another proceeding under the sway of *anánke*, which would be as inexplicably as they are inextricably woven into one another. Accordingly, I could in principle formulate such questions as follows: I would creatively transform myself by assuming the better self *graciously* offered to me in my imagination by God, an appropriation carried out by means of a process that may be given succinct expression by saying that it involves a temporal shift from the future perfect subjunctive, proper to the possibility being offered,[85] to the future perfect indicative, characteristic of projection in worldly action,[86] to the present time in which the execution of a plan would eventuate. And all of this would unfold, of course, according to "rule", on the assumption that I opt for the possibility offered to me, instead of averting or neutralizing it.

What is involved here is, as before, the principle of pitch (i.e., the self-exercise of the ends characteristic of one's *enérgeia*), even if it is enacted by the mediation of God's grace. Hopkins's poetic thought and diction conveys this point admirably:

> Each mortal thing does one thing and the same:
> Deals out that being indoors each one dwells;
> Selves — goes its self; *myself* it speaks and spells,
> Crying *What I do is me: for that I came*.[87]

Anything natural consists in selving; a man amounts to going his own self. In other words, every finite entity — human or not — is the performing (or doing) of its own essence, both generically and individually. One can accept this assertion on account of the following grounds, with which we have been working: 1. the distinction between—and the reciprocal grounding of—universal nature (species-being or *Gattungswesen*) and individual essence;[88] 2. the correlation of the concept of "basic or originary pitch or condition of *enérgeia*" and the notion of derivative or founded "modulation" of pitch (if understood as endowment). Now, the selving or self-performance of an entity is the meaning of Creation, or the faithfulness characteristic of the Divine *fiat*, which, according to orthodox belief, is not obliterated but perfected by grace, when the latter overcomes it. Carrying itself out according to *inlaw*, each thing nonetheless belongs to one universe or "system" of mutuality and interpenetration effected on the basis of the gradations of *enérgeia*. I am for thinghood, and thinghood is for me, and things are for one another in causal exchange, very much like the reciprocity of morphology and syntax in speech (except that with things the impenetrability of materiality is involved),[89] for the self-exercise of the universal nature and individuality of each thing or person[90] "*myself* . . . speaks and spells", and so do I for the self of each thing or person I encounter, for we cry to one another, whether in silence or in utterance, what each one is, thus constituting and re-constituting at every turn the living grammar and melody of the universe.

Notes

1 Cf. Plato, *Sophist*, 246 a 4.

2 This is of course an *ideal* limit of the human experiential spectrum, one in terms of which the structures and "lawfulness" of history would be accommodated only with difficulty; moreover, it abstracts from salvific considerations and the regimen of supernatural grace, for in this perspective the life of man is considered only insofar as it unfolds on the basis of human nature alone. This notwithstanding, I will here take no position as to its efficaciousness and actuality. It may very well be just as a mere notional possibility that can only be realized subject to modalizations within some particular order of concretion. Cf. *infra*, n. 4; *vide* Henri de Lubac, *The Mystery of the Supernatural*, trans. R. Sheed (New York: Herder and Herder, 1967).

3 Karl Rahner, "Beatific Vision", *Sacramentum mundi*, ed. K. Rahner *et al.* (New York: Herder and Herder, 1964), I, p. 153, col. 2; cf. Benedict XII, "De visione Dei beatifica et de novissimis" in Heinrich Denziger, *Enchiridion symbolorum*, ed. J. B. Umberg, 27th. ed. enlarged (Barcelona: Herder, 1951), No. 530, p. 230; *vide* Heribert Fischer, "Mysticism", *Sacramentum mundi*, IV, p. 138, col. 1, where grace and faith are identified as constituting together the formal medium of the beatific vision, and F. Wulf, "Mystique" in *Encyclopédie de la foi*, ed. H. Fries (Paris: Cerf, 1966), III, p. 171, where it is said that Adam's "knowledge of God, according to the theologians, lies between the ordinary knowledge of faith and the beatific vision in heaven".

4 Cf. Edmund Husserl, *Ideas Pertaining to a Pure Phenomenology and to a Phenomenological Philosophy*, I, trans. F. Kersten (The Hague: Martinus Nijhoff, 1982), § 104.

5 F. Wulf, "Mystique", § 2B, *op. cit.*, p. 173. The experiential familiarity with God of which the author speaks here is seemingly what Maritain, following St. Thomas Aquinas (*Summa theologiae*, I, q. 1, art. 6, *ad* 3; II-II, q. 45, art. 2), refers to as "knowledge by connaturality". [Cf. Jacques Maritain, *Distinguish to Unite or the Degrees of Knowledge*, trans. G. B. Phelan (New York: Scribner's Sons, 1959), pp. 260 ff.] This sort of knowledge is clearly analogical, for it takes various forms with reference to "a *basic* type", namely, one's acquaintanceship with the practical ends of life. [Cf. J. Maritain, "L'expérience mystique naturelle et le vide", *Oeuvres (1912-1939)*, ed. H. Bars (Bruges: Desclée de Brouwer, 1975), pp. 1126 f.] The other forms of connaturality are the following: the intellectual (*ibid.*, pp. 1127 ff.) or way *per modum cognitionis* (p. 1130), the poetical (pp. 1132 f.), and the mystical *stricto sensu* (pp. 1133 ff.), which, however different from one another they may be in terms of the *formal medium* of exercise each of them requires (i.e., inclination,

concept, creation, and love, respectively; cf. *ibid.*, pp. 1145-46 and *passim*), may nonetheless combine with the basic type and with one another in one and the same nexus and performance of a person's life, and even influence one another as a result.

6   J. Maritain, "L'expérience mystique . . . ", *op. cit.*, p. 1126. (Please note that Maritain does not capitalize "absolute" to allow for two possible forms of mysticism, namely, the natural and the supernatural). This notion presupposes, of course, some kind of *a priori* receptivity on man's part with regard to the absolute, but this should come as no surprise, since, after all, this is true of any possible human experience in relation to its specifying object proper. This is perhaps suggested by Fischer's remarks to the effect that the *scintilla animae*, or the light of faith and grace, is "where the soul is a unity before developing in multiplicity . . .", if one takes these words to the limit, for, as he later adds, a "theology of mysticism will also have to include in its investigations the radical subjectivity of man as the *recipient* of grace. Hence an adequate theological anthropology [and, I would add, an antecedent and grounding philosophical anthropology] become . . . of equally great importance". (H. Fischer, "Mysticism", *op. cit.*, p. 137, col. 2; the emphasis is mine). This notwithstanding, one should not construe mystical experience as if it were a necessary or even a possible consequence deriving solely or primarily from man's nature (and the law based thereupon) on the occasion of man's encounter with the Divine. This could not possibly be the case, for (supernatural) mystical experience presupposes man's faith and his actuation by grace, and this in turn is conditioned by human finitude and the Trinitarian nature of God's inner life, all of which forecloses that alternative. Consistent with this, one is to assert that "mystical contemplation is always experienced as a gift". [Karl Rahner and Herbert Vorgrimler, "Mysticism", *Theological Dictionary*, ed. C. Ernst, trans. R. Strachan (New York: Herder and Herder, 1965), p. 302]. Cf. the definition of "mysticism" in *The Compact Edition of the Oxford English Dictionary* (New York: Oxford University Press, 1971), I, p. 1889: " . . . belief in the possibility of union with the Divine nature by means of ecstatic contemplation . . ." For critical remarks, both positive and negative, concerning this nominal definition, *vide* Gregory Vlastos, *Socrates, Ironist and Moral Philosopher* (Ithaca: Cornell University Press, 1991), p. 78.

7   J. Maritain, "L'expérience mystique . . . ", *op. cit.*, p. 1133.

8   Cf. Pseudo-Dionysus the Areopagite, *The Mystical Theology*, cc. 3 ff. in *Dionysus the Areopagite on the Divine Names and the Mystical Theology*, trans. C. E. Rolt (New York: The Macmillan Co., 1957), pp. 196 ff.

9   J. Maritain, "L'expérience mystique . . .", *op. cit.* This lived dimension of mysticism does not require, it seems to me, an express belief in the realization of the union.

10   Cf. K. Rahner *et al.*, "Mysticism", *op. cit.*, p. 301.

11   Cf. H. Fischer, "Mysticism", *op. cit.*, p. 137, col. 2.

12   J. Maritain, "L'expérience mystique . . . ", *op cit.*, p. 1133. This formula is in agreement with the following essential-descriptive definition of mysticism: " . . .

the interior meeting and union of a man with the divine infinity that sustains him and all other being . . ." (K. Rahner *et al.*, "Mysticism", *op. cit.*, p. 301).

13 Cf. *John* 17, vv. 11 and 14.

14 K. Rahner *et al.*, "Mysticism", *op. cit.*, p. 302. Cf. F. Wulf, "Mystique", *op. cit.*, p. 171: "Abraham . . . , Jacob . . . , Moses . . . , Elijah . . . , Isaiah . . . , Jeremiah . . . had the impression of being directly touched and grasped by God, of being face to face with Him . . . , without however being at all able to contemplate his face directly . . ."

15 F. Wulf, "Mystique", *op. cit.*, p. 169.

16 J. Maritain, "L'expérience mystique . . .", *op. cit.*, p. 1134. In other words, man's love of charity for God, which is inspired in us by God's own constitutive love as a mirroring of Himself in our lives brought about by the mediation of Christ, is the formal medium by which man could "achieve" the effective familiarity with God that is characteristic of mysticism.

17 Cf. *supra*, p. 258.

18 Cf. *supra*, p. 258.

19 Cf. *supra*, p. 257.

20 Cf. *supra*, p. 258.

21 Cf. Gerard Manley Hopkins, "Comments on the Spiritual Exercises of St. Ignatius of Loyola", *The Notebooks and Papers of Gerard Manley Hopkins*, ed. Humphry House (London: Oxford University Press, 1937), p. 309.

22 *The Compact Edition of the Oxford English Dictionary*, II, p. 912, col. 1, No. 11.

23 *Ibid.*, col. 2, No. 14 (*obsolete*).

24 *Ibid.*, No. 19 (*rare* except in "at the pitch of one's voice").

25 *Ibid.*, col. 3, No. 22.

26 *Ibid.*, No. 23.

27 Cf. *ibid.*, p. 914, col. 3, No. 17.

28 G. M. Hopkins, "Comments . . .", *op. cit.*, p. 310. For an interesting though perhaps misleading presentation of some of Hopkins's relevant concepts, cf. Gerald L. Bruns, "The Idea of Energy in the Writings of Gerard Manley Hopkins", *Renascence*, XXIX (1976), pp. 25 ff.

29 Aristotle, *Physics*, 201 a 29, trans. R. Hope (Lincoln: University of Nebraska, 1961), p. 42.

30 Cf. *ibid.*, a 30 f.

31 Cf. Aristotle, *Metaphysics*, 1048 b 18-24; *Physics*, 201 b 31 f.

32 Cf. Aristotle, *Metaphysics*, 1050 a 23.

33 Aristotle, *De anima*, 417 b 6-7. Cf. *infra*, n. 67.

34 Cf. G. M. Hopkins, "Comments . . .", *op. cit.*, p. 309.

35 *Ibid.* Cf. *infra*, p. 266.

36 Cf. G. M. Hopkins, "Comments . . .", *op. cit.*

37 *Ibid.*

38 *Ibid.*

39 Cf. *ibid.*, pp. 309 ff.

40 *Ibid.*, p. 309.

41 *Ibid.*

42 *Ibid.*

43 Cf. *ibid.* *Vide* Aristotle, *Metaphysics*, 1072 b 21.

44 G. M. Hopkins, "Comments . . .", *op. cit.*, p. 309.

45 *Ibid.*

46 Cf. E. Husserl, *Cartesian Meditations*, trans. D. Cairns (The Hague: Martinus Nijhoff, 1960), § 14.

47 Hopkins's keen awareness of the unity and duality of human experience is communicated to us by him both thetically and expressively. As a thesis, he presents it thus: "What you look hard at seems to look hard at you". [*The Journals and Papers of Gerard Manley Hopkins*, ed. H. House and G. Storey, 1959, p. 204, *apud* Robert B. Martin, *Gerard Manley Hopkins. A Very Private Life* (New York: G. P. Putnam's Sons, 1991), p. 203]. Expressively, he embodies it in what Martin characterizes as a "curious syntactical habit", namely, the distinctive employment of the dangling participle, which cannot amount to "a simple, igno-rant mistake" (*ibid.*), for it is used not only deliberately, but also as a means to convey a nexus of experience that cannot be genuinely communicated otherwise, except by stepping out of the mode of poetry *lato sensu* and having recourse to universal and necessary theses (as happened in the procedure which we have just seen Hopkins avail himself of). Martin gives two wonderful examples of this prac-tice of concretization as followed by Hopkins: a. "In returning the sky in the west was in a great wide winged or shelved rack of rice-white fine pelleted fretting" (*The Journals* . . . , p. 216; *apud* R. B. Martin, *ibid.*), wherein Hopkins "achieves", contends Martin quite rightly, "a kind of obliteration of distinction between self and sky" (*ibid.*); b. " . . . by watching hard the banks began to sail upstream . . ." (*The Journals* . . . , p. 200; *apud* R. B. Martin, *ibid.*; the emphasis is Martin's), a formula-

tion by which Hopkins, as Martin points out, adopts "the viewpoint of the water" (*ibid.*). In neither case does one however find Hopkins characterized by the attitudes of naïveté or carelessness; on the contrary, he is quite conscious of the distinction between his experiencing self and the object experienced (i.e., the sky or the river and its banks), but he chooses to underscore the unity and mutuality of both sides of experience, thus running counter to the usual abstractive or differentiating proclivities embedded in ordinary language and everyday attitudes — hence his special use of the dangling participle.

48 G. M. Hopkins, "Comments . . .", *op. cit.*, p. 324.

49 Cf. *supra*, p. 261 and n. 26.

50 G. M. Hopkins, "Comments . . .", *op. cit.* Cf. St. Thomas Aquinas, *Summa theologiae*, I-II, q. 6, art. 1, *ad* 3; *vide* Hans Urs von Balthasar, *Herrlichkeit. Eine theologische Ästhetik*, 2nd. ed. (Einsiedeln: Johannes Verlag, 1984), II-2, "Hopkins", ii.

51 G. M. Hopkins, "Comments . . .", *op cit.*, p. 325.

52 Cf. Plato, *Meno*, 77 b - 78 b; *Protagoras*, 358 c; *Gorgias*, 468 c; W. K. C. Guthrie, *A History of Greek Philosophy* (Cambridge at the University Press, 1969), III, pp. 450 ff; G. X. Santas, *Socrates* (London: Routledge & Kegan Paul, 1979), cc. 6-7; St. Augustine, *The Enchiridion*, cc. 11 ff.; G. M. Hopkins, "Comments . . .", *op. cit.*, p. 326.

53 Cf. St. Thomas Aquinas, *De veritate*, q. 1, art. 1, *Respondeo;* Francisco Suárez, *Disputationes metaphysicae*, III, ii, 3; *Handbuch philosophischer Grundbegriffe*, ed. H. Krings *et al.* (Munich: Kösel Verlag, 1973), "Das Gute"; *vide* H. Urs von Balthasar, *op. cit.*

54 G. M. Hopkins, "Comments . . .", *op. cit.* p. 325.

55 *Ibid.*

56 Cf. *infra*, p. 269 for the synonymous expression "originary form of moral consciousness", which is the equivalent of these cosmological formulae in the area of moral conduct taken as a distinct human prerogative.

57 Cf. *supra*, p. 262.

58 Oded Balaban, "Praxis and Po[f]esis in Aristotle's Practical Philosophy", *The Journal of Value Inquiry*, 1989, 1, "Praxis - 1".

59 *Ibid.*, n. 14.

60 Cf. *supra*, p. 261 and n. 26.

61 Cf. Plato, *Republic*, 349 c 10 and F. M. Cornford's remarks on p. 33 of his edition and translation of this work (New York: Oxford University Press, 1945), especially for the concepts of limit (*péras*) and measure (*métron*) and their relevance to tuning (*harmonía*). For the Pythagorean origin of these notions, cf. Frederick Copleston, *A History of Philosophy* (London: Burns and Oates, 1961), I, p. 33;

John Burnet, *Greek Philosophy* (London: Macmillan, 1964), pp. 35 ff.; W. K. C. Guthrie, *A History of Greek Philosophy*, I (1962), pp. 220 ff.; Rodolfo Mondolfo, *El pensamiento antiguo*, 3rd. ed. rev. (Buenos Aires: Losada, 1942), I, pp. 55-57.

62 This is Spinoza's Aristotelian notion of *conatus* (cf. Spinoza, *Ethics*, iii, props. 6-8) as applied in this context to man, who, among all finite entities, is the only one to require rational projection in action in order to achieve himself. For the notion of self-coincidence as one of the essential conditions of happiness, or the ultimate goal of man, cf. José Ortega y Gasset, "Pidiendo un Goethe desde dentro", *Obras Completas*, Centenary Edition (Madrid: Revista de Occidente / Alianza Editorial, 1983), IV, pp. 406-407, where one can find his insightful commentary on Goethe's notion of the "rectitude" of something, which is its state of conformity to the individual (*was ihm gemäss ist*) as mediated by the individual's *entelechy*; "En torno a Galileo", *ibid.*, V, p. 88; *Goya* in *op. cit.*, VII, pp. 552-53, where Ortega presents the conjunction of the concept of self-coincidence and the notion of one's coincidence with the prevailing circum-stance; *La idea de principio en Leibniz y la evolución de la teoría deductiva* in *op. cit.* , VIII, p. 86, where he considers the possibility that self-coincidence may be impossible in our this-worldly circumstance.

63 Aristotle, *Categories*, trans. J. L. Ackrill, c. 5, 4 a 5-7 in *The Complete Works of Aristotle*, rev. Oxford trans., ed. J. Barnes (Princeton: Princeton University Press, 1984), I, p. 7.

64 For the Aristotelian and Graeco-Christian roots of this "energetic" or "dynamic" sense of *being* (taking "energetic" in a Greek sense and "dynamic" with modern connotations), cf. Xavier Zubiri, "El ser sobrenatural, Dios y la deificación en la teología paulina", *Naturaleza, Historia, Dios*, 5th ed. (Madrid: Editora Nacional, 1963), pp. 409 ff.

65 Cf. *supra*, p. 263.

66 G. M. Hopkins, "Comments . . .", *op. cit.*, p. 328. Cf. John Duns Scotus, *Opus oxoniense*, ii, disp. 3, q. 6, n. 15, where he denies that *haecceitas* or the principle of individuation (as exercised) is either matter or form, or the composite of both, for it is rather the *ultima ratio entis*, or the essence of the thing insofar as the essence itself is individual, a fact which thus guarantees that the thing be no mere *multiplicity* of determinations and components. Accordingly, *haecceitas* (as meant) is an ultimate *difference* or denominative term that is irreducibly simple, designating as it does the reality of the thing to the extent that it is individual. Cf. J. D. Scotus, *Quaestiones subtilissimae in Metaphysicam Aristotelis*, q. 5, n. 61; *vide* also "Notes" in J. D. Scotus, *Philosophical Writings*, trans. A. Wolter (Indianapolis: Hackett, 1987), p. 166, n. 3.

67 For the concept of *inlaw*, cf. *infra*, pp. 271-72. *Vide* Aristotle, *De anima*, 417 b 6-7. [Aristotle, *Traité de l'âme*, Greek text and French trans. by G. Rodier (Paris: Ernest Leroux, 1900), I, p. 98]. Aristotle's radical formulation is *eis autó gàr he epídosis kaì eis entelékheian*, or "being in reality a development [*epídosis*] into its true self or actuality [*entelékheia*]". (*On the Soul*, trans. J. A. Smith in *The Complete Works of Aristotle*, rev. Oxford trans., I, p. 664).

68 Cf. Antonio Rodríguez Huéscar, *La innovación metafísica de Ortega. Crítica y superación del idealismo* (Madrid: Ministerio de Educación y Ciencia, 1982), Part 2, "Complejidad", pp. 121 ff. As meant in the present context, the complexity or complication in question works both at the universal and individual levels in terms of concretions resulting from the "systematically" interconnective events occuring in my life, insofar as the latter encompasses both myself and otherness. *Vide* José Ortega y Gasset, *Meditaciones del Quijote*, with a "Commentary" by Julián Marías (Madrid: Universidad de Puerto Rico at Revista de Occidente, 1957), p. 43 ("Commentary", pp. 266-68).

69 For a fuller development of these questions, it would be necessary to bring up and expound Hopkins's elusive and original concept of *inscape*. As Martin says, Hopkins believed that "when one understands a person, an object, or even an idea, through close study, that which is studied radiates back a meaning, one that is certainly unique because each manifestation of the world is somehow different from any other, so that no two meanings can be precisely the same. *Inscape* is that meaning, the inner coherence of the *individual*, distinguishing it from any other example. It is perceived only through close examination or empathy, but it is not dependent on being recognized; rather it is inherent in everything in the world, even when we fail to notice it" (*op. cit.*, p. 205; the emphasis is mine). I have permitted myself this lengthy quotation, nearly descriptive in approach, because I cannot go here into the analysis of the important concept of inscape, requiring as it does the close examination of texts taken from Hopkins's prose and poetry. For further elaborations of this notion, cf. Marjorie D. Coogan, "Inscape and Instress: Further Analogies with Scotus", PMLA, LXV (1950), pp. 66 ff. and, above all, Bernadette Waterman Ward's remarkable piece, "Philosophy and Inscape: Hopkins and the *Formalitas* of Duns Scotus", *Texas Studies in Literature and Language*, XXXII, No. 2 (Summer 1990), pp. 214 ff.

70 Cf. *supra*, p. 266.

71 G. M. Hopkins, "Comments . . .", *op. cit.*, p. 325.

72 *Ibid.*, p. 332. Cf. H. Urs von Balthasar, *op. cit.*

73 Cf. *The Compact Edition of the Oxford English Dictionary*, III (1987), p. 98, "Burl", sb. 2, No. 1.

74 G. M. Hopkins, "Comments . . .", *op. cit.*, p. 329.

75 *Ibid.*, p. 332.

76 Cf. *ibid.*, pp. 328-29 and 330. For the roots and the important role of imagination in the English theological, philosophical, and literary tradition, insofar as it decisively influenced Hopkins, *vide* H. Urs von Balthasar, *op. cit.*, "Hopkins", i.

77 G. M. Hopkins, "Comments . . .", *op. cit.* p. 332.

78 *Ibid.* Cf. H. Urs von Balthasar, *op. cit.*, "Hopkins", ii.

79 G. M. Hopkins, "Comments . . .", *op. cit.*

80 *Gerard Manley Hopkins*, ed. Catherine Phillips (Oxford: Oxford University Press, 1986), p. 129.

81 *Ibid.*, first stanza. One is to note here the connection established between "name", a signifier of essence, and "fling". Furthermore, one should not overlook the fact that the link of which Hopkins speaks has been translated to the domain of expression, even if it is true that one is still at its inception, namely, at the level of sound and its production, which is nonetheless the antechamber of *lógos*. For the nominal nexus between being and casting or flinging forward, and the metaphysical hypothesis in verification that is suggested thereby, cf. *supra*, pp. 261-62 and n. 27.

82 G. M. Hopkins, "Comments . . .", *op. cit.*, p. 314.

83 *Ibid.*, p. 315. The concept of *inlaw* is highly reminiscent of Leibniz's monadological multiple centering of the universe and its reverberations in the realm of consciousness. Cf. G. W. Leibniz, *On Nature in Itself*, 6, *Die philosophischen Schriften von G. W. Leibniz*, ed. C. I. Gerhardt (Berlin: 1875-90), IV, p. 507 (*vide* also II, p. 263); *Discours de métaphysique et correspondance avec Arnauld*, ed. and comm. G. le Roy (Paris: J. Vrin, 1974), §§ 9-10 and 13; Aron Gurwitsch, *Leibniz. Philosophie des Panlogismus* (Berlin: Walter de Gruyter, 1974), c. 6, § 5; Martial Gueroult, *Leibniz. Dynamique et métaphysique* (Paris: Aubier-Montaigne, 1967), p. 175.

84 Cf. *supra*, p. 265.

85 Cf. *supra*, p. 270; *vide* H. Urs von Balthasar, *op. cit.*, "Hopkins", ii.

86 Cf. Alfred Schutz, *The Phenomenology of the Social World*, trans. G. Walsh and F. Lehnert (Evanston: Northwestern University Press, 1967), §§ 9 ff. and 17.

87 This is the first stanza of "As kingfishers catch fire" in *Gerard Manley Hopkins*, ed. C. Phillips, p. 129. Please note the deliberate peculiarity of Hopkins's diction. For instance, he may use verbs as if they were nouns, or nouns in the way of verbs, as he does here ("selves"), and he may even employ verbs in a special way too, as when, for example, he transforms an intransitive into a transitive verb (as it also happens here in the case of "goes"). And I say "deliberate" not only because he does so intentionally for some historical or philological reason, or due to a requirement justified by his poetics, but also and above all by virtue of philosophico-theological theses and analyses, as we already have had the occasion to notice and are about to see again in what follows. Cf. Denis Donoghue, "The Flight of Gerard Manley Hopkins", *The New York Review of Books*, XXXVIII, No. 13 (July 18, 1991), p. 17.

88 Cf. *supra*, pp. 266 ff. For the concept of *Gattungswesen* or species-being, cf. Ludwig Feuerbach, *The Essence of Christianity*, trans. G. Eliot (New York: Harper & Brothers, 1957), c. 1, § 1, pp. 1-2: "But what is this essential difference between man and the brute? . . . [It is] consciousness . . . [taken] in the strict sense . . . [which] is present only in a being [man] to whom his species, his essential nature, is an object of thought . . . [It is a consciousness] akin to science. Where there is this higher consciousness there is a *capability* of science. Science is the

cognisance of the species" (the emphasis is mine). Going beyond Feuerbach, however, one must say that, for Hopkins, consciousness as man's *Gattungswesen* is not exclusively or primarily theoretical, and that our way of access to it — *pace* Marx — is *individual* consciousness *and* action (though rooted, no doubt, in social life and history), for the individual and universal levels of human essence are not only *in via* but are also reciprocally grounding. [*Vide* Karl Marx, *Early Writings*, trans. and ed. T. B. Bottomore (New York: McGraw-Hill, 1961), "On the Jewish Question", pp. 13 and 26; "Economic and Philosophic Manuscripts":   i. "Alienated Labor", pp. 126 ff. and iii. "Private Property and Communism", pp. 154, 158, 202, and 208]. All this notwithstanding, it is to be noted that, in his employment of the noun "self", in his use of the verbal form "selve" (cf., e.g., "Comments . . .", *op. cit.*, p. 315 and *passim*), and in his management of their derivatives, Hopkins does not necessarily or primarily have in mind synonyms of "ego", "soul", "consciousness", "mental content", and the like. Those words *may* certainly be taken in these senses when Hopkins refers to *man* or some aspect of him, but for the most part, however, he avails himself of such terms as co-extensive with being when taken intrinsically and *in actu exercito*, i.e., as signifying pitch or *enérgeia* as gathered by and arising as *inlaw*. Consistent with this, he speaks of something that exists subsistently as being selved or pitched, whether it is human or not. Finally, he will go as far as coining "selfbeing" to refer to human nature as exercised individually, or as the activity and product of the dialectic of freedom and necessity, and of the interplay of universal and individual nature, when man is taken according to his full historical and ontological wealth. Cf. G. M. Hopkins, "Comments . . .", *op. cit.*, p. 309.

89 Cf. my paper, "Perceptual Consciousness, Materiality and Idealism", *Analecta Husserliana*, XXXIV (1991), pp. 299 ff.

90 *Vide* G. M. Hopkins, "Comments . . .", *op. cit.*, p. 328; cf. *supra*, pp. 268 f.

Simone Weil on Necessity

Helmut Kohlenberger

Intellectual commitment and passionate participation in the real conditions of social life led Simone Weil into the world of labor, even though she has been educated in elite schools in Paris. Besides her teaching activity (starting in 1931) she collaborated in study circles organized by labor unions and took part in demonstrations. From December 1934 until August 1935 she worked in several factories. She described in detail the mechanized working conditions and showed the extent to which a factory worker became a part in a machine. Thus did Simone Weil learn the decisive lesson of social life. It was no empty phrase when she emphasized throughout her life the central place of physical labor for an orderly social system. With respect to the shocking condition of the workers, who counted for nothing even though politics were conducted in their name, it appeared to her that her task was to think appropriately on work. For Simone Weil, that meant to think of work as something necessary.

As a first step, this thought serves to expose the contrast between the real working conditions and the situation of the workers on the one hand, and the mythologization of work propounded especially by Marxism on the other. Always for Simone Weil the contradiction between social reality and mythologization was a massive stumbling-block. Her aim was to winnow out everything that was unreal.

With complete pertinence, Marx had analyzed the oppression of the worker in the production process. Workers are drawn into the production mechanism and become as means in the framework of the increasingly automatizing production of the means of production. Marx in no way makes it clear how at one stroke the victims of production are to become the masters of production. So strongly was he enmeshed in the blind belief in progress that he believed he could derive revolutionary hope from the production process itself. He inappropriately connected the scientific with the religious manner of speaking. Thus, the revolution became "the opium of the people" — a kind of devotion traditionally reserved for religion. The Workers became the modern Deity which soon became victimized—as Christ, and were driven deeper into oppression. The organs of government (army, police, bureaucracy), at a remove from the people, remained unexplained in Marxism, as did the phenomenon of war. The less these realities entered into revolutionary theory, the more effective they proved to be in actual experience. For Simone Weil, this outcome in no way signifies the surrender of the lowly in the face of the predominance of mechanization, of force. The revolutionary spirit ought not to disappear even if the oppression had ceased. For it serves to grasp the greatness of human work and to free it from all ideological presuppositions combined with the modern 'religion' of the self-creation of man by means of revolutionary processes.

By work, necessities for human life are made. Human beings can live only within the framework of the necessities that they make. On that account, work is a goal unto itself and does not serve any secondary objectives. Man is condemned to work just as he is condemned to death. By working, man accomplishes a "supreme act of total obedience."[1] Neither work nor death are the objects of free choice, but rather of either revolt or consent. "Immediately after the consent to death, the consent to the law that renders work indispensable to the conservation of life is the most perfect act of obedience that it is given to man to accomplish."[2] In work, the necessities of human life are made in a violent action against nature and against man himself. Simone Weil talks outright about a twofold conduct of war: "The organization of all society reflects the conditions of this twofold war, against human beings and against nature."[3]

It is self-evident that one needs a materialistic mode of thinking in order to understand the conditions of this conduct of war. Action runs into limits in matter, yet therein order and necessity are displayed. "Matter is something that imposes an inevitable order upon our actions. Everything is matter, except for *thought* which perceives necessity. Materialism is inconceivable without the notion of spirit."[4] It is in work that man comes into his own. Simone Weil does not hesitate, with Proudhon, to speak of the victim of work: "There is no true sacrifice outside of work, since it involves the exercise of man's highest faculties."[5]

Yet in the modern state since Richelieu, especially in socialism, man is separated from his own kind by work. A general uprooting became widespread, manifesting itself primarily in false notions of greatness, in a weakening of the sense of justice, in the idolization of money and in the lack of a religious dimension. In the Revolution of 1789 law was absolutized, yet at the same time its presumed dimension of obligation was loosened. A fundamental clarification of disordered relationships is seen by Simone Weil only if the obligation is acknowledged that proceeds from human nature itself. From it derives the recognition of all of man's vital needs, the physical as well as the spiritual. Among the needs of the body are nourishment, sleep and warmth; among the needs of the soul belong order, freedom, obedience, responsibility, equality, order of precedence, honor, punishment, freedom of opinion, security, readiness for risk, property and truth.[6] These needs of the soul are not at all abstractly conceived; rather, they are determined by a participation endowed by nature in collective living, a participation resulting from location, from birth, from vocational environment and from close circumstances. Nonetheless, this participation is not something immediate. It is rooted in the individualization of every human being, which in turn is based upon the fact that every person is an image of God. Each one acknowledges the needs of the other, who like himself is an image of God. Therein lies the meaning of love for neighbor.

Participation in the life of another means in the first place the acceptance of the creatureliness of oneself and of the other. This creatureliness fundamentally signifies loneliness. Through compassion I am bound to the other as creature. Through compassion I serve the needs of the other. It is the only way in which I am empowered to accept the other's creatureliness. On that account, Christ healed and gave food. In the extreme case, through compassion we touch upon the dimension of truth and affliction. For Simone Weil, truth and affliction belong together. In normal living and talking, the two do not emerge. In truth and affliction we are seized by something alien, indeed we are outright destroyed. In this context Simone Weil speaks about the death of the soul—also about that this death must in each instance precede physical death. "Only the supernatural action of grace causes a soul to go beyond its own destruction to the place where it acquires for itself the sort of attentiveness that alone enables it to be attentive to truth and affliction. It is the same for both objects. It is an intense, pure, fixed, gratuitous and generous attention. And this attention is love."[7]

Nietzsche also was also struck by the point that suffering places man "in our ultimate depth."[8] However, for him this experience of nothingness signifies the retreat "into the mute, rigid, and deaf yielding, forgetting and extinguishing of oneself."[9] In this view, compassion is plainly the "practice of nihilism,"[10] and serves only to advance the decadence of life. Compassion operates contagiously: in the stead of life there emerge redemption, blessedness and other substitutes for nothingness. Nietzsche saw in antiquity a dignified connection with compassion: Aristotle held tragedy to be purgative. However, in Christianity, suffering was no longer something great in itself. The Christian knows too much and believes he can explain it. The specific dignity of suffering was lost.

Simone Weil places suffering in creatureliness, and therefore in man's constitutive loneliness as God's image. In suffering she recognizes God's otherness and our separation from him. The decisive idea, however, is that, precisely in his loneliness, the suffering human being takes part in God's creation. This change in the perception of suffering is due to the view of creation as a renunciation on God's part of being everything. "For, by creating, God renounces being everything; he relinquishes a bit of being to that which is other than himself. Creation is renunciation for love."[11] In this idea something suddenly emerges that calls to mind the cabalistic teaching of Tsimtsum. In this teaching creation is regarded as the self-limiting of God, which precedes the illumination of the creature with divine light. In it is detected one of the few serious attempts to set creation from nothing against the emanation teaching with its pantheistic consequences.[12] However the connection between Simone Weil's thought and the doctrine of Tsimtsum is to be judged, one will in any event take hold of the liberating element in this thought, that the greatness of man—precisely at its hardest point, in suffering—consists in sharing in the self-limitation of God. Nietzsche's line from "Thus Spake Zarathustra" sounds like a reflective echo: "Truly, there must be much more bitter dying in your lives, O you who create!"[13] Here it is—as already in the previously mentioned connections—as if Nietzsche wanted to give a narcissistic twist, which degenerates into a hollow pathos and leads into nothingness, to an inescapable insight which Simone Weil acknowledges.

The perception of the connection between suffering and creatureliness leads into the inescapable. We bear our own existence, not that of some other person. Necessity is then suffered. "The consent to necessity is pure love and in some way even an excess of love . . . Whatever one's declared belief with regard to religious matters, including atheism, wherever there is complete, authentic and unconditional consent to necessity, there is the fullness of the love of God, and nowhere else. This consent continues the sharing in the cross of Christ."[14]

No longer can we speak of modernity, technology, and liberalism as the solid ground of everything. The experience of the necessary— in suffering—becomes set against the modern emphasis on man's self-responsibility for the world and on his political achievement of liberty. In this way Simone Weil anticipated judgments drawn from a modern type of necessity experience derived from the self-referential reconstruction of the world. Nietzsche, after all, proclaimed as the "new gospel" that "Everything is necessity — thus states the new knowledge; and this knowledge itself is necessity."[15] Nietzsche intends to show "that we ourselves in our most purposeful actions do nothing more than play the game of necessity."[16] He thereby returns to the Stoic ideal of *amor fati* (the love of fate). In it he sees the "formula for greatness in man . . . not merely to put up with necessity, nor even less to conceal it — all idealism is mendacity in the face of the necessary — but rather to *love* it . . . "[17]

Nietzsche is dealing with *amor fati* in a Dionysian way — loving his own suffering, which for Simone Weil is pure obedience before God. The order of the world ought to be loved since it is pure obedience to God . . . everything that comes our way in the course of our lives, having been led by the total obedience of this universe to God, puts us into contact with the absolute good which constitutes the divine will; for this reason, everything without exception, joys and pains indiscriminately, ought to be welcomed with the same interior attitude of love and gratitude."[18] *Amor fati* for Simone Weil is precisely this love for the order of the world. With heightened interpretation, she identifies *fatum* and Logos: she interprets the message of the Gospel of John in the sense of a necessity of events that overcomes the motif of reward and punishment, a necessity that influences the workings of divine grace. The just and the unjust receive sunshine and rain in the same measure. "And if you save your greetings for your brothers, are you doing anything exceptional? Even the pagans do as much, do they not? You must therefore be perfect just as your heavenly Father is perfect" (Matt 5:47 f.). Simone Weil does not hesitate to identify the love of John for Christ with the acknowledgement of the necessity of mathematical truths. "One could never prove that something as absurd as consent to necessity might be possible. One can only attest it. There are indeed souls who consent."[19]

Notwithstanding, this recognition of necessity in no manner signifies the acceptance of force and violence — on the contrary. Here it is a matter of purely immaterial relations, which do not submit to the limiting temporal constitution of our existence. In necessity, the superiority of the world order over earthly needs and over the limitations by force and violence is acknowledged. This acknowledgement in obedience is often the suffering of limitation.

From the superiority of the order of the world, there issues for Simone Weil her great respect for mathematics and science, which display the world's beauty in a symbolic interpretation, and which do not fall under the power of an irresponsible frivolous juggling of possibilities. The transparency in our action of an order at a remove from our grasp remains crucial.

To the dimension of the holy, in which the human soul has a share, Simone Weil is surpassingly sensitive. To the extent that the soul belongs to the holy, it is withdrawn from a sphere belonging to the person, which necessarily opens itself only to solitude. The human soul has thereby left collective existence and beyond that, the dimension of the personal. Nothing is as opposed to the holy as is the collective, especially since the collective has the tendency to become a false imitation of the holy, a terrestrial god.[20] Simone Weil expressly emphasizes that not even the Church is exempt from this danger of the collective form of existence. The mingling of devotion to the Spirit of truth, in the sense of the Gospel of John, with the totalitarian claims of an organization has historically had some advantages but mostly disadvantages.[21]

With a view to Nietzsche, it was stated in this regard that antiquity was repeated at the peak of modernity. Reminiscent of this, there is manifest in Simone Weil a justification for speaking of tragedy in the horizon of the event of the Cross. It has multiple stages: already in the Church the uprooting was taking hold just as it had encroached upon Europe and outward to the whole modern world.[22] In the modern world of labor, especially in socialism, it has reached an unbearable level. It is not a mistake to see in the technological reconstruction of the world an imitation of the holy that is absolutely destructive. Seen in this manner, the modern world calls to mind as a collective the tragic hero who in complete freedom has taken his destiny upon himself and hastens his downfall.

With respect to this situation, Simone Weil reminds us about the loneliness of man taking part in God's creation. The tragic fate of modernity is not an optional (avoidable) event. In it there occurs the radicalization of the uprootedness that is a constitutive element of human nature: alienation. It stands in the sign of the Cross. It does not behoove us to unravel the threads of this fate.

Notes

1 *L'Enracinement. Prélude à une déclaration des devoirs envers l'être humain* (Gallimard, Paris 1949), p. 378.

2 *Ibid.*, 379 f.

3 *Le matérialisme historique* (1934), in: *Oeuvres complètes* II (Gallimard, Paris 1988), p. 331.

4 *Sur la pensée et le travail* (1932-1933), in: *Oeuvres complètes* I (Gallimard, Paris 1988), p. 378 f.

5 *Ibid.*, p. 378.

6 Cf. *L'Enracinement,* Première Partie.

7 *Ecrits de Londres et dernières lettres* (Gallimard, Paris 1957), p. 36.

8 *Nietzsche contra Wagner*, Epilog (1), *Werke*, ed. K. Schlechta (Hanser, Munich 1969), vol. II, p. 1059.

9 *Ibid.*

10 *Der Antichrist* (7), *Werke*, vol. II, p. 1168.

11 *Intuitions préchrétiennes* (Fayard, Paris 1985), p. 148.

12 Cf. G. Scholem, *Major Trends in Jewish Mysticism* (Thames & Hudson, London 1955) p. 260 ff. and often elsewhere. On the connection between S. Weil and the Cabala, cf. W. Rabi, "La conception weilienne de la création. Rencontre avec la Kabbale juive," in: *Simone Weil. Philosophe, historienne et mystique*, ed. G. Kahn (Paris 1978).

13 *Also sprach Zarathustra*, Zweiter Teil, *Auf den glückseligen Inseln*, *Werke* vol. II, p. 345.

14 *Intuitions*, p. 148 f.

15 *Menschliches, Allzumenschliches* vol. I (107), *Werke* I, p. 514.

16 *Morgenröte*, Zweites Buch (130), *Werke* I, 1102.

17 *Ecce homo, Warum ich so klug bin* (10), *Werke* II, p. 1098.

18 *L'Enracinement*, p. 363 f.

19 *Intuitions*, p. 150.

20 *Ecrits de Londres*, p. 18.

21 *Lettre à un religieux* (Gallimard, Paris 1951), no. 14.

22 *Ibid.*, no. 9.

Postscript: in the foregoing text, reference was made repeatedly to Nietzsche. Simone Weil was no reader of Nietzsche. She remarked once that reading Nietzsche was unbearable for her (in a letter to André Weil, cf. Simone Fraisse, "*Die Nation im Denken Simone Weils*," in: *Simone Weil—Philosophie, Religion, Politik*, ed. H.R. Schlette and A.-A. Devaux (J. Knecht, Frankfurt am Main 1985, p. 251, note 8). However, it makes sense to compare Nietzsche and Simone Weil, since both think in terms of the extreme situation of misery, yet they view it in diametrically opposite ways.

Section III

Islamic Mysticism

Situating Islamic "Mysticism": Between Written Traditions and Popular Spirituality

James W.Morris

Those who write about Islamic "mysticism" for all but specialized scholarly audiences are usually referring to a small selection of classical Arabic and Persian writings translated into Western languages, or to the handful of traditions of spiritual practice from the Muslim world that have become known even more recently in the West. In that situation the risks of serious misunderstanding, for an uninformed audience, are almost unavoidable, especially where some sort of comparative perspective is assumed. In the hope of helping non-Islamicists to avoid some of those common pitfalls, this essay is devoted to outlining some of the most basic features of the actual contexts of teaching and devotion within which those Islamic texts most often characterized as "mystical" were originally written and studied.

I. Introduction: The Concept of *Walaya*

Perhaps the most fundamental dimension of this problem is beautifully summarized in the following *hadîth qudsî*, one of the most frequently cited of those extra-Qur'anic "divine sayings":

> (God said:) "For Me, the most blessed of My friends[1] is the person of faith who is unburdened (by possessions), who takes pleasure in prayer, who carries out well his devotion to his Lord and eagerly serves Him in secret. He is concealed among the people; no one points him out. His sustenance is barely sufficient, and he is content with that . . . . His death comes quickly, there are few mourners, and his estate is small."[2]

Now the living presence of the "Friend of God" or *walî* (pl. *awliyâ'*), in one manifestation or another — whether it be Muhammad and his Family or certain Companions, any of the earlier prophets, the Shiite Imams, or the many pious Muslims who have come to be recognized posthumously as "saints" — has for centuries been a central focus of popular religious and devotional life in much of the Islamic world.[3]

But the true *walî*, as this hadîth stresses, is most often publicly "invisible" in this life, outwardly indistinguishable from many other normally devout Muslim men and women. And even after death, for those *awliyâ'* whose mission of sanctity or "proximity" to God (*walâya*) has become more widely recognized, the mysterious reality of their ongoing influence likewise remains invisible to most people, revealing itself directly only at the appropriate moments in *individual*, highly personalized means of contact: through dreams, visions, intuitions and spiritual acts of Grace (*karamât*) or special blessings that only appear to "those with the eyes to see."

Thus this famous hadîth suggests two basic considerations that should be kept in mind whenever one encounters the written works usually associated with Islamic "mysticism". The first point is that with rare exceptions such texts were *not* originally meant to be studied by themselves. Usually they were understood, by their author and audience alike, to be only secondary or accessory means to their aim (and often their source): the *awliyâ'* – taken in the broadest sense, including the prophets and Imams – and the gradual realization of that spiritual condition of *walâya*, or "closeness to God", embodied in such individuals.[4]   The second, closely related point is that such "mystical" writings in their original context – and especially those works written in languages other than classical Arabic – were often quite inseparable from the whole range of "popular" religion, from the faith so diversely lived and practiced by the mass of the Muslim population (in contrast to the versions represented by the Arabic traditional religious sciences and the claims of their learned urban male interpreters). In fact in many regions of the Muslim world that faith was originally spread and inculcated almost entirely by such popular "mystical" writings and their even more widespread oral equivalents, or rather above all by the saints and other religious teachers who conveyed (and often created) both that literature and the music and other forms of spiritual practice that typically accompanied it.

If one keeps both those essential points in mind, it is easy to understand the practical and historical reasons behind the profusion of personalities and spiritual methods, symbols, practices, and beliefs that one discovers already in the lives of the classical exemplars of Islamic mysticism in Baghdad and Khorasan in the 3rd century (A. H.). But those same considerations also help us to appreciate the deep sense of disillusionment and failure, of something gone profoundly wrong, whenever the spiritual dimension of Islam has come to be identified with any particular, exclusive set of such historical forms.[5]   That recurrent realization was summed up in the frequently echoed response of the Khurasani mystic al-Qûshanjî (d. 348/959) to a disciple's naive question "What is Sufism (*taṣawwuf*)?":

"(Today it's) a name without reality; but it used to be a reality without a name."[6]

Whether name or reality, the unavoidable problem for students of religion is that there is still so little accessible literature that one can rely on to provide either of these essential contexts for understanding the wider religious functions and meaning of the many written—and the far more extensive unwritten—forms and expressions of Islamic mysticism.

II. The Qur'an and the Islamic Humanities

Interestingly enough, there is a fairly simple experiment that quickly reveals both the origins of the many genres of Islamic "mystical" literature and the key to the contexts within which they originally functioned. If one simply makes a serious effort to communicate *in English* (or in any other non-Islamic language) something of the inner meanings and deeper message of the Arabic Qur'ân[7] to a cross-section of a given community—from children to adults, both women and men, with all their practical occupations, personal concerns, educational backgrounds, and spiritual and intellectual aptitudes—one quickly finds oneself obliged to recreate, in today's idiom, virtually the full spectrum of what is usually called Islamic "mystical" literature, both theoretical and practical. Hence the typologies of form and audience outlined in the following sections are clearly determined by the necessary interplay between (a) particular topics or teachings drawn (directly or indirectly) from the Qur'ân; (b) the attitudes, expectations and capabilities of each particular audience; and (c) the individual teacher's own perceptiveness and creative ability—using words, music, drama, and all the other instruments of human communication—to evoke in each member of their audience the indispensable immediate awareness of those ever-renewed theophanies "in the world and in their souls"[8] which will actually bring that spiritual message alive.

Now if we may borrow the term "*Islamic humanities*" to describe the whole socially embedded and historically changing matrix of cultural forms—institutions, epics, myths and folktales, rituals, poetry, music, codes of right behavior (*adab*) and implicit values and expectations—through which that transmission of spiritual teaching actually takes place within each Muslim family or local social group, then it is clear that the religious literatures traditionally associated with Islamic "mysticism" have indeed played a central (although by no means exclusive) role in that process of spiritual education for the majority of Muslims living in any period.[9]   And it is equally clear that the immense corpus of hadîth (in both their Sunni and Shiite forms) constitute the paradigmatic example, the "prototype" as it were, for the subsequent creative development of all the Islamic humanities.[10] Whatever their historical authenticity, the complex corpus of hadîth marvelously illustrates both the central Islamic assumption of the true "embodiment" of the spiritual teaching in the archetypal example of the *walî* (in this case the Prophet or Imams) and the fruitful, but problematic refractions of that living teaching through the particular perspectives and understandings of the many generations of individuals receiving and transmitting it. All the forms and dilemmas of later "mystical literature", and of the Islamic humanities more generally, are already reflected and often beautifully dramatized in that vast literature of hadîth.

At this point non-Islamicist readers might well object that all of this must be so obvious as scarcely to require mentioning. The problem, however, is that this "self-evident" observation happens to run counter to some of the most fundamental paradigms, both normative and historical, underlying the classical Arabic "religious sciences" as they were written down and elaborated by small influential groups of learned religious scholars (the *ᶜulamâ'*) in the scattered cities of the Muslim world from the 3rd/9th century onward. From the perspective of those scholarly paradigms, the revelation of the Qur'ân was considered as inseparable, both temporally and normatively, from the equally "revealed" teachings recorded and conveyed by the hadîth and—in practice—from the related auxiliary Arabic linguistic and interpretive sciences. Together these Arabic textual studies came to be viewed by this small group of learned interpreters as constituting religious "Knowledge" (*ᶜilm*) *par excellence*, the joint and unique foundations or "sources" (*uṣûl*) from which they could then derive, in a variety of ways, their own authoritative standards of properly Islamic practice and belief.[11]

Thus the learned elite purveyors of those Arabic religious disciplines, while constituting themselves as the (self-appointed) authoritative interpreters of that wider Prophetic legacy, at the same time at least theoretically conceived of the immense majority of their fellow Muslims—especially such groups as women and illiterate rural and tribal peoples—as condemned to a doubly degenerate state of belief and practice. For according to their twofold "trickle-down" model of Islam,[12] even the most learned and zealously pious students of these Arabic sources would necessarily come to be increasingly removed from the pure ideal represented by the short-lived Medinan community (or the earliest Imams), while the vast majority of Muslims could only imitate, at an even further remove, the various models of belief and behavior developed and expounded by this handful of learned interpreters.

From the standpoint of those later learned men, the Islamic humanities (both oral and written) and their representatives and creators could represent at best only an approximation to (or inevitable "compromise" with) their own authoritative standards of properly religious knowledge and behavior. At worst, of course, the popular Islamic humanities, especially in their oral and non-learned forms, tended to appear from that viewpoint as "deviant" and igno-rant "survivals" of pre-Islamic "customs," as the unmentionable – if sometimes practically unavoidable – "superstitions" and "popular" or even "nominal" religion of women and children, illiterate peasants and the masses of uncultured, only partly "Islamicized" tribal peoples.[13]

But that immense majority of less learned Muslims in the past, in all the regions of the Islamic world, certainly did not have to wait for the insights of modern students of religion, or the discoveries of modern ethnologists and social historians, to expose the many theological and historical fallacies and the ill-concealed political and cultural pretensions of that scripturalist paradigm of the *ʿulamā'*. Thus most of the types of "theoretical" mystical writings discussed below, for example, were in fact created precisely to defend the prac-tices and presuppositions of the wider Islamic humanities – whether in their high-cultural and learned, or their oral and popular forms – by transforming or even replacing influential versions of that religious paradigm, either by exposing its theological and metaphysi-cal inadequacies or by articulating the alternative spiritual claims of particular representatives of the *awliyā'*. And of course in many parts of the Islamic world people went on creating and living out the more practical local forms of the Islamic humanities, as they do today, with-out overly worrying about the disputes and alternative visions of those often far-off urban male learned elites.[14]

Here again, the great obstacle for students of religion approaching the *texts* of Islamic "mysticism" is that any adequate phenomeno-logical description of their social and historical *contexts* – assumed by the original authors and audiences alike – is still often inaccessible to non-specialists. The invaluable contributions of recent studies of the social history of all periods and regions of the Islamic world in revealing those local contexts, and especially in highlighting the immense lacunae in our knowledge of earlier Islam societies and the actual religious lives and practice (most notably of women and tribal peoples) outside a handful of urban cultural centers, have not even begun to be assimilated in surveys of Islam intended for non-specialists.[15] And the equally important detailed descriptions of individual local Muslim communities (usually rural or tribal) by anthropologists and ethnographers in this century likewise have typically been carried out, in all but a handful of exceptional cases, in unfortunate ignorance of the historical depth and cultural complexities of the Islamic humanities and the widespread interplay of their localized forms with more learned traditions, especially those associated with Islamic mysticism.[16]

The fundamental relevance of the growing evidence from these disciplines for situating Islamic "mysticism" can be stated very simply: the closer one looks at the actual lives of individual Muslim women and men in any period (including the learned male scholarly elites), the harder it is to discern any indigenous literary or cultural category or social institutions (*including* those associated with "Sufism") that could somehow be singled out as uniquely or authoritatively representing "Islamic mysticism". At best, as in the fitting title of A. Schimmel's classic study, one can speak broadly of the "mystical *dimensions*" of virtually every aspect of Islamic life and culture in the pre-modern world. Time and again, when one looks at the actual historical contexts, it turns out that what have often been identified as "mystical" practices or writings were in fact integrally embedded in the wider Islamic humanities, or what outside observers have often so revealingly labeled as "popular" — i.e., *actually lived* — religion and spirituality.

To give only a few examples directly illustrating the following discussion of the types of mystical literature, the repeated invocation of divine Names (the prayer of *dhikr*, or "remembrance" of God) turns out to be not simply a central "Sufi" ritual, but in some areas an important part of funerals and a common stage in the religious education of young people, who learn (even before the canonical prayers) the "Most Beautiful Names" and their recitation with the aid of prayer beads — a practice carried on throughout life without presupposing any official affiliation to a particular Sufi order. Likewise periodical visitations (*ziyârât*) to the shrines and tombs of saints (and prophets, Imams, and some of their descendants) and associated festivals have long been an integral part of ritual and family life in virtually every region, with more widespread participation even today than the Hajj which typically figures so prominently in textbook accounts of Islam. And even more common and spiritually significant — if less visible — are the diverse practices of offerings, prayers, sacrifices and vows in connection with those dreams, spiritual visions, intuitions and blessings that are each individual's decisive proof of the effective (and affective) power of a given *walî*. Finally, at least in traditional settings throughout much of the Eastern Islamic world, "mystical" and devotional poetry (frequently in conjunction with music) is often not just an incidental ornament or illustration of some more learned Islamic teaching, but in fact the primary vehicle for discovering and formulating the "mystical" dimension of the spiritually significant experiences and situations constantly arising in everyday life.[17] There those compelling vernacular poetic literatures and vast repertoire of popular stories about the prophets and saints are the equally complex equivalent in the Islamic humanities of the multitude of spiritually significant tales and legends—likewise only partially "scriptural"—whose reminders are built into the stained glass windows and elaborate stonework of Chartres and other medieval cathedrals.[18]

III. Types of Mystical Writing:　Texts and Contexts

The following basic typology should help to bring out the importance of the actual contexts of the various writings often associated with Islamic "mysticism", contexts which are rarely discussed in adequate detail in the still limited set of translations or analytical discussions of those texts available to non-Islamicists. This schematic analysis is based on an extremely simplified consideration of the main audiences and subjects of that literature, a procedure that is subject to several important qualifications mentioned below. A few reliable English translations are cited as illustrations in each case, as an aid to those working in related fields who might wish to use such texts in teaching or comparative studies.

The most fundamental distinction one immediately encounters in considering Islamic "mystical" texts is that between works addressed to the relatively small network of scholars conversant with the learned traditions of the religious and "rational" (i.e., philosophic, scientific, medical, etc.) sciences, which were usually written in classical Arabic[19]—works that we may broadly characterize as "*theoretical*" in their format and audience—and a vastly more complex and diverse literature of the Islamic humanities, both written and predominantly oral, in a multitude of languages, intended for the *practical spiritual instruction* or edification of far wider audiences. These latter, more practical types of writing typically share a common concern with directly communicating, in a locally meaningful form, essential spiritual teachings of the Qur'an and hadîth.[20]

The selection of writings included in the following categories roughly corresponds to the broad set of subjects that are commonly associated with "Islamic mysticism" in modern translations and discussions by students of other religious traditions. But in reality this standard selection is somewhat arbitrary and artificially limited in a number of crucial respects that must constantly be kept in mind if one is to appreciate the distinctive roles of these specific types of writing within the much wider complex of the Islamic humanities and their actual religious functions in particular local contexts.

To begin with, the typology of "mystical" writings outlined here does not directly include the traditional complex of Arabic "religious sciences" (*fiqh, kalâm, usûl al-fiqh, tafsîr, hadîth,* related linguistic and historical studies, Arabic calligraphy, and the like), even though all of those disciplines have frequently been used and construed as important, even integral aspects of mystical or spiritual paths in various Islamic contexts by some of the learned elite to whom they were directly accessible.[21] More importantly, we have left out of consideration here the vast realm of supposedly "non-religious" local literatures[22]—e.g., forms of epic poetry, "folk-tales", proverbs and fables, traditional (family, tribal, etc.) genealogies, histories and legends, etc.—and related practices, even though those forms of the Islamic humanities are frequently central to the actual understanding and symbolic articulation of religious and spiritual experience in each local context.   Hence the following typology of audiences and subjects, it should be stressed, is *not* directly based on any traditional literary genres: one could give both prose and poetic illustrations, in both written and oral expression, for each category of "mystical" writing outlined below. And certainly many of the classic, most lastingly and widely influential vehicles of the Islamic humanities (such as the hadîth themselves, the *Ihyâ' ʿUlûm al-Dîn* of Ghazâlî, or the epic accomplishments of poets like Rumi, Attar and Hafez) include virtually all of the following categories.

Even more fundamentally, the actual spiritual functions of the limited types of *writing* discussed below in practice overlap and intersect with a far more extensive and diverse network of other forms of local practices, rituals, iconographies, social patterns and cultural assumptions which can differ radically from one family, quarter, village or tribe even to its nearest neighbors. Whether any aspect of a particular Islamic socio-cultural context (including its written and oral literatures) actually operates as—or is perceived as—"mystical" (or "religious", "Islamic", etc.) raises thorny questions of *individual* realization and broader cultural definition that are at least as complex and controversial in those local contexts as are their more familiar metaphysical and scholarly counterparts. Within the major urban centers of Iran, for example, such widespread rituals and practices as the ceremonies surrounding the solar New Year (*Now Rûz*)—or the recitation of Ferdowsi's epic *Shâhnâmeh* (and its popular retellings); the extraordinary intertwinings of polite language (*ta'ârrof*) and social etiquette and norms; the *zûr-khâneh* (men's "gym"); the craft guilds and bazaar associations; mastery of *shekasteh* or other scripts; diverse items of dress; or the host of special foods and offerings whose preparation is prescribed for even relatively minor passages in life—have all taken on "mystical" meanings for individual Muslims and even for wider communities at different times.[23]   And if one looks more closely, it turns out that the same dynamic, creative processes go on today—likewise with virtually no traditionally learned or formally "Islamic" literary input, and often without public documentary manifestations—within the families and communities of African American (and other American) Muslims today.[24]

Finally it should be obvious that the actual "mystical" or spiritual functioning of any of these forms of the Islamic humanities—at least in any deeper and consistently meaningful sense—still depends above all on the very different ways in which individual Muslims actively appropriate and experience them. At least for each of the "practical" categories of mystical writing, one could easily cite a long continuum of illustrations stretching from undeniably spiritual expressions to relatively banal, traditionally "folkloric" or even more grossly "superstitious" and mundane uses.[25] (Perhaps that essential contrast is most obvious in the remarkable range of cultural and individual uses of the "occult sciences", like alchemy, astrology or numerology, and of their psychic and cosmological symbolism.) In fact, just as with the full corpus of hadîth, one often tends to find the ostensible "extremes" of that spectrum of spiritual realization contained *within* the same literary work, or expressed at times in the life and activities of a single individual.

IV. Practical Types

—"Music" in the broadest possible sense[26]—including the various forms and ritual circumstances of Qur'an recitation; all the expressions of group prayer ceremonies (*dhikr*), whether chanted or accompanied by instruments; as a common setting for the classics of mystical lyric poetry; at saints' shrines and festivals; and within a host of other religious rituals and life-cycle ceremonies—remains fundamental to any serious phenomenology of religious and mystical life in most Muslim societies, and to even the most elementary understanding of the Islamic humanities. Fortunately, students of religion now have at their disposal, even without travelling, a rapidly growing range of recordings and descriptive studies sufficient to give some idea of the centrality of music in a wide variety of Islamic spiritual paths and disciplines, especially in those rural, tribal and "popular" contexts so often neglected in general works on Islam.[27]

As a revealing contrast, studies of architecture and other visual arts as manifestations of the Islamic humanities—and more particularly in their relations to mystical and spiritual dimensions of Islam—have apparently been greatly limited by the art-historical disciplines' classical focus on a canon of "great" works or monuments associated with a select group of urban centers of patronage, trade and power, as well as by highly inappropriate, culturally limited definitions of what constitutes "fine" and minor or "decorative" (or "civilized" and "primitive") arts.[28]　Certainly scholars are now paying increased attention to such relatively obvious phenomena as the interactions between mystical thought and literature and miniature paintings often produced in the same court settings, or to the social and political dimensions of Islamic "mystical" movements from the 13th through the 19th centuries, as their deeply rooted popular influences were mirrored in the fortunes of dynasties and the widespread official construction and endowment of saints' shrines, tombs, khanegahs, and the like.　But the more widespread popular reflections and subtle influences of mystical teachings and practice in such culturally diverse forms as calligraphy (in all Islamic languages) and the aesthetics and iconography of textiles, clothing, jewelry, utensils, ceramics, and carpets; in tombs; and in the plethora of more "rustic" mosques, zâwiyas, Imâmzâdehs or jamkhânehs—especially as those physical creations interacted with particular local customs and social patterns—has yet to attract the same level of scholarly attention, above all with regard to those aspects that would most interest the student of religions.[29]　Thus, apart from important studies of a few pre-modern cities and famous monuments, something as primordial as the concrete expression of the sacred and physical *space* of Islamic spirituality and mystical practice in non-urban settings, from West Africa to China and Indonesia, necessarily continues to be another mystery to all those (including many Islamic scholars) who have not been privileged to travel and live in those unique local contexts and communities.

—Reflecting the central focus in popular Islamic spirituality on sacred-human mediating figures (the *awliyâ'*, Imams, prophets and especially Muhammad and his Family and Companions) already discussed above, by far the largest category of mystical literature (including corresponding oral forms) consists of what could very broadly be called *"devotional"* literature: prayers, invocations, blessings and praises, and (at least in Shiite contexts) rites of mourning and elegies typically directed toward, or else produced by, those central theophanic figures.[30] In fact the importance of those human spiritual exemplars is so overwhelming in virtually every sphere of Islamic spirituality[31] that in practice it is extremely difficult to separate this category of spiritual writing and practice from almost all of the other "mystical" forms of the Islamic humanities discussed below; those other types of writing can all be understood (and often were consciously intended) as extended commentaries on one or another of these exemplary spiritual archetypes. The remarkable lack of translations[32] of this kind of literature (not to mention in-depth studies of its actual religious functions in specific local contexts) may in part reflect the relative predominance of its oral or "popular", vernacular forms and more particularly its associations with that (supposedly) "silent majority" — i.e., Muslim *women* — whose actual experience and practice of the spiritual life is still so strikingly absent from most of the available scholarly literature on Islamic religion.

— It would certainly be tempting, especially for students of comparative mysticism and spirituality, to try to separate out from the above category texts concerned more specifically with the actual practice of methods of contemplation, meditation, visualization and related disciplines pursued in the Sufi orders and other "mystical" forms of Islamic religion.[33] The fact that such an effort would be doomed to failure even in the original languages reflects two fundamental and quite distinctive features of Islamic spirituality — both deeply rooted in the central mystery of the unique language and rhetoric of the Qur'an — whose significance will be discussed in more detail at the end of this essay. First, from the time of Muhammad down to the present day, "mystical" or spiritual practices in Islam, despite all their diversity and changing forms, have typically *not* been viewed or portrayed as clearly distinct from the archetypal Prophetic model of constant prayer, devotion, awareness, vigil, fasting, and retreat — i.e., from the actualization of those more universal spiritual virtues which are the constant subject and aim of the Qur'an itself. Secondly, for reasons also discussed below, detailed attempts to record or prescribe those spiritual practices in *written* form seem to have been virtually nonexistent. Even if translations were more widely available, the relatively few written works on such central mystical practices that do exist — such as summary accounts of the particular prayers and litanies associated with certain Sufi orders, catalogues of divine Names used for *dhikr*, or brief instructions on breathing or visualization—typically give no inkling of the complex, highly individualized application and adaptations of such procedures under the guidance of an accomplished master, nor of the critical process of their integration within the less "esoteric" (but no less indispensable) ethical and ritual forms shared with surrounding communities.

—Perhaps the next most common form of Islamic mystical literature, and one equally inextricable from the wider complex of Islamic humanities, is that of *lives of the saints* (and Imams and prophets). The formal grounding and inspiration of that immense and constantly accumulating mystical literature in the earlier Arabic prototypes of hadîth, the *Sîra* (Prophetic biography and legend) and the parallel popular genre of "stories of the prophets" should need no explanation.[34] But whether in the epic masterworks of Rumi and Attar or in the endlessly transformed oral versions of those often universal stories,[35] it is remarkable how consistently the focus remains—as already in the hadîth—on the *archetypal*, on spiritually significant incidents or anecdotes intended to "illustrate" a more general, recurrent teaching.   The absence of any tradition of self-consciously *individualized* spiritual "autobiography" providing a detailed and psychologically realistic account of the actual processes of spiritual teaching and initiation[36] is another of those distinctive characteristics of Islamic mystical *writing* whose origins and deeper significance will be explored in the concluding sections of this study.

—The broad category of ecstatic sayings and metaphysical paradoxes (*shatahât* or Sufi "koans"), parables, aphorisms, and mystical tales[37]—drawn both from exemplars in the Qur'an, hadîth and prophetic tales, and from the accumulated wisdom of every preceding religious tradition—represents a familiar, abundant type of Islamic mystical literature in which it is often extremely difficult to draw any rigid boundaries between written and oral teaching, between commonplace proverbs and profound spiritual intuitions. To be sure, many such riddles, stories and poems are clearly protreptic, designed simply to awaken their readers' awareness of and interest in pursuing the deeper meaning behind the outward forms of religion and everyday experience. But again we have almost no scholarly literature that would adequately convey the complex higher religious functions of those short, easily memorable tales and sayings either as they are skillfully used by an accomplished master or as they resonate inwardly when their meaning is awakened in conjunction with the appropriate meditation or critical moment of spiritual insight.

—Another important category of Islamic mystical writing, which has only begun to be explored, consists of more *practical guides* to spiritual life, whether focused on the "rules" of proper behavior (*adab*) to be followed by Sufi novices, outlines of the "stages of the path" and spiritual psychology, or in actual letters of direction or students' "transcriptions" (*malfûzât*) of a master's oral teaching to certain disciples.[38] Once again, students of comparative religion who gain some familiarity with the Islamic works of this type are likely to be somewhat disappointed; for in most cases, including the translations just cited, such writings tend to be repetitive and relatively elementary, or too sketchy and fragmentary to be fully meaningful. Rarely will one find, for example, any detailed, phenomenologically adequate account of the particular Islamic uses of fasting, prayers, vigil and spiritual retreat, or of the awareness and appropriate interpretation of dreams, intuitions, and other spiritually significant events which in reality are so central to actual situations of instruction and spiritual guidance.

— Certainly the most problematic, but nonetheless extremely widespread and influential, category of Islamic mystical literature is the diverse group of so-called "occult sciences," including such complex fields as the multi-dimensional sciences of letters and numerology (*jafr* and *ʿilm al-hurûf*); alchemy; astrology; talismans; chiromancy; and so forth.[39] This sort of writing and associated practice—in many cases reflecting a common symbolic and cosmological heritage shared with late Antiquity and the medieval West—spans an enormous range of manifestations in most Islamic societies, from highly theoretical treatments and profound mystical elaborations (detailing cosmological or subtle psychological processes) to popular "superstitions" and their own pragmatic uses. For a variety of reasons, neither of those extremes has yet been subject to much sustained scholarly attention in the Islamic context, while recent religious modernists and reformers have typically considered both learned and popular manifestations of these disciplines to be embarrassing relics of a backward, "pre-scientific" superstitious mentality. Thus accounts of Islamic mysticism and related arts and poetry for modern audiences have naturally tended to neglect the decisive importance of their communication of a "sacred canopy" of common cosmological symbols (including the omnipresent letters of the *sacred alphabet*) in accounting for the wider efficacy and persuasiveness of many expressions of the traditional Islamic humanities across the whole cultural spectrum from court poetry and learned sciences to the most remote local oral traditions.[40]

— Finally, there is the broad category of more direct expression, often in lyrical or even ecstatic poetic form, of actual mystical or spiritual experiences—a category which, because of its relative familiarity of subject and expression, has been a consistent favorite of modern Western translators.[41] The popularity and immediacy of such classic texts, however, should not automatically be taken as an index of either their representative qualities or their adequacy for depicting the broader spectrum of Islamic "mystical" practices and presuppositions. To take only one striking example, the predominance in Rumi's lyric poetry of universal images drawn directly from nature — even if those symbols are almost always intended as revelatory commentaries on familiar mystical themes from the Qur'an and hadîth — surely helps explain the widespread appeal of his writing, especially to contemporary literary tastes. But the relative directness and simplicity of some of Rumi's poetry is far from typical of the highly stylized, formalistic rhetorical conventions of much later Islamic mystical poetry, with its complex, entirely untranslatable play of musical associations on a multidimensional repertoire of symbolic and metaphysical archetypes (again often scriptural in origin) shared by writer and audience (whether learned or "illiterate") alike. In those later, highly influential traditions, as exemplified in the incomparable Persian lyrics of Hafez, poetry comes to be seen less as a vehicle of communication of some particular "original" individual insight than as a subtle mirror reflecting and revealing the deeper, archetypal dimensions of each reader's/listener's own momentary spiritual state. So again it turns out that the more genuinely religious and "mystical" (i.e., not merely conventional) dimensions of that central type of Islamic literature — whether in its learned or vernacular expressions — can only be discerned in light of highly complex practical and cultural contexts that are typically assumed, rather than openly stated.

V. The Islamic Context of "Theoretical" Mystical Writings

It is important to note that the four broad types of "mystical" writing distinguished under this heading are relatively later phenomena in Islamic thought, since in both their Sunni and Shiite forms they presuppose the early foundational teachings of Muhammad and the Imams; then the broader development and spread of the earliest Arabic exemplars of the Islamic humanities (hadîth, Sîra, stories of the prophets, etc.);[42] and finally the gradual intellectual "crystallization" or increasingly sophisticated theoretical articulation in classical Arabic — throughout the 3rd and 4th centuries of the Islamic era, in a few urban centers of the Abbasid empire — of *alternative learned understandings* of the proper implications and interpretations (social, political, spiritual and intellectual) of that accrued body of diverse religious traditions. During that period several schools of what have been loosely (and somewhat misleadingly) called Islamic "theology" gradually developed a shared vocabulary for articulating different visions of the Arabic religious sciences, while Farabi and others (including many translators) were likewise developing an Arabic philosophic language capable of expressing the universal insights and pretensions of the inherited Hellenistic scientific and philosophic traditions. The remarkably successful creative melding of those two conceptual universes by the philosopher Avicenna (d. 429/1037) eventually resulted in a complex shared philosophico-theological language which was used by most later Muslim intellectuals, until the present century, to articulate and defend their alternative visions of the proper theoretical and practical understandings of Islamic tradition. The most famous and lastingly influential "theoretical" expositions of Islamic mysticism—including especially those by Ibn ʿArabî (d. 1240) and Ghazâlî (d. 1111), whose works are still widely read throughout the Islamic world today—both drew upon and further transformed that distinctive philosophic and theological vocabulary, which was freely adapted by most subsequent mystical writers in each of the four categories below.

Thus the place of these "theoretical" forms of Islamic mystical writing within this larger intellectual development—and more significantly, their relation to the more widespread popular and practical manifestations of mystical and spiritual teaching—was radically different from the role of outwardly similar intellectual forms developed in other religious or civilizational contexts. First, unlike the case of Hindu or Buddhist traditions, "mystical *philosophy*" (or theosophy) in a thoroughly speculative or primarily intellectual form hardly exists in the Islamic context. And those theoretical mystical writings that were produced in later periods were themselves rarely the inspiration of the far more extensive practical and devotional forms of mysticism spread by the Islamic humanities. On the contrary, even the types of theoretical writings discussed below appear relatively late and among a small intellectual elite, presupposing the complex of highly elaborated and deeply rooted practical mystical traditions they propose to justify or explain. Likewise these distinctively Islamic forms of theoretical mystical writing did *not* historically grow out of earlier "non-mystical" forms of religious tradition, nor are they typically conceived or presented as special "interpretations" or further spiritual dimensions of such non-mystical religious forms,[43] as in at least some historical presentations of kabbalah, for example.

Instead, when one examines these texts more closely, it turns out that the majority of more theoretical writings about Islamic mysticism are in fact primarily self-consciously *"political"* works directed toward influential elites of urban religious intellectuals. Through the presumed authority and wider educational influences of those intellectual elites, these writings were typically intended to affect, transform or protect the relative positions and wider social implementation of what their authors considered more properly or effectively spiritual understandings of the local forms of Islamic tradition and practice. As such, they usually involved intellectual debate *against* justifications of alternative socio-political interpretations (or "abuses") of the same body of learned religious tradition. Hence in each case the actual practical implications of those seminal texts, both in their original historical contexts and in the controversies which have often swirled around them down through the centuries, only become clear when we can isolate in sufficient detail both the particular intended audience and the specific issues of interpretation and practice in question.[44] Whether they are viewed historically, practically or intellectually, the classic works of theoretical mystical writing in Islam thus appear as the proverbial "tip of the iceberg" in relation to the profuse forms of mystical and spiritual practice developed and spread independently by the much larger body of the Islamic humanities in each local context.[45]

Now the disproportionate emphasis of earlier Western translations and secondary studies on such theoretical expositions of Islamic mysticism is quite understandable in terms of the pioneering European scholars' natural interests in Islamic materials apparently comparable to their own "mystical" traditions, as well as the inherited expectations of their own audiences: the philosophic and theological vocabulary of those selected "mystical" texts is (or at least once was) more familiar to learned Western readers than the unfamiliar symbolic universes and complex socio-cultural presuppositions of the more widespread practical forms of the Islamic humanities. But the legacy of that problematic initial definition of "Islamic mysticism" has been to reinforce a potent combination of theological presuppositions and questionable historical paradigms that together have largely blocked a more adequate scholarly perception of Islamic "mysticism" (including the Islamic humanities)—and which by the same token have tended to obscure presentations of Islamic religious life more generally. Some of the resulting misunderstandings are still so deeply rooted that it is necessary to point out how they differ from the actual perspectives of the authors of both practical and more theoretical mystical writings in Islam.

To begin with, neither those Muslim authors nor their opponents tend to single out some *separate* realm of mystical or spiritual activities or experiences within the wider social and ontological domains of religion: typically there is no essential separation claimed or assumed between "letter" and "spirit", "law" and "grace", ritual and realization, etc. (The highly distinctive social and literary forms and assumptions peculiar to the various forms of Islamic "esotericism" discussed in section VII below are of a very different order.) Secondly, the fundamental focus shared by these theoretical writings — i.e., the realization of the spiritual virtues and their relation to the metaphysical ground and destiny of human souls — is itself at the very center of the explicit, "exoteric" Qur'anic text. Thus any sort of text or practice one might associate with Islamic "mysticism" almost inevitably turns out to be nothing more than a *reminder or actualization* (within a particular socio-cultural setting) of unduly neglected fundamental aspects of those explicit scriptural teachings. The intimate, often inseparable relation between the outward forms and sacred-human exemplars of Islamic mysticism and those of popular religion, as well as the creative, ongoing development of the Islamic humanities in the most diverse cultural and social contexts, are rooted in the way those manifold cultural expressions return directly to the Qur'anic archetype and its explicitly metaphysical, trans-historical perspectives. More often than not the "theoretical" writers of Sufism or esoteric Shiism were simply articulating the theological and philosophic explanations (and scriptural justifications) for what *ordinary* Muslims (not just "mystics") were actually *doing*.

Thirdly, the fundamental issue at stake between virtually all the "theoretical" proponents of Islamic mysticism, both in Sunni and Shiite settings, and their opponents usually turns out to be the extremely practical — and indeed religiously unavoidable — question of the nature of the *human spiritual exemplars*[46] through which the full meaning of the revelation can be known and realized: i.e., *who* are those special persons (whether in this world or the "unseen"), and *how* can one best either locate and contact them (so as to follow their guidance and seek their aid and intercession) or else develop the spiritual qualities necessary to move toward that same state of perfection? Again, one may note (a) the fundamental continuities between Islamic "mysticism" and popular religious expressions on this point; and (b) the fact that this issue is likewise central to the Qur'anic teaching concerning the ongoing, universal realities and perennial spiritual functions of all the divine Messengers, prophets and angels.[47] So it should not be entirely surprising if in reality the differences of perception (and corresponding practice) between any two Muslim "mystics" concerning this fundamental religious question were (and still are) often at least as conspicuous as the differences separating either of them from many other groups of less avowedly mystical Muslims.

Finally, one can hardly exaggerate the determinative influence for the subsequent development of Islamic mysticism (including Shiite esotericism) — and for the evolution of the Islamic humanities more generally — of the *unique historical circumstances* (political, cultural and even geographical) which at critical moments prevented any single model or claimant from achieving anything approaching exclusive legitimacy for their claims to religio-political authority.[48] Far more than the few (and in fact not totally hostile) Qur'anic allusions to earlier clerical, kingly and monastic religious institutions,[49] it was the historically effective stalemate between the many competing paradigms of religious legitimacy during the first four formative centuries of Islam that kept the exemplary Muslim mystics of those periods from being either suppressed or routinely institutionalized (e.g., in monastic foundations, etc.) by any of those contending claims to religious authority. And it was the extreme fragmentation and instability of all but the most local political authorities for much of the next five centuries that allowed the *awliyâ'* (of very different sorts) and eventually the related Islamic humanities to take on their increasingly preeminent role in popular religious life and imagination from Africa to Central and South Asia.[50] Thus while non-Muslim observers from many backgrounds have continued to read their own models of "religion" and religious authority — including equally inappropriate notions of "orthodoxy" and "orthopraxy" — into the most diverse Islamic settings, modern historical research increasingly reminds us of the remarkable extent to which those decisive religious questions have actually remained creatively unsettled in past Islamic contexts, just as they so often still are today. Almost without exception, the masterpieces of Islamic mystical writing have been created in just such highly unsettled historical situations.

VI. "Theoretical" Types of Mystical Writing

— The first common type of "theoretical" mystical writings to appear (in Sunni circles, at least) were relatively *"defensive"* or apologetic Arabic treatises, directed toward other elite religious scholars, proposing to demonstrate the consistency of already widespread popular Sufi practices and teachings with the particular religious standards and conceptions of that learned elite,[51] while often attempting at the same time to establish religiously appropriate standards for judging (and controlling) the various manifestations and perceived social or spiritual "dangers" of those popular spiritual movements.[52] The religious problems and paradigms isolated at this early stage — e.g., the alternative attitudes toward the exemplary case of al-Hallaj's teaching and martyrdom, or the tragic events of Kerbala — tended to be repeated in such scholarly writings for centuries.

— A second, far more complex category would include more ambitiously *"offensive"* writings aimed at explaining and revealing the centrality of the spiritual life and practices of the various mystical groups and the decisive importance of the *awliyâ'* (however understood) for properly interpreting and living out other learned forms of Islam — such as various Arabic religious sciences, or even the rational and philosophic sciences — ordinarily conceived of as being relatively separate from those spiritual matters. In a way, one could say that this type of Arabic mystical writings were essentially a more scholarly equivalent of what the spiritually oriented practical Islamic humanities were actually intended to do for Muslims in other walks of life. By far the most elaborate and historically influential illustration of this type of Islamic mystical writing is the immense summa of Ibn 'Arabi's "Meccan Illuminations",[53] which discusses in endless detail the deeper spiritual meanings contained within all the scriptural sources and later religious (or even secular) elaborations of Islamic tradition. That work's persuasiveness and comprehensiveness eventually won its author the honorific title of "the Greatest Teacher" (*al-shaykh al-akbar*), and made it a primary source for most later Islamic writings of this sort — as well as for some of the more openly universalist philosophic expositions in the fourth category below.

— A third, very broad category would include actual intellectual or symbolic explanations of various dimensions of spiritual experience and their epistemological and ontological underpinnings, growing directly out of the need to understand and communicate the recurrent realities of the spiritual Path. An immensely complex creative effort of reflection in this direction already underlies the elaboration of the profuse technical vocabularies of even the earliest generations of Sufi teachers and comparable Shiite figures.[54] But it is typical of the wider social expression and essentially *practical* orientation of Islamic mysticism that the pursuit of any purely theoretical inquiry in these fields seems to have been reined in early on by a strong sense of the spiritual and social pitfalls of such intellectual activity pursued as an end in itself. Instead, one more typically finds such topics dealt with indirectly in the more "practical" types of mystical writing discussed above in terms of refined allusions to classical scriptural symbols or spiritually revealing anecdotes: in such works the pure theoretical impulse is constantly turned back toward what is instead portrayed as its proper, comprehensive human context of spiritual realization.

— Finally, there are those theoretical works whose authors have attempted more comprehensive, openly universal philosophic accounts, in both ontological and epistemological terms, of the central insights and related practices of one or more forms of Islamic "mysticism".[55] Those monumental philosophic achievements — associated with such celebrated and diverse thinkers as Avicenna, Suhrâwardî, Ibn Sabᶜîn, Mullâ Ṣadrâ and the many commentators of Ibn ᶜArabî — became widely studied by intellectuals during later periods of Islamic history, especially within the complex multi-cultural, multi-confessional socio-religious worlds of the Mogul and Ottoman empires, with their significant resemblances (at least at the elite level) to our own world-cultural situation today.[56] But one cannot too strongly emphasize that even those more original theoretical explorations were ordinarily not conceived of as opening a privileged form of intellectual access to mystical or spiritual realization, nor indeed even as being necessary for such realization by themselves. For in most cases such writings presuppose the same wider *practical* contexts and methods of realization shared with the more popular expressions of Islamic spirituality. And indeed the most striking evidence of the ongoing cultural significance of the Islamic humanities, in both Arab and later Eastern contexts, is the fact that each of the authors of this theoretical type of Islamic mystical writing was obliged to turn to the alternative of more accessible popular forms of expression — whether Persian-language mystical tales and religious commentaries in the cases of Avicenna, Suhrâwardî, and Mullâ Ṣadrâ; or Arabic mystical poetry in the cases of Ibn ᶜArabî and of Ibn Sabᶜîn's disciples — in order to reach out and influence wider, more popular circles beyond the learned religious elites.

VII. Spiritual Teaching and the Limits of Writing

By now our outline of the various types of Islamic mystical writing should have highlighted several distinctive characteristics that carry across many of the above categories and are in fact peculiar to virtually all the *written* expressions of Islamic mysticism. First, the great majority of those writings, when viewed in their original cultural setting, turn out to have been consciously directed either toward specific religio-intellectual elites not necessarily involved in any special spiritual disciplines (in the case of many "theoretical" writings) or toward other Muslims who were only potential mystical "beginners" — i.e., not readers who were already actively engaged in spiritual disciplines under the guidance of a master. Secondly, a further distinctive sign of this situation is the widespread reluctance in Islamic mystical writings to speak in concrete detail about such fundamental practical dimensions of the spiritual Path as meditation, retreat, fasting, prayers, vigil, dream visions, and so forth. Finally, an even more striking characteristic (at least for modern Western readers) is the peculiar reluctance of these Islamic mystics to write in an openly personal manner about their concrete individual experiences and insights.[57] Instead Muslim mystical writers of virtually all times, places and literary genres typically prefer to *allude* to those more personal dimensions of their experience through archetypal symbols drawn from scriptural and other traditional sources. An unfortunate consequence of these recurrent features of reticence and discretion, for students of religion unfamiliar with their deeper social and practical contexts, is that initial acquaintance with the *literature* of Islamic mysticism may give a quite misleading impression of repetitiveness, relative (intellectual) superficiality or simplification, and even conventionality.[58]

In fact, each of these particular literary characteristics (like their close parallels in the other artistic expressions of the Islamic humanities) can only be understood in terms of the ways such writings were intended to operate in their original social and cultural contexts. These mystical texts are only the most visible aspects of a wider *assumption of "esotericism"* rooted in three foundational features of Islamic religious culture (both popular and elite) already cited at the beginning of this essay. The first of these is the remarkable centrality of "mystical" aims and practices in the Qur'ân, where the spiritual life is portrayed as the primordial essence of Religion (*Dîn*, the universal God-soul relationship), combined with the (apparently utopian) insistence that those spiritual realities be explicitly expressed and realized in the *everyday* lives of *all* people of faith, following the Prophet's own example. The second key feature is the constant focus, beginning already with the archetypal cases of Muhammad and the other prophets (and of the Imams, for Shiites), on the practically decisive need for a living divine-human connection and exemplar (i.e., the *walî* or "Friend of God" in the broadest sense, whether in this world or accessible spiritually) who can properly guide each Muslim's specific realization of those broad Qur'anic injunctions. And the third essential point, discussed at some length above, is the profound integration of virtually all expressions of Islamic "mysticism" within the Islamic humanities and the surrounding local forms of popular religion.

Integration, however, is not the same as identity. And the outward "invisibility" of the Friend of God described in the famous hadîth with which we began beautifully expresses the inner paradoxes and tensions—and the profound limits of any writing—inherent in the distinctively "esoteric" context of spiritual teaching assumed by most forms of Islamic mysticism. For from that perspective the ultimate purpose of mystical writing, as of all the associated spiritual methods, conditions and ways of life, was rarely conceived or presented as a particular *new* set of beliefs or social practices that could somehow be stated or applied "literally" and unambiguously.[59] Instead, within the Qur'anic framework and its ongoing socio-cultural expressions (including all the related Islamic humanities), that aim could only be portrayed as a *transformed insight or realization* of *existing*, publicly accessible doctrines, norms and forms of experience—and as a trans-formation in principle (or degree) potentially accessible to *all*.[60] Hence both the tenacious (and in the long run generally successful) resistance to any widespread institutionalization of religiously sepa-rate, exclusivist mystical sects or distinct sub-religions within the wider Islamic community,[61] and the equally typical persistence of Muslim mystics' attempts to share their theoretical and practical spiri-tual insights (especially by means of the Islamic humanities) in forms ultimately accessible in some degree to all members of the wider Muslim community.

The second profound limitation on mystical writing, whose wider importance has already been discussed, was the almost universal assumption that the spiritual goal set forth by the Qur'an could only be fully realized within the context of *ongoing personal association* between each disciple and an accomplished master (whether on earth or accessible spiritually, including all the prophets).[62] As suggested by the frequent recourse to images drawn from alchemy, that essential spiritual process was not seen as involving the "concealment" of anything that could be communicated unambiguously to all comers. For virtually all Islamic mystics, it is precisely the true *understanding* of the scriptural symbols (and not those images themselves) that is "esoteric". From their perspective, the sacred texts themselves convey the Truth quite literally—so it is the disciple who must be gradually transformed, through the guidance and teaching of a master, in order eventually to grasp that *literal* sense,[63] to rediscover the essential connections between the sacred symbols and the corre-sponding realities and consequences in his or her own experience.

And finally, the fundamental principle underlying both of the above points and all their practical and literary consequences was Muslim mystics' characteristic awareness of the irreducible *hierarchy of human spiritual capacities and predispositions* (at least at any given moment), and their corresponding perception of the Qur'an and hadîth as being carefully and appropriately addressed to this full, incontrovertible range of human types and possibilities. In this situation only a genuine master, it was assumed, could properly judge the readiness and aptitude of each individual student with regard to the relevant aspects of their character and spiritual development.

Now the above points, presented in this fashion, might seem abstract and even—for those without firsthand contact with the spiritual traditions in question—a sort of relic from another age.[64] But already at the purely textual level, even the most skeptical readers can begin to appreciate the importance and actual functioning of these integral relationships between "mystical" text, master, and spiritual practice in the Islamic context by focusing in on two subjects— indeed two inescapable "mysteries"—whose practical existential importance, within any religious tradition, is as self-evident as their prominent position in Qur'anic teaching. In both of these cases, inquisitive readers can begin to appreciate more fully what is ordinarily *not* stated in Islamic mystical texts, and the possible reasons why certain matters are only discussed orally within the context of actual spiritual guidance and disciplines, simply by considering the alternative conceptions and possibilities more openly discussed in other religious traditions.

The first of those two subjects is the deeper grounds of the interplay between individual spiritual capacities and advancement (and eventually the very meaning of divine "Justice") and the ultimate consequences of each individual's actions in the "other world". In the Islamic context the meaning (and relative human importance) of this reality is conveyed by the detailed, remarkably complex eschatological symbolism which is probably the single most frequent subject of the Qur'an. The second recurrent subject is that of the "spiritual hierarchy": of the deeper relationship between the timeless spiritual realities of the divine intermediaries discussed repeatedly in the Qur'an and hadîth (prophets, angels, saints, etc.) and their particular earthly manifestations both in history and as those figures are encountered more directly by each individual in the course of their spiritual itinerary.

Even a passing acquaintance with the treatment of these issues in the history of religions, whether in Islamic or other contexts, should be sufficient to suggest some of the ethical, social and political reasons for the persistent refusal of even the greatest and most respected Islamic mystics to *write* more openly than the Qur'an, or to speak more publicly than the Prophet, concerning these two central spiritual mysteries.

VIII. The Invisibility of the Saints

Whatever one's spiritual outlook and interests, the points we have outlined concerning the inner relations between Islamic mystical writings and the wider Islamic humanities, and their particular social manifestations within each Muslim community, are neglected, yet *historically* decisive phenomena that should be of the utmost interest to serious students of Islamic history, culture, religion and society. Like the "invisibility" of the Friends of God described in the celebrated hadîth with which we began, the very unfamiliarity of those perspectives to our own ways of thinking and viewing the world should at least suggest the possibility of realities, or at least new angles of vision, yet to be discovered.

A striking illustration of that possibility is provided by two short works by the great Muslim mystic Ibn ᶜArabî which have been partially translated under the title *Sufis of Andalusia*.[65] They give one cautionary lesson with regard to the highly problematic relations between texts (of any sort) and the available portrayals of Islamic history and religion. Among the surviving monuments and literary records of Muslim Spain in the late 12th century (apart from Ibn ᶜArabî's own voluminous writings), there is very little in the Arabic poetry, political chronicles, biographies of learned legal and religious scholars, or the celebrated works of a philosopher like Averroes, to suggest any particular social significance, or indeed even much conscious awareness, of what later came to be viewed as "Sufism". Islamic "mysticism," in that later, more institutionalized and self-consciously distinctive sense, is in fact almost invisible in the writings of those learned and privileged elites. Yet Ibn ᶜArabî recounts in the most moving terms his own decisive personal encounters, over a few years of his youth, with dozens of men *and women*, from every region and walk of life, learned and illiterate, outwardly "religious" and less obviously so, whose extraordinary spiritual powers and influences were exercised almost entirely within the web of "ordinary" social and religious life and practice, visible in many instances only to those few specially motivated individuals who cared to seek them out.

The broader historical lessons that can be drawn from this telling example must surely be kept in mind when reading about any aspect of Islamic religion or culture. As for Ibn ᶜArabî, he was making a different point.[66]

Notes

1 *awliyâ'î* (singular *walî*): i.e., those who are "close to" God, probably alluding to the famous Qur'anic verses 10:62-64: ". . . the friends of God, they have no fear and they do not grieve . . . theirs is the Good News in this lower life and in the next (life) . . . that is the Tremendous Attainment". The same Arabic term – which also carries significant connotations of "protector", "guardian" and even "governor" – also appears as one of the more frequent Names of God (at 2:257; 3:68; 45:19; etc.).

In the influential poetic classics of the later Islamic humanities, this complex of Arabic terms is conveyed above all by the recurrent, intentionally ambiguous references to the "Beloved" or "Friend" (Persian *Yâr* or *Dûst*, and their equivalents in Turkish, Urdu, Malay, etc.). There this relationship of *walâya/wilâya* becomes the central metaphor for the divine-human relationship and the theophanic nature of all nature and experience.

2 This hadîth is included, with minor variations, in the canonical collections of Tirmidhî, Ibn Mâja, and Ibn Hanbal. See the full text and notes in W. A. Graham, *Divine Word and Prophetic Word in Early Islam* (The Hague, 1977), pp. 120-121.

3 Throughout this paper it should be kept in mind that the English word "saint" (and its equivalents in other Christian contexts) is quite inadequate to convey either the centrality or the fluidity of the implicit associations and spiritual connections which are typically perceived in Islamic devotional contexts – e.g., in prayers at a specific shrine, or within a given Sufi path – between the divine *al-Walî* (*Yâr, Dûst*, etc.) and the wide spectrum of human and spiritual exemplars who are typically available to each individual Muslim or local community. And even within Islamic religious scholarship, the learned theological explanations of these central popular devotional practices (e.g., in terms of functions like *wasîla*, *shifâ'a, wilâya*, spiritual "hierarchies," and the like) usually depend on drawing firm distinctions and conceptual boundaries that scarcely reflect the intimate spiritual realities of actual prayer and devotional life.

4 Perhaps the most visible and significant illustration of this point is the fact that many of the "founders" and eponyms of major Sufi tariqas were either relatively anonymous (at least in terms of contemporary written historical documentation), nearly illiterate, or authors of relatively few "mystical" texts. The same relative anonymity often holds true as well for those innumerable local saints (and in Shiite settings, relatives of the Imams) whose shrines are the objects of pilgrimage and popular devotions throughout the Islamic world: the manifestations of their *walâya* are not sought in writing, and the "proofs" of their presence are not handed down in books.

5 A typical sign of this phenomenon recurring in different contexts throughout Islamic history is the characteristic progressive socio-linguistic *devaluation* of technical terms once used to refer to "mystics" as soon as the practices or institutions connected with those forms of spirituality have become popularly routinized and "corrupted" (from the perspective of different elites). To take only a few illustrations from the Persianate cultural sphere at very different periods, there is the early succession from *ʿâbid* to *zâhid* to *ʿârif*; the eventually even more widespread pejorative connotations of words like *darvîsh, faqîr* and *sûfî* (often coexisting with other positive meanings); and the post-Safavid Shiite scholarly opposition of terms like *tasawwuf* (or *mutasawwifa*) – in either case associated with Sunni or "folk", rural religious movements – to *ʿirfân* (true "gnosis").

6 The dictum is repeated in two of the most famous Persian works on Sufism, Hujwîrî's (d. ca. 465/1071) *Kashf al-Maḥjûb* (tr. R. A. Nicholson, London, 1911, p. 44), and Jâmî's (d. 1492) biographical dictionary, *Nafaḥât al-'Uns* (ed. M. Tawhîdîpûr, Tehran, 1336 h.s./1957, pp. 255-56), apparently based on a more direct account in the earlier Arabic *Ṭabaqât* of Sulamî (d. 412/1021).

7 To date, even the best English "translations" of the Qur'an bear roughly the same relation to the recited Arabic original as program notes to the actual performance of a classical symphony. The inadequacies of those efforts – which reflect the difficulties of the challenge, more than the talents of the translators – only highlight the extraordinary creativity and originality (and the frequently Qur'anic inspiration) of the great masters of the poetic and musical traditions of the Islamic humanities discussed below.

    Similarly, anyone performing this experiment in a Western language relatively untouched by Islamic culture will quickly discover the profound ways in which traditionally Islamic languages from the most diverse linguistic families (e.g., Persian, Turkish, Swahili, or Malay) have in fact become thoroughly permeated in their vocabulary and wider conceptual and symbolic universes by language and symbols drawn from the Qur'an and hadîth.

8 A reference to the famous verses at 41:53, "We shall show them Our Signs on the horizons and in their souls" (or "within themselves"), perhaps the most frequently cited Qur'anic proof-text for the perennial *human* manifestations of the divine *walâya*.

9 As discussed in more detail below, it is essential to keep in mind that the religiously relevant "literatures", in almost any Islamic context – and particularly for the women, villagers, peasants and tribespeople who have constituted the vast majority of Muslims in the world until this century – have been predominantly *oral* and *vernacular*, in creative, locally meaningful cultural forms that can seldom be understood simply as "diluted" versions of any of the learned Arabic sciences. The fundamental, ongoing religious importance of the *awliyâ'* – whether physically present or through the spiritual archetypes communicated by those local "literatures" – can only be grasped in light of their role in those specific, concrete contexts of individual spiritual teaching and practice.

    The contemporary situation of thousands of African-American Muslims in the process of discovering and elaborating their own authentic forms of Islam – typically with only a quite limited contact with external traditions of Islamic literature and learning—is actually remarkably representative of the local situations historians discover, wherever sufficient evidence exists, as they move beyond the learned, urban and courtly circles that were until recently the primary subjects of Islamic history.

10 In addition, from the point of view of the Islamic humanities, particularly at the level of popular, oral culture, the early religious forms of "tales of the prophets" (*qiṣaṣ al-anbiyâ'*), along with similar stories about the life of Muhammad (the *sîra*) and the Shiite Imams, are at least equally as important in forming Muslims' images and understandings of the *awliyâ'* and their teachings as the accounts preserved in the form of hadîth, despite the fact that such forms of "popular" literature were later accorded much lower religious status in the opinion of religious scholars.

11 For understandable reasons, subsequent learned Muslim scholars, whatever their school, have rarely cared to point out to what an extent even the earliest, most widely respected Arabic works of legal interpretation, Qur'ânic commentary, and biographies of Muhammad are inextricably grounded in an immensely complex body of oral traditions (by no means limited to the hadîth) written down many decades or even centuries after the events they recount. More inexcusably, the naive repetition of this particular paradigm of Islamic religious scholarship in most non-specialized modern Western accounts of the religion of Islam has of course tended to obscure the multitude of competing, at least equally influential visions of religious authority, "knowledge", tradition and practice which have in fact informed the historical landscape of so many Islamic societies from the death of Muhammad down to the present day.

12 A particularly extreme (and historically influential) case of this religio-historical paradigm is beautifully illustrated in the polemic work translated by M. U. Memon as *Ibn Taymîya's Struggle against Popular Religion* (Mouton/The Hague, 1976).

13 We have intentionally highlighted these key code-words of modern Islamicist political ideologies—too often naively repeated in uninformed scholarly as well as journalistic discourse—to help suggest the curious process of hybridization through which historically alien religious conceptions, most often reflecting Western Protestant or Marxist cultural paradigms, have been grafted with traditional paradigms of Islamic scholarship to give rise to such peculiar categories and typifications of various Muslim peoples. The essential point to bear in mind is that such ideologically motivated accounts clearly have very little to do with how Muslims in general (and more particularly those groups thus typified) have actually viewed their faith and relations to God.

14 See the particularly insightful illustration of this much wider phenomenon, in the case of one mountain village during the recent "Islamic Revolution," in R. Loeffler's *Islam in Practice: Religious Beliefs in a Persian Village* (Albany, 1988) and E. Friedl's *Women of Deh Koh: Lives in an Iranian Village* (Washington, 1989). For similar phenomena in a wide variety of more urban, Arab contexts, see the revealing anecdotes throughout M. Gilsenan's *Recognizing Islam* (London, 1983). Closer to home, the pioneering research of Beverly McCloud (n. 24 below) provides fascinating firsthand descriptions of the same creative elaboration of meaningfully Islamic forms—often in conscious opposition to alien cultural models of custom and behavior—among small communities of African-American

Muslim women with only the most tenuous contacts to learned Arabic tradition of religious scholarship.

15   The amazing coexistence of scholarly handbooks on Islamic religion conveying, if anything, increasingly ideological and ahistorical portrayals of "Islam" (in terms of supposedly normative doctrines, practices, etc.) at precisely the same time as hundreds of detailed historical studies, in both Western and Islamic languages, have come to highlight the grave limits and constantly shifting motives and meanings of such idealized paradigms in any particular period and locale, is a curious paradox deserving its own study in the sociology of knowledge.

For students of *religion* interested in delving into that already immense recent historical literature—and for the time being, given the absence of reliable historical syntheses (especially with regard to popular culture and non-urban populations), no serious understanding of Islam, including Islamic "mysticism," is really possible without immersing oneself in many such detailed local studies—two important cautions are in order. First, many of those recent historical inquiries are linked to the development of new nation-states and a naturally renewed interest by local scholars in their national "roots" and in "popular" movements conceived in modern national terms. The common danger in all such cases is an inadequate awareness of the wider relevance and interconnections of many areas of Islamic culture in pre-modern times, both of learned religious literature and of the written and oral Islamic humanities, in ways that usually transcend contemporary national, regional and linguistic boundaries. In the West this problem is aggravated by even more artificial recent "area studies" divisions in scholarly treatments of the Islamic cultures in question.

The second, less obvious, major barrier for students of Islamic religion, is that historical studies with rare exceptions focus on what is viewed as politically or historically "significant" and unusual "behavior"—i.e., on what stands out, often in terms of violence, rebellion, etc.—and *not* on the "longue durée" and the more universal, by definition almost "invisible," spiritual dimensions of religious life. In the present context, for example, the pitfalls of this outlook are especially obvious in the focus of many studies of "Islamic mysticism" on the charismatic leaders of Sufi orders functioning as *political* leaders of anti-colonial resistance in the 19th century (e.g., the Mahdi in the Sudan, the Sanusiya in Libya, ᶜAbd al-Qâdir in Algeria, Shâmil in the Caucasus, etc.), or on the equally striking case of Shah Ismail and the Safavid movement. For a student of Islamic *religion*, such studies often do not even pose the key questions: the "charisma" of religio-political leaders, as we know from experience, can be demonic or divine; and the thousands of "saints" who do correspond to Muhammad's description (n. 2 above), whose teaching and example gives meaning to Islam and continues to guide other Muslims' lives throughout the world, rarely enter anyone's historical chronicles (at least until after their death).

16   Since the very existence and multiple functions of the local Islamic humanities, much less their central role in the actual religious life of Muslims everywhere, are not even acknowledged in most non-specialist introductions to Islamic religion, anthropologists working in every area of the Muslim world have tended to assume the historicist paradigm of the ᶜ*ulamâ* represents a descriptive as well as (polemically) normative account of "Islam"—and thus have inevitably found it irrelevant (or hostile) to what they actually do observe in many local oral or writ-

ten cultures somehow "remote" from the representatives of that elite learned Arabic tradition. The resulting difficulties in perceiving the centrally "Islamic" character of a multitude of local practices and attitudes conveyed by and centering on the *awliyâ'* have only been aggravated by further intellectual interference from more recent Islamicist ideologies and other, often competing, nationalist accounts of the same local cultural phenomena.

Students of Islamic religion, however, face a much more daunting obstacle in attempting to "translate" the data of anthropological and ethnographic studies into *religiously* meaningful terms in a way that will reveal the essential interconnections between specific local practices and the more learned, "mystical" forms of the Islamic humanities. Since the meaningfulness of those local forms (literary, poetic, musical, etc.) depends on their capacity to *awaken*, within each participant, the awareness and practice of the universal spiritual virtues which are the heart of the Qur'ânic focus on *Dîn* ("Religion" in the sense of the intimate relationship between each soul and God), they are likely to be quite opaque to observers who are not looking for them or who are unwilling actually to enter into that spiritual life. Since there is ordinarily nothing in the liberal arts background or professional training and preoccupations of anthropologists that would lead them to take that central dimension of the Islamic humanities seriously, it should not be surprising if even the best available ethnographic material on the religious life of Muslims (including "mystical" groups and practices) in any part of the world is rarely very accurate or helpful in communicating the spiritual life and experience of the individuals it attempts to describe. In fact, works of "fiction" from the same Muslim societies are typically far more effective in communicating the religious content and meaning of the local Islamic humanities.

17   To give a few more particular illustrations from the Persianate cultural sphere (from southern Iraq to Tadjikistan and northern Pakistan), one could mention the frequent divinatory consultation (*fa'l*) of the mystical poetry of Hafez in any life-situation requiring spiritual guidance; the central place of the *Dîvân* of Hafez on the *haft sîn* table at the center of the monthlong New Year's celebrations (*Now Rûz*); or the preeminent place of Rumi's *Dîvân-i Shams-i Tabrîz* (alongside the Qur'an) in mosques of Ismaili Shiite communities throughout that region. In such situations even the most "illiterate" villager often knows thousands of verses of these mystical poets by heart, recalling the appropriate ones whenever the corresponding experience arises.

Only those who are aware of the pervasive spiritual functions of these locally rooted Islamic humanities, or of their vernacular equivalents throughout other parts of the Islamic world, can begin to appreciate the devastating religious and cultural impact (potentially deeper than many earlier invasions, or even the script "reforms" of an Ataturk or Stalin) of the recent replacement of those local Islamic humanities in so many areas by newly invented national ideologies (Islamicist or other) and compulsory public "education" in them.

18   G. John Renard's forthcoming study of *Islam and the Heroic Image: Themes in Literature and the Visual Arts* (Columbia, SC, 1992), is a remarkably comprehensive synthesis of the corresponding visual and epic "iconography" of the local Islamic humanities, including relevant "mystical" dimensions, in many regions of the Islamic world, from West Africa to Indonesia. See also the forthcoming volume by

A. Schimmel, et al., *The Popular Muhammad: The Person of Muhammad in Muslim Folk Poetry* (Columbia, 1992).

19   Or occasionally in Persian (or Ottoman Turkish), which often functioned as the *lingua franca* of intellectual and religious elites in many regions of the Eastern Islamic world down to the present century. It should also be stressed that many of learned, "theoretical" Arabic texts in question were (and are) equally inaccessible to Arabic speakers without years of initiation and study of those learned traditions—and that Arabic-speaking regions had their own local "Islamic humanities" (both oral and sometimes written), which have only very recently begun to interest students of religion.

20   These practical spiritual writings, it should be noted, are usually quite distinct from the a wide range of vernacular works intended for the "popularization" or vulgar assimilation of the learned Arabic religious and rational sciences. The spiritual, aesthetic and ethical sophistication that typifies the adaptation of the traditional Islamic humanities in their local contexts, where (reflecting the Qur'ânic perspective) they are integrally adapted to the spiritual capacities and life-situation of each individual, offers a particularly radical contrast with the alien models of "religious education" and "Islamicization" adopted by the national systems of compulsory public education in certain modern Muslim states.

21   Those possibilities are well illustrated in some of the well-known later writings of al-Ghazâlî, and even more voluminously throughout the works of Ibn ʿArabî.

22   I.e., all the literatures and other ethically and aesthetically significant local activities and customs which don't happen to fit within the historicist and scripturalist paradigms of the ʿulamâ discussed above. This artificial separation from the whole local complex of the Islamic humanities is especially devastating for anyone attempting to discover the actual spiritual dimensions of Muslim women's religious lives (since, not surprisingly, they do not necessarily mirror learned urban male accounts of what is "Islamic") or looking at anthropological work on religion in Muslim peasant or tribal communities outside the "Middle East".

For two major forthcoming works that break down these barriers and begin to explore the unexamined religious dimensions of these Islamic humanities, see n. 18 above.

23   For an impressive portrait of those religious realities in an urban, educated setting, see such memoirs as S. M. A. Jamâlzâdeh's *Isfahan is Half the World* (Princeton, 1983), or—for a woman's perspective—S. Guppy's more recent *The Blindfold Horse: Memories of a Persian Childhood* (Boston, 1988). For the very different religious world of villagers not far away, see the work by R. Loeffler cited at n. 14 above.

24   See the Ph. D. dissertation of Beverly McCloud (Temple University, Dept. of Religion, 1991) on the religious lives of three generations of Muslim women from five local African-American Islamic communities in Philadelphia. The total absence of published documentation on the actual *religious* life of those thriving, decades-old and quite indigenously American contemporary Muslim communities should serve as a sufficient caution to those who might assume that the fundamental problems

of perception and presentation of Islamic religion and mysticism highlighted in this paper are simply the result of distance (in time or space) and relative unfamiliarity of *foreign* Muslim communities and religious practices. On the other hand, if the religious lives of these thousands of Muslim neighbors and colleagues have remained quite literally "invisible" to American religious scholarship for decades, hopefully that should suggest something of the reliability of portraits (and prejudices) drawn from far more distant worlds and vastly more limited and problematic sources.

25 This continuum of radically different spiritual perspectives, within the essentially common oral religious culture and background of a single Iranian village, is beautifully illustrated by the various individual world-views portrayed in the major work by R. Loeffler cited at n. 14 above.

26 We must stress the phenomenological *inclusiveness* of this dimension of Islamic "mysticism" because so many textbook accounts of this subject in Islamic contexts have unfortunately portrayed as either (unquestionably) normative or descriptive a multitude of highly problematic legal/theological categories and opinions: e.g., between "permitted" chanting or recitation of divine Names and "illicit" forms of singing or instrumental music; or between "religious" or "Islamic" ceremonies and "folk" customs or "local" rituals. Such widespread misconceptions of the Islamic humanities do beautifully illustrate the presuppositions and dangerous limitations of the historicist and scripturalist paradigms of certain *ʿulamā* discussed above.

27 The pioneering work that comes closest to conveying the religious and spiritual dimensions of such music — truly a model in this field of Islamic studies — is E. H. Waugh's superb *The Munshidin of Egypt: Their World and Their Song* (Columbia, SC, 1989). Two other excellent recent studies of even more explicitly "mystical" Islamic music and associated rituals, in related, yet very different religious worlds, are R. Burckhardt Qureshi's *Sufi Music of India and Pakistan: Sound, Context and Meaning in Qawwali* (Cambridge, 1986, with cassette tapes); and *The Art of Persian Music*, by J. During, et al. (Washington, 1991, with compact disc).

For Qur'ân recitation, which is an indispensable key to the understanding and genesis of so many of the visual and musical forms of the Islamic humanities, see K. Nelson, *The Art of Reciting the Qur'ân* (Austin, 1985), and chapters 7-9 of W. Graham's *Beyond the Written Word: Oral Aspects of Scripture in the History of Religion* (Cambridge, 1987).

Despite the publicly visible importance of *dance* in the local Islamic humanities throughout great parts of the Islamic world, whether in sessions of Sufi *dhikr* and other undeniably "religious" ceremonies involving spiritual states and trances, or in celebrations of weddings and other major feasts, useful ethnographic films and documentaries (not to mention articles or books) in this area are still extremely rare. Again the virtual nonexistence of serious studies of this subject perfectly illustrates the insidious role of the above-mentioned learned paradigms of Islamic religion in concealing key elements in even the most elementary phenomenology of Muslim spiritual life in those many regions where such dance forms are religiously important, as well as in blocking any appreciation of the typical inter-penetration of "mystical," Sufi practices and wider customary forms of popular religiosity in such Islamic settings (including the lives of contemporary American Muslims).

28 Of course even those visual arts which are clearly "major" in the more familiar
    Islamic contexts (calligraphy, ceramics, textile design, metalwork, carpets, books
    and their illumination, etc.) are typically not at the center of aesthetic reflection
    and esteem in the West. But even more striking in these art-historical disciplines
    is the unquestioned persistence of distinctions mirroring the earlier paradigmatic
    opposition of learned Arabic literatures and understandings of Islam to "popular",
    "local", "customary", or even "folkloric" forms of religious experience. Thus the
    artistic and aesthetic visual expressions of the Islamic humanities among suppos-
    edly "peripheral" Muslims in (not coincidentally) largely peasant or tribal areas
    like Indonesia and Malaysia, Central Asia, the Balkans and Caucasus, Kurdistan,
    West Africa, or the Swahili coast are typically ignored or at best mentioned in
    passing in virtually all textbook treatments of "Islamic art". Two remarkable
    recent exceptions which highlight many of those unwarranted assumptions and
    their blinding effects are L. Prussin's *Hatumere: Islamic Design in West Africa*
    (Berkeley, 1985), and the forthcoming study by J. Renard, *Islam and the Heroic
    Image: Themes in Literature and the Visual Arts* (Columbia, SC, 1992).

29 This area is especially relevant to our understanding and appreciation of the
    deeper spiritual roots and socio-cultural influences of Islamic "mysticism". Most
    obviously, in the actual practice of all these arts and music (in Islam as elsewhere)
    subtle "aesthetic" and "spiritual" values and disciplines are often inseparable. And
    in the everyday life of most Muslims, the deeper interpenetrations of spiritual life
    and the Islamic humanities were typically far more widely and profoundly
    mediated by these particular *aesthetic forms* – e.g., a few beautiful lines of calligra-
    phy ("religious" or not); the properly moving recitation of the Qur'an; the satis-
    fying shape, color and decoration of a vessel for ablutions, a bookstand, or a set of
    prayer beads; the ornamentation of a mosque or saint's shrine; the inner layout of
    one's own house; or the complex religious associations of a simple reed pen – than
    by nominally or self-consciously "religious" concepts and teachings.   The
    widespread neglect of this fundamental religiously mediating function of the
    popular Islamic humanities has led to a remarkable unconsciousness of the full
    extent of the profound religious and spiritual consequences simply of the most
    physical dimensions of "modernization," which may be even deeper than the trans-
    forming effects of national "religious education" discussed above.

30 One of the essential spiritual consequences of the continuum of *walāya* (the inner
    "proximity" connecting God, the *awliyâ'*, and each soul) is that in "repeating" any
    of the prayers and invocations of the prophets, Imams and saints – as preemi-
    nently in the universal daily ritual recitations of the Qur'an itself – the Muslim
    worshipper is not simply reproducing or imitating *someone else's* prayers and
    devotions. Instead, what is ultimately aimed at and presupposed, in each of these
    endlessly diverse devotional forms, is a profound state of co-participation, if not
    spiritual union, with that divine Source.
        In the Shiite ʿAshûrâ commemorations, of course, that inner spiritual connec-
    tion is often sought (or manifested) in more physically palpable forms. In partic-
    ular, the dramatic annual re-enactments of the martyrdom of Imam Husayn in
    Twelver Shiite communities, which so remarkably illustrate the complex role of
    the Islamic humanities at the interface between learned Arabic and local religious
    traditions, have attracted a great deal of scholarly attention in recent years. See
    e.g., the pioneering work of M. Ayoub, *Redemptive Suffering in Islam: A Study of the*

devotional aspects of ᶜAshūrā in Twelver Shiism (The Hague, 1978); and P. Chelkowski, ed., *Ta'ziyeh: Ritual and Drama in Iran* (N.Y., 1979).

31 Certainly this is no less true in most parts of the Islamic world, at the level of *actual*, observable religious and spiritual life, than with the roles of the corresponding sacred-human theophanies in Christian, Buddhist or Hindu spiritual practice. Again there is little or nothing in books about Islam intended for non-specialist readers that would even begin to suggest the importance and complexity of that dimension of Muslim spiritual life—although the widespread reactions underlying the "Rushdie Affair" may at least have suggested the popular centrality and sensitivity of this spiritual reality in certain Islamic contexts.

Along similar lines, one may note the even more egregious lack of focus on *female* spiritual archetypes (e.g., Fatima, Zaynab, Aisha, Khadija, and especially Mary—whose Qur'ânic description sounds disconcertingly "Catholic" to many Protestant readers) in the religious lives of Muslim women from the most diverse cultural settings. (In this regard, see the recent pioneering article by E. B. Findly, "Religious Resources for Secular Power: The Case of Nûr Jahân", pp. 129-148 in *Colby Library Quarterly* XXV/1989.)

Above all, the peculiar domination of accounts of "Islam" by the theological categories and conceptions of small groups of learned religious scholars—or by the even more unrepresentative slogans of modern ideologists—apparently explains the refusal of most handbooks to recognize even the most obvious phenomena of Muslim spiritual life: namely, that depending on the particular devotional context, Muhammad, Ali, Husayn, Abbâs, Abd al-Qâdir, Muᶜîn al-Dîn Chishtî, and a host of other *awliyâ'* are appealed to *directly* and intimately, on the same terms and in the same diverse life-contexts, as with the devotional roles of Jesus, various bodhisattvas, and similar theophanies in other religious traditions. (For those who have not been able to witness this directly, the best approach is simply to observe the "lyrics" of virtually any of the available recordings of Islamic mystical and spiritual music, especially from ceremonies taking place in "traditional", less modernized rural or tribal contexts.)

32 The most comprehensive popular introduction remains C. E. Padwick, *Muslim Devotions* (London, 1960), while A. Schimmel's *And Muhammad is His Messenger: The Veneration of the Prophet in Islamic Piety* (Chapel Hill, 1985) provides profuse illustrations of these central religious expressions from many regions of the Islamic world, to be supplemented by the two major forthcoming studies cited in n. 18 above. See also W. Thackston's translations of Abdullah Ansari's classic Persian *Munâjât (Intimate Conversations*: N.Y., 1978 [Classics of Western Spirituality]).

Probably the most useful and sensitive introduction to this subject for the student of religions is to be found in W. C. Chittick's recent translation of Zayn al-ᶜAbidin's *al-Sahîfa al-Sajjâdîya: The Psalms of Islam* (London, 1988), especially the introductory explanations on "Prayer in Islam". However, what has so far been translated or studied is no way indicative of the volume and importance of such works in actual Islamic humanities, "mystical" or otherwise. The most fundamental gaps remain the lack of reliable and readable, adequately annotated English translations of the major collections of hadîth (both Sunni and Shiite) and of Ali's *Nahj al-Balâgha*.

33 As for more "theoretical" accounts of those spiritual practices, combining meta-
    physical explanation and elaborate scriptural justifications, by far most complete
    and elaborate (and historically influential) versions in Islam are the detailed treat-
    ments of those subjects by al-Ghazâlî (in his famous "Revival of the Religious
    Sciences" (*Ihyâ ʿUlûm al-Dîn*), now being systematically translated by the Islamic
    Texts Society, Cambridge) and by the famous Andalusian mystic Ibn ʿArabî in his
    "Meccan Illuminations" (*K. al-Futûhât al-Makkîya*), discussed in sections V and VI
    below.

34 For Muhammad and his Companions, see Ibn Ishâq (trans. A. Guillaume), *The
    Life of Muhammad: A Translation of Ibn Ishâq's 'Sîrat Rasûl Allâh'* (Oxford, 1955),
    and the adaptation of Ibn Ishâq by M. Lings, *Muhammad: His Life Based on the
    Earliest Sources*, which is more readable and especially sensitive to those dimen-
    sions which are central to Islamic spirituality and mysticism. For the early Shiite
    Imams, see Shaykh al-Mufid (trans. I. K. A. Howard), *Kitâb al-Irshâd: The Book of
    Guidance* (London, 1981). And for the "tales of the prophets" genre, see al-Kisâ'î
    (trans. W. Thackston), *The Tales of the Prophets of al-Kisâ'î* (Boston, 1978); and J.
    Knappert, *Islamic Legends: Histories of the Heroes, Saints and Prophets of Islam*, (2
    vols., Leiden, 1985) — the second volume largely devoted to stories of Islamic
    saints and famous Sufis, especially ʿAbd al-Qâdir Jîlânî, from many parts of the
    Muslim world.

        It is important to note that Muslims in the most disparate cultural settings
    (apart from the religiously learned elite) rarely distinguish in their awareness of
    spiritually significant *stories* between those conveyed by the local Islamic humani-
    ties, and those having their sources directly in the Quran or hadîth. Indeed the
    same spiritually significant stories are often told of or attributed to Muhammad,
    Ali, other saints and prophets, and heroes drawn from local vernacular epics and
    legends: see the many illustrations in J. Renard's forthcoming study cited at n. 18
    above.

35 A widely accessible hagiographical work introducing the most famous spiritual
    exemplars of the early Sufi tradition is F. Attâr (abridged trans. by A. J. Arberry),
    Muslim Saints and Mystics: Episodes from the Tadhkirat al-Auliyâ' (London, 1966).
    M. Sells is preparing a forthcoming volume of translated selections from many of
    the classical figures and texts of early Islamic mystical hagiography for the
    "Classics of Western Spirituality" series (Paulist Press). In English, two extensive
    illustrations of the integration of such stories in contexts of Islamic mystical
    teaching are Attâr's *The Conference of the Birds* (trans. M. Darbandi and D. Davis,
    London, 1984), and R. A. Nicholson's 3-volume translation of *The Mathnawî of
    Jalâlu'ddîn Rûmî* (London, repr. 1977).

        Unfortunately, there are still no widely accessible studies of particular local
    Islamic communities that adequately communicate the essential process of
    "spiritual contextualization" provided by the Islamic humanities in their local
    (usually oral) contexts, the way "illiterate" individuals are often extraordinarily
    sophisticated in making the essential connections between each particular mystical
    story or saying (whatever its source) and the specific type of life-event or inner
    experience to which it is spiritually or ethically applicable.

36 Even such remarkable Shiite texts as the early Ismaili initiatic dialogue of *The
    Master and Disciple* (see our forthcoming Arabic edition and translation) do not

really provide such an illustration: while the dramatic setting in that dialogue is clearly drawn, it is quite typically directed to bringing out the archetypal character of essential Qur'anic passages, such as the encounter of Moses and Khezr.

The handful of invaluable translations that do provide a more realistic picture of the actual processes of spiritual teaching and direction in very different Islamic cultural settings are not really exceptions to the above "rule" concerning the distinctive nature and limits of mystical *writing* throughout the Muslim world, since each of those books in fact reflects the extraordinary recording, by a contemporary observer, of typical cases of *oral* transmission and recounting of teachings and experiences which ordinarily would have remained an "invisible" and unrecorded part of the process of spiritual guidance between a master and disciple. See the relevant sections of M. Lings, *A Sufi Saint of the Twentieth Century, Shaykh Ahmad al-'Alawi* (London/Berkeley, 1971); L. Brenner, *West African Sufi: The Religious Heritage & Spiritual Search of Cerno Bokar Saalif Taal* (London/Berkeley, 1984), especially the translated "spiritual discourses", pp. 157-192; and our translation (in preparation) of Nur Ali Elahi, *Athâr al-Haqq* (Tehran, 1366 h.s., 708 pp.).

37 See, for example, Ibn ʿAtâ'allâh (trans. V. Danner), *The Book of Wisdom* (New York, 1978); al-Junayd (trans. A. H. Abdel-Kader), *The Life, Personality and Writings of Al-Junayd* (London, repr. 1976), pp. 120-183; as well as the forthcoming volume of translations by M. Sells cited at n. 35; and S. Suhrawardi (trans. W. Thackston), *The Mystical and Visionary Treatises of Suhrawardi* (London, 1982). At the more popular, oral level such spiritual sayings and riddles are woven throughout all the previously mentioned hagiographic tales of the saints and prophets, and even into the multitude of popular "jokes" and comic stories concerning such figures as Jûhâ or "Mulla/Khoja Nasruddin".

The most glaring gap for this major genre of Islamic mystical writing is surely the lack of a complete English translation of any of the major collections of (and commentaries on) the *Shataḥât*, the "metaphysical paradoxes" of the early Sufis discussed by C. Ernst in *Words of Ecstasy in Sufism* (Albany, 1985). Already in the Islamic world the profound linguistic difficulties involved with translating (as opposed to paraphrasing and explicating) such works in any language is reflected in the vast commentary literature, in several Islamic languages, relating to each of the above-mentioned types of mystical writing.

38 See, for example, Ibn Abbad (trans. J. Renard), *Ibn Abbad of Ronda: Letters of Spiritual Direction* (N.Y., 1986); S. Maneri (tr. Paul Jackson), *The Hundred Letters* (N.Y., 1980); N. Razi (tr. H. Algar). *The Path of God's Bondsmen from Origin to Return (Mirsâd al-ʿIbâd)* (N.Y., 1982); and U. Suhrawardi (transl. W. Clarke, from the Persian tr. by M. Kashani), *A Dervish Textbook from the ʿAwârifu-l-Maʿârif . . .* (London, repr. 1980). All of Ibn ʿArabî's writings, including the recent English translations of selections from his immense *al-Futûḥât al-Makkîya*, contain extensive illustrations of all three of these types of practical mystical writing. However, a great deal of this more practical spiritual literature remains to be explored even in its original manuscript form, especially for later periods in such vast areas as Muslim India, Ottoman Turkey, sub-Saharan Africa, etc.; one can thus expect some of the most interesting new studies in the areas of Islamic spirituality and mysticism to emerge from investigations of this broad range of practical Sufi literature.

39   The virtual absence of English-language studies and translations of such materials
      in no way reflects their relative importance in earlier forms of Islamic spirituality
      and mysticism. See our forthcoming review article of a number of recent French
      studies in this field in the *Journal of the American Oriental Society*, and the vast
      amount of manuscript material (including only texts exclusively devoted to these
      subjects) in the bio-bibliographic survey volumes on early Arabic alchemy and
      astrology in F. Sezgin's *Geschichte des Arabischen Schrifttums*.
          The most revealing introduction to the widespread uses of this genre in
      Islamic mysticism is the chapter by D. Gril (in French) on Ibn ᶜArabî's under-
      standing of the "science of letters", pp. 385-487 in the recent bilingual anthology
      from Ibn ᶜArabî's *The Meccan Illuminations/Les Illuminations de la Mecque*, (Paris,
      1989).

40   See the representative illustration of these types of symbolism throughout our
      translation of "Ibn ᶜArabî's Spiritual Ascension" (ch. 367 of the *Futûḥât*), pp. 351-
      438 and 574-607 in *The Meccan Illuminations/Les Illuminations de la Mecque*, (Paris,
      1989). Materials of this type pose recurrent dilemmas for translators of Islamic
      religious writings into any modern language, since the related frameworks of
      cosmology, astrology, physics, physiology and numerology were often universally
      assumed in both learned and popular Islamic understandings even of the Qur'ân
      (and of the many hadîth on related cosmological matters) until modern times.
      Hence an adequate translation of such texts requires complex footnotes and
      detailed explanations, for the modern reader, of matters which were often implic-
      itly assumed by pre-modern writers and audiences alike (very often in the Latin
      West as well): the situation is somewhat like attempting to explain a baseball
      sportscast (where the most complex rules and statistical categories are "obvious"
      to a numerically illiterate first-grader) to someone unfamiliar with that sport.

41   Some of the more poetically approachable English translations, among a number
      of recent efforts, are the recent collaborative translations of Rûmî by J. Moyne and
      C. Barks, including *Open Secret* (versions from the *Rubâ'îyât*) and *Unseen Rain*
      (translations from the *Dîvân-i Shams-i Tabrîz*), (Putney, VT, 1984 and 1986). The
      immense bibliography of translations and studies of Rumi is also summarized in
      two complementary introductory and background volumes, W. C. Chittick's *The
      Sufi Path of Love: The Spiritual Teachings of Rûmî* (Albany, 1983) and A. Schim-
      mel's *The Triumphal Sun: A Study of the Works of Jalâluddîn Rûmî* (London, 1980).
          The familiarity for Western audiences of Rumi's mystical symbolism
      (especially its frequently direct appeals to our experience of nature, or concrete
      images drawn from everyday life) and the *relative* lack of symbolic (though not
      musical) complexity of his poetic language helps to explain his great appeal to
      Western translators. (Similar points could be made about the popular Turkish
      mystical poetry of Yunus Emre: cf. *The Drop That Became The Sea: Lyric Poems of
      Yunus Emre*, tr. K. Helminski and R. Algan, Putney, VT, 1989.) However, it
      should be stressed that the mystical symbolism and poetic structures in the classi-
      cal poetic expressions of the later Islamic humanities, at least in the Eastern
      Islamic world, are usually far more complex and indeed impossible to translate (at
      least as effective English poetry). Cf. the many attempts at translating the incom-
      parable Persian lyrics of Hafez, or the works of S. N. al-Attas on early Malay
      Islamic mystical poetry, including *The Mysticism of Hamza al-Fanṣûrî* (Kuala
      Lumpur, 1970).

42   The actual processes of formation of "Islam" as a separate, self-consciously universal world religion during these first three centuries are still largely unexplored, or
      at best at the stage of working hypotheses in each of the relevant fields. (There is
      as yet nothing even remotely approaching the efforts that have been expended,
      for example, on exploring the comparable historical origins of early Christianity
      and rabbinic Judaism.) However, more detailed historical investigations can only
      show in much greater detail how what eventually came to be seen as "classical"
      learned Arabic religious disciplines actually represent only the earliest *written*
      stages of the Islamic humanities, reflecting the same processes of creative (and
      originally oral) individual expressions of Qur'ânic teachings in the context of the
      remarkable variety of pre-existing local cultural and religious traditions within the
      vast area of the initial Arab conquests. Again the existing hadîth collections—
      especially the still virtually unexplored materials on the early Shiite Imams—
      clearly represent many stages and facets of that long creative process.

43   The only even remote approximation to such an approach, at any point in Islamic
      history, is possibly to be found in certain rare forms of later (Nizari) Ismaili
      Shiism, in an extreme reaction by a threatened religious minority that at times
      came to present its Sunni Seljuk opponents as exclusively "exotericist". However,
      even in that case, as everywhere else in Islam, any such attempts to *separate* an
      "exoteric" *zâhir* from a spiritual or mystical *bâṭin* ran up against the basic fact that
      in the Qur'ân itself explicitly "mystical", insistently universal teachings about the
      spiritual reality and destiny of human beings provide the primary context even for
      the (relatively few) specific "mundane" religious prescriptions.

      Hence the more recurrently typical Islamic phenomenon—which continues to
      puzzle outsiders arriving with different expectations of "mysticism"—of a combination of exclusivist, even fanatical adherence to particular socially or scripturally
      "exoteric" versions of Islam combined with a curious insistence on highly original
      "mystical" forms of exegesis and spiritual practice.   See, for example, in
      completely different Muslim traditions, such representative cases as the famous
      Hanbali Sufis Anṣârî of Herat and ᶜAbd al-Qâdir Jîlânî; the Shiite hadîth-based
      spirituality of the Shaykhî movement in Qajar Iran and Iraq; and the more recent
      Naqshbandî Sufi tariqa.

44   The most prominent and enduring example of this process is the ongoing role of
      the works of the great 13th-century Andalusian mystic Ibn ᶜArabî at the political
      and cultural interface between the learned Arabic sciences and various local
      expressions of the Islamic humanities down to the present day. Ibn ᶜArabî's lasting impact on the Islamic humanities throughout the Eastern Islamic world is
      outlined in our 3-part monograph on "Ibn ᶜArabî and His Interpreters", in the
      Journal of the American Oriental Society 107-108 (1986-87), while "Ibn ᶜArabî's
      'Esotericism': The Problem of Spiritual Authority", in *Studia Islamica* LXXI
      (1990), outlines the philosophic and religious principles underlying the ongoing
      controversies surrounding those mystical texts.

45   Of course the most widely read of the learned Arabic, "theoretical" works on
      Islamic mysticism—above all the writings of Ibn ᶜArabî and Ghazâlî—were at the
      same time extremely influential, both directly and indirectly, within all the more
      practical categories of spiritual writing already discussed above.

46 This basic distinguishing factor is operative whether those spiritual intermediaries are understood to be directly accessible in this material world, or in the spiritual world through dreams, visions, *karamât* and *barakât* (particular evidentiary "acts of grace" and "blessings") received through one or another of the *awliyâ'* (including the prophets). The range of possibilities and combinations of these intermediary figures (in either world) in the spiritual life and experience of any given Muslim is typically extremely broad and often only loosely connected with visible sociological or historical considerations. See the vivid *contemporary* illustrations of these phenomena in the visions recorded in M. Lings' *A Sufi Saint of the Twentieth Century* (Berkeley, 1971) and in K. Ewing, "The dream of spiritual initiation . . . among Pakistani sufis," in *American Ethnologist*, vol. 17 (1990), as well as the profuse illustrations of such dreams and visions of the *awliyâ'* throughout the classical Sufi works already cited.

47 As Ibn ʿArabî and other Muslim mystics have repeatedly stressed, that broader Qur'anic teaching concerning the spiritual intermediaries also underlies the assumptions of the ʿulamâ about the inseparability of the Qur'ânic message from the life and example of (at least) Muhammad—conceptions which are axiomatic for all the Arabic "religious sciences" claiming a religious authority for their interpretations of the corpus of hadîth. Within the context of the *Sunni* religious sciences see the detailed explanations of this point, drawn from Ibn ʿArabî's magnum opus, in *The Meccan Illuminations/Les Illuminations de la Mecque* (Paris, 1989), and W. C. Chittick, *The Sufi Path of Knowledge: Ibn al-ʿArabî's Metaphysics of the Imagination* (Albany, 1989).

48 This is certainly not intended to deny the recurrent attempts (amply illustrated in virtually every generation down to the present day) to institutionalize virtually every conceivable human form of religious authority: e.g., Umayyad divine kingship; Shiite sacred priestship; clerical legalism; tribal factionalism (often combined with various forms of charismatic religious leadership); radically egalitarian antinomianism; Messianic personalism; the enlightened philosopher-king; sectarian "ethnic" minorities; etc. Here again, what is remarkable is how the manifold historical and *contemporary* illustrations of this decisive fact—and the remarkable ways those alternative forms of authority actually combine and co-exist in specific Muslim settings—are strangely absent from the many handbooks claiming to describe "Islamic religion."

49 At most, those Qur'ânic passages have offered ammunition to *critics* of one or another of the religious models of authority in question. They certainly have never stopped the contending claimants of religious authority—even in cases grossly illustrating the Qur'ânic criticisms—from attempting to institutionalize their conceptions wherever political circumstances have permitted.

50 In Islamic history, as with humanity generally, there are ample illustrations of the principle that strong central governments prefer honoring dead saints to putting up with living ones. During this period, the frequent lack of inherent religious legitimacy of even the most powerful (often Turkic) local military regimes, throughout the central Islamic lands, typically led them to play off popular charismatic ("mystical") leaders and institutions against influential *ʿulamâ* and other contending religious authorities. Detailed social-historical studies over the

past three decades have added immensely to our understanding of these socio-religious processes in particular urban, rural and tribal Muslim contexts, although the largely intuitive summary of M. G. S. Hodgson, *The Venture of Islam* (Chicago, 1973), vol. 2, remains perhaps the best available survey for non-specialists. The contrasting attitudes and actions of *modern* Islamic nation-states of all ideological colors toward both Sufism and other traditional forms of popular Islamic religion likewise vividly illustrate the profound influence of changing local political frameworks on the visible social expressions of Islamic "mysticism".

51 Certainly the most widely translated illustration of this category is Ghazâlî's *al-Munqidh min al-Ḍalâl* ("The Deliverer from Error . . .") and other related works – e.g., in the version by R. J. McCarthy, *Freedom and Fulfillment: An Annotated Translation of Al-Ghazâlî's al-Munqidh min al-Ḍalâl and Other Relevant Works* . . . (Boston, 1980), with an extensive bibliography of other translations and studies of his works.

52 In Sunni circles, those more worldly and spiritual concerns alike were often expressed in discussions centering on the symbolic role of the early Sufi martyr al-Ḥallâj: see the monumental study by L. Massignon, (tr. H. Mason), *The Passion of al-Ḥallâj, Mystic and Martyr of Islam* (Princeton, 1982, 4 volumes), and the more accessible summary in C. Ernst, *Words of Ecstasy in Sufism* (Albany, 1985). In approaching the recurrent critiques by *ʿulamâ* (whether Shiite or Sunni) of "Sufism" and related popular movements it is essential to keep in mind that a key dimension of the widespread popular respect for *awliyâ'* (of all sorts) in Muslim rural and tribal settings, from the earliest Islamic periods (various Kharijite leaders and Shiite claimants) down to the present day, was the ever-present potential for protests, revolts, coalitions and invasions coalescing around such charismatic figures and their religio-political claims. Such immediate socio-political concerns are often more important than any deeper religious or theological issues in the long line of "theoretical" critiques of Sufi and related movements by Muslim scholars working in those contexts (including contemporary Islamic states). The constant reminders in such polemic theoretical works (whether for or against "mystical" tenets) of the public dangers of antinomianism and millenarianism are typically more concerned with the potential socio-political consequences of such popular movements – and their potential impact on the urban elite of scholars and merchants – than with the more profound individual spiritual dangers that are highlighted in *practical* spiritual works intended for mystics and Sufis themselves.

53 The growing number of translated sources available in English include the two anthologies from the *Meccan Illuminations* already cited at n. 47 above (including extensive bibliographies) and *The Bezels of Wisdom* (tr. R. W. J. Austin; New York, 1980).

54 In English, see Massignon's work on al-Ḥallâj cited at n. 52, and G. Bowering's *The Mystical Vision of Existence in Classical Islam: The Qur'anic Hermeneutics of the Sufi Sahl At-Tustarî (d. 283/896)* (Berlin/New York, 1980). The fundamental historical contributions of early Shiite esotericism (especially Jaʿfar al-Ṣâdiq) in this area have been much less explored – partly because the earliest Shiite hadîth sources pose a variety of problems for modern Shiite Uṣûli clergy. For illustra-

tions of this category of mystical writing in a Shiite setting, see H. Corbin, *Spiritual Body and Celestial Earth: From Mazdean Iran to Shi'ite Iran* (Princeton, 1977), pp. 109-170.

55   In earlier periods works of this category were apparently attempted in an assort-
     ment of gnostic, hermetic and Neoplatonic vocabularies drawn from earlier tradi-
     tions. After Avicenna, Muslim authors—including such key mystical writers as
     Suhrawardî, Ghazâlî and Ibn ᶜArabî—almost always used versions of his creative
     combination of Aristotelean terminology, Ptolemaic cosmology, and kalâm
     theological vocabulary to express their own insights. For Avicenna's own role and
     motivations in this wider historical development, see our discussion of "The
     Philosopher-Prophet in Avicenna's Political Philosophy," in *The Political Aspects of
     Islamic Philosophy* (Cambridge, 1992). J. Michot's study of *La destinée de l'homme
     selon Avicenne: Le retour à Dieu (maᶜâd) et l'imagination,* (Louvain, 1987) provides
     extensive translations from the later Islamic mystical philosophers inspired by
     Avicenna.

56   For Suhrawardî see the forthcoming translation of his *The Philosophy of Illumina-
     tion (Ḥikmat al-Ishrâq)* by J. Walbridge and H. Ziai. For the Shiite mystical
     philosopher Mullâ Sadrâ, see our study of *The Wisdom of the Throne: An Introduc-
     tion to the Philosophy of Mullâ Ṣadrâ* (Princeton, 1981). For Ibn ᶜArabî and his
     interpreters and their far-reaching influences on the Islamic humanities through-
     out the Muslim world, see the translations and historical surveys cited at notes 40,
     44 and 47 above.

57   The rare partial exceptions to this rule, like Suhrawardî or Ibn ᶜArabî, are all the
     more striking—and their exceptional personal openness is often related (as in
     these two instances) to such writers' unusual assertion of a particular divine
     "mission" differentiating their case from that of other Muslims. However, there is
     certainly no lack of "individuality" in this mystical literature: instead the aesthetic
     ideal here, as in many other fields of Islamic art, was to express one's individual
     experiences through highly nuanced allusions to a vast repertoire of scriptural
     and legendary archetypes and symbols conveyed by the local Islamic humanities.
     See the illustrations of this convention of the high-cultural Islamic humanities in
     our discussions of Mullâ Ṣadrâ's "spiritual autobiography", in the study cited in
     the preceding note, and in S. F. Dale's "Steppe Humanism: The Autobiographical
     Writings of Ẓâhir al-Dîn Muhammad Babur, 1483-1530", pp. 37-58 in *Interna-
     tional Journal of Middle East Studies* 22 (1990).

58   It is likewise no coincidence if initial encounters with the central Islamic arts and
     humanities more generally—e.g., calligraphy, poetry, both learned and popular
     religious music, carpets, architecture, etc.—sometimes lead to similar reactions. In
     addition to the obvious unfamiliarity of much of their symbolism and religious
     references, those creations typically presuppose a common aesthetic and meta-
     physical outlook in their audiences—centering on the theophanic re-creation of
     shared spiritual archetypes—and the practical social contexts in which their
     explicitly contemplative functions could actually be realized. See the remarkably
     sensitive illustration of these essential points in W. Andrews' *Poetry's Voice, Society's
     Song: Ottoman Lyric Poetry* (Seattle, 1985).

59 The closest approaches to such an exclusivist attitude (both intellectually and socially), in some forms of Shiism from early centuries down to the present, inevitably led to the "sectarian" social consequences largely limited to Shiite groups in Islam—consequences which are *not* at all typical of the most influential forms of Islamic mysticism. And even within later Shiite sectarian communities, "mystics" or esotericists typically formulated their teachings and pursued their practical activities in ways closely paralleling the situation of mystics working within wider Sunni settings.

60 The resulting social and institutional fluidity of "mystics" and Sufis in most periods, with their profusion of orders, paths, and competing local shaykhs, has more typically resembled the indeterminate, constantly evolving relationship of contemporary "Twelve-step" spiritual programs to their surrounding American and European communities more than it has any rigid institutional models drawn from the later periods of Christian or Buddhist monasticism. Again and again, as already discussed at n. 5 above, one can observe in Islamic history the recurrent pattern of an almost automatic religious discrediting of those spiritual movements which took on the accoutrements of "successful" political, social, or economic institutionalization in ways that would thereby cut them off from the rest of the local Muslim community.

61 Even the widespread Sufi ṭarīqas of the 13th-19th centuries and their modern survivals have rarely been constituted as separate sects or "orders" in the institutional sense familiar, for example, in Catholicism. Instead they are typically voluntary associations (whose members remain immersed in the daily life of the surrounding Muslim community), local in their membership, surrounding a particular local leader, and more often that not dissolving or splitting up at the death of each locally accepted guide. Frequently they are in active competition with a range of similar local groups, with considerable movement from one guide to another; meetings may be held in homes or neighborhood mosques, with no special institutional locale required. In revealing contrast, the undoubtedly sectarian organization of Shiite groups in many Islamic contexts has usually occurred under very particular situations of extreme political hostility and persecution—situations which have normally had nothing to do with any particularly "mystical" activities or tendencies.

62 Of course this does not rule out certain extremely rare cases of individuals claiming to have reached spiritual enlightenment through direct divine intervention (the *majdhûb*)—e.g., as was claimed in various ways by Ibn ʿArabî and his famous 19th-century Algerian follower, ʿAbd al-Qâdir. But it is revealing that even these exceptional individuals, before undertaking to teach others, first consciously undertook to pass through the "normal" stages of the spiritual path under the guidance of other masters: see M. Chodkiewicz, *Emir Abd el-Kader: Ecrits spirituels* (Paris, 1982) and *Le Sceau des saints* (Paris, 1986), and the longer biography by C. Addas, *Ibn ʿArabî ou la quête du Soufre Rouge* (Paris, 1989).

63 This typical attitude of Islamic spirituality—which is sufficiently contrary to models carried over from other religious contexts that it has frequently led to serious misunderstandings—obviously reflects the overt and irreducibly symbolic and musical character of the Qur'anic text, which so often pointedly defies any

translation or "obvious" understanding. Perhaps even more important for the predominance of this particular structure of writing and oral teaching in Islam is the repeated insistence, throughout the Qur'ân and in dozens of hadîth constantly cited by Sufis and other Muslims, that the prophets (*awliyâ'*, Imams, etc.) and angels *are* here now, and that most people are simply unconscious of their spiritual presence (as of the ever-present "unseen world", *al-ghayb*, more generally).

64 See the timely autobiographical illustrations of these points, within a contemporary Turkish Sufi order, in Part I of L. Hixon's *Heart of the Qur'ân* (Wheaton, IL, 1988). For all its sketchiness, that firsthand account reveals far more about the typical functioning of the above principles than most of the translated Sufi literature cited above. For similar contemporary illustrations of the processes of oral teaching in more traditional Islamic settings in Senegal, Algeria and Iran, see the translations cited at n. 36 above.

65 Tr. R. W. J. Austin, Oxford, 1971. For a more detailed analysis of the spiritual and personal significance, and the social-historical background, of those encounters, see the two pioneering French studies cited at n. 62 above (both forthcoming in English translation by the Islamic Texts Society, Cambridge).

66 See the remarkable contemporary illustration of *that* point — as of so many other central teachings of the Islamic humanities — in Wim Wenders' *Der Himmel über Berlin* (1987: distributed in English and French as "Wings of Desire").

Typologies of Islamic Mysticism

Parviz Morewedge

I. Context, methodology, and a summary

In scholarship dealing with Middle Eastern texts two methodological perspectives are often encountered. The first consists in transmitting a body of knowledge without the writer proposing any new constructs. The second method — the analytical constructive — consists in the author constructing his own pragmatic schema which he uses to draw form different traditions so as to make manifest those general trends and patterns imbedded in various contexts of inquiry.

Since the present study focuses on typologies of Islamic mysticism this requires that we investigate different traditions and select what is common in the salient features so that we can proceed with our enterprise of constructing our proposed model. It must be admitted that one shortcoming of this method is that of not describing any particular trend of Islamic Mysticism but of only preparing a schema which possibly provides a better reading of the texts in question.

This paper offers a typology of "monistic sufism" in its ontic, epistemic and pragmatic dimensions. It clarifies this typology by: (1) differentiating the ontology of "the unity of being, *al-wahdat al-wujūd*", from notions of ultimate being in Greek philosophy, as well as from the God of monotheism; (2) by constructing three monistic meanings of the self (*nafs*) which are incompatible with theistic sufism; and (3) by depicting the archetypal representations of the mediator-figure sage (*murshid*) which are peculiar to monistic sufism.

Even though the presence of a monistic trend in sufism has been recognized by previous investigators, a comprehensive philosophical typology of "monistic sufism," has never been presented and sufism has never been discussed in the context of contemporary scholarship on mysticism using the tools of western philosophical analysis. Our study attempts to do both.

We focus on primary Persian and Arabic texts, using our own translation of the works of the most important sufic metaphysical poets: Attar, Rumi and Shabasteri and two major theoreticians of Islamic mysticism: Avicenna and Nasafi.

Let us begin by examining the most popular typologies of mysticism which are attributed to R. C. Zaehner, who uses them to criticize

Aldous Huxley's views on mysticism as expressed in *The Doors of Perception*. Some drugged states, Huxley suggests, are conducive to the salvation achieved in, or said to be enjoyed in mystic and religious experiences. Specifically, he recommends that,[1]

> . . . the mescaline experience is what Catholic theologians call "a gratuitous grace," [and is] not necessary to salvation but potentially helpful and to be accepted thankfully, if made available.

Supporting his position by a thorough examination of the classics of mysticism, Zaehner dissociates Catholic theology from any such "drug-related" program. He introduces several prima facie classifications including two typologies: "monistic or nature oriented," and "theistic." In the former, the self is supposed to be "integrated" into an ultimate being, an entity which is not identified with the God of monotheism. In this vein, Zaehner notes, "The nature mystic identifies himself with the whole of Nature, and in his exalted moments sees himself as being one with Nature and as having passed beyond good and evil."[2] In the latter meaning, the soul may have grace through being "isolated," a grace which is necessary for salvation. Zaehner describes this option, as follows, " . . . isolation . . . means the isolation of what Christians call man's mortal soul from all its purely psycho-physical adjuncts."[3] Zaehner's findings make a significant impact on the study of mysticism. For example, Rist refers to Zaehner's *Mysticism Sacred and Profane*, as " . . . a book whose importance for the study of mysticism is so great as to make much of what has previously been written look like pointless maundering."[4] Many ambiguities in "pre-Zaehner" scholarship may be eliminated by an examination of the writings of Otto, Kingsland, Hughes and Inge.[5] Moreover, several "post-Zaehner," disputes in mysticism can be deciphered by his typologies as the writings of Stace, Staal, Smart and others show.[6] In our view his system holds up well under critical scrutiny. At least two cases which reject Zaehner's typology, those of Stace and Staal, pose no serious objection to the scheme under consideration.[7]

In a previous study we accused Zaehner of offering a circular argument in his reasoning against the legitimacy of the doctrine of "integration" held by the sufi monists.[8] The present essay contains a refinement of his typology based on its application to sufic texts. Three results emerge from this application, which we shall now present:

(1) The Islamic tradition includes no doctrine of *nature* mysticism that is charged with being against religion. Islam had neither

Nietzsche nor Freud. Instead, the split shows in the contrast between the ontology of "pure monism," in which God is immanent in nature, and the type of monotheism which embraces the dualistic ontology of a transcendent God and the world of creation (*ᶜālam-i khalq*). Logically, the former corresponds to Zaehner's "monistic," or "nature," mysticism, while the latter qualifies as "theistic" mysticism.

(2) Another problematic matter is the nature of the self-soul. A reading of the most sophisticated sufic poets, such as Rumi, Shabasteri, and Attar, reveals distinct meanings of the soul-self. We offer three different constructs of the self for the sufi monist. The monist integrates himself into god or a deified nature rather into a secular one. The theists of Islam follow Zaehner's scheme of "isolation."

(3) With respect to the theory of action and language, monistic sufis interpret religious rituals, icons and actions as only one family of archetypal presentation, without preference for religious ones. This attitude is evident in the case of the mediator figure, which links the finite and the infinite.[9] Accordingly, Avicenna points to three isomorphic representations of the same archetype of the mediator figure: in the language of religion (*bi zabān-i sharī ᶜat*), Gabriel (or the Holy Ghost), in mysticism the sage (*pīr*), and in philosophy what its practitioners call the active intelligence (*al-ᶜagl-i al-faᶜᶜāl*).[10] Avicenna distinguishes carefully between the single designatum (the archetype) and the different names given to it by the corresponding traditions. Having outlined our general theses, let us proceed next to the three contexts in which our concept of "monistic sufism" is analyzed.

III. The Monistic Ontology of the "Unity of Being," (al-waḥdat al-wujūd) in Nature Sufism

Let us examine the significance of the notion of unity of being in all forms of mysticism, the monistic version of unity, and a paradigm case of treatment of this notion in a sufic text.

III.1 The Concept of the Unity of Being
"The Unity of Being," most mystics and their interpreters agree, is the crux of all mysticism. In agreement with this method, Stace takes "the unifying vision," expressed as "All is One," to be the first core of

mysticism.[11]   Inge notes that "The Unity of all existence is a fundamental doctrine of Mysticism."[12]   Others, such as James, Underhill, and Staal, agree with this choice.[13]   In devotional mysticism, the existential meaning of this doctrine refers to the integration of the self with the Divine or another ultimate being. Psychologically this move may be plotted on many axes, such as a return to the origin (*arche, aṣl*) as stated by Rumi and Eliade, or as a return to one's mother as stated by Freud.[14] Regardless of its ontic validity, there is a psychological basis for this tendency. Mysticism is only one response to the most existential and inner problem of man, namely alienation. Since "mystical bliss or peace" is sought as a solution to "alienation," all mystics aim towards an affinity with whatever may be the "ultimate being" of their peculiar system.

Both mystics and their interpreters are often ambiguous when they refer to this ultimate being with which the self is to become united. In the context of devotional dimension of mysticism, this ambiguity does not cause any problem. Therapeutically, God, Who is Our Father in Heaven, our biological father, a therapist, mother nature, or any other type of support system is called on to play the same role, namely to give us comfort. Philosophically, however, the ambiguous object of unity in mysticism has distinct metaphysical meanings. They are: (i) the ultimate system in a philosophical system, such as the Form of the Good in Plato's ontology; (ii) some metaphysical sense of being (*hastī, to ehn eh en*), existence *(wujūd, to de ti)*, Braham, *(ule)*; (iii) the transcendent God of monotheism; and (iv) the phenomenological self-world. Let us examine if these choices are incompatible with one another.

III.2 The Ultimate Being in Sufic Monism and Greek Philosophy

The ultimate being of classical Greek philosophy cannot be used without modification by any mystic, for the following reasons: (a) with the exception of Parmenides, no Greek advocated a pure monism that is compatible with monistic sufism, and (b) the ultimate being in the system of the Greek philosophy lacks the intentional predicates needed for the devotional aspect of any mysticism. Neither Plato's Form of the Good, nor Aristotle's First Mover, can be the object of mystical union. Plato's Form of the Good is not a conscious entity and cannot partake of an existential dialogue, or a prayer. Moreover, Platonic Forms are fixed, and particular souls cannot be integrated with them.   The same type of problem is involved in applying Aristotle's first mover, which is a substance, to the domain of mysticism. The concept of the "mystical union" cannot be formulated in the substance-event language of the Aristotelian metaphysics. Unlike processes, substances do not blend into each other. We have argued elsewhere that the One of Plotinus, was modified extensively in Islamic mysticism for it is different from the ultimate being of the muslim mystics.[15] For illustration let us enumerate the distinctions between the One of Neoplatonism and the Necessary Existent in the system of Avicenna.

(1) In his major metaphysical texts such as *Al-Shifā* and *The Dānish Nāma*, Avicenna begins the concept of being and proceeds to the Aristotelian categories.[16] Moreover, he embraces and expands Aristotle's categories in his logic. In contrast, Plotinus rejects the categories. (*Enneads* VI 1 [1-24]). Consequently the two respective metaphysical systems are very distinct.

(2) Avicenna accepts the categories in the preliminary phase of metaphysical analysis. But he does not follow an Aristotelian model which places the unmoved mover in the category of substance. Instead, Avicenna states that the Necessary Existent is a kind of "being," in the spite of the fact that it is neither a substance nor an accident.[17] For the Neoplatonists the One is not a being but beyond being. Plotinus notes that the One generates being (*Ennead*, V 2). Proclus places both the One and God beyond being.[18]

(3) Avicenna's Necessary Existent is conscious of itself.[19] In contrast, the One of Plotinus' is not conscious of itself (*Enneads* VI 9 (9), chap. 6 III 9 [13], chaps. 7, 9, and VI 1 [9]).

(4) Specifically, Plotinus holds that numbers are substantial and associates them with the soul (*The Enneads* VI [6] 5), whereas Avicenna considers numbers as accidents.[20]

(5) Plotinus separates the realm of universals as intelligibles from the realm of particulars as sensibles. With respect to the problem of universals, the Neoplatonists are classified as realists. Avicenna's position on the universals is against simple realism.[21]

(6) Avicenna explicitly rejects Porphyry's doctrine of identification of the knower and the known and mentions Porphyry by name.[22] He knows the specifics of Neoplatonist epistemology, he identifies it by name and rejects it.

(7) While we have no social or political philosophy in Neoplatonism, Avicenna's *Al-Shifā* deals with prophecy with respect to the
position of the ideal-ruler.[23]

(8) Unlike Plotinus, Avicenna, does not follow asceticism either in
his philosophy or personal life. For example, Avicenna was a
physician, indulged extensively in physical pleasures and was
active in his political life.

In sum, in the light of these considerations, the entire Neoplatonic
Greek perspective is alien to the system of Avicenna who is the major
theoretician of sufism.

III.3 "Being-qua-being" and the Ultimate Being of the Monists

The next candidate for the notion of "being-qua-being," is not a
substance but a transcendental term.   E. A. Moody has clarified
Ockham's classical interpretation of this concept.   The six transcendental terms [are:] "*ens* (that which is), *res* (thing), *aliquid* (something),
unum (that which is one or 'individual'), *verum* (that which is, *qua*
intelligible), and *bonum* (that which is *qua* desirable).   These are
predicates of absolute universality, predicable convertible of each
other, and predicable significantly and *per se* of every significant
term."[24]   The theoreticians of sufism, such as Avicenna and Tusi,
followed Aristotle in placing "being (*hastī*)," as the primary object of
metaphysics and "the categories (*al-maqūlāt*)," as specifications of
"being."   They signified "being," (*hastī*), in the Ockhamean-Moody
sense of "transcendental term;" thus, it is a concept which is totally
different from the God of monotheism, or the object of unification
with the self in nature mysticism.   It is merely a concept that
expresses what the designata of all meaningful terms have in
common.[25]   Muslim philosophers of mysticism are well aware of this
fact. For example, Avicenna never takes '*hastī*' to be a morally significant concept.   It is only a notion which along with the modalities
(necessity, contingency, and impossibility), comes to mind on the first
level, prior to any other set of concepts.[26]   Gilson provides the
following plausible explanation for this choice, "Since being is thinkable apart from actual existence, whereas actual existence is not
thinkable from being, philosophers . . . [posit] being minus actual
existence as the first principle of metaphysics."[27]

In Western literature there is much confusion on the part of both
mystics and philosophers of mysticism about the identity of "God," or

"the One," with "Being." Otto's observation illustrates the confusion about these categories.[28]

> Not only mysticism but the personalistic scholasticism also defines God as Being . . . Deus est sum esse, . . . ; He does not have being as other things have their being . . . He is His own being and is also that which in the highest sense can alone be called Being. Eckhart, however, goes a step further still: "Esse est Deus." Being is not predicated of God, . . . , God is predicated of Being; Esse is thereby logically the first concept of speculation.

This type of confusion disappears if we take the following perspective. In sufic monism, any existent entity in a theophanic sense displays iconically the Divine. Al-Ghazali's restatement of the common view that "There is only one God," means for the mystic that "There is nothing but God."[29] But God here as the ultimate cause of all actualized entities may be identified as the Necessary Existent (*wujūd*) but not as pure being (*hastī*).

III.4 Distinctions between the One of Nature Sufism and the God of Monotheism

Zaehner observes correctly that the theistic mystic should isolate himself from, "the phenomenal world or, as the theist puts it, from all that is not God."[30] The purpose of the union sought by the theist is not an identification with God; as Zaehner notes, "The Christian mystic, if he is orthodox, will not go so far as to say that he actually is God in any absolute and unqualified sense."[31] It follows that a theist cannot identify his God with all existents, for in theism God is distinct from the rest of the world. By contrast, the monistic mystic may have a vision of one being and then identify himself with the One-God-Nature. Consequently, the two definitions of the ultimate being in theism and monism cannot be the same, and theistic and monistic mystics cannot refer to the same entity as the object of their union.

In Islamic mysticism, the two types of mystics agree on their apparent religious fervor, but disagree on the following metaphysical position questions. First what is the basis of the metaphysical system? Is the system an "introverted type of mysticism," and phenomenological in which the self-world, or a Heideggerean *Dasein* is the primary being, replacing the traditional notion of substance? Or is the metaphysics an "extroverted type of mysticism," according to which the ultimate reality is the world-nature with or without a transcendent God?[32] The first option follows an idealistic or a phenomenological type of epistemology; the second option holds the epistemology of naive realism. Second is the ultimate being of the system transcendent or immanent, as specified by the following logical distinction: is it logically possible for a transcendent God to exist, while the world does not exist? For nature mystics, an immanent ultimate being co-exists with the world only by the mediacy of the universe.

In the Islamic intellectual tradition, this opposition between monism and theism began when philosophers advocated various versions of Neoplatonic emanationism in opposition to the orthodox doctrine of creation.[33] Muslim philosophers often refer to the Necessary Existent (*al-wājib al-wujūd*), and not to God (*allāh, khudā, Īzad*) as the ultimate being of their ontological systems. This concept often implies a "necessity" which does not partake of "will," "consciousness," and many "intentional" predicates. Its "knowledge," and "love," are translated into "necessity of being an existent," since there cannot be any duality of predicates in the ultimate being. If one logically examines the systems of Al-Fārābī, Avicenna, Averroes, Suhrawardi, and Mulla Sadra, one arrives at the following non-monotheistic doctrine: it is impossible for the Necessary Being (*al-wājib al-wujūd*) to exist while the rest of the world is unactualized. The statement "The Necessary Being (*al-Wājib al-Wujūd*) Is, and the rest of the world is not," is a contradiction in Islamic metaphysics. In these systems, the ultimate being is like a sun, while the rest of the world, necessarily emanates from it as light emanates from the Sun; the latter is a necessary by-product of the former. Categorically the world is contingent since its cause is a self-necessity; but conditionally, the world is a necessity. Hobben makes the following correct observation with respect to Avicenna: "the whole system of emanation from God is not a free creation but a production and emanation according to a determined monism of existence and being."[34] Gilson makes the same observation "Yet, Avicenna, does not consider his God as having created the world by an act of will. As has been said, the world flows from God's intrinsic necessity, according to the laws of intelligible necessity."[35] The view of the philosophers of emanation stands in radical contrast to the Muslim orthodox view that the existence of creatures is due solely to the grace of God without any logical necessity; God does not have to create the world. Creatures exist only due to His grace (*Karama*).[36] Similarly, in Judaism and Christianity God is transcendent and independent of the world. In his sober moments, Al-Ghazali has to revert to the early Muslim occasionalism in order to sustain the supremacy of God.[37]

III.4 Some Paradigm Cases of Monism in Sufic Literature

The theoreticians of Islamic mysticism were keenly aware of the ontological distinction between the monism and pluralism of a transcendent God with a created continent world. They commonly labeled the general problem as the notion of "*al-waḥdat al-wujūd*," meaning the unity of being.[38] According to their distinctions, there was rarely any type of mysticism that made explicit separation between "nature" and the "religious." Instead they elaborated on the categories of "monism" and "pluralism." In sufic poetry, one finds repeatedly the identification of God with absolute being. Jami, a sufi poet, reflects on the sufic meaning of the phrase that "there is exactly one God;" he asserts that what is called God by the pluralists (*mushrikān*) is nothing but the absolute existent (*hastī-i muṭlaq*).[39] Jami writes as follows,[40]

> The [actual] agent (*fāᶜil*) is the *Ḥagg* [God, Truth, Reality]; others as a mere instrument. Existence, being the effect of *Ḥagg* is a unity;/ All others [the apparent duality] is a mere image and conjecture.

A systematic account of the different metaphysics of sufism is found in the works of Nasafi, who occupies the essentialist position in the essence-existence controversy.[41] He begins with a sufic version of Aristotle's dictum about the primacy of first substances, i.e., particular existents.[42] His first illustration is the doctrine, ascribed to Avicenna, that the mark of an existent is that it is the object of phenomenological reference (*ishāra*). His second version is ascribed to Muhammad who was asked: "What is it? to be an existent?" (*wujūd chīst?*), and who answered rhetorically, "What is, other than an existent?"[43] He presents a charming allegory about the search for an existent, in the form of a story about a school of fish in the sea, who were attempting to understand the meaning of "water;" because meaning is clarified by the use of a limit and a differentia, "being an existent" cannot be experienced.[44]

In his *Kashf al-Haqāyīq*, Nasafi, identifies the following schools, with respect to the topic of unity (*tawḥīd*).[45] The pluralists are called (*ahl-i-aktharat*) and the monists are named (*ahl-i-wahdat*). The pluralists comprise the followers of religious law (*ahl-i-sharīᶜat*) and the philosophers (*ahl-i-ḥikmat*).[46] The former divide being into (i) that which is an eternal (*al-qadīm*), and thus a non-created God, and (ii) that which is ephemeral (*hadīth*), and which is created. Among the latter are philosophers who divide being into two types of entities: (i) contingent beings and (ii) a being who is necessary in itself, the cause of all contingent existents, the first cause, and the absolute fixed agent.[47]

The monists are divided into what he calls the religious unitarians (*ahl-i-wahdat*) and a peculiar group he labels the followers of (*hulūl*) (incarnation) and (*itihād*) (harmony). The former hold that there is only one existent which is God and that nothing else exists but God.

The followers of incarnation and harmony are of the opinion that being can be discussed only in terms of light (*nūr*) and its manifestations (*mazhar*). They point to the light as God and to its manifestations as the creation.[48] They consider man an indestructible aspect of the Divine. In this vein, Nasafi points out that for the illuminationist monists, the essence of humanity (*haqīqat-i-ādamī*) is immortal, unchangeable, death, being darkness, applies only to the physical mold of humanity; darkness is not a substance but a mere privation of light.[49]

IV. Three Phases of the Self in Monistic Sufism

The elements of the typology of Islamic monistic mysticism may also be identified through an account of the analyses of the concept of the self, a prominent topic in philosophy and mysticism. As Wittgenstein asserts, "What brings the self into philosophy is the fact that 'the world is my world'."[50] It is for these reasons that in all traditions "knowledge of the self" is often the first step in the philosophical or mystical inquiry. In Christianity, Augustine reminds us that the primary object of his inquiry is the search for God and his soul-self.[51] Its importance in Islamic mysticism is reflected in the archaic Arab proverb, often quoted by Al-Ghazali, "He Who Knows His Soul, Knows His God." This proverb points to the Augustinian doctrine of "the inner teacher," namely, the mediator figure between God and the Self, for the monistic sufis plays the same role in the self realization process. The cardinal difference between the monist's and the pluralist's vision of the self is well delineated by Otto.[52]

> All religion, indeed, seeks the transcendent . . . it strives thereby to pass beyond the natural and merely creaturely . . . But however close the relationship is thought to be, there remains the chasm between the creator and created. Even in the final consummation of his fellowship the cleft is unbridged and unbridgeable. In the mysticism of Eckhart and Sankara, however, the soul seeks out to pass out of the region of the created to the being and dignity of God himself.

Even though all mystics speak of the encounter between man and his God, the specifics of this encounter are used to circumscribe the typologies of mysticism. Accordingly, James states that in religious mysticism, there is a " . . . sudden realization of the immediate presence of God."[53] James goes on to note that in Christian mystical theology the method acceptable to the Church is that of 'orison' or meditation, the methodical elevation of the soul towards God."[54] Margaret Smith notes that "The concept of the final state of the mystic who has passed away from self and entered into union with god, and henceforth lives in Him, is expressed in much the same terms by Sufi and Christian mystics alike."[55] But in religious mysticism, as Smith points out, the key element is asceticism. "Between Mysticism and the ascetic spirit which led to the development of the monastic life there is a close connection."[56]

Monistic sufis, however, view the self, not in terms of asceticism or isolation, but rather in terms of what Zaehner calls "integration." Here we have three logically independent concepts of the self: (1) the self is embedded in the process of travelling through the path of the realization (*ṭarīqa*) and perfection of the human being, the last phase of which is integration of the self-soul with the ultimate being in a mystical union; (2) the self as the boundary of the world, the ground of being, or the subject of all possible experiences—what changes here is the world perspective, from an alienated, separated (*tafrīq*) to a harmonious, collected union (*jam͑*); and finally (3) the self as a macrocosm, a monad—which is a self-contained perspective.

Let us examine specific aspects of each of the views. The first view, formulated in the context of the path of self-realization and terminating in mystical union has been most popular among the Muslim mystics. The two aspects of the union are: (i) the annihilation of the ego-dimension of the self (*fanā'*), and (ii) the eternal persistence of a dimension of the self which is united with the one (*baqā'*). As Attar affirms, there is an integral connection between these two phases of the self. He notes that "Until you do not surrender (the self-ego) to annihilation (*fanā'*), you cannot correctly integrate yourself in eternal persistence."[57] He explicitly advocates that a mystic should give up his particular status as a unique existent (*nīst show*), if he wishes to partake of the true universal Existent.[58] Both Attar and Rumi, employ the same theme in different poems, that the death of the self-ego is a necessary prelude to the birth of the new self.[59] Both emphasize that the soul-ego is totally absorbed in the ultimate being. Attar illustrates the process by relating how a particle of light (*zarrih*) becomes molded into (*mahvast*) the sun; Rumi in the same manner uses various analogies, including "the flight of the bird," and "the baptism of life into an endless ocean."[60] Theoretically this view is best expressed in terms of a metaphysics of processes, which, unlike the Aristotelian substance-event language, allows for the union of the alienated self and the Divine Ultimate Being.[61] It is for this reason that Avicenna, the most logically oriented theoretician of Islamic mysticism, states explicitly that his Necessary Existent (*al-wājib al-wujūd*) or God is not a substance, but the beholder of the world.[62]

The difference between the first view of the self and the orthodox Islamic view is this. In the former, a person may assert with Al-Hallaj and Abu Yazid that God-Truth-Reality (*al-Ḥagg*) and the Ego are ultimately one and the same; in this model God is not a transcendent being, but the partaker of the last phase of the self. Such a position is unacceptable to all monotheistic traditions.

Whereas the first model focuses on the ontological dimensions of the sufic view of the self, the second emphasizes the epistemic perspective. According to this view, the self is the ground of all experience, the subject to which the word is disclosed. That some notion of self is presupposed in all experience has been recognized by many philosophers. Kant, for instance, states: " . . . I am conscious to myself a priori of a necessary synthesis of representations – to be entitled the original synthetic unity of apperception – under which all representations that are given to me must stand, but under which they have also first to be brought by means of a synthesis."[63] In a similar vein, Wittgenstein notes that, "The world and life are one," and, "The subject does not belong to the world; rather, it is a limit of the world."[64] Kant and Wittgenstein support a popular theme in philosophy: that (a) the experience of the existence of any entity other than the self is dependent on some presupposition relating to the existence of the subject of the experience, that (b) no limit or boundary of the self can ever be experienced, and that (c) the soul-subject-self is, in some sense epistemically prior to any other possible entity. Philosophers of mysticism embed this notion of the self in its spiritual extension. Inge, recognized for his erudition in the field of Christian mysticism, clarifies this notion by stating that "What is really apprehended is not the Absolute, but a kind of 'form of formlessness,' not an idea of the Infinite but the indefinite."[65] In the Islamic tradition, the self as the totality of the transcendental conditions of all experiences is closely associated with God. Al-Ghazali, the recognized champion of theistic mysticism, asserts in the beginning of his text on *The Alchemy of Happiness* that the key to the gnosis of God lies in the gnosis of the self.[66] Accordingly to him, human happiness lies in the gnosis of God because happiness (*sacᶜādat*) and pleasure (*lizzat*) are produced when the subject receives what is in perfect accord with its nature. Since God is the very being and cause of man, His knowledge constitutes our ultimate self-knowledge and thus the ultimate happiness.[67] Accordingly, our highest happiness and pleasure lies in our union (*paiwand*) with the Necessary Existent.[68] Whereas physical pleasures are always finite, spiritual pleasures have no limit and provide us with an immediate experience of the limitlessness. In the metaphysical poem of Shabasteri, the following refinements of this theme are observed. "Since I am in my own essence the measure (the criterion of what reality is), I cannot know (or experience) that which is my shadow (or is outside of my own mind)."[69] But his notion of "the I (*man*)", is not that is the personal soul. In another poem, he states "I, we, you and He are one and the same existent, since there can be no (ultimate) distinction in unity (*waḥdat*)."[70] Accordingly, he offers to correct Al-Hallaj's saying that "I am the Ultimate Truth (*al-Ḥaqq*), as follows: "There is no existent other than the Ultimate Truth (*al-Ḥaqq*); if you wish to assert, 'I am the Truth-Reality,' say "It (God-the Ultimate) is the Ultimate Truth."[71] This version of the sufic view of the self is embedded in an extreme sense of monism which is incompatible with any theistic doctrine.

The third view which is analogous to Leibniz' monadology holds that each microcosm mirrors the world in its entire history, in accordance with the so-called predicate-in-substance principle.[72] Inge points to the prevalence of this doctrine in Christianity.[73] The Islamic version finds expression in the writings of many philosophers, among them Shabasteri, who states that "the universe is a person and a person a universe." He draws out the philosophical implications of this principle in a series of analogies: (i) each drop of water reveals hundreds of seas; (ii) each part of dust manifests thousands of human souls; (iii) the point of the immediate present gathers all of the universe within it; (iv) from any point on the periphery of the circle, thousands of figures can be constructed.[74] This perspective is often placed in the context of a mystic's embracing a sense of eternity of his incarnation of the Divine through love. This attitude is embedded in the joy of presence intimated by the dancing dervishes who follow Rumi. The dance celebrates an existentialistic joy and ecstasy that is far removed from the ascetic sober monastic mysticism observed in the Far East, in Christianity and in the spirit of martyrdom found in Shiism. In fact, Rumi's poems sustain such a doctrine as for instance, when he pleads; "Since your life is experienced in a temporal and a physical context, choose to be in a noble place and spend your time."[75] For him a dog in love is better than a smart lion who is not a lover; moreover, he advises that one should not count that portion of life which passes without love, for love is the fountain of youth and should be ingrained in life.[76] He observes further that while intelligence educates the body, joyous, perpetual love intoxicates the very essence and generator of the body.[77] Similarly, Shabasteri notes: "Open the (significance of the) essence of any drop, and note a hundred pure oceans emerge from it; observe correctly any particle of dust, and in it appear (potentially) one thousand Adams.[78] In sum, in its third variation the self in Islamic monistic sufism is the microcosm of the universe. In its primitive version, this system consists of the immediate existential feeling tones of the mystic, who displays a spirit of joy and bliss. Presupposed in this is a theophanic system, which makes the process of mystical experience not an accidental dimension of the universe, but its metaphysical center. The immediacy of the mystics' present state (*ḥāl*), is the actualization and concretion of the eternal laws. This emphasis on the importance of the presence is more akin to Bergson's notion of *duree*, than to a monotheistic tradition usually associated with passive asceticism and piety.[79] Even though this view of the self is not predominant in sufism, its presence in Rumi and Khayyam and among some sufi groups demands that it be recognized.

It follows that any perspectives of the self outlined above may be used to differentiate monistic from theistic types of mysticism. The theistic theory emphasizes God as the sole origin of the self. The monistic view takes God as the last phase of the self in the process of self-realization (*ṭarīqa*). The logic of our argument is not limited to the Islamic case. Inge, who supports a Christian version of mysticism, is keenly aware of this problem when he notes that[80]

> If the Son of God is regarded as an all embracing and all-pervading cosmic principle, the "mystic union" of the believer with Christ becomes something much closer than the ethical harmony of two mutually exclusive wills.

The problem, Inge realizes, is whether there is a human personality distinct, even if not separate, from God. For him, as for any religious mystic the answer has to be affirmative because he holds that ". . . it is only on the analogy of human personality that we can conceive of the perfect personality of God."[81]

V. The Pragmatics of Signs (*Mithāl, Tilisms*)

As we have shown, mystics express their views in allegories and universally archetypal symbols embracing a variety of experiences.[82] Let us take the celebrated case of the flight of the bird. In mysticism, the bird stands for the soul, while the flight depicts the imagery of the ascent or the return of the soul to its origin, which is the converse of the emanation process. To a believer the flight of the bird may signify perhaps the separation of the soul from the body; to a naturalist, a follower of Lucretius's metaphysics, it may refer to the integration of the body into the physical realm of nature. In sufism — unlike religion — there are no sacred texts or extensionally determined ritual for salvation. Instead, one encounters numerous biographies of wise men and women, including the prophets, who function as mystical paradigms. For instance, the sage (*murshid*) functions as a paradigm for the mystical novice. Through participation in the praxis (*ʿamāl*) of mysticism, habits and attitudes are first experienced and then internalized in a manner similar to the process of the "imitation" of "Christ-like behavior" in Christianity. Spurgeon, who affirms that symbolism is of immense importance to mysticism," provides another reason when she contends that, "This necessity for symbolism is an integral part of belief in unity . . . [for example as] falling leaves are a symbol of human mortality, because they are examples of the same law as that which it symbolizes."[83] Another reason for the wide use of symbolism is philosophical. As H. A. Wolfson shows, the problem of the Divine Predicates plays a central role in the Islamic intellectual tradition. The only intellectually affirmative predicate of God is existence, God being, "He Whose Essence is no other than being an Existent."[84] Since existence is a transcendental concept, the only path left even to the theistic mystics is the method of symbolic theology, clothed in the language of allegory.[85]

There are logically distinct interpretations of this trend. First, in agreement with the medieval doctrine of symbolic theology, one may argue that since God is transcendent, man can communicate his religious experience at best by means of an icon. Second, from a phenomenological perspective, there is no normative priority for either the religious, the mystical or the philosophical perspectives. There is one structure of reality, analogously, just as each game must have a set of rules, or each formal syntax must have rules of formation, deduction and interpretation.[86] Each perspective becomes a peculiar concretion of the general principle. It may be argued that such a Wittgensteinean interpretation is only a modern invention and cannot be applied to medieval Muslim writers. But the textual evidence at hand supports our contention. In his work entitled *The Perfect Man (al-Insān al-Kāmil)*, Nasafi states explicitly that the mediator figure has many names, some religious, some mystical, and others mythical.[87] A number of allegorical treatises written by technical philosophers, such as Avicenna and Suhrawardi, lend additional supports to the view that the theoretical founders of Islamic mysticism consider archetypal tools to be the primary medium for the expression of mysticism. Third, even though the sufis of a monistic creed may consider themselves "religious," or "spiritual," in some sense, their views in fact lie outside of the monotheistic orthodoxy of Islam. According to this perspective, Al-Ghazali surmised correcting that what started as a theoretical modification of Greek philosophy in Islam lead in fact to a tradition that was not in harmony with Islamic orthodoxy.[88]

But there is a delicate difference between the application and the concept of symbolism. Religions impose a close net of disciplined rituals on followers, irrespective of the peculiarity of one believer and another. As a rule, clergy are not in a position to vary the general doctrines of the religion for a specific believer. In some creeds, like Catholicism, a mechanism like confession may be present to allow for confidential communication between the clergy and the believer. But even in confession, a priest has to follow the specific rules postulated by the Holy See. In contrast to the practice of monotheistic religions, the sufic master may impose different tasks on the mystic based on the specific character of the individual at hand. For this reason, monistic mysticism, when applied to a naturalistic context, is akin to a kind of psychotherapy, as exemplified by the Jungian method of individuation. Zaehner, for a similar reason, observed sharp similarities shared by the medieval philosophies of sufis, e.g. Avicenna, and Carl G. Jung, a twentieth century depth psychologist: "Thus, for Avicenna as for Jung, integration of personality was man's first aim on earth, and his lower soul does not seem to differ greatly from Jung's collective unconscious."[89] But the medieval Muslim mystic did not see himself as a naturalistic therapist. Instead, he considered himself as the most important step on the mystical ladder – the spiritual dimension of religion. For example, Shabasteri writes that "Religious law (*sharīʿat*) is the skin, the kernel-seed is truth (*haqīqat*); mystical way is between them."[90]

Illustrative of the peculiarity of religious ritual is Muhammad Jawvani's *Manahej Al-Sayfiyyah*, where strict obedience to tradition is enjoined on believers, extending even to personal cleansing rituals, as, for instance, the placement of feet and hands – the believer must first place his left foot forward and wash the right hand with the left.[91] The body of this text, however, goes beyond prescriptive rituals in its interpretation of their mystical meaning. For example, while the devotee thanks "the God of the world," he should understand that he is appreciating the limitless grace of God as a spectator of creatures who are dependent on with respect to their realization, persistence, and relative place in the order of universe.[92]

It is beyond the scope of this investigation to ascertain whether or not the use of mystical symbolism follows a fixed pattern. We can, however, delineate this pattern with a few examples. In another study we have given account of the mystical use of the light motif in the sufic poetry of Rumi.[93] In addition to light, we note that the bird in flight is used as a vehicle to express the relationship of both the soul and the mediator figure in the works of Nasafi, Rumi, Avicenna, and Attar. An investigation of the symbolism of the mediator figure encapsulates the variation between theistic and monistic mysticisms.

The significance of the mediator figure has been recognized in sufism by many investigators. Staal writes[94]

> In Islam it is the foundation of the *silsila* or "spiritual lineage." The teacher (*murshid, shaikh, pir*), does not merely initiate the novice (*murid, ganduz*) but guides him throughout. He is the real *Ka'ba* to which the pupils turn.

The mediator figure has many facets. Suhrawardi lists two names for the sage. What is called by the religious believer (*sharic*), the holy intelligence [*Ruh al-Qudus*, the holy Ghost] is designated by philosophers as the active intelligence [*al-aql-i al-faccāl*]; Suhrawardi, in fact, calls it a light, which is related to us as a father [*pidar*].[95] Attar states in *Mantiq al-Tair* that in the last phase the thirty birds (souls in a mystical journey) recognized that they, themselves (*khīsh*) were the *Simurq* (which is the Griffen).[96] What is the philosophical implication of this doctrine? Very simply this: man is identical with the prophet and with God. — Logically this is an anti monotheistic creed, as no orthodox Muslim would ever identify himself as Muhammad, or as God. Analogously a Jew can not say, "I am Moses, or God"; nor can the Christian identify himself as God-Christ.

VI. Concluding Remarks; the basis of our topology

In sum, we note that both conceptual analysis and textual examinations warrant that we postulate the two primary typologies of mysticism, with the following qualifications. (i) For the religious mystics God transcends the world ontologically, while for the monistic mystic man's last phase of self-realization is a phenomenological incarnation of a God-like perspective. (ii) For the theistic mystic the way of salvation leads only to a harmony with the religious law following a prophet who is chosen by God (in Islam and Judaism), or is the Son of God in Christianity. As Margaret Smith notes, this variation of Islamic mysticism is akin to its Christian sources.[97]

> When we come to consider the origins of those mystical doctrines found in Orthodox Islam, it seems evident that they must, to a considerable extent, be derived from similar doctrines in Christianity . . .

In monistic mysticism, however, this mediator figure is the image of God within us, identified as the hidden self. Finally, (iii) whereas theists may give mystical meaning to religious rituals and icons, monistic mystics regard religious symbolism, and ritual as a family of archetypal representations illustrating archetypal truth which finds its parallels in philosophy and mysticism.

Notes

1 Aldous Huxley, *The Doors of Perception*, (N.Y.: Harper and Row, 1954), p. 73. Huxley's major point in the text is that immediate existential perception is the most significant window to the soul-world. Zaehner, R. C., *Mysticism, Sacred and Profane*, (London, Oxford and New York: Oxford University Press, 1957). (hereafter *MSP*) focuses only on Huxley's unwarranted remarks about drugs. He notes: "It should be said at the outset that this book owes its genesis to Mr. Aldous Huxley" (p. ix.). There is no question that Zaehner, being a scholar of oriental languages, uses his knowledge to refute Huxley's interesting insights about a human experience which has no basis in world mysticism.

2 R. C. Zaehner, *MSP*, p. 108. Zaehner in fact states that there are two kinds of "nature mysticism:" (a) the pan-en-henic, which is the sense of union with all creation, and (b) the psychological phenomenon of integration, which according to Jung, is a synthesis of the female/male as well as the evil/good dimensions of the self (p. 118). But obviously the two are interrelated. (a) is merely the ontological dimension of nature mysticism, while '(b)' depicts the specific process within which "nature mysticism" is achieved.

3 R. C. Zaehner, *MSP*, p. 128. Here, according to Zaehner, the soul is purified, like a new-born child.

4 J. M. Rist, *Plotinus: The Road to Reality*, (Cambridge: Cambridge University Press, 1967), p. 214.

5 Cf W. R. Inge, *Christian Mysticism*, (New York: Meridian, 1956), pp. 302-332. Here Inge attempts to clarify the notion of "nature mysticism." He classifies St. Francis of Assisi as a nature mystic, who is supposedly marked by a "tender reverence for nature." According to Inge all Platonists, including Plotinus, adhere to this view. Cf R. Otto, *Mysticism, East and West: A Comparative Analysis of the Nature of Mysticism*, (New York, 1926), Part A Chap. vii. Here Otto distinguishes between "soul-mysticism," and "God-mysticism;" the former corresponds to Zaehner's view of the monist who attempts to incarnate God within his soul, while the latter corresponds to a "theistic" view of a transcendent God. Cf T. H. Hughes, *The Philosophical Basis of Mysticism*, (Edinburgh: T. & T. Clark, 1937). Hughes distinguishes between Nature, on the one hand, and philosophical and religious types of mysticisms, on the other, identifying the last type as the primary one. He asserts that the mark of "philosophical mysticism" is "the transcendence of God over the world" (p. 16). His account would place most of the philosophical mystics of Islam, like Avicenna, outside the category of philosophical mysticism. Cf. W. Kingsland, *Rational Mysticism*, (London: Allen and Unwin, 1924). Kingsland considers religion primarily in terms of "a spiritual quality of life" (p. 234).

For him it is distinguished from mysticism by many factors, e.g., its consciousness of a "duality" versus the "identity" of the mystic's vision. (p. 259). This account would leave the theistic mystics out of the body of mysticism, since their adherence to "isolation" would make them religious and not mystical.

6 Cf. W. T. Stace, *Mysticism and Philosophy*, (London: Macmillan, 1960). Stace postulates two kinds of mysticisms: extroverted and introverted and holds that "nature mysticism" is a useless classification (p. 80). In addition, Stace, makes a distinction between a mystical experience and an interpretation of that experience (see p. 35). He attacks Zaehner on holding that Christians and Hindus are different; Stace shows that the Christian and the Hindu mystics have the same primary mystical experience but differ on the interpretations of their beliefs. There is a problem however with Stace's own classification; it cannot be applied to any theistic type of mysticism. When he examines the relation between religion and mysticism, he focuses on organized religions and comes to the conclusion that mysticism may exist apart from monotheistic religions. Cf. F. Staal, *Exploring Mysticism*, (California, 1975). Staal accuses Zaehner of being "the best contemporary example of the dogmatic approach to the study of mysticism . . . " (p. 67). Staal points out that Zaehner's preference for "theistic" mysticism makes him read monist texts inaccurately. Staal also objects to Zaehner's positions on drugs that they effect our body and not the mind, and further objects that the effects on us are beyond our control. Staal does not refer anywhere to Zaehner's observation that, unlike mysticism drugs cause a bad experience (trip).

7 Stace's major distinction between "extroverted" and "introverted" could be subsumed under the devotional and the speculative dimensions and types mentioned by Zaehner. His main objection to Zaehner's work lies in criticizing him for not adhering to the difference between a mystic's experience and an interpretation of that experience (see W. T. Stace, *Mysticism and Philosophy*, p. 37). If Stace were correct in this objection his criticism would not be applicable to the basis of Zaehner's typology but to its refinement. Staal, in *Exploring Mysticism*, accuses Zaehner of being a religious dogmatist who misreads the texts in order to condemn non-religious mystics (see pp. 67-69). Moreover, he objects to Zaehner's position on the topic of drugs and mysticism (see pp. 184-86). None of these objections is directed towards Zaehner's theoretical constructs of types of mysticism. N. Smart in, *Mysticism and Philosophical Analysis*, S. Katz ed. (NY: Oxford, 1978) supports Staal's criticism of Zaehner (see pp. 13-15). His objection, however, is not relevant to Zaehner's theoretical point and focuses only on Zaehner's Christian perspective, which is recognized by Zaehner himself.

8 See "Sufism, Neoplatonism and Zaehner's Theistic Theory of Mysticism," in P. Morewedge, *Islamic Philosophy and Mysticism* (Delmar, 1981).

9 Cf. P. Morewedge, "A Philosophical Interpretation of Rumi's Mystical Poetry: Light, the Mediator, and the Way," in *The Scholar and the Saint*, P. J. Chelkowski, ed. (New York, 1975), pp. 186-216. The mediator figure in religion links the finite man to the infinite God, e.g., "logos," or Christ.

10 *Avicenna et le Recit Visionaire*, ed. H. Corbin, (Tehran, 1952), pp. 6-7.

11 W. T. Stace, *Philosophy and Mysticism*, p. 79.

12 Inge, *Christian Mysticism*, p. 28.

13 C. F. E. Spurgeon, *Mysticism in English Literature*, (Cambridge, 1922). She notes that the most important mark of mysticism consists of " . . . an attitude of mind founded upon an intuitive or experienced conviction of unity, of oneness, of alikeness in all things" (see p. 3). Underhill takes the object of the mystic's quest as a union with the absolute; cf. *Mysticism*, (New York, 1970), p. 70. A. Schimmel notes that *unio mystica* is the goal of all mystical quest (p. 4). However, according to her this union (*al-waḥdat al-wujud*) is not a substantial unity, but a vision of the mystic (Cf. A. Schimmel, *Mystical Dimensions of Islam*, (Chapel Hill, 1975), p. 367.

14 *The Mathnawi*, ed. Kh. Mirkhani (Tehran, 1337 A.H.) p. 2. The Arabic-Persian word '*aṣl*' has the same meaning as the Greek '*arche*,' which means the archetypal or proto-type dimension of an entity, or its cause. The '*aṣl*' of a person signifies his efficient as well as his final cause, which is the One of those mystics.

15 See *Islamic Philosophy and Mysticism*, ed. P. Morewedge (Albany, 1980), and *Neoplatonism and Islamic Thoughts*, ed. P. Morewedge (Albany: SUNY Press, forthcoming).

16 Ibn Sina, *Al-Shifā' Al-Ilāhīyyāt (La Metaphysique)*, ed. G. C. Anawati, M. Y. Moussa, S. Dunya, and S. Zaid, 2 vols. (Cairo, 1960), vol. I, pp. 112, 93; *The Metaphysical of Avicenna (Ibn Sinā)*, ed. P. Morewedge, pp. 30-33.

17 (*Dānish Nāma*), Chap. 3.

18 Proclus, *The Elements of Theology*, ed., tr. R. R. Dodd (London, 1953), p. 101.

19 *Danish Nama*, p. 100 and Ibn Sina, *Al-Ishārāt wa-l-Tanbīhāt*, ed. S. Dunya (Cairo, 1960), vol. III, p. 279.

20 *Danish Nama*, chap. 12, *Al-Shifa'*, bk. 5 Chap. 1-2.

21 Avicenna states "It becomes evident, then, that the idea of universality, for the very reason that it is a universal, is not an actual existent except in thought . . . Its reality, however, both exists in thought and is external to thought, for the reality of humanity and of blackness both exist in thought and is external to thought in things." *Danish Nama*, p. 53. Also, see Marmura, M. "Avicenna's Chapter on the Universals in the Isagoge of his Shifa'," in *Islam: Past Influence and Present Challenge*, ed. A. Welch and P. Cachia (Edinburgh, 1979), pp. 34-56.

22 See J. Finnegan, "Avicenna's Refutation of Porphyrius," *Avicenna Commemoration Volume*, (Calcutta, 1956), pp. 187-204.

23 See Galston, M., "Realism and Idealism in Avicenna's Political Philosophy," *Review of Politics XLI* (1979), 561-577. Also, *Medieval Political Philosophy*, eds. Lerner, R. and Mahdi, M. (New York, 1963).

24 E. Moody, *The Logic of William of Ockham*, (New York, 1965), p. 46.

25 According to Avicenna, being "*hastī*" applies to any contingency (e.g. the prophet Abraham), a necessity (i.e. The Necessary Existent), or even an impossibility (e.g.

"a round square"). Only caused contingencies and the Necessary being are existents. So, each existent is a being, but not every being is an existent.

26 See Ibn Sina, *Dānish Nāme-i alāi (Ilāhiyyāt)* (Tehran, 1371 A. H.), chapter 3. see our translation of this text, P. Morewedge, *The Metaphysical of Avicenna (Ibn Sīnā)* (New York and London, 1973).

27 E. Gilson, *Being and Some Philosophers* (Toronto, 1952) p. 3.

28 R. Otto, *Mysticism, East and West*, p. 22.

29 Al-Ghazali, *Mishkat al-Anwar*, trans. W. H. Gairdner (Lahore, 1952), p. 60.

30 R. C. Zaehner, *MSP*, p. 33.

31 Ibid., p. 32.

32 Obviously Hallaj knew that from a physical perspective he could not identify himself with *al-Ḥaqq* (reality, truth, God). So, his identification with *al-Ḥaqq*, is meaningful only in a phenomenological or a symbolic context which belongs to "extroverted mysticism."

33 See P. Morewedge, "The Logic of Emanationism and Sufism in Ibn Sina, Part I," *Journal of the American Oriental Society*, 91, No. 4 (October-December 1971), pp. 467-476, and Part II, 92, No. 1 (January-March 1972), pp. 1-8.

34 J. J. Hobben, "Avicenna and Mysticism," in *Avicenna Commemoration Volume*, (Calcutta, 1956), p. 216.

35 E. Gilson, *Being and Some Philosophers* (Toronto, 1952), p. 58.

36 *The Qur'an* surah xi, 6-8.

37 M. Fakhry, *Islamic Occasionalism* (London, 1958). Also Ghazali explicitly asserts the creation doctrine in *Tahafut al-Falāsifah*, tr. S. A. Kamali (Lahore, 1963), p. 185.

38 For a detailed treatment of Jami's position as an example of the Muslim's preoccupation with the doctrine of *al-waḥdat al-wujūd*, see Heer, "Al-Jami'e Treatise on Existence," in *Islamic Philosophical Theology*, ed. P. Morewedge (Albany, 1979), pp. 223-256.

39 Jami, *Mathnawi*, (Tehran, n.d.), p. 22.

40 *Divān-i Kāmil-i Jāmi*, H. Rida, ed. (Tehran, 1962), p. 14.

41 M. Damghani in his introduction to Aziz a-Din Nasafi's *Kashf al-Haqayiq* (Tehran, 1344 A. H.), stated that Nasafi is a follower of Ibn Arabi (p. 14). We do not observe much similarity between them; in the context of the essence-existence controveresy, Ibn Arabi's position emphasizes existence, whereas Nasafi's views uphold the priority of existence. See, our "Greek Sources of Some Near Eastern

Philosophies of Being and Existence," in *Philosophies of Existence, Ancient and Medieval*, P. Morewedge, ed. (New York, 1982), pp. 285-336.

42 Cf. Aristotle, *Physics* 192 a22-34, and *Metaphysics* 1029 a20-26, and 1042 a27-28. Our quotations from the works of Aristotle are taken from *The Works of Aristotle*, ed. W. D. Ross, (Oxford, 1908-52).

43 *Kashf al-Haqayiq*, pp. 30-31.

44 The problem may be illustrated both syntactically and phenomenologically. Syntactically, a species is defined by its genus and differentia. So, a transcendental term has no definition. Phenomenologically, a transcendental condition of experience such as temporality cannot be experienced as an object; instead, it is presupposed in every experience.

45 Ibid., p. 31.

46 Ibid., pp. 148-150.

47 Nasafi, *Kashf al-Haqayiq*, p. 150.

48 Ibid., p. 150.

49 Ibid., p. 156.

50 L. Wittgenstein, *Tractatus Logico-Philosophicus*, D. F. Pears and B. F. McGinnes, eds. (London, 1961), p. 117, 5.641.

51 Augustine, *Soliloquies* 2.7.1, in *Basic Writings of Saint Augustine* I, ed. W. J. Oates (New York, 1948), p. 262.

52 Al-Ghazali, *Kimiya-iSa'dat*, (Tehran, 1319 A. H.), vol. I, p. 9.

53 *Varieties of Religious Experiences*, p. 393.

54 Ibid., p. 406.

55 M. Smith, *Studies in Early Mysticism in the Near and Middle East* (London, 1939), p. 253.

56 Ibid., p. 10.

57 Attar, *Mantiq at-Tair* (Tehran, 1319 A. H.), poem 4289.

58 Ibid., poem 4239.

59 Attar, *Mantiq at-Tair*, poem 2364. Attar notes that we are born in order to die. All quotations of Rumi's work are from our own translation of the Persian texts *Shams* refers to *Divan-i Shams*, B. Furuzanfar ed. (Tehran, 1336-46), 10 vols., and *Mathnawi* designates R. A. Nicholason's edition and translation of *Mathnawi* (London, 1925-40), 6 vols. Cf. *Mathnawi* VIII, 519, p. 88. Rumi states that "When I die, do not say that he died. Instead, by death he became alive and The Friend took him"

(Mathnawi VIII, 519, p. 88). The Friend, here refers to the messenger who takes the mystic to the Ultimate Being.

60 Attar, poem 4159; See Rumi, *Shams* IV, 2653 for the bird analogy, and Shams 6180 for the allegory of life drowning in the baptism of itself in the eternal ocean.

61 In the relation of mystical union, the two terms in the field of relation, i.e., "man" and "the ultimate being," are modified without being destroyed. Since the only substantial changes are generation and destruction, the Aristotelian substance-event language is not a suitable ontology for the idea of "mystical union."

62 Cf. *Danish Name*, chapters 24-26.

63 *Immanuel Kant's Critique of Pure Reason*, trans. N. K. Smith (London, 1953), p. 155.

64 Wittgenstein, *Tractatus Logico-Philosophicus*, p. 117.

65 Inge, *Christian Mysticism*, p. 98.

66 *Kimia-yi Sa'adat*, p. 9.

67 Ibid., p. 33.

68 *Danish Name*, chapter 37.

69 M. Shabasteri, *Gulshan-i Raz*, Nurbakhsh ed. (Tehran, 2535 S. H.); cf. poem 126, p. 31.

70 Ibid., poem 117, p. 31.

71 Shabasteri, p. 32.

72 See C. D. Broad, "Leibniz' Predicate-in-Notion Principle and Some of Its Alleged Consequences," *Theoria*, v. 15, March 1949, pp. 54-70. According to Broad, Leibniz' model implies that each predicate is either a truth of reason or a truth of fact which follows from the principle of sufficient reason. Consequently, the actual state of the world is only categorically contingent but hypothetically a necessary. This view is very close to the position of Avicenna. See H. A. Davidson, "Avicenna's Proof of the Existence of God as a Necessary Being," in *Islamic Philosophical Theology*, P. Morewedge, ed. (Albany, 1979), pp. 165-187.

73 Inge states, "The theory that man is a macrocosm . . . is a favorite doctrine of the mystics . . . It follows that the Incarnation, the central fact of human history, must have its analogue in the experience of the individual. We shall find that this doctrine of the birth of an infinite Christ in the soul is of immense importance in the systems of Eckhart, Tauler, and our Cambridge Platonist" (*Christian Mysticism*, p. 35).

74 Shabasteri, pp. 12-13.

75 *Shams* III, p. 47, 12261.

76 *Shams* III, 12491, p. 59; *Shams* III, 11609, p. 28.

77 *Mathnawi*, poems 2835-7.

78 Shabasteri, p. 13, poems 42-43.

79 H. Bergson states, "Duration is the continuous progress of the past which gnows into the future which swells as it advances." *Creative Evolution* (New York, 1944), p. 7. Thus the immediate human experience, marked by the duration of a temporal passage is the ultimate primitive term of the metaphysical system of the process of self-realization in sufism. The notion of time in this view is in harmony with the Platonic imagery in The Timeaus that "time," is "a moving image of eternity" (37d5). But this passage is not disconnected from the eternal laws. As A. E. Taylor comments, "The sensible world is a thing of passage, but it never passes away; its passage fills all time, and, of course, the formal laws of its structure remains the same through out." *A Commentary on Plato's Timeaus* (Oxford, 1962), p. 187.

80 Inge, *Christian Mysticism*, p. 29.

81 Ibid., p. 30.

82 See P. Morewedge, "A Philosophical Interpretation of Rumi's Mystical Poetry." We have shown how in Rumi a set of related light-symbols (Sun, fire, heat, mirror) are used to depict mystical themes.

83 C. F. E. Spurgeon, *Mysticism in English Literature*, pp. 8-9.

84 See H. A. Wolfson, "Avicenna, Al-Ghazali, and Averroes on Divine Attributes," in *Homenaje a Millas-Vallicrosa* (Barcelona, 1956), pp. 545-571.

85 The argument in the language of medieval Islamic theology is presented as follows. Since God is finite, It has no limit; thus, It cannot be a body (with a surface as its limit). So, God cannot be experienced by the senses. Moreover, since God is not-finite, the actual infinite cannot be conceived. No immediate experience of God is possible. Thus, all references to It must be allegorical.

86 See R. Carnap, *Introduction to Symbolic Logic and Its Application*, trans. W. H. Meyer and J. Wilkinson (New York, 1958). This text is a very useful example of how Carnap attempts to show that formal systems have isomorphic structures, e.g., a set of signs and three distinct types of rules. In a similar way, when spirituality is introduced into social games or communications, like religion and mysticism, similar archetypal patterns appear. For example, for the Hebrews the figure is the body of the chosen people, for the Christians Christ, for the Muslims the Qur'an, for the Communists the communist party, for the patient the therapist, and for the mystic the sage. The functional rules of all of these figures are identical, as they provide the link between a person and the ultimate being which promises salvation.

87 A. Nasafi, *Al-Insan al-Kamil*, M. Mole ed. (Tehran, 1983), pp. 4-5.

88 Note that Averroes is very clever in placing al-Ghazali against the sufis, as follows: "Ghazali aserts in this book [*Tahafut al-Falasafi*] that no Muslim believes in a purely spiritual resurrection and in another book [*Balance of Action*] that the sufis hold it" (Averroes' *Tahafut al-Tahafut*, tr. S. Van Den Bergh (London, 1969), v. I, p. 362). Zaehner accuses al-Ghazali of holding a monistic position in *Mishkat al-Anwar* (See *Mysticism, Sacred and Profane*, p. 159).

89 Cf. *Mysticism, Sacred and Profane*, p. 106.

90 *MSP*, p. 106.

91 M. E. Joveini, *Manahej Al-Sayfiyyah*, N. M. Heravi, ed. (Tehran, 1363 A. H.), p. 53.

92 Ibid., p. 57.

93 P. Morewedge, "A Philosophical Interpretation of Rumi's Mystical Poetry."

94 Staal, *Exploring Mysticism*, p. 144.

95 Suhrawardi, *Haikel al-Nur*, in *Oeuvres Philosophiques et Mystiques*, S. H. Nasr, ed. (Tehran, 1977), s. v. 3, pp. 96-97.

96 *Mantiq al-Tair*, p. 235.

97 *Early Mysticism in the Near and Middle East*, p. 149.

Ethical Standards and the Vision of Oneness: The Case of Ibn al-'Arabî

William C. Chittick

Those spiritual masters whom the Sufi tradition has looked back upon with reverence have considered the Shari'a—the revealed Law—as the foundation of the path to God. But many of these same masters have been criticized by Muslim jurists and theologians for their anti-nomian views. In the case of Ibn al-'Arabî (d. 1240)—the "Greatest Master"—and his followers, these criticisms often take the form of attacking the doctrine of the "Oneness of Being" (*wahdat al-wujûd*).[1] According to critics, those who uphold this doctrine fail to distinguish between good and evil and claim to stand beyond the revealed Law. A contemporary scholar expresses these criticisms succinctly when he says in regard to Ibn al-'Arabî, "A thoroughly monistic system, no matter how pious and conscientious it may claim to be, can not, by its very nature, take seriously the objective validity of moral standards."[2]

Why then does Ibn al-'Arabî—along with many other Sufis who predate and follow him and to whom a "thoroughly monistic system" might easily be attributed—insist on the necessity of the Shari'a? Why, in fact, is a "mysticism" founded upon the practice of the revealed Law normative for all Islamic history, whatever the deviations which on occasion have occurred? There are no doubt many possible approaches to answering these questions. I look at Ibn al-'Arabî's teachings on ethics and suggest one of these approaches.

Ethics in Ibn al-'Arabî

However we define ethical and moral standards, little of what Ibn al-'Arabî has to say in his enormous corpus of writings is unrelated to them. It is impossible in a short paper even to begin to sort out the principles or details of Ibn al-'Arabî's ethical views. Instead I will only attempt to show what he understands by the single term *akhlâq*, the word normally used for "ethics" in the philosophical vocabulary, and then suggest the manner in which he finds a grounding for *akhlâq* in an ontology that can fairly be described by the term "Oneness of

Being." The actualization of *akhlâq* within the context of this ontology will then be seen to depend upon the observance of the Law.

Though Ibn al-'Arabî's analysis of ethics shares many common characteristics with discussions of ethics by Muslim philosophers (who based their writings largely on works translated from Greek), he finds his basic point of reference and the ultimate source for most of his key terminology in the Koran and the sayings of the Prophet Muhammad (the Hadith). In discussing almost anything at all, Ibn al-'Arabî displays a constant concern to go back to the thing's "root" (*asl*) or "reality" (*haqîqa*), which is the divine attribute or name from which it comes forth and which is mentioned in the Koran and the Hadith. He frequently reminds his readers that these attributes or names are not concrete things, but providential designations for the relationships which exist between the Divine Reality and the things of the "cosmos" (*al-'âlam*, which is defined as "everything other than God"). The divine names provide human beings with knowledge of their own connection with the absolute and immutable ground of everything that exists. Without the names—or without the revelation that provides them—people would wander in a sea of uncertainties and relativities.

The Arabic word *akhlâq* or "ethics" is the plural of *khuluq*, which means both "character" and "character trait". It is used twice in the Koran (in the singular) and repeatedly in the Hadith (often in the plural). One Koranic instance was especially suggestive for later commentators. Addressing the Prophet, God says, "Surely you have a *khuluq azîm*" (68:4). English translators have rendered these two words with expressions such as "mighty morality," "sublime nature," "tremendous nature," "sublime morals," "sublime morality," and "tremendous character." Such translations of the term *khuluq* attempt to bring out its moral and ethical connotations on the one hand and its ontological roots on the other, for the word is separated only by pronunciation (not in the way it is written) from the term *khalq*, which means "creation". For Ibn al-'Arabî, the term's ontological side is fundamental. The Prophet's "tremendous character" has to do not only with his inward goodness and the way this was reflected in his dealings with people, but also with the degree to which he had realized the potentialities of his own primordial nature, rooted in the Being of God.

The Origin of Noble Character Traits

In the general Islamic view, made completely explicit by Ibn al-'Arabî, noble character traits (*makârim al-akhlâq*) belong truly to God and only metaphorically to human beings. Everything good comes from God, and moral traits such as generosity, justice, patience, forbearance, etc., are no exception. The Koran confirms this point by the names it ascribes to God: Generous, Just, Patient, Pardoner, Clement, Thankful, and so on. Hence, as Ibn al-'Arabî declares,

> God is more worthy of noble attributes than the servant. Or rather, they belong to Him in reality and to the servant only by His grace in bestowing them. (II 617.26)[3]

Ibn al-'Arabî often discusses Koranic verses or hadiths which mention God's noble qualities. He concludes that

> God never praises a noble character trait unless He Himself is more worthy of observing it toward His creatures, and He never blames a base character trait unless the Divine Side is further away from it [than are human beings]. (I 285.8)

These "character traits of God" (*akhlâq Allâh*) are the same as "God's names" (*asmâ' Allâh*), and Ibn al-'Arabî uses the two expressions interchangeably. This follows naturally from the fact that so many of the divine names revealed in the Koran are also the names of noble human traits. Moreover, how can a Muslim answer the question, "What are God's character traits?", if not by listing the "most beautiful names" (*al-asmâ' al-ḥusnâ*) mentioned in the Koran?

Ibn al-'Arabî often employs the terminology of the Peripatetic philosophers like Avicenna in referring to God. Hence God is the Necessary Being (*wâjib al-wujûd*), while everything else that may be said to exist is a possible thing (*mumkin*). In Ibn al-'Arabî's way of thinking, *wujûd* (Being, existence, or the fact of being found)[4] belongs in the final analysis only to God. At best the possible thing can be said to have received *wujûd* on loan. But what is important in the present context is that Ibn al-'Arabî prefers the religious to the philosophical terminology in explaining the nature of God's *wujûd*. The answer to the question, "What are the attributes of *wujûd*?", is given by listing the names of God. Generosity, justice, forbearance, pardon, gratitude and all the other divine character traits are intrinsic to *wujûd*. The human task is not to devise some ethical system or to debate about the meaning of morality, but simply "to be, to exist, to be found." Through the purification of one's *wujûd*, or through allowing the divine Sun to shine through the limitations of the human individuality, a person brings about the manifestation of the noble character traits as a matter of course. They are already present in the nature of *wujûd* itself.

The Divine Form

Few teachings are as fundamental to Sufi anthropology as the idea that God created the human being in His own image or "form" (*ṣûra*). Ibn al-'Arabî pays close attention to the fact that in the prophetic saying, "God created Adam upon His own form," the name Allah is employed, not, for example, Creator or Forgiver or Vengeful. The name Allah is known as the "all-comprehensive name" (*al-ism al-jâmi'*), since it comprises within itself the meaning of all God's names and is referred to by all of them. One says, "Allah is Merciful, Allah is Lord, Allah is Creator," and so on. Hence God created Adam in the form of Allah, the universal name that embraces all names, not in the form of some specific name such as Knowing, Willing, Powerful, Merciful, Vengeful, or Forgiving.[5]

Not only the human being but also the whole cosmos was created in the form of Allah and therefore in the form of all the names. In Ibn al-'Arabî's terms, both the human being and the cosmos are loci of manifestation (*maẓhar, majlâ*) for all the divine names, since within them are found the traces (*âthâr*) and properties (*aḥkâm*) of God's life, knowledge, desire, power, speech, generosity, justice, and so on. But in the cosmos these traces and properties are found divided up among the things of the universe in a "differentiated" manner (*tafṣîl*), while in the human being they are found in their entirety in each individual in an "undifferentiated" way (*ijmâl*).

Since human beings, like the universe, display the properties of God's names, every name that is attributed to God can also, in some respect, be attributed to humans. It is this peculiar characteristic that sets them apart from all other individual creatures and makes them capable, for example, of carrying the "Trust" (mentioned in Koran 33:72) and serving as God's "vicegerents" or representatives (*khalîfa*) in the earth. Sufis see a direct Koranic reference to man's being made in God's form in the verse, "God taught Adam the names, all of them" (2:31), a verse that comes immediately after the statement that God had decided to place Adam in the earth as His vicegerent.

> The human being is the locus of manifestation for the divine names and comprehends the realities of the whole cosmos, whether angels, celestial spheres, corporeal bodies, nature, inanimate objects, or animals—all this in addition to the knowledge of the divine names that pertains exclusively to him. (I 125.29)
>
> The human being, who is "Adam," consists of the sum total (*majmû'*) of the cosmos . . . . God arranged in Adam everything outside of and other than Himself . . . . All the divine names are related to him. Nothing of them eludes him. Hence Adam appeared in the form of the name "Allah," since it is this name which comprises all the divine names. (II 124.1)

Human Perfection

The divine names are identical with the divine character traits, while human beings were created in the form of God, comprehending all the names. Hence human beings were created with all God's character traits. However, nobility of character is in fact not easy to come by. Many human beings are not even aware that it exists, not to speak of possessing it themselves. When we pay closer attention to what Ibn al-'Arabî means when he says that human beings are made in the divine form, we realize that he draws a clear dividing line between what is potential in human beings and what is actual.

It is well known that one of Ibn al-'Arabî's favorite topics is "perfect man" (*al-insân al-kâmil*), a term which denotes a complex metaphysical, cosmological, and spiritual reality. Without touching upon various cosmological dimensions of this doctrine, we can say that perfect man represents the ideal human situation which all people should strive to achieve. Only those who have attained to perfection may truly be said to be created in God's form, since only they have actualized the potentialities latent in the primordial human nature (*fiṭra*).

Ibn al-'Arabî is fully aware that perfection is a relative affair, and he devotes a great deal of attention to the various kinds, levels, and degrees of perfection. Fully actualized perfection — absolute perfection (*al-kamâl al-muṭlaq*) — is found only in the Divine Being, while human perfection always accepts increase, whether in this world or the next, since the finite can never attain to the infinite. Hence, even in the case of the most perfect of perfect men, there is no question of a static situation.

> The "perfect" is that which does not accept any increase. But we increase in knowledge in this world and in the next, so we are linked to imperfection. Hence our perfection depends upon the existence of imperfection within it. Hence we have a single perfection, but God has two perfections, an absolute perfection, and another perfection concerning which He says, "[And We shall assuredly try you] until We know [which of you struggle and are steadfast]"[6] (Koran 47:31). Our copy (*nuskha* [i.e, of God's perfection]) is from the perfection of "until We know", not from the absolute perfection. (II 543.13)

Most people live at the level of what Ibn al-'Arabî refers to as "animal men" (*al-insân al-ḥayawân*), since they have not gone beyond the elementary possibilities of the human state.

> Within the human being are gathered the potentialities (*quwâ*) of the whole cosmos and of the divine names in their perfection. Hence there is no existent more perfect than perfect man. But if a person does not reach perfection in this

world, he is a rational animal, a part of the [divine] form, nothing more. He does not reach the degree of the human being. On the contrary, his relationship to the human being is the relationship of a corpse to a human being; the corpse is a human being in shape, not in reality, since in fact it lacks all potentialities. So also is the one who has not reached perfection. The human being's perfection is through the vicegerency, so anyone who does not possess the merit of all the divine names is not a vicegerent. (II 441.3)

Only those human beings who have attained to perfection can truly be said to be created in God's form. Within them the divine names—or the all-comprehensive name Allah—display their full range of properties to the extent possible on the ontological level envisaged. Since the names represent all the possibilities of deployment and manifestation possessed by that nondelimited *wujûd* which is God, they display *wujûd* in its full splendor. The specifically human qualities can be explained by this manifestation of all the names. In the microcosm, the combination of all ontological potentialities in a single individual means that human beings can develop in any possible mode of existence, whether this mode be perceived as "good" or "evil."

An example may serve to make this infinite potentiality of human beings clear: God knows all things, as the Koran often reminds us. Made in God's form, the human being has the potentiality to know all things. Naturally there are fundamental differences between the divine knowledge and human knowledge, but to the extent that the human being's knowledge is not hindered by the limitations of contingent existence, it is infinitely expandable. The whole of human history is there to prove this statement. Anything known by any human being at any time and place is, in principle, knowable by every human being, given a healthy mind and various other external conditions. Human beings forget, grow old, and die, but it is a matter of common experience that knowledge accepts only accidental bounds; the basic act of knowing accepts no principial limits. The underlying ethos and goals of modern science clearly express the basic human intuition that everything can be known.

In a given human being, knowledge will be "perfected" to the extent that everything knowable comes to be known; in the context of Islam, what is knowable is fundamentally God, His names, His angels, His scriptures, His prophets, and the various branches and ramifications of this metacosmic and cosmic knowledge. Real knowledge is achieved when God is known and when the things are known with a view toward their roots in God. To the extent such knowledge is actualized, it will, as a matter of course, include knowledge of the nature of the cosmos and its contents, since all these are "signs" (*âyât*) of God. Ibn al-'Arabî and other Sufis would consider what passes for knowledge in modern science as a veil over real knowledge, since it has not been integrated into a wider view tying phenomena back to their roots in absolute *wujûd*. It is concerned fundamentally with the peripheral matters of existence, not the essential.

In most people, knowledge is not brought to "perfection." At most one or two possibilities or modes of knowing are developed to some degree. In the majority of cases knowledge remains largely a virtuality, even by contemporary standards.   Formal education is not completed, the demands of social status prove more attractive than learning, the need to make a comfortable livelihood overcomes intellectual potential, and so on. But from Ibn al-'Arabî's viewpoint, even those who develop various possibilities of knowing usually do so in a wrong-headed manner. Instead of devoting themselves to the roots of things in God, they become engrossed with the branches; instead of searching out the First Cause, they dissect secondary causes to no ultimate end; instead of seeing inward meanings (*ma'ânî*), they fix their gaze on outward forms (*suwar*). The result is the tremendous proliferation of facts that we see before us; the human potential for unlimited knowledge is being actualized, but in a bewildering variety of peripheral modes.

One could undertake a similar analysis of any of the divine names. God is Desiring, Powerful, Speaking, Hearing, Seeing, Forgiving, Vengeful, Grateful, and so on. In the Sufi view, a perfect human being will have actualized all the divine names to the extent possible and in the appropriate manner, given certain individual limitations having to do with the corporeal body, time, place, environment, and so on—though inwardly, in the spiritual realm, these limitations count for less than they do outwardly. To use a common analogy, the light of the sun—which represents the inward world of the Divine Spirit—is one, but the courtyards of the bodily houses display the light in different shapes.

The actualization of the divine names, it was just said, must take place in the "appropriate" manner. Another analogy can make clear the basic problem, which is intimately connected with ethics: The goal of human life is to actualize pure white light by putting together an indefinite number of colored lights of varying intensities. How do we prevent ourselves from ending up with too much red, too much green, too much blue? What is the measure by which we can gauge the different colors and put them together harmoniously?

When we look at the divine names, we see that many of them are mutually contradictory. God is the Forgiver and the Avenger, the Merciful and the Wrathful, the Life-giver and the Slayer, the Abaser and the Exalter. Given that human beings must actualize these names, how can the opposite qualities be harmonized in a single personality? According to Ibn al-'Arabî, the divine names reach an equilibrium in the highest stage of human perfection such that perfect man is uncolored and nondelimited by any name whatsoever, like the Divine Essence itself.[7]

> In the case of perfect man, the names hinder one another, and this mutual hindrance leads to their leaving no trace in him who has this attribute. Hence he remains purified of all traces just like the Absolute Essence, which is not delimited by names and attributes. (II 615.23)

Much of Ibn al-'Arabî's writing has to do with the manner in which human beings can become full and harmonious loci of manifestation for all the divine names and thereby possess in the appropriate manner all the divine character traits. In every case his advice is fundamentally the same: In order to attain the full perfection of their character traits, human beings must return to the right balance among the qualities as found in the divine names, and this balance is set down in the Koran and the Hadith. In other words, the Shari'a or revealed Law provides the necessary practical guidelines for establishing equilibrium among the divine names and character traits. Having established this equilibrium, human beings will have actualized the form in which they were created.

The process of actualizing the divine form is described in many ways, but in the present context, I wish to discuss a single term, since, among all the terms that could be mentioned, it demonstrates most clearly the connection between the divine names and human character traits. The term is *takhalluq*, the fifth verbal noun from the root *kh.l.q.*, from which we have *akhlâq*, "character traits." *Takhalluq* means "to assume (i.e., the character traits of)". The most famous usage of the word in Sufi texts is the command, often attributed to the Prophet, "Assume the character traits of God!" (*takhallaqû bi akhlâq Allâh*). Ibn al-'Arabî quotes the following hadith: "God has three hundred character traits. He who assumes one of them as his own will enter paradise."

In Ibn al-'Arabî's vocabulary "assuming the traits of the divine names" (*al-takhalluq bi'l-asmâ' al-ilâhiyya*) and "assuming the divine character traits" (*al-takhalluq bi'l-akhlâq al-ilâhiyya*) are synonymous terms. Moreover, he sometimes gives to the word *takhalluq* a meaning that goes outside the ethical sphere altogether, though it points to the ontological root of character traits. For example: "To God belong the Most Beautiful Names, and to the cosmos belongs manifestation through them by assuming their traits" (II 438.23). This is reminiscent of his oft-repeated axiom, "There is nothing in existence but God,"[8] and of its expanded form, "There is nothing in existence but God, His names, and His acts" (III 68.12).

> There is no existent who is named by all the divine names except the human being. Moreover, he has been charged to assume them as character traits. (II 603.4)
>
> The servant sincere in his love for his Lord assumes the traits of His names. Hence he assumes the trait of independence (*ghinā*) from other than God, might ('*izz*) through God, bestowal ('*aṭā*') with the hand of God, preserving (*ḥifẓ*) with the eye of God. The men of knowledge (*al-'ulamā*') know about assuming the traits of God's names and have written many books about it. Since they loved God, they qualified themselves with His attributes to the degree appropriate for them. (II 596.14)

The Root of Base Character Traits

Up until this point, there is nothing unusual about Ibn al-'Arabî's description of character traits as being rooted in the divine names. Much of what he says is implied if not stated explicitly in earlier texts. But so far we have not really begun investigating the second part of our topic, which is the relationship of character traits to the doctrine of *waḥdat al-wujûd* or "Oneness of Being."[9] For present purposes, we can say that the Oneness of Being implies that every existing thing, by the very fact of its existence, manifests absolute and nondelimited *wujûd*, i.e., God. In other terms, everything in the universe is a locus of manifestation for the divine names. There is only one *wujûd*, and to speak of many "*wujûds*" is merely a manner of speaking, one that is justified by our normal if imperfect perception of the nature of the cosmos. But ultimately, everything that may be called *wujûd* in whatever form it appears is in fact the nondelimited *wujûd* of God. That which delineates the specific properties of those things described as possessing *wujûd* is the mode under which the *wujûd* of the Real manifests Itself because of the laws of Its own nature — laws which revelation summarizes in terms of the divine names.

Such a description of the cosmos necessarily sees everything as stemming ultimately from God, even the "evil" that is found within it. Of course there are all sorts of ways to avoid attributing evil directly to God, and Ibn al-'Arabî employs most of them. For example, he devotes a tremendous amount of space to discussing "nonexistence" ('*adam*) and the manner in which it "dilutes" as it were the intensity of *wujûd*, so that whatever defect is found in existence must be attributed to the side of nonexistence, not to nondelimited *wujûd*.

When it comes to the question of human activity, the situation is extremely complex. For one thing, every act does in fact manifest an ontological quality, or else it could not occur. There is something positive and affirmative about activity. Are not the very creatures known as God's "acts" (*af'âl*) in Islamic theology? How then do we deal with human character traits? Ibn al-'Arabî does not shy away from the demands of his own logic. Though on one level he can say, as he does in the passage quoted above and many others, that character traits which are blameworthy (*madhmûm*) for human beings are even more blameworthy for God, on deeper analysis he has to admit that even the most blameworthy traits arise out of the nature of existence itself, which is nothing but the self-manifestation of the divine *wujûd*.

> All character traits are divine attributes. Hence all of them are noble, and all are found in the human being's fundamental makeup . . . . God is the Necessary *wujûd* through Himself, while the human being has *wujûd* through his Lord. Hence he acquires *wujûd* from Him, so he acquires character traits from Him. (II 241.28)

In other words Ibn al-'Arabî affirms that base character traits as well as noble character traits have their roots in *wujûd* and that, in fact, what we call base character traits are really noble. But in no sense does this lead him to some sort of antinomian position. Nowhere does he suggest, for example, that since everything comes from God, it makes no difference how we act. Quite the contrary, the very fact that all character traits come from God leads Ibn al-'Arabî to affirm even more strongly that there is no possible way of leading a correct life outside the guidance of the prophets, who also come from God and who show how to make all our character traits praiseworthy.

Ibn al-'Arabî's basic argument concerning prophetic guidance goes back to his position on the nature of existent things. All things in the cosmos are but the properties and traces of the divine names, which themselves are but designations for the relationships that exist between nondelimited *wujûd* and the things. This means that in the last analysis there is nothing in existence but various modalities of *wujûd*, or various relationships and attributions. There is no plurality of existent things, but one of relationships. Anything in the cosmos that we want to analyze is a relationship between other things. There are no fixed entities, only the flux of changing attributions. Character traits are no different from anything else. Hence, if the attributions change, character traits can be transformed from base to noble.

Ibn al-'Arabî commonly makes these points in connection with the prophetic saying, "I was sent to complete the noble character traits." Character traits were incomplete, he says, because many of the noble character traits had been left out of the lists set down by the earlier prophets. What Muhammad did was to "complete" them by adding all the base character traits to the noble character traits. This took place because his revealed Law transforms the blameworthy traits into praiseworthy ones. It does this by changing the manner in which the so-called base character traits are employed (*maṣraf*).

> Rational proofs, unveiling, and gnosis all show us that there is nothing in the cosmos except the character traits of God. Hence there are no base character traits. Therefore the Messenger of God . . . gave news that he had been sent to complete the noble character traits, since they are the character traits of God. Hence he joined what had been called "base character traits" to the noble character traits, and as a result, all became noble. He who understands what is meant by the revealed Law sees that the Prophet did not leave a single base character trait in the cosmos. (II 363.25)
>
> The attributes found in the human being's fundamental makeup do not change, since they are intrinsic to this world's plane and his specific constitution. These include cowardice, avarice, envy, greed, talebearing, arrogance, harshness, seeking subjugation, and the like. Since no one can set out to change them, God explained various uses for them toward which they can be turned through injunctions of the divine Law. If the soul turns the properties of these attributes toward these uses, it will be felicitous [in the next world] and attain to high degrees. Hence the soul should be cowardly toward committing forbidden things because of the loss it can expect. It should have avarice toward its religion. It should envy him who spends his property [in the way of religion] and him who seeks knowledge. It should be greedy toward good and try to spread it among the people. It should tell the tale of good just as the garden tells the tale of the sweet-smelling flowers within it. It should be arrogant in God toward him who is arrogant toward God's command. It should be harsh in its words and activities in the places where it knows God approves of that. It should seek the subjugation of him who is hostile toward God and resists Him. Such a soul does not leave its own attributes, but it turns them toward uses for which its Lord, His angels, and His messengers have praised it. Hence the revealed Law has brought only that which aids nature . . . . So people perish only when they are controlled by egocentric desires. (II 687.12)[10]

Servanthood

In the previous section blameworthy character traits were looked upon from the human side, without any attempt to attribute them directly to specific divine names. Another way to approach the same problem is to analyze specific divine names whose attribution to human beings will cause obvious difficulties. While Ibn al-'Arabî says that perfect man assumes the character traits of all the divine names, he acknowledges that in practice assuming the traits of certain names would conflict with our normal ideas about noble character traits, e.g., names such as the Arrogant, the Inaccessible, the Majestic, the Slayer, the Conqueror, the Avenger, the Terrible in Punishment. How can a person assume these traits without turning into a monster? The simple answer is that he has to do so in proper measure, or in equilibrium with other names, and that the scale by which the names can be weighed in proper measure is the revealed Law.

Ibn al-'Arabî states the problem in relation to God's attribute of arrogance or greatness (*kibriyâ'*) as follows:

> Everything in the cosmos has a divine root, but if the servant should become qualified by a divine root, this is not necessarily praiseworthy. For example, without doubt arrogance has a divine root. But if the servant becomes qualified by it, makes himself a branch of it, and employs it internally, everyone agrees that this is blameworthy in every respect. (III 36.25)

Ibn al-'Arabî explains in a variety of ways how it is possible to assume the character traits of the divine names without falling into disequilibrium and deviation. Here a brief allusion to one of the most basic of his teachings will have to suffice: The spiritual station in which a human being attains to perfect equilibrium in relation to the divine attributes and is able to manifest them in the correct proportions is known as servanthood (*'ubûdiyya*). This is fundamentally an ontological situation, arising out of the "possibility" (*imkân*) of the created things, i.e., the fact that creatures have received their existence and attributes on loan from God. Ibn al-'Arabî equates the philosophical term "possibility" with the Koranic expression "poverty" (*faqr*). By their very essences all existent things are poor toward and in need of God, while God has no need for anything in existence. "O people! You are the poor toward God, and God, He is the Independent, the Praiseworthy" (Koran 35:15). The basic human task is to come to a full understanding and realization of the radical poverty of all things, especially themselves; acting in accordance with this understanding will then be called servanthood, and there is no higher station to which a person can aspire, since this is the station where all things dwell in their proper place and all ignorance and illusion are effaced.

In one passage Ibn al-'Arabî discusses the Trust given to the human being by God, identifying it with the divine form and the resulting all-comprehensiveness of the human reality. Then he explains that like any trust, this Trust is a burden, and the only way to gain release from the burden is to give the burden back to God by surrendering to the dictates of servanthood.

> Do you not see that when someone deposits property with a person, he finds that it weighs him down? Guarding and preserving it are a burden for him. If its owner says to him, "I give this to you and it no longer belongs to me," the carry-

ing of that property becomes easy for him, and he becomes tremendously happy, honoring the person who gave it to him.

   In the same way God's attributes are a Trust with the servant. The servant never ceases being aware that they are a trust with him. He is weighed down by watching over them: How should he employ them? Where should he put them to use? He fears lest he use them in the way their true owner might use them. When this weighs him down, he returns them to their owner and remains happy and burden-free in servanthood, which is his own characteristic, or rather, his reality, since anything in addition to that may disappear from him. (II 631.4)

In Ibn al-'Arabî's view, the perfect human being must combine the poverty of servanthood with the full display of the divine attributes demanded by his being created in God's form. This is achieved only by the messengers, the prophets, and the greatest "friends of God" (*awliyâ' Allâh*). It is the goal of human existence, yet it is rarely actualized. Even for those who have set out on the path to achieve it, it poses many dangers. The divine deception (*al-makr al-ilâhî*), about which the Koran often warns, will sometimes manifest itself to those attempting to attain to perfection. The only escape is to cling to the station of servanthood. In one passage Ibn al-'Arabî describes the various difficult ascents (*'aqaba*) which the spiritual traveler must pass over in achieving this station.

   If God does not favor this servant through protection and guarding and does not fix his feet in this difficult ascent by keeping his vision fixed upon his servanthood while he manifests the form of God . . . , then his feet will slip and what he possesses of God's form will come between him and his vision of his servanthood . . . . This derives from the divine deception. He who wants protection from the divine deception must cling to his servanthood and its concomitants in every state. (III 147.6)

The first concomitant of "servanthood" is that the human being must "serve" the Divine Reality. In the Koran God says, "I created jinn and mankind only to serve [or "to worship"] Me" (51:56). This service or worship has an ontological dimension (called "essential worship") whereby all things serve God through their mode of existence, and a second, moral and religious dimension (called "accidental worship") whereby human beings employ their free will and choose whether or not to follow the Law. Hence observance of the Law makes possible the perfection of servanthood and the eschatological fruit of this perfection, which is known as "felicity" (*sa'âda*). Neglecting the Law throws the human being into error, deviation, and ultimate "wretchedness" (*shaqâwa*).

   Perfect man manifests the divine form while being firmly fixed in servanthood. Through affirming his radical ontological deprivation, or his absolute nothingness in face of the Necessary Being, he fixes himself in the distance from his Lord that his possibility and contingency demand. He submits himself absolutely to the requirements of the Necessary Being, as set down in revelation, which represents God's guidance for mankind in this plane of existence. Yet, paradoxically, through his knowledge of his true situation and his maintenance of absolute distance, perfect man is brought into God's proximity. Ibn al-'Arabî points to the happy combination of distance and proximity, of servanthood and manifesting the names of God, by quoting two apparently contradictory sayings from the famous Sufi Abû Yazîd Bistâmî:

> Servanthood is not a state of proximity. That which brings the servant near to his Lord is his knowledge that he is His servant, not the servanthood itself. Servanthood demands distance from the Master, but the servant's knowledge of servanthood requires nearness to Him. When Abû Yazîd became bewildered about proximity and did not know how he should gain nearness to his Lord, God said to him in his inmost consciousness, "O Abû Yazîd! Come near to Me through that which I do not possess: lowliness and poverty." Hence God negated from Himself these two attributes, lowliness and poverty. That which He negates from Himself is an attribute of distance from Him. So when those attributes which demand distance arise in someone, they determine his situation, and they demand distance.
>
> At another time Abû Yazîd said to his Lord, "Through what should I gain proximity to Thee?" God said to him, "Leave aside your self and come!" Once he abandons himself, he will have abandoned the property of servanthood, since servanthood is identical with distance from Masterhood and the servant is far from the Master.
>
> Hence in lowliness and poverty Abû Yazîd sought proximity through servanthood, while in abandoning self he sought proximity through assuming the character traits of God. (II 561.14)

Notes

1   This doctrine is often said to have been formulated for the first time by Ibn al-'Arabî. However, the term itself is not found in his works, though it is present in the works of some of his followers, and many Sufis before Ibn al-'Arabî expressed the same idea. Cf. Chittick, "Rumi and *Wahdat al-wujûd*," in A. Banani and G. Sabagh (eds.), *The Heritage of Rumi* (Cambridge: Cambridge University Press, forthcoming).

2   Fazlur Rahman, *Islam*, 2nd ed. (Chicago: University of Chicago Press, 1979), p. 146.

3   References throughout are to *al-Futûhât al-makkiyya* (Cairo: 1911), volume, page, and line number.

4   One of the difficulties we face in discussing Ibn al-'Arabî's views is how to translate *wujûd*. Either "Being" or "existence" presents us with problems, not the least of them the fact that Western thought does not agree on what we are talking about by the use of such terms. For present purposes, we can say that *wujûd* refers to the fact that something is "found" (the literal sense of the term) in the real world, in whatever mode it may be found. God is identical with *wujûd* since He is that which cannot not be found (at least by Himself), while everything else possesses what may be referred to as *wujûd* in respect of the fact that God has given *wujûd* to it. For detailed discussions of the meaning of *wujûd* in Ibn al-'Arabî's thought, cf. Chittick, *Sufi Path of Knowledge*, pp. 3, 6, 80-81, 133, 212, 226-227 et passim.

5   If human beings had been created in the form of one of the specific divine names, this would have limited their reality and made it impossible for them to have knowledge of all things. Cf. Chittick, *Sufi Path of Knowledge*, p. 304.

6   Ibn al-'Arabî often points to this and similar verses to illustrate some of the "mysteries" of the divine knowledge. The Koran reiterates in several places that God knows all things, even the leaves that fall from the trees. So how could He not know him who struggles and him who does not? What is at issue in such verses concerns the testing and trial (*ibtilâ'*) of mankind so that they and others will be able to perceive their own natures. Cf. *Futûhât* II 515, 534, 537, 543, 692; III 111, 134.

7   On this highest stage of human perfection, referred to by such names as the "station of no station," cf. Chittick, *Sufi Path of Knowledge*, chap. 20.

8   E.g., I 272.15, 279.6; II 114.1, 148.17, 160.4. Al-Ghazâli among others says the same thing (*Ihyâ 'ulûm al-dîn* IV.6.8; [Cairo: Matba 'at al-'Âmirat al-Sharafiyya, 1326-27/1908-09], IV, p. 230).

9 For detailed explanations of the meaning of this concept, see Chittick, *Sufi Path of Knowledge*; idem, "Rumi and *Wahdat al-Wujûd*"; idem, "Ebno'l-'Arabî's Doctrine of the Oneness of Being," *Sufi* [London], 4 (1989-90), pp. 6-14.

10 For two more passages making the same points, cf. I 350.10; II 198.28.

The Voice of Love
Mystical Poetry in Islam:
Maulānā Jalāluddīn Rūmī
(1207-1273)

Annemarie Schimmel

One of the central problems for mystics in all religion is to express their experiences. How to speak of the Ineffable, or even to define the different steps on the path which, as they hope, will lead them to the highest bliss, that is to union with the object of their longing? After lifting the numberless veils that separate the creature from the Creator, they had again to weave veils of words before the all too radiant Reality which one can not see without dying. Should God be described by way of showing Him as the Ultimate Cause of everything (*via causalitatis*), the Creator, Sustainer, and Judge, or should one rather try to use the *via eminentiae*, summed up best in the Islamic formula *Allāhu akbar*, "God is greater (than anything imaginable)", even greater than the truth one reaches by non-rational means, or would the final solution of all these problems be to express Him by the *via negationis*, that was so dear to the mystics in all religions, be they the authors of the Upanishads or Dionysius Areopagita?

The Sufis were well aware of these difficulties and developed in the early centuries of Islamic history a cryptic language — expressions which were as it were coded and whose real meaning only those could grasp who had undergone the proper initiation. The Arabic language is an ideal vehicle for such an undertaking, for the generally three-consonantal root of a word can be enlarged or its consonants can be permutated, and each root carries with it almost inexhaustible cross relations just as the sound of a lute string evokes other cognate sounds.

The greatest achievements of the early Arabic Sufis were, however, not poetical works, poetry being looked at rather unkindly due to the Koranic verdict against the poets at the end of Sūra 26; they concentrated upon prose and expressed their concerns in sentences of extreme brevity, pressing deep wisdom into three or four words. One should beware of taking such aphoristic sentences always at face value, as some translators into Western languages did; one should also beware of systematizing such sayings in order to understand them logically. Rather, it may well be that these seemingly paradoxical and contradictory statements were meant to be a kind of *koan*, which suddenly opens the way to a non-rational and non-intellectual understanding.

The poetical fragments left by the early Sufis are rather brief and concise; some short verses were used with musical accompaniment during the *samāᶜ*, the concerts in which the mystics found some relaxation from their intense ascetic practices. Enjoying the sweet and bitter love songs they could easily understand them as pointing to their love of God, for "the metaphor is the bridge toward Reality."

The most famous early Sufi verses were written by Ḥallāj, the martyr mystic who was cruelly executed in Baghdad on March 26, 922 and whose suffering and death "at the hands of the establishment" have made him a role model not only for many Sufis but also for progressive writers to our day. In the folk poetry of the Indus Valley and of Anatolia, in the songs of Bengali Sufis or Panjabi ecstatics the name of "Mansūr" Ḥallāj is repeated over and over again, conjuring up his longing for martyrdom to reach his goal, the disappearance of his I, his creatureliness, which forms a veil between him and the uncreated, eternal Beloved. High poetry in Iran, Turkey and India has taken up his brief allegory of the moth which, attracted by the candle, casts itself into the flame and reaches union with it to be transformed into something higher, to experience (to use Goethe's expression) the *Stirb und werde*, "Die and become", for this is the way of love. Ḥallāj's verse, popular as it was, is certainly not 'great' poetry, but it contains a number of aspects that are typical of mystical literature, such as the expression of timelessness in the state of ecstasy, of *fanā*, "annihilation" or *Entwerden* when the mystic breaks through the "infidel's girdle" of created, serial time to reach the Divine Eternal Now. In his famous poem *Uqtulūnī yā thiqātī*

> Kill me, oh my trustworthy friends,
> for in my being killed is my life . . . ,

Ḥallāj sings in the central part:

> Verily I am an old man (or "master", *shaikh*)
> in the highest ranks, then I became an infant
> in the bosoms of the nursing women . . . .
> My mother gave birth to her father —
> Verily, that is a miracle
> and my daughters, after being

my daughters are my sisters.
This is not the work of Time,
no, and not of adultery . . .

This tendency to express one's return to the time when there was no time, when one has "become as one was before one was" (as Junaid said) is well-known among the Sufis, and has been expressed by Turkish singers such as Yunus Emre (d. ca. 1321) and in India, where cross relations with the *ultābhaṅsi* songs of the *bhaktas* can be established. One finds it also in high Sufi literature such as the great Arabic *Tā'iyya* by Ibn al-Fāriḍ, (d. 1235 in Cairo), who is regarded as the only truly great Sufi poet of the Arabs. Ibn al-Fāriḍ used all the inherited rhetorical forms of classical Arabic poetry and one wonders how his elaborate verses, comparable to the work of a fastidious goldsmith, could have been sung in ecstasy. Yet, this is perfectly possible, and such inspired poetry can be found to this day. When one has seen how Turkish mystical songs were "born" (*doğuş*) from the lips of an illiterate man who sang his verses with traditional imagery under the flood of inspiration (*Yeni Yunus Emre* in Adana) one can well imagine how earlier, greater Sufi poets, deeply steeped in the religious, poetical, and rhetorical tradition of their respective languages were able to sing of the unspeakable with superbly skillful verses even while in a rapture that accounts for a tendency to turn upside down traditional imagery. This can be observed best in the writings of the greatest mystical poet of the Muslim world, Maulānā Jalāluddīn Rūmī (1207-1273):

When the parrot 'Soul' chews sugar,
Suddenly I become intoxicated and chew the parrot (D 1526).

Parrots are always "sugar chewing" in Persian literature, and the green parrot is a soul bird, connected thanks to his green color, with Paradise, where those clad in green, *sabzpūsh*, live. Could there be a greater ecstatic confusion than chewing the parrot as though he were sugar?

Rumi's poetry abounds in such images. His life is exemplary for a mystic's development: born in the area of Balkh as son of a mystically minded father, whose work is filled with expressions of the constant presence of God, the Beloved, near every atom of the body and the soul, he reached Anatolia (*Rūm*, hence his surname *Rūmī*) after long wanderings, settled in Konya, and succeeded his father as professor in 1231. After his initiation into the mystical path his whole life was changed by the meeting with the wandering dervish Shamsuddīn of Tabriz in the fall of 1244. When Shams disappeared Maulānā was suddenly transformed into a poet, and time and again he asked himself:

> I was ascetic and intelligent, a striving man—
> My healthy state—why did you fly away, say, like a bird? (D 2245).

Shams returned to disappear forever in December 1248, and Maulānā finally realized that the beloved lived in himself "radiant as the moon", as his son, Sultan Valad, tells. The poems written in that period now bear the pen name not of Rūmī himself, but of Shams, for he was the true inspirator while Maulānā, as he admitted in his prose work *Fīhi mā fīhi*, did basically not care for poetry. But:

> Where am I? Where is poetry? But that Turk breathes into me: "Ho, who are you?" (D 1949)

This line, with the question in Turkish, translates Maulānā's feelings: it was not he who sang but the breath of the Friend, manifested through Shams, moved him—he was only the reed flute that sings when the breath of the player touches it (just as God breathed into Adam to give him life, Sura 15/29). His whole work grew through this inspirational process, whether it was the nearly 40,000 verses of lyrical poetry in the *Dīvān-i Shams* or the 25,000 verses of the *Mathnavī*, the great mystico-didactic poem which he began on the behest of his favorite disciple, Ḥusāmuddīn Chelebi, in 1256.

Rumi was, however, not the inventor of these poetical forms in Persian literature; Sanā'ī of Ghazna (d. 1131) had introduced the form of rhyming couplets (*mathnavi*) as a vehicle for didactic poetry, and his *Ḥadīqat al-ḥaqīqa* set the model for this type of literature which was to become extremely popular in the Persianate world. Its greatest master was Farīduddīn 'Aṭṭār, (d. ca. 1220 in Nishapur), whose mystical epics have never lost their attractiveness: the *Manṭiq uṭ-ṭair*, "The Birds' Language", tells of the pilgrimage of the thirty birds, *sī murgh*, to the King of Birds, the *Sīmurgh*, and at the end of their journey through seven valleys they realize that they themselves are identical with the Divine Bird. Similarly, the seeker who is the hero of the *Muṣībatnāma*, "The Book of Affliction", undergoes the forty days' seclusion and finally is taught by the Prophet of Islam that he should delve into the ocean of his soul to find God there.

Besides the *mathnavi*, Persian mystics used the lyrical form, the *ghazal*, a rather short poem (ideally 7-14 verses), which is held together by monorhyme, and is an ideal vehicle for love poetry—the imagery of human love could be used to express the mysteries of Divine Love, and the constant oscillation between the two levels of experience makes Persian and Turkish poetry so delightful but also so difficult to translate correctly. Sometimes, especially in hymnical praise of the Creator or the Prophet Muhammad, the lightful model of the believers, the poets would use the *qaṣīda*, the long poem which, again maintaining the monorhyme, could extend over dozens if not hundreds of lines. The short quatrain, *rubāʿī*, with its rhyme scheme *aaxa*, (known in the West through FitzGerald's free version of Omar Khayyam's *Rubāʿiyyāt*) was often used in musical sessions.

Maulānā Rūmī made use of all these forms, and his development is reflected in the form and content of his poems. The early *ghazals*, still without disclosing the beloved's name, are filled with images, often weird, often paradoxical, glowing and ecstatic; at a later point, after having "burnt" himself completely in the love of Shams, he found some spiritual rest in the friendship with Ṣalāḥuddīn Zarkūb, a goldsmith, to whom a number of lyrics are devoted, but it was his third friend, his disciple Ḥusāmuddīn, who inspired him to dictate his *Mathnavī*, and therefore Rūmī says at an early stage of the great poem:

> I think of rhymes, but my beloved says:
> "Don't think of anything but of my face!"

The *Mathnavī* is replete with stories, anecdotes, mystical tales, proverbs, and forms almost an encyclopedia of Muslim literature and life in thirteenth century Anatolia, and with its often very concrete and matter-of-fact descriptions of daily life it enables us to sketch a picture of medieval Anatolian life as well as of the wealth of mystical ideas known to Rūmī. He, however, never attempted to give a theoretical introduction into Sufism, or into the states and stations on the path, nor does he systematically discuss theosophical problems; he simply sang, forced by an irresistible power, often without knowing what and how he was composing. Time and again he faced the problem of expressing his feelings in human language, but, he asks, what are these languages but husks? The story of the Arab, the Turk, the Greek and the Persian who asked for *ʿinab, üzüm, istafil* and *angūr* respectively only to discover that they all wanted grapes (M II 3681 ff.), is a typical point in case. And therefore Maulānā tells his listeners:

> Whether you are Arab or Greek or Turk—
> Learn the tongue without tongues! (D 1183)

He sometimes complains of the difficulties posed by the rigid application of the Arabic metrical forms as expressed in catchwords:

This *mufta ʿilun mufta ʿilun* has killed me!

Or he closes a poem with the Arabic line:

My friend and physician fills the cup — leave
the *fāʿilun mufta ʿilun* and *fāʿilatun* and *faʿl*!

And it may well happen that a poem that begins with verses of
incredible strength and breathtaking energy all of a sudden tapers off
when the inspiration fades away, and then follow a number of verses
which, kept together only through the thread of the rhyme, sound flat
and insipid and apparently serve only to keep the poet's mind from
suddenly falling into the bottomless empty room.

A typical aspect of such inspired verse, particularly in Rūmī, is the
application of repetitions, and of metrical forms that can be easily
split into smaller units — one should never forget that most of
Maulānā's poetry was born from the sound of music and the movement of the whirling dance in which the enraptured mystic was
carried out of the gravitation of the earth to reach — at least in his
mind — higher and higher spheres to circle finally around the eternal
sun. A typical example of this poetry is D 1785 with its beginning:

Biyā biyā dildār-i man dildār-i man
dar ā dar ā dar kār-i man dar kār-i man
Tū-ī tu-ī gulzār-i man gulzār-i man,
bi-gū bi-gū asrār-i man asrār-i man
Come, come, my beloved, my beloved,
Enter, enter into my work, my work!
You are, you are my rosegarden, my rosegarden!
Tell, tell my secrets, my secrets!

One knows sometimes which sensual experience underlies a
poem — Maulānā might hear a word that sparked off an association, as
in the story according to which a peddlar passed by his house, calling
out in Turkish *Tilkü, tilkü,* "Fox, fox" to sell some fur, whereupon
Rūmī immediately began to sing a poem that began with the words
Dil kū? Dil kū? "Where is the heart, where is the heart?" The view of
something unusual, the smell of certain foodstuff, could inspire him
to weave these experiences into his verse, and thus his lyrics abound
in images taken from the life in home, street, and garden.

Then, again, he tried to tell of his visionary experiences, and it
would be worth while to have all of them properly analyzed. One
may think of the extended descriptions of Daqūqī's visions in the
Mathnavi (Vol III 1985 ff), the transformation of seven candles into
seven trees into seven men etc., or of the poem dated Nov. 26, 1256,

the eve of a Mongol attack on Konya; but probably the best known account of a vision is the poem describing the moon that appeared on the sky in the morning to carry the seeker's heart as a falcon carries his prey, until he sees the primordial ocean:

> The ocean was all filled with foam
> and every fleck of this foam
> produced a figure like this,
> and was a body like that,
> and every body-shaped fleck
> that heard a sign from the sea,
> it melted and then returned
> into the ocean of souls . . .

The whole world is filled with signs from which the seeker can understand God's working — God, who reveals Himself through the interplay of *jalāl*, Majesty, and *jamāl*, Beauty, both of which form the warp and woof of the universe, constituting as it were the garment which hides and yet reveals the invisible, unfathomable Divine Self. Whatever the mystic may see, it points to the One. As the early Sufis would sing:

> And in everything there is a witness
> that points to His being One!

The gardens manifest the miracle of His creation; the blossom in spring, kissed by the morning breeze, resembles the Virgin Mary who, touched by Gabriel, the "faithful spirit" was to bring a precious fruit, i.e. Jesus. Every narcissus is an eye to look out for the beloved; every rose reflects the beauty of the beloved's face — is not the red rose a sign of God's glory, as the Prophet said according to a tradition? Or was it created, as legend tells, from the drops of the Prophet's perspiration that fell down during his nightly journey, *miʿrāj*, and is therefore impregnated with the Prophet's fragrance? The violet sits on the green prayer rug of the lawn, wrapped in the dark blue garb of an ascetic, and places its head on its knees as though meditating while the lily wields the white sword to fight the creatures of winter and the material world. Every spring is a resurrection, every animal, too, participates in it, and when the dark crows, symbols of the hibernal world of matter, disappear, the nightingales, soul birds *par excellence*, can again sing of their longing for the eternal rosegarden. The mystic who is able to discover this Divine manifestation in everything, appears, in a late scene of the *Mathnavī*, as comparable to Zulaikhā, Potiphar's wife, who was madly in love with Yūsuf (Joseph) as Sura 12 tells. In this scene — written not long before his

death—Rūmī allows us a glimpse into his way of using symbols: at
the beginning of the *Mathnavī* he had rebuked young Ḥusāmuddīn
who wanted to know more about Shams, and told him that it was
better to tell the secret of the beloved in the stories of other people;
the *bū-yi pīrahan-i Yūsuf*, the fragrance of Yūsuf's shirt, which healed
his father's blindness, would be enough to heal the spiritually blind.
His own poetry, as he states in a lyrical passage, is like fragrance, a
fragrance that cures those whose eyes cannot see the beloved. Thus,
he takes up the story of Yūsuf and Zulaikhā once more at the end of
his life after not mentioning Shams of Tabriz throughout the entire
Mathnavī. But now the reader sees how Zulaikhā hid Yūsuf's name in
everything:

> And when she said: The wax is melting softly!
> That was to say: My friend was kind to me.
> And when she said: Look how the moon is rising!
> And when she said: The willow is now green!
> And when she said: The leaves there are a-trembling.
> And when she said: How nicely burns the rue! . . .
> And when she said: The birds sang for the roses!
> And when she said: Beat firmly all my rugs!1
> And when she said: The bread is all unsalted!
> And when she said: The spheres are going wrong . . .
> She praised something—that meant "His sweet embracing";
> She blamed something, that meant: "He's far away:" . . .

How many names she might pile up, her intention was only the
beloved, and his name was her furcoat in the cold of winter, and was
her food in times of famine. Thus, the seeker sees the traces of God
everywhere, and whatever he says is nothing but an expression of his
relation with the Divine Beloved, whose love is greater and more
powerful than anything imaginable.

Rumi's poetry is born out of this love, a love which to describe he
uses hundreds and hundreds of comparisons. It is the power that
resembles black lions or strong dragons, that is kindly like a mother
and cruel like a policeman enacting confiscations by applying all
kinds of tortures; it is fire and is the ocean, it is a cutpurse and a
majestic ruler, a wondrous tree and the worm that hollows out the
tree—in short, Rūmī finds the most unexpected comparisons for this
power which uprooted him so completely from the peaceful life of a
scholar and teacher. Does not Love take the lover's brains and bodies
and hearts like nuts to braise them in its mortar so that they turn into
precious oil? Is it not like a shopholder who deals with intestines,
livers, lungs, brains as they are taken from the suffering lovers? And
the lover is happy to lick the vessels of Love's dogs, or to become

blood, or "to sit with the dogs at the door of fidelity." In such descriptions, Rumi uses paradoxes and invents seemingly absurd images. In an ecstatic poem with the beginning:

> When love comes: "Do you hand over your soul to me?"
> Why don't you immediately say: "Yes, yes!"

he relies on an old oriental superstition, i.e. that ostrichs live on fiery charcoals, and he sees Love:

> Love like a tower of light,
> Inside the tower of light: what a fire!
> Like ostrichs, the souls around this tower:
> Their food: a very tasty fire!

It is natural that in this world of Love the intellectual faculties are of no use. Intellect is required in the beginning of the path; it is a solid guide who teaches the child how to behave and where to go, it is the police officer who can guide the visitor to the king's palace but is left at the gate because only "the eunuch Grief" is admitted to the chamber of loving union. But strange things can happen to intellect: when Love enters the city:

> Prison became Paradise through the clamor of Love:
> Mr. Justice Intellect drunken on the judge's bench!
> They came to Professor Reason to ask:
> "Why has this terrible riot happened in Islam?"
> Mufti First Intellect answered with a *fatwā*:
> "This is the moment of resurrection—where is [the difference between] licit and
>   illicit?" . . . .

It can be even worse: when the Sultan Love arrives he hangs Intellect like a thief even though he was a king before, and even though Intellect may be a Plato in his own right, Love takes a mace and hits him over the head . . . But there is some hope: even though Intellect, as a good ascetic, recedes into a corner when Love brings wine and roast, he may just eat one grain from Love's bait and immediately lose all his plumage, or meekly crawl in the dust of Love's vestibule. He may even taste some opium from Love's hand, and when asked what happened to him he has a good answer:

> I asked: "Dear Intellect, where are you?"
>   And Intellect replied:
> "Since I've turned into wine, why should I
>   behave like sour grapes?" (D 2924).

For nothing can return to its previous state; the road leads upward, and life is a constant journey to higher and loftier spheres—ideas most impressively expressed in Rūmī's story of the chickpeas in the *Mathnavi* (Vol. III 4158 ff.) where the vegetables, suffering in the boiling water, are told by the housewife that to be cooked is necessary for their becoming edible; thus they will, in the course of time, become part and parcel of human beings and participate in the spiritual life. Did not Ḥallāj say, as Maulānā quotes him in this connection:

> Kill me, oh my trustworthy friends,
> for in my being killed is my life?

In tens of thousands of verses Rūmī has tried to express his experience of the highest rapture; carried away by the strong falcon Love, his heart beheld the infinite glory of God and His manifestations in the universe, beheld also the whirling dance of atoms and stars, a dance which permeates the world ever since the day of creation, when the not-yet-created beings heard God's address: "Am I not your Lord?" and, answering, "Yes" (Sura 7/172) they entered Being in an ecstatic dance to become trees and flowers and humans (D 1832).

Maulānā saw all this, and tried to convey his visions to his listeners, not because he wanted it but because he was compelled to do it, forced by the beloved who would "split his mouth" when he failed to sing a *ghazal*. And yet, it is not in vain that many of his *ghazals* end with the call *Khāmūsh*, "Quiet", for like all mystics Rūmī knew all too well that only by complete silence the seeker can turn into laud and praise for the Lord. He has expressed this feeling that even the most beautiful expression proves that there is still a trace of selfishness in the lover in a beautiful image: the material world is the world of winter, and love and union is the fire which transforms the snow and ice into veritable water of life. But:

> In the essence of annihilation I said: "O king of all kings,
> All images have melted in this fire!"
> He spoke: "Your address is still a remnant of this snow—
> As long as the snow remains, the red rose is hidden!" (D 1033)

Both the word about God, the poem, and the word to God, prayer, end in complete silence. Only the nightingale that is separated from the rose, can sing. Union, however, is without words, without voice—perhaps some fragrance may reach those that are left outside the sanctissimum.

Bibliographical Notes

D *Dīvān-i kabīr ya kulliyāt-i Shams*, 10 vols. ed. Badīʿuzzamān Furuzānfar, Tehran University, 1957-76.

M. *Mathnawī-yi maʿnawī*, ed. Reynold A. Nicholson, 8 vols., with translation and commentary, London, Luzac, 1925-1940.

Fīhi mā fīhi, ed. Badi'uzzamān Furūzānfar, Tehran 1951.
Translation: *Discourses of Rumi*, tr. Arthur John Arberry, London: John Murray, 1961.
German: *Von allem und vom Einen*, tr. Annemarie Schimmel, Munich 1988.

William C. Chittick, *The Sufi Path of Love*. Albany, SUNY Press, 1984.

Fritz Meier, *Bahā-i Walad*. Leiden 1989.

Hellmut Ritter, "Maulānā Calāleddin Rūmī und sein Kreis." *Der Islam* 46 (1942).

ders. *Das Meer der Seele. Gott, Mensch und Welt in den Geschichten Farīd-addin ʿAṭṭārs*. Leiden 1955, 2nd. ed. 1976.

Annemarie Schimmel, *Mystical Dimensions of Islam*. Chapel Hill: University of North Carolina Press, 1975 and often.

_____, *The Triumphal Sun. A study of life and work of Mowlānā Jalāloddīn* Rumi. London-The Hague, East-West Publications, 1978.

_____, *As through a Veil. Mystical Poetry in Islam*. New York: Columbia University Press, 1982.

_____, *Look, that is Love* (translations from Rūmī's poetry), Boston, Shambhala, 1991.

_____, *I am Wind, you are Fire*. Boston, Shambhala, 1992.

Bridal Symbolism in Ismāᶜīli Mystical Literature of Indo-Pakistan

Ali S. Asani

Evelyn Underhill, in her classic study of mysticism, while discussing the difficulties mystics encounter in communicating their spiritual experiences, writes:

> . . . . it is not strange that certain maps, artistic representations or symbolic representations should have come into being which describe or suggest the special experiences of the mystical consciousness and the doctrines to which these experiences have given birth. Many of these maps have an uncouth, even an impious appearance in the eyes of those unacquainted with the facts which they (the mystics) attempt to translate. . . . [1]

These comments are particularly applicable to descriptions of the crowning point of the mystical experience – the union of the soul with the Absolute. Like most esoteric states, the unitive experience is essentially ineffable and beyond the realm of ordinary human language. Yet, when constrained to describe it, many mystics frequently resort to the metaphor of the spiritual marriage of the soul with God. This particular metaphor, a special favorite of those for whom mysticism is an intimate and personal mode of communion[2], has been used, since the earliest periods of human religious history, to evoke the consummating event of the spiritual quest.[3] Admittedly, most mystics have been cognizant of the dangers of employing this particular symbolic expression: it is liable to be misunderstood or misinterpreted by the uninitiated and provides opportunity for harsh criticism from those who view the mystic path with disfavor.[4]

The popularity of spiritual marriage as a symbol among mystics of all periods and cultures is not difficult to explain. Mystics, though aware of the inadequacy of symbols and images as vehicles of expression, nevertheless employed them to provide material clothing for the spiritual. Only in this manner could they hint at or suggest to their fellows, albeit imperfectly, the nature of their experience. In their search for symbols best suited to represent the business of "being in love with the Absolute", it was but natural for them to turn to the sphere of human love and marriage. Both worldly experiences offer parallels to the mutual love and permanent bond that ties the soul to God. Moreover, the conception of marriage in many medieval (and some modern societies) with its aspects of duty, perpetuity, finality and loving obedience, "make it an apt image of a spiritual state in which humility, intimacy, and love were the dominant characteristics."[5]

Our concern here is with the application of the spiritual marriage symbolism in a rather unusual Islamic context, specifically, within the mystical literature of a small Shii Muslim group—the Nizārī Ismāᶜīlīs. The Nizārī Ismāᶜīlīs are well-known in the contemporary Muslim world as members of a community whose spiritual leader (*Imām*) is the Aga Khan. They are widely-dispersed in over 25 countries including those of the Middle East, South and Central Asia, East Africa, and, in recent times, Europe and North America. We do not have the space here to discuss the checkered religious and political history of the Nizārī Ismāᶜīlī movement nor can we dwell into the complex historical background of the particular Nizārī Ismāᶜīlī subgroup that will interest us here—the Khojas, as the Nizārī Ismāᶜīlīs of Indo-Pakistan are popularly known.[6] We do however, have to point out two distinctive characteristics of Nizārī Ismāᶜīlī theology.

Firstly, the Nizārī Ismāᶜīlīs believe, in common with other Shiites, that the message of Islam can be truly understood and implemented by the Muslim community only under the leadership of a divinely-guided *Imām*. This *Imām*, Shii Muslims declare, must be a specifically designated descendant of the Prophet Muḥammad through his daughter Fāṭimah and his cousin and son-in-law ᶜAlī. At present, the Nizārī Ismāᶜīlīs remain the only Shii group with a physically manifest *Imām*, namely, Aga Khan IV, acclaimed as the forty-ninth direct descendant of the Prophet Muhammad. The contemporary community's conceptions of the *Imām* are a conglomeration of beliefs transmitted through the centuries, interpreted and adapted by each generation in diverse cultural milieus. However, through the flux of change and diversity, obedience and devotion to the *Imām* have remained cardinal pillars of faith. For Nizārī Ismāᶜīlīs, only the *Imām*'s spiritual insight and knowledge can provide the faithful with the correct interpretation (*taᵓwīl*) that penetrates beyond the formal and literal meaning of the Divine Word embodied in the Qurᵓan.[7] Secondly, the Nizārī Ismāᶜīlīs are notable for the precedence they give the *bāṭin*, the esoteric or spiritual aspects of the faith over the *ẓāhir*, the esoteric or external. Their literature has been perennially preoccupied with the spiritual life of the human soul especially its search to escape from the shackles of material bondage and fulfill its ultimate destiny. This, according to the Qurᵓanic saying "From God we are and to Him we return"

(II:156), is for the soul to return to its origin in God. Such a spiritual journey, according to Ismaili thought, is only feasible by means of the spiritual relationship that exists between the inner reality of the individual believer and the inner reality of the *Imām* as epiphany of divine light (*nūr*). As keeper of the mysteries of the *bāṭin* (the esoteric), the *Imām* becomes not only the guide but also the object of the spiritual quest.[8] The *ism-i aᶜẓam* (the Greatest Name) given by the *Imām* to each disciple (*murīd*) for use in meditation (*dhikr*) is in this respect of critical importance.[9]

Clearly, the *Imām* is the focus, and even the fountainhead of mystical life in the community. He is the sole connecting link with the "other", standing as he does on the threshold between the temporal world and the world of spiritual reality.[10] Each aspirant desiring to enter the spiritual path must necessarily concentrate on cultivating his or her own individual spiritual relationship with the *Imām*. It is a relationship that is based on mutual love and devotion, its personal dimension being enhanced by the presence of a visible and living *Imām*. Love and devotion to the *Imām* are, in fact, among the Nizārī Ismāᶜīlīs necessary conditions for the attainment of spiritual vision (*dīdār*) and mystical union for which the believer yearns.[11]

The relationship of the *Imām* to his disciple (*murīd*) as well as the quest for spiritual enlightenment in the context of this relationship have been central themes in the community's literature. Nizārī Ismāᶜīlī literature is far from being a homogeneous corpus. It is as linguistically diverse as the community itself, with each cultural region producing its own distinctive literary artifacts.[12] In the Indian sub-continent, the Nizārī Ismāᶜīlī tradition developed a unique literary genre consisting of approximately 800 hymn-like poems, called *ginān*s.[13] Composed in several Indic vernaculars, they are meant to be sung in various Indian *rāga*s (musical modes). Tradition attributes authorship of the *ginān*s to preacher-saints (*dāᶜī*s or *pīr*s) sent from Iran to India by Nizārī Ismāᶜīlī Imams for the purpose of propagating the faith. The *ginān*s, though probably dating back to medieval times, continue till today as one of the mainstays of religious life of the Nizārī Ismāᶜīlī community of Indo-Pakistan; their poetic appeal forms the main content of religious experience within the community.

The *Imām-murīd* relationship, with its mystical and emotional elements, is the subject of many a *ginān*. The mystical experiences that the *pīr*s, the authors of these religious poems, underwent in the course of developing their own spiritual relationships with the *Imām*, were eternalized in poetic form. Indeed, certain *ginān*s can be considered to be literary expressions of mystical experiences. At the same time, these mystical *ginān*s play an important role in nurturing an individual's understanding of the nature of his or her relationship with the *Imām*. The ultimate goal of this relationship, as portrayed in the *ginās*, is *dīdār* (vision) of the *Imām*. *Dīdār* is not conceived of in anthropomorphic terms; rather it refers to the inner, mystical vision of the *Imām*'s spiritual light (*nūr*).[14] It is this vision that re-unites the soul with the lofty and sublime origin from which it is separated. Without the experience of the *Imām's dīdār*, life is painfully incomplete.

The most common symbolic expression used in the *ginān* literature for the *Imām-murīd* relationship is that of the woman separated from her beloved — the woman representing the pining human soul, while the beloved represents the *Imām* as divine epiphany. Typical of this use of the woman-soul is the *ginān* "*Tamakū sadhāre soh din*", ("The day that you left") attributed to the fourteenth century Pīr Ṣadr ad-Dīn. This poem, in the form of a woman's lament at the departure of her beloved, highlights the agonies of separation in a language that is intended to inspire the novice on the spiritual journey.

> Beloved, the day of Your departure has long since passed.
> My merciful Lord, my Creator, my Master,
> Anxiously I await you.
> O my Beloved, how will I spend the day without You?[15]

The utter selflessness, humility and devotion that are necessary prerequisites for success on the spiritual path are also strikingly portrayed in the *ginās* by the symbol of the woman as a wife awaiting the return of her husband. It is not uncommon to find *ginās* using Indic terms for "husband, lord" (*nar, nāth, swāmī*) in reference to the *Imām*. This symbol of the wife is best exemplified in the *ginān* "*Swāmī rājo more man thī na viserejī*" ("My heart will never forget the Master, the King") also attributed Pir Ṣadr ad-Dīn, in which the woman-soul is portrayed as performing her "wifely-duties" towards her Husband.[16] The idea of servitude is also expressed by representing the soul as the servant or slave of the Lord. A popular *ginān* "*Darshan dīyo morā nāth*", ("Grant me *darshan*, my lord"), composed by a female saint Imām Begum, is based entirely on this theme, with the supplicating servant craving for *dīdār/darshan* (vision) of the Lord.[17] In accord with the tendency to portray the human soul as a female, the servant/slave, too, is always a *dāsī* (a female slave), never a *dās* or male slave.

Yet the most dramatic symbol employed in the *ginās* recalls the image of the woman separated from her beloved. More precisely, the woman-soul is likened to a bride awaiting her marriage. A host of terms and rituals, normally associated with the marriage ceremony in

Indian society, are used to garb the spiritual experience with a form
that arouses immediate associations and is readily understood. The
ginān that best reflects the use of the image of the bride and the spiritual marriage is in the form of a supplication (*ventī*). It is attributed to
a male author of the fifteenth century, Pīr Ḥasan Kabīr ad-Dīn, who
portrays himself as a bride longing for her divine Bridegroom.[18]
Comprising of 50 verses in the Gujarati language, the *ginān* is often
published under the evocative title, *Rūhānī Visāl*, "spiritual union."[19]
The emotions aroused by the exquisite use of symbols in this *ginān* as
well as the wistful and plaintive *rāg* (melody) in which it is sung have
undoubtedly contributed to its immense popularity within the
community. In Indo-Pakistan it is sung particularly during occasions
when the *jamāᶜat* (congregation) decides to make a special effort, for a
period of seven days, towards meditating deeply on their *ism-i aᶜẓam*,
for union with Divine. These occasions, *satāḍās*, are seen as periods of
spiritual regeneration and renewed resolution to strive for spiritual
progress. The *ginān* is not used during the *dhikr* (meditation) itself;
for this, each individual uses the *ism-i aᶜẓam* given to him by the *Imām*.
The *ginān* is sung, however, just before the meditation session to
create an appropriate spiritual atmosphere and evoke a mood
suitable to this significant occasion.

The central concept that underlies the *ginān Ruhānī Visāl*[20] is one of
a primordial covenant between the yearning soul and the Beloved.
The *ginān* begins with an invocation to the absolute and indescribable
Lord, the origin of all beings who have been separated from Him
through the process of creation and earthly manifestation. To this
typically gnostic theme is added another element. The fifth verse
alludes to a primordial gathering, obviously of great significance:

> Whoever in that crowd (gathering) recognized You,
> Him You will select [to marry?] (5)

The soul, longing to be united with her Lord, reminds Him of a
promise that was made between them and urges Him to fulfill the
promise, since she has been waiting too long:

> Lord, my attention is fixed on You;
> It is you who occupy my thoughts.
> How can I capture another?
> Lord, come back and fulfill Your promise to me
> Do not forsake me, even for a single moment. (28)

The concepts of a primordial gathering and a promise in this *ginān*
refer to a verse in the Qur'an (7:172), where God called the future
humanity out of the loins of the yet uncreated Adam and addressed

them with the words, "Am I not your Lord (*alastu bi rabbikum*)?" and they answered, "Yes, we witness it (*balā shahidnā*)". The idea of this primordial covenant between God and man is one that has made a deep impression on the outlook of Muslim mystics.[21] This event in pre-eternity commemorates the establishment of a lasting bond or relationship between God and His creation. It is a relationship that the Islamic mystic conceives of being based on love and obedience. In the words of Henry Corbin, "The religious conscience of Islam is centered upon a fact of meta-history."[22]

> The goal of the mystic is to return to the experience of the "Day of *Alastu*", when only God existed, before He led future creatures out of the abyss of not-being and endowed them with life, love and understanding so that they might face Him again at the end of time.[23]

The motif of the primordial covenant, so characteristic of Islamic mysticism in general, is represented in our *ginān* by the use of symbols and imagery normally associated with betrothal and marriage. The most obvious of these symbols is the *nikāḥ*, the marriage rite among Muslims. The spiritual state of yearning and longing for divine union is compared to a woman's longing to get married.

> For ages on end I have been waiting anxiously
> But yet the *nikāḥ* has not been performed! (7)

To add a dramatic note to the quality of longing, the woman is described as being in the bloom of youth (*bhar joban*) and unable to wait any longer for the wedding. In mystical terms, the bloom of youth refers to the state in which the soul feels it is mature for divine union. It is a state which is achieved through a long and painful process of spiritual evolution, during which the impure and wayward soul (in Sufi terminology, the *nafs al-ammārah*) is purified and tamed. It is only after the wayward soul is completely broken and transformed through the dynamic force of divine love that she is mature and "ripe" enough to be accepted into the presence of the Husband. Thus, the term for bloom of youth (*bhar joban*) in this *ginān* refers to a state similar to the Sufi *nafs al-muṭmaᶜinnah*, "the soul at peace". According to Islamic thought, it is in this state that the *nafs* is ready to be "called home to its Lord."[24]

> Lord, sobbing and sighing, I plead with You.
> My heart pines in longing
> O Lord! come soon
> Lest (it is too late and) bloom of youth fade away (39)

In keeping with the overall theme of the covenant, the marriage is portrayed as one that has been promised to the woman by her Beloved. The use of the terms *dūhāg* and *sūhāg* in this connection are particularly significant. *Dūhāg*, depicting the state of waiting that elapses between the time the bride-to-be receives news of her approaching (and traditionally arranged) marriage and the performance of the marriage ceremony, corresponds to a period of formal engagement. *Sūhāg*, on the other hand, corresponds to a state of married bliss. In the *ginān*, the soul complains about the lengthy period of time that she has passed in the unfulfilled state of *dūhāg* and urges the Beloved to remedy the situation:

> O Lord, for how long must I stay alone?
> The days pass in *dūhāg* (separation)
> Transform my state of *dūhāg* to that of *sūhāg*
> Master of the fourteen heavens, preserve my honour (12)

Again, the woman-soul reminds her Beloved that she has been entrusted to Him by her parents, and she exhorts Him to fulfill this trust by marrying her (verses 17, 19). Having been committed to marriage with the Beloved, the woman reminds Him that preservation of her honour (*lāj*), a goal so important in Indian society, depends on the fulfillment of the promise. Here the relationship with the Lord is not seen as one that is hindered by other competing relationships. It is a unique association that goes back to pre-eternity, innate and natural to the soul. The marriage or union marking the culmination of this relationship has been promised, even guaranteed; it is inevitable that the Beloved fulfill the promise. His only freedom is in determining the time for the inevitable marriage. The relationship, as a binding contract between two parties, thus downplays the importance of the free gift of divine grace without rejecting it completely.

In verse 29, the bride-soul observes, in desperation, that she cannot marry anyone else, for the coconut, which is a public declaration of the bridegroom's honorable intentions and commitment of marriage, has already been sent to her. Having willingly accepted the Beloved's proposal, now it would be disgraceful for her to look at another. It is only the Beloved who can soothe the agonies of the soul. The soul, in its search for divine union, must be willing to sacrifice and risk everything for the sake of the Beloved. Hence the bride-soul in our *ginān*, in a very bold move, leaves her parental home and comes to the Beloved's residence with a water pot (*hail*) on her head. Through this Gujarati custom which permits young women to choose their own spouses, the bride offers herself of her own accord to her Beloved. If rejected, she runs the risk of losing all honor and standing in society and perhaps ruining her chances of ever receiving a marriage offer. She pleads with the Beloved to accept her offering, and hence herself, by taking down the water pot from on top of her head (verse 8). This offer of love also indicates that the marriage is important not just for the sake of preserving the woman's honour and the mere fulfillment of a contract, but it is fervently desired by the soul as an end in itself.

An important facet of the pleas for marriage is the constant use of terms associated with the rites and rituals of the marriage ceremony. The bridegroom is urged to come and collect the bride from her parental home with the traditional marriage procession while she, in anticipation, beautifies herself with *ambar* (clothes) and *ābhūshan* (ornaments) (verse 34). The theme of the bride preparing herself for the Beloved is a significant allusion to an important facet of the mystical path – the preparation the soul has to undertake before it is ready to experience the unitive experience.[25] The Beloved is also urged to set up a *chorī*, or boundary of sacredness, within which the marriage is to take place. Significantly, in this *ginān*, the *chorī* is to be set up in the midst of the universe, giving the marriage a cosmological tone (verse 44). Another verse (22) refers to the *chauk (chok) bāzār*, an ornamental square of colored flour in which a bride and bridegroom are seated for a short while for a certain number of days before the wedding. The soul ascends to the *chauk* remembering the name of the Lord – a significant hint at the value of practising meditation with the word or *ism-i aʿzam* given to the disciple by the Imām. In later verses of the *ginān*, the importance of repeating the name of the Lord becomes apparent: the image of the bride constantly thinking about her Beloved correlates with the practice of meditation – "breath upon breath I contemplate" (verse 35). Through the power of the name, all obstacles on the spiritual path are removed and salvation (union with the Divine) is attained.

The role played by the parents represents symbolically the role of the world in the spiritual quest. The parents and relatives, rather than being obstacles on the path to spiritual fulfillment, seem to play a supportive role in the bride's pleas for marriage. For the sake of the family honor, they urge their daughter to get married, and do not want to keep her any longer than is necessary in the family home (verse 13). It is the parents who entrusted their daughter to her husband-to-be, arranged the marriage (verse 17) and they are perfectly happy to see it actualized (verse 42). While this may be in stark contrast to the views of "ascetic" forms of mysticism which regarded the world and family as obstacles to the spiritual path, it alludes to a fundamental propensity in Ismāʿīlī thought to regard the material world to exist in a state of complementarity with the spiritual. The world of matter is the arena in which the context for a spiritual life is shaped; without acting in it, the spiritual quest is regarded as unworthy.[26]

The synthesis between the spiritual and the material in a mystical symbol has often led to the conclusion that mystical love poetry refers to earthly love. Poetry composed by Persian mystics has sometimes been interpreted in this manner. In the *ginān "Rūhānī Visāl"*, despite the use of imagery of human love and marriage, there can be no doubt of its religious and spiritual character. This lack of ambiguity is partly achieved by the absence of any erotic images and symbols. It is also the result of the overall cosmological tone of the *ginān* and the inclusion of clear spiritual advice, especially in the last verses. (46-49) Denouncing ignorance, the bride-soul pleads with the believers (Gujarati *rikhīsaro*; Arabic *mu'mins*) to acquire virtue, meditate regularly and love the Lord, i.e. the *Imām*, so that divine union may be achieved. True knowledge is taken to mean that which enables the soul to keep its attention on the Lord. The lack of knowledge, and indulgence in activities such as backbiting, remove the fixation of the mind on the Lord and hence are hazardous to the attainment of bliss. The soul is dear to the Lord when He knows not only that she thinks of Him constantly but also that she is aware of Him in every one of her actions. Hence the traditional Indian image of the loving, devoted wife, constantly thinking about her Beloved, is an excellent means of portraying the psychological orientation necessary in the spiritual quest.

The symbols of the bride and marriage are by no means the only symbols used in the *gināns* in connection with the mystical experience. A host of other symbols from the world of nature that depict states of dependence, selflessness and devotion are also employed quite effectively. An especially popular one among the *pīrs* was the symbol of the fish writhing in agony when it is out of the water. Love, as symbolized by water, is portrayed through this symbol as the emotive principle of life.[27] Symbols exalting in the efficacy of an inner mode of worship and interiorized religion as against the mindless performance of external rituals are also emphasized in consonance with the traditional Ismaili preoccupation to correlate the interior with the exterior, the spiritual with the material, the *zāhir* with the *bāṭin*.[28] Within this rich treasure of symbols and images, however, the symbol of the woman separated from her lover or the bride longing for her groom is pre-eminent in its importance. So strongly has the human soul of the *ginãns* been glued to this symbol, that the *pīrs*, the mostly male composers, often reversed gender when they spoke for the soul and its experiences. Typically, the composer of the *ginãn* "*Rūhānī Visāl*", says in its final stanza:

> Pīr Ḥasan Kabīrdīn [Kabīr ad-Dīn], becoming a woman, supplicates;
> And holds the hand of her husband ʿAlī.

The *pīr* specifically states that he has taken on a feminine role to petition ʿAlī, the first Shii *Imām* of history, who here symbolically represents the institution of Imamat. This gender reversal is noteworthy, for, it implies that gender itself is endowed with religious significance. Adopting a feminine consciousness seems to lead to a fuller spiritual experience; selfless devotion and love are conceived as more innate to the feminine mode. This is of course of considerable importance in our understanding of the psychology of the religious experience. It raises the question of finding out in what way the feminization of the male believer and the use of the marriage symbol is institutionalized through ritual. These are issues certainly worthy of analysis but beyond the scope of this article.[29]

The *ginãn* literature of the Nizārī Ismāʿīlīs of Indo-Pakistan has its own place within a cultural and religious context beyond the specific confines of the community. Its cultural context was that of premodern North India, specifically the regional cultures of Sind, Gujarat and Punjab. In its religious context, it belongs to the vast corpus of Islamic mystical literatures produced in the subcontinent by a large number of mystically-inclined Muslim groups. The literature's partiality to and preference for the use of bridal symbolism can best be appreciated by considering it within both these contexts.

By casting the soul in the *ginãns* in the feminine mode, the *pīrs*, though representatives of an Islamic movement with strong historical and political links to the Perso-Arabic world, demonstrated an awareness and sensitivity to cultural and literary conventions of their Indian audience. While the woman-soul or bride symbolism of the *ginãns* seems unique in the broader corpus of Ismāʿīlī literature, it is extremely common and popular in Indian literature. Medieval Indian poets of the Hindu *bhakti* tradition, under the influence of the Krishna devotional movement of Northern India, almost always wrote their poems from the point of view of *gopīs*, the young women who herded cows and were madly in love with Krishna.[30] Being male in traditional North Indian society meant superior social standing — a standing that in devotional poetry could only be a prerogative associated with the Divine. Indeed, according to Hindu ideals of marriage, the husband was representative of divine power. Moreover, the Hindu tradition perceived women as innately closer to the intimacy and naturalness of spirit that it is the purpose of *bhakti* to cultivate.[31] Thus it was only logical for Mīrābāī, medieval India's foremost female poet-saint, to declare that in the presence of the Lord Krishna all of humanity is reduced to woman-hood.[32] To become a woman before Krishna was, indeed, the goal of spiritual life among some Vaishnavite devotional cults.[33]

To what extent do the woman-soul and the bride-soul symbols found in the Ismaili *ginān* literature fit into the topography of other Islamic mystical literatures? Annemarie Schimmel has remarked that in classical Sufi poetry from the Arab and Iranian world, the woman is, with a few exceptions, almost always a negative symbol, representing something that is dangerous to the spiritual health of the soul.[34] Many a Sufi would agree with the statement of the great Islamic mystic, Mawlānā Jalāl ad-Dīn Rūmī, "first and last my fall is through woman."[35] The situation changes dramatically, however, when we move to the Indian subcontinent and examine Sufi poetry written in the indigenous languages such as Hindi, Sindhi, Punjabi, etc. In this type of poetry, it is conventional to represent the soul as a woman, either as a *virahinī* (a woman yearning to be reunited with her lover), a faithful wife or a loving bride.[36] In some regions such as Punjab and Sind, Sufi poets identified themselves with the heroines from the many folk romances which they endowed with mystical interpretation. They depicted these heroines in the long and painful search for the union with the Beloved.[37] The soul explicitly portrayed as a bride also makes her appearance as a symbol in many *qawwālīs*, the popular songs recited at the shrines of Muslim saints in the subcontinent. Thus, in a *qawwālī* attributed to Amir Khusrau (d. 1325), the renowned poet of the Chishti order, expresses his mystical love through a young bride longing to offer herself up in utter devotion to her groom.[38] Bridal symbolism also occurs in the poetry of some of the earliest Sufi poets writing in Urdu. Again, in the provinces of Sind and Punjab, one frequently finds in poems of the *bārahmāsa* genre that the poet identifies himself as a bride waiting to be reunited with God or with the bridegroom of Medina, that is, the Prophet Muḥammad.[39] Seen with this larger context, the highly-developed use of bridal-soul symbolism in the *gināns* falls into perspective. Clearly, like the *Ismāᶜīlī pīrs*, other Muslim authors also felt the need to indigenize their symbolism to the literary tastes of their local Indian audiences. The symbol of the longing woman or the bride, taken over from Hindu devotional poetry, is a powerful one in which many of the emotions experienced by the soul in its quest for union can be intensely compressed and tenderly expressed. It was, on the whole, a perfect "Indian" vehicle in which Indo-Muslim mystics, Shii and Sunni alike, could convey their message most effectively and with maximum impact on their audiences.

Notes

1 Evelyn Underhill, *Mysticism. A Study in the Nature and Development of Man's Spiritual Consciousness*, 12th ed. (New York: E. P. Dutton, 1930; paperback, 1961) 125.

2 *Ibid.*, 128.

3 Mircea Eliade et al., eds. *Encylopaedia of Religion* (New York: Macmillan Publishing Company, 1987), s.v. "Mystical Union" by Ileana Marcoulesco.

4 Evelyn Underhill points out that the other common form of expressing mystical union, favoured by mystics she calls the "transcedent-metaphysical" types, is deification—a form of expression considered at least as dangerous as that of the spiritual marriage. *Ibid.*, 415.

5 *Ibid.*, 163. Underhill notes the interesting case of the mystic Richard St. Victor who found the symbolism of marriage so appropriate to the spiritual life that he devised a daring and detailed application of it by identifying the soul's mystical development to four stages of betrothal, marriage, union or wedlock and fruitfulness. 139-140.

6 General summations of Ismāʿīlī history will be found in the following: *Encylopaedia of Islam*, s.v. "Ismāʿīlīyya" (by W. Madelung); Aziz Esmail and Azim Nanji, "The Ismāʿīlīs in History," in *Ismāʿīlī Contributions to Islamic Culture*, ed. S. H. Nasr (Tehran: Imperial Iranian Academy of Philosophy, 1977) 225-65. For the Nizārī Ismāʿīlī movement in general, see M. G. S. Hodgson, *The Order of the Assassins* (The Hague: Mouton, 1955) and the article by the same author, "The Ismāʿīlī State," in *The Cambridge History of Iran*, vol. 5, ed. J. A. Boyle (Cambridge: University Press, 1968) 422-82. For the Nizārī Ismāʿīlīs of the Indian subcontinent, see Azim Nanji, *The Nizārī Ismāʿīlī Tradition in the Indo-Pakistan Subcontinent* (New York: Caravan Books, 1978); Aziz Esmail, "Satpanth Ismailism and Modern Changes Within it with Special Reference to East Africa" (Ph. D. diss., University of Edinburgh, 1971) and Ali S. Asani, "The Khojahs of Indo-Pakistan: The Quest for an Islamic Identity," *Journal of the Institute of Muslim Minority Affairs*, 8, No. 1: 31-41.

7 Azim Nanji, "Ismāʿīlism," in *Islamic Spirituality: Foundations*, ed. by S. H. Nasr, vol. 19 of *World Spirituality: An Encyclopedic History of the Religious Quest* (New York: Crossroad, 1987) 185.

8 For an overview of spirituality among the Ismāʿīlīs, see Henry Corbin, "De la Gnose Antique à la Gnose Ismaélienne," *Oriente e Occidente nel Medioevo* (Rome: Accademia Nazionale dei Lincei, 1957); "Epiphanie Divine et Naissance Spir-

ituelle dans la Gnose Ismaélienne," *Eranos Jahrbuch* 23 (1954); "Le Temps
Cyclique dans le Mazdéisme et dans l'Ismaélisme," *Eranos Jahrbuch* 20 (1951);
"Herméneutique Spirituelle Comparée," *Eranos Jahrbuch* 33 (1964). The first
three essays have been translated by R. Mannheim and J. Morris in *Cyclical Time
and Ismāʿīlī Gnosis* (London: Kegan Paul International and Islamic Publications,
1983). See also Azim Nanji, "Ismāʿīlism."

9 The *ism-i aʿẓam*, or *bol*, as it is popularly known, is a sacred word, usually from the
Islamic Beautiful Names of God, given to a Nizārī Ismāʿīlī by the *Imām* for use in
dhikr (meditation). The receiving of the *ism-i aʿẓam* marks the initiation of the
believer into spiritual life. Each believer is given a personal *ism-i aʿẓam* by the
Imām, a further expression of the intimacy of the *Imām-murīd* relationship. Once
the disciple receives his or her *ism-i aʿẓam*, he or she is expected to sit in meditation every day between 4-5 a.m. As the disciple advances in meditation, he or she
may eventually exhaust the spiritual potential of a specific *ism-i aʿẓam*; in this case
he or she receives a new one which is more appropriate for a more advanced spiritual stage. This practice of spiritual initiation by the *ism-i aʿẓam* is similar to Sufi
practices.

10 Aziz Esmail, "Satpanth Ismailism," 459-460.

11 The bond of love between the *Imām* and his followers is readily apparent to
anyone who is acquainted with modern Nizārī Ismāʿīlī communities. Nizārī
Ismāʿīlis consider the *Imām* to be their "spiritual father and mother", while the
Imām in turn refers to his followers as "my beloved spiritual children". It is crucial
to bear in mind this spiritual basis for the love and devotion shown to the *Imām*
for it goes a long way in explaining the centrality of the Imamate for Ismailis, and
why they have upheld their faith in the *Imām* despite severe persecution.

12 Some of the languages in which Ismāʿīlī literature is recorded include: Arabic,
Persian, Urdu, Hindustani, Sindhi, Gujarati, Punjabi, Burushaski, Shina and
Khowar.

13 For detailed discussions of this literary genre, see W. Ivanow, "Satpanth," in
Collectanea, I, (Leiden: E. J. Brill, 1948) 36-39; Azim Nanji, *The Nizārī Ismāʿīlī
Tradition*, Aziz Esmail, "Satpanth Ismailism," and Ali S. Asani, "The Ismaili *Gināns*
as Devotional Literature," in *Devotional Literature in South Asia*, ed. R. S. McGregor
(Cambridge: Cambridge University Press, 1992), 101-112.

14 Aziz Esmail, "Satpanth Ismailism," 60.

15 Translated from text in D. Velji, *72 Ginans. Part I: Transliteration of Holy Ginans*
(Nairobi: Shia Imami Ismailia Association for Kenya, 1972) 3-5.

16 Text, in Roman transliteration, in *Wonderful Tradition* (Kampala: Shia Imami
Ismailia Association for Uganda, 1968) 20.

17 Text in *Wonderful Tradition*, 40-41.

18 According to Aziz Esmail, *gināns* attributed to Pīr Ḥasan Kabīr ad-Dīn are marked
by an acute sense of contriteness and dereliction, which finds expression in

numerous and intense prayers and outbursts of passionate longing for beatific vision. "Satpanth Ismailism," 33.

19 *Rūhānī Visāl. Venti Pīr Hasan Kabīrdīn.* (Karachi: Ismailia Association for Pakistan, 1976).

20 The text of the *ginān* used in this analysis is contained in the edition referred to above. As is the case with most printed *ginān* texts, it has not been critically edited and hence may vary in minor details from versions found in original manuscripts. This does not, however, affect its use in this study for the text is faithful in its representation of the symbolism associated with the *Imām-murīd* relationship.

21 Annemarie Schimmel, *Mystical Dimensions of Islam* (Chapel Hill: University of North Carolina, 1975) 24.

22 H. Corbin, *Histoire de la Philosophie Islamique* (Paris: Gallimard, 1964) 16.

23 Annemarie Schimmel, *ibid.* See also p. 184 of the same work. Love-intoxicated Sufis such as Ibn al-Fārid and Gīsūdarāz refer to true lovers drinking the wine of love at the day of the covenant, while Maulānā Rūmī represents the pre-eternal covenant by the image of the *samāʿ* or mystic dance:

A call reached Not-Being; Not-Being said:
"Yes, yes.
I shall put my foot on that side, fresh and green and joyful."
It heard the *alast*; it came forth running and intoxicated,
It was Not-Being and became Being (manifested in) tulips and willows and sweet
    basil.

24 *Ibid.*, 112.

25 Cf. verse 51 from the *ginān Sloko nāno* where the *pīr* addresses the woman-soul embarking on the mystic journey:

Strive for the Truth,
And decorate yourself with the Truth;
Take love as the *kohl* (make-up) for the eye,
And place the Beloved as a garland around the neck.

Text from *Shrī Nakalaṅk Shāstra. Pīr Sadardīnno saloko nāno.* 1st ed. (Bombay: The Recreation Club Institute, 1923) 10.

26 Azim Nanji, "Ismāʿīlism," 197.

27 A typical example of the use of the fish symbol occurs in the *ginān Huñ re pīyāsī* ("I am thirsty").

28 A. Nanji, *The Nizārī Ismāʿīlī Tradition*, 178.

29 It would be interesting to look into the implications of the woman symbol from the viewpoint of Jungian psychology. For a discussion of this symbol in Gnostic thought, see Wayne A. Meeks, "The Image of the Androgyne: Some Uses of a

Symbol in Earliest Christianity," *History of Religions* 13, no. 3. See also M. Eliade, *The Two and The One* (New York: Harper and Row, 1965) 78-122.

30 For a discussion of gender reversal in this tradition, see John Hawley, "Images of Gender in the Poetry of Krishna," in *Gender and Religion: On the Complexity of Symbols*. ed. Caroline Bynum et al. (Boston: Beacon Press, 1986) 231-256.

31 *Ibid.*, 238.

32 *Ibid.*, 235.

33 *Ibid.*, 236.

34 *Mystical Dimensions of Islam*, 428. In the Arabic and Persian mystical literature, the only representation of the longing soul in the image of a woman occurs in the rare cases of Mary, the mother of Jesus, and Zulaykha, the wife of Potiphar.

35 *Ibid.*, 429.

36 *Ibid.*, 434; Lajwanti Rama Krishna, *Panjabi Sufi Poets A.D. 1460-1900* repr. ed. (Karachi: Indus Publications, 1977) xxi; and Ali S. Asani, "Sufi Poetry in the Folk Tradition of Indo-Pakistan," *Religion and Literature* 20, no. 1 (1988): 85-86.

37 See Annemarie Schimmel, *Pain and Grace: A Study of Two Mystical Writers of Eighteenth Century Muslim India* (Leiden: E. J. Brill, 1976) and Lajwanti Ram Krishna, *Panjabi Sufi Poets*.

38 Regula Qureshi, *Sufi Music of India and Pakistan. Sound, Context and Meaning in Qawwali* (Cambridge: Cambridge University Press, 1986) 26.

39 Annemarie Schimmel, *And Muhammad is His Messenger* (Chapel Hill and London: University of North Carolina Press, 1985) 212-213.

Index